CHARLES HUDSON·

THE
SOUTHEASTERN
INDIANS

THE UNIVERSITY OF TENNESSEE PRESS

Frontispiece, Various Indians living along the Mississippi River. Drawing by A. DeBatz, 1735. Courtesy,
Peabody Museum, Harvard University.

Library of Congress Cataloging in Publication Data

Hudson, Charles M
  The Southeastern Indians.

  Bibliography: p.
  Includes index.
  1. Indians of North America—Southern States. I. Title.
  E78.S65H82   975'.004'97   75-30729
  ISBN 0-87049-187-3

FOR *Frank J. Essene*

They are ingenious, witty, cunning, and deceitful; very faithful indeed to their own tribes, but privately dishonest, and mischievous to the Europeans and Christians. Their being honest and harmless to each other, may be through fear of resentment and reprisal—which is unavoidable in case of any injury. They are very close, and retentive of their secrets; never forget injuries; revengeful of blood, to a degree of distraction. They are timorous, and, consequently, cautious; very jealous of encroachments from their Christian neighbors; and, likewise, content with freedom, in every turn of fortune. They are possessed of a strong comprehensive judgment, —can form surprisingly crafty schemes, and conduct them with equal caution, silence, and address; they admit none but distinguished warriors, and beloved men, into their councils. They are slow, but very persevering in their undertakings—commonly temperate in eating, but excessively immoderate in drinking.—They often transform themselves by liquor into the likeness of mad foaming bears. The women in general, are of a mild, amiable, soft disposition: exceedingly modest in their behavior, and very seldom noisy, either in the single, or married state.

JAMES ADAIR, *History of the American Indians*, 1776, p. 5.

PREFACE

This book is meant to be a comprehensive introduction to the native people of the Southeastern United States. It is comprehensive in that it traces the main outlines of their prehistory, social institutions, and history, but it is introductory in that I have not entered into fine points of interpretation. More than any of the native people in North America, the Southeastern Indians have been the victims of scholarly neglect; and above all I have wanted to bring them to life, to sketch them boldly and vividly. The intricacies of specialist uncertainties would have blurred the images I have sought to make plain. Hence this book is more the first word on the subject than the last word.

The Southeastern Indians profoundly affected the South as a region and the history that transpired there. Accordingly, these aboriginal Southerners are of interest not only to anthropologists and historians, but to anyone who wants to deepen his understanding of the South. I have therefore written with the lay reader in mind, avoiding technical language wherever possible.

This book is not intended to be a contribution to theory, but it has been shaped by two theoretical assumptions which ought to be made explicit. First, I take the point of view that social anthropology, particularly at the descriptive level, is rather more like social history than it is like the natural sciences. Second, I take the "neointellectualist" point of view that as social anthropologists we ought to regard the beliefs of preliterate people as serious attempts at explanation and not merely as bits of custom to be explained away by one or another of our theories.

As in social history, one of the fundamental theoretical and methodological problems in social anthropology is how to combine the synchronic analysis of a social system with the diachronic shifts and changes of the historical process. I do not presume to solve this problem, but my attempt to cope with it explains the somewhat peculiar structure of this book. The reader will find that I have sandwiched a synchronic analysis of the fundamental Southeastern Indian social institutions between two diachronic segments. After the preliminaries of chapter 1, there is presented in chapter 2 a survey of Southeastern prehistory and earliest European exploration. Then follows in chapters 3 through 7 a description of the major social institutions before they were fundamentally changed by European invaders. Finally, chapter 8 again becomes historical in tracing the history of the Southeastern Indians from the era of European colonization to the present day. This structure has enabled me to eschew the ethnographic present, wherein one speaks of customs long dead as if they were still viable, and more importantly it has enabled me to join together for the first time the prehistory, social anthropology, and history of the Southeastern Indians into a whole fabric.

Because I assume that the beliefs of the Southeastern Indians ought to be taken seriously, I begin the synchronic reconstruction with an analysis of their belief system—rather than ending with it, as is so often done. It is by absorbing something of their view of the world that we can see the sense of their social institutions, and I have quoted their myths extensively to allow them to speak for themselves.

As far as I was able, I have tried to see the world as the Southeastern Indians saw it, and I have tried to infuse their view of things into this book. Some readers will grant more credence to this world view than others. I myself do not believe that Southeastern Indian rainmakers could cause the rain to fall, although at times I may sound as if I did. On the other hand, I do believe that their priests and medicine men were able to alleviate the suffering of their patients far more effectively than most of us are prepared to accept. They used herbal medicines rather successfully, and they were probably able to cure "psychosomatic" and "sociosomatic" disorders more effectively than the medical, social, and psychiatric therapists in our own society.

In the six years it has taken me to research and write this book I have incurred many debts. It would have been much the poorer without the criticism and advice of David Hally and James Crawford. H. Eugene Hodges has influenced my view of the Southeastern Indians and of the South more than he knows. I owe a special debt to Charles Fairbanks, Raymond D. Fogelson, and Arrell M. Gibson, who read the manuscript from first to last, giving me helpful criticism. James H. Howard, Duane King, and John H. Peterson, Jr., gave me benefit of their knowledge of the Southeastern Indians and the use of unpublished materials, obviating a number of errors that would otherwise have been made. For reading parts of the manuscript and for giving me advice on particular matters I want to thank Ronald Butler, William Merrill, Theda Perdue, Bradford Rockwood, Bruce Smith, Abraham Tesser, and William McKee Evans.

The task of assembling the maps and illustrations for this book proved to be a far greater task than I had anticipated. I am grateful to James Ingram and his cartographic staff at the University of Georgia for drawing the maps. The photographic staff of the University of Georgia Libraries—Marvin Sexton, Geneva Rice, and Joyce Colquitt—came to my aid expertly and efficiently. William C. Sturtevant took time out from a burdensome work schedule to locate some particularly crucial photographs. And I am grateful to the following for helping me locate and obtain photographs: Charles A. Isetts, Robert McGaw, Marilyn Pennington, Ernie Robertson, Ted Guthe, Carol Speight, Charles Faulkner, Richard Jefferies, Clarence H. Webb, Thomas H. Hartig, Frederick Dockstader, Philip Phillips, Ben Harrison, William H. Sears, Leland Ferguson, John D. Combes, David L. DeJarnette, Keith Fleming, Archibald Hanna, James R. Glenn, Samuel Proctor, and Helen Wallis.

Some of the maps which appear in this book have been adapted from the work of others: map 2 is adapted from Nevin M. Fenneman's "Physical Divisions of the United States," U. S. Department of the Interior, 1946; map 4 from James B. Griffin's "Eastern North American Archaeology: A Survey," *Science* 156(1967):185; map 7 from Grant Foreman's *Indian Removal* (Norman, Oklahoma: Univ. of Oklahoma Press, 1932); and map 8 from the Bureau of Indian Affairs Indian Land Areas Map, 1971.

The University of Tennessee Press received a grant from the Andrew W. Mellon Foundation and the American Council of

Learned Societies supporting publication of this book. A portion of the writing was done while I held an appointment at the Institute for Behavioral Research at the University of Georgia.

I am mindful that Stephen F. Cox stopped by for a cup of coffee more years ago than I care to remember and waited patiently while a small book grew into a big book. My debt to my wife, Joyce Rockwood, is enormous. She took time out from her own writing to edit, criticize, discuss, and buoy me up in moments of frustration and despair.

C. H.
Danielsville, Georgia
October 1975

ORTHOGRAPHIC NOTE

Over the years scholars have devised several writing systems for Southeastern Indian languages. The older systems are faulty in that they, on the one hand, use too many symbols and, on the other, fail to symbolize some features of the languages. Modern systems of writing are far more likely to use a parsimonious but adequate number of symbols, but the lists of symbols used by modern linguists often differ in small ways. Instead of attempting to try to reconcile all these differences, I have adopted the expedient of citing forms as I have found them.

In a few instances I have anglicized Indian words which enjoyed some currency in the historic past or still do today: e.g., *miko*, *chunkey*, *coontie*, *sofkee*, and *chickee*. And I have anglicized a few additional words which I have used repeatedly: e.g., Cherokee *tlanuwa* and *uktena*, both mythical monsters, and *ulunsuti*, a miraculous Cherokee divining crystal.

The following symbols will be unfamiliar to readers who are unacquainted with phonetic notation. They have the values indicated.

ə, ȧ = Schwa. The sound of *u* in *but*.

Λ = A nasalized schwa, with approximately the sound of the French indefinite article *un*.

ŭ = Schwa in Muskogean languages.

â = The sound of *aw* in *law*.

û = The sound of *oo* in *foot*.

tc, č = A voiceless affricate with approximately the sound of *ch* in *cheese*.

thl, ł = A voiceless *l*. English has no equivalent. It is enunciated with the tongue in place for an *l*, but the vocal cords do not vibrate. It is rather like the sound of *hl*.

ꝑ = Glottal stop. Not a significant sound in English. But it regularly occurs unperceived as a slight catch in the throat when vowels are uttered in sequence, as in *a, e, i, o*.

. , :, ⁻ = Long vowel.

˅ = Short vowel, in Cherokee.

ˊ = Rising Pitch.

ˋ = Falling pitch.

( ) = Indicates a sound which may or may not be present.

CONTENTS

ILLUSTRATIONS

xvi

Kinship Diagrams

Maps

THE SOUTHEASTERN INDIANS·

CHAPTER ONE

INTRODUCTION

The native people of the American South—the Southeastern Indians—possessed the richest culture of any of the native people north of Mexico. It was richest by almost any measure. At the time Europeans first came to the New World, the Southeastern Indians lived on the fruits of an economy which combined farming with hunting and gathering; they organized themselves into relatively complex political units; they built large towns and monumental ceremonial centers; and they possessed a rich symbolism and an expressive art style. But hardly any of this has left an impression on our historical memory. The average American has some notion of the Powhatan Indians of Virginia and of the role they played in our early colonial history; he has a clear but stereotyped concept of the Indians who lived on the Great Plains; he may know something about the Navajo and Pueblo Indians of the Southwest; but he knows little or nothing about the Southeastern Indians.

All people have blind spots in their memory of the past, but the Southeastern Indians are the victims of a virtual amnesia in our historical consciousness.[1] And this amnesia has afflicted Southerners as much as it has people in other parts of the United States. This is particularly surprising in light of the fact that an unusually large number of Southerners, both black and white, claim to have some Indian blood in their veins. Almost invariably they say that it comes from an Indian grandmother (usually a "Cherokee"), and they are generally proud of it, though occasionally ambivalent toward it.[2]

The Southeastern Indians have not been completely eradicated from our sense of the past. Some people have a negative stereotype of them—an image of the marauding frontier Cherokee or Creek (they were always marauding), savagely bloodying the heads of idyllic pioneers. And some have a positive stereotype of them—an image of the noble but childishly naïve Five Civilized Tribes. (Among Indians, as among no other people, nobility and naïveté always went together.) Some Southerners, both black and white, know a few "Indian" herbal remedies. And many have heard about the suffering of the Southeastern Indians when they were forcibly and cruelly "removed" from their lands and driven west of the Mississippi River. All of these notions reflect historical fact, but none of them tells us much about the true nature of the aboriginal people of the Southeastern United States. They do not tell us what the Southeastern Indians were like as people, or how they lived their day-to-day lives.

The Indians of the Southeast have been inadequately portrayed both by historians and by anthropologists. The reasons for this failure are many. One general problem has been that the Indian cultures were so different from European cultures that it has been difficult for European intellectuals to translate the life experience of Indians into terms a layman can readily understand; this problem still exists today, but it was even more acute when European colonization first began.[3] But perhaps the foremost reason for our ignorance about the Southeastern Indians is simply that many of them were killed, their societies disrupted, and their cultures greatly changed before the day when educated people thought the Indian cultures were worth studying. The social and cultural dislocation suffered by the Southeastern Indians was both severe and rapid; indeed, some evidence suggests that some of the Southeastern Indians experienced social and cultural breakdown even before Hernando de Soto's exploration of the South. For example, when de Soto reached the province of Cofitachequi in central South Carolina in 1540, he found whole villages that had been emptied two years earlier by a virulent epidemic.[4] This disease could have come from the people who belonged to Lucas Vázquez de Ayllón's colony, which was established in 1526 somewhere in the vicinity of the Cape Fear River, and which failed within six months because of starvation and disease. Even at an earlier date the Indians could have contracted diseases for which they had no resistance from European ships briefly touching the coast or from shipwrecked sailors.[5] The shock of this initial contact with Europeans and their microbes must have been severe, but it is not yet possible to assess its effects with certainty.

4

The Southeastern Indians were socially diverse but culturally similar people who lived in the American South, or, more precisely, in the Southeastern Culture Area (Map 1), a region bounded on the east by the Atlantic Ocean, on the south by the Gulf of Mexico, on the west by the dry country beyond the Trinity River in Texas, and on the north by the colder climate of the upper Mississippi and Ohio River valleys. Drawn on a modern map, the Southeastern Culture Area (the Southeast, for short) includes the present states of Georgia, Florida, South Carolina, western North Carolina, Alabama, Mississippi, Louisiana, southern and eastern Arkansas, Tennessee, and the portions of the states of Missouri, Illinois, and Kentucky that border the Mississippi River. John R. Swanton estimates the population of the Southeast to have been about 170,000 at the time of European contact,[6] but more recent estimates place the figure far higher, at perhaps ten times Swanton's figure.[7]

In the earliest period of European exploration and colonization, the Southeast was inhabited by such people as the Timucuans and Apalachees of northern Florida and southern Georgia; the Guales of coastal Georgia; the Yamasees of the South Carolina and Georgia back country; and the Natchez, Houmas, and Chitimachas of the lower Mississippi River. These were some of the first groups to feel the crunch of European colonization, with the result that many of them were exterminated or absorbed by other groups in a relatively short time, and many of their names disappear from history. Later the Southeast was dominated by the Cherokees of the southern Appalachian Mountains, including the Lower Towns on the headwaters of the Savannah River, the Middle Towns of the headwaters of the Little Tennessee River, and the Upper Towns (Overhill and Valley) of the lower Little Tennessee River and the headwaters of the Hiwassee River;[8] the Catawbas, a collection of diverse Indians in the back country of South Carolina;[9] the Chickasaws of northern Mississippi and southwestern Tennessee;[10] the Caddos, who made their homes in Louisiana and Arkansas;[11] the Choctaws of southern Mississippi;[12] the Upper Creeks, Alabamas, and Koasatis of the Coosa, Tallapoosa, and Alabama rivers, and the Lower Creeks and Yuchis of the lower Chattahoochee River, these constituting powerful political alliances;[13] and the Seminoles, composed of several groups of Creek Indians who moved into Florida in the eighteenth and early nineteenth centuries.[14]

5

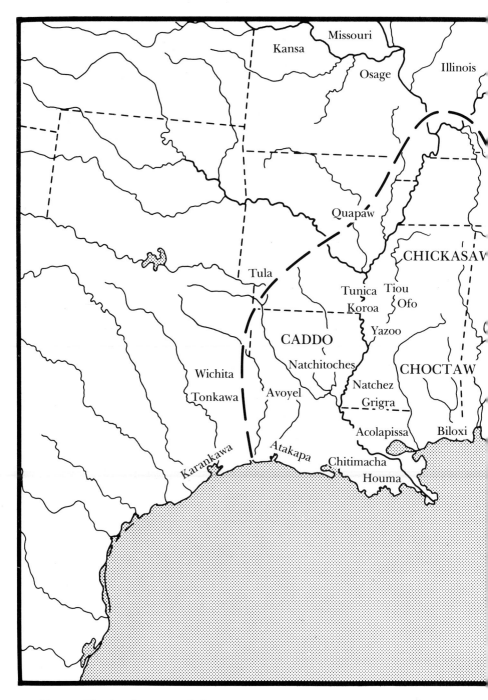

Map 1. The Southeastern Culture Area.

6

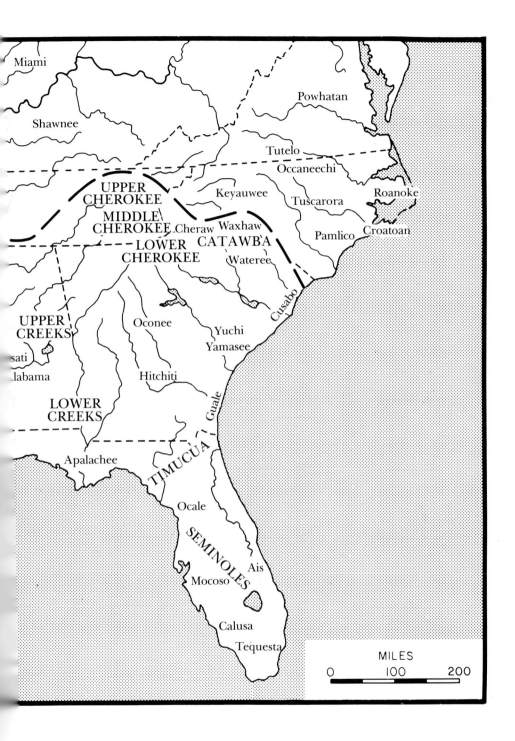

Miami

Shawnee

Powhatan

Tutelo

Occaneechi

UPPER
CHEROKEE

Keyauwee

Roanoke

MIDDLE
CHEROKEE Cheraw Waxhaw

Tuscarora

LOWER
CHEROKEE CATAWBA

Pamlico

Croatoan

Wateree

Cusabo

UPPER
CREEKS

Oconee

Yuchi
Yamasee

sati

labama

Hitchiti

Guale

LOWER
CREEKS

TIMUCUA

Apalachee

Ocale

SEMINOLES

Ais

Mocoso

Calusa

Tequesta

MILES

0   100   200

This list only includes those societies that were historically prominent. The Southeast included many smaller cultural groups about whom we know very little. For some of these cultures, such as the Avoyels, Grigras, and Acolapissas of Louisiana; the Yazoos of Mississippi; the Congarees of South Carolina; and the Ocales of northern Florida; we know little more than their names. They are so poorly documented we are likely never to know much more about them, except in those fortunate instances in which the archaeologists and ethnohistorians succeed in digging additional information out of the ground and out of the archives.

Around the boundaries of the Southeast were a number of Indian groups who resembled the Southeastern Indians in some respects but not in others. They were marginal to the Southeastern Culture Area. The Calusas, Ais, Tequestas, and other people living in southern Florida differed sharply from the Southeastern Indians in that they did not practice agriculture, but lived entirely from fishing, collecting shellfish, and gathering wild vegetable foods. Because their territory was so rich in seafood, the Calusas, like the Indians of the North Pacific Coast, had a denser and more highly stratified population than is usually the case among people who make their living solely from hunting, fishing, and gathering.[15] The Calusas and their neighbors were perhaps the most marginal of all the peoples on the edges of the Southeastern Culture Area.

In the northeastern corner of the Southeastern Culture Area lay a series of Indian groups who combined farming with hunting and gathering, as did the Southeastern Indians, but who were never much affected by the last great cultural development in the Southeast in the late prehistoric period—the Mississippian tradition. Until about the time of European contact, these groups were culturally influenced not from the south, but from the north.[16] These were people like the Tutelos, Occaneechis, and Keyauwees of the Carolina piedmont and coastal plain. Some of these small groups are known to have spoken Siouan languages, but for the most part their linguistic affiliations are unknown. Also marginal were the Tuscaroras, who spoke a language related to Cherokee and who lived on the Roanoke, Neuse, Tar, and Pamlico rivers in North Carolina. After suffering crushing defeat in a war with the colonists and allied Indians in 1711–13, the Tuscaroras moved north where they were accepted among the Iroquois. Even more remote from the Southeast were the Powhatans and other coastal Algonkians of North Carolina and Virginia, who practiced agriculture, but perhaps less intensively than the Southeastern Indians, relying more heavily on fish and shellfish.[17]

On the western margin of the Southeastern Culture Area lay a series of Indian societies which might with some justification be included within the Southeast—namely, the Caddoan-speaking Wichitas and Pawnees and the Siouan-speaking Quapaws, Osages, Missouris, and Omahas. The cultures of these people took shape as variants of the Mississippian tradition, and they carried their agricultural way of life up the western tributaries of the Mississippi River. Here they lived in fortified villages in a rather uneasy relationship with hunters and gatherers who lived on the grass-covered plains away from the river valleys—people who in the eighteenth and nineteenth centuries borrowed the horse from the Europeans and developed the nomadic culture of the familiar Plains Indians. Thus in the late prehistoric period two sharply different cultures lived in the eastern plains—nomadic buffalo-hunters and Mississippian riverine agriculturalists. By building their way of life around the horse, with all the mobility and military advantage the horse conferred, the buffalo-hunters were able to stand up to encroaching white settlers more effectively than the agriculturalists were able to do, and they have dominated our image of the Plains Indians ever since.[18]

A case can also be made for including the Algonkian-speaking Shawnees in the Southeastern Culture Area. Although they lived in Kentucky and Ohio on the northeastern margin of the area of the Mississippian tradition for most of their history, some evidence indicates that one band of Shawnees moved south and took up residence on the Savannah River in the early 1700s. The whites called them "Savanoes," whence comes the name of the river and city in Georgia. After remaining there a few years, some of them moved down to live among the Lower Creeks on the Chattahoochee River, and others moved north to Lancaster County, Pennsylvania. Still later the Shawnees who had moved to the Chattahoochee moved north to live among the Upper Creeks, where they were joined by yet another group of Shawnees who moved down from the north. Later the great Shawnee leader Tecumseh was born of a Shawnee father and a Creek mother.[19]

The Southeastern Indians differed from each other in many respects, including the languages they spoke, but they did share many broad cultural and social similarities. This basic similarity is evident in the accounts of the de Soto expedition of 1539–43. Beginning in northern Florida, de Soto and his men marched through the heart of the Southeast all the way to western Arkansas and eastern Texas (see map 5). They repeatedly remarked in their accounts that all of the Southeastern Indians were alike. Even the Timucuans seemed to them to be similar to the other Southeastern Indians in many respects, although in retrospect they do not seem to have possessed the characteristic Mississippian Culture of the Indians further north and west. It was only when de Soto and his men encountered the Caddoan-speaking Tulas of western Arkansas that they met people who differed markedly from the people they previously encountered. Unlike the Southeastern Indians who lived in large communities and depended on agriculture for much of their food, the Tulas lived in smaller communities and depended to a large degree on hunting buffalo for food, and they raised relatively little corn.[20] De Soto's men also found cultural differences in east Texas, where they encountered people who lived in encampments of tiny houses and who made their living largely by hunting and gathering wild food.[21] On the Atlantic coast a cultural boundary evidently existed between Winyaw Bay, as described by the Indian Francisco of Chicora,[22] and the people near Cape Fear, as described by Giovanni da Verrazzano.[23] Although both of these descriptions are far too brief to allow us to draw firm conclusions from them, the societies around Winyaw Bay sound like Mississippian peoples found elsewhere in the Southeast, while those further north appear to have been different.

It would be a mistake to put too much faith in any map depicting the Southeastern Culture Area. Any boundaries drawn are inevitably somewhat arbitrary because all of the aboriginal people east of the Rocky Mountains and north of the Gulf of Mexico to the boreal forest of Canada shared many cultural features.[24] This situation must in large measure be a consequence of the domination of this part of the continent by the Mississippi River and its tributaries, along whose banks many social and cultural innovations developed and diffused from one group to another in prehistoric times.

Although the Southeastern Indians possessed cultural and social features which prevailed more widely in North America, they did live in an area which has a rather distinctive set of physiographic, biotic, and climatic features. Specifically, the Southeast is an area in which there are rich but limited fields of easily tilled river-bottom soil, an abundant variety of woodland animals and vegetable foods, and a warm, wet climate. More than anything else, these features underlay the distinctiveness of the Southeastern way of life.

We will see in chapter 8 that descendants of the Southeastern Indians live today in isolated parts of the Southeast, and even more of them live in Oklahoma, the place to which they were "removed." While remaining distinctive in some respects, these modern Southeastern Indians are for the most part culturally contemporary. This book is not primarily about them, but about their ancestors. It would be a marvelous thing if we could have a full account of the Southeastern Indians at the time of de Soto's exploration in the sixteenth century, when they were near the height of their cultural development. We know from archaeological evidence that Southeastern cultural patterns were more widespread then, extending far up the Mississippi River and its tributaries. But de Soto's chroniclers recorded far too little information for such an account. Their visit was brief and cruel, and they were only interested in the Indians as a means to quick wealth.

We have no choice but to rely on later historical sources. Important among these are the writings of John Lawson, a British colonist who traveled through the Carolina piedmont in 1700; of Le Page du Pratz, a Frenchman who spent several years along the lower Mississippi River in the early eighteenth century; of James Adair, who lived and traded with the Indians, particularly the Chickasaws, from 1735 until 1768; of Jean-Bernard Bossu, a French naval officer who traveled in the Mississippi Valley and through present-day Alabama from 1751 to 1762; of Lieutenant Henry Timberlake, a young British soldier who visited the Cherokees during the French and Indian War; of Bernard Romans, a surveyor for the British in Florida and Georgia in the late 1760's and early 1770's; of William Bartram, a naturalist who toured the Southeast in 1773–77, leaving a superbly written account of his observations; of Benjamin Hawkins, an intelligent administrator among the Creeks in the late eighteenth and early nineteenth centuries; and of William O. Tuggle, who served as a lawyer for the Creeks from 1879 to 1883, and who collected a series of Creek oral traditions.

Later we have the work of the anthropologist James Mooney, who did field work among the eastern Cherokees chiefly from 1887 to 1890, leaving us a lucid, thoughtful account of their oral traditions and religious beliefs. Later still, we have the work of the anthropologist John R. Swanton, who did field work among several groups of Southeastern Indians in the early decades of this century, most notably among the Creeks in 1911 and 1912. In addition to collecting firsthand materials on his own, Swanton made a comprehensive search through the most important historical documents, gleaning relevant information and publishing it in several reports and bulletins of the Bureau of American Ethnology. Another anthropologist who did firsthand fieldwork was Frank Speck, whose most important research was with the Cherokees, Yuchis, Catawbas, and Taskigi Creeks. Additional information on the ancient Southeastern Indians comes to us from the archaeologists, who dig their records of the past from the earth. As the archaeologists continue their research in the Southeast, we are able to compare the information they retrieve with the historical record, thus correcting, amplifying, and verifying it.[25]

When one's goal is to see the world as the Indians saw it, the most valuable information comes not from these European and Anglo-American observers and scholars, but from the Indians who told the anthropologists about their cultures. In a true sense they were the last repositories of the world of the Southeastern Indians. These were people like George W. Grayson, Zachariah Cook, and Jackson Lewis, the Creeks who gave Swanton most of his information; and Samuel Blue of the Catawbas, on whom Frank Speck primarily relied. But the most outstanding of these Indians who kept their culture alive was the Cherokee wise man Swimmer, to whom James Mooney was indebted for some of his best knowledge of Cherokee culture. Speaking no English, Swimmer not only recited to Mooney the basic Cherokee oral traditions, but he handed over to him a book in which he had written many sacred formulas in the Cherokee script perfected by Sequoyah in 1819.[26]

Mooney's deepest understanding of the Cherokees came from Swimmer (fig. 1). Because of Swimmer, Mooney was one of the first

12

Figure 1. Swimmer. The Cherokee from whom James Mooney obtained much of his information. 1888. Negative no. 1008. Courtesy, Smithsonian Institution, National Anthropological Archives.

anthropologists to realize fully that the American Indians held consistent systems of beliefs. He wrote: "When we are willing to admit that the Indian has a religion which he holds sacred, even though it be different from our own, we can then admire the consistency of the theory, the particularity of the ceremonial and the beauty of the expression. So far from being a jumble of crudities, there is a wonderful completeness about the whole system which is not surpassed even by the ceremonial religions of the East."[27] At Swimmer's death, Mooney wrote: "Peace to his ashes and sorrow for his going, for with him perished half the tradition of a people."[28]

In reconstructing the basic social institutions of the Southeastern Indians, it would be ideal to have at hand full documentary information for a relatively brief span of time—say the last decade of the eighteenth century; and it would be ideal to have roughly comparable amounts of information on *all* the social institutions of *all* the various Southeastern tribes. If this were the case one could be sure that one was dealing with whole social entities, and one could formulate precise generalizations about the Southeastern Indians. Unfortunately, this cannot be the case. The documentation is uneven with respect both to time and to cultural coverage.

Compromise is therefore necessary, and the compromise that has been adopted in this book has been that of using the richest information available. This treatment means, for example, that some of the chapters are based on documents whose dates are separated by a century or more. It means that the chapter on the Southeastern Indian belief system is drawn almost exclusively from documents on the Cherokees, while the chapter on social organization is largely based on documents on the Creeks. And since the Old South was a plural society, it is possible that some of our documentation on the Southeastern Indians is not so unaffected by European and African influences as one would wish. But in the end it is to be hoped that the fullness made possible by this approach will in some measure compensate for its historical unevenness.

REGIONS OF THE SOUTHEAST

The Southeastern Culture Area included parts of three distinct natural regions (map 2): the coastal plain, the southern piedmont, and the southern end of the Appalachian Highlands.[29] The Ozark-

14

Ouachita Highlands of Arkansas and Missouri and the dry plains of eastern Texas formed a western boundary to the Southeastern Culture Area, and the interior low plateaus of Kentucky and Tennessee and the interior plains of Illinois formed a northern boundary, although not a sharp one, since people possessing general Southeastern culture patterns lived further north along the Mississippi River and its tributaries in late prehistoric times.

More than three-fourths of the Southeastern Culture Area lay in the coastal plain, whose flat expanses are covered by longleaf and slash pines, interspersed with magnolia, cypress, and live oak. It is an area of sluggish, meandering rivers feeding innumerable swamps, some of vast size, thickly covered with cypress and cane, two important raw materials to the Southeastern Indians. Because of its resistance to rot, cypress was favored for posts and for dugout canoes. Although we generally regard cane as a nuisance, the Indians used it to make a great variety of things both large and small.

The coastal plain was rich with edible wild vegetables and fruits, including blackberries, palmetto, gooseberries, grapes, certain varieties of acorns, prickly pears, sea grapes, and several plants from which the Indians obtained roots. Spanish moss was abundant as well as useful. The Indians used it as tinder, braided it into cord, and in some places the women fashioned skirts out of it.

Many mammals and birds lived in the coastal plain and were hunted by the Indians. Here, as elsewhere in the Southeast, the deer was the most important game animal. Its flesh was used as food; its skin for clothing and leather articles; its horns were made into arrow points and glue; its hooves were made into rattles; and its bones were fashioned into a variety of articles. The bear was another important source of food and skins, and from the fat of the bear the Indians extracted an oil which they ate and used also for other purposes. Some of the needs of the Indians were met by smaller animals, including the beaver, otter, raccoon, muskrat, opossum, squirrel, and rabbit. These same animals were also hunted by several carnivores living in the region: the cougar, the bobcat, the fox, and the wolf. Turkeys thrived in the coastal plain and provided an important source of food and feathers. In certain seasons of the year immense numbers of waterfowl were present in the coastal plain, particularly along the Mississippi flyway. Many other coastal plain animals, such as snakes, turtles, terrapins, alligators, crawfish,

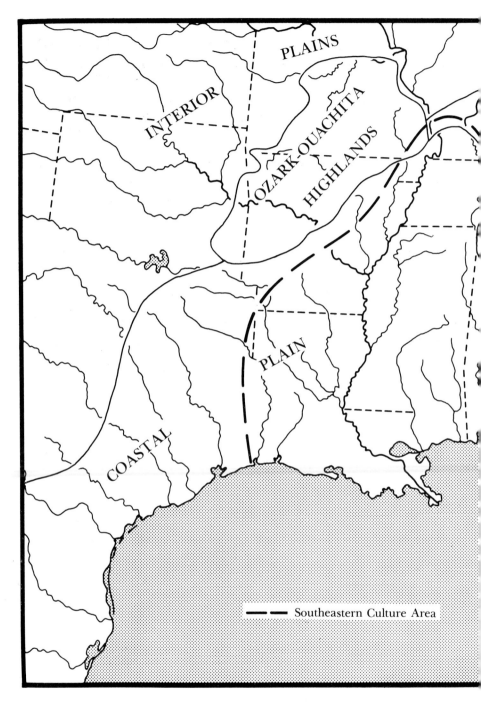

PLAINS

INTERIOR

OZARK-OUACHITA

HIGHLANDS

PLAIN

COASTAL

— — — Southeastern Culture Area

Map 2. Regions of the Southeast.

16

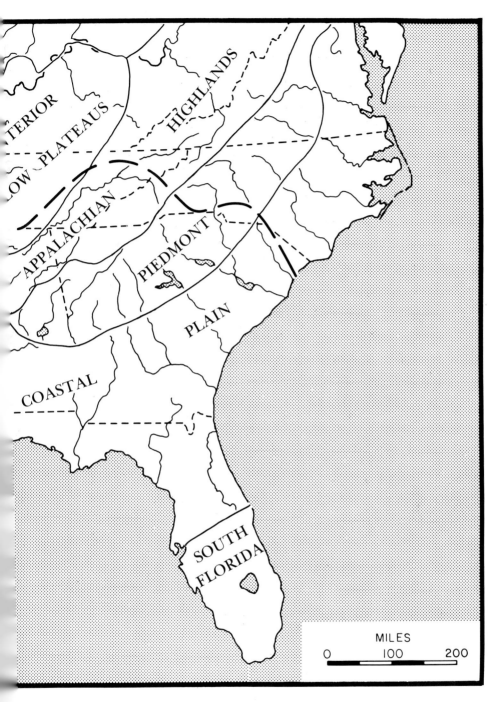

INTERIOR LOW PLATEAUS

HIGHLANDS

APPALACHIAN

PIEDMONT

PLAIN

COASTAL

SOUTH FLORIDA

MILES

0   100   200

crabs, clams, mussels, and oysters, were used for food and for other purposes.

In late prehistoric times the Southeastern Indians probably conceived of the coastal plain as consisting of several distinct regions. The lower Mississippi River with its deep alluvial soils and its oak-gum-cypress forests is distinctive; the richest alluvial soils are here, but flint and other kinds of stone useful to the Indians were usually missing, and periodic flooding must have been a problem. The lower Mississippi River has the highest flood potential of any part of interior North America.[30] De Soto's soldiers were told by an old woman that the Mississippi River had a great flood every fourteen years. And the river did in fact flood while they were there. According to one account the river began to rise in mid-March of 1543, and it did not crest until forty days later, the water covering everything except the tops of the trees. The river did not return to its banks until the end of May.[31] This account may have been colored by the well-known Biblical event, though not by much, judging from the flooding in this area in more recent times. Other rivers in the coastal plain must have had similar periodic flooding along their lower courses. On the upper Mississippi River the Indians would have had the advantage of the rich alluvial soils without the disadvantage of such severe flooding. The disadvantage of the upper Mississippi River, on the other hand, was that this area did not enjoy the longer growing season of the region further south.

The Indians probably also distinguished the Atlantic and Gulf coasts and all of northern Florida from the rest of the coastal plain. Along the coast the land is swampy, much of it covered with standing water. It evidently was not ideal for Indian agriculture, although both the Apalachees and the Timucuans grew the same crops as were grown elsewhere in the Southeast, though perhaps less intensively. The advantage of the coastline itself was that it was capable of providing abundant food in the form of fish, shellfish, and along the eastern coastline of Florida, whales, which the Indians occasionally killed and ate. Perhaps for this reason the aboriginal population was denser around coastal lagoons than in the interior of the coastal plain. The greatest disadvantage of the coast was the great swarms of mosquitoes during the warm part of the year. Alvar Nuñez Cabeza de Vaca, marooned on the Gulf Coast in the sixteenth century, wrote that three kinds of mosquitoes infested the coast, "all very bad and troublesome." On the islands along the Gulf Coast the Indians would build big fires out of damp and rotten wood, and even though the smoke from these fires was often so thick as to keep them from sleeping, it was worth the discomfort if it kept the mosquitoes away. Cabeza de Vaca says that the Indians were sometimes so badly bitten they looked like lepers.[32]

South Florida, below a line drawn from Charlotte Harbor to the Cape Kennedy (Canaveral) region, is also distinct. Here the land is decidedly swampy, with as much as 50 percent of it covered by standing water. Great portions are covered by everglades, palmetto prairie, and mangrove swamp. Here the climate is nearly tropical, with 300 to 330 freeze-free days per year.[33] As we have already seen, the Indians living in this region were marginal to the Southeastern Culture Area.

The second important region for the Southeastern Indians was the piedmont, a band of hilly uplands between the Appalachian Mountains on the one side and the coastal plain on the other. The piedmont is separated from the coastal plain by the "fall line," an imaginary line drawn through the shoals and rapids of the rivers as they fall abruptly from the uplands to the flat coastal plain. The territory lying immediately to either side of the fall line was an important region in itself. Some of the most populous societies in the prehistoric Southeast lay along this line, the reason being that from this vantage point the Indians could exploit the natural resources of the coastal plain, the piedmont, and the fall line itself. The best freshwater fishing in the Southeast was at the fall line, where in certain seasons fish could be taken in vast numbers as they swam upstream to spawn.[34]

The dominant trees in the piedmont were oak and hickory, but also abundant were the short-leaf pine and many hardwoods, such as sassafras, poplar, hackberry, sycamore, sweet gum, and persimmon. Contrary to popular opinion, many parts of the Southeast were not virgin forest when Europeans first arrived. The Indians actually modified the forest cover far out of proportion to their numbers. They repeatedly burned off large portions of the forest to create grazing lands, artificially stimulating the number of deer. Large herds of deer are mentioned in the earliest accounts of the Southeast.[35] The Indians also used fire as a hunting technique to concentrate game so that it could be killed easily, and they burned their agricultural fields in late winter in preparation for planting. As a consequence of all this burning, the forest cover of the piedmont was broken by large expanses of grassland containing scattered giant oaks and large herds of deer.[36]

Bison are occasionally mentioned in the early historical records of the Southeast. De Soto, for example, reports having seen "cow horns" in a village in northern Georgia, but he does not report actually seeing bison on the hoof until he crossed the Mississippi River. Bison did occur in the Southeast, but so infrequently that they were more a curiosity than a dependable source of food.[37]

Many of the animals of the coastal plain also lived in the piedmont. One important piedmont bird was the passenger pigeon, now extinct, but formerly existing in vast flocks that darkened the sky when they flew.

The southern end of the densely forested, rugged Appalachian Mountains was the third region included in the Southeastern Culture Area. These mountains were the homeland of the historic Cherokees, who hunted in the mountain forests and farmed in the narrow, alluvial river valleys. The mountains provided an abundance of turkey, deer, bear, and a variety of other animals. The mountains were a favorite habitat of the eagle, whose feathers were prized above those of all other birds. This region was particularly rich in wood and tree products. Poplar trees, which grew to enormous size, were used to make dugout canoes. The mountains provided inexhaustible supplies of chestnuts, hickory nuts, hazelnuts, walnuts, butternuts, chinquapins, and other nuts, all rich in food value. The mountains were also the source of various kinds of minerals used by the Indians, including mica, steatite, and several kinds of quartz crystals.

Most of the Southeastern Culture Area enjoys a mild climate. In most of the area the average July temperature is between 80°F. and 90°F., while the average January temperature is 35°F. to 40°F. in the extreme northern part of the area and 55°F. to 65°F. in the southern part.[38] Southwesterly winds prevail in the Southeast, bringing in abundant rainfall averaging 48 to 64 inches per year in most places, but with the piedmont getting only 40 to 48 inches per year. In the western part of the Southeast annual precipitation falls off very sharply, setting off the dry plains and forming the western boundary of the Southeastern Culture Area. With few exceptions, the Southeastern Culture Area falls within the area of the eastern United States getting over 40 inches of rainfall per year.[39] The Southeast enjoys quite a long growing season—from 240 days along the fall line to as many as 270 days along the Gulf and south Atlantic coasts—a factor of great importance in aboriginal agriculture. Further north in the piedmont the growing season shortens to about 210 days per year. The northern limit of the Southeast was generally set at the region where the growing season is less than 180 days per year.[40] The exception to these conditions is the Appalachian Mountains, where it is cooler, averaging only about 70°F. in July, and wetter, averaging 64 to 96 inches of rainfall per year. In fact, the southern part of the Appalachians is the wettest place in the eastern United States. Summer rains, particularly in the mountains, are accompanied by vivid flashes of lightning and awesome thunderclaps, all of which, as we shall later see, had their place in the religious beliefs of the Southeastern Indians. A good description of one of these summer storms comes to us from William Bartram. He describes a storm that came up as he was traveling on horseback in what is now northeastern Georgia, near the present town of Clayton.

> It was now after noon; I approached a charming vale, amidst sublimely high forests, awful shades! darkness gathers around, far distant thunder rolls over the trembling hills; the black clouds with august majesty and power, moves slowly forwards, shading regions of towering hills, and threatening all the destructions of a thunder storm; all around is now still as death, not a whisper is heard, but a total inactivity and silence seems to pervade the earth; the birds afraid to utter a chirrup, and in low tremulous voices take leave of each other, seeking covert and safety; every insect is silenced, and nothing heard but the roaring of the approaching [storm]; the mighty cloud now expands its sable wings, extending from North to South, and is driven irresistibly on by the tumultuous winds, spreading its livid wings around the gloomy concave, armed with terrors of thunder and fiery shafts of lightning; now the lofty forests bend low beneath its fury, their limbs and wavy boughs are tossed about and catch hold of each other; the mountains tremble and seem to reel about, and the ancient hills to be shaken to their foundations: the furious storm sweeps along, smoking through the vale and over the resounding hills; the face of the earth is obscured by the deluge descending from the firmament, and I am deafened by the din of thunder; the tempestuous scene damps my spirits, and my horse sinks under me at the tremendous peals, as I hasten on for the plain.[41]

Bartram's language is too extravagantly romantic for modern tastes, but he does succeed in describing a feeling for weather that few of us can today appreciate. Our technology has insulated us from the weather. Our houses and buildings protect us from it, and we usually travel in vehicles which also protect us. Only people who are frequently exposed to the weather and its effects—such as hunters, fishermen, backpackers, gardeners, bird watchers, and cyclists— can appreciate something of the Indians' regard for weather.

It should be clear that these three regions of the Southeast are here defined primarily according to criteria used by modern geographers. The differences we have observed among and within the three regions were probably important to the Southeastern Indians, but they need not have coincided in any simple way with the categories and concepts with which they conceptualized their natural surroundings. The aspects of the natural world which interested the Southeastern Indians were no doubt different from those which interest us. Perhaps in the future, through additional historical, ecological, and archaeological research, we may come to have a more accurate appreciation of the natural regions of the Southeast as the Indians themselves conceived of them.

LANGUAGES

Many languages were spoken by the Indians of the aboriginal Southeast. In fact, linguistic diversity in the Southeast was comparable to that in the California-Oregon and Northwest Coast area, the most linguistically diverse area in North America.[42] Some of the languages spoken in the Southeast were closely related to each other, some of them as closely as English is to German, so that a person speaking one of the languages could easily learn the other and in so doing discover many similarities between them. Other languages in the Southeast were more distantly related to each other but were still in the same language family, as, for example, English and Russian are in the same language family. Still other languages belonged to different language families, and they were as different from each other as English is different from Japanese.

Quite a few of the languages that were once spoken in the Southeast are now extinct. For some of these—such as the languages spoken by the Avoyels, Taensas, Koroas, Grigras, Tious, Yamasees,

Ais, Tequestas, Calusas, and many, many others—we have no record at all.[43] For others, such as Timucua, we have record of only a small number of words or a few pages of text; too little, in fact, to allow us to relate them to other languages with confidence. Still other languages, such as Catawba, are more fully documented, but one wishes that more had been learned about them before they became extinct.

Most of the adequately documented languages of the Southeast can be classified into five language families: Algonkian, Muskogean, Iroquoian, Siouan, and Caddoan. The Algonkian family includes languages spoken over a vast area of the central and northeastern parts of the United States, along the northern Atlantic Coast, and far into central Canada, including such languages as Cree, Menominee, Fox, Delaware, and Penobscot. One language of the Algonkian family, Shawnee, was present in the Southeast proper, but unfortunately the role of the Shawnees in the Southeast is not as clear as one would wish. Also speaking Algonkian languages were the Powhatans and Pamlicos of Virginia, who were marginal to the Southeast; but other Algonkian-speakers may have lived further south along the Carolina coast.

The Muskogean family, on the other hand, was the most important language family in the Southeast. Once spoken in Louisiana, Mississippi, Alabama, Georgia, and adjacent areas, it includes five closely related groups of languages: Choctaw-Chickasaw, Apalachee, Alabama-Koasati, Mikasuki-Hitchiti, and Muskogee-Seminole. Some of these languages, such as Muskogee (Creek), are today spoken by several thousand people, while others, such as Alabama-Koasati, are spoken by only a few hundred people. Still others are extinct. In addition we know of four language isolates—Tunica, Natchez, Atakapa, and Chitimacha—that are remotely related to the Muskogean family. All four of them are extinct or nearly so. Many place-names in Alabama, such as Tuscaloosa, Tuskegee, and Talladega, are derived from Muskogean words. The word *Alabama* itself is, of course, Muskogean. Also, many names of rivers in Alabama and Georgia are derived from Muskogean words, including Tombigbee, Coosa, Tallapoosa, Chattahoochee, and Ocmulgee.

In its number of contemporary speakers the Iroquoian family is second in importance to the Muskogean family, though it may not have been so in the late prehistoric period. It includes Cherokee, which in historic times had several closely related dialects with thousands of speakers, and Tuscarora, which was once spoken by a much smaller number of people in the coastal plain of North Carolina. Many place-names in Tennessee and Georgia are derived from Cherokee words. Examples are Chilhowee, Conasauga, Chickamauga, Tellico—all in Tennessee—and the word *Tennessee* itself; in Georgia we have Kennesaw, Coosawatee, Hiawassee, Tallulah, Toccoa, and Dahlonega, to name just a few.

The Siouan language family embraces an extensive series of languages that were spoken in historic times in the plains. More pertinent here is a group of closely related Siouan languages—Osage, Omaha, Ponca, Quapaw, and Kansa, the Dhegiha languages—which were spoken on the western fringe of the Southeastern Culture Area. At the time of European contact, the speakers of these languages were more in the Southeastern sphere of influence than they were later, after they acquired the horse and took up life on the plains. Languages in the Southeast which were definitely Siouan were Tutelo, Biloxi, and Ofo. Two language isolates, Yuchi and Catawba, clearly belong in the Southeast, but their linguistic status is not altogether clear. Many linguists have concluded that Catawba is more closely related to Siouan than to any other language family, and some linguists have concluded that it is Siouan. Yuchi appears to be distantly related to Siouan.

The Caddoan languages were spoken in the southwestern fringe of the Southeast.[44] The Caddoan family is composed of four major languages: Caddo, Pawnee, Wichita, and Kitsai. The Caddo language itself was spoken by basically Southeastern people who lived in Louisiana and Arkansas. In the past Caddo consisted of several dialects, though they were probably all mutually intelligible. The other Caddoan languages—Pawnee, Wichita, and Kitsai—were spoken by people whose cultures were similar to the Indians of the eastern plains. Caddo is the most divergent of all the Caddoan languages, perhaps because the Caddos were so much in the Southeastern sphere of influence.

In addition to their mother tongues, some Southeastern Indians also used a lingua franca called the Mobilian trade jargon or the Chickasaw trade jargon. This was used as a means of communication by the speakers of different Indian languages, and it was also used in historic times as a means of communication between Indians, on the one hand, and white and black speakers of European languages on the other. This jargon was formed by using words mainly from Choctaw (perhaps from the Chickasaw dialect) along with a few words from Alabama or Koasati. Like most other jargons it used a simplified grammar. The time when the Mobilian trade jargon first came into use is not known. Perhaps it dates back to prehistoric times, or perhaps it was devised during the days of early European exploration and trade.[45]

One further linguistic development by Southeastern Indians must be mentioned, namely Sequoyah's invention of a syllabary for writing Cherokee. Judging from how rarely systems of writing have been invented in the history of mankind, this was truly a remarkable achievement. Sequoyah, who spoke no English, worked on his syllabary for several years before finally perfecting it in 1819. He used a few letters from the Roman alphabet, and perhaps a few from Greek and possibly from the Fraktur alphabet of the Moravian missionaries, but the linguistic values he assigned to them were his own. He initially used eighty-six symbols, but later abandoned one of them to make a total of eighty-five symbols: one symbol represents the English *s* sound, six symbols represent vowel sounds, and the rest of them represent various combinations of consonants and vowels (fig. 2). For example, Sequoyah signed his own name:

Literally, this has the value *s–si–gwo–ya*.

With great wisdom, Sequoyah realized that one of the most important advantages of the whites over the Indians was their ability to put their words down on paper. He poured all of his energy into inventing this system of writing. He let his farm go to waste, neglected his family, and began to be seen as a deviant in the eyes of his own people. So aberrant was his behavior in accordance with conventional Cherokee standards, he was eventually tried for the crime of witchcraft. But in 1819 he exonerated himself by proving before a group of Cherokee elders that any speaker of Cherokee could quickly learn to read and write the language using his syllabary. Within a few years thousands of Cherokees became literate. With

CHEROKEE ALPHABET.

CHARACTERS SYSTEMATICALLY ARRANGED WITH THE SOUNDS.

D a	R e	T i	♃ o	Ⴍ u	ᴑ v
ⴹ ga ꝏ ka	Ⱶ ge	Ᵹ gi	A go	J gu	E gv
ⴽ ha	ꝓ he	ⱥ hi	Ⱶ ho	Γ hu	ⴗ hv
W la	♂ le	ℓ li	G lo	M lu	ⴺ lv
ⴏ ma	ꝺ me	H mi	♅ mo	ⴘ mu	
θ na ꞇ hna ɢ nah	ⴉ ne	ɦ ni	Z no	ⴅ nu	ᴖ nv
ⴚ qua	ⴝ que	ⴃ qui	ⵣ quo	ⴝ quu	ꜱ quv
ꞷ s ꝟ sa	ⴄ se	ᵬ si	ⴲ so	ꝑ su	R sv
Ⴑ da W ta	ꙅ de ⴲ te	ⴊ di ⴊ ti	V to	ꙅ du	ꝯ dv
ⴼ dla ⴋ tla	L tle	C tli	ⴝ tlo	ⴐ tlu	P tlv
G tsa	ꝟ tse	Ⱶ tsi	K tso	J tsu	ꜿ tsv
Ꝯ wa	ꙍ we	θ wi	ꙍ wo	Ᵹ wu	6 wv
ꙍ ya	ꝓ ye	ⴺ yi	ꝑ yo	Ᏻ yu·	B yv

SOUNDS REPRESENTED BY VOWELS.

a   as *a* in *father,* or short as *a* in *rival,*
e   as *a* in *hate,* or short as *e* in *met,*
i   as *i* in *pique,* or short as *i* in *pin,*
o   as *o* in *note,* but as approaching to *aw* in *law,*
u   as *oo* in *moon,* or short as *u* in *pull,*
v   as *u* in *but,* nasalized.

CONSONANT SOUNDS.

g is sounded hard, approaching to k; sometimes before e, i, o, u and v, its sound is k. d has a sound between the English d and t; sometimes, before o, u and v, its sound is t, when written before l and s the same analogy prevails. All other letters as in English.

Syllables beginning with g, except ga, have sometimes the power of k; syllables written with tl, except tla, sometimes vary to dl.

Figure 2. Sequoyah's syllabary. Courtesy, University of Georgia Libraries.

some help from outside, the Cherokees established a press in 1828 and began publishing their own newspaper, *The Cherokee Phoenix,* in English and Cherokee. Between 1828 and 1835 they published portions of the Bible translated into Cherokee, the laws passed by their council, political pamphlets, a hymnbook, and other documents.[46] This was the syllabary used by Swimmer and other Cherokee wise men to write down their religious formulas (fig. 3). Clearly, the Cherokees had the beginnings of a sacred literature.

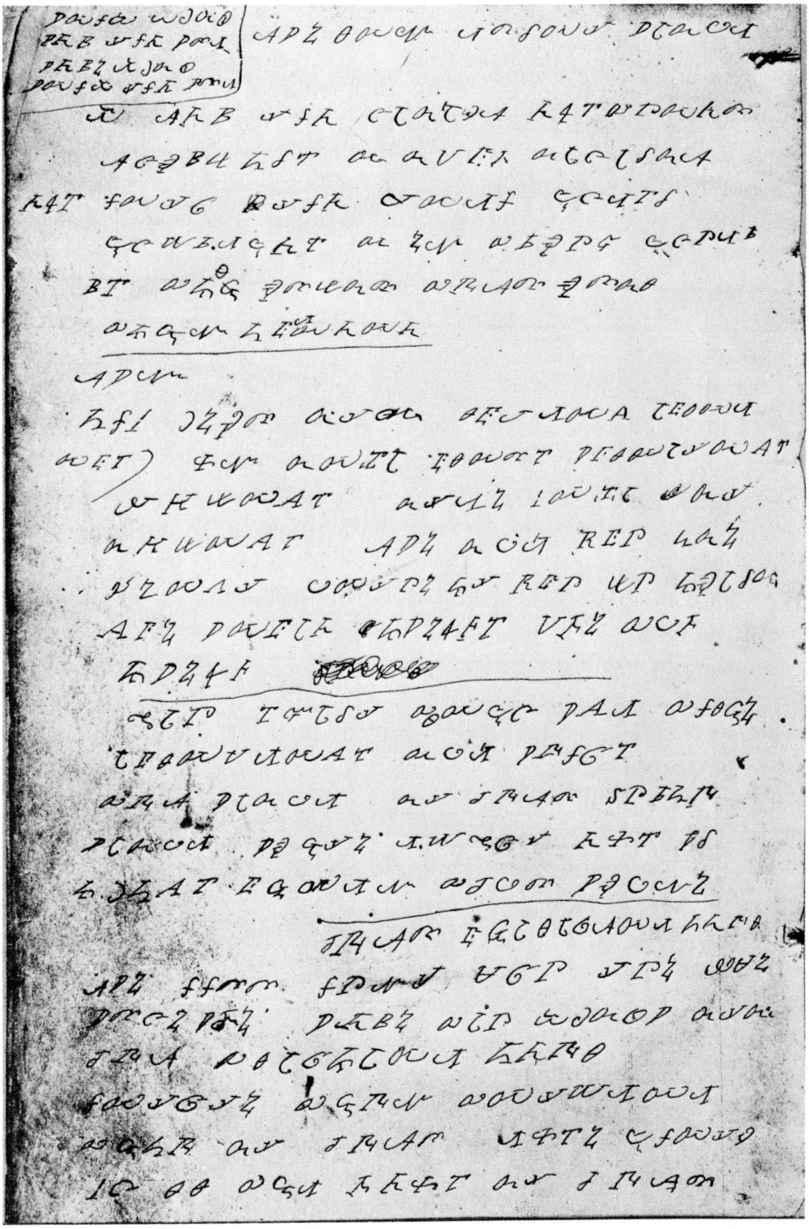

Figure 3. A page from the notebook of Gahuni, a Cherokee medicine man. He died around 1858. An English translation of this formula for treating arthritis may be seen in James Mooney's "Sacred Formulas of the Cherokees," pp. 349–51. Negative no. 998–b–1. Courtesy, Smithsonian Institution, National Anthropological Archives.

THE INDIANS AND THEIR ANCESTORS

For reasons that are not well understood, archaeologists have been able to unearth very few finds of old skeletal remains in the New World. None of those which have been found are much older than about 10,000 B.C., and none of them are significantly different from living Indian populations.[47] However, although truly old skeletal remains are lacking, we shall see in the following chapter that archaeologists have discovered what are taken to be tools that may indicate that man first came to the New World as long ago as 30,000 or 40,000 B.C.

We usually think of the native peoples of North and South America as a single racial stock, and with some justification. They are, in fact, an unusually homogenous population, and this assumption is consistent with the recency with which they entered the New World and their subsequent isolation from genes in the Old World. But small differences do exist among the Indians, and some of these were observed by the very first European observers. For example, in 1524, Giovanni da Verrazzano describes the Indians of the Atlantic Coast, from the South Carolina–North Carolina boundary northward, as being " . . . rather broad in the face: but not all, for we saw many with angular faces."[48] Some of these differences undoubtedly arose as a result of random change and natural selection after they came to the New World. However, some anthropologists feel that there are too many differences among the Indians to be wholly accounted for in this way. They argue that there must have been more than one migration of people to the New World, and these migrations may have consisted of people who belonged to significantly different populations.

Until fairly recently it was thought that the American Indians were a variety of Asiatic Mongoloids. We shall see in the next chapter that there is little doubt that American Indians are descended from men who came over from Asia; and, in fact, the Eskimos, who were the last people to come over from Asia, do bear a strong resemblance to Asiatic Mongoloids. The same is true of the Athapaskan-speaking Indians of interior Alaska, western Canada, and a small portion of the Southwestern United States; but they, too, are relatively recent arrivals. In other places, including the Southeast, American Indians do not resemble modern Asiatic Mongoloids very strongly. This difference is understandable, however, in view of generally accepted evidence that the Asiatic Mongoloids did not emerge as a racial type until relatively late times. Thus the first people who came to the New World were of a racial stock that was either ancestral to the Asiatic Mongoloids or that coexisted with the stock which was ancestral to them.

The skeletons uncovered by archaeologists in the Southeast can be classified into two varieties, an earlier "Iswanid" type and a later "Walcolid" type.[49] Both of these types are thought to have evolved from the racial stock of the earlier migrants. The Iswanid type had a relatively long, narrow cranium, and the skull and other features were rather small. Many have been recovered from early prehistoric sites, such as Indian Knoll in Kentucky and Eva in Tennessee. Since all of the old human remains in the New World are long-headed, it is probable that the Iswanid type in the Southeast is genetically descended from the earliest inhabitants. In contrast, the Walcolid type had a round, broad cranium, large in size, with a smaller nose and a rather large, rugged face. These Walcolid types occurred in late prehistoric times. Apparently, this Walcolid type is not a new migration from Asia, but rather a form that gradually evolved out of the earlier long-headed type. The skeletons that archaeologists have recovered from historic sites on the Virginia coast and adjacent areas and from the piedmont of North Carolina are generally Iswanid, while those from sites further south and west are generally Walcolid. There are, however, many exceptions. At the late prehistoric site at Moundville, Alabama, most of the skulls were round-headed, while a minority were long-headed.[50]

Early European observers in the Southeast often remarked on the large size of male Indians. They described them as being frequently over six feet tall and seldom below five feet eight or ten inches. This was quite large by European standards of the time because Europeans then were smaller than they are today. On the other hand, several observers commented on the small stature of Creek women, who were said seldom to exceed five feet. James Adair noted that the Chickasaws were much taller than the Choctaws, a surprising difference in light of the fact that they lived near each other, were culturally similar, and spoke mutually intelligible languages. William Bartram, writing in the late eighteenth century, described the Cherokees as being the tallest of all, and as having skin of a lighter color than the Creeks. The skin color of the Southeastern Indians was described in colors that ranged from olive to dark-copper. The fact is that the Indians are not heavily pigmented, but they have the capacity to tan darkly with exposure to sunlight, and this undoubtedly explains why the Cherokees in their cloudy country were lighter in color than the Creeks in sunny Alabama and Georgia. The hair of the Southeastern Indians was straight and black or dark brown, and their noses were often aquiline.

In addition to admiring the large size of the Indians, early Europeans often admired the physical development and endurance of the men. Their limbs were well proportioned, and their legs were particularly strongly developed. Clay McCauley, writing in the latter part of the nineteenth century, tells of an eleven-year-old Seminole boy who went out hunting, killed a deer which dressed down to fifty pounds, and carried gun, equipment, and deer several miles back to camp. Europeans were also impressed with the Indians' bearing: they stood straight, walked with dignity and confidence, and possessed a good sense of balance.

Like people everywhere, the Southeastern Indians tried to improve on nature. The men in particular were fond of painting designs on their bodies and faces (see fig. 62), and both sexes made extensive use of body tattooing (see figs. 48, 56, 73, 79). This was especially practiced by Creek and Cherokee warriors, who tattooed on their bodies the figures of scrolls, flowers, animals, stars, crescents, and the sun, with the latter usually placed in the center of their chests. The serpent was frequently used as a design. The Creek chiefs, in particular, were elaborately tattooed with well-executed designs around their legs, arms, and body, dividing them into zones (see fig. 27). Along the lower Mississippi River tattooing was not only an ornament but a mark of distinction or social standing. Some of the Indians made tattoos by pricking the flesh with garfish teeth dipped in soot from pitch pine, thus imparting a black or dark-blue color. They used the mineral cinnabar (mercuric sulphide) for red designs. In some places tattooing was done with five or six needles tied to a small piece of wood in such a way that all the points were aligned like the teeth of a comb; the design was first traced on the body in charcoal, then the pigment pricked in with this instrument. In the recent past the Southeastern Indians used an instrument like this not to tattoo, but to administer ritual scratching before participation

30

in important events like the ball game, as described in chapter 7 (see fig. 98).[51]

For Europeans the most striking way in which Indians modified their bodies was by artificially flattening their heads. They did this by binding their infants to cradle boards made of wood or basketry in such a way that they were perfectly immobile. A child was bound to his cradle board until he was about one year old, though he spent more and more time free each day until at last he was left off the cradle board altogether. The head of the infant was flattened by binding it back against the cradle board (fig. 4).[52] This practice flattened both the back of the skull and the forehead, making it slope backward and, in John Lawson's words, making "the Eyes stand a prodigious Way asunder, and the Hair hang over the Forehead like the Eaves of a House, which seems very frightful."[53] Some of the Indians explained the custom by saying that they believed it improved eyesight, making a man a better hunter (fig. 5). Others did it because they thought it looked handsome. They contemptuously referred to Europeans as "long heads." This artificial head-shaping was so extensively practiced in the late prehistoric period that it has been argued that it was this rather than biology that produced the "Walcolid" physical type.[54] If so, then these round-headed individuals were simply Iswanids whose heads had been culturally modified.

This custom of head-flattening strikes us as bizarre, even disgusting, confirming perhaps for some the expectation that savages, after all, are savages. But is this really so different from our use of orthodontics? Do we not send our children to practitioners who sometimes pull out perfectly healthy teeth to make room for the others, binding them all in outlandish metal and rubber contraptions, inflicting considerable discomfort and even pain, all for the purpose of producing unnaturally straight teeth?

After the Southeast was invaded by whites from Europe who also brought in blacks from Africa, genetic admixture with Indians began, and it continues today (see figs. 62, 110). According to one study, present-day Cherokees show a substantial genetic mixture with whites, and present-day Catawbas show about 50 percent white admixture. In contrast, the Seminoles of Florida are predominantly Indian, with some individuals having small amounts of white and

31

Figure 4. Baked clay effigy of an infant on a cradle board. Recovered from a Mississippian stone box grave near Nashville, Tennessee. The infant's skull shows frontal cranial deformation. Courtesy, Thruston Collection, Vanderbilt University.

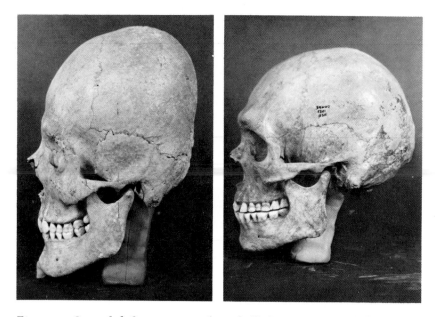

Figure 5. Cranial deformation. *Left:* a skull showing occipital flattening, from a Mississippian stone box grave near Nashville. *Right:* a normal Indian skull from a late-eighteenth-century site in Walworth County, South Dakota. Courtesy, Dr. William M. Bass, Department of Anthropology, University of Tennessee.

black admixture. Indian genes also show up in many of the unusual "racial isolates" or "little races" of the Southeast, groups like the Brass Ankles, the Haliwas, and the Melungeons.[55]

CHAPTER TWO

PREHISTORY

AND EARLY HISTORY

Our earliest information on man in the Southeast comes from the archaeologists. Because the prehistoric people of the Southeast lacked writing, we can never know much about such intangible parts of their culture as the languages they spoke, the way they reckoned kinship, or the deities they believed in. But by digging into the earth and recovering their material remains—the traces of their houses, their tools, and especially the remains of their garbage—archaeologists can make careful inferences and tell us much about the way they obtained their food, something about how they lived, and especially how their cultures developed and changed through several millennia of prehistory. In some cases, particularly in the late prehistoric period, archaeologists can even tell us something about the ideology or world view of the Southeastern Indians.

In the Southeast, archaeologists have not only had the difficult task of reconstructing the prehistory of the Southeastern Indians and their ancestors, they have also had to correct some extremely persistent myths about the prehistory of the Southeast. The landscape of the Southeast is dotted with many large mounds and earthworks. Although Hernando de Soto and a few other Europeans in the Southeast at an early date observed the Indians using these mounds, subsequently these observations were more or less forgotten, and when the mounds were rediscovered in the popular press in the early nineteenth century, the authorities of the day attempted to explain where they came from. Few people believed that they could have been built by the ancestors of the Indians who still lived in the Southeast at that time. Some of the mounds are truly enormous in size, and almost everybody assumed that Indians were lazy by nature. By around 1830 the most widely accepted interpretation was that the mounds had been built by a more or less civilized race of "Mound Builders" who had come to the Southeast from elsewhere. According to different theories, these Mound Builders were immigrant "Tyrian Phoenicians, Assyrians, ancient Egyptians, Canaanites, Israelites, Trojans, Romans, Etruscans, Greeks, Scythians, Tartars, Chinese Buddhists, Hindus, Mandingoes or other Africans, Madagascans, the early Irish, Welsh, Norsemen, Basques, Portuguese, French, Spaniards, Huns, or survivors of the Lost Continents of Mu or Atlantis, the last a uniquely difficult theory to debate, since their alleged great civilizations conveniently sank beneath the ocean some eleven thousand or more years ago, with Plato possibly the earliest authority we have for their existence."[1] In several of the theories the Mound Builders are said to have lived by tilling the soil until they were killed off by the Indians, who were said to be a horde of savages who subsisted mainly by hunting and gathering wild foods.[2]

The reasons why these Mound Builder theories became so popular are not entirely clear, but they obviously fulfilled some need in nineteenth-century American thought. The **Mound** Builder theme was taken up by poets of the day, and also by novelists and pseudo-scientists who created around the Mound Builders an early form of science fiction. The details of the Mound Builder theories were argued by learned scholars and by clergymen. It has been suggested that one reason why the Mound Builder theories became so popular was that they could be used as a justification for the way the Southeastern Indians were treated in the early decades of the nineteenth century. "Removing" them and seizing their lands seemed less unjust when viewed against the story of their having done the same thing to the Mound Builders.[3] The Mound Builder myth began to decline in the late nineteenth and early twentieth centuries, when scientific archaeology began. But it is not dead even today; it still lives in science fiction, and in recent years yet another attempt has been made to prove that the Southeastern Indians are descended at least in part from Mediterranean people who sailed across the Atlantic in the second millennium B.C.[4] The archaeologist has a most difficult time combating such spectacular and curiously popular theories, no matter how ill-founded they actually are.

Even though the archaeologist can tell us a surprising amount about the past, he can rarely describe known societies with definite names. Extracting his information from particular "sites" (maps 3 and 4)—the physical remains of campsites, villages, ceremonial centers, and so on—the archaeologist usually talks in terms of general cultural forms or patterns. Thus the archaeologist is not so much interested in particular artifacts as he is in "types" of artifacts, including such diverse things as the shapes in which javelin points were made, the floor plans of houses, and patterns of religious symbolism. When the archaeologist can describe several of these types and prove that they are associated with each other, he can speak in terms of cultures and phases, and these can be lumped into a "tradition"—a general cultural pattern which endured for some time in a particular location. In the Southeast, archaeologists distinguish four traditions: Paleo-Indian, Archaic, Woodland, and Mississippian.[5] These traditions followed each other through time, though earlier ones lingered on in marginal places as new ones took shape elsewhere.

THE FIRST MEN IN THE NEW WORLD

No remains of extinct forms of men (like *Homo sapiens neandertalensis*) have been found in the New World, nor is there much expectation that any will ever be found, although it is not prudent to rule out this possibility altogether. However, the evidence we now have indicates that all of the fundamental biological and cultural events in human evolution occurred in the Old World. By about 30,000 years ago every part of the Old World was peopled by races of men who were physically similar to races of men living today. Culturally, they were Upper Paleolithic, using a variety of specialized, well-made stone and bone tools, and subsisting by hunting large animals, many of which are now extinct. Consistent with this evidence is the fact that all of the earliest skeletal remains that have been discovered in the New World are similar to living races of men.

The first men in the New World came out of Siberia and across the Bering Strait land bridge into Alaska during the Pleistocene geological period—the Ice Age. The Pleistocene period lasted about two million years, and during this time the ice advanced and retreated at least four times. Each time the ice advanced, glaciers moved down from the northern and mountainous regions of North America, temperatures fell, and in some places precipitation increased, so that areas which had been deserts became covered with swamps and lush meadows of grass. At the same time, because of the huge quantities of water locked in the glaciers, the sea level fell and the Bering Strait land bridge became exposed, forming an avenue as much as 1,300 miles wide connecting Siberia and Alaska. When the glaciers retreated, the water was again released, the Bering Strait land bridge was slowly inundated, and the swamps reverted back to deserts and dry plains.

The last advance of the ice began about 70,000 years ago and lasted until about 10,000 years ago, when climatic conditions similar to those prevailing today began to occur. Man first came to North America during this last advance of the ice. During this 60,000-year period the temperature warmed and cooled several times, fluctuating, with the glaciers advancing and retreating, and with the sea level rising and falling. It is known that the Bering Strait land bridge was exposed at least twice during this last glacial period: it was exposed between 50,000 years ago and 40,000 years ago and again between 28,000 and 10,000 years ago. During the first of these land bridges the weather was only moderately cold, but the land bridge was narrow; during the second exposure of the land bridge the weather was colder, but the land bridge was wider.

Archaeologists have established beyond a reasonable doubt that men were widespread in the Americas in the latter years of this second land bridge; there is some evidence that they were present during the early years of the second land bridge, and that they could have traveled from Alaska to North America through an ice-free corridor.[6] More recently the archaeologists are turning up indications that men *may* also have come to North America across the first land bridge—that is, around 50,000 to 40,000 years ago. The evidence for this first migration is a series of what appear to be crude tools—flakes, scrapers, and pebble-choppers—that were presumably formed by striking and flaking stone. None of these tools appear to have been hafted to a handle or shaft, hence they have come to be known as the "pre-projectile point complex." These objects have been found in several places in North America and South America, but unfortunately they have been found mainly on the surface of the ground, making it difficult for archaeologists to determine how old they are. A number of these stone objects—the "Lively complex"

—have been found on the surface of the ground in northern Alabama.[7] In a few places they have been found in the same general vicinity as the bones of animals which lived in the Pleistocene period.

Some of the best evidence uncovered so far on the extreme antiquity of man in the New World has come from Flea Cave in highland Peru. At the deepest level of this cave archaeologists have found a series of crude stone sidescrapers, choppers, cleavers, and spokeshave scrapers which have been carbon–14 dated to about 20,000 years ago. Above this level archaeologists have found several distinct tool complexes along with the bones of extinct animals such as *Megatherium*, a large, ground-dwelling sloth. What this discovery may mean is that if men were in Peru 20,000 years ago, they must have been in North America at an earlier date. These tools are similar to those found in China and Siberia at an earlier date.[8]

The most intriguing "pre-projectile" find so far in North America is the Calico site in San Bernardino County, California. This site, found under a deep overburden of sand and gravel, contains stone objects which some have interpreted as a hearth, hammerstones, stone flakes with edges which were apparently worked, and pieces of "exotic" jasper, agate, and quartz which originated at some distance from the Calico site.

But the site is controversial. For one thing, geological estimates of its antiquity range from 30,000 to as much as 500,000 years ago— immensely older than any other prehistoric site in the New World. More important, all of the flaking and chipping of the pieces of stone could have been produced by ordinary geological processes—the action of wind, water, gravity, lightning, and so on. The "hearth" could also have been produced by natural forces, and so too the presence of the seemingly "exotic" jasper, agate, and quartz. The stone objects exhibit a continuous transition between what some consider to be artifacts, to probable artifacts, to possible artifacts, to non-artifacts. This is precisely the kind of variation natural causes would have produced.[9] The Calico site, and indeed the argument for the extreme antiquity of man in the New World, must be regarded as hypothetical until more conclusive evidence is found.

THE PALEO-INDIAN TRADITION

If the evidence for man's presence in the New World at a very early date is not yet convincing, the evidence for man's presence in North America at 11,000 to 11,500 years ago is overwhelming. Evidence from many archaeological sites indicate that North America was populated at this time by people whom we call Paleo-Indians, people whose culture was reminiscent of Old World Upper Paleolithic cultures which had spread across central Asia all the way to Japan by 15,000 years ago. One of the questions archaeologists ask is whether the skillfully made lance-shaped spear points used by the Paleo-Indians were invented in North America or whether the technology was brought here from the Old World. All of these points are bifacial—shaped on both sides—and many of them are "fluted," with shallow grooves chipped along their lower faces. Many archaeologists now feel that they were an indigenous New World development, but that some of their features may have come from the Old World.[10] For example, some spear points at the Upper Paleolithic site at Kostyenki in the western U.S.S.R. have thinned, concave bases with some fluting like those on the lance-shaped points of the New World.

The Paleo-Indians lived in the grassy and swampy plains of North America at the close of the Pleistocene period. Much of their livelihood was gained from the specialized hunting of such large animals as the mammoth, camel, horse, and an archaic form of bison (*Bison antiquus*), all of which are now extinct. The earliest example of the lance-shaped points used by the Paleo-Indians is the Clovis point, widely found east of the Rocky Mountains (see fig. 7). This is a large point with grooves running from the base up one-half or less the length of the point. The edges on both sides near the base of the point were purposefully dulled, probably to keep them from cutting through the bindings with which they were attached to the spear shaft. In fact, it now appears that Clovis points were hafted to a bone foreshaft (fig. 6). At the Anzik site in southwestern Montana archaeologists discovered several fluted points along with slender shafts made of mammal bone. The ends of these foreshafts are beveled and inscribed with cross hatching. A black material, probably resin, still adheres to some of the foreshafts, suggesting that the points were both bound and glued to them. These foreshafts were probably set into a socketed wooden spear handle, so that it could be thrust into an animal and then pulled free, leaving the foreshaft imbedded in the animal's flesh. Each hunter probably carried sev-

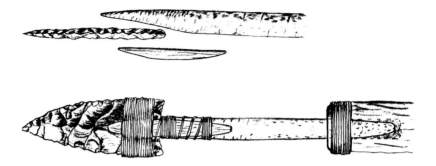

Figure 6. Clovis point and bone foreshaft. The socket in the wooden spear shaft is conjectural. *Science*, vol. 186 (11 October 1974), p. 149, fig. 3A. Copyright 1974 by the American Association for the Advancement of Science. Courtesy, Robson Bonnichsen and *Science*.

eral of these foreshafts along with a single spear handle, so that the handle could be repeatedly armed and thrust into an animal. The foreshafts, with their sharp stone blades, may have also been used as knives in butchering the animal.[11]

The Paleo-Indians either threw their spears at the animals or thrust them in at close range. Probably it was the latter, for the skill of most simple hunting people lies not in hitting the animal from a distance, but in getting so close to the animal that they cannot miss. A favorite strategy of most people of simple technology who hunt large game animals is to wound the animal and then follow and harass it until it wearies to the point that they can get close enough to kill it. One technique for wounding a large animal was to creep up on it while it was drinking water. Ambush seems to have been the principal Paleo-Indian means of attack. They very often set up their camps on ridges or slopes of hills overlooking watering spots, thus allowing them to keep these places under constant surveillance. They apparently made little use of caves or rock shelters. Other camp sites were located near natural traps, such as cliffs or box canyons.[12]

Another effective big-game hunting technique of the later Paleo-Indians was to stampede a herd of animals over a precipice or into a gully to their deaths. A Paleo-Indian site in Colorado gives us an amazingly complete picture of one such kill which took place around 6,500 B.C., just at the end of the Paleo-Indian tradition. Archaeologists studied the arrangement and condition of the bison bones found at the site and were able to draw the following conclusions. It was in late May or early June when hunters from a band of perhaps 150 people crept up on a large herd of bison. They probably approached from the north, downwind from the herd, and their plan was to stampede the bison south into a gully which would lie across their path from east to west. The gully was at its deepest and widest part about 7 feet deep and 12 feet wide; the bison would be killed as they fell on top of one another, crushing and disabling all but the ones near the top. Some of the hunters formed east and probably west flanks near the gully to keep the bison from veering around the trap. The Indians were successful in their strategy, and about 200 bison were killed in the trap. The butchering took place on the spot, and the hunters seem to have followed very much the same procedure as was used by the Plains Indians in the historic past. Some of the tongues and probably some of the internal organs were eaten on the spot, and the rest of the meat was probably taken back to the camp to be consumed in the next couple of weeks or to be dried for future use. About 75 per cent of the kill was butchered. The band probably would not have had to kill more game for another month or more.[13]

There can be no doubt that the Paleo-Indians were good at hunting large animals. The mammoth, the horse, and the camel all disappeared from North America around 9,000 to 8,000 B.C. *Bison antiquus* survived for about one thousand years longer, when it too became extinct. It is possible that the Paleo-Indians played a role in the extinction of these large animals. In coming to the New World, the Paleo-Indians entered a vast hunter's paradise in which the animals had had no experience with men and hence had not had through the ages the chance to develop defensive behavioral adaptations against them. Also there were few ecological pressures to hold down the human population. Most important in this regard was the fact that the Paleo-Indians' long, cold trek through the Arctic had acted as a disease filter: most of the illnesses which afflicted men in the Old World were left behind. The Paleo-Indian population may have increased very rapidly, perhaps reaching saturation in 500 to 800 years, and they may have swept through the Americas in a kind of front, killing large numbers of Pleistocene animals along the way. It may have taken no more than one thousand years for them to reach the utmost southern tip of South America. As the population "front" moved through, smaller numbers of men would likely have been left behind to occupy niches throughout the American continents.[14]

In contrast to the rather detailed evidence on the Paleo-Indian way of life in the western United States, where erosion and sparse vegetation expose sites for easy discovery, the picture of the eastern United States is much less complete. Many thousands of Clovis points have been found in the east, particularly in an area that includes most of what is today Kentucky, Tennessee, and Ohio.[15] Unfortunately, almost all of these were found on the surface of the ground or in the beds of streams so that their dating remains in doubt. Also, in the Southeast no fluted points have been found in direct association with the bones of extinct animals. It has been established, however, that in the Southeast these fluted points are found in areas where mammoth bones are frequently found. Large lance-shaped points, some of which resemble Clovis points, have been found in better archaeological contexts in Pennsylvania, Massachusetts, and Virginia. In the later part of the Paleo-Indian period in the Southeast, the projectile points began to take on a new appearance as the flutes became less prominent and the bases became increasingly concave, often producing widely flaring ears. Examples are the Cumberland, Quad, and Dalton points (fig. 7). Although they have not been able to prove it, many archaeologists believe that all of these types of points were derived from the earlier Paleo-Indian points.

All of this talk about projectile points does not mean that these were the only kind of tools the Paleo-Indians possessed. It is just that these are the most easily recognizable tools both on the surface of the ground and at the kill sites, where the Paleo-Indians killed and butchered large animals. But at sites where the Paleo-Indians presumably lived, such as the Williamson site in Virginia, archaeologists have found a variety of tools, such as small scrapers, spokeshave scrapers, knives, and gravers. The Paleo-Indians also used bone to make tools, but bone does not survive the passage of time nearly as well as does stone.[16] It is almost certain, moreover, that these people that we characterize as hunters of big game had sources of food other than large animals. But here again it is a matter of preservation of the evidence, for the remains of smaller game and wild vegetable foods do not endure as well as the remains of larger

42

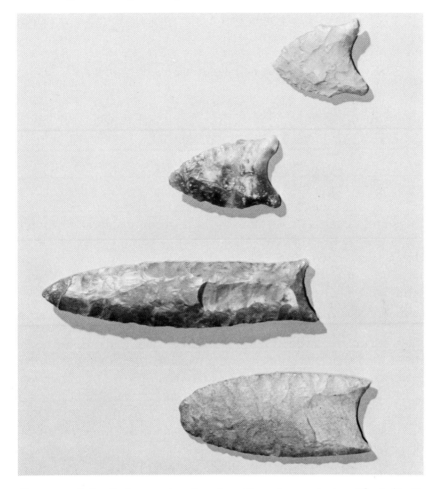

Figure 7. Paleo-Indian projectile points. *From bottom to top:* Clovis (6.56 cm. long); Cumberland; Quad; Dalton. Courtesy, Frank H. McClung Museum, University of Tennessee.

animals. It is possible, in fact, that the Paleo-Indians relied on small game and vegetable foods rather heavily.

Apart from the way they made their living, we know relatively little about the Paleo-Indians. But new facts are being discovered all the time. At the Anzik site, along with Clovis points and bone foreshafts, archaeologists unearthed the skeletal remains of two subadults. A large number of artifacts were interred with them, and

43

the bodies and the artifacts had been sprinkled with red ocher (hematite). The bone foreshafts show signs of having been intentionally broken before they were laid in the graves. We can infer from this that the Paleo-Indians had ritual means of coping with death, and that they may have had some notion of an afterlife. All of these burial customs—the use of red ocher, the interment of material objects with the corpse, and the intentional breaking of grave goods—existed in the Southeast throughout the prehistoric period.

THE ARCHAIC TRADITION

At the close of the Pleistocene period the ice receded and the large cold-adapted animals became extinct. As this happened the Paleo-Indian hunting tradition gradually declined. In its place, at around 8,000 B.C., a new tradition—the Archaic—began to take shape in the eastern United States.[17] Instead of a primary reliance on hunting large animals, the Archaic tradition was both diversified and efficient, being based on the gathering of vegetable foods, particularly acorns and hickory nuts, fishing, and the hunting and trapping of small woodland animals. People in the Archaic became increasingly sedentary, making their living in smaller and smaller territories, and they became increasingly efficient in exploiting all the food resources the environment had to offer. The Archaic tradition left its mark on all subsequent cultures in the Southeast.

The Archaic tradition was more complex than the Paleo-Indian tradition. Archaic projectile points were made in a wide variety of shapes, but frequently they had stemmed bases, notches for attachment to shafts, and barbs (fig. 8). Choppers and scrapers of chipped stone continued into the Archaic with relatively little change from Paleo-Indian contexts.[18] It was in the Archaic tradition that the Indians began making artifacts out of polished stone (fig. 9). Some of these artifacts were purely practical, such as milling stones for grinding seeds, stone adzes for working wood, gouges, and grooved axes; others were artistically pleasing as well as utilitarian, such as finely polished stone objects used as weights on weapons (see fig. 12); and late in the Archaic quite a few stone artifacts—like pendants, plummets, and beads—were purely for decoration, pleasure, or ritual. The variety of these polished stone tools and ornaments increased as time went on in the Archaic.[19]

The Archaic tradition eventually dominated a vast area of North

Figure 8. Archaic chipped stone artifacts. *Left:* chopper (11.6 cm. long). *Above center:* end scraper. *Upper right:* stemmed point, side-notched point. *Below center:* adze. *Lower right:* Eva type point. Courtesy, Frank H. McClung Museum, University of Tennessee.

America from the plains eastward to the Atlantic Coast, and from central Canada southward to the Gulf Coast. The Archaic does not seem to have been introduced by a new group of people coming from elsewhere. But the details of the origin and early development of the Archaic tradition are not altogether clear. Some archaeologists believe that the Archaic developed out of an early unspecialized hunting and gathering tradition. Other archaeologists believe that the Archaic developed gradually out of the Paleo-Indian tradition, pointing out that with the exception of the projectile points, many of the tools remained the same.[20] Archaeological evidence for the latter argument has been found in sites in Alabama, Florida, and North Carolina in which late Paleo-Indian artifacts have been found at the bottom of deeply stratified Archaic sites.[21] Russell Cave in Alabama, a site which has been preserved as a national park, is an

Figure 9. Archaic polished stone artifacts. *Left:* pestle (25.5 cm. long). *Upper row, left to right:* grooved axe; stone pendant; muller; nut stone. *Below:* mortar. Courtesy, Frank H. McClung Museum, University of Tennessee.

example of a habitation site that was favored by Indians through all the phases of Southeastern prehistory. In this large cave some materials related to late Paleo-Indian cultures have been found beneath a deep layer of Archaic materials. While Paleo-Indian sites are always thin, deep Archaic sites have been discovered in several caves and rock shelters, along rivers and streams, and along the old shores of lakes.

It should be understood that the change from Paleo-Indian to Archaic did not happen suddenly. Some evidence indicates that early Archaic people continued to hunt large animals where they could. And in the West particularly, some people persisted unchanged in the Paleo-Indian tradition after the Archaic tradition had begun.[22]

46

Eva, a shell and earth midden located on an old channel of the lower Tennessee River, is a particularly rich Archaic site.[23] Beginning around 5,000 B.C., this site was occupied for a period of several thousand years, although perhaps not continuously. The Archaic people hunted and gathered a wide variety of foods seasonally; this means that some of them moved from one site to another during the year, fishing and collecting shellfish in one place, collecting nuts in another, and hunting in still another. They made great use of freshwater mussels, and they caught fish using well-formed bone fishhooks (fig. 10). They also ate a variety of vegetable foods, such as berries, several kinds of nuts, and certain roots. The people used specialized tools to process their vegetable foods, including nutstones for cracking nuts, and mortars and pestles for grinding up seeds and other foods (see fig. 9).

The people who lived at the Eva site hunted a great many animals, including deer, elk, bear, fox, wolf, squirrel, raccoon, opossum, beaver, otter, turkey, and other birds. Of these, the deer was by far the most important food source; around 90 percent of all the mammal bones in the site were from deer. The deer was obviously the most important game animal, and it continued to be most important throughout the entirety of Southeastern prehistory. The Archaic people killed large animals with javelins or short spears ejected from spear-throwers. The spear-thrower is a wooden shaft about two feet long with a hook on one end. This hook, often carved out of deer antler, was placed behind the end of the spear so that both the spear and the spear-thrower were held in the throwing hand. When the spear was hurled, this spear-thrower effectively increased the length of the hunter's arm, greatly increasing the force with which the spear could be thrown (fig. 11). These spear-throwers frequently had weights ("bannerstones" and "boatstones") of finely polished stone attached to their shafts (fig. 12). The function of these weights is uncertain. They may have enhanced the velocity of the spears which were cast from them, or they may have made the spear-thrower suitable for secondary use as a war club. The darts, or spears, were tipped with rather large stone points with stemmed or notched bases. After the kill, game was dressed and cut up with large stone knives, and the hides were processed with scrapers and further worked with bone awls and needles. These awls and needles may

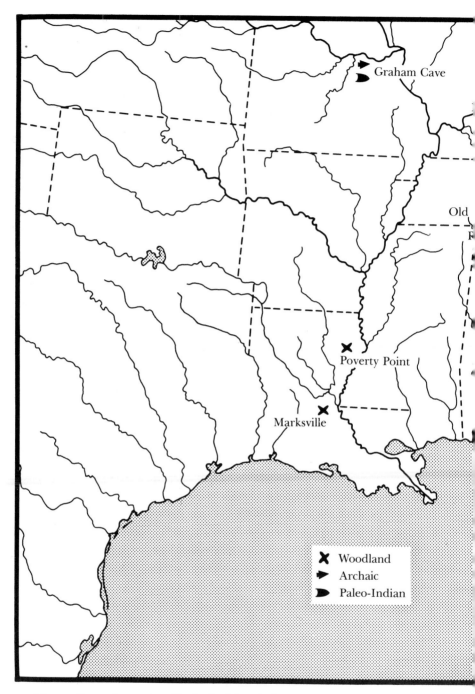

Map *3*. Some Important Early Prehistoric Sites.

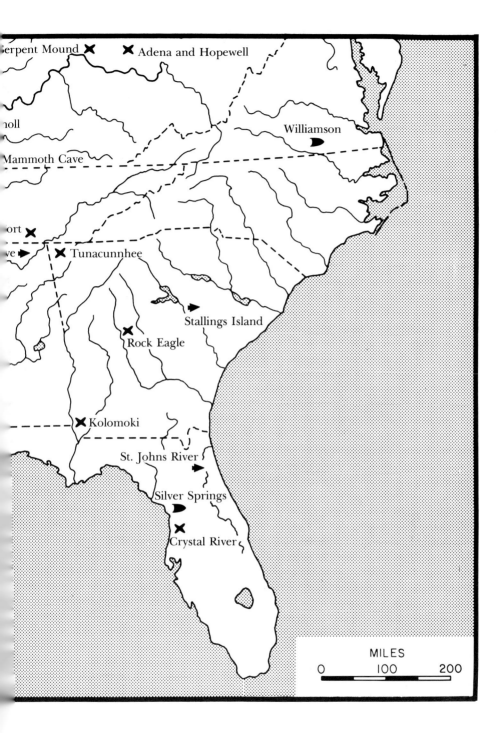

erpent Mound ✖   ✖ Adena and Hopewell

noll

Mammoth Cave

Williamson ➤

ort ✖

ve ➤   ✖ Tunacunnhee

Stallings Island ➤

✖
Rock Eagle

✖ Kolomoki

St. Johns River
➤

Silver Springs
➤
✖
Crystal River

MILES

0   100   200

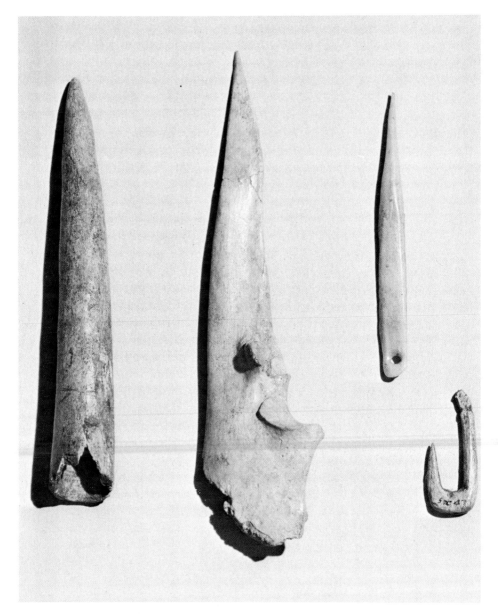

Figure 10. Archaic bone artifacts. *Left:* antler projectile point. *Center:* deer ulna awl. *Right:* needle, fishhook. Courtesy, Frank H. McClung Museum, University of Tennessee.

have been used to make basketry as well (see fig. 10).[24] The skeletons of rather large dogs—possibly hunting dogs—have also been discovered at the Eva site.

The Archaic people are thought to have exploited a definite territory, and they were therefore more closely tied to a particular area than the Paleo-Indians were. Because they adapted to local resources, regional differences developed and led to several distinct

Figure 11. Use of the spear thrower. Courtesy, *South Carolina Wildlife*.

Figure 12. Polished stone spear thrower weights. Courtesy, Frank H. McClung Museum, University of Tennessee.

cultural variations within the broad Archaic tradition. Some of these differences were important. For example, some of the earliest pottery in North America has been found at the important Archaic site of Stallings Island, located in the Savannah River near Augusta, Georgia. Like the Eva site, Stallings Island contains a shell midden of enormous size; it is about 500 feet wide, 1,500 feet long, and from 6 to 12 feet deep. At the lower levels archaeologists have found typical Archaic grooved axes, spear-thrower weights, mortars for grinding food, and projectile points, along with decorative bone pins, shell beads, and bone and stone pendants. But in the upper levels of the midden, they have found pottery dating to about 2,000 B.C. Subsequently, additional finds of the same sort of pottery turned up at sites along the lower Savannah River and on islands along the Georgia coast. The pottery is in the form of open bowls, with thick walls decorated with incised lines and punched indentations made by pressing a small pointed tool into the wet clay before firing. This is fiber-tempered pottery, which means that fibers from grass, roots, Spanish moss, and other materials were placed in the clay, and the clay was thereby strengthened for firing (fig. 13).

52

Archaeologists are not sure of the precise point of earliest occurrence of this fiber-tempered pottery. It could have been the Savannah River area, or it could have been the area of the St. Johns River in Florida.[25] The St. Johns River area was extraordinarily rich in the kinds of food preferred by the Archaic people, and they made good use of it. Extensive shell middens contain a full array of Archaic artifacts, including fiber-tempered pottery. The pottery of the St. Johns area was more elaborately decorated than the Stallings Island ware, with incised chevrons, diamonds, or squares on the outside of the bowls. Fiber-tempered pottery also shows up along the Tennessee River at a somewhat later date, where it was decorated with stamped designs of one kind or another.

The phase of the Archaic tradition that prevailed along the Savannah River area also reached somewhat further northward into the piedmont. In general, however, the Archaic people of the northern piedmont were more similar to people to the west and to the north of them than to those in the southern piedmont. Indeed, in the Archaic period people in the piedmont from South Carolina to southern New England were generally similar to each other. They used similar banana-shaped or prism-shaped spear-thrower weights, large stemmed or notched projectile points, and a semilunar knife. The technique of making fiber-tempered pottery never went very far northward in the piedmont. Instead, people in the northern piedmont continued making containers out of steatite or soapstone, a soft, easily worked mineral, long after the occurrence of pottery further south. From this time forward, people in the northern

Figure 13. Fiber-tempered potsherds. The irregular markings on the surfaces were caused by the fibers. Courtesy, Frank H. McClung Museum, University of Tennessee.

piedmont region remained somewhat distinct from people further south in the southern piedmont and coastal plain. When pottery did abruptly appear around A.D. 400 in the northern piedmont, it resembled pottery in the northeast. Until about A.D. 1500, new ideas from the Southeast were adopted slowly in the northern piedmont, if at all.[26]

To summarize, the Archaic tradition represents the successful adaptation of the people of the Southeast to the warmer weather and forest flora and fauna that marked the close of the Pleistocene. As the large animals disappeared, these people learned to make their living by using all that their environment had to offer: fish, fresh-water mussels, nuts, seeds, and a wide variety of woodland animals. In addition to these purely practical innovations, the Archaic people apparently invented the technique of polishing stone (see fig. 9). This technique was also used in Asia and in South America, but the Archaic people of the Southeast seem to have come up with it on their own. They did, of course, make practical implements out of polished stone, but the craftsmanship that went into some of the spear-thrower weights, for example, exceeded mere utility. In addition, they may also have invented fiber-tempered pottery independently.

The increasingly efficient hunting and gathering techniques which developed in the Archaic allowed the Indians time for other pursuits. A number of objects used for personal adornment were unearthed at the Eva site. In the early period these were beads made out of bird bones, perforated dog, bobcat, and bear canine teeth, and stone pendants. One burial had with it a necklace made from the vertebrae of a large rattlesnake strung together in place.

Tubular stone pipes which were presumably used for smoking show up in the later occupation of the Eva site (fig. 14). This does not, however, necessarily mean that they smoked tobacco in these pipes. The tobacco (*Nicotiana rustica* L.) used by the Southeastern Indians was native to the central Andes, and we do not know when it first reached the eastern United States. We do know that the Indians of the upper Great Lakes smoked twenty-seven different native plant substances, including shining willow bark (*Salix lucida* Muhl.), red willow bark (*Cornus amonmum* Mill.), smooth sumac leaves (*Rhus glabra* L.), staghorn sumac leaves (*Rhus typhina* L.), fragrant goldenrod flowers (*Solidago graminifolia* [L.] Salisb.), Philadelphia

Figure 14. Archaic tubular stone pipe. Courtesy, Frank H. McClung Museum, University of Tennessee.

fleabane flowers (*Erigeron philadelphicus* L.), and others. In historic times the Indians believed that many of these aroused the scent glands in does, and they were thus smoked by men who hunted deer.[27]

In the Archaic era, proper burial of the dead became an important matter. At the Eva site, adult corpses were bound in a tightly flexed position and placed in small pits, and they were probably wrapped in some kind of covering. Children and infants were treated in the same way, except that very young infants were apparently bound to their cradle boards, in an extended or partly flexed position. And about one third of the burials were accompanied by such things as red ocher, weapons, tools, and the bodies of their dogs. This growing concern with proper burial of the dead was a prelude to the impressive mortuary practices which characterize the next era in aboriginal Southeastern prehistory.

THE WOODLAND TRADITION

This new tradition—the Woodland—began to take shape in the eastern United States, most notably along the Mississippi and Ohio rivers, around 1,000 B.C.; it lasted, with modifications, until around A.D. 700. The Woodland tradition entailed both a change in the ideology of the Indians and a change in their subsistence pattern, but in both cases the changes appear to have gradually developed out of antecedents in the Archaic tradition. This tradition was a combination of new culture traits into a pattern peculiar to eastern North America; in fact, it was probably the most distinctive, the most completely indigenous culture ever to exist in eastern North America.[28] All other cultures, earlier and later, were either present elsewhere or influenced from elsewhere.

The people of the Woodland tradition followed the same hunting and gathering way of life that their ancestors had established earlier. In the Woodland tradition, however, they developed more and more refinements in ways of doing things as they learned to exploit particular foods of their local regions more efficiently. In the deciduous forest region of the middle Southeast, for example, the collection and use of nuts evidently became increasingly important. Extensive use was made of underground pits, probably to store nuts and seeds which the people were gathering in large quantities.[29] Such storage must have allowed a somewhat more sedentary life, and it is during this time that we have the first clear evidence for sturdy, relatively permanent houses. The people must have continued to move about exploiting their environment in some kind of seasonal cycle, for even in much later times Europeans observed whole villages moving in search of better hunting. However, it does seem that Woodland people lived in small settlements which were more permanent than before.

The several innovations which characterize the Woodland tradition evidently grew out of the established patterns of the Archaic, although some of them may have been prodded along the way by indirect influences from Mesoamerica. During this time pottery became widespread, and its form and decoration became locally stylized. The rudiments of agriculture began to emerge as a supplement to the old established hunting and gathering way of life. And burial customs which were gaining importance in the Archaic tradition were followed in the Woodland tradition by amazingly elaborate burials of certain individuals. These elaborate mortuary customs included the most impressive of all the innovations of the Woodland people, the building of a great many monumental earthworks, some of them truly enormous in size.

The earthworks built by the Indians in the Woodland tradition varied both in form and function. Some were only a few feet high while others were immense; one instance of these is the Poverty Point site in Louisiana, a site so huge and complex that its full extent was not wholly recognized until the days of aerial observation. Many of the Woodland mounds were burial mounds which were constructed over human bones or cremated remains, or in other cases over bodies buried in substantial log tombs. Sometimes the mounds covered only one burial, sometimes several, and sometimes there were dozens of burials scattered throughout the mounds. Earth was carried to the mounds a basketful at a time as the mounds were built. The burials were usually accompanied by elaborate grave goods, such as pottery, jewelry, and sheets of mica cut in various shapes. After about 100 B.C. these burial mounds became very widespread in the eastern United States.

Other earthworks were not burial mounds, and in fact we do not know what they were for. In some cases the earth was piled high into mounds, in other cases it was built up into shapes of animals, and in still other cases it was used to make large enclosures. These enclosures are sometimes geometric, and they sometimes surround groups of burial mounds. Some formations found from this period were made by piling up rocks rather than dirt.

Many of these earthworks which were not burial mounds are scattered throughout the eastern United States today and are usually regarded by the local people as great mysteries. Many stories exist about their origin, one of the most popular being that they were made by the Mound Builders, who, as we have already seen, were believed to have been a mysterious race of men who somehow appeared and then disappeared from this continent ages ago. The most widespread popular belief about the function of these earthworks is that they served as forts, since most of them consist at least in part of some kind of enclosure. However, the embankments are rarely, if ever, substantial enough to keep anyone out, and it is doubtful that they served this purpose.

One rather imposing structure of this sort is Old Stone Fort near Manchester, Tennessee (fig. 15). This site resembles sites found in Georgia, Alabama, Kentucky, and Missouri, and also to the north along the Ohio River. Archaeological research has established that it was built in the first three or four centuries of the Christian era. The site is situated on a natural plateau where the two forks of the Duck River come together. It comprises an area of about fifty acres bounded on two sides by steep cliffs and on the other sides by rambling walls made of loosely piled stone covered with earth. Altogether the several segments of the wall measure 4,600 feet in length. The enclosure has only one entrance, a complex structure consisting of a corridor of parallel earthen walls leading in to a wall across the end of the corridor with an exit to the side. The function or

Figure 15. Old Stone Fort. Courtesy, University of Tennessee Press.

purpose of this complex entrance is not understood. The purpose of the enclosure is also unknown. No pottery and only a handful of stone artifacts have been found in the enclosure, and none of these were definitely made by the people who built the walls. Since no refuse has been found within the enclosure, it evidently was not used as the site for a community. The walls are only four or five feet high, and therefore would have had limited effectiveness as a defensive fortification. Most archaeologists believe instead that the enclosure must have been used seasonally, perhaps only once a year, for ceremonial purposes, though it must be admitted that no direct evidence for ceremonial activity has ever been found.[30]

Some of the animal effigy mounds that were built by Indians of the Woodland tradition can still be seen today. One of the most impressive is the Serpent Mound, built atop a steep bluff in southern Ohio (fig. 16). This is a carefully constructed earthen structure built to represent the body of a snake, complete with several curves, a coiled tail, and a rather complex head. From head to tail it measures 737 linear feet. The body of the serpent averages about 20 feet wide and 4 or 5 feet high. Because of its great length and the curves of its body, a man standing at one end of the serpent cannot see the other end. Archaeologists do not know why the Indians built this mound.

Another effigy mound that can still be seen is at the Rock Eagle site in Georgia. Here rocks were piled into the shape of a bird, perhaps an eagle or a buzzard. Here again archaeologists have no clue to its use. We know so little about these "mystery" mounds because the Indians left little or nothing in the vicinity of each of them for archaeologists to work with. For some of the other areas of life in the Woodland period, however, our knowledge and understanding are relatively good.

The evidence that we have shows that the Woodland tradition was a time of transition from an exclusively hunting and gathering way of life to a way of life in which agriculture played a larger role. In the Woodland tradition the Indians were exploiting two kinds of plants—native and tropical. The native plants—all exploited for their seeds—were sunflower (*Helianthus annuus* L.), sumpweed (*Iva annua* L.), chenopodium (possibly *Chenopodium bushianum*), pigweed (*Amaranthus* sp.), knotweed or smartweed (*Polygonum* sp.), giant ragweed (*Ambrosia trifida* L.), and maygrass or canary grass (*Phalaris caroliniana* Walt.). Seeds of all of these (except giant

Figure 16. Aerial photograph of the Serpent Mound. Courtesy, National Geographic Society and the Ohio Historical Society.

ragweed) were found at Salts Cave, a remarkable early Woodland site in the Mammoth Cave region of Kentucky, where organic materials, including a mummified body, human feces, baskets made of twilled split cane, slippers made of twilled vegetable fiber (fig. 17), and torches made of bundles of cane, were preserved as if in a time vault. The same seeds found at Salts Cave have been found in other late Archaic and early Woodland sites in Illinois, Indiana, Ohio, Kentucky, and Tennessee.

Some of these plants evidently constitute an old "Eastern Agricultural Complex" which possibly began in the eastern United States in the early second millenium B.C. The shape and conformity of late Archaic and early Woodland sunflower seeds indicate that they were cultivated rather than simply gathered, and the size of sumpweed seeds, some of them as much as three times the size of present-day species of sumpweed, strongly suggests that it, too, was cultivated. A large-seeded variety of chenopodium has been found, suggesting that it may also have been cultivated, but the evidence is less compelling than for sunflower or sumpweed. The large-seeded sumpweed is now extinct, this in itself being evidence that it was in fact domesticated and dependent on man for its propagation. Seeds from the other native plants—pigweed, smartweed, canary grass,

Figure 17. Woodland slipper made of twilled fibers. Mammoth Cave, Kentucky. Negative no. MNH 2303. Department of Anthropology, National Museum of Natural History, Smithsonian Institution.

and giant ragweed—may have been gathered in quantity rather than cultivated. There is evidence that seeds were stored for use in winter and spring.

It was during the Woodland tradition that the Indians first began to show a decided preference for living near the flood plains of rivers. It was in the flood plains that all of these native seed-bearing plants thrived. All of them depend upon some external factor, such as flooding or soil disturbances by man, to eliminate their competitors and to expose raw soil. The poorer the drainage, the more these plants would have thrived. Here, conditions were ideal for intensive seed-collecting to lead gradually to intentional cultivation —agriculture.

Late in the second millennium B.C., late Archaic people added to their native plants two tropical plants which had been domesticated south of what is now the Mexican border and which had diffused northward. These were the bottle gourd (*Lagenaria siceraria* Standl.) and squash (*Cucurbita pepo* L.). Both of these are highly productive and easy to cultivate, and they would have thrived in the flood plains and in rubbish heaps in the villages. The Woodland Indians probably used the gourds as containers. The squash also produced a hard rind which they used as a container, and they ate squash seeds, though these were evidently not terribly important in their diet.

Another tropical cultigen, corn, was acquired by Woodland people around 200 B.C., considerably later than gourds and squash. This was a type of corn commonly called "tropical flint," characterized by small ears and ten to fourteen (occasionally sixteen) rows of kernels. We do not know how successful it was outside its warm homeland or how intensively the Woodland people cultivated it. But from what we do know thus far, it does not seem likely that corn in the Woodland period was of such paramount importance as a food as it was later to become.

One of the archaeological puzzles in the eastern United States is that corn disappears from archaeological sites around A.D. 400 and does not reappear until around A.D. 900, when the Mississippian tradition began. One possible explanation is that the climate became both cooler and moister during this period, shortening the growing season to such a degree that tropical flint corn could not be cultivated.[31]

Along with these cultivated foods, the Woodland people continued to rely on gathered plant foods for much of their diet. From charred remains and from remains in dry caves, archaeologists have compiled a long list of wild plant foods utilized by Woodland people: hickory nuts, walnuts, butternuts, acorns, hazelnuts, beechnuts, chestnuts, chinquapins, grapes, persimmons, raspberries, blackberries, strawberries, blueberries, honey locust pods, and pawpaws; and there were undoubtedly many others which have left no trace.[32]

Some archaeologists point to the large mounds and earthworks of the Woodland tradition as indirect evidence for agriculture's being important during this time, saying that these structures could not have been built by a people who subsisted solely by hunting and gathering wild foods. Other archaeologists argue, on the other hand, that the eastern United States was a rich environment abounding in a variety of wild vegetable and animal foods, and that efficient exploitation of these resources could have produced a surplus of food great enough to allow the leisure to produce these monumental earthworks.[33] The Indians exploited their natural environment fully. The historic Indians of the Great Lakes area used 275 species of plants for medicine, 130 species for food, 31 species for magical purposes, 27 species for smoking, 25 species as dyes, 18 species for beverages and as flavoring, and 52 species for various other purposes.[34] The role of agriculture in the Woodland tradition will undoubtedly be argued for many years to come.

It was during the Woodland tradition that pottery became widespread in the Southeast. Regional variations in form and decoration arose, but there were also some pottery traits that were shared by different regions. Any such sharing of traits in artifactual remains is looked upon with interest by prehistorians because it offers a clue to the interaction of people and ideas.

The pottery of the Woodland tradition was usually tempered with crushed rock or grit instead of vegetable fibers, and it was finished with several characteristic surface decorations. Cord-marking and fabric-marking were produced by paddling the wet clay surface of a vessel with a paddle or stick wrapped with cord or fabric. Surface decoration similar to this was introduced into Alaska from Asia around 1,000 B.C., and it is therefore possible that it diffused from Alaska to the eastern United States.[35] Stamped pottery was made in a similar way, only the wooden paddles had designs carved directly into them, and these designs were then stamped into the wet clay. Some of the stamped designs were quite elaborate (fig. 18). Other decorations consisted of incised or punctated lines made with a sharply pointed instrument. A variety of designs were made in this way, including bird and serpent motifs. This is especially noteworthy because bird and serpent symbolism continues on into late prehistoric and historic times as an important element in the belief system of the Southeastern Indians. Some of the finest pieces of pottery that we have from the Woodland tradition were found in burial mounds. Some of these vessels were ceremonially "killed" by knocking holes in them before they were placed in the graves. Others were obviously made for such ceremonial purposes because they had holes neatly cut through the walls of the vessel as part of the design (see fig. 26).

Of the other objects from the Woodland tradition that have been uncovered by archaeologists, some of the most characteristic are what might be called luxury items. Included among these are reel-shaped and bar-shaped gorgets made from stone or copper (fig. 19). Gorgets are flat objects designed to be worn on a cord around the neck. Ear spools were also objects of personal adornment. They were fashioned from stone or copper or carved from wood, sometimes with a thin copper sheet covering the wood. The Indians slit

Figure 18. Woodland potsherds. *Left to right:* cord-marked, fabric-marked, check-stamped. Courtesy, Frank H. McClung Museum, University of Tennessee.

the lower margins of their ears and stretched them until the ear spools could be slipped into place. Fresh-water pearls were valued for their beauty; they were strung for necklaces and bracelets and also sewed into clothing as beads.

Panpipes, apparently a kind of musical instrument, were sometimes placed in graves (fig. 20). Quite a different kind of grave artifact

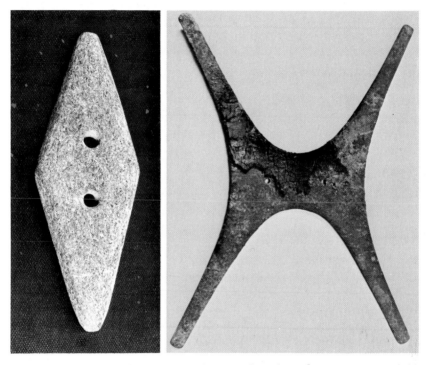

Figure 19. Woodland gorgets. *Left:* stone bar-shaped gorget. Tunacunnhee site. Courtesy, Laboratory of Archaeology, University of Georgia. *Right:* copper reel-shaped gorget, Hazlett Mound, Locking County, Ohio. Courtesy, Ohio Historical Society.

were platform pipes, used for smoking. These pipes were carved from stone or made of pottery with stem holes drilled through small platforms which held plain bowls or bowls in the form of small, exquisitely carved animal effigies, many of which are truly admirable in their detailed likenesses of the animals they represent (fig. 21).[36]

An extensive trade network appears to have developed during the

Figure 20. Copper panpipe. Tunacunnhee site. Courtesy, Laboratory of Archaeology, University of Georgia.

Woodland period. At present we know virtually nothing about how it was organized, but we do know that many exotic materials from far away places were interred with bodies in burials. There was much use of copper of the freely occurring kind that is found in abundance around the Great Lakes and in lesser quantities in isolated parts of the Southeast. Mica from the Appalachian Mountains was used throughout most of the Southeast, as were sea shells and fossilized sharks' teeth from the Atlantic and Gulf coasts. Grizzly bear canine teeth and obsidian (volcanic glass) from the Rocky Mountains also show up in some sites.

The Southeast as a whole did not develop in the same way at the same time during the Woodland tradition. Rather, the people of different regions developed at different times cultures which were in some ways unique to their particular area but which also shared many of the traits we have seen to be characteristic of the Woodland tradition as a whole.

The Poverty Point culture in Louisiana and Mississippi was one such region. The people who lived here between about 1300 B.C. and 200 B.C. were probably the first people in North America to build large mounds and earthworks, and they did it most spectacularly. At the Poverty Point site itself, in northeastern Louisiana, they made the principal mound 640 feet from north to south and 70 feet in

66

height. Their village, occupying an area of more than two-thirds of a mile in diameter, was built upon a series of six concentrically arranged ridges, 4 to 6 feet in height, which were laid out in an octagonal pattern and separated by aisles that radiated from the center of the village like the spokes of a wheel. The ridges were built

Figure 21. Platform pipes. *Above:* plain pipe, Tunacunnhee site. Courtesy, Laboratory of Archaeology, University of Georgia. *Below:* frog effigy pipe, Mound City Group, Ross County, Ohio. Courtesy, Ohio Historical Society.

up out of village site debris. One unique feature of Poverty Point and related sites is the occurrence of a great quantity—perhaps millions—of small fired clay objects made in the shape of cylinders, melons, cones, squeezed shapes, and crude human and animal figures; archaeologists think that because stone is absent in this area, these were used in place of stones to line the pits in which food was cooked (fig. 22).

The Poverty Point site is an early mound complex which has few of the traits characteristic of mound complexes found in other regions later in the Woodland tradition. In most respects the Poverty Point people were Archaic, as in their use of the spear-thrower and darts with heavy stemmed and notched points. Pottery was not widely used. Most containers were carved out of soapstone (steatite) and sandstone. Of the few pieces of pottery that have been found, most are fiber-tempered. Fragments of basketry have also been found. At the present time the Poverty Point mound complex appears to be so unlike any other archaeological site that it is not yet possible to place it firmly with respect to other mound sites in North America.[37]

In contrast, there developed in the Ohio River valley at a slightly later time a cultural complex which more or less epitomized the Woodland tradition. There were actually two developments in this region: Adena, dating from about 1,000 B.C. to about A.D. 200, and Hopewell, which sprang up alongside Adena at around 300 B.C., became more elaborate and widespread, and outlasted it, finally declining around A.D. 600.[38]

Located primarily within 150 miles of Chillicothe, Ohio, Adena sites usually contain cone-shaped burial mounds, often built over bodies which were interred in rectangular log tombs. In some cases the bodies were placed in buildings which were then burned, and in other cases the bodies were cremated in circular or elliptical clay basins dug into the earth. Among the objects placed in the graves were bar-shaped and reel-shaped stone gorgets, imported copper fashioned into gorgets and other body adornments, tubular-shaped smoking pipes (fig. 23), small stone tablets with stylized animals (usually birds) or curvilinear geometrical designs carved on them (fig. 24), and the remains of what appear to have been animal masks.[39]

Adena sites occasionally contain earthen-walled enclosures averaging about 100 yards in diameter. Although these are often

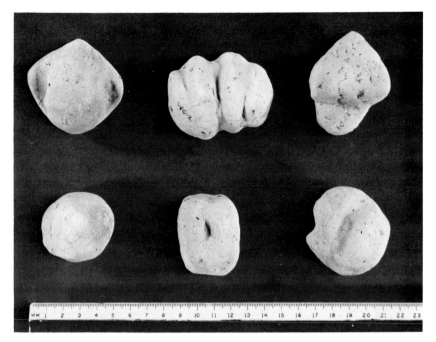

Figure 22. Poverty Point objects. *Top row, left to right:* biconal grooved; cylindrical with lateral grooves; biconal, extruded. *Bottom row, left to right:* biconal plain; melon-shaped; cross-grooved. Courtesy, Clarence H. Webb; photograph by Gordon W. Maxcey.

referred to as forts, the walls are generally too low to have provided much defense. The Adena people built circular houses that were anywhere from 18 to 60 feet in diameter. The walls were made by setting pairs of wooden posts into the ground at an angle of about 11 degrees so that the tops leaned outward. This angle kept water from running down the walls, and along with the overhanging cone-shaped bark roof, gave some protection to the walls against decay. The outer edge of the roof was held up by wall posts, and its apex was supported by a rectangular frame held in place by four large posts in the center of the house floor. Sometimes the Adena people built a U-shaped screen between the inner posts of the frame with the open side facing the doorway. Thus as the wind came through the door, it was diverted by the screen and rose, carrying the smoke through a smoke hole in the apex of the roof (fig. 25).[40]

Figure 23. Adena tubular pipe. It is thought to represent a dwarf. Note the ear spools. Courtesy, Ohio Historical Society.

70

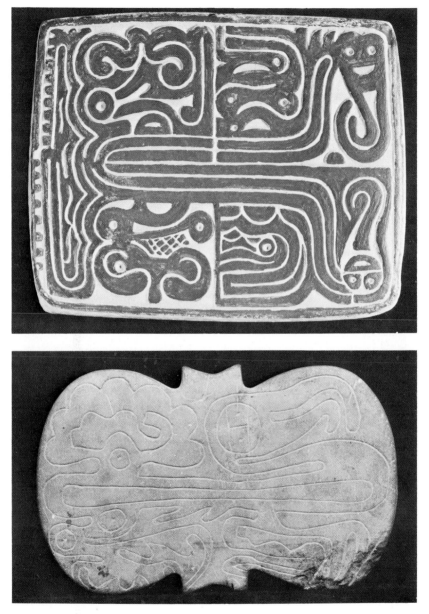

Figure 24. Stone Adena tablets. Both show representations of stylized birds of prey. *Upper:* the Wilmington tablet, Sparks Mound, Clinton County, Ohio. *Lower:* the Berlin Tablet, Jackson County, Ohio. Courtesy, Ohio Historical Society.

The Hopewell culture evidently took shape in Illinois and Ohio, and from there it spread widely in all directions, including southward into the Southeast.[41] Hopewell people built elaborate earthworks, some of them enclosing as many as eighty acres, with earthen embankments as high as twelve feet. Often these enclosures were built in geometric patterns—squares, circles, and octagons—which sometimes were connected by pairs of parallel earthen walls. The burial mounds contained a greater variety of grave goods than those left by the Adena people, including quantities of fresh-water pearls, pan pipes, ear spools, effigy platform pipes, and pottery. Also included were figures cut out of sheets of mica and copper and other objects made from such imported materials as sea shells, grizzly bear teeth, fossilized shark teeth, and obsidian. There is little evidence

Figure 25. Partly conjectural model of an Adena house. Courtesy, Ohio Historical Society.

that Hopewell people lived inside their impressive earthwork enclosures, though occasionally they did. But it is believed that they usually only came to the earthworks for ceremonies and that they lived not far away in small settlements along the rivers and streams.

As Hopewell gradually declined in the north, a somewhat different variant of the Woodland tradition—the Gulf culture—developed in the lower Mississippi valley and along the Gulf Coast. One of the most impressive Gulf sites is Kolomoki in southern Georgia. Covering over three hundred acres, this site contains a large mound, presumably a temple mound, measuring a little over 56 feet high at its highest point, and with a base measuring 325 feet by 200 feet. Directly to the west of the temple mound lie two burial mounds. Both of these, though quite large, were evidently built in a single brief ceremonial period in an effort that is estimated to have involved the labor of perhaps one thousand people. Each mound contained centrally the skeleton of an individual accompanied with elaborate grave goods in a log-lined grave which was covered entirely with rocks. Later stages of the mound contained additional skeletons, perhaps of individuals who were killed as retainers to accompany the dead. One of the burial mounds contained in its earliest stage a platform raised upon posts, perhaps similar to the raised platforms erected by the Natchez in connection with their mortuary ceremonials. At one point in the construction of the mounds large quantities of pottery vessels, pottery effigies (opossum, snake, deer, cougar, and birds, mostly owls) (fig. 26), sheets of mica, conch shells, and what appear to be "trophy" skulls, as well as bundles of human long bones, and ashes of cremated human remains were placed along the eastern sides of the mounds. Many of the vessels were "killed" by having a hole knocked through the bottom, or else a hole was cut through the vessel before it was fired. It is believed that the entire contents of the temple were cleaned out and placed in the burial mounds.

Several graves also contained small "cymbals" made of copper and meteoric iron. These were found near the ears of the dead person, around the neck, at the chin, and at the waist. Thus they were used as ornaments in a variety of ways. This use of the cymbals is confirmed in early European drawings of Indians in this area who are depicted with small circular objects attached to various parts of their bodies (fig. 27).

Figure 26. Kolomoki pottery effigies. *Top:* horned owl. *Bottom:* crested bird. Both are coated with red pigment. Courtesy, Laboratory of Archaeology, University of Georgia.

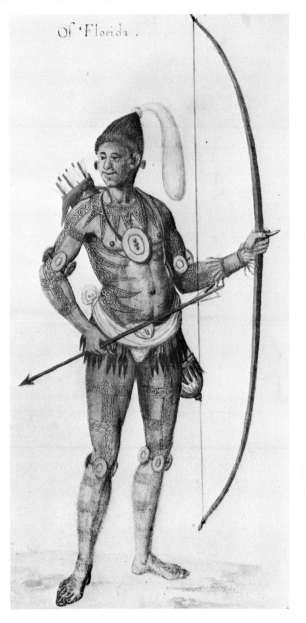

Figure 27. Indian man of Florida. John White drawing probably copied from an original painting by Jacques Le Moyne de Morgues. The man wears a metal gorget about his neck and metal cymbals attached to his arms and legs. Courtesy, Trustees of the British Museum.

The temple mound at Kolomoki is entirely surrounded by a large open space, or plaza. Although little definite information is known about the Kolomoki houses themselves, they are thought to have been arranged in a semicircle around the plaza. One smaller mound to the south of the temple mound apparently served as the foundation for a huge post, two to three feet in diameter, probably like those used in a game played by the Timucuans and other Southeastern Indians. No direct evidence for agriculture has been found at Kolomoki; it is possible that it was absent, though agriculture was definitely practiced somewhat later, in historic times, in this area. There is, however, ample evidence of hunting, with deer and turkey being the favorite game animals.[42]

The Gulf culture lasted into historic times. The chroniclers of the de Soto expedition described several groups of Indians, including the Timucuans, who had some features in common with it. The Calusas of southwestern Florida are perhaps an even better example of a people who represented the last cultural remnants of the early Gulf culture. Clearly outside the Mississippian sphere of influence, the Calusas did no farming, but lived instead by gathering wild foods, particularly by fishing and collecting shellfish which are so abundant in this area. Huge shell middens occur throughout the Calusa area. One of these, a shell midden on Key Marco, measured 1,700 feet by 1,900 feet, reaching a height of 12 to 15 feet. The Calusas used the bow and arrow, but they also retained the spear-thrower, and according to the Spanish they were accurate at throwing their darts. By a remarkable accident of preservation, several spear-throwers and many other wooden objects were recovered from the muck at Key Marco.

The main Calusa village was Calos, located on Mound Key in Estero Bay, whence their head chief wielded some sort of dominance over about fifty villages from Lake Okeechobee southward to the Keys. The chiefs of these villages paid the head chief at Calos "tribute" in the form of exotic feathers, mats, deerskins, food, and precious metals and captives from wrecked Spanish ships. The head chief had several wives and at least some of his wives came from villages which were subject to him. He wore special regalia and expected deference from all his people. The Calusas built large mounds and other unusual earthworks with semicircular ridges, corridors between parallel ridges, and ditches which are at least

the highest cultural achievement in the Southeast, and for that matter in all of North America. The population increased, and towns grew up that were larger, more permanent, and more secularized than the large religious centers of the Woodland tradition. Some Mississippian towns, such as Cahokia in Illinois and Moundville in Alabama, were larger than even the huge Poverty Point site. This is not to say that all Mississippian sites were large, for archaeologists have excavated many small ones, but there are more large sites found for the Mississippian period than for any previous time.[46]

Perhaps the most characteristic feature of the Mississippian tradition was the building of flat-topped, pyramidal earthen mounds that served as the foundations for temples or mortuaries, chiefs' houses, and other important buildings. De Soto and his men observed the manner in which these mounds were built. According to his chroniclers, dirt was carried up a basketful at a time, emptied out, and then stamped down with great force until it had the desired consistency. They noted that the sides of the mounds were so steep that it was difficult for a man to climb them. Therefore, a more gently sloped earthen ramp was usually built up the face of a mound to give easy access to the top (see fig. 31). De Soto and his men had no difficulty riding their horses up these ramps, which they described as being from fifteen to twenty feet wide, with log steps laid crosswise. Archaeological research has shown that the buildings atop these mounds were periodically destroyed, either intentionally or by accident, and a mantle of earth was then laid over the entire mound, thus enlarging it; some mounds were enlarged as many as eight or ten times, or even more. The mounds frequently faced a large open plaza which served as a playing field, a ceremonial area, and a village commons. One of these mound and plaza complexes may be seen today at the reconstructed Chucalissa village near Memphis, Tennessee.[47] Around the boundaries of Mississippian plazas were additional mounds, public buildings, and houses.[48] Priests sometimes stood on the mounds to address crowds of people who assembled on important occasions, as for example, to deliver a eulogy on the occasion of re-interring the bones of a dead person.[49] Not all Mississippian mounds were truncated pyramids. Some of them had a circular ground plan; others were long and ridge-shaped.

One characteristic of Mississippian sites was that they were invariably built near the courses or old channels of rivers and streams where the best soil for their kind of agriculture was found. They were also frequently surrounded by defensive structures. Ditches were often dug around the perimeter of the town, presumably for defense, and in some cases they were filled with water. As described by the de Soto chroniclers, the town of Pacaha, on the west bank of the Mississippi River, was almost completely surrounded by a man-made ditch filled with water from a canal cut to the river.[50] With or without ditches, many Mississippian towns were surrounded by palisades made of large posts set vertically into the earth. Other poles were attached to these horizontally, and the whole thing was covered with a thick coating of mud and straw plaster. Built into the walls at regular intervals were defensive towers manned by sentinels, or in time of battle, by seven or eight archers (fig. 28). According to the de Soto chroniclers, the town of the Alabamas was laid out in a perfect square, with walls four hundred feet long; on one side this fort was entered via three doors so low a horse could not get through, and the other side by a gate opening onto a steep river bank which was difficult to climb. The Alabama fort also contained interior defensive walls so that if one was taken by the enemy the next one could be defended.[51] Other towns had palisades built according to more irregular plans which incorporated advantageous features of the terrain.

Figure 28. Town Creek. A reconstructed South Appalachian Mississippian site with palisade, defensive towers, and a temple mound. A stream runs behind the trees in the left background. Courtesy, North Carolina Division of Archives and History.

Within particular regions Mississippian sites are often differentiated both in size and in social function. Typically, a single large site with one or more mounds served as the center of the society. In some cases, as at Cahokia, this large site served both as a ceremonial center and a population center. In other cases, as at Spiro or Town Creek, the large site was only a ceremonial center with a small resident population. Most of the members of the society lived within a few miles of the large site in small villages that were sometimes fortified. Still other members of the society lived out near the agricultural fields in small, unfortified homesteads.

The temple mounds and defensive structures indicate that the Mississippian tradition entailed new religious and social elements, and that there were also important economic changes. The Mississippian people began to rely on agriculture—particularly the cultivation of corn, beans, and squash—for a large portion of their food, even though hunting and gathering remained important. Following precedents set in the Woodland period, Mississippian people practiced agriculture along the river valleys, always with their villages and towns located nearby. Their main agricultural tools were the digging stick and a short-handled hoe with a blade made of chipped flint (fig. 29) or the shoulder blade of a large mammal, such as an elk or bison.

Woodland people cultivated small-eared, many-rowed, tropical flint corn between about 200 B.C. and A.D. 400, about which time corn disappears or becomes exceedingly scarce in the eastern United States. Tropical flint grows best in a dry climate with a moderately long growing season. A moist, cool climate in the late Woodland period could have made its cultivation difficult. Corn reappears in the early Mississippian period, around A.D. 800 to A.D. 1000. Though the Mississippian people resumed cultivation of a corn descended from the early tropical flint, by about A. D. 1200 most of the corn grown in the eastern United States was a new variety. This new variety, eastern flint, has its kernels in paired rows, usually with eight rows in all but sometimes with ten or twelve. Eastern flint is thought to have been domesticated in highland Guatemala, whence it presumably spread northward to the Southwest and thence to the Southeast. The advantage of this corn was that it would thrive in moist soil and in a relatively cool climate. This made it ideal for cultivation in the eastern United States.

80

Figure 29. Mississippian flint hoe. The wide end of the blade was polished through use. Courtesy, Frank H. McClung Museum, University of Tennessee.

Present-day commercial corn is a relatively recent hybrid developed from this eastern flint and a many-rowed dent corn native to Mexico.

Beans showed up in Mississippian sites at about the same time the eastern flint corn does. And the Indians continued cultivating gourds and squashes which were presumably descended from varieties cultivated throughout the Woodland tradition. The precise nature of the differences between Woodland and Mississippian agriculture are not well understood. The new hardy variety of corn was undoubtedly more productive than the older tropical flint. Perhaps more important was the combination of corn and beans, whose nutrients complement each other. Together they provide a reasonably good vegetable diet; separately they do not. After this Mississippian agricultural complex took shape, the cultivation of the old native plants—sunflower, sumpweed, and others—apparently declined.

In addition to corn, beans, and squash, Mesoamerican affinities were apparently present in Mississippian religious architecture, but how they came to be there is not clear. The difficulty is that there are no temple mounds in a vast area between central Mexico and the Southeast, and in fact the absence of large rivers and alluvial soils in the western coastal plain may have constituted an ecological barrier between central Mexico and the Southeast. Also, no evidence has been found of direct Mesoamerican intrusion into the Southeast. The influence must have come from occasional immigration of people and the diffusion of ideas from Mesoamerica. At the same time, archaeological evidence indicates that the Mississippian tradition itself was spread within the Southeast partly by diffusion of ideas but also by intrusive movements of people out from the Mississippi valley, and distinguishing between these two kinds of diffusion is by no means easy.[52]

Evidence of intrusive movements of Mississippian people has been found at several sites on the periphery of the area that came under Mississippian domination. Around A.D. 900, for example, a group of Mississippian people moved up the Illinois River and displaced Woodland people occupying the Dickson Mounds site. They remained here until about A.D. 1300, when they abandoned the site for reasons that have not yet been explained. Perhaps their agricultural practices exhausted the soil, or they may have run out of convenient firewood, or perhaps the climate was not entirely suitable for successful Mississippian agriculture. Much the same thing seems to have happened at the Aztalan site in Wisconsin, the northernmost extension of the Mississippian tradition. The area was settled around A.D. 1000 by people coming up from further south. They selected a site on a tributary of the Rock River. Here they built a village surrounded by a strong, fortified palisade with walls measuring from 12 to 19 feet high; it surrounded not only the village but the ceremonial center and agricultural fields as well. In addition, the village contained several inner palisades (like those at the

Alabama fort), so that the village could be defended one area at a time. The people remained here for about 200 years, at which time the entire village burned down and was never rebuilt.

Additional evidence of a movement of people exists at several other sites in the Southeast. For example, at the Town Creek site near Mount Gilead, North Carolina, on a tributary of the upper Pee Dee River, we have evidence that Mississippian people settled the site around A. D. 1300, building villages and tilling fields of corn (see fig. 28). They built their villages up and down the river, fortifying them with palisades, and they built a palisaded ceremonial center with a temple mound with a square building on top. (This small ceremonial center, now reconstructed for the public, is an excellent example of Mississippian architecture.) They remained in this territory for a century or so after which time it reverted back to its original inhabitants, a number of small Woodland hill tribes.[53] Another possible example of an intrusive Mississippian community, here intruding into the area of the Gulf culture, is the Fort Walton culture in northwest Florida. The Fort Walton site itself contains a low mound which probably served as a ceremonial center for a number of small villages in the area. The Fort Walton culture may be that of one of the ancestors of the Lower Creeks, who are believed to have invaded the area in the sixteenth century.[54]

Another intrusive Mississippian population settled at what is now Ocmulgee National Park at Macon, Georgia. It is located on the Ocmulgee River, on the fall line. Here at about A.D. 900 a group of people bearing the early Mississippian cultural tradition came in and displaced the people of the late Woodland tradition who were living there. We are fairly sure that this was indeed an invasion because the pottery and many other artifacts that belonged to the new people were so completely different from those of the former inhabitants that it is unlikely that they evolved from them. These new Mississippian people built a large town on a bluff beside the Ocmulgee River and encircled it with two ditches for fortification. Their fields, of course, were in the bottoms along the river. They built several mounds, one of which was a large burial mound and two others of which were large temple mounds.

One interesting feature of the Macon Plateau site is an "earth lodge," a men's winter council house, which has been reconstructed from the archaeological evidence and can be seen today by visitors to the park. It is a circular building about forty-two feet in diameter, made of pine logs and covered with earth so that from the outside it looks like a small mound. On the floor of the council house and located opposite the entrance is an earthen platform in the shape of a hawk or falcon, its head oriented toward the circular fire basin in the center of the building. A low clay bench is built around the wall containing seats for forty-seven people. Three more seats are located on the tail of the earthen platform, which is also against the wall, thus completing the circle of seats. Presumably, these three seats were reserved for important men.

For reasons unknown to us, the Macon Plateau people suddenly disappeared from the area around A.D. 1100. The site remained unoccupied until the late prehistoric period, when around A.D. 1400 a town which archaeologists call Lamar was set up about three miles south of the abandoned town. The artifacts left by the inhabitants of Lamar reveal a continuity with the people whom the Macon Plateau intruders had originally pushed out. Their earlier culture had not been destroyed by the invaders, but it had been changed to incorporate many Mississippian elements. Their town, located on a hammock deep in the river swamp, was palisaded, and their agricultural fields were situated in the river bottoms. In the town were two temple mounds which faced each other across an open plaza. One of these was circular and was mounted by means of a spiral ramp running counterclockwise around its perimeter.

The Mississippian tradition reached a high development around A.D. 1200, influencing almost all the cultures in the Southeast. As time went on, the territory of the Mississippian tradition expanded, and some of the large ceremonial sites were made even larger. Monk's mound at the Cahokia site, for example, was enlarged until it finally stood 100 feet high with a base of 710 feet east-west and about 1,000 feet north-south, containing almost 22 million cubic feet of earth fill. Monk's mound was built between A.D. 900 and 1200. Over 100 smaller mounds are situated within five square miles of the large mound, and many other even smaller mounds have been destroyed in recent years by farmers, builders, and developers. Many of these mounds appear to have been built in clusters in accordance with a plan. A series of culturally similar but smaller sites are strung along the Mississippi River in Missouri, Tennessee, and Arkansas. Fortified Mississippian sites were also built along the banks of the Ohio River, as may be seen at the Angel site near Evansville, Indiana.[55]

In central and western Tennessee and northern Georgia, the Mississippian tradition had the familiar temple mounds with ramps. The towns were generally fortified, enclosing clusters of rectangular houses. The most elaborate stone work in the Southeast comes from this area. These people made large ceremonial flints in the shape of swords or knives, "batons," and several other intriguing shapes (see fig. 88). Complete axes carved out of a single piece of stone were obviously used for ceremonial purposes (see fig. 89). In addition, several stone statues of men and women have been found. These are rather realistic depictions of sitting or kneeling figures, averaging about two feet in height. Particularly fine examples of these statues representing a man and a woman have been found at the Etowah mounds in northern Georgia (see fig. 92). Indeed, some of the finest examples of Southeastern art have been recovered from the Etowah site.[56] In addition to the statues, archaeologists at Etowah have recovered fine monolithic axes, a polished stone disc with scalloped edges, an elaborate headdress made from pieces of copper, and large copper plaques with men impersonating falcons embossed on them (see fig. 93). Later the people of Etowah made a kind of pottery called Lamar, whose dominant forms were bowls and large jars with complicated-stamp patterns, often with incising and other decorations on the rims (fig. 30). This Lamar pottery also occurs at the previously mentioned Lamar site near Macon, at the Naccoochee mound in northern Georgia, at the Hollywood mound near Augusta, Georgia, at the Irene mound near Savannah, Georgia, and northward into the Carolina piedmont.[57]

Second in size only to Cahokia, Moundville is a large Mississippian site situated south of Tuscaloosa, Alabama, on a high bluff overlooking the Black Warrior River (fig. 31). The site covers around 300 acres, including twenty flat-topped pyramidal mounds grouped in and around a plaza and with a village area surrounding this. Like other Mississippian sites it had a defensive palisade around it. Smaller sites, villages and homesteads, culturally related to Moundville extend up and down the river for several miles. All of these sites are located near rich, easily tilled sandy soils in the flood plain of the river. A rich collection of artifacts has been recovered at Mound-

Figure 30. Lamar plain ware. Bartow County, Georgia. Courtesy, Laboratory of Archaeology, University of Georgia.

ville, including shell gorgets with etched designs, embossed copper pendants (see fig. 60), monolithic axes, engraved stone discs, and exquisite pottery in such forms as jars (see fig. 85), beakers, small-mouthed water bottles, and elbow-form pipes.[58]

   Similar artifacts and a strikingly similar series of symbolic forms appear in several sites in the Southeast in the late prehistoric period. They are collectively referred to as the Southern Cult or the Southeastern Ceremonial Complex because they presumably imply a set of shared religious beliefs which were held by Mississippian people.[59] This complex includes similar ceremonial costumes, ritual objects, and religious symbols. This symbolism shows up particularly on pottery and shell gorgets. The designs include the Greek cross (usually enclosed in a circle) (see figs. 37, 38), the swastika, a circle with scalloped or rayed edges, human hands with eyes in the

86

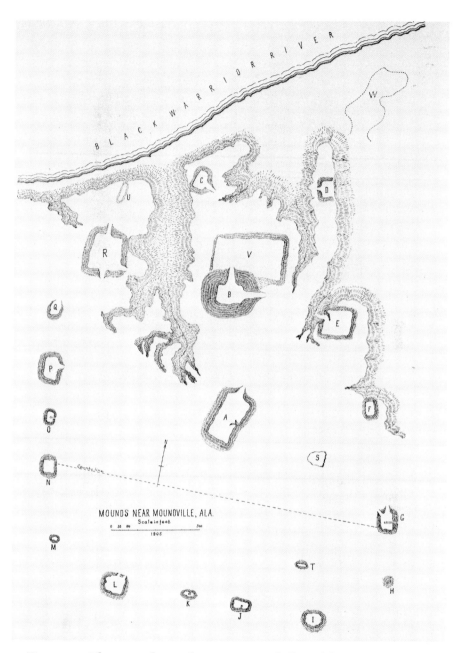

Figure 31. The mound complex near Moundville, Alabama. Note the ramps up the sides of the mounds. From Clarence B. Moore, "Moundville Revisited." *Journal of the Academy of Natural Sciences of Philadelphia*, second series, vol. 13, pt. 3 (1907), frontispiece.

palms (see fig. 90), the feathered serpent (see fig. 45), the forked eye—a human eye embellished with a chevron, zig-zag, or other V-shaped design (figs. 32, 34, 36), the spiral, an oval with a bar through its center (see fig. 35), a curious "bi-lobed arrow" (fig. 32), and human skulls and long bones. The Southeastern Ceremonial Complex also entailed the use of ritual objects, such as a bi-pointed knife (see fig. 46), monolithic axes (see fig. 89), "batons" chipped out of flint (fig. 32), several kinds of exquisitely made stone and copper celts (see fig. 58), trophy heads (fig. 32), scalloped stone discs (see fig. 90), and large ceremonial flints in several unusual shapes (see fig. 88). The human figures in Southeastern Ceremonial Complex art are depicted wearing ear spools, necklaces with pendants made from columellas taken from large conch shells (see fig. 35), forelocks with one or more large beads threaded on them (fig. 32), hair knots at the backs of their heads (fig. 32), belts with tassels on the ends, and peculiar pointed pouches or aprons (fig. 32). These symbolic elements are most often found at the large Mississippian sites, such as Etowah, Moundville, and as far away as the Spiro site in Oklahoma. Smaller amounts of Southeastern Ceremonial Complex materials have been found at lesser towns, such as Hiwassee Island in Tennessee. Each of these towns seems to have been the center of a political entity perhaps comparable to the Creek *tálwa* of historic times, to be described in chapter 4.

The undeniable similarity of some of the Southeastern Ceremonial Complex symbols to symbols used in Mesoamerica suggests that Mesoamerican influences in the Southeast went beyond corn, beans, squash, temple mounds, and a few additional items of material culture. Most of the similarities involve symbols which in Mesoamerica are associated with agriculture and fertility, and may in fact have come to the Southeast along with corn and beans.[60] But whether these symbols retained their original meanings after adoption in the Southeast is uncertain. Many of the symbols in the Southeastern Ceremonial Complex, perhaps most of them, were related not to fertility, but to war and conjury.

The bearers of some elements of Mesoamerican culture may have been *pochtecas*, traveling Aztec traders, whose presence in North America may be supported by the fact that curious shell and copper masks of a "long-nosed god" have been discovered at many Mississippian sites (fig. 33). It so happens that the god of the *pochtecas* was

Figure 32. Mississippian shell gorget with Southeastern Ceremonial Complex motifs. The man wears a beaded forelock, forked-eye design, a bi-lobed arrow stuck through his hair knot, and a pointed pouch. In his right hand he holds a trophy head; in his left a "baton" war club. Courtesy, Museum of the American Indian, Heye Foundation.

Yacatecuhtli, who is often portrayed with a long nose.[61] The adventures of the Spaniard Cabeza de Vaca suggest the way in which such long distances could have been traveled. As Cabeza de Vaca made his way along the Gulf Coast from Florida to Mexico he had two roles open to him as he encountered new people: priest (and healer) and trader. And there is no reason why the *pochtecas* could not have combined the two roles, enabling them to pass in safety through

89

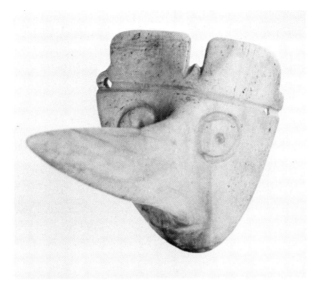

Figure 33. Miniature Long Nose God mask made of shell. Sumner County, Tennessee. Courtesy, Museum of the American Indian, Heye Foundation.

societies which were at war with each other. After enduring incredible hardship among the Indians at Galveston Bay, Cabeza de Vaca escaped and set out across Texas, northern Mexico, and down the west coast to what is now Sinaloa. At times he was followed by hundreds of Indians in a remarkable procession. When Cabeza de Vaca healed people, they gave him all their possessions, which he in turn distributed among his followers. The more he cured, the more wealth he was given for redistribution and the more the Indians were in awe of him.[62]

As archaeologists accumulate more and more detailed information about the Mississippian tradition, they are realizing that it was more complex than it at first seemed. It is now obvious, for example, that the Mississippian tradition was not everywhere the same. Its highest development was in the environs of where it first developed, the Middle Mississippi area. This includes what is now southern Illinois, southwestern Indiana, eastern Missouri, western Kentucky, most of Tennessee, northeastern Arkansas, northern Mississippi, and northern Alabama. Middle Mississippian sites are large, covering many acres, and were permanently inhabited. Some of the sites

90

have as much as ten feet of midden. The houses were generally rectangular with wattle and daub construction and wall trenches (wall posts set in trenches instead of individual holes), and they were frequently built in rows, as if along streets. Middle Mississippian pottery is characteristically tempered with pulverized shell, smooth surfaced, and decorated by painting or incising.

A variant, South Appalachian Mississippian, occurred in Georgia, South Carolina, and the western fringe of North Carolina. Here the familiar Mississippian flat-topped pyramidal mounds were built, but the pottery is quite distinctive, with complicated-stamp surface decoration. The South Appalachian Mississippian variant was evidently a local Woodland culture which was modified by borrowing from the Mississippian cultures to the west. Another variant, Caddoan Mississippian, occurred in western Louisiana and Arkansas, and in eastern Texas and Oklahoma. Here again the familiar temple mounds were built, but burial mounds were also important. Caddoan pottery is distinctive in that shell-tempering was not used until very late in the prehistoric period. The Caddoan people lived not in large villages, but in scattered, small hamlets, as did their descendants, the Caddoans of the historic period. The large mound sites in the Caddoan area were evidently ceremonial centers rather than habitation sites. Still another variant of the Mississippian tradition —Plaquemine—existed in southern Mississippi. Here the pottery was not shell-tempered and the settlements were small and dispersed. Plaquemine mound sites are quite large, but they were evidently limited to ceremonial functions because no substantial population lived on the site throughout the year.

To the north the influence of the Middle Mississippian tradition was more tenuous. After A.D. 1100 the Oneota culture developed on the upper tributaries of the Mississippi River and along the upper course of the Missouri River. Oneota people made shell-tempered pottery, but they built no mounds, and their villages were not fortified. Agriculture was evidently less important here because of the northerly climate. The Oneota culture is thought to have been ancestral to the culture of the Chiwere Sioux—the Iowa, Oto, Winnebago, and Missouri Indians of the historic period. The ancestors of the Dhegiha Sioux—the historic Poncas, Omahas, Osages, Quapaws, and Kansas—were possibly Middle Mississippian peoples. The Dhegiha Sioux lived in the Great Plains in historic times,

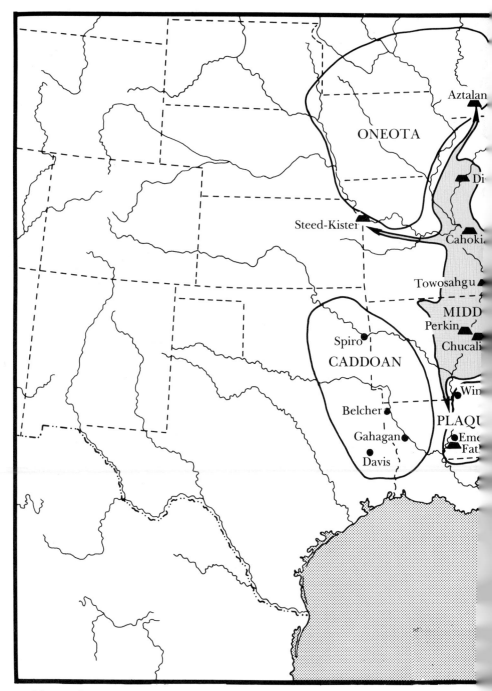

Map 4. Some Important Mississippian Sites.

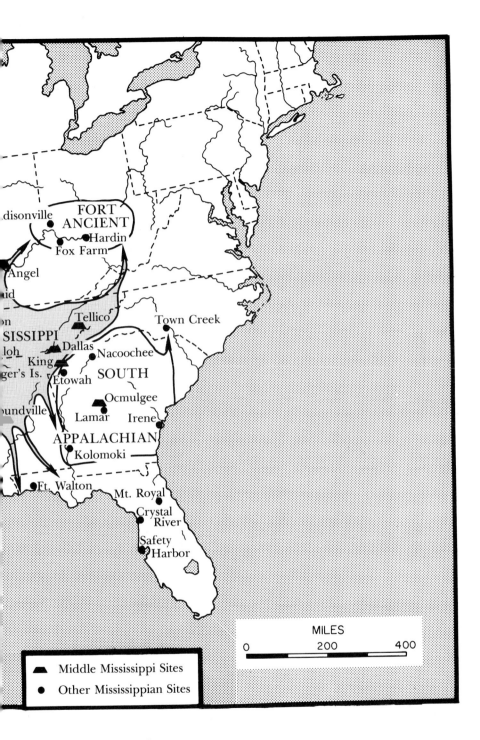

FORT
ANCIENT

disonville
Hardin
Fox Farm

Angel

id

SISSIPPI
loh
King
ger's Is.
Etowah
undville

Tellico
Dallas
Nacoochee
SOUTH
Ocmulgee
Lamar
Irene
APPALACHIAN
Kolomoki

Town Creek

Ft. Walton
Mt. Royal
Crystal
River
Safety
Harbor

MILES

0   200   400

▲ Middle Mississippi Sites
● Other Mississippian Sites

but there is evidence that they had previously lived to the east near the Mississippi River.

The Middle Mississippian culture also influenced the Fort Ancient culture that existed in northeastern Kentucky, southern Ohio, and western West Virginia from about A.D. 1400 to about A.D. 1650. Here the pottery was tempered with shell or grit, and the surfaces of the vessels were either smooth or cord-marked. Fort Ancient sites have turned up a few large flint "swords" along with other materials related to the Southeastern Ceremonial Complex. The Fort Ancient people are thought to have been ancestral to the Shawnees of the historic period. In the latter half of the seventeenth century, the Shawnees lived in several scattered bands further south and west, perhaps because they were driven from their homeland by the Iroquois.

It is far easier to establish linkages between late Mississippian archaeological complexes and named historic groups of Indians around the margins of the Southeast than in the Southeast proper. When Hernando de Soto explored the Southeast in 1539–43, he saw full-blown Mississippian cultures. But the precise route de Soto followed is by no means certain, and the names of places and peoples noted down by his chroniclers cannot always be tied in with later social and linguistic groups. Almost one and one-half centuries passed between de Soto's *entrada* and the time when the Southeastern Indians—the Cherokees, Catawbas, Creeks, Chickasaws, Choctaws, and smaller groups—entered the historic era. At this time they no longer built mounds; the old Mississippian religion and social order was a thing of the past; and many groups of people had been uprooted from their homelands. Archaeologists and ethnohistorians are now making some headway in establishing linkages between archaeology and history in the Southeast, but for the present little more can be said with certainty than that most of the Southeastern Indians described in this book are the descendants of South Appalachian and Middle Mississippian ancestors.

It can almost be said that the more archaeologists learn about the Mississippian tradition the less they understand. Once it was thought that the Mississippian tradition was based on intensive agriculture, and that it got its initial push from a strong influence from Mesoamerica. But it now appears that while agriculture was important to Mississippian people, so was hunting and gathering.

94

The relative importance of agriculture versus hunting and gathering probably varied from time to time and from one Mississippian culture to another, and we may never be able adequately to measure this variability. All things being equal, Mississippian sites tend to occur where there were (1) substantial areas of riverine soil (i.e., well-drained, sandy loam soils, particularly where these soils were annually renewed by inundation); (2) a long, moist growing season; and (3) good hunting, particularly for deer and turkey. Several Mississippian settlements in marginal locations—e.g., Aztalan, Dickson, and Town Creek—appear to have been short lived. Perhaps they were short lived because one or more of these variables was found wanting.

But even if agriculture did not rule the hearts and souls of Mississippian people, it was important to them. Indeed, the relative scarcity of riverine soil may help to explain the process by which the Mississippian tradition took shape and expanded. The theory that the Mississippian tradition was the consequence of a Mesoamerican push is no longer acceptable. The borrowing of eastern flint corn and beans was important, but it now appears that the Mississippian tradition was largely built out of local cultural materials. What was new in the Mississippian tradition was a more centralized political structure, and it is almost certain that this was a local development and not an import from Mesoamerica.

How did it happen that Woodland communities relinquished some of their autonomy to become part of a centralized chiefdom? One theory that has been proposed is that after the Indians began to specialize in the cultivation of scarce riverine soils, they became environmentally circumscribed. In many parts of the world, it has been observed that environmental circumscription of this sort has led to political centralization, namely chiefdoms or states. To the Indians of the Woodland tradition, this riverine soil was desirable, but evidently not crucial. Thus if Village A came into conflict with a stronger Village B, A could simply move away to safety. But once riverine soil became all important, and particularly after most of the riverine soil in any particular area was already under cultivation, Village A could not so easily remove itself from B's proximity. An alternative for A might be to secure itself beneath the mantle of a chief powerful enough to effect harmony between the conflicting villages. The result would be a welding together of A and B under the influence of the chief, enabling all involved to stand more strongly against mutual outside foes.

It could also happen that entire chiefdoms might come into conflict with each other, and if as a consequence they fell under the sway of a single strong chiefdom, they would then have attained something approaching state organization. If this latter development actually occurred anywhere in the Mississippian tradition, it would have been at Cahokia. The American Bottom was a rich area where Mississippian people could flourish, but here environmental circumscription was especially great. Expansion was limited on the north, east, and west by climatic conditions too cold or dry for Mississippian agriculture and by decreasing availability of large areas of the necessary riverine soil. There may have been some migration to the south, but by and large the river bottoms here were already occupied by thriving late Woodland or early Mississippian peoples. With such pressures on a burgeoning population, it was likely no accident that the great Cahokia political entity developed where it did.[63]

It should not be inferred from this that the Mississippian tradition spread solely by Mississippian people pushing each other to new riverine frontiers. This did sometimes happen, as we know from Mississippian sites that are clearly intrusive. But there was a second way in which the Mississippian tradition could have spread. All things being equal, centralization breeds centralization. Because centralization confers a military advantage, anywhere Mississippian societies impinged on Woodland societies, it would have been to the latter's advantage to become more centralized, and in so doing they may have adopted aspects of the Mississippian tradition. The South Appalachian cultures may have developed in this fashion.

The Mississippian tradition did not reach into every part of the Southeast. Indeed, at the time of early European contact, there were parts of the Southeast in which the material culture was much like that of Woodland or even Archaic peoples. This was particularly true of territory adjacent to the Texas Gulf Coast, an area whose soil was unsuitable for Mississippian agriculture and an area that was marginal to the spread of new ideas and practices.[64] The people of the northern piedmont and the coast of the Middle Atlantic states were similarly isolated. And as the survivors of the de Soto expedition neared the mouth of the Mississippi River, they were attacked by people who still used the spear-thrower and the javelin. The Woodland tradition lingered on in other places, as in the culture of the Menominees of Wisconsin and the Iroquois of New York State. And as we have already seen, the cultures in Florida and along parts of the Gulf Coast persisted into historic times with only relatively minor Mississippian influence. The Natchez of the lower Mississippi River were basically Mississippian, but perhaps with vestiges of the old Gulf culture.[65]

EUROPEAN EXPLORATION

When Christopher Columbus set foot on the shores of the New World, paving the way for European adventurers to invade and colonize the Americas, the consequences proved great both for the Europeans and for the native people of the New World. Never in the history of the world have cultures so different and so unprepared for each other come into such ineluctable collision. On the one side were the Europeans, with a centuries-old literate tradition behind them, able to accumulate massive quantities of knowledge and to disseminate it through the printed word, to create complex social organizations with precisely specified tasks, and to plan complicated social strategies far into the future. On the other side were the Indians, relying on delicately structured oral traditions, living out their lives in tautly organized social structures, and making their livings in balanced ecological systems worked out over centuries of intensive experience in their home territories.

The American Indians and their homeland were so new to the Europeans, so outside the realm of their best knowledge, that it took over one and one-half centuries for anything approaching a full realization of the new reality to sink in. Africa and Asia were poorly known to Europeans, but they were not new, and when new knowledge of Africa and Asia began reaching Europe it did not challenge fundamental assumptions in the European world view. But there was too much in the New World to comprehend. For the first century or so after the colonization of the New World began, Europeans were little interested in reading about it, preferring instead to read about Turks and Asians.[66] When compared to their accumulated knowledge of people and places in the Old World, the information from the New World seemed weird, unbelievable,

97

irrelevant—it could not be accommodated in familiar categories of understanding. In many ways the European mind was closed against experience. To a surprising degree, the first Europeans in the New World saw what they expected to see.[67]

The first extensive reports from the New World came from the Spanish friars who had to learn native languages and inquire into native cultures and religions in order to be effective missionaries. As these reports reached Europe, intellectuals not only had to fit America as a geographical entity into their image of the physical world, they also had to find a place for the Indians among their categories of human beings, and they had to fit America as a historical entity into the European conception of world history. They were able to make none of these intellectual adjustments immediately. The classical geography of Greece and Rome held on for a remarkably long time while fresh knowledge from the New World eroded it bit by bit.

The problem of where the Indians fitted in as human beings— indeed whether they were human beings at all—was argued throughout the sixteenth century. Since the Indians could not be directly accounted for in Judeo-Christian or classical works, Europeans tried to categorize them in terms of two general classifications of mankind: (1) Christian/heathen and (2) civil/barbarian, with "civil" meaning having benefit of European literate knowledge and social graces, and "barbarian" meaning not having benefit of these.[68] Skin color was at this time relatively unimportant as a way of classifying people. In time it became clear that the Indians of North America were human beings, but they were neither Christian nor civil. In time the Europeans realized that barbarians were of many sorts, ranging from people only a little less civil than Europeans to rude forest-dwellers. Heathens also were of several sorts, in that some of them were more amenable to Christianity than others. The debate continued. Some argued that even if the Indians seemed unintelligent and stupid, this could merely be a product of their upbringing, in much the same way that European peasants were made stupid.

A more serious conceptual problem arose when they realized that a European peasant could be a Christian but a barbarian at the same time. And by the same token, an Indian convert could be a barbarian but also a Christian. Obviously, the two sets of categories did not coincide in any satisfying way, and the Europeans were forced to examine some of their basic assumptions. In the end, they generally decided that people could be rational without being Christian and that higher and lower grades of civilization existed in the world, in different stages of development, ranging from the Chinese on the high end to the savage whose dwelling-place was like that of an animal on the low end. Ultimately, they succeeded in devising a new frame of reference, the forerunner of what anthropologists today call the theory of social evolution.[69]

What the Indians thought of the invading Europeans is far more difficult to determine. Because the Indians lacked writing, the only documentation for the early period is European, and we find only a tantalizing bit of evidence here and there. In general, though, when the Indians first met Europeans, they were friendly and curious, but sometimes apprehensive; they evidently became hostile through experience. In 1524, Giovanni da Verrazzano explored the eastern coast of North America from the Carolinas all the way northward to Newfoundland. When he encountered Indians who had no previous contact with Europeans, they would sometimes run into the woods and hide, but more often they came out to marvel at the Europeans and their white skins and strange clothing. But Verrazzano himself helped change their initial attitudes. At one point in his narrative he casually mentions that his men seized an eight-year-old boy to take him back to France as a specimen. It was not until he reached the coast of Maine, which had previously been visited by English and Portuguese explorers and fishermen that Verrazzano met Indians who were "full of crudity and vices, and were so barbarous that we could never make any communication with them, however many signs we made to them." Evidently, these Indians had already had some experience in trading with Europeans, because they would only accept "knives, hooks for fishing, and sharp metal" in exchange for their goods, refusing the more useless trifles which were offered to them. When Verrazzano's men tried to go inland, the Indians of the coast of Maine shot arrows at them.[70]

From accounts of the de Soto expedition a few years later, we learn that the Indians at first regarded the Spaniards as human beings who would react in predictable, human ways. In one incident, while de Soto was marching northward through Florida, some Indians came peaceably into his camp. Suddenly, one of them took

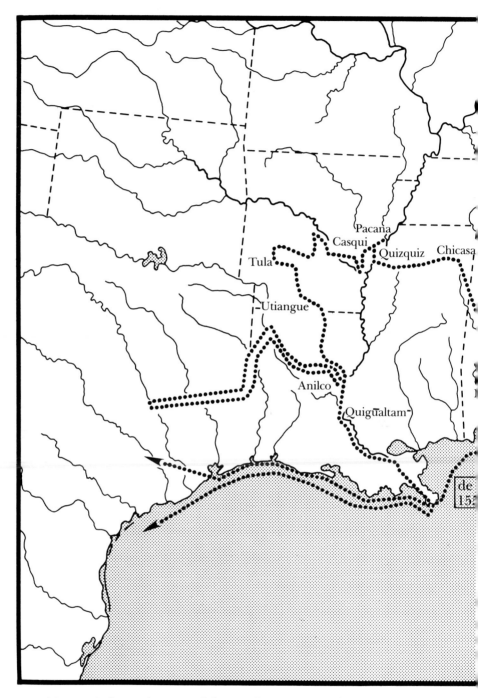

Map 5. Early Exploration of the Southeast.

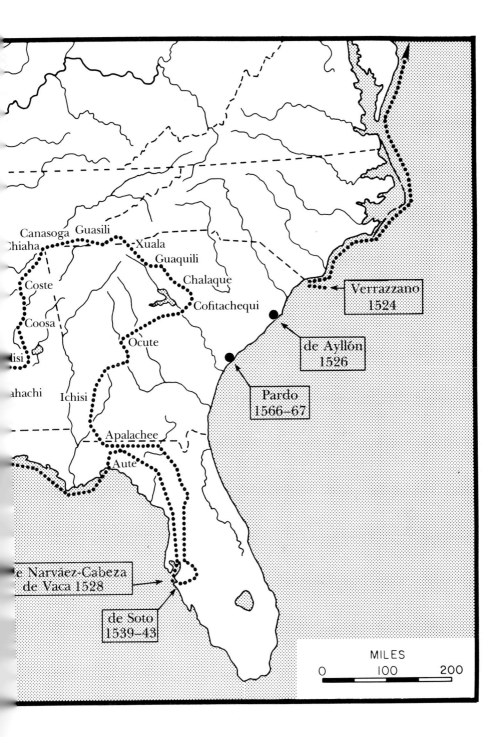

Canasoga Guasili
Chiaha   Xuala
                 Guaquili
   Coste   Chalaque
                 Cofitachequi
   Coosa
                        Verrazzano
                        1524
...isi   Ocute
                            de Ayllón
...hachi   Ichisi   1526

                    Pardo
                    1566–67
          Apalachee
          Aute

e Narváez-Cabeza
de Vaca 1528

      de Soto
      1539–43

                         MILES

                    0   100   200

101

his bow and struck a Spaniard across the back, and then ran away into the woods. His intention was not to kill or injure the Spaniard, but to challenge him to give chase and possibly to do combat, and of course the Spaniard, if he should fail to catch him, would be angered and humiliated, this being counted a victory in Indian warfare. This was evidently an indigenous warfare pattern, and the Indian expected the Spaniard to understand it as any human being would. But the Spaniard sent a huge Irish hound after the Indian either to maim or to kill him.[71] By the time de Soto's men reached Mabila in southern Alabama the Indians, profiting from bitter experience, had redefined them. In an elaborately planned surprise attack, the Indians tried to crush the expedition in one bold stroke, and they very nearly succeeded.

At times the Indians appear not to have appreciated the enormity of the advantage the Europeans gained from their science and technology. When John Lawson was traveling to the back country of South Carolina in 1699–1700, he met a trader who told him about an incident in which some Sewee Indians equipped a fleet of dugout canoes with sails and set out for England, where they expected to get a better rate of exchange for their furs and skins. But before they had gotten far their canoes foundered. Some of them drowned while others were picked up by an English ship and sold into slavery in the West Indies.[72]

On other occasions the Indians were uncomfortably accurate in their appraisal of European beliefs and values. When John Wesley, the founder of Methodism, visited Georgia in 1735–37 to convert the Indians to Christianity, he asked Chicoli, an old Creek chief, what he thought he was made for, implying that his earthly existence was short as compared to eternity. To this Chicoli replied:

> He that is above knows what he made us for. We know nothing. We are in the dark. But white men know much. And yet white men build great houses, as if they were to live for ever. But white men cannot live for ever. In a little time, white men will be dust as well as I.[73]

John Wesley returned to England without having converted the Southeastern Indians to Christianity.

Early Explorers. Although the Norse voyagers visited the northern coast of North America between 1000 and 1013, there is no evidence that any of them visited the southern coast, and it is unlikely that any of those who visited the northern coast had any effect on the Southeastern Indians, unless, of course, they introduced diseases which reached the Southeast.[74] Neither Christopher Columbus (1492) nor John Cabot (1497–98) had any contact with the Southeastern Indians. The first meeting between Europeans and Southeastern Indians for which we have adequate documentation came in 1513 with the Spaniard, Juan Ponce de León, who landed on the Florida Coast and got a decidedly hostile reception from the Indians. In fact, the hostility of the Indians suggests that they either had some previous experience with Europeans, or else some knowledge of their motives.[75] When Ponce de León returned to Florida in 1521 to establish a colony, possibly near Charlotte Harbor, the Indians again attacked, driving his party off and mortally wounding him.[76]

All of the early Spanish explorers in the Southeast were dominated by a single motive—to acquire something they could take away as wealth. The first salable objects they could lay their hands on were human beings, and in 1521 a party led by a captain of Lucas Vázquez de Ayllón came ashore on the south Atlantic coast in the vicinity of Winyaw Bay, South Carolina, where they were greeted by the Indians. Inviting the Indians out to visit their two ships, the Spaniards promptly enslaved them and then embarked for Santo Domingo. One ship foundered and sank en route, killing all on board, and many of the prisoners on the other ship fell ill and died, refusing to eat Spanish food. In an act of mercy, Spanish authorities forced the captors to set the survivors free, but most of the Indians later died. Only one managed both to survive and later to rejoin his own people. This was a man whom the Spaniards named Francisco of Chicora. Ayllón took him to Spain where he met and was interviewed by the great historian Peter Martyr (Pietro Martire d'Anghiera). Largely from what he learned from Francisco, Martyr put together the first lengthy description of a North American Indian group, including it in his book *De Orbe Novo*. Although parts of this description are distorted, either through Martyr's inability to comprehend what Francisco told him, or through Francisco's deliberate distortion, the main features of the description accord with subsequent descriptions of Southeastern Indians.[77]

The next explorer of any consequence was Giovanni da Verrazzano, who set sail from France in January, 1524, in search of a southwest passage to the Pacific Ocean. After fifty days en route he touched the coast of North America near 34 degrees north latitude, just south of Cape Fear. Verrazzano realized that he had landed not upon the coast of Asia, but on the coast of a "new land." From here he sailed up the coast, occasionally going ashore for short visits. He mapped the coast all the way to the Cape Breton–Newfoundland area, and he wrote a brief but valuable account of the people and the land he observed. Even though Verrazzano and his men could not communicate with the Indians through language, he nevertheless felt justified in coming to the following conclusion:

> We think they have neither religion nor laws, that they do not know of a first Cause or Author, that they do not worship the sky, the stars, the sun, the moon, or other planets, nor do they even practice any kind of idolatry; we do not know whether they offer any sacrifices or other prayers, nor are there any temples or churches of prayer among their peoples. We consider that they have no religion and that they live in absolute freedom, and that everything they do proceeds from Ignorance; for they are very easily persuaded, and they imitated everything that they saw us Christians do with regard to divine worship, with the same fervor and enthusiasm that we did.[78]

This account must rank as one of the most extravagant examples of European ethnocentrism ever. It is tempered only by the fact that it does come early, before Europeans had begun to come to grips intellectually with the New World and its people.

The Spanish continued attempting to establish colonies in the Southeast, and they continued to fail. In 1526, Lucas Vázquez de Ayllón with about 500 settlers attempted to establish a colony on the south Atlantic Coast, probably near Winyaw Bay. The Indian, Francisco of Chicora, acted as a guide for Ayllón, but he soon escaped and presumably returned to his own people. Within six months the settlement failed; many of the Spaniards sickened and died, including Ayllón. About 150 people survived to return to the West Indies.

Any of several diseases could have caused the deaths of Ayllón's colonists. Smallpox first broke out on Santo Domingo in the Caribbean in December 1518 or January 1519. Along with it came other diseases, such as measles, typhus, tuberculosis, chicken pox, and influenza. The Europeans had been exposed to these diseases for many centuries, and they had acquired a resistance to them, so that when they fell ill from them, they frequently recovered. But given the inadequate food supply and the crowded conditions in Ayllón's colony, these illnesses would have produced a higher than average mortality rate.

As we have seen, the ancestors of the Southeastern Indians left the diseases of the Old World behind as they entered the New World in the late Pleistocene. But there was no escaping the ultimate consequence, and when Old World diseases did at last reach their shores, the people of the New World met with disaster.

Smallpox was the most terrible of the new diseases. It is caused by a virus that is communicated through the air by means of droplets or dust particles, entering any new host who happens to breathe them into his lungs. It is extremely communicable, especially under crowded conditions. Among the previously unexposed New World populations it would have infected almost every single individual, and 30 percent or more of those infected would have died. After an incubation period of about twelve days, the victim of smallpox suffers from high fever and vomiting, and three or four days later his body becomes covered with skin eruptions. For those who survive the disease, the eruptions dry up in about a week or ten days, and the scabs fall off leaving disfiguring pockmarks, particularly if the eruptions have been scratched. Some are made blind by the disease. Those who survive are immune for a period of several years.[79] By any measure, the initial damage done to the Southeastern Indians by European diseases was far greater than anything Europeans could have inflicted with weapons and military suppression.

Another attempt to colonize the Southeast came in 1528 when Pánfilo de Narváez attempted to conquer the Indians living on the west coast of the Florida peninsula. He landed with a party of about three hundred in Timucuan territory, near Tampa Bay. Narváez and his men did not find this location to their liking, however, and they began moving northward toward the territory of the Apalachee Indians. The Indians to the south had told them that here they would find great quantities of gold and ample crops of corn in the fields.

As soon as they entered Apalachee territory they did indeed find much larger supplies of corn than they found to the south, but they also encountered determined resistance from the Apalachee Indians.[80] The houses of the Apalachees were scattered throughout the countryside. What the Spaniards supposed to be the main village contained forty houses built in an open space sheltered by large trees. All through this country their travel was made difficult by large trees that had been felled by some great storm, probably a hurricane. Narváez appropriated the main village—from which the Apalachees had fled—for his own use. The Apalachees stepped up their raids, picking off Narváez's men and horses one by one. Narváez explored the territory to the north of the village and found it thinly populated. When it became obvious that their colony could not succeed, the Spaniards pulled themselves together and marched southward toward the Gulf. In nine days they reached the village of Aute, where they found that the Indians had burned down all their houses to keep the Spaniards from using them, though they did not burn their fields of corn, beans, and squash, all newly ripe and ready for harvest.[81] The Indians of Aute kept Narváez's party under constant attack. Many of the Spaniards were ill. In desperation they abandoned Aute and marched southward along the course of a river toward the Gulf Coast.

Using improvised materials and tools, they built five barges. They boarded these and set sail to the west, attempting to skirt the Gulf Coast and return to Mexico. But soon they began to run short on food and water. The Indians they met along the coast were apparently hunters and gatherers who lived "poor and miserable" lives as compared to the agriculturalists in the interior. Gradually the Spaniards died—some from disease, others from starvation, others from periodic attacks by the Indians, and still others were drowned when their barges foundered and sank. In time several men, including the remarkable Cabeza de Vaca, found themselves marooned on an island off the coast of Louisiana or Texas. In all probability it was Galveston Island. Here their lives with the Indians (probably Karankawas) were incredibly hard, with frequent periods of famine. The Indians more or less forced them to become medicine men. As such they combined Indian techniques of breathing on the sick person, making small incisions and sucking out small amounts of blood, using massage, and applying fire, with Catholic prayers and ritual actions, such as making the sign of the cross and reciting the Pater Noster, the Ave Maria, and other prayers. In return, the Indians took care of them.[82] Cabeza de Vaca later became a trader and was allowed to move freely among the various groups, most of whom were at war with each other.

After six years, Cabeza de Vaca and three other survivors—Andrés Dorantes, Alonso del Castillo Maldonado, and Estévanico, a black man—escaped and journeyed all the way across what is now Texas and Mexico to Culiacán on the western coast of Mexico, where they rejoined their countrymen. It was an amazing journey, one of the great adventure stories of all times.

For anyone interested in keeping a body count, it would seem that up to this time roughly equal loss of life through combat was suffered on both sides, with the Spanish perhaps suffering somewhat greater losses. However, though the evidence is not conclusive, it is probable that even at this early time the Indians were suffering considerable loss of life from new diseases. Narváez found some evidence of depopulation in West Florida, and even better evidence was found by the next Spanish explorer, Hernando de Soto.

Hernando de Soto. Of all the early exploratory expeditions into the Southeast, the most important by every measure was the expedition of Hernando de Soto. Having attained the rank of captain by the time he was twenty years old, de Soto played an active role in the conquest of the Inca Empire in Peru. He became wealthy from this adventure, but not content; he wanted more. Early explorers had found occasional evidence of gold in the Southeast, and this proof whetted de Soto's appetite for another Inca Empire and accomplishments equal to those of Pizzaro and Cortes.

On May 18, 1539, he set sail from Havana with an army of 600 men along with a contingent of camp followers, servants, and slaves, numbering perhaps an additional hundred. The expedition was outfitted with about 220 horses, a large herd of hogs to be used as food, some mules, and several large, savage Irish hounds to hunt down and kill Indians. He had men and materials sufficient to equip an army and to found a new colony.

De Soto landed at Tampa Bay and immediately came upon virtually the only stroke of good fortune he had on the entire expedition. His party happened upon a Spaniard, Juan Ortiz, who had been a member of the Narváez expedition, and who had been captured by Indians. He had lived with them for eleven years and was able to speak fluently one of their languages—probably a Timucuan language. He served as de Soto's interpreter as they traveled through Timucuan territory, and later on he served as the last link in a chain

of interpreters. For example, when they entered Apalachee territory they had to locate an Indian who could translate Apalachee into
Timucuan, and Ortiz could then translate from Timucuan into
Spanish. Later in the expedition there were three or more links in
the chain of translation.[83] In addition to serving as interpreter, Ortiz
probably served as a kind of anthropological advisor to de Soto,
although his knowledge of Timucuan Florida was probably not an
infallible guide to what they encountered in the interior.

Not finding the Tampa Bay region attractive, de Soto immediately
began moving north. As they passed through a series of small
Timucuan groups, they encountered increasing resistance from the
Indians. This was probably a consequence of de Soto's brutality. He
burned villages needlessly, and when his Indian guides did not
perform to his liking, he threw them to the Irish hounds to be torn
apart and killed.[84] Generally speaking, the further they moved
north and inland, into the Mississippian heartland, the more populous and the more strongly centralized were the societies they
encountered. The territories of these groups were frequently separated by large rivers and by unpopulated areas. The expedition was
barely under way when they reached northern Florida, but already
they were beginning to run low on the supplies of cheese and biscuit
they brought along for food, and so they began to rely on the stores of
corn and vegetables they could plunder from the Indians. They were
meat-hungry for the duration of the expedition. Early in the expedition they took to killing and eating every dog they could find in the
Indian villages.[85]

Some of the Indians simply abandoned their villages and let de
Soto pass through. Others harassed his expedition as it moved
through their territory. In early October, de Soto entered the
territory of the Apalachee Indians, who had so successfully driven
out the Narváez expedition eleven years earlier. Like Narváez, de
Soto did not find adequate supplies of native food until he entered
Apalachee territory, and this was also where his soldiers met their
first serious military challenge. Having constructed ingenious fortified impediments against the Spaniards and thereby slowing down
their movements, the Apalachees launched a well organized attack
against them as they moved through a difficult swamp crossing. The
Apalachees fought the Spaniards every step of the way to the tribe's
main town. The Spaniards retaliated by killing everybody they could

lay their hands on. But the Apalachees continued to harass them day and night, never allowing them to rest.

The territory of the Apalachees lay on an ecological frontier. De Soto's men found the terrain to the north of the Apalachees free of swamps and heavy forest, but to the south the swamps were so dense that they were difficult to penetrate.[86] Perhaps this explains why they found a greater abundance of deer here than further south. They spent the winter of 1539–40 in Apalachee territory, even though the Indians continued to put constant pressure on them, harassing them and picking them off one by one. The Spaniards were deeply impressed with the reckless courage of the Indians.

In early March, de Soto and his men again began moving northward, entering the southwestern corner of Georgia. Their goal was to reach the province of Cofitachequi, where the Indians had told them they would find precious metals. Traveling rapidly, they passed through several villages without resistance. When they approached the village of Ichisi, they were met by women clad in skirts and mantles made out of white mulberry fiber, who gave them corn cakes and bunches of small green onions to eat.[87] Where they could, they forced the Indians into service carrying their gear and supplies. But even so, when they entered the town of Ocute, which is thought to have been on the Ocmulgee River, they were welcomed by the Indians. De Soto learned that the territory of Ocute bordered that of Cofitachequi, but that a vast wilderness (possibly the territory from the Ocmulgee River to beyond the Savannah River) lay in between and required two weeks to cross. A chief, Patofa, supplied guides and burden bearers, and he proposed that he would bring along a large number of warriors and the two would ally in an assault against Cofitachequi.

However, as their travels through the wilderness progressed, it became clear that the Indians were somewhat confused about the best route. De Soto and his Indian companions soon became unsure in their movements, their food ran out, and their way was impeded because the streams and rivers were flooded, making it necessary for them to build bridges and barges. The forests were very dense and difficult to get through.

When they reached the first small town in Cofitachequi, Patofa and his men robbed the temple, desecrated it, and killed and scalped every person they could catch. Patofa repeated these actions in several additional towns, and then he and his men returned home.[88]

It would appear that the Indians of Ocute were seeking revenge from Cofitachequi (see chap. 4). When they were satisfied with the vengeance they had wreaked, they left. The fact that they were unsure of the way to Cofitachequi suggests that in their conflict with that province they were more often the attacked than the attackers, and that de Soto provided them with a rare chance to turn the tables.

The main town of Cofitachequi is thought to have been located at Silver Bluff, near Augusta, Georgia, on the South Carolina side of the Savannah River, or else on the headwaters of the Santee River in South Carolina. Cofitachequi was apparently an unusual society. For one thing, the official welcome to de Soto was given by a woman—the "Lady of Cofitachequi." She was carried to the river on a litter covered with delicate, white cloth and then taken across to the Spaniards in a large, ornate dugout canoe. One of the Indians carried a special stool for her to sit on as she talked with de Soto, and a Spaniard of the expedition romantically compared her to Cleopatra, noting that she was "brown but well proportioned."[89] She told de Soto that there was little food because her people had been afflicted by a terrible plague that had caused many deaths. Perhaps this was from diseases introduced by Ayllón's people fourteen years earlier. De Soto expected to find gold and silver, but when he asked for it, the people brought him the closest thing they had—pieces of copper and large slabs of mica. The only articles they possessed of any value were quantities of fresh-water pearls, and even these were much inferior to salt-water pearls.

Cofitachequi was one of the most impressive Indian societies de Soto encountered. When the Spaniards crossed the river, the people of Cofitachequi gave them presents of well tanned skins, "blankets," strips of venison, dry wafers, and a large quantity of "very good salt." The people wore unusual leggings and moccasins, and they wore matchcoats made of "sable" and "wild cat" (probably cougar) skins. They were described by the Spaniards as being "clean and polite." In one of their temples the Spaniards found beads, rosaries, and "Biscayan" axes, which had evidently been carried inland from Ayllón's ill-fated colony.[90]

About three or four miles from the main village lay Talomico, the religious center and perhaps political center of the society, a town said to contain five hundred houses built on a bluff overlooking a gorge of a river. This town contained one of the most impressive examples of native architecture that de Soto witnessed. The town itself was deserted, probably because of the depopulation caused by the plague. The buildings were larger and more carefully constructed than buildings in other villages in Cofitachequi. The main temple was particularly impressive. Situated on a high mound, it was 100 feet long and 40 feet wide, with a lofty roof covered with finely made cane mats. Inside and out the roof was decorated with conch shells and strings of fresh-water pearls.[91]

Entrance to the temple was through large doors. Just inside, the entrance was lined with paired rows of massive, life-like wooden statues. There were six pairs in all. The first pair carried maces with diamond-shaped heads, reminiscent of the "batons" depicted in Southeastern Ceremonial Complex motifs.[92] The second pair held wooden "broadswords" like those in the Southeastern Ceremonial Complex.[93] The third pair held clubs made of two parts connected with a swivel, like flax swingles.[94] The fourth pair held "battle-axes"; the fifth pair held bows and arrows; and the sixth pair held pikes with copper spear points. All of the statues held their weapons threateningly, as if they were about to use them on intruders. The room also contained numerous statues of men and women. Carved wooden chests containing the remains of dead notables rested on low benches along the walls. The room also contained "breastplates like corselets and head pieces made of rawhide" (see fig. 91), round and oval-shaped shields, chests filled with pearls, and bundles of furs and skins.[95] Around the temple there were eight small "annexes." These annexes were filled with different kinds of weapons and shields. Many of these weapons were decorated with strands of pearls, strips of colored leather, or with strips of copper.[96]

After plundering the temple of all its pearls, de Soto and his men left, heading northwest and taking with them by force the Lady of Cofitachequi. They traveled along the banks of a river and came next to a territory called "Chalaque," perhaps the Muskogean word *čilo·kkitá*, "people of a different speech." This and several other settlements they passed through seem to have been affiliated in some way with Cofitachequi. In all of them there was a scarcity of corn.[97] This may have been owing to the disruption of the plague.

In late May of 1540, the de Soto expedition crossed the Blue Ridge

Mountains into Cherokee territory. The surprising ease and rapidity with which their Indian guides led them across the mountains suggests that they traveled a trail that provided frequent and probably friendly contact between the Indians on the eastern side of the mountains and the Cherokees on the western side. In fact, it is probable that then as later the Cherokees were living on both sides of the mountains. The ease with which the Spaniards moved through this area may also indicate that the Cherokees had been weakened by smallpox or some other European disease. In Cherokee territory the expedition is thought to have followed the course of the Hiwassee River to the village of Canasoga. Then they swung southward to Chiaha and Coste and southward again to the upper reaches of the Coosa River in northern Alabama, where they once more encountered Muskogean-speaking people. Here they found plenty of corn. Chiaha and Coste seem to have been frontier towns that helped protect the Muskogean-speakers from the Cherokees in the mountains. According to one of de Soto's chroniclers, Chiaha was the first place they encountered a palisaded village, and both Chiaha and Coste were built on islands.[98]

In mid-July, de Soto entered the province of Coosa (whose descendants were the Upper Creeks of later times). Here his party was met by the principal chief, who was carried on a litter in great state, accompanied by several hundred warriors. Coosa at this time was one of the most powerful social entities in the Southeast. The dense population suggests that European diseases had not yet reached this far into the interior. De Soto had heard of the existence of Coosa several months earlier. The expedition remained there for about one month while their relations with the Indians steadily deteriorated. In the end they seized the chief and several of his men, putting them in iron collars and chains and forcing them to serve as burden bearers, and then they slowly moved southward during September, visiting towns and villages of Muskogean-speaking people along the banks of the Coosa River. At each town they demanded bearers and women. Talisi, the last town in Coosa, was fortified with a wood and earth palisade, and it lay surrounded by fields of corn in a sharp bend of the river, so that it was almost completely encircled by water.

In early October they entered the territory of Tascalusa, an Indian leader more imposing than any de Soto had previously encountered. Entering the town of Atahachi, they found Tascalusa seated on cushions on a "kind of balcony" atop a mound on one side of the plaza. He wore a kind of coif or turban, which signified his authority, and a handsome feather cape that reached all the way to his feet. An attendant stood by holding a sunshade in the form of a very large round "fly fan" decorated with a white cross on a black field. The Spaniards described it as being like the emblem of the Knights of the Order of St. John of Rhodes. When de Soto walked up to meet Tascalusa, he remained seated "as if he had been a king." After a while a number of Indians came into the plaza to dance.[99]

Later, de Soto placed Tascalusa under arrest and demanded four hundred burden bearers and one hundred women. Tascalusa gave him the bearers and told him he would have the women once they reached the town of Mabila. On the way they came to a village where they learned that a Greek and a black man from Narváez's expedition had been killed when they put ashore during their attempt to reach Mexico.[100] All along the way, Tascalusa was accompanied by an attendant shielding him from the sun with a sunshade. As they approached Mabila some Indians came out and gave Tascalusa some chestnut bread to eat.

Although the exact site of Mabila has not been discovered, it is thought to have been located between the lower Alabama and Tombigbee rivers. The town was situated on a clear, level plain, surrounded by a strong palisade that stood "as high as three men." It was built of heavy vertical posts with smaller poles tied to these in horizontal courses on both sides, and the whole thing plastered with mud mixed with grass. Defensive towers that could each hold seven or eight warriors were situated at fifty-foot intervals along the wall. Inside there was a plaza with houses and buildings around it.

The Indians evidently had planned for some time to attack de Soto at Mabila. It was a surprise attack with the Indians suddenly swarming from their hiding places in great numbers and driving most of the Spaniards outside the gates. The Indians killed all the horses they could lay their hands on, and a pitched battle raged for several hours. Then the Spaniards managed to counterattack and to regain entry to the town. They fell on the Indians and killed most of them, burning many to death by setting fire to the houses. Here, as throughout the expedition, it was the horses that won the battle for the Spaniards. The Indians were superior to Spanish foot soldiers, but they were no match against the cavalry. Even though the

Indians had "pikes," they did not know how to use them effectively against the horses.

As the fight at Mabila progressed and the Spaniards gained the upper hand, the Indians fought even more furiously, and eventually suicidally. More than 20 Spaniards died in the battle, most of them struck by arrows in the face or in the neck, where their armor of quilted cotton left them unprotected. Another 20 or so died later of wounds they sustained in the battle. In addition, more than forty horses were killed. Virtually all of de Soto's men were wounded, many of them more than once. The Indians suffered a staggering loss that is variously estimated at from 2,500 to 5,000 dead. Tascalusa's son (or, what is more likely, his sister's son) was killed, and perhaps Tascalusa himself was killed.

The battle of Mabila was the turning point in the de Soto expedition. His soldiers were wounded almost to a man, they had lost the pearls they stole from Cofitachequi, they lost most of their clothing, and they were short on food. They had found no wealth to speak of, and they were coming to realize that the Southeastern Indians were not like the Indians of Mexico and Peru: "They [began to think] that it was impossible to dominate such bellicose people or to subjugate men who were so free, and that because of what they had seen up until that time, they felt they could never make the Indians come under their yoke and dominion either by force or by trickery, for rather than do so these people would all permit themselves to be slain."[101]

De Soto's men grew mutinous, and even though he knew that he was within one hundred miles of the Gulf Coast and safety, he determined to turn north once again in a desperate attempt to salvage something from the expedition. He realized that he was on the verge of losing everything. If his army disintegrated, he would never command another. After pausing to allow the wounds of his men to heal, he again struck out northward, burning Indian villages as he went through Choctaw territory in the middle of November.

De Soto continued northward and then westward through what is now Mississippi, entering Chickasaw country in late December. Here they camped for the winter. But by now the Indians had figured out more effective tactics. They could not raid the Spanish as they could other Indians; and it was foolhardy for them to mount a massive attack against the Spanish and their horses, as at Mabila.

What the Chickasaws did was to harass the expedition continually, attacking mainly in the night. In one particularly severe night attack, the Chickasaws dealt them a near-mortal blow. About one dozen Spaniards were killed and fifty or sixty of their precious horses were lost.

In late April 1541, de Soto and his men set out once more toward the west. In early May they came upon a village they called Quizquiz (possibly Tunica-speakers), on the eastern bank of the Mississippi River. Here they stopped long enough to build barges, which they used to cross the river into what is now Arkansas; and as they worked, thousands of Indians gathered on the opposite shore to threaten them. Across the river, in the town of Casqui, they saw the remains of buffalo for the first time. Casqui and the nearby town of Pacaha had the strongest fortifications of any town they had seen.[102] As they moved further west and south they encountered the Tulas, who lived on the western margin of the Southeastern Culture Area. Their main source of food was the buffalo, and unlike the Indians the Spaniards encountered all through the Southeast, they raised little corn. In November they settled in Utiangue, a palisaded town in southern Arkansas, where they spent a hard, cold winter. Here, Juan Ortiz, their interpreter, died.

In early March 1542, they again began to move south. In late March, at a place called Anilco, in eastern Louisiana, they found larger stores of corn than they had found at Coosa or at Apalachee. It was also the most densely populated region they had seen. De Soto destroyed several towns along the western bank of the Mississippi River. Then, according to the chroniclers, he became despondent, caught fever, fell progressively more ill, and died in May 1542.

Luis de Moscoso de Alvarado assumed command. The previous summer and winter the Indians had told them that they had heard of another Spanish expedition conquering Indians to the west. Evidently, the Indians had got word of Coronado and his exploration of the Southwest, which began in 1540. Desiring to join up with his countrymen, Moscoso set out due west. They again encountered Caddoan-speaking Indians and eventually the Tonkawas. The land grew progressively arid, and they were soon forced to eat grass and roots. They began encountering Indians who did not live in large, compact villages, but rather in small huts with no more than four or five huts to a community. They grew no corn, subsisting mainly by hunting buffalo. Moreover, by constantly lying in ambush for the Spaniards, they inflicted painful losses on them. They would prepare a careful ambush, rise up and shoot arrows, and then run away to safety. These attacks were constant, day and night.

Now desperate, Moscoso determined to return to the Mississippi River, where he knew he could get Indian corn. They returned there to spend their final winter. They built seven small boats and began sailing down the river in early July. A few days later they were attacked by the chief of the Quigualtams, who had formed an alliance with other Indians, laying aside for this occasion their traditional hostilities. Some of them were probably ancestors of the Natchez. An immense fleet of Indians in large canoes followed the Spaniards down the river harassing them for over one week and doing considerable damage. When they reached the Gulf Coast, they were attacked for the first time by people who used six-foot javelins thrown from spear-throwers.[103] On July 18 they departed the Southeast for Mexico, and on September 10, 1543, about three hundred survivors reached the port of Panuco. From here, some of them returned to Spain, others went to Peru, and some remained in Mexico.

Later Explorers. Other men explored the Southeast after de Soto, but none with such drama nor with such telling consequences for the Indians. In July 1559, Tristán de Luna led an expedition of 300 soldiers along with 1,200 women, white retainers, and Indian servants from Mexico. They established a post at the Indian village of Ochuse near Pensacola Bay. De Luna was supposed to explore westward to the Mississippi River and to find a route linking Coosa with the Atlantic Coast, but he succeeded in none of this. The de Luna expedition began running short on food, and in February 1560 they moved inland, where some of them reached the Coosa Indians and got corn, beans, and squash from them. According to de Luna and his men, the Indians all along the Alabama River were depleted as a result of their encounter with de Soto and probably from diseases as well. The de Luna expedition soon failed, and most of the survivors returned home in April 1561.[104]

In the 1560s the Spanish became fearful that the French were planning to establish colonies on the eastern seaboard of North America, whence they could both attack Spanish shipping and explore the interior, perhaps finding an overland route to the Spanish silver mines in northern Mexico. In 1565 the Spanish founded St. Augustine, and in 1566 they strengthened their tiny outpost at Santa Elena, near Beaufort, South Carolina, and they commissioned Captain Juan Pardo to explore, missionize, and secure the interior. In November 1566, Pardo set out with 300 men, along with another contingent of 125 men under Sergeant Hernando Boyano. For seven days they traveled through the coastal plain, for some 90 to 100 miles, through territory which was evidently only sparsely populated. Then they reached Guiamae (de Soto's Aymay), and a few miles further they found Cofitachequi.

From here they moved northward into the piedmont, where they found meadowlike country with many springs. They passed through Tagaya, Issa (later called Essaw), and finally Xuala, previously visited by de Soto. From the site of Xuala, they could see the Blue Ridge Mountains. Here they built a small garrison, naming it San Juan de Xuala. Leaving Boyano and his detachment at the garrison, Pardo set out eastward and southward along the stream on which Xuala was located. They passed through the village of Quihanaqui and thence to Guatari, a seat of power, evidently governed by two female chiefs. Here they built another small outpost. Then, getting word that Santa Elena might be in danger, Pardo returned to the coast.

In the meantime, Boyano aligned himself with the Xuala Indians and began attacking the Cherokees in the mountains. One of the Cherokee leaders sent word that he was coming over to kill and eat the Spaniards and Boyano's dog as well. Boyano and his men then traveled through the mountains for four days, finding and attacking the Cherokees in a palisaded town. They destroyed the town, killing many. From here Boyano moved on past the town of Cauchi, past the town of Tanasqui, which was protected on one side by a strong palisade with towers and presumably by a river on the other sides. From here they went to Chiaha, previously visited by de Soto. Here the soil was unusually fertile, and there were many villages on the creeks and rivers.

Then Pardo returned from Santa Elena and joined Boyano at Chiaha. Together they set out again traveling south and west to the towns of Chalaume and Satapo, but here they met opposition from the Indians and they turned back. However, Pardo's interpreter continued on until he reached a town in Coosa, where he found drawings of Spaniards and horses on the walls of Indian houses, as well as coats of mail and Spanish weapons. They built small garrisons at Chiaha, Cauchi, and Guiamae, leaving from fifteen to twenty soldiers in each. But the Spanish were subsequently unable to maintain these outposts, and they were either destroyed by the Indians or abandoned.[105]

Although de Soto discovered the Mississippi River for the Europeans, the French explored it. In 1673, Joliet and Marquette traveled by canoe down the Mississippi River to a Quapaw town near the mouth of the Arkansas River. And in 1682, La Salle descended all the way to the mouth of the river, taking possession of the land in the name of the king of France. In 1690, Tonti came down the river, stopping at the Taensa village on Lake St. Joseph, and crossing over to the town of Natchitoches on the Red River.

The British were far more prosaic in their exploration than were the Spanish and French. Sir John Hawkins sailed along the Florida and Carolina coast in 1565, writing a brief account of his observations. After Jamestown and other settlements were finally established, John Lederer explored the Virginia back country in 1669 and 1670, going southward into the piedmont for some distance, although the true extent of his exploration is controversial. In 1671, Thomas Batts and Robert Fallam of Virginia also explored southward into the piedmont. And in 1673, James Needham and Gabriel Arthur, also from Virginia, penetrated even further into the back country and into the Appalachian Mountains, where they visited the Cherokees, finding that they possessed some European goods they had evidently acquired from the Spanish. These explorations paved the way for the Virginia traders, who followed very aggressively on their heels. By 1700, English traders penetrated all the way to the Quapaw country on the banks of the Mississippi River.[106]

What did the Europeans gain from their exploration and the carnage that went along with it? They learned, first of all, that there was no easy avenue to wealth in North America. De Soto apparently found evidence of the gold deposits in northern Georgia, but it would have to be mined. They also learned that the Indians could not be conquered and pacified in the way that the Spanish were able to conquer Mesoamerica and South America. Perhaps the most important gain for the Europeans from this early exploration, small as it now seems, was that they were able gradually to put together a cartographic conception of eastern North America. By about 1700 reasonably good descriptive maps were available for the Southeast, although truly modern mapping with refined instruments did not begin until after 1750.[107]

And what, we may ask, did the Southeastern Indians gain? Salvation for their souls? A desire for enlightenment? An appreciation of the achievements of European civilization? None of these. What they got was their first taste of a people so reckless with human lives that they were willing to pit entire armies against each other, in open combat, with fearful losses of life on both sides. They got their first taste of a people who would kidnap, enslave, and burn their villages out of pique because their sheets of copper and slabs of mica were not precious enough. They got their first taste of a people who wished to take from them everything they possessed and who would one day dig up their very graves for the value of what they contained.

CHAPTER THREE

THE BELIEF SYSTEM

Like all other people in the world, the Southeastern Indians interpreted most of the humdrum, everyday events in their lives in terms of ordinary, common sense beliefs and knowledge. This does not mean that the common sense beliefs and knowledge of the Southeastern Indians resembled our own common sense beliefs and knowledge in a point-by-point fashion, but rather that it was knowledge which was generally shared by all normal adults. At the same time, again like all other people, the Southeastern Indians encountered in the course of their lives some events and conditions which they could not explain in terms of common sense, and these are precisely the events and conditions their belief system explained.

It is useful to think of this Southeastern Indian belief system as a kind of theory. Just as a theory in our natural sciences explains a certain range of phenomena, a belief system explains unusual events in everyday life, though it is expressed in terms we generally call religious or magical. But to regard the belief system of the Southeastern Indians as being merely religious or magical is to fail to appreciate it. The fact is, the categories and beliefs of the Southeastern Indians represented the world as they believed it existed, and this included both the natural and the supernatural, the normal and the abnormal, and the sacred and the profane. The social arrangements, customary practices, and rituals of the Southeastern Indians make sense only when viewed against the ideological background of their belief system.

Anthropologists who have studied the belief systems of living preliterate people have found that the spiritual beings they believe in often display a dazzling complexity. But it is a complexity that has a system behind it, so that complex appearances can often be accounted for in terms of a few basic categories and principles.

Moreover, these categories and principles usually fit together in a way that is more complete and ordered than anything in our own experience. In a rather literal sense, in preliterate belief systems everything is related to everything else. The interrelated structure of the Southeastern Indian belief system is the key to understanding their almost obsessive concern with purity and pollution. We will see in chapter 6 that most of their rituals and ceremonies were means of keeping their categories pure and of ridding them of pollution after it occurred. Moreover, like other preliterate and protoliterate peoples, the Southeastern Indians placed a special value and meaning on the anomalies and abominations that occurred along the margins and in the interstices of their classification system, the things and creatures which happened to have the attributes of two or more categories.[1] If there is a single word which epitomizes the Southeastern Indian belief system, it is "order." They insisted that things be the way they thought they were supposed to be.

Unfortunately, we cannot hope to reconstruct the Southeastern belief system in the fullness of its original form. Unlike anthropologists who may spend up to ten or even twenty years analyzing the belief system of a single living preliterate people, we who study the Southeast are largely limited to what we can learn from the documentary information collected by early naturalists, historians, and anthropologists. When an anthropologist working with living preliterate people is puzzled about the precise nature of a category or belief, he can ask someone to explain it to him. But fieldwork with contemporary Southeastern Indians cannot supply the information that we need about their ancestors who lived so long ago, and so to answer our most important questions we must rely on historical documents. Although we shall be forever in the dark about some details, enough information was collected by early observers like John Lawson, James Adair, and William Bartram, and by anthropologists like James Mooney and John R. Swanton to allow us at least to reconstruct the outlines of the Southeastern belief system.

It is regrettable that we can never know how much diversity existed among the belief systems of various Southeastern societies. We do know from the archaeological record and from accounts left by the earliest Europeans who had contact with the Southeastern Indians that there were in fact substantial cultural similarities among these societies in late prehistoric and protohistoric times. We also know that when some of the Southeastern Indians began to be dislocated by European diseases, slave-raiders, and wars, they took up residence with other Southeastern peoples with considerable ease, and this implies that they thought in much the same terms even when they spoke different languages. The Natchez, for example, after being driven out of the lower Mississippi valley by the French went to live with Creeks, Chickasaws, Catawbas, and Cherokees. And it is notable that James Mooney and John Swanton who collected Southeastern oral traditions in the late nineteenth and early twentieth centuries often remarked on the large number of motifs and stories that were common all over the Southeast. In some cases, the Indians with whom Mooney and Swanton worked explicitly said that they learned some of their oral traditions from storytellers who were from other Southeastern societies.[2]

THE COSMOS: BASIC CATEGORIES AND CONCEPTS

The Southeastern Indians conceived of This World as a great, flat island resting rather precariously on the surface of the waters, suspended from the vault of the sky by four cords attached at each of the cardinal directions. Most of them evidently thought that the island was circular in shape, but that it was crosscut by the four cardinal directions, and it is reasonable to assume that each Southeastern society conceived of itself as occupying the center of the circle.[3] It is also reasonable to assume that the circle and cross motif of the Southeastern Ceremonial Complex represents This World, the four directions, and the center (fig. 34).[4] Above This World was the sky vault, an inverted bowl of solid rock which rose and fell twice each day, at dawn and at dusk, so that the sun and moon could pass beneath it.[5] When the sun passed up and under the inside of the sky vault it was day; while it was returning back to its starting place in the east it was night.

The Southeastern cosmos consisted of three worlds: in addition to This World, an Upper World existed above the sky vault, and an Under World existed beneath the earth and the waters. This World was believed to have seven levels. Although the way in which these levels were arranged probably varied in different parts of the Southeast, the Cherokees evidently thought they all existed in This World, between the Under World and the Upper World, with the

Figure 34. Shell gorget with the circle and cross motif. Spiro, Oklahoma. Courtesy, Museum of the American Indian, Heye Foundation.

first level nearest the Under World and the seventh level nearest the Upper World. Thus, the Cherokees may have conceived of the sky vault as not a spherical bowl, but rather as a bowl whose sides were composed of a series of concentric, stepped levels.[6] This stepped sky vault may be represented above a bird-man engraved on a shell drinking cup found at Spiro (fig. 35). Perhaps it represents a bird-man deity flying above the earth.[7]

In the beginning, just two worlds existed: the Upper World and the Under World. This World, the world on which the Indians lived, was created later. The Upper World epitomized order and expecta-

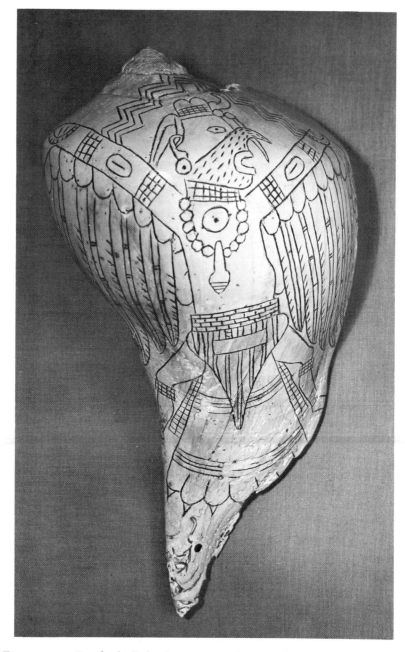

Figure 35a. Conch shell drinking cup with incised design. Spiro, Oklahoma. Courtesy, Museum of the American Indian, Heye Foundation.

124

Figure 35b. Bird-man deity or a man costumed as a bird. Drawn from the conch shell cup in Figure 35a. Note the conch shell columella necklace and barred ovals. Courtesy, Museum of the American Indian, Heye Foundation.

bleness, while the Under World epitomized disorder and change, and This World stood somewhere between perfect order and complete chaos.

In the Upper World things existed in a grander and purer form than they did in This World. We will probably never entirely understand the precise nature of the more remote Southeastern deities who dwelled in the Upper World. The Sun and the Moon, for example, were of the Upper World, but their sexual identities are inconsistent. The Sun, the source of all warmth, light, and life, was one of the principal gods, but whereas some of the Southeastern Indians regarded the Sun as male, the Cherokees generally considered the Sun to be female. The Cherokees called the Sun "the apportioner," referring to her dividing night and day, and perhaps life and death as well. The Creeks called their principal deity "the master of breath."[8] The earthly representative and ally of the Sun was sacred fire, the principal symbol of purity. If anyone did anything wrong in the presence of sacred fire, it would immediately inform the Sun of this wrongdoing, and the Sun might punish the offender.[9] The Choctaws believed that the Sun watched them with its great blazing eye, and so long as the eye was on them they were all right, but if the eye was not on them they were doomed. The Cherokees believed that sacred fire, like the Sun, was an old woman. Out of respect, they fed her a portion of each meal; if neglected, they thought she might come at night in the guise of an owl or whippoorwill and take vengeance on them.[10] Successful hunters would throw into the fire a piece of meat (usually liver) from any game they killed. One could be stricken by disease as a consequence of urinating into a fire, spitting into it, or throwing into it anything that had saliva on it. The Cherokees addressed fire by the epithets "Ancient White" and "Ancient Red."[11] Some Southeastern Indians built their sacred fire by resting four logs together in the shape of a cross, so that the fire burned in the center; others built sacred fire by arranging small pieces of wood or dry cane in a circle or spiral, so that the sacred fire burned in a circular path. Thus the circle and cross motif also symbolized sacred fire.[12]

The Cherokees believed that the Moon was the Sun's brother, with the clear implication that an incestuous relationship existed between them.[13] In the Southeastern belief system the Moon was sometimes associated with rain and with menstruation, and with fertility generally, but it was not as important a deity as the Sun. When an eclipse of the Moon occurred, the Indians believed that it was being swallowed by a giant frog in the Upper World. They would all run out of their houses yelling and making noise to frighten away the frog.[14] It goes without saying that they always succeeded, thereby saving the moon from destruction.

The Cherokees addressed both the Sun (and sacred fire) and the

Moon as "our grandparent." As we shall see in chapter 4, the kinship system of the Southeastern Indians was more than just a means of ordering social relationships among kinsmen. It was a conceptual model which shaped their thinking about relationships in other realms. By addressing the Sun and Moon as "our grandparent," the Cherokees meant that the Sun and Moon stood in a relationship of respect and affection, as their remote ancestors. Their metaphorical use of "elder brother," "younger brother," "mother," and so on also implied relationships modeled on kin relationships in their social world.

Another important Cherokee deity was Thunder or *Kanati*, the Red Man, who lived above the sky vault in the east. The Red Man's voice was heavy, rolling crashes of thunder, while lighter, metallic sounding thunder was the voice of his two sons, the Thunder Boys, also called the Little Red Men. The Indians regarded the Red Man as their friend. He sometimes killed white men with lightning, but never Indians, unless of course they treated him disrespectfully. The Red Man was opposed to the Black Man, who lived above the sky vault in the west. Although the Red Man was usually a source of aid and comfort, he became angry when men took his name in vain by calling him "red" in everyday speech; consequently, in everyday speech the Cherokees called him "white," calling him by his real name only on ceremonial occasions.[15]

Creatures in the Upper World were much larger than those in This World, and although the Upper World had many of the same features that were found in This World, such as chiefs, councils, and town houses, the beings of the Upper World were not subject to all of the rules that limited ordinary people in their behavior. They could therefore do remarkable things, such as transforming themselves into other shapes. In contrast, beings in the Under World were often ghosts or monsters, and things in the Under World often had inverted properties—just the opposite of normal things in This World. The seasons, for example, were the opposite of seasons in This World, so that when it was warm in This World it was cold in the Under World. Under World beings sometimes wore rattlesnakes around their necks and wrists instead of necklaces and bracelets. The Under World was peopled by cannibals, ghosts, man-killer witches, monsters, and various thunder spirits.

The Upper World represented structure, expectableness,

boundaries, limits, periodicity, order, stability, and past time. The Under World represented inversions, madness, invention, fertility, disorder, change, and future time. The Southeastern Indians lived in between, in This World, trying to strike a balance.[16] For example, sacred fire, which represented the Sun and the Upper World, was thought to be opposed to water, especially water in springs and rivers, which represented the Under World, and it was up to man to see that these two substances were always kept apart. Therefore, it was forbidden to pour water onto sacred fire. The Cherokees regarded the river as a deity, calling him the Long Man, ". . . a giant with his head in the foothills of the mountains and his foot far down in the lowland, pressing always, resistless and without stop, to a certain goal, and speaking in murmurs which only the priest may interpret."[17]

The Southeastern Indians believed that things were not always as they are now, and in early times many of the large animals and beings of the Upper World came down to live in This World. But This World grew to be progressively a less ideal place to live, and one by one the great animals and beings went back to the Upper World, leaving their inferior images behind to be the ordinary animals and spirits with which the Southeastern Indians were familiar. As this happened, This World became populated by three great categories of nonspiritual beings: men, animals, and plants. Men and animals were opposed to each other, with enmity existing between them, while plants were the friends of man. We shall presently see that this triad of men, animals, and plants figured prominently in the Cherokee theory of disease and medicine.

There were three major categories of animals: the four-footed animals, epitomized by the deer; the birds, who because of flight were associated with the Upper World, and who were epitomized by the bald eagle; and thirdly, vermin, such as snakes, lizards, frogs, fish, perhaps insects, and other animals associated with the Under World and epitomized by the rattlesnake. The position of insects in this scheme is uncertain: if they were not a separate order, they were probably categorized with the vermin. Each of these major categories was broken down into subcategories to such a degree that the Indians had names for all of the species that were important to them.

Many animals had specific symbolic values in Southeastern thinking. Birds were especially important, and this importance is reflected in the many bird motifs in the Southeastern Ceremonial Complex. Most important of all were the falcons, and probably the peregrine falcon (*Falco peregrinus*) in particular, the swiftest of all the birds, who flies high and dives down at its prey with partly folded wings at an estimated speed of 180 miles per hour. Unlike the hawk, which kills by grasping and impaling its prey with its talons, the keen-eyed falcon dives down on its unsuspecting prey and strikes so powerful a blow with its feet or talons that the prey is often killed outright, much as an enemy would fall beneath the blow of a warrior's war club. Representations of peregrine falcons on sheets of thin copper have been found at several Mississippian sites, and the forked-eye design of the Southeastern Ceremonial Complex evidently is modeled after falcon eye markings (fig. 36).[18] Within the memory of John Swanton's informants, Creek hunters used to carry a buckskin pouch containing a sacred crystal (to be discussed presently) and some red ocher pigment. They would take out this pouch, open it up to the rays of the sun, and then take the pigment and make horizontal and vertical marks about their eyes—what must have been a forked-eye design—the purpose being to improve their vision.[19] This falcon also served as the model of the Tlanuwa, the monstrous bird of prey in Cherokee oral traditions, who was said to swoop down and kill its victims with its sharp breast.[20] Some of the Southeastern Ceremonial Complex motifs of men, possibly dancers, dressed as birds may in fact represent this Tlanuwa.[21]

The Cherokees saw nothing inconsistent in the fact that the bald eagle (*Haliaetus leucocephalus leucocephalus* L.), the near relative of the falcon, symbolized peace, the perfect order of the Upper World. Perhaps they thought of the bald eagle, who flies serenely above all other creatures, as the white-haired grandparent of the falcons. Their word for the red-tailed hawk (*Buteo jamaicensis borealis* Gmelin) literally means "love-sick," because to the Cherokees his call is a lonely sounding whistle. Perhaps because the kingfisher (*Megaceryle alcyon alcyon* L.) is able to fly down to the water and reach beneath it to pluck up a fish, Cherokee priests or conjurers would invoke it to pluck out objects which had been magically intruded into their patients' bodies, making them ill. While for us the turkey buzzard (*Cathartesaura septentrionalis* Wied) symbolizes death, for the Cherokees it symbolized healing, because the turkey buzzard is able to expose itself to dead things

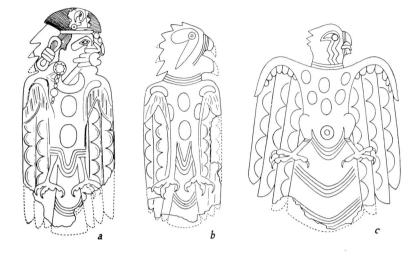

Figure 36. Spotted falcons with the forked-eye motif embossed on copper plates. *a.* An anthropomorphic falcon from Dunklin County, Missouri. *b.* A spotted falcon from Dunklin County, Missouri. *c.* A spotted falcon from near Peoria, Illinois. From Charles C. Willoughby, "History and Symbolism of the Muskhogeans," in *Etowah Papers*, Phillips Academy, edited by Warren K. Moorehead. New Haven: Yale University Press, 1932, fig. 8, p. 22. Courtesy, Yale University Press and R. S. Peabody Foundation for Archaeology.

with impunity. The long-eared owl (*Asio otus wilsonianus* Lesson), whom the Cherokees call *tski•li*, was an ill omen, a witch, a repulsive being. The red-bellied woodpecker (*Centurus carolinus carolinus* L.), whom the Cherokees call *dalala*, was a swift and cunning bird who symbolized war, perhaps because his red head looks as if it had been scalped.[22] The pileated or ivory-billed woodpecker depicted in the Southeastern Ceremonial Complex motifs may have had a similar meaning (figs. 37, 58).[23] Another bird that occasionally shows up in the Southeastern Ceremonial Complex, the turkey, whose black hair-like neck feathers resemble a human scalp, was also associated with men and with warfare. One of the war whoops of the Southeastern Indians was an imitation of a turkey gobble.[24]

This World was sometimes frequented by Under World monsters who came out of the rivers, lakes, waterfalls, and mountain caves, all of these being entrances to the Under World. They lurked around lonely spots like mountain passes, making mischief or even causing great misfortunes for people. There were giant frogs and giant lizards among these monsters, but the most horrible of all was the monster the Cherokees called Uktena, a creature combining features of all three categories of normal animals. It had the scaly body of a large serpent, as big around as a tree trunk, with rings or spots of color along its entire body, but it had deer horns on its head, and it

Figure 37. Shell gorget with pileated or ivory-billed woodpecker motif. From William H. Holmes, "Art in Shell of the Ancient Americans." *Second Annual Report of the Bureau of American Ethnology.* Washington, D. C., 1883, opp. p. 282.

had wings like a bird. On its forehead it had a bright diamond-shaped crest that gave off blinding flashes of light. A similar monster existed in the beliefs of most Southeastern Indians. The Koasatis, for example, called him "snake-crawfish," a snake with horns. The symbolic significance of the Uktena will be discussed a few pages hence. In many parts of the Southeast the Indians believed that the streams were inhabited by "tie-snakes." These were believed to be powerful snakes that would crawl up on land to wrap themselves around their victims and pull them under the water.

The Cherokees attached much significance to the four cardinal directions, associating each of them with a series of social values. Actually, these seem to have been two sets of opposites. In one opposition, the east was the direction of the Sun, the color red, sacred fire, blood, and life and success; its opposite, the west, was associated with the Moon, the souls of the dead, the color black, and death. In the other opposed pair, the north was associated with cold, the color blue (and purple), and trouble and defeat; while its opposite, the south, was associated with warmth, the color white, peace, and happiness. The Cherokees also gave a propitious value to brown, assigning it to the upward direction, and yellow, like blue, was associated with trouble, though the direction to which it was assigned is not clear. A full complement of spiritual beings dwelt in the Upper World in each of the four quarters. Thus there was a Red Man, Red Bear, Red Sparrow Hawk, and so on in the east; a Black Man, Black Bear, Black Sparrow Hawk, and so on in the west.[25] The Creeks used the same four cardinal colors with much the same values, but the directions with which they were associated were somewhat different. As with the Cherokees, black was associated with the west, but white was associated with the east, red (and yellow) with the north, and blue with the south.[26]

These, then, are the broad categories of the belief system of the Southeastern Indians—their mental furniture. In the following story, collected by James Mooney, the Cherokees tell how their world began.

How the World was Made. The earth is a great island floating in a sea of water, and suspended at each of the four cardinal points by a cord hanging down from the sky vault, which is of solid rock. When the world grows old and worn out, the people will die and the cords will break and let the earth sink down into the ocean, and all will be water again. The Indians are afraid of this.

When all was water, the animals were above in [the Upper World], beyond the arch; but it was very much crowded, and they were wanting more room. They wondered what was below the water, and at last . . . "Beaver's Grandchild," the little Water-beetle, offered to go and see if it could learn. It darted in every direction over the surface of the water, but could find no firm place to rest. Then it dived to the bottom and came up with some soft mud, which began to grow and spread on every side until it became the island which we call the earth. It was afterward fastened to the sky with four cords, but no one remembers who did this.

At first the earth was flat and very soft and wet. The animals were anxious to get down, and sent out different birds to see if it was yet dry, but they found no place to alight and came back again to [the Upper World]. At last it seemed to be time, and they sent out the Buzzard and told him to go and make ready for them. This was the Great Buzzard, the father of all the buzzards we see now. He flew all over the earth, low down near the ground, and it was still soft. When he reached the Cherokee country, he was very tired, and his wings began to flap and strike the ground, and whenever they struck the earth there was a valley, and where they turned up again there was a mountain. When the animals above saw this, they were afraid that the whole world would be mountains, so they called him back, but the Cherokee country remains full of mountains to this day.

When the earth was dry and the animals came down, it was still dark, so they got the sun and set it in a track to go every day across the island from east to west, just overhead. It was too hot this way, and . . . the Red Crawfish had his shell scorched a bright red, so that his meat was spoiled; and the Cherokee do not eat it. The conjurers put the sun another hand-breadth higher in the air, but it was still too hot. They raised it another time, and another, until it was seven hand-breadths high and just under the sky arch. Then it was right, and they left it so. This is why the conjurers call the highest place . . . "the seventh height," because it is seven hand-breadths above the earth. Every day the sun goes along under this arch, and returns at night to the upper side to the starting place.

There is another world under this, and it is like ours in everything—animals, plants, and people—save that the seasons are different. The streams that come down from the mountains are the trails by which we reach this underworld, and the springs at their heads are the doorways by which we enter it, but to do this one must fast and go to water and have one of the underground people for a guide. We know that the seasons in the underworld are different from ours, because the water in the springs is always warmer in winter and cooler in summer than the outer air.

When the animals and plants were first made—we do not know by whom—they were told to watch and keep awake for seven nights, just as young men now fast and keep awake when they pray to their medicine. They tried to do this, and nearly all were awake through the first night, but the next night several dropped off to sleep, and the third night others were asleep, and then others, until, on the seventh night, of all the animals only the owl, the [cougar], and one or two more were still awake. To these were given the power to see and to go about in the dark, and to make prey of the birds and animals which must sleep at night. Of the trees only the cedar, the pine, the spruce, the holly, and the laurel were awake to the end, and to them it was given to be always green and to be greatest for medicine, but to the others it was said: "Because you have not endured to the end you shall lose your hair every winter."

Men came after the animals and plants. At first there were only a brother and sister until he struck her with a fish and told her to multiply, and so it was. In seven days a child was born to her, and thereafter every seven days another, and they increased very fast until there was danger that the world could not keep them. Then it was made that a woman should have only one child in a year, and it has been so ever since.[27]

The numbers four and seven occur repeatedly in Cherokee myths and rituals. As such, they are not merely magic numbers but expressive of the Southeastern belief system. Perhaps it could be said that four represented everything in the known world, all the familiar forces in the cosmos. Seven, on the other hand, represented the highest degree of ritual purity and sacredness to which anything could aspire. In fact, it represented a degree to which most men, animals, and plants could not attain. As we have just seen, it was a level which only the owl and the cougar attained, and it should be noted that both had special significance for the Cherokees as for most Southeastern Indians; and it was a level attained only by cedar, pine, spruce, holly, and laurel, all of which were important in Cherokee ceremonials.[28] Cedar, an aromatic, rot resistant wood with a distinctive red and white color, was most sacred of all. It was the wood used to make the litters on which the honored dead at Cahokia and Spiro were carried.

In the next Cherokee story, man acquires fire and sets himself apart from the animals. His ally and intermediary in this exploit is the little water spider, who frequently shows up in Southeastern Ceremonial Complex motifs, often with a circle and cross on her back representing sacred fire.

The First Fire. In the beginning there was no fire, and the world was cold, until the Thunders . . . , who lived up in the Upper World, sent their lightning and put fire into the bottom of a hollow sycamore tree which grew on an island. The animals knew it was there, because they could see the smoke coming out at the top, but they could not get to it on account of the water, so they held a council to decide what to do. This was a long time ago.

Every animal that could fly or swim was anxious to go after the fire. The Raven offered, and because he was so large and strong they thought he could surely do the work, so he was sent first. He flew high and far across the water and alighted on the sycamore tree, but while he was wondering what to do next, the heat had scorched all his feathers black, and he was frightened and came back without the fire. The little Screech-owl . . . volunteered to go, and reached the place safely, but while he was looking down into the hollow tree a blast of hot air came up and nearly burned out his eyes. He managed to fly home as best he could, but it was a long time before he could see well, and his eyes are red to this day. Then the Hooting Owl . . . and the Horned Owl . . . went, but by the time they got to the hollow tree the fire was burning so fiercely that the smoke nearly blinded them, and the ashes carried up by the wind made white rings about their eyes. They had to come home again without the fire, but with all their rubbing they were never able to get rid of the white rings.

Now no more of the birds would venture, and so the little . . . snake, the black racer, said he would go through the water and bring back some fire. He swam across to the island and crawled through the grass to the tree, and went in by a small hole at the bottom. The heat and smoke were too much for him, too, and after dodging about blindly over the hot ashes until he was almost on fire himself he managed by good luck to get out again at the same hole, but his body had been scorched black, and he has ever since had the habit of darting and doubling on his track as if trying to escape from close quarters. He came back, and the great blacksnake . . . "The Climber," offered to go for fire. He swam over to the island and climbed up the tree on the outside, as the blacksnake always does, but when he put his head down into the hole the smoke choked him so that he fell into the burning stump, and before he could climb out again he was as black as [the black racer].

Now they held another council, for still there was no fire, and the world was cold, but birds, snakes, and four-footed animals, all had some excuse for not going, because they were all afraid to venture near the burning sycamore, until at last . . . (the Water Spider) said she would go. This is not the water spider that looks like a mosquito, but the other one, with black downy hair and red stripes on her body. She can run on top of the water or dive to the bottom, so there would be no trouble to get over to the island, but the question was, How could she bring back the fire? "I'll manage that," said the Water Spider; so she spun a thread from her body and wove it into a *tusti* bowl, which she fastened on her back (fig. 38). Then she crossed over to the island and through the grass to where the fire was still burning. She put one little coal of fire into her bowl, and came back with it, and ever since we have had fire, and the Water Spider still keeps her *tusti* bowl.[29]

The Southeastern Indians lived between two worlds that were neither wholly friendly nor wholly hostile toward them. But the Upper World and the Under World were opposed to each other. This is why the Tlanuwa and the Uktena were mortal enemies. The Indian often found himself in the middle of this cosmic conflict, and could sometimes play one side off against the other.

The Nest of the Tlanuwa. On the north bank of the Little Tennessee River, in a bend below the mouth of Citico Creek in Blount County, Tennessee, is a high cliff hanging over the water, and about halfway up the face of the rock is a cave with two openings. The rock projects outward above the cave, so that the mouth can not be seen from above, and it seems impossible to reach the cave either from above or below. There are white streaks in the rock from the cave down to the water. The Cherokee call it . . . "the place of the Tlanuwa," or great mythic hawk.[30]

In the old time, away back soon after the creation, a pair of Tlanuwas had their nest in this cave. The streaks in the rock were made by the droppings from the nest. They were immense birds, larger than any that live now, and very strong and savage. They were forever flying up and down the river, and used to come into the settlements and carry off dogs and even young children playing near the houses. No one could reach the nest to kill them, and when the people tried to shoot them the arrows only glanced off and were seized and carried away in the talons of the Tlanuwas.

At last the people went to a great medicine man, who promised to help them. Some were afraid that if he failed to kill the Tlanuwas they would take revenge on the people, but the medicine man said he could fix that.

136

Figure 38. Shell gorget with water spider motif. From William H. Holmes, "Art in Shell of the Ancient Americans." *Second Annual Report of the Bureau of American Ethnology.* Washington D. C., 1883, opp. p. 288.

He made a long rope of linn bark, just as the Cherokee still do, with loops in it for his feet, and had the people let him down from the top of the cliff at a time when he knew that the old birds were away. When he came opposite the mouth of the cave he still could not reach it, because the rock above hung over, so he swung himself backward and forward several times until the rope swung near enough for him to pull himself into the cave with a hooked stick that he carried, which he managed to fasten in some bushes growing at the entrance. In the nest he found four young ones, and on the floor of the cave were the bones of all sorts of animals that had been carried there by the hawks. He pulled the young ones out of the nest and threw them over the cliff into the deep water below, where a great Uktena serpent that lived there finished them. Just then he saw the two old ones coming, and had hardly time to climb up again to the top of the rock before they reached the nest.

When they found the nest empty they were furious, and circled round and round in the air until they saw the snake put up its head from the water. Then they darted straight downward, and while one seized the snake in his talons and flew far up in the sky with it, his mate struck at it and bit off piece after piece until nothing was left (fig. 39). They were so high up that when the pieces fell they made holes in the rock, which are

Figure 39. Shell gorget with tlanuwa-like bird doing combat with an anomalous monster. The latter is probably a water cougar. Bell County, Texas. Courtesy, Museum of the American Indian, Heye Foundation

still to be seen there, at the place which we call "Where the Tlanuwa cut it up," opposite the mouth of Citico. Then the two Tlanuwas circled up and up until they went out of sight, and they have never been seen since.[31]

Like preliterate people elsewhere, the Southeastern Indians were particularly interested in anomalies and abominations, beings which fell into two or more of their categories.[32] These anomalies and abominations were singled out for special symbolic values, and they played important roles in their oral traditions. The animal that fell into both the human category and the four-footed animal category was the bear, an animal which is four-footed, but which often walks upright on two legs, and it frequently eats the same kinds of food men eat.[33] We shall presently see that the Cherokees used to tell a story about a clan of people turning into bears, and the bear shows up in the Cherokee oral tradition about the origin of disease and medicine, which is itself primarily concerned with the opposition between men and animals.

The boundary between bird and four-footed animal categories was overlapped by two anomalous animals: the bat, a four-footed animal that has wings, and the flying squirrel, another four-footed animal that "flies." We shall see that both the bat and the flying squirrel figure prominently in the Cherokee oral tradition about a ball game between birds and four-footed animals, a story which expresses the opposition between birds and four-footed animals and the superiority of the former over the latter.

The case for anomalous animals marking a boundary between the four-footed animals and the vermin associated with the Under World is not quite so clear. But a case can be made for the frog (fig. 40) and the turtle (fig. 41), both of whom are four-footed animals who spend a lot of time under water. The turtle is particularly important in Cherokee stories about men who visited the Under World. Moreover, both the frog and the turtle were favored in Mississippian art. Pottery vessels, for example, were sometimes made in the shape of frogs. One suspects that the beaver and the otter were anomalous in the same way that frogs and turtles were.

The boundary between the animal and plant domains was overlapped by two odd plants, the Venus flytrap (*Dionaea muscipula*) and the pitcher plant (*Sarracenia purpurea*), both of which are anomalous because they trap and "digest" insects. Hence they are plants which, like men, subsist by "hunting." The Cherokees called the roots of these plants *yú•gwila*, and they imputed extraordinary powers to them. They believed, for example, that when hidden away these roots had the power to move physically from one place to another.[34]

Within the bird category they may have distinguished between birds of the air and birds of the water. If so, both the wood duck and the kingfisher would have been anomalous. The wood duck is unlike other ducks in that it nests not on the ground but in a tree hollow like a bird of the air. And the wood duck has a particularly furtive way of

Figure 40. Frog effigy jar. Mississippi County, Arkansas. Courtesy, Museum of the American Indian, Heye Foundation.

140

Figure 41. A rattle carved in the form of a turtle. Made of cedar and covered with a thin sheet of copper. Spiro, Oklahoma. Courtesy, Museum of the American Indian, Heye Foundation.

flying to its nest—it almost seems to disappear into thin air. The wood duck often shows up in Mississippian pottery motifs, and the Natchez covered the stems of some of their pipes with the feathered skins of wood ducks (fig. 42). The kingfisher would have been anomalous for opposite reasons—it is a bird of the air that drops down to invade the water and pluck up a fish. The kingfisher shows up in Mississippian motifs, and Cherokee priests often invoked Kingfisher to come and pluck out objects which had been magically "intruded" into their patients.

A different kind of anomaly may be seen in living things which defied categories of time. We recall that in the Cherokee oral tradition about the creation, the animals who remained awake for seven nights were the owl and the cougar, both of whom are anomalous in that they can see at night and are nocturnal in their habits. Appropriately, the Cherokees had a particular regard for owls; in fact, the Cherokee word *tski•li*, which means "long-eared owl," also means "witch" (fig. 43). The Cherokees are not alone in thinking the owl peculiar. Wherever people and owls occur together, the people realize that the owls neither look nor act like other birds. When an owl walks he looks a bit like an old man walking with his hands behind his back. The long-eared owl, with feathered tufts on his head, in dim light can easily be mistaken for a cat perched on a limb. But it is the owl's eyes that are so uncanny. They are quite large, and they are directly in front, like a man's, and they can be closed one at a time. Even though the owl's keen vision can see slight movements of small animals in poor light, his vision is limited in other respects. He cannot move his eyeballs in their sockets, and therefore he probably sees two images. His vision is not stereoscopic, and therefore he cannot easily judge distance. This is why an owl bobbles his head up and down and from side to side in a most peculiar way when he is trying to determine the distance of something. Moreover, the only way an owl can look at you is piercingly, with acute ferocity.[35]

The cougar is another peculiar animal (fig. 44, 82). The cougar is so secret in its habits that even students of animal behavior are rarely able to observe it in the wild. When a cougar screams at night, it frequently sounds like a woman screaming. The Southeastern Indian's special regard for the cougar goes back to early Mississippian times: at the Ocmulgee site archaeologists unearthed two cougars'

Figure 42. Wood duck effigy bowl. Recovered near Nashville, Tennessee. Courtesy, Thruston Collection, Vanderbilt University.

Figure 43. Owl effigy bottle. From Noel Cemetery in Nashville, Tennessee. Courtesy, Thruston Collection, Vanderbilt University. Photograph by Peggy Wrenne.

lower jaws that had been carefully covered with thin sheets of copper and used as part of a headdress. The cougar also shows up on Mississippian shell drinking cups and gorgets.[36]

Plants as well as animals defy normal categories of time. We recall that in the Cherokee oral tradition about the creation, the plants that remained awake for seven nights were the cedar, pine, spruce, laurel, and holly trees. All of these are anomalous because they keep their leaves the year around, and as one might expect they are among the most important plants in Cherokee medicine and ceremony.

Figure 44. Cougars incised on a conch shell drinking cup. Their feet resemble those of a bird of prey; hence they may represent anomalous monsters. Spiro, Oklahoma. Courtesy, Museum of the American Indian, Heye Foundation.

The most abominable creature of all was the Uktena (figs. 45, 90), with the attributes of the serpent (a creature associated with the Under World), the deer (a creature of This World), and the bird (a creature associated with the Upper World).[37] It was modeled after the snake, a creature which practically all people in the world regard as peculiar. The snake is born from an egg, like a bird, but birds hate

144

Figure 45. Uktena-like monster incised on a Moundville pot. From Clarence B. Moore, "Moundville Revisited." *Journal of the Academy of Natural Sciences of Philadelphia*, second series, vol. 13, pt. 3(1907), fig. 58, p. 374.

snakes, as anyone knows who has seen a snake invade a bluejay's territory. One can encounter a snake in all realms—swimming in the water, crawling on the land, and hanging from a tree limb. To compound the anomaly even further, the Uktena was believed to have originally been a man who was thus transformed and given the task of killing the Sun, the most sacred Southeastern deity, who had sent down a plague to destroy man. But the Uktena failed miserably in this task and was subsequently full of jealousy and resentment for men. Uktenas were believed to inhabit deep pools of water and also high mountain passes, on the boundaries of the Cherokee world, where they would kill people whenever they could.[38] Merely to see an Uktena brought misfortune to a man, and to smell an Uktena's breath brought death.[39] As one might expect, Uktenas were repelled by fire, a thing of the Upper World.

Uktenas are frequently depicted in Southeastern Ceremonia Complex motifs inscribed on shell gorgets and pottery.[40] On othei gorgets men are represented with antlers, wings, birdlike claws instead of hands, and wearing breechcloths that perhaps represent spotted snake skins (fig. 46).[41] Since the Yuchis in the early 1900s still performed a dance in honor of the Uktena, one suspects that the men depicted on these gorgets were dancers playing the part of the Uktena.[42] In some of these gorgets, the Uktena has not the head nor horns of a deer, but the head of a cougar; and probably represents the Water Cougar, an anomalous creature similar to the Uktena.[43]

Figure 46. Anthropomorphic serpents or men impersonating uktena-like monsters on a conch shell drinking cup. The coiled serpent below has horns on its head and beads about its neck and tail. Note the tasseled belts and bi-pointed knives. Spiro, Oklahoma. Courtesy, Museum of the American Indian, Heye Foundation.

The Water Cougar of the Florida Seminoles had "four legs, no feet, long hair, and a long fish-like tail, and . . . [left] the water to hunt on land."[44] The Water Cougar had a controlling influence on water and Under World creatures, and he stood in opposition to beings of the Upper World. Thus the Uktena and the Water Cougar were more or less equivalent. Why the Southeastern Indians should have believed in the existence of two such monsters is unclear.

It should be understood that the Uktena was quite real to the Cherokees. In fact, they spoke of the Uktena in such vivid terms to James Adair that he was convinced that the Uktena really existed.

Between the heads of the northern branch of the lower Cherake river, and the heads of that of Tuckasehchee, winding round in a long course by

146

the late Fort-Loudon, and afterwards into the Mississippi, there is, both in the nature and circumstances, a great phaenomenon—Between two high mountains, nearly covered with old mossy rocks, lofty cedars, and pines, in the valleys of which the beams of the sun reflect a powerful heat, there are, as the natives affirm, some bright old inhabitants, or rattle snakes, of a more enormous size than is mentioned in history. They are so large and unwieldy, that they take a circle, almost as wide as their length, to crawl round in their shortest orbit; but bountiful nature compensates the heavy motion of their bodies, for as they say, no living creature moves within the reach of their sight, but they can draw it to them; which is agreeable to what we observe, through the whole system of animated beings. Nature endues them with proper capacities to sustain life;—as they cannot support themselves, by their speed, or cunning to spring from an ambushcade, it is needful they should have the bewitching craft of their eyes and forked tongues.

The description the Indians give us of their colour, is as various as what we are told of the camelion, that seems to the spectator to change its colour, by every different position he may view it in; which proceeds from the piercing rays of light that blaze from their foreheads, so as to dazzle the eyes, from whatever quarter they post themselves—for in each of their heads, there is a large carbuncle, which not only repels, but they affirm, sullies the meridian beams of the sun. They reckon it so dangerous to disturb those creatures, that no temptation can induce them to betray their secret recess to the prophane. They call them and all of the rattle-snake kind, kings, or chieftains of the snakes; and they allow one such to every different species of the brute creation . . . .[45]

Adair also tells of an old trader who tried to bribe the Cherokees into telling him where he could see an Uktena, but they refused, saying that if he were to kill one of them it would make the "inferior species of the serpentine tribe" angry, and this would expose the Cherokees to the danger of being bitten by snakes.[46]

Although it may seem paradoxical, these anomalous beings in the Southeastern Indian belief system were byproducts of their search for order, and intellectually they helped sustain that order. One of the outstanding characteristics of the belief systems of preliterate people is the diligence with which they protect the fundamental notions of their belief system and the integrity of their classification system from disproof or even serious challenge.[47] This strikes us as odd because an important principle in our own scientific world view—though one which we often try to avoid—is that our own categories and theories should be constantly tested, and if disproven, then replaced with more adequate categories and theories. Because of our ability to store information in written form and on magnetic tapes, we have an incredibly large number of categories with which to classify the things in the world around us. If we encounter something which does not neatly fit into a preexisting category, then we simply create a new one.

But among preliterate people like the Southeastern Indians, who had to carry all their categories in their heads, the case was quite different. Lacking writing, the number of categories at their disposal was tiny as compared to ours. And given such a small number of categories, they necessarily encountered things which did not neatly fit, things which fell into two or more categories. Thus anomalies and abominations were inevitable. But instead of throwing their classification system asunder, the Southeastern Indians held up the bear, the owl, the cougar, and so on, as special animals, investing them with special meaning in their world view. Moreover, they created the Uktena and the Water Cougar, creatures even more anomalous than the bear, the owl, and the cougar, making them at the same time objects of fear and power. And so by deliberately holding these anomalies up to public view, they shored up the integrity of their classification system.[48]

In keeping with this concern with categorical tidiness, the Southeastern Indians believed that if a person mixed things from opposed categories, the result was sure to be some form of chaos. Therefore many rules ("tabus") in Cherokee society had to do with avoiding the mixing of categories, or pollution, while many of their ceremonies were intended to dispel pollution once it had occurred. This rule against mixing categories is an important part of the Cherokee myth about Kanati, the first man, and Selu, the first woman. In the story, Selu washes in the river game killed by Kanati, thus mixing blood with water.[49] As a consequence, from the blood a boy called Wild Boy (also called "Blood-Clot Boy" or "Orphan" in other parts of the Southeast) comes into existence claiming to be Selu's son and claiming to be the elder brother of her own son, even though he came into existence after her own son was born. Thus, Wild Boy was anomalous in two ways: in his strange birth and in his peculiar relationship with his "brother." One of the most important features of Wild Boy is that he came from the water, and water is associated with disorder, innovation, and fertility; thus, Wild Boy was always breaking rules

148

and doing new things. In addition to the anomalous origin of Wild Boy, Kanati and Selu were possibly brother and sister, making the other son the fruit of an incestuous union, so that he too was an anomaly.

The Origin of Corn and Game. When I was a boy this is what the old men told me they had heard when they were boys.

Long years ago, soon after the world was made, a hunter and his wife lived at Pilot Knob with their only child, a little boy. The father's name was Kanati (the Lucky Hunter), and his wife was called Selu (Corn). No matter when Kanati went into the wood, he never failed to bring back a load of game, which his wife would cut up and prepare, washing off the blood from the meat in the river near the house. The little boy used to play down by the river every day, and one morning the old people thought they heard laughing and talking in the bushes as though there were two children there. When the boy came home at night his parents asked him who had been playing with him all day. "He comes out of the water," said the boy, "and he calls himself my elder brother. He says his mother was cruel to him and threw him into the river." Then they knew that the strange boy had sprung from the blood of the game which Selu had washed off at the river's edge.

Every day when the little boy went out to play the other would join him, but as he always went back again into the water the old people never had a chance to see him. At last one evening Kanati said to his son, "Tomorrow, when the other boy comes to play, get him to wrestle with you, and when you have your arms around him hold on to him and call for us." The boy promised to do as he was told, so the next day as soon as his playmate appeared he challenged him to a wrestling match. The other agreed at once, but as soon as they had their arms around each other, Kanati's boy began to scream for his father. The old folks came running down, and as soon as the Wild Boy saw them he struggled to free himself and cried out, "Let me go; you threw me away!" but his brother held on until the parents reached the spot, when they seized the Wild Boy and took him home with them. They kept him in the house until they had tamed him, but he was always wild and artful in his disposition, and was the leader of his brother in every mischief. It was not long until the old people discovered that he had magic powers, and they called him . . . (He-who-grew-up-wild).

Whenever Kanati went into the mountains he always brought back a fat buck or doe, or maybe a couple of turkeys. One day the Wild Boy said to his brother, "I wonder where our father gets all that game; let's follow him next time and find out." A few days afterward Kanati took a bow and some feathers in his hand and started off toward the west. The boys waited a little while and then went after him, keeping out of sight until they saw him go into a swamp where there were a great many of the small reeds that hunters use to make arrowshafts. Then the Wild Boy changed himself into a puff of bird's down, which the wind took up and carried until it alighted upon Kanati's shoulder just as he entered the swamp, but Kanati knew nothing about it. The old man cut reeds, fitted the feathers to them and made some arrows, and the Wild Boy—in his other shape—thought, "I wonder what those things are for?" When Kanati had his arrows finished he came out of the swamp and went on again. The wind blew the down from his shoulder, and it fell in the woods, when the Wild Boy took his right shape again and went back and told his brother what he had seen. Keeping out of sight of their father, they followed him up the mountain until he stopped at a certain place and lifted a large rock. At once there ran out a buck, which Kanati shot, and then lifting it upon his back he started for home again. "Oho!" exclaimed the boys, "he keeps all the deer shut up in that hole, and whenever he wants meat he just lets one out and kills it with those things he made in the swamp." They hurried and reached home before their father, who had the heavy deer to carry, and he never knew that they had followed.

A few days later the boys went back to the swamp, cut some reeds and made seven arrows, and then started up the mountain to where their father kept the game. When they got to the place, they raised the rock and a deer came running out. Just as they drew back to shoot it, another came out, and then another and another, until the boys got confused and forgot what they were about. In those days all the deer had their tails hanging down like other animals, but as a buck was running past, the Wild Boy struck its tail with his arrow so that it pointed upward. The boys thought this good sport, and when the next one ran past the Wild Boy struck its tail so that it stood straight up, and his brother struck the next one so hard with his arrow that the deer's tail was almost curled over his back. The deer carries his tail this way ever since. The deer came running past until the last one had come out of the hole and escaped into the forest. Then came droves of raccoons, rabbits, and all the other four-footed animals—all but the bear, because there was no bear then. Last came great flocks of turkeys, pigeons, and partridges that darkened the air like a cloud and made such a noise with their wings that Kanati, sitting at home, heard the sound like distant thunder on the mountains and said to himself, "My bad boys have got into trouble; I must go and see what they are doing."

So he went up the mountain, and when he came to the place where he kept the game he found the two boys standing by the rock, and all the birds and animals were gone. Kanati was furious, but without saying a word he went down into the cave and kicked the covers off four jars in one corner, when out swarmed bedbugs, fleas, lice, and gnats, and got all over the boys. They screamed with pain and fright and tried to beat off the insects, but the thousands of vermin crawled over them and bit and stung them until both dropped down nearly dead. Kanati stood looking on until he thought they had been punished enough, when he knocked off the vermin and made the boys a talk. "Now, you rascals," said he, "you have always had plenty to eat and never had to work for it. Whenever you were hungry all I had to do was to come up here and get a deer or a turkey and bring it home for your mother to cook; but now you have let out all the animals, and after this when you want a deer to eat you will have to hunt all over the woods for it, and then maybe not find one. Go home now to your mother, while I see if I can find something to eat for supper."

When the boys got home again they were very tired and hungry and asked their mother for something to eat. "There is no meat," said Selu, "but wait a little while and I'll get you something." So she took a basket and started out to the storehouse. This storehouse was built upon poles high up from the ground, to keep it out of the reach of animals, and there was a ladder to climb up by, and one door, but no other opening. Every day when Selu got ready to cook the dinner she would go out to the storehouse with a basket and bring it back full of corn and beans. The boys had never been inside the storehouse, so wondered [*sic*] where all the corn and beans could come from, as the house was not a very large one; so as soon as Selu went out of the door the Wild Boy said to his brother, "Let's go and see what she does." They ran around and climbed up at the back of the storehouse and pulled out a piece of clay from between the logs, so that they could look in. There they saw Selu standing in the middle of the room with the basket in front of her on the floor. Leaning over the basket, she rubbed her stomach—*so*—and the basket was half full of corn. Then she rubbed her armpits—*so*—and the basket was full to the top with beans. The boys looked at each other and said, "This will never do; our mother is a witch. If we eat any of that it will poison us. We must kill her."

When the boys came back into the house, she knew their thoughts before they spoke. "So you are going to kill me?" said Selu. "Yes," said the boys, "you are a witch." "Well," said their mother, "when you have killed me, clear a large piece of ground in front of the house and drag my body seven times around the circle. Then drag me seven times over the ground inside the circle, and stay up all night and watch, and in the morning you will have plenty of corn." The boys killed her with their clubs, and cut off her head and put it up on the roof of the house with her face turned to the west, and told her to look for her husband. Then they set to work to clear the ground in front of the house, but instead of clearing the whole piece they cleared only seven little spots. This is why corn now grows only in a few places instead of over the whole world. They dragged the body of Selu around the circle, and wherever her blood fell on the ground the corn sprang up. But instead of dragging her body seven times across the ground they dragged it over only twice, which is the reason the Indians still work their crop but twice. The two brothers sat up and watched their corn all night, and in the morning it was full grown and ripe.

When Kanati came home at last, he looked around, but could not see Selu anywhere, and asked the boys where was their mother. "She was a witch, and we killed her," said the boys; "there is her head up there on top of the house." When he saw his wife's head on the roof, he was very angry, and said, "I won't stay with you any longer; I am going to the Wolf people." So he started off, but before he had gone far the Wild Boy changed himself again to a tuft of down, which fell on Kanati's shoulder. When Kanati reached the settlement of the Wolf people, they were holding a council in the townhouse. He went in and sat down with the tuft of bird's down on his shoulder, but he never noticed it. When the Wolf chief asked him his business, he said: "I have two bad boys at home, and I want you to go in seven days from now and play ball against them." Although Kanati spoke as though he wanted them to play a game of ball, the Wolves knew that he meant for them to go and kill the two boys. They promised to go. Then the bird's down blew off from Kanati's shoulder, and the smoke carried it up through the hole in the roof of the townhouse. When it came down on the ground outside, the Wild Boy took his right shape again and went home and told his brother all that he had heard in the townhouse. But when Kanati left the Wolf people, he did not return home, but went on farther.

The boys then began to get ready for the Wolves, and the Wild Boy—the magician—told his brother what to do. They ran around the house in a wide circle until they had made a trail all around it excepting on the side from which the Wolves would come, where they left a small open space. Then they made four large bundles of arrows and placed them at four different points on the outside of the circle, after which they hid themselves in the woods and waited for the Wolves.[50] In a day or two a whole party of Wolves came and surrounded the house to kill the boys. The Wolves did not notice the trail around the house, because they came in where the boys had left the opening, but the moment they went inside the circle the trail changed to a high brush fence and shut them in. Then the boys on the outside took their arrows and began shooting them down, and as the Wolves could not jump over the fence they were all killed, excepting a few that escaped through the opening into a great swamp close by. The boys ran around the swamp, and a circle of fire sprang up in their tracks and set fire to the grass and bushes and burned up nearly all the other Wolves. Only two or three got away, and from these have come all the wolves that are now in the world.

Soon afterward some strangers from a distance, who had heard that the brothers had a wonderful grain from which they made bread, came to ask for some, for none but Selu and her family had ever known corn before. The boys gave them seven grains of corn, which they told them to plant the next night on their way home, sitting up all night to watch the corn, which would have seven ripe ears in the morning. These they were to plant the next night and watch in the same way, and so on every night until they reached home, when they would have corn enough to supply the whole people. The strangers lived seven days' journey away. They took the seven grains and watched all through the darkness until morning, when they saw seven tall stalks, each stalk bearing a ripened ear. They gathered the ears and went on their way. The next night they planted all their corn, and guarded it as before until daybreak, when they found an abundant increase. But the way was long and the sun was hot, and the people grew tired. On the last night before reaching home they fell asleep, and in the morning the corn they had planted had not even sprouted. They brought with them to their settlement what corn they had left and planted it, and with care and attention were able to raise a crop. But ever since the corn must be watched and tended through half the year, which before would grow and ripen in a night.

As Kanati did not return, the boys at last concluded to go and find him. The Wild Boy took a gaming wheel and rolled it toward the Darkening land.[51] In a little while the wheel came rolling back, and the boys knew their father was not there. He rolled it to the south and to the north, and each time the wheel came back to him, and they knew their father was not there. Then he rolled it toward the Sunland, and it did not return. "Our father is there," said the Wild Boy, "let us go and find him." So the two brothers set off toward the east, and after traveling a long time they came upon Kanati walking along with a little dog by his side. "You bad boys," said their father, "have you come here?" "Yes," they answered, "we always accomplish what we start out to do—we are men."[52] "This dog overtook me four days ago," then said Kanati, but the boys knew that the dog was the wheel which they had sent after him to find him. "Well," said Kanati, "as you have found me, we may as well travel together, but I shall take the lead."

Soon they came to a swamp, and Kanati told them there was something dangerous there and they must keep away from it. He went on ahead, but as soon as he was out of sight the Wild Boy said to his brother, "Come and let us see what is in the swamp." They went in together, and in the middle of the swamp they found a large [cougar] asleep. The Wild Boy got out an arrow and shot the [cougar] in the side of the head. The cougar turned his head and the other boy shot him on that side. He turned his head away again and the two brothers shot together—*tust, tust, tust!* But the [cougar] was not hurt by the arrows and paid no more attention to the boys. They came out of the swamp and soon overtook Kanati, waiting for them. "Did you find it?" asked Kanati. "Yes," said the boys, "we found it, but it never hurt us. We are men." Kanati was surprised, but said nothing, and they went on again.[53]

After a while he turned to them and said, "Now you must be careful. We are coming to a tribe called the . . . ("Roasters," i.e., cannibals), and if they get you they will put you into a pot and feast on you." Then he went on ahead. Soon the boys came to a tree which had been struck by lightning, and the Wild Boy directed his brother to gather some of the splinters from the tree and told him what to do with them. In a little while they came to the settlement of the cannibals, who, as soon as they saw the boys, came running out, crying, "Good, here are two nice fat strangers. Now we'll have a grand feast!" They caught the boys and dragged them into the townhouse, and sent word to all the people of the settlement to come to the feast. They made up a great fire, put water into a large pot and set it to boiling, and then seized the Wild Boy and put him down into it. His brother was not in the least frightened and made no attempt to escape, but quietly knelt down and began putting the splinters into the fire, as if to make it burn better. When the cannibals thought the meat was about ready they lifted the pot from the fire, and that instant a blinding light filled the townhouse, and the lightning began to dart from one side to the other, striking down the cannibals until not one of them was left alive. Then the lightning went up through the smoke-hole, and the next moment there were the two boys standing outside the townhouse as though nothing had happened. They went on and soon met Kanati, who seemed much surprised to see them, and said "What! are you here again?" "O, yes, we never give up. We are great men!" "What did the cannibals do to you?" "We met them and they brought us to their townhouse, but they never hurt us." Kanati said nothing more, and they went on.[54]

* * * * * * *

He soon got out of sight of the boys, but they kept on until they came to the end of the world, where the sun comes out. The sky was just coming down when they got there, but they waited until it went up again, and then they went through and climbed up on the other side.

There they found Kanati and Selu sitting together. The old folk received them kindly and were glad to see them, telling them they might stay there a while, but then they must go to live where the sun goes down. The boys stayed with their parents seven days and then went on toward the Darkening land, where they are now. We call them "The Little Men," and when they talk to each other we hear low rolling thunder in the west.

*   *   *   *   *   *   *

After Kanati's boys had let the deer out from the cave where their father used to keep them, the hunters tramped about in the woods for a long time without finding any game, so that the people were very hungry. At last they heard that the Thunder Boys were now living in the far west, beyond the sun door, and that if they were sent for they could bring back the game. So they sent messengers for them, and the boys came and sat down in the middle of the townhouse and began to sing.

At the first song there was a roaring sound like a strong wind in the northwest, and it grew louder and nearer as the boys sang on, until at the seventh song a whole herd of deer, led by a large buck, came out from the woods. The boys had told the people to be ready with their bows and arrows, and when the song was ended and all the deer were close around the townhouse, the hunters shot into them and killed as many as they needed before the herd could get back into the timber.

Then the Thunder Boys went back to the Darkening land, but before they left they taught the people the seven songs with which to call the deer. It all happened so long ago that the songs are now forgotten—all but two, which the hunters still sing whenever they go after deer.[55]

Like the Garden of Eden episode in the Old Testament, the Thunder Boys explained why the Cherokees did not live in an ideal world.[56] Both were braggarts—reckless rule-breakers who brought uncertainty into a perfectly orderly world. But although they made it difficult for man in the beginning, they later served as intermediaries between man and the Upper World. When a person was faced with an insoluble problem or a terrifying threat, the Thunder Boys might step in with a helping hand.

The circle, a recurrent motif in the story of Kanati and Selu, is one of the basic symbolic forms in the Southeast. Many ceremonies involved movement in a circular path, usually with the direction specified. As we have already seen, many of the shell gorgets the Southeastern Indians wore about their necks were circular. Winter council houses, such as the one at Ocmulgee (the "earthlodge") had circular floor plans. And in the council house itself, a fire was often built in the center of the earthen floor by arranging pieces of pine or dry cane cut about two feet long in continuous X's to form a circle, so that the fire continually burned in a circular path.

The story of Kanati and Selu clearly expresses the way in which the Southeastern Indians regarded hunting and agriculture. Hunting was a man's occupation, while agriculture was a woman's occupation. Indeed, the story makes it clear that Selu gave birth to corn and other vegetables, and it was through her death that they were made available to man, much as a seed "dies" when it is placed in the earth. Because she was a spiritual being, after being killed Selu later came back to life and went to the Upper World. The Cherokees sometimes referred to corn in a metaphorical sense as "Old Woman." Other Cherokee stories tell of corn stalks at night being transformed into beautiful young women. Similar stories about the origin of corn were told throughout the Southeast.

To understand these oral traditions properly one must realize that the Cherokees and other Southeastern Indians thought in terms of two different kinds of time. We can call these "ancient time" (Cherokee *hilahiyu*) and "recent time." In ancient time events commonly occurred which only rarely occurred in recent time, and beings existing then were not subject to the rules and limitations that usually constrained ordinary people in recent time. Men, animals, and plants, for example, spoke the same language in ancient time. Moreover, these rules and limitations which are now in effect were themselves created in ancient time. Thus the story of Kanati and Selu explains why corn grows not everywhere but only in patches; why men can only raise two crops of corn in a season instead of seven; why corn takes a whole season to grow instead of a single night; and why man must hunt for game and often fail to find it. In contrast, events in recent time are the events of everyday life, subject to all the rules and limitations of everyday life.

The Southeastern Indians believed that a balanced opposition existed between the great cosmic categories. The next oral tradition explains how men, animals, and plants are interrelated. Men must necessarily hunt to live, and as long as they have a properly respectful attitude toward the animals they kill, the animals are not offended. But when men kill animals disrespectfully or carelessly, the animals are offended and exact vengeance on men by causing them to have diseases specific to their offenses. However, when diseases occur, men can use plants, which men seldom offend, as medicine to cure the diseases. Thus this theory of medicine of the Southeastern Indians recognizes elaborate correspondences between animals, diseases, and herbal medicines.

Origin of Disease and Medicine. In the old days the beasts, birds, fishes, insects, and plants could all talk, and they and the people lived together in peace and friendship. But as time went on the people increased so rapidly that their settlements spread over the whole earth, and the poor animals found themselves beginning to be cramped for room. This was bad enough, but to make it worse Man invented bows, knives, blowguns, spears, and hooks, and began to slaughter the larger animals, birds, and fishes for their flesh or their skins, while the smaller creatures, such as the frogs and worms, were crushed and trodden upon without thought, out of pure carelessness or contempt. So the animals resolved to consult upon measures for their common safety.

The Bears were the first to meet in council in their townhouse under Kuwa'hi mountain, the "Mulberry place," and the old White Bear chief presided. After each in turn had complained of the way in which Man killed their friends, ate their flesh, and used their skins for his own purposes, it was decided to begin war at once against him. Some one asked what weapons Man used to destroy them. "Bows and arrows, of course," cried all the Bears in chorus. "And what are they made of?" was the next question. "The bow of wood, and the string of our entrails," replied one of the Bears. It was then proposed that they make a bow and some arrows and see if they could not use the same weapons against Man himself. So one Bear got a nice piece of locust wood and another sacrificed himself for the good of the rest in order to furnish a piece of his entrails for the string. But when everything was ready and the first Bear stepped up to make the trial, it was found that in letting the arrow fly after drawing back the bow, his long claws caught the string and spoiled the shot. This was annoying, but some one suggested that they might trim his claws, which was accordingly done, and on the second trial it was found that the arrow went straight to the mark. But here the chief, the old White Bear, objected, saying it was necessary that they should have long claws in order to be able to climb trees. "One of us has already died to furnish the bowstring, and if we now cut off our claws we must all starve together. It is better to trust to the teeth and claws that nature gave us, for it is plain that man's weapons were not intended for us."

No one could think of any better plan, so the old chief dismissed the council and the Bears dispersed to the woods and thickets without having concerted any way to prevent the increase of the human race.

Had the result of the council been otherwise, we should now be at war with the Bears, but as it is, the hunter does not even ask the Bear's pardon when he kills one.

The Deer next held a council under their chief, the Little Deer, and after some talk decided to send rheumatism to every hunter who should kill one of them unless he took care to ask their pardon for the offense. They sent notice of their decision to the nearest settlement of Indians and told them at the same time what to do when necessity forced them to kill one of the Deer tribe. Now, whenever the hunter shoots a Deer, the Little Deer, who is swift as the wind and can not be wounded, turns quickly up to the spot and, bending over the blood-stains, asks the spirit of the Deer if it has heard the prayer of the hunter for pardon. If the reply be "Yes," all is well, and the Little Deer goes on his way; but if the reply be "No," he follows the trail of the hunter, guided by the drops of blood on the ground, until he arrives at his cabin in the settlement, when the Little Deer enters invisibly and strikes the hunter with rheumatism, so that he becomes at once a helpless cripple. No hunter who has regard for his health ever fails to ask pardon of the Deer for killing it, although some hunters who have not learned the prayer may try to turn aside the Little Deer from his pursuit by building a fire behind them in the trail.

Next came the Fishes and Reptiles, who had their own complaints against Man. They held their council together and determined to make their victims dream of snakes twining about them in slimy folds and blowing foul breath in their faces, or to make them dream of eating raw or decaying fish, so they would lose appetite, sicken, and die. This is why people dream about snakes and fish.

Finally the Birds, Insects, and smaller animals came together for the same purpose, and the Grubworm was chief of the council. It was decided that each in turn should give an opinion, and then they would vote on the question as to whether or not Man was guilty. Seven votes should be enough to condemn him. One after another denounced Man's cruelty and injustice toward the other animals and voted in favor of his death. The Frog spoke first, saying: "We must do something to check the increase of the race, or people will become so numerous that we shall be crowded from off the earth. See how they have kicked me about because I'm ugly, as they say, until my back is covered with sores"; and here he showed the spots on his skin. Next came the Bird—no one remembers now which one it was—who condemned Man "because he burns my feet off," meaning the way in which the hunter barbecues birds by impaling them on a stick set over the fire, so that their feathers and tender feet are singed off. Others followed in the same strain. The Ground-squirrel alone ventured to say a good word for Man, who seldom hurt him because he was so small, but this made the others so angry that they fell upon the Ground-squirrel and tore him with their claws, and the stripes are on his back to this day.

They began to devise and name so many new diseases, one after another, that had not their invention at last failed them, no one of the human race would have been able to survive. The Grubworm grew constantly more pleased as the name of each disease was called off, until at last they reached the end of the list, when some one proposed to make menstruation sometimes fatal to women. On this he rose up in his place and cried: "*Wadan!* [Thanks!] I'm glad some more of them will die, for they are getting so thick that they tread on me." The thought fairly made him shake with joy, so that he fell over backward and could not get on his feet again, but had to wriggle off on his back, as the Grubworm has done ever since.[57]

When the Plants, who were friendly to Man, heard what had been done by the animals, they determined to defeat the latters' evil designs. Each Tree, Shrub, and Herb, down even to the Grasses and Mosses, agreed to furnish a cure for some one of the diseases named, and each said: "I shall appear to help Man when he calls upon me in his need." Thus came medicine; and the plants, every one of which has its use if we only knew it, furnish the remedy to counteract the evil wrought by the revengeful animals. Even weeds were made for some good purpose, which we must find out for ourselves. When the doctor does not know what medicine to use for a sick man the spirit of the plant tells him.[58]

This story gives us some insight into the Cherokee concept of natural balance. While the industrialized nations have for so long assumed that nature exists for man to use in any way he sees fit, and that nature is infinitely forgiving, the Cherokees recognized that man had to exploit nature in order to live, but that man should do so carefully, and that nature was not infinitely forgiving. If mistreated, nature could strike back. This story also shows that the Cherokees realized that man tends to abuse nature, and that man can become too populous, and that when he does nature suffers. Although this Cherokee concept of natural balance is expressed in an unfamiliar idiom, their concept of natural balance would seem to have a long-term superiority over our own.[59] It is we, after all, who are now realizing that we cannot exploit natural resources indefinitely and that the very process of exploitation itself degrades the quality of our lives.

This remarkable oral tradition contains a second notion which is worthy of our intellectual admiration. It clearly contains a highly general theoretical orientation which directs man not to be wary of the pharmacological properties of plants, but rather to experiment with them and find out how they can be used to help man. Many plants do make good medicine (e.g., quinine, morphine, reserpine, digitalis, salisylic acid, and caffeine, to name a few), even when measured by the most stringent canons of modern medicine. In fact, some of the organic molecules in plants have amazingly specific effects on the central nervous system, and it is reasonable to hypothesize that these pharmacological properties of plants have come about through the process of adaptation: they are chemical defenses against animals.[60] Some few of these effects are, of course, lethal. But in other cases they relieve pain, promote healing, or produce a change in a person's psychological mood. The point of all this is that given the level of technology available to the Cherokees, it is impossible to imagine a more intelligent approach to discovering medicines. The Chinese see its wisdom even today. Ironically, along with acupuncture our medical people are now examining Chinese herbs, which can be imported and sold for high prices, while an ancient, indigenous Southeastern Indian herbalism languishes in obscurity at our doorstep.

In the Cherokee world view the animals were divided into categories patterned after the same kinship and social principles that prevailed in human society. Men and animals were not sharply separated, worlds apart, as they are in our thinking. Thus the relationships among animals were patterned after human relationships, and by the same token the basic Indian kinship groups—the clans—were named after animals and natural phenomena. The Indians who belonged to the deer clan were literally "people of the deer." This does not mean that the Indians confused people with deer; it means that the categories they used to classify deer with respect to other animals could be used to classify one clan of people with respect to other clans.

But even though men and animals were interrelated, men were still set apart. Above all other animals, the bear represents the nature of the division between people and animals. According to a Cherokee oral tradition, bears are descended from a Cherokee clan who decided that they would prefer to live in the company of animals where they would never go hungry rather than face the toil and uncertainties of human existence. In Southeastern Indian thought, part of being human was eating human food. Thus in their oral traditions men who went to live and eat with animals or spiritual beings generally died after returning and eating human food for several days.

Origin of the Bear: The Bear Songs. Long ago there was a Cherokee clan called the Ani-Tsaguhi, and in one family of this clan was a boy who used to leave home and be gone all day in the mountains. After a while he went oftener and stayed longer, until at last he would not eat in the house at all, but started off at daybreak and did not come back until night. His parents scolded, but that did no good, and the boy still went every day until they noticed that long brown hair was beginning to grow out all over his body. Then they wondered and asked him why it was that he wanted to be so much in the woods that he would not even eat at home. Said the boy, "I find plenty to eat there, and it is better than the corn and beans we have in the settlements, and pretty soon I am going into the woods to stay all the time." His parents were worried and begged him not to leave them, but he said, "It is better there than here, and you see I am beginning to be different already, so that I can not live here any longer. If you will come with me, there is plenty for all of us and you will never have to work for it; but if you want to come you must first fast seven days."

The father and mother talked it over and then told the headmen of the clan. They held a council about the matter and after everything had been said they decided: "Here we must work hard and have not always enough. There he says there is always plenty without work. We will go with him." So they fasted seven days, and on the seventh morning all the Ani-Tsaguhi left the settlement and started for the mountains as the boy led the way.

When the people of the other towns heard of it they were very sorry and sent their headmen to persuade the Ani-Tsaguhi to stay at home and not go into the woods to live. The messengers found them already on the way, and were surprised to notice that their bodies were beginning to be covered with hair like that of animals, because for seven days they had not taken human food and their nature was changing. The Ani-Tsaguhi would not come back, but said, "We are going where there is always plenty to eat. Hereafter we shall be called *yanu* (bears), and when you yourselves are hungry come into the woods and call us and we shall come to give you our own flesh. You need not be afraid to kill us, for we shall live always." Then they taught the messengers the songs with which to call them, and the bear hunters have these songs still. When they had finished the songs the Ani-Tsaguhi started on again and the messengers

161

turned back to the settlements, but after going a little way they looked back and saw a drove of bears going into the woods.[61]

Here we clearly see the anomalous position of the bear in Cherokee thought. He usually played the role of a good-natured but awkward buffoon. Perhaps because bears were originally people, who were degraded into bears because of their own laziness, the Cherokees did not have to take ritual precautions when they killed one.

Each four-footed animal had its peculiar characteristics which were reflected in the oral traditions. The rabbit, for example, was a trickster and a deceiver; he was malicious, but he was often beaten at his own game by his intended victims. The rabbit was an enthusiastic ladies' man, gaining access to them by trickery. Because the rabbit easily becomes confused when running, ball players would not eat their flesh. The Southeastern Indians told many stories illustrating the natures of the various animals, as in the following Creek story about Rabbit as trickster, seducer, and polygynist.

How Rabbit won His Wife's Sister for His Second Wife. Rabbit was lying down with his head in his wife's lap and she was gently rubbing it. Presently her sister, who lived with them, a beautiful girl, rose and said, "I must go after the water," and went out.

Then Rabbit jumped up and said to his wife, "I must go and attend to my business." He ran across the stream and hid in some low bushes.

Then the girl came to the stream and began to get water. Rabbit in a disguised voice asked her from his concealment:

"Is Par-soak-ly-ah (Pasikola, his own name) at home?"

"Yes," she replied, looking in the direction of the voice, but not seeing the Rabbit.

"Tell Par-soak-ly-ah that all the people have agreed to undertake a big bear hunt, and they have sent me to tell him to be sure to come. He must go ahead and select a camp and build a fire. No man is to carry his wife, but every man must take his wife's sister."

The girl ran to the house, and Rabbit ran around a different way, and, when the girl came in, he was lying with his head in his wife's lap.

The girl related what she had heard, except the point about every man carrying his wife's sister. Then Rabbit waited a while and said, "Is that all?" She then told it all. Rabbit's wife said:

"I will stay at home. You must go, my sister, on the bear hunt. Both of you must go." Then Rabbit's wife made all things ready for them, and Rabbit and the girl went to the appointed place, reaching it just before the sun went down.

Rabbit built a fire and swept the ground. He expressed great wonder that the other hunters did not come.

"I am disappointed," said he, and running to a log, he jumped on it, and looked in every direction to see if the hunters could be seen.

The sun went down and Rabbit complained bitterly that the hunters had not come.

As it grew dark he said, "Let us go to sleep. You make your bed on that side of the fire and I will make mine on this side."

He had selected a place for the girl where there was an anthill, and when she lay down she could not sleep. She tossed and scratched but could not sleep. Then Rabbit began his wooing, and succeeded in winning his second bride.[62]

Rabbit was not only a polygynist, but a sororal polygynist, marrying sisters; but more on this in chapter 4.

Other stories explain how the animals first acquired their distinctive features, as in the following Choctaw story about the opossum.

> *Why the Possum Grins.* "Did you ever hear why the possum grins?"
> "No."
> "Well the wolf was nearly starved to death [and] as he couldn't get anything to eat, he went to a pond [and] drank water. This didn't satisfy him. He went along [and] looking way up a tree he saw the possum eating persimmons.
> 'How do you get up there?'
> 'I climb up but sometimes the simmons fall down on the ground [and] I pick them up.'
> 'I wish I had some.'
> 'Well, you go way off yonder [and] run with all your might [and] butt your head against the tree [and] shake some down.'
> "The wolf did as directed, came with all his might, hit the tree [and] killed himself. The possum was so delighted at his death that he has never stopped laughing. He laughs [and] grins yet."[63]

One of the most highly prized birds in the Southeast was the bald eagle, the symbol of peace. The tail feathers were particularly valued because they were absolutely necessary for some of the rituals. The killing of an eagle concerned an entire village, and it could only be undertaken by a professional eagle killer who knew the prayers necessary to keep the eagle from taking vengeance on the village. Reflecting the opposition between birds and snakes—the

Upper World and the Under World—the Indians believed that the eagle could only be killed in the late fall or winter, when snakes had retired to their dens. Killing an eagle in summer was thought to bring frost which would kill the corn. If anyone dreamed of an eagle or of eagle feathers, he had to sponsor an eagle dance, else someone in his family would die. Only the men with the greatest social standing were permitted to wear eagle feathers or to carry them at a dance. Because birds were associated with the Upper World, the Cherokees believed them to be superior to the four-footed animals, as may be seen in the following story.[64]

The Ball Game of the Birds and Animals. Once the animals challenged the birds to a great ballplay, and the birds accepted. The leaders made the arrangements and fixed the day, and when the time came both parties met at the place for the ball dance, the animals on a smooth grassy bottom near the river and the birds in the treetops over by the ridge. The captain of the animals was the Bear, who was so strong and heavy that he could pull down anyone who got in his way. All along the road to the ball ground he was tossing up great logs to show his strength and boasting of what he would do to the birds when the game began. The Terrapin, too—not the little one we have now, but the great original Terrapin— was with the animals. His shell was so hard that the heaviest blow could not hurt him, and he kept rising up on his hind legs and dropping heavily again to the ground, bragging that this was the way he would crush any bird that tried to take the ball from him. Then there was the Deer, who could outrun every other animal. Altogether it was a fine company.

The birds had the Eagle for their captain, with the Hawk and the great Tlanuwa, all swift and strong of flight, but still they were a little afraid of the animals. The dance was over and they were all pruning their feathers up in the trees and waiting for the captain to give the word when here came two little things hardly larger than field mice climbing up the tree in which sat perched the bird captain. At last they reached the top, and creeping along the limb to where the Eagle captain sat they asked to be allowed to join in the game. The captain looked at them, and seeing that they were four-footed, he asked why they did not go to the animals, where they belonged. The little things said that they had, but the animals had made fun of them and driven them off because they were so small. Then the bird captain pitied them and wanted to take them.

But how could they join the birds when they had no wings? The Eagle, the Hawk, and the others consulted, and at last it was decided to make some wings for the little fellows. They tried for a long time to think of something that might do, until someone happened to remember the drum they had used in the dance. The head was of ground-hog skin and maybe they could cut off a corner and make wings of it. So they took two pieces of leather from the drumhead and cut them into shape for wings, and stretched them with cane splints and fastened them on to the forelegs of one of the small animals, and in this way came *Tlameha*, the Bat. They threw the ball to him and told him to catch it, and by the way he dodged and circled about, keeping the ball always in the air and never letting it fall to the ground, the birds soon saw that he would be one of their best men.[65]

Now they wanted to fix the other little animal, but they had used up all their leather to make wings for the Bat, and there was no time to send for more. Somebody said that they might do it by stretching his skin, so two large birds took hold from opposite sides with their strong bills, and by pulling at his fur for several minutes they managed to stretch the skin on each side between the fore and hind feet, until they had *Tewa*, the Flying Squirrel. To try him the bird captain threw up the ball, when the Flying Squirrel sprang off the limb after it, caught it in his teeth and carried it through the air to another tree nearly across the bottom.

When they were all ready the signal was given and the game began, but almost at the first toss the Flying Squirrel caught the ball and carried it up to a tree, from which he threw it to the birds, who kept it in the air for some time until it dropped. The Bear rushed to get it, but the Martin darted after it and threw it to the Bat, who was flying near the ground, and by his dodging and doubling kept it out of the way of even the Deer, until he fiinally threw it in between the posts and won the game for the birds.

The Bear and the Terrapin, who had boasted of what they would do, never got a chance even to touch the ball. For saving the ball when it dropped, the birds afterwards gave the Martin a gourd in which to build his nest, and he still has it.[66]

Snakes were thought by the Cherokees to be different from all other animals. The Creeks, Hitchitis, Alabamas, and other South-eastern Indians told stories of men who were transformed into snakes, often as a punishment for eating polluted food. In a Creek story, for example, a man was transformed into a snake because he mixed the brains of a snake, a squirrel, and a turkey, thereby mixing the three realms of animals. Snakes were associated with the Under World, with a particularly close connection with lightning, thunder, and rain, and they had influence over other plants and animals. Snakes, deer, and ginseng, a root used as medicine, were said to be allies. The Cherokees never killed a snake unless they needed it for medicine or some other important purpose, and then they only did so with elaborate ritual precautions. James Adair tells of killing a large rattlesnake, whereupon his Indian companion became very upset and predicted that they would soon be in danger, and as it so happened, their lives were soon threatened by a party of warriors from the Creek town of Okchai.[67] Any man who carelessly or impolitely killed a snake would soon be surrounded by snakes with glistening eyes and darting tongues, and he would inevitably go mad. When a man dreamed of being bitten by a snake he was treated as if he had actually been bitten. Certain acts, such as the town house dance, made the snake angry and perhaps jealous; for this reason the town house or eagle dance was performed in the fall, when snakes were in their dens. The Chickasaws and Choctaws thought of the snake as a treacherous creature, and they said of a deceitful person that he had a snake's tongue.[68]

The rattlesnake was chief of all the snakes. He was once a man, but he was transformed into a rattlesnake and given the task of saving the human race from extermination by a disease sent down by the Sun. Whereas Uktena had failed in this task, Rattlesnake succeeded, and the Indians regarded him highly. He was said to be "Thunder's necklace." The Indians used the teeth, rattles, and flesh of the rattlesnake in a variety of ways. Curers used the teeth to scratch their patients and cure certain diseases. Ball players tied the rattles on their heads to frighten their opponents, and they sometimes ate bits of the flesh to make themselves fierce. The flesh also protected one against certain diseases, but it was used sparingly because it was apt to make one hot tempered. The oil was thought to be good for rheumatism and sore joints.

The Under World where the snakes belonged was an ambiguous world. It was a world of monsters and a source of danger, but it was also the source of water, fertility, and a means for coping with evil. The Uktena was feared as an anomalous monster, but like preliterate and protoliterate people in other parts of the world, the Cherokees seized upon that which was most horrible as an important source of power.[69] Like most of the Indians of the Southeast, the Cherokees believed that their priests and conjurers were able to see into the future by gazing into certain crystals. According to Cherokee oral tradition, the most powerful crystal of all was the *Ulunsuti* (literally, "transparent"), the crest that blazed on an Uktena's head. One had to risk one's life to obtain one of these, but it was thought to be worth the risk. Inferior crystals could be had from the mere scales of an Uktena.

The Uktena and the Ulunsuti. Long ago—[in ancient time]—when the Sun became angry at the people on earth and sent a sickness to destroy them, the Little Men changed a man into a monster snake, which they called Uktena, "The Keen-eyed," and sent him to kill her. He failed to do the work, and the Rattlesnake had to be sent instead, which made the Uktena so jealous and angry that the people were afraid of him and had him taken up to the Upper World, to stay with the other dangerous things. He left others behind him, though, nearly as large and dangerous as himself, and they hide now in deep pools in the river and about lonely passes in the high mountains, the places which the Cherokee call "Where the Uktena stays."

Those who know say that the Uktena is a great snake, as large around as a tree trunk, with horns on its head, and a bright, blazing crest like a diamond upon its forehead, and scales glittering like sparks of fire. It has rings or spots of color along its whole length, and can not be wounded except by shooting in the seventh spot from the head, because under this spot are its heart and its life. The blazing diamond is called *Ulunsuti*, "Transparent," and he who can win it may become the greatest wonder worker of the tribe, but it is worth a man's life to attempt it, for whoever is seen by the Uktena is so dazed by the bright light that he runs toward the snake instead of trying to escape. Even to see the Uktena asleep is death, not to the hunter himself, but to *his family*.

Of all the daring warriors who have started out in search of the Ulunsuti only . . . [Ground-hog's Mother, a great magician] ever came back successful.[70] The East Cherokee still keep the one which he brought. It is like a large transparent crystal, nearly the shape of a cartridge bullet, with a blood-red streak running through the center from top to bottom. The owner keeps it wrapped in a whole deerskin, inside an earthen jar hidden away in a secret cave in the mountains. Every seven days he feeds it with the blood of small game, rubbing the blood all over the crystal as soon as the animal has been killed. Twice a year it must have the blood of a deer or some other large animal. Should he forget to feed it at the proper time it would come out from its cave at night in a shape of fire and fly through the air to slake its thirst with the lifeblood of the conjurer or some one of his people. He may save himself from this danger by telling it, when he puts it away, that he will not need it again for a long time. It will then go quietly to sleep and feel no hunger until it is again brought out to be consulted. Then it must be fed again with blood before it is used.

167

No white man must ever see it and no person but the owner will venture near it for fear of sudden death. Even the conjurer who keeps it is afraid of it, and changes its hiding place every once in a while so that it can not learn the way out. When he dies it will be buried with him. Otherwise it will come out of its cave, like a blazing star, to search for his grave, night after night for seven years, when, if still not able to find him, it will go back to sleep forever where he has placed it.

Whoever owns the Ulunsuti is sure of success in hunting, love, rain-making, and every other business, but its great use is in life prophecy. When it is consulted for this purpose the future is seen mirrored in the clear crystal as a tree is reflected in the quiet stream below, and the conjurer knows whether the sick man will recover, whether the warrior will return from battle, or whether the youth will live to be old.[71]

The Cherokee concern with keeping things separate and in their proper sphere can clearly be seen in the manner in which the crystals had to be treated. That is, they had to be kept wrapped in a deerskin, placed in an earthen jar, and kept in a cave, as befitted things of the Under World. Similarly, when an eagle was killed and its feathers taken for use in rituals, the feathers had to be kept wrapped in a deerskin and placed in a small, round feather house, built especially for this purpose, on the edge of the dance ground.

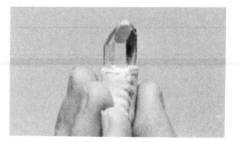

Figure 47. A Western Cherokee divining crystal. The lower portion is covered with white buckskin. In the collection of James H. Howard.

Quartz crystals have been found by archaeologists at Spiro and at many other Mississippian sites, though they are frequently not reported because they are unworked, and archaeologists perhaps have not fully appreciated their significance (fig. 47). The Creeks call them *sapiyá*, and as we have already seen, the Creek hunter carried his crystal and some red ocher in a deerskin pouch. When applied to his face, the pigment was believed both to enhance his eyesight and to attract game. The pigment could also be used to attract members of the opposite sex, but using it to excess was thought to cause the user to go insane. The Florida Seminoles once believed that such crystals could be used to ward off bullets, and earlier we are probably safe in concluding that they were believed to bring a man success in warfare as well as in rainmaking, hunting, and lovemaking.[72] Perhaps the Mississippian hand-and-eye design represents a crystal held in a man's hand, symbolizing the ability to see into the future, although this interpretation must remain conjectural until other evidence presents itself.[73]

PEOPLE AND SPIRITS

The oral traditions of the Southeastern Indians mostly tell of events which occurred in ancient time, in the remote past, when the world was different from the way it is now. But this does not mean that spirits lived only in ancient time; on the contrary, they were very much present in the everyday world of the Southeastern Indians. Moreover, it is not terribly accurate to think of these spiritual personages as being "supernatural." They were far different from ordinary human beings and animals, but they were very much a part of the "natural" world. This does not mean, however, that a Southeastern Indian attached no more importance to his experience with a spiritual being than with an ordinary human being or animal; this experience with spiritual beings was of special importance, but it was a kind of experience that most ordinary people had at some time or another in their lives.

The Cherokees lived in a world that included several categories of spiritual beings. The great spirits of the Upper World—the Sun, the Moon, the Great Thunder (Kanati), Corn (Selu), and others—rarely intervened in everyday matters. In contrast, lesser spiritual beings, most of whom lived in the Under World, used to intervene more frequently. One such group of spirits was the Immortals. The Immortals were invisible, except when they wanted to be seen. They looked rather like ordinary Cherokees, and people in the stories about them generally confused them with Cherokees from other settlements. The Immortals lived in town houses within the mountains, and especially in the bald mountains, on whose high peaks no timber ever grows. They also lived under the Nikwasi mound at what is now Franklin, North Carolina, and some of them lived underwater. They were friendly beings who looked after tired hunters and lost children, inviting them down into their town houses. They were fond of drumming and dancing, and the Indians often heard them inside the bald mountains, which actually do occasionally emit rumbling sounds. The Immortals often aided the Cherokees against their adversaries.

The Spirit Defenders of Nikwasi. Long ago a powerful unknown tribe invaded the country from the southeast, killing people and destroying settlements wherever they went. No leader could stand against them, and in a little while they had wasted all the lower settlements and advanced into the mountains. The warriors of the old town of Nikwasi, on the head of the Little Tennessee, gathered their wives and children into the townhouse and kept scouts constantly on the lookout for the presence of danger. One morning just before daybreak the spies saw the enemy approaching and at once gave the alarm. The Nikwasi men seized their arms and rushed out to meet the attack, but after a long, hard fight they found themselves overpowered and began to retreat, when suddenly a stranger stood among them and shouted to the chief to call off his men and he himself would drive back the enemy. From the dress and language of the stranger the Nikwasi people thought him a chief who had come with reinforcements from the Overhill settlements in Tennessee. They fell back along the trail, and as they came near the townhouse they saw a great company of warriors coming out from the side of the mound as through an open doorway. Then they knew that their friends were . . . the Immortals, although no one had ever heard before that they lived under Nikwasi mound.

The [Immortals] poured out by hundreds, armed and painted for the fight, and the most curious thing about it all was that they became invisible as soon as they were fairly outside of the settlement, so that although the enemy saw the glancing arrow or the rushing tomahawk, and felt the stroke, he could not see who sent it. Before such invisible foes the invaders soon had to retreat, going first south along the ridge to where [it] joins the main ridge which separates the French Broad from the Tuckasegee, and then turning with it to the northeast. As they retreated they tried to shield themselves behind rocks and trees, but the [Immortals'] arrows went around the rocks and killed them from the other side, and they could find no hiding place. All along the ridge they fell, until when they reached the head of Tuckasegee not more than half a dozen were left alive, and in despair they sat down and cried out for mercy. Ever since then the Cherokee have called the place *Dayulsunyi,* "Where they cried." Then the [Immortals'] chief told them they had deserved their punishment for attacking a peaceful tribe, and he spared their lives and told them to go home and take the news to their people. This was the Indian custom, always to spare a few to carry back the news of defeat. They went home toward the north and the [Immortals] went back to the mound.

And they are still there, because, in the last war [i.e., the Civil War], when a strong party of Federal troops came to surprise a handful of Confederates posted there they saw so many soldiers guarding the town that they were afraid and went away without making an attack.[74]

Another Cherokee category of spiritual beings, the Little People, were more frequently encountered than the Immortals. Like the Immortals, they were invisible except when they wanted to be seen. They were physically well formed, but like European leprechauns and fairies they were no higher than a man's knee, and their hair grew long, like Trolls, reaching almost to the ground. They lived not in town houses, but in rock shelters and caves in the mountain side, in laurel thickets, in broom sage, and out in the open. Like the Immortals, they were fond of drumming and dancing, and they would help children who were lost in the woods. But they were mischievous, playing tricks on people which sometimes caused great harm. One had to deal with the Little People with some care. They did not like to be disturbed, and anyone who did so might suffer a psychological or physical illness. The Little People could cause a person to become temporarily bewildered, or even to become insane. For this reason, when the Indians heard the Little People outside their houses at night, they would not go out and try to see them. Moreover, if anyone did see them, he could not tell anybody, because to do so would bring death. When a hunter found something in the woods, like a knife, that perhaps belonged to the Little People, before he could pick it up he had to say, "Little People, I want to take this."[75]

The Little People had to be treated carefully, and the same was true for all of the other spiritual beings. If these spiritual beings were slighted or treated disrespectfully, they would become resentful, and the offender would be stricken with disease. This was especially true when dealing with ghosts. The Southeastern Indians believed that each individual had a soul that lived on as a ghost after death. Ghosts were believed to have the ability to materialize so that some individuals could see them though others could not.[76] When a person died, all the people in the village shouted and made noise in an attempt to frighten the ghost up to the western sky. If a ghost were allowed to stay around, it could cause people to fall ill or even die. Sometimes a ghost would become lonely and come back from the West to haunt his relatives, causing them to fall ill.[77] The Indians would not eat food that had been left out overnight for fear that ghosts had touched it. And the ghost of a man whose murder had not been avenged was thought to haunt the eaves of his house until his murderer or his murderer's relatives had shed equal blood.

Other creatures who lived in the world of the Southeastern Indians also had souls that had to be treated carefully. If an animal was properly killed, death was only a temporary thing; the animal was reincarnated in identical form. But as we have seen, if the hunter did not take the necessary ritual precautions, the ghost of the slain animal took vengeance on the hunter by inflicting him with a disease such as rheumatism, dysentery, swollen joints, or violent head-aches. Even the ghosts of insects, which one could hardly avoid killing, would establish colonies in a victim causing ulcers, blisters, and swellings.[78] Most of the diseases caused by animal ghosts were said to be "intruders." The ghosts were believed to intrude them-selves into a person and cause the disease. Sometimes they would lie dormant for some time before the disease appeared. Thus when a patient fell ill, a priest had to inquire into his behavior for the preceding several months or even years.

Although the spirits of the Upper World rarely injected them-selves into human affairs, they were often called upon to help cure diseases. As a rule, a spirit which caused a disease was not called upon to take it away; rather, a rival spirit was called upon to come and do combat. The Sun was often called upon to cure disease, and a priest usually asked the Sun's permission before gathering medici-nal herbs. Fire, the Sun's earthly representative, was also fre-quently called upon to fight disease. Since fire was a thing of the Upper World, it was used in curing diseases caused by animals of the Under World, including turtles, snakes, and fish. When a medicine had to be drunk, it was often strengthened with the power of fire by dropping four or seven live coals into it.

Rivers also figured prominently in the Cherokee spirit world. The river was called "Long Man" or "Long Snake." The head of the Long Snake was thought to be in the mountains and his tail in the low-lands. The river was associated with the moon, and on every new moon, including those in winter, the Cherokees used to go to the bank of the river where a priest officiated and everybody plunged in. This was to ensure long life, implying that the snake, which annually sheds its skin, is associated with longevity. Usually this ritual took place at a bend of the river where they could face upstream toward the rising sun. Just as Fire could be offended, so could the river.

GOOD AND EVIL

When faced with the problem of making sense out of the great disasters and calamities of their lives, the Southeastern Indians explained relatively little in terms of what we regard as chance or accident. There was a reason why things went wrong. Many of the things which went wrong they explained as having come about because people in their communities broke rules of ritual separation or propriety; when such rules were broken, men suffered. This was the working of supernatural justice, in which good men were rewarded and evil men punished by gods and spirits. This was especially true for men, who had to keep the rules with great diligence, else they could endanger the success of their comrades in warfare. When a man was caught in an immoral act, his fellows would reproach and ridicule him so unmercifully he might contemplate or resort to suicide.[79] They were especially likely to explain loss of life in warfare as having been caused by one or more of their warriors having been impure.[80]

Illness, like death in warfare, was often explained in this fashion. In 1738, for example, a devastating smallpox epidemic struck the Cherokees, killing almost half of them.

At first it made slow advances, and as it was a foreign, and to them a strange disease, they were so deficient in proper skill, that they alternately applied a regimen of hot and cold things, to those who were infected. The old magi and religious physicians who were consulted on so alarming a crisis, reported the sickness had been sent among them, on account of the adulterous intercourses of their young married people, who the past year, had in a most notorious manner, violated their ancient laws of marriage in every thicket, and broke down and polluted many of their honest neighbours bean-plots, by their heinous crimes, which would cost a great deal of trouble to purify again. To those flagitious [*sic*] crimes they ascribed the present disease, as a necessary effect of the divine anger; and indeed the religious men chanced to suffer the most in

173

their small fields, as being contiguous to the town house, where they usually met at night to dance, when their corn was out of the stalks; upon this pique, they shewed their priest-craft.[81]

Sin and impurity were serious matters among the Southeastern Indians. They affected not only the well-being of the sinner, but of his entire community and society as well. Living, as we do, in more or less impersonal communities, it is difficult for most of us to imagine what it would have been like to live in such a morally intense community.

In addition to explaining misfortunes in terms of supernatural justice, which was somewhat predictable, or at least intelligible, because it was meted out with respect to a known body of rules, the Southeastern Indians occasionally suffered from disasters which could not be explained in this way. It sometimes happened that good men kept the rules but suffered horrible calamities, and it sometimes happened that evil men broke the rules but prospered. These "wild" events the Southeastern Indians explained as having been caused by witchcraft.

The Southeastern Indians believed that serious misfortunes, illness, and even death could be caused by the action of witches. This belief should not be confused with our own popular notion of witches as old women who come out once a year to ride their broomsticks on Halloween night, nor has it anything to do with contemporary "witch" cults. Basically, witchcraft is the theory that one's serious troubles are caused by other people, even by kinsmen and close neighbors, working through mystical means. With witchcraft we enter a realm of human affairs that is full of hidden meanings, deceit, and ambiguity. Many, perhaps most, preliterate societies all over the world believe that people can harm other people through witchcraft; indeed, this theory of why things go wrong in human affairs is so widespread in the world that it must fit the facts of life in a small-scale society exceedingly well. Until one can understand witchcraft as both a rational and even reasonable way of explaining and manipulating human behavior in a small-scale society, one cannot understand it at all. By "rational" I mean that it proceeds logically from certain assumptions, even though we ourselves might find these assumptions unacceptable or unreasonable. By "reasonable" I mean that if one can lay aside, for the moment, one's own cultural assumptions, one can see that witchcraft is a theory of

174

behavior especially appropriate for life in small-scale societies.

This matter requires further explanation. In a small-scale society, such as those in which the Southeastern Indians lived, a person lived out his entire life among the same small group of people. It is difficult for us to appreciate all that this entails. Unlike our society, in which most of a person's relationships with others are specific and limited to one area of life—as with teacher, doctor, boss, grocer, and so on—in a small-scale society people relate to each other in many different ways. In our society if a person's relationship with another person deteriorates, there is no great problem (unless it is a member of the immediate family), but in a small-scale society a single troubled relationship, even with someone who is not a kinsman, can affect many areas of a person's life. Moreover, in the context of such intensive relationships, people come to read each other's behavior very closely, and consequently ambiguity and doubt about the intentions of others is inevitable. James Adair, for example, tells how closely the Indians guarded their own affairs, while they pried into his affairs so avidly that privacy was impossible.[82] Jealousy can be particularly damaging in such societies, and jealousy and ambiguity lie at the heart of witchcraft. One can think of witchcraft as an ideological outgrowth of: "What did he mean by that? Did he really mean that, or did he mean just the opposite?"[83]

The Cherokee notions of witchcraft were epitomized in their beliefs about man-killers. There were several kinds of man-killers. A race of water cannibals, for example, was believed to live in the bottoms of deep rivers and would come in early morning just after daybreak to shoot their victim with invisible arrows and carry the body beneath the water to feast upon it. The confusing thing was that they would leave the image of the dead person behind. Everybody would think it was the person himself; but within seven days the image would weaken and die. They were particularly fond of children, so that Cherokee parents would always try to awaken their children just before daybreak, saying, "The *hunters* are among you," this being an oblique reference to the water cannibals.[84]

The Cherokees also believed there to be an old man and woman who were man-killers. The old people were clad in stone so that they were very hard to kill. The old woman was called Spear-finger. Consistent with the ambiguity intrinsic in witchcraft beliefs, Spear-finger had the ability to change herself into any shape—

raven, owl, cat, purple light, or another person. Thus one's next door neighbor could actually be Spear-finger.

Spear-finger. Long, long ago—[in ancient time]—there dwelt in the mountains a terrible ogress, a woman monster, whose food was human livers. She could take on any shape or appearance to suit her purpose, but in her right form she looked very much like an old woman, excepting that her whole body was covered with a skin as hard as a rock that no weapon could wound or penetrate, and that on her right hand she had a long, stony forefinger of bone, like an awl or spearhead, with which she stabbed everyone to whom she could get near enough. On account of this fact she was called . . . "Spear-finger," and on account of her stony skin she was sometimes called . . . "Stone-dress." There was another stone-clothed monster that killed people, but that is a different story.

Spear-finger had such powers over stone that she could easily lift and carry immense rocks, and could cement them together by merely striking one against another. To get over the rough country more easily she undertook to build a great rock bridge through the air from . . . the "Tree rock," on Hiwassee, over to . . . Whiteside mountain on the Blue Ridge, and had it well started from the top of the "Tree rock" when the lightning struck it and scattered the fragments along the whole ridge, where the pieces can still be seen by those who go there.[85] She used to range all over the mountains about the heads of the streams and in the dark passes of Nantahala, always hungry and looking for victims. Her favorite haunt on the Tennessee side was about the gap on the trail where Chilhowee mountain comes down to the river.

Sometimes an old woman would approach along the trail where the children were picking strawberries or playing near the village, and would say to them coaxingly, "Come, my grandchildren, come to your granny and let granny dress your hair." When some little girl ran up and laid her head on the old woman's lap to be petted and combed the old witch would gently run her fingers through the child's hair until it went to sleep, when she would stab the little one through the heart or back of the neck with the long awl finger, which she had kept hidden under her robe. Then she would take out the liver and eat it.

She would enter a house by taking the appearance of one of the family who happened to have gone out for a short time, and would watch her chance to stab some one with her long finger and take out his liver. She could stab him without being noticed, and often the victim did not even know it himself at the time—for it left no wound and caused no pain—but went on about his affairs, until all at once he felt weak and began gradually to pine away, and was always sure to die, because Spear-finger had taken his liver.

When the Cherokee went out in the fall, according to their custom, to burn the leaves off from the mountains in order to get the chestnuts on the ground, they were never safe, for the old witch was always on the lookout, and as soon as she saw the smoke rise she knew there were Indians there and sneaked up to try to surprise one alone. So as well as they could they tried to keep together, and were very cautious of allowing any stranger to approach the camp. But if one went down to the spring for a drink they never knew but it might be the liver eater that came back and sat with them.

Sometimes she took her proper form, and once or twice, when far out from the settlements, a solitary hunter had seen an old woman, with a queer-looking hand, going through the woods sings low to herself:

> *Uwéla nátsĭkû'. Sú să' saí.*
> Liver, I eat it. Sú să' saí.

It was rather a pretty song, but it chilled his blood, for he knew it was the liver eater, and he hurried away, silently, before she might see him.

At last a great council was held to devise some means to get rid of Spear-finger before she should destroy everybody. The people came from all around, and after much talk it was decided that the best way would be to trap her in a pitfall where all the warriors could attack her at once. So they dug a deep pitfall across the trail and covered it over with earth and grass as if the ground had never been disturbed. Then they kindled a large fire of brush near the trail and hid themselves in the laurels, because they knew she would come as soon as she saw the smoke.

Sure enough they soon saw an old woman coming along the trail. She looked like an old woman whom they knew well in the village, and although several of the wiser men wanted to shoot at her, the others interfered, because they did not want to hurt one of their own people. The old woman came slowly along the trail, with one hand under her blanket, until she stepped upon the pitfall and tumbled through the brush top into the deep hole below. Then, at once, she showed her true nature, and instead of the feeble old woman there was the terrible Spear-finger with her stony skin, and her sharp awl finger reaching out in every direction for some one to stab.

The hunters rushed out from the thicket and surrounded the pit, but shoot as true and as often as they could, their arrows struck the stony mail of the witch only to be broken and fall useless at her feet, while she taunted them and tried to climb out of the pit to get at them. They kept out of her way, but were only wasting their arrows when a small bird . . . , the titmouse, perched on a tree overhead and began to sing "*un, un, un.*" They thought it was saying *únahŭ'*, heart, meaning that

177

they should aim at the heart of the stone witch. They directed their arrows where the heart should be, but the arrows only glanced off with the flint heads broken.

Then they caught the titmouse and cut off its tongue, so that ever since its tongue is short and everybody knows it is a liar. When the hunters let it go it flew straight up into the sky until it was out of sight and never came back again. The titmouse that we know now is only an image of the other.

They kept up the fight without result until another bird, little . . . chickadee, flew down from a tree and alighted upon the witch's right hand. The warriors took this as a sign that they must aim there, and they were right, for her heart was on the inside of her hand, which she kept doubled into a fist, this same awl hand with which she had stabbed so many people. Now she was frightened in earnest, and began to rush furiously at them with her long awl finger and to jump about in the pit to dodge the arrows, until at last a lucky arrow struck just where the awl joined her wrist and she fell down dead.

Ever since the chickadee is known as a truth teller, and when a man is away on a journey, if this bird comes and perches near the house and chirps its song, his friends know he will soon be safe home.[86]

The songs of the Carolina chickadee (*Parus carolinensis*) and the tufted titmouse (*Parus bicolor*) closely resemble each other, and it is easy to confuse the two, just as it is sometimes easy to confuse falsehood with truth.[87] Other evidence suggests that many birds had specific meanings as omens for the Southeastern Indians. The Timucuans believed that if a person were startled by the cry of a bluejay it meant that someone was coming to visit him or something unusual was about to happen; that it was a bad omen to see an owl, and especially bad to frighten one from its perch; and that if a person saw a woodpecker he should keep quiet lest he suffer a nosebleed.[88] James Adair tells of being in the woods with an Indian war party, when all of them became visibly anxious and agitated at the song of a certain "small uncommon bird."[89]

The story of Spear-finger, the man-killer, makes clear the ambivalent and anomalous nature of witchcraft. Even her heart was not in the right place. Her ability to transform herself into any shape meant that what appeared to be one's neighbor might actually be a horrible monster intent upon killing people by stealing their livers. In a world with witches one could never be sure.

It should be realized that just because Spear-finger was killed in

178

this story, this did not mean that she was dead forever. Spear-finger was no ordinary being, and mere death did not put an end to her. Perhaps the closest analogy in our own culture is the old Dracula movies in which Dracula was inevitably killed in the end, but no one thought it surprising for him to turn up later in another movie.

One of the main reasons that witches attacked a person was that the witch wanted to add the life of the victim to his own. For this reason the Cherokees believed that witches were often very old individuals. At the same time, old people among the Cherokees were both respected and powerful; but they were sometimes distrusted, just as we sometimes distrust people in power in our own society. People who were seriously ill or otherwise feeble or decrepit were especially vulnerable to attack by a witch, because they were so easy to overcome. This is one of the reasons why relatives would sit up all night with people who were ill. Women in labor and young infants were also likely victims. One of the most horrible of the man-killer witches was Raven Mocker. The following story is Cherokee, but similar stories were told by other Southeastern Indians.

> *The Raven Mocker.* Of all the Cherokee wizard or witches the most dreaded is the Raven Mocker . . . , the one that robs the dying man of life. They are of either sex and there is no sure way to know one, though they usually look withered and old, because they have added so many lives to their own.
>
> At night, when some one is sick or dying in the settlement, the Raven Mocker goes to the place to take the life. He flies through the air in fiery shape, with arms outstretched like wings, and sparks trailing behind, and a rushing sound like the noise of a strong wind. Every little while as he flies he makes the cry like the cry of a raven when it "dives" in the air—not like the common raven cry—and those who hear it are afraid, because they know that some man's life will soon go out.[90] When the Raven Mocker comes to the house he finds others of his kind waiting there, and unless there is a doctor on guard who knows how to drive them away they go inside, all invisible, and frighten and torment the sick man until they kill him. Sometimes to do this they even lift him from the bed and throw him on the floor, but his friends who are with him think he is only struggling for breath.
>
> After the witches kill him they take out his heart and eat it, and so add to their own lives as many days or years as they have taken from his. No one in the room can see them, and there is no scar where they take out the heart, but yet there is no heart left in the body. Only one who has the

179

right medicine can recognize a Raven Mocker, and if such a man stays in the room with the sick person these witches are afraid to come in, and retreat as soon as they see him, because when one of them is recognized in his right shape he must die within seven days. There was once a man named Gunskaliski, who had this medicine and used to hunt for Raven Mockers, and killed several. When the friends of a dying person know that there is no more hope they always try to have one of these medicine men stay in the house and watch the body until it is buried, because after burial the witches do not steal the heart.

The other witches are jealous of the Raven Mockers and afraid to come into the same house with one. Once a man who had the witch medicine was watching by a sick man and saw these other witches outside trying to get in. All at once they heard a Raven Mocker cry overhead and the others scattered "like a flock of pigeons when the hawk swoops." When at last a Raven Mocker dies these other witches sometimes take revenge by digging up the body and abusing it.

The following is told on the reservation as an actual happening:

A young man had been out on a hunting trip and was on his way home when night came on while he was still a long distance from the settlement. He knew of a house not far off the trail where an old man and his wife lived, so he turned in that direction to look for a place to sleep until morning. When he got to the house there was nobody in it. He looked into the asi [A small, heavily insulated house, used in cold weather.] and found no one there either. He thought maybe they had gone after water, and so stretched himself out in the farther corner to sleep. Very soon he heard a raven cry outside, and in a little while afterwards the old man came into the asi and sat down by the fire without noticing the young man, who kept still in the dark corner. Soon there was another raven cry outside, and the old man said to himself, "Now my wife is coming," and sure enough in a little while the old woman came in and sat down by her husband. Then the young man knew they were Raven Mockers and he was frightened and kept very quiet.

Said the old man to his wife, "Well, what luck did you have?" "None," said the old woman, "there were too many doctors watching. What luck did you have?" "I got what I went for," said the old man, "there is no reason to fail, but you never have luck. Take this and cook it and let's have something to eat." She fixed the fire and then the young man smelled meat roasting and thought it smelled sweeter than any meat he had ever tasted. He peeped out from one eye, and it looked like a man's heart roasting on a stick.

Suddenly the old woman said to her husband, "Who is over in the corner?" "Nobody," said the old man. "Yes, there is," said the old woman, "I hear him snoring," and she stirred the fire until it blazed and lighted up the whole place, and there was the young man lying in the corner. He kept quiet and pretended to be asleep. The old man made a noise at the fire to wake him, but still he pretended to sleep. Then the old man came over and shook him, and he sat up and rubbed his eyes as if he had been asleep all the time.

Now it was near daylight and the old woman was out in the other house getting breakfast ready, but the hunter could hear her crying to herself. "Why is your wife crying?" he asked the old man. "Oh, she has lost some of her friends lately and feels lonesome," said her husband; but the young man knew that she was crying because he had heard them talking.

When they came out to breakfast the old man put a bowl of corn mush before him and said, "This is all we have—we have had no meat for a long time." After breakfast the young man started on again, but when he had gone a little way the old man ran after him with a fine piece of beadwork and gave it to him, saying, "Take this, and don't tell anybody what you heard last night, because my wife and I are always quarreling that way." The young man took the piece, but when he came to the first creek he threw it into the water and then went on to the settlement.[91] There he told the whole story, and a party of warriors started back with him to kill the Raven Mockers. When they reached the place it was seven days after the first night. They found the old man and his wife lying dead in the house, so they set fire to it and burned it and the witches together.[92]

These oral traditions about man-killing monsters should not lead one to think that the Southeastern Indians lived in paralyzing terror of witchcraft, for witchcraft was a topic of day-to-day conversation, a part of the fabric of their lives, and one could not be terrified of such a pervasive force in human affairs.[93] The Southeastern Indians used the notion of witchcraft to explain the kind of events that some people in our society explain with the notion of fate, and which others explain, to a more limited degree, with the notion of the unconscious self, and we are terrified neither of fate nor of the unconscious self.

Though much misfortune was attributed to witchcraft, the Southeastern Indians did not use it to account for every small failure, accident, or disappointment. If an inept hunter failed to come back with game, his failure would be seen as a reflection of his ineptitude. But if an expert hunter repeatedly failed to kill game, then he might suspect that his failure was caused by witchcraft. Witchcraft explained "wild" events that could not be explained in terms of a person's conformity to the moral code.

Perhaps it would not be going too far to say that with respect to the Southeastern Indian belief system, witches were anomalous in the human realm in much the way that the frog, the bat, and the snake were anomalies in the animal realm. That is to say, a witch looked like an ordinary human being, but his evil nature placed him outside the human realm. The Cherokees say of a man that he is *dugu:gho:dá*, a word which connotes that he is just, righteous, straight, honest, true, and upright. They say of a man that he is *u:da:nʌ:ti*, a man with soul, heart, or feeling. But they say of a witch that he is *u:ne:gu:tso:dá*, so heartlessly evil as to be beyond forgiveness. An ordinary man might commit a thoughtless, illegal, or immoral act and still be forgiven. But there is no forgiveness for a witch, for his evil is intrinsic to his being.[94]

A witch was not what he or she appeared to be, and a person could never be sure when he was dealing with one. Consistent with this idea, a witch frequently caused a person to fall ill by "changing his saliva." Saliva was thought to be as important a part of one's physiology as blood was, and keeping one's saliva pure was important for good health. The symptom of changed saliva was acute depression. A witch might also attack his victim by changing an apparently mild disease into a serious or fatal disease. The danger of this is that it could deceive the medicine man or conjurer and lead him to prescribe the wrong cure.[95] With witches one could never be sure. Witches were the epitome of uncertainty in human affairs.

In a sense, ordinary witches were more threatening than the man-killer witches. Spear-finger, for example, possessed known attributes, and one could take precautions against her, but ordinary witches were more difficult to evade or counteract. The Cherokees believed that witches were made, not born. They believed that a person could bring up his child to be a witch by isolating him from visitors and by feeding him not milk from his mother's breast but the liquid from fermented hominy.[96] But if people in the community heard that a mother was raising her child in this way, they would attempt to slip the baby some food which had been prepared by a menstruating woman, and this would nullify what the mother was attempting.[97]

Another way to become a witch was to drink a decoction made from duck-root (*Sagittaria latifolia* Willd.), which looks like a beetle-like insect with the stem of the plant growing out of its mouth. In spring and early summer this plant is said to have purple fire dropping from its stem, and purple is the color of witchcraft. If a person fasted and drank a liquid made from this root on four successive days, it enabled him to transform himself into the form of any animal of This World; if he fasted and drank it for seven days it enabled him to transform himself into any animal of This World, the Upper World, or the Under World, and it enabled him to fly through the air and dive under the ground.[98]

Whether any Cherokee parent was evil enough to turn his own child into a witch is not known. In all probability, this was simply the Cherokee theory of where witches came from rather than an actual practice. It was thought, however, that children who were raised in this way became highly competent, self-reliant individuals—who might be called "inner-directed"—but the danger was that they might go too far in this and become socially disruptive, and in some cases even witches. Thus through the best of motives, the belief may have been that some parents accidentally caused their children to become witches.[99] As for Cherokee priests, they often used duck-root in the prescribed manner to enable themselves to discover the identity of witches and thwart their evil plans.

The Cherokees believed that in some cases the soul of a witch traveled about at night in the form of a small flame or spark floating through the air. One of the harmless little spirit people of the Cherokees was "Fire-carrier," so called because he carried a little light with him at night. But the Cherokees did not know what he looked like because a light at night usually meant that there was a witch on the prowl, and they were afraid to look.[100] This is simply another instance of how witchcraft was based on fear, mistrust, and suspicion. Indeed, witchcraft was an expression of all these human frailties.

Our concern here has been to describe the way in which the belief in witchcraft fitted into the belief system of the Southeastern Indians, and to attempt to surmount our own cultural biases in order to see how witchcraft beliefs are a "rational" and even "reasonable" way of explaining human behavior in small-scale communities. Witchcraft was, of course, not only a theory or set of beliefs, but also a way of behaving. It was acted out as well as thought out. This behavioral aspect of witchcraft among the Southeastern Indians will be discussed in chapter 6.

CHAPTER FOUR

SOCIAL ORGANIZATION

The basic building blocks of the Southeastern Indian belief system consisted of categories and sets of categories comprising a classification system, this being the fundamental stuff of all belief systems, whether preliterate, like that of the aboriginal Southeast, or literate, like our own. But preliterate belief systems are distinctive in several respects. In preliterate belief systems, what we ourselves regard as distinct domains or areas of classification are often linked together and mutually adjusted to each other so that they smoothly coincide. We have already seen, for example, that in the Southeast, directions of the compass were linked with colors, social values, and opposed forces in the cosmos.

Another distinctive feature of preliterate belief systems is that certain sets of categories are used to classify not just a single domain of phenomena, as is the case with our Linnean classification of plants or animals, but rather the sets of categories are used to classify phenomena which to us seem unrelated. It is for this reason that an understanding of the kinship system of the Southeastern Indians is essential for an understanding of both their social life and their view of the world. The life of the Southeastern Indian was largely regulated by his kinship system. It provided him with a set of readymade categories that determined who his enemies were, who his allies were, whom he could and could not marry, and to whom he could leave his property and his social prerogatives after he died. The Southeastern Indian lived in a world of kinsmen, and a man without kinsmen was like a man without a country.

Basically, then, the Southeastern Indian kinship system was a way of classifying relatives of various kinds. But the use of kinship as a classificatory system went far beyond this. Kin relationships were used as a model for the way in which the Southeastern Indians thought about relationships between discrete kinship groups, between different towns, and even between wholly different societies and cultures. For example, when the Spaniard Menéndez visited the Calusas, Tequestas, and Tocobagas of South Florida in the late sixteenth century, they addressed him as "elder brother," thus placing themselves in the position of "younger brother," and elder brothers were supposed to be kind and protective toward their younger brothers.[1] Later, in the middle of the eighteenth century, Malachi, an important Creek chief, spoke of the Chickasaws as his "younger brothers" and of his own people as their "elder brothers."[2] Moreover, as we saw in the last chapter, the kinship system even served as a model for conceptualizing relationships between different animal species. Kinship was a kind of mentality that pervaded many areas of life.

One can scarcely overemphasize the importance of kinship in the social life of the Southeastern Indians. But kinship was not all there was to their social life: there was the added dimension of politics and law, concerned with relationships among kin groups, towns, and larger political units. The Southeastern Indians defined political relationships in basically opposed terms: they all consisted of various definitions of friend as opposed to enemy. There were, moreover, several kinds of friends and enemies. The different kinds of friends were defined in terms of the kind of support an individual could expect from them, and the various kinds of enemies were defined in terms of the kind of conflict they might suffer from them.

KINSHIP

Kinship among the Southeastern Indians was matrilineal, with kinsmen tracing their relationships to each other through women. One basic feature of matrilineal kinship must be clear from the start. This is that in a matrilineal system an individual's "blood" relatives are not both on his mother's side and his father's side of the family, but only those relatives—both male and female—on his mother's side traced through women. Diagram 1 will help the reader identify these relatives. In kinship diagrams, anthropologists use the following conventions: a triangle represents a male; a circle represents a female; a horizontal line represents the relationship between brothers and sisters; a vertical line represents the parent-child relationship; and an equivalency sign represents marriage. One individual, usually a male, is arbitrarily designated as *Ego*, as a point of reference. In diagram 1, Ego's matrilineal "blood" relatives are shaded.

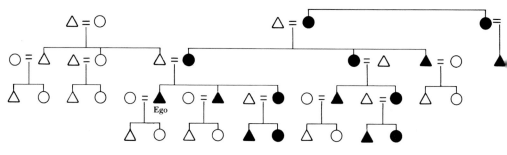

Diagram 1. Matrilineal descent.

As diagram 1 makes clear, Ego's closest relatives in a matrilineal descent system are his mother and her sisters and brothers, mother's mother, and the children of these female relatives, including, of course, Ego's own brothers and sisters. One outstanding feature of a matrilineal kinship system is that the children of Ego's male relatives are not his "blood" relatives, and this also holds for a male Ego's own children. The children of Ego's female relatives, however, are his blood relatives. Another startling feature is that Ego's father is not a blood relative, nor are his father's people. This does not mean that Ego's children, his father, and his father's people are unimportant to him—they are. But it does mean that they are not kinsmen in the sense that his brothers and sisters, or his mother, or his mother's brother are.

Several other facts about matrilineal kinship need to be made plain before one can understand the kinship organization of the Southeastern Indians. One is that even though they traced their descent through women, and even though women occupied honored places in their society, this did not mean that women had charge of the society. Although houses, land, and certain other kinds of property were owned and controlled by a matrilineal group of relatives, most of the effective political power lay in the hands of men, and the important decisions were generally made by men. Some exceptions did occur. We have already seen that both Hernando de Soto and Juan Pardo encountered in the course of their explorations female chiefs with considerable power. Later, the "beloved women" among both the Cherokees and the Creeks were people of influence. For example, in 1774, when the Creeks were on the verge of going to war against the English colonists, a Cherokee beloved woman at Sugartown sent a message to a Creek beloved woman at Coweta urging the Creeks to remain at peace.[3] But for the most part women were influential rather than powerful, and they were more inclined to sway opinion behind the scenes than out in the open.

Another peculiarity of the matrilineal kinship system is that a particularly close relationship exists between a woman and her brother; in some ways she is closer to her brother than she is to her husband. This relationship with her brother carries over to her children; in matrilineal societies a boy respects his mother's brother in much the way a boy in other kinds of societies respects his father (fig. 48): He looks to his mother's brother to teach him much of what he needs to know as a man, and when he is sick he looks to his mother's brother to comfort him. The other side of the relationship is that the mother's brother has authority over his sister's children and is responsible for disciplining them. Although this seems odd at first, it is not at all odd when we realize that the mother's brother is the boy's closest senior male blood relative.

The question that inevitably arises is, what if a woman has no brother? Would this not put Ego in the position of having no mother's brother? The answer is that in the matrilineal kinship system of the Southeastern Indians Ego used the same kinship term to refer to all of his matrilineal male relatives in his mother's generation as he would use to refer to mother's own brothers, and thus Ego would normally have many "mother's brothers" (see diagrams 1 and 4). Beyond this, the precise way in which the Southeastern Indians parceled out authority and responsibility between mothers' brothers and sisters' sons is not well understood. But it is likely that in any particular instance, one of Ego's mother's brothers, more senior and more respected than the others, would be given the main responsibility for disciplining and looking after the general welfare of all the boys he called "sister's son."

Another inevitable question is, would this kinship system not frustrate the affection and loyalty of a father for his own children? The answer is that to some extent it probably did. In fact, a considerable body of eighteenth-century historical evidence indicates that among the Southeastern Indians titles, wealth, and social prerogatives were sometimes passed from father to son. The British colonists were, of course, culturally biased in favor of a father passing down wealth and position to his own children, but this British influence does not necessarily explain this seemingly anomalous father-son relationship among the Southeastern Indians at such an early date. As time went on, however, the Southeastern Indians did gradually abandon their matrilineal kinship system in favor of one closer to our own.[4]

Like many other people who trace descent matrilineally, the Creeks (and most other Southeastern Indians) used the "Crow" type of cousin terminology, so called because the Crow Indians of the American Plains first provided anthropologists with a classic example of this pattern of kinship terms. In the Crow type of terminology Ego refers to his mother's brother's children with the same terms he uses to refer to his own children, and he refers to father's sister's children with the same terms he uses to refer to his father and to his father's sister.[5] The Creek terminology is shown in diagram 2. This terminology strikes us as illogical because on the mother's side it seems to take terms from the generation below Ego and applies them to his own generation, so that he must call his maternal cousins *kputci* "son" and *tchusti* "daughter." And on the father's side it seems to take terms from the generation above Ego and applies them to his own generation, so that he must call his paternal cousins *ɬki* "father" and *posi* "father's sister."

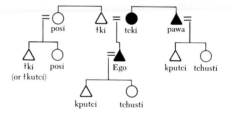

Diagram 2. Creek cousin terms.

This peculiar terminology only makes sense when we realize that our own kinship categories such as "father," "son," "daughter," and so on cannot be applied to kinship systems in other cultures in the sense in which we use them in our own culture. In a matrilineal kinship system this problem of translating kinship terms comes from

188

the fact that we are dealing with *groups* or *categories* of matrilineal kinsmen rather than with individuals. Thus the Creek word *ɬki* means "father," but it also means "a male of father's lineage" of any age. At the same time, Ego generally referred to his own father as *ɬki*, while calling the other males of father's lineage "little father"—*ɬkutci*, adding to *ɬk(i)* the diminutive *-utci*. Similarly, *posi* means "father's sister," but it more generally means "a female of father's lineage," and it has other meanings which we need not go into here. The important thing is that all of the men of father's lineage are called *ɬki* (or *ɬkutci*), and all of them do in fact stand in a kind of father relationship to Ego. The pattern of cousin terms used by the Cherokees was basically the same, except that a Cherokee used a single term, "child," to refer to children of both sexes in his lineage.[6]

Applying this principle of the importance of categories and groups to Ego's mother's side, in diagram 2 *kputci* means "the son of a man of my lineage" and *tchusti* means "the daughter of a man of my lineage." And looking at the relationship from the other end, Ego (along with his male kinsmen) is a kind of father to all of the people he calls *kputci* and *tchusti*.

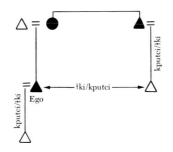

Diagram 3. Creek reciprocal kinship terms.

Diagram 3 illustrates the reciprocal nature of these categories. Ego refers to his mother's brother's son as "son," and he in turn refers to Ego with the same term he uses to refer to his own father.

The basic kinship group among the Southeastern Indians was the matrilineal lineage or matrilineage. This was a group of matrilineal kinsmen who could trace descent from a known ancestress and most of whom lived in the same locality, owning property, and sharing certain ceremonial rights.

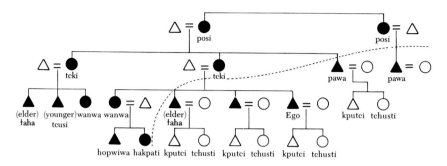

Diagram 4. The Creek matrilineage.

The Creek matrilineage consisted of an old ancestress *posi* (as we have seen, *posi* also meant "female of father's lineage," but more on this later), her children, her daughters' children, and her daughters' daughters' children.[7] The husbands of these women lived in the lineage households, but the husbands' closest affiliations were with their sisters, who lived in their own lineage households elsewhere in the village. Similarly, the adult males of the lineage who were married lived with their wives in their wives' households. The only males belonging to the lineage who lived on lineage property were the unmarried sons. Each Creek town was composed of about four to ten lineages or groups of lineages. In diagram 4 relatives to the left of the dotted line are members of the matrilineage living in one place, while the males to the right of the dotted line are married and living elsewhere.

We are now in a better position to understand how the Creeks and other Southeastern Indians were able to classify almost all of the people in their social universe in terms of a few kinship categories. A Creek male not only referred to his own mother as *tcki*, but also to all of her sisters, generally using a diminutive meaning "little mother" (*tckutci*). Mother's brothers were all called *pawa*, with one of them serving as headman of the lineage. The children of mother and her sisters were referred to by men as *łaha* "elder brother," *tcusi* "younger brother," and *wánwa* "sister." The children of elder brother and younger brother were not lineal kinsmen of Ego, so they were categorized with Ego's children and the children of mother's brother. Sister's children, on the other hand, were important lineal relatives, and Ego referred to them as *hopwiwa* "sister's son" and *hákpati* "sister's daughter." As we have already seen, the relation

190

between a man and his sister's children was a very important one.

The kinship terms used by a female differed in several important respects from the terms used by a male.

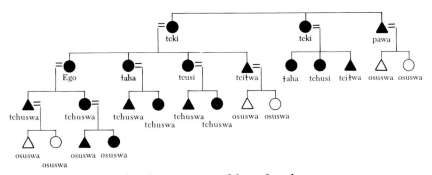

Diagram 5. Creek kinship terms used by a female.

A female speaker applied the term *taha* to her elder sister and to her mother's sisters' daughters of comparable age, and *tcusi* to her younger sisters and to other females according to the same pattern. Thus *taha* literally means "elder sibling of my sex," and *tcusi* literally means "younger sibling of my sex." She called all her brothers *tcitwa*, applying the same term to her mother's sisters' sons. She called all the children of her lineage *tchuswa*, "child." In contrast, she called the children of the men of her lineage *osuswa*, a term she also applied to her own grandchildren and to others in that same generation.

A Creek Indian used this set of kinship categories to classify his known relatives, and this was sometimes a considerable number. But the application of these kinship categories went much further than this. In addition to matrilineages, the Creeks, Cherokees, and other Southeastern Indians reckoned kinship in terms of matrilineal clans. A clan was a category of people who believed themselves to be blood relatives, but who could not actually trace their relationships to each other through known ancestral links. Each clan was associated with a particular animal or natural phenomenon (e.g., Deer, Bear, Wolf, Wind) from which it took its name and from which it derived certain symbolic associations. Thus the Bear clan consisted of all the people who belonged to Bear lineages; a member of a particular Bear lineage could trace his relationships to all the other members of his lineage, but he might not be able to trace his relationship to a member of a Bear lineage from a distant village. Still, they were of the Bear clan, and kinship terms were extended to all members of the clan. Thus if a male member of a Bear lineage met a male member of a Bear lineage from a distant town, he would call him *taha* if he were about the same age as his older brother, *tcusi* if he were about the same age as his younger brother, *pawa* if he were about the same age as his mother's brother, and so on. It is important to realize that while lineages were real social groups functioning on a day-to-day basis, clans were not so much social groups as *categories* of people who believed themselves to be of one "blood." Clans rarely if ever assembled together as a group, though before European contact they may have done so on ceremonial occasions, such as the Green Corn Ceremony to be described in chapter 6.

In a very general sense we can think of a clan as "consisting" of a series of lineages scattered about in various towns. For example, early in the twentieth century the Oklahoma Creek town of Talladega contained, among others, lineages representing the Bear, Wind, Bird, Deer, and Cougar clans. All of these clans were likewise represented in the contemporary Creek town of Kantcati. If a man of the Bear lineage in Talladega happened to visit Kantcati, he could go to a household of the Bear lineage where the members would extend hospitality to him, saying "come to your home." They would do this even if they had never seen him before. They might secretly resent having to extend hospitality to him, but they would do it nonetheless. The visitor would address all of these clansmen with kinship terms. He would refer to the senior women as *tcki*, "mother"; to their brothers as *pawa*, "mother's brother"; to their elder sons as *taha*, "elder brother"; and so on. Extending the use of kinship categories to clansmen meant that these categories could be used to refer to hundreds of individuals instead of just a few.

These kinship terminologies were not only guides to classifying relatives of remote degree, they also served as a guide to interacting with them. Thus a Cherokee had to show respect and deference to anyone he called "father," "mother," "child," or "mother's brother." On the other hand, he could joke in a rough and satirical way with anyone he called "brother," and he had to protect from harm anyone he called "younger brother," and if harm were done he was expected to seek revenge. He had to be especially polite to anyone he called "sister." In marked contrast to the respect he had to show to "father" and "mother," he could be especially free with almost anyone he called "grandfather" or "grandmother," the main exception being that he had to show respect for father's father. In fact, the freedom a Cherokee man had in his relationship with his "grandmothers" was often a prelude to sexual intercourse or marriage, and the Cherokees sometimes married their "grandmothers." This is not at all odd when one realizes that a Cherokee called *all* the females, from infant to octogenarian, in father's father's clan and mother's father's clan "grandmother," and it should be noted that they were not blood relatives.[8]

Unlike the lineage, the clan was not an economic unit; it did not own property. But both the lineage and the clan were exogamous. This meant that an individual could not marry a person who belonged to the same lineage or clan, even though they might be distant cousins by our standards. And conversely it meant that people who were close kin by our standards could marry. For example, if a man married two women of different clans, the children of these women would belong to the clans of their mothers, and the members of one could marry members of the other.

The members of a clan had special regard for the animal or phenomenon from which they took their name. The Creeks had a vague notion that a person should not kill or eat his clan animal, though this was often a matter of jest rather than a serious prohibition. One Creek convention was that to one's fellow clansmen one spoke disparagingly of one's own clan animal, but this was with the understanding that what was said was meant in the opposite sense. However, if one spoke disparagingly of another clan's animal, he might be subject to a fine or some other sanction by that clan. The Creeks had some notion of being descended from their clan animals, but it was more figurative than literal. Animal names for the clans were more a classificatory device than a belief in animal ancestry.

The clan was the most important social entity to which a person belonged. Membership in a clan was more important than membership in anything else. An alien had no rights, no legal security, unless he was adopted into a clan. For example, if a war party happened to capture an enemy and the captive was not adopted by a clan, then any sort of torture could be inflicted upon him. But if he were adopted into one of his captors' clans, then no one could touch him for fear of suffering vengeance from the adopting clan. The rights of clansmanship were so fundamental they were seldom if ever challenged.[9]

The Creeks believed that their clans, like all their important social institutions, originated in the ancient past. The following story was collected by John R. Swanton early in this century.

> When the Creek Indians came to know anything of themselves, it was to find that they had been for a long series of generations completely buried and covered as it were in a dense fog impenetrable to their powers of vision. Being unable to see, they were dependent on their other senses, especially that of touch, in their efforts to obtain subsistence.
>
> In their quest for food the people very naturally became separated, straying away from each other in groups, and each group was aware of the existence and locality of its neighbors only by calling to them through the obscuring fog, each adopting the precaution not to stray out of calling distance of some other of the scattered groups.
>
> After a great while there arose a wind from the east that gradually drove the fog from the land. The group of people who first saw clearly the land and the various objects of nature, now rendered visible by the dissipating fog, were given the name of the Wind clan. It is related that, among the many things they were now able to see, the first animate objects observed by the people of the Wind clan were a skunk and a rabbit which appear to have accompanied them during their existence in the obscuring fog. While the people did not adopt either of these as their [clan symbol], they did declare them their nearest and dearest friends. So well is this understood by the full blood Creek Indian, that it is universally understood to be the duty of the sons of the Wind clansmen always to extend to these animals protection and defense from physical injury and ridicule, saying "They are my fathers."[10]
>
> As the fog continued to recede and disappear before the driving east wind, other groups of people came to light; and, as each looked about, it adopted as the [symbol] of the clan by which it would thereafter be known, the first live animal which had emerged from the fog along with it.
>
> In this manner three other clans—the Beaver, the Bear, and the Bird—were established, who, together with the Wind, have always been known as . . . [Hathagálgi] (the Whites) and recognized as leaders in the establishment and maintenance of peace in the nation. The Wolf clan is kindred to the Bear clan, but without the political prestige of the latter. All the other clans, which are very numerous, were formed in the same manner, and are known as . . . [Tcilokogálgi] (speakers of a different language) as distinguished from the [Hathagálgi], or Whites.[11]

In addition to accounting for the origin of the Creek clans in general, this myth also accounts for the origins of the most important of them—the Beaver, the Bear, the Bird, and especially the Wind clan. It also mentions the division between the Whites (*Hathagálgi*) and the "speakers of different languages" (*Tcilokogálgi*), and I shall later discuss the significance of this division.

When a Creek lineage became too large and unwieldy to function properly, or when irreconcilable differences arose among the members of a lineage, the lineage underwent segmentation. That is, the lineage split, and one part of it moved off to live somewhere else. After segmentation, where there was once a single lineage, there were now two lineages, one senior and the other junior, one "mother" and the other "daughter." Although actual instances of this process are not adequately documented in the historical record, it must have happened frequently, for this is the only way one can explain how it was that the same clan was represented by lineages in many different towns.

In addition, we have some evidence for the way in which new clans came into existence. The Creeks regarded sexual relationships between a man and woman of the same clan as being incestuous, even though the couple might have been distant cousins by our standards. Incest was a crime that was very severely punished— even by death. But John Swanton heard of one case involving a man and a woman of the Toad clan, in which both of the offenders were well regarded in the community. Instead of punishing them, the town council met and designated the woman as the first of a new clan, the Mole clan, thereby making the sexual relationship legitimate. It is probable, however, that both "Toad" and "Mole" were humorous names which therefore carried a social stigma. Swanton was told that many of the small clans originated in this way. This process may be the explanation for the existence of over fifty clans among the Muskogees, Hitchitis, Alabamas, Natchez, Yuchis, Timucuas, and Chickasaws, although it is likely that this proliferation of clans was not a normal process but was produced by social disruption following European colonization.[12]

Some of these clans were quite small, and their constituent lineages were correspondingly small in number. This seems to be the reason why some lineages linked themselves together in exogamous relationships. For example, if through disease or war the

Potato lineage in a particular town became too small to function properly, it linked itself with, say, the Raccoon lineage. The children of the two clans grew up regarding themselves as brothers and sisters and, hence, were forbidden to have sexual intercourse. Linkages between particular clans sometimes occurred widely, but not universally. The Raccoon and Potato clans, for example, were in fact linked together in many Creek towns; but in some they were separated. These linked clans thought of themselves as standing in a mother's brother–sister's son relationship. The stronger clan usually took the position of sister's son, and the weaker clan took the position of mother's brother. The reason for the weaker clan having what would seem to be the dominant position in this metaphorical relationship is not clear, but it may have been a form of politeness.

The Creeks drew on their belief system for explanations of particular instances of linked clans, but some of the explanations seem somewhat contrived. The Bear and Wolf clans were often paired, it was said, because both had claws. But by this principle the Cougar clan should have been linked to them, and it never was. The Cougar and Deer clans were often paired because "the story is that [Cougar] and Deer lived together as friends, but at noon [Cougar] jumped upon Deer and killed him. So the [Cougar] and Deer clans are one until noon and after that separate. Until noon the same terms of relationship are extended over both clans." This story illustrates the fragile nature of the rule of exogamy as applied to the two groups. The Creeks told several stories about how the link between two lineages was broken when a man and a woman of the linked lineages were discovered having sexual relations. In such cases the link between the two lineages would be severed and their fire, the symbol of purity, was said to be put out. But in some cases the two lineages were said to be, as with the previously mentioned Cougar and Deer lineages, "one until noon, but separate afterwards."[13]

MARRIAGE

Much of a Southeastern Indian's social life was shaped by descent, the fact of being born into a particular clan. Another social fact of life that strongly affected most of his remaining social relationships was marriage. As we shall presently see, it is a mistake to think of marriage among the Southeastern Indians as being closely similar to marriage in our society. Just as one must think in terms of categories and groups in order to understand matrilineal kinship, one must think in terms of categories and groups in order to understand marriage as it was practiced in the Southeast.

We have already seen that the Southeastern Indians recognized rules of exogamy which made it illegal for a person to marry or have sexual relationships with another of his or her own lineage or clan.[14] The penalty for breaking this rule was said to be death, although it is unlikely that the rule was often broken until fairly late in the historic period, when Southeastern Indian societies began to break down. For the Creeks a person was also forbidden to marry anyone in the father's lineage. Thus a man could not marry any woman called *tcki*, "mother"; *posi*, "grandmother"; *wànwa*, "sister"; or *hàkpati*, "sister's daughter."

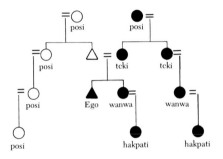

Diagram 6. Forbidden marriage partners for a Creek male.

It is obvious from diagram 6 that there were entire categories of women whom Ego could not marry. Marriages were as much relationships between kin groups as they were relationships between individuals. If a boy became interested in a particular girl, he did not speak to her or to her parents directly; instead he sent his mother's sister to speak to the girl's mother's sister to explore the possibility of marriage. Afterwards, the girl's mother's sister would discuss the matter with other members of the girl's lineage—particularly with the girl's mother—often without the girl's being formally told about the negotiations, although informally she probably did know about it or expect it to occur. If her lineage viewed the matter favorably, word would be sent to the boy's lineage.[15]

Even though a girl's lineage might encourage her to marry a particular boy, her consent was necessary before the marriage could take place. Marriages were arranged but not forced. The Creek way of allowing her to express her wishes was to inform her of the boy's desires and to invite him to visit her household. A bowl of sofkee (Seminole *sá•fki*, "boiled hominy meal") was placed near a corn crib in sight of her house. If she allowed the boy to steal up and eat a spoonful of the sofkee, this was taken as an expression of her willingness to marry him; but if she ran out and stopped him from taking the sofkee, it meant that she did not want to marry him. In this way she could reject him indirectly, without humiliating him. The fathers of both the boy and the girl, not being blood relatives, were not formally consulted when the marriage was arranged, though they might be told about the negotiations as an act of politeness.

After an expression of willingness from the girl and her lineage was obtained, the boy assembled with the help of his lineage a collection of gifts which were presented by his lineage to the girl's lineage. If accepted, the boy and girl could begin having sexual relations. Even after this began, the girl often continued living in her parents' household for a time. In some cases she slept in the corn crib, with the boy sneaking in to spend the night with her. The boy could generally escape being sanctioned by her lineage by the simple expedient of being up and gone by dawn the next day. The Southeastern Indians' favorite places for sexual episodes were corn cribs, corn fields, and bean patches. After the boy had built a house and raised a crop, again with the help of his lineage, the marriage ceremony could be performed. The ceremony itself was fairly simple. The boy went out in the woods and killed a deer or a bear, showing that he could provide meat, and therefore was a man. In the company of his lineage, the boy then presented the meat of the butchered animal to the girl, and she in turn presented him with an ear of corn or some food she had cooked, showing that she could provide vegetable food and therefore was a woman. In some cases they exchanged bean poles—pieces of wood or cane around which bean vines twined—these evidently symbolizing sexual union. After this they were considered married, and the house became the girl's property.

But this did not mean that the marriage was absolutely binding. The couple remained married until the performance of the next Green Corn Ceremony, the most important religious ceremony of the year, when the new crop of late corn was celebrated and social relationships in the entire society were realigned or adjusted. If the

198

marriage was unsatisfactory at the time of the Green Corn Ceremony, it was dissolved and the boy moved back in with his lineage.

The custom of polygyny—the marriage of a man to two or more
women—was widely practiced in the Southeast. The Creeks placed
a high value on having several wives or concubines, though only the
wealthier men could afford it. A concubine was a woman from whom
a man gained sexual rights by purchase. The Creeks thus distinguished between marrying a woman and "buying" a woman. Although a relationship with a concubine had to be approved by the
woman's lineage, it did not place all the constraints of marriage on
the man. A man could take neither a concubine nor a second wife
without his first or principal wife's permission. If he did not obtain
her permission in taking a concubine, he could be accused of adultery, in which case the wife's kinsmen might punish the offending
man and woman by beating and mutilation. If he tried to bring in a
second wife against his first wife's will, she and her female relatives
might beat the girl and scratch her face. If the first wife chose to do
this, however, she had to separate from her husband, and the new
wife became her ex-husband's principal wife.

It should be realized that only a wealthy man could afford plural
wives, and when he did have several wives, it frequently took the
form of sororal polygyny; that is, a man married several sisters, or
even a woman and her daughters by a previous marriage. The
advantage of this arrangement was that sisters and mother and
daughter usually got along better with each other than did unrelated
women. With sororal polygyny, the wives would usually consent to
continue living in the same house or in adjacent houses, but co-
wives who were not sisters lived in separate dwellings.[16] One of the
wives, usually the first, was the principal wife who had authority
over the others. If a second wife was not of the same lineage as the
first wife, she would have to move away from her own lineage if she
wanted to live with her husband. A woman usually was reluctant to
do this, always preferring to live in her mother's household. In any
case, her children claimed descent from her clan and their allegiance
was there.

This custom of polygyny—and particularly sororal polygyny—
explains the logic behind other conventions in the Creek kinship
terminology. In Creek kinship terminology a man called his
mother's brother's wife *hatcawa*, and he called his wife's sister by

the same term. In terms of matrilineal ideology, with its insistence on distinguishing similar relatives by a single term, this terminology initially seems puzzling. But the logic behind it becomes clear when we examine some of their marriage customs. There is some evidence that Southeastern Indian lineages established preferential marriage relationships with other lineages, with most of the men from lineage A marrying women from lineage B.[17] With this arrangement it makes sense for a Creek man to use the same term for wife's sister and mother's brother's wife because they would belong to the same lineage. On the other side of it, father's brother could well be married to mother's sister, so it made sense to call her *tcki*, "mother," and her children by the same terms he used for his mother's children and his mother's sister's children. Following this same logic, mother's sister's husband was called *ƚki*, "father."[18]

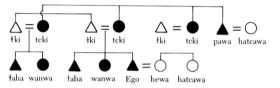

Diagram 7. Creek relatives by marriage.

Among the Creeks as among other matrilineal people, marriages were somewhat fragile and divorce was rather common. Marriage was not a binding contract. For some of the Southeastern Indians marriages were renewed annually at the Green Corn Ceremony or in some other ceremonial way. Among some of the Creeks, a man's claim on his wife's fidelity was annually renewed by having his own kinsmen hoe out the corn fields of his wife or wives. Sometimes a woman would decide that she wanted a divorce because her husband treated her too harshly. A Creek man could divorce his wife if she were lazy, quarrelsome, or disobedient, but adultery was the most common ground for divorce. Before marriage a Creek girl enjoyed considerable sexual freedom, and any sexual relationships she had with unmarried men were not considered adulterous. But after she was married she was expected to be faithful. If caught in adultery she was likely to be beaten by her husband's relatives, with or without his consent, and in some cases they would take a knife— sometimes a dull knife—and cut off the ears of the woman and her lover.[19] Usually the marriage was thereby dissolved, but the woman retained possession of her house and land, and she retained custody of her children. For a certain period of time, however, she was forbidden to have sexual relations with any man except the lover with whom she had been caught. There was little chance after this that any man would ever take her for his wife, though she could probably find someone who would "buy" her as a concubine. When a divorce took place in some Southeastern groups, both the man and the woman had to wait until after the Green Corn Ceremony before they could remarry; in other societies only the woman had to wait until after the Green Corn Ceremony. But the Cherokees were far different. A Cherokee woman, whether married or single, could more or less go to bed with whomever she chose, and her husband could do little or nothing about it. The Cherokee woman had the same sexual freedom that a Cherokee man had.[20]

Among the Creeks, when a person was widowed, he or she was supposed to mourn until four of the annual Green Corn Ceremonies had been performed. A widow was not supposed to take care of her hair and was supposed to dress in unattractive clothing for the entire period. In some cases the body of her husband was buried in the floor of her house, and she had to sleep over his grave. She was supposed to lament her husband's death audibly and loudly each morning for one year. James Adair wryly observed that this motivated a woman to take good care of her husband because she dreaded the prospect of being a widow.[21] Men were forbidden to stand in water upstream from a widow, and when the wind was blowing they were forbidden to walk on her windward side. Both of these acts were presumably overtures to adultery and were sometimes regarded as being acts of adultery. After the four-year period was over, the deceased husband's female relatives would bathe the woman and dress her in new clothes and lead her to a dance. After this, she could remarry whomever she pleased.

This four-year rule could be circumvented in several ways. A man could be released from it by marrying a woman of his deceased wife's lineage, and a woman could be released by marrying a man of her deceased husband's lineage. This is another expression of the fact that marriages were not so much relationships between individuals as they were enduring relationships between groups of people, and it further illustrates the logic behind Creek kinship terminology.

Another way out was that the widow could appeal to her deceased husband's lineage to have mercy and release her from the mourning period. They could do so if they chose. Furthermore, a widow or widower could elope with a new spouse, and if they could elude the dead spouse's kinsmen until after a Green Corn Ceremony had been performed, they could return and live in society without fear of punishment.[22]

THE CHIEFDOM

In the eighteenth century, and probably earlier, the Southeastern Indians were organized into a series of chiefdoms. The Creek word for chiefdom was *tálwa*, the Hitchiti word was *okli*, and the Choctaw word was *okla*. Following the usage of early European explorers, soldiers, and traders, these words traditionally have been translated to mean "town," but "chiefdom," in the technical sense used by anthropologists, is a far better word. A chiefdom is a type of political organization which stands midway between the egalitarian, highly decentralized tribal organization of the Iroquois, Hopis, and Navajos on the one hand, and the highly centralized state organization of the Incas of Peru and the Aztecs of the Valley of Mexico on the other. The king of the Incas was so powerful he could order one of his subjects to be put to death more or less arbitrarily, particularly if the subject were poor. In a tribe, on the other hand, everyone is as poor (and as rich) as everyone else, and their leaders are little more than men of influence. In a state wrongs against individuals are punished by legitimate agents of the state, but in a tribe wrongs against individuals are punished by the wronged individual's kin group, and this often causes feuds among the kin groups which weaken the social fabric. The local communities of a state are held together "organically" by complex social and economic dependencies, with rulers living in cities and their subjects living in towns and villages. The local communities of a tribe are self-sufficient. They are held together "mechanically" (and far more weakly) by virtue of their members belonging to clans, age-grades, and other associations which crosscut local communities.[23]

The best evidence we have indicates that the degree of centralization of authority in the Southeastern chiefdoms stood somewhere between the tribe and the state. As the name implies, the Southeastern chiefdoms had chiefs, but in historic times these chiefs led

202

their people more than they commanded them. These chiefdoms were not completely egalitarian, but neither were they stratified into classes of people who differed greatly in hereditary wealth. Within a chiefdom, Southeastern Indian men ranked themselves in terms of a strict hierarchy, from highest to lowest, partly with respect to age, and partly with respect to their accomplishments as warriors, leaders of men, and as religious and medical practitioners. These men were most determined in their pursuit of rank, and they avidly bedecked themselves with symbols of their attainments and standing. These symbols included names or titles, tattooed designs on their bodies, and the seats they occupied in their council houses. James Adair tells us that if a man were foolish enough to take a seat in the council house which was above his rank, he would be peppered with humiliating catcalls and would immediately take a more appropriate seat; and Adair tells us that Indians who tattooed themselves with designs to which they were not entitled were forced to go through the painful process of removing them.[24] Most of the icons and artifacts of the Southeastern Ceremonial Complex must have been used to symbolize positions in this male hierarchy.[25] The Indians identified themselves so passionately with their symbols that they took them with them to their graves, as has been abundantly demonstrated by the archaeologists.[26] Some evidence suggests that the wives of important men shared their rank. Among the Natchez, for example, the women with the most extensive body tattooing were the wives of important men.

It should be understood that not all of these chiefdoms comprised comparable numbers of people, nor were they equally centralized. Chiefdoms may have small populations or large, and their chiefs may be relatively weak or strong. Moreover, at the time of de Soto's exploration of the Southeast, some of the Southeastern Indians may have been organized into something other than chiefdoms. Some of the small groups of people on the margins of the Southeast, such as the people along the western Gulf coast and in the northern piedmont, may have been organized into tribes, lacking chiefs altogether or else having chiefs in a very weak sense.

A more interesting possibility is that at the time of de Soto, some of the Southeastern Indians may have had what were either very powerful chiefdoms or perhaps very small primitive states. This is indicated by the fact that some of the Indians showed such great

Figure 48. Tomochichi and his "nephew," Tooanahowi. Tomochichi was a Creek chief who played an important role in early Georgia history; the boy was probably his sister's son. Taken from a portrait by William Verelst in 1734. Negative no. 1129–A. Courtesy, Smithsonian Institution, National Anthropological Archives.

loyalty to their chiefs. When de Soto reached the vicinity of Cofitachequi, he was unable to get anyone to tell him where the chief was, even though he tortured several Indians to death by burning.[27] Some of the Southeastern Indian leaders, such as the Lady of Cofitachequi and Tascalusa, were treated with extreme deference, carried on litters (fig. 49), and surrounded by retainers and assistants. The fierce military encounter at Mabila in which thousands of Indians mounted a surprise attack against de Soto would seem to indicate centralized planning which exceeded the capability of chiefdoms in the ordinary sense. Finally, the mere size of sites such as Moundville and Cahokia make one think of similar sites built by the people of primitive states in Mesoamerica.

We also have evidence indicating that the power of Southeastern chiefs declined after European colonization gained a foothold. Most of the earliest observers in the Southeast reported that the chiefs had great power. This was said of the people de Soto observed, the French said it of the Natchez, and the Spanish said it of the Calusas. But by the middle of the eighteenth century, no Indian leader possessed such power. In fact, James Adair was so struck by this discrepancy that he argued that the early descriptions of chiefly power were simply wrong, having been produced by the exaggeratedly autocratic mentality of the French and Spanish Catholics.[28] But it may have been Adair who was wrong. If powerful chiefdoms or small primitive states did exist in the Southeast in Mississippian times, they were probably not very stable, as is the case in such societies elsewhere in the world, the reason being that their local communities remained almost completely self-sufficient.[29] Thus if a village, town, or affiliated chiefdom were cut off from the seat of

Figure 49. The Natchez Great Sun carried on a litter. From LePage Du Pratz, *Histoire de la Louisiane*, Paris, 1758, vol. 2, opp. p. 367. Courtesy, University of Georgia Libraries.

power, it probably made little difference in the day-to-day lives of the people.

If this interpretation is correct, and if some of the Southeastern Indians did have truly powerful chiefdoms or primitive states at the height of the Mississippian period, it may explain something which has always been puzzling about the Southeastern Ceremonial Complex. That is, after this symbolic complex developed and spread over all the territory from northern Florida to St. Louis, Missouri, and Spiro, Oklahoma, why do the material symbols and artifacts associated with it suddenly disappear from the archaeological record in the late prehistoric and early historic period? And why in historic times did the Indians no longer build mounds, even though for a time they used the old ones?[30] It would seem reasonable to suppose that these aspects of Southeastern Indian culture were closely associated with the highest levels of hierarchy in the powerful chiefdoms or primitive states and would have fallen away if these top levels were to have collapsed. There is evidence that this began to happen in some parts of the Southeast well before the arrival of the Europeans. Where in other parts the hierarchy remained, the European invasion brought it to an end. For these chiefdoms the collapse would likely have begun when the first foreign diseases swept the land. Yet, the Southeastern Ceremonial Complex could not have existed unless Indians at all levels had shared symbols, categories of understanding, and knowledge, so that it is not surprising to find "survivals" of the Southeastern Ceremonial Complex even in comparatively recent times. Moreover, the far more modest chiefdoms of the eighteenth century and later were almost certainly organized along the same general lines as most of the villages and towns of the Mississippian tradition. We can perhaps use the analogy of a two-story house in a tornado, where the small, ornate upper story is blown away, leaving all the lower rooms more or less intact.

This older, more centralized political order survived into the eighteenth century only among Indians along the lower Mississippi River, such as the Natchez, who are known to us from the observations and reports of French colonists between 1700 and 1731. The Natchez political structure was more or less like that of other Southeastern Indians in later times, to be described a few pages hence. But the Natchez were different in that their religious and civil chief, the Great Sun, commanded more veneration and had more power than chiefs in later times. The Great Sun came from the Sun family, and probably from a special Sun lineage, although the documentation on this point is incomplete. As elsewhere in the Southeast, succession to the office of Great Sun was matrilineal: the Great Sun was succeeded by the son of his sister, the particular sister who was called "White Woman." Even though the French were good observers in some respects, they did not succeed in understanding the principles of matrilineal organization and exogamy which must have been practiced by the Natchez as it was practiced by all the other major Southeastern groups. Instead, shaped by their own experience in a sharply hierarchical society, the French interpreted the Natchez social order as hierarchical in much the same sense as theirs, with the Suns as a noble "class."

But the French could not help but see that the Natchez "class system" failed to conform to their own in several important respects. Unlike French nobility, who almost always married within their class, a Sun man or woman (because of exogamy) could not marry another Sun, and unlike French nobility, only the offspring of Sun women were Suns. Because the children of Sun males were not Suns (they must have taken the clan membership of their mothers, who were not Suns), the French concluded that the children of male Suns declined in class. Pulling together the pieces of this combination of ethnocentrism and valid observation, John R. Swanton collated it all into a model of the Natchez "class system," which seemed unique in the entire world, and which has confused anthropologists and historians to the present day.

According to Swanton's model, the Natchez were divided into two classes: an upper class divided into three smaller ranked classes— Suns, Nobles, and Honored People—and a lower class whose members were called "Stinkards." The male and female members of all three of the upper classes had to marry Stinkards, and those Stinkards not marrying into the upper classes presumably had to marry among themselves. A female Sun could divorce her husband at will, and if he were unfaithful she was said to have had the power to have him killed; but the female Suns could be as promiscuous as they wished. As we have already seen, the children of female Suns were Suns, but the children of male Suns were said by the French to decline to the rank of Nobles, and the children of male Nobles were said to decline to the rank of Honored People, and the children of male Honored People were said to become Stinkards. The French observed an inconsistency in the system in that only the rights and social honor of Suns were completely hereditary, whereas other positions in the society could be filled by a male of any "class" who could ascend the class structure by warlike exploits and other acts of merit. The French were also puzzled by the fact that status recently acquired was no less esteemed than status acquired in the past. Over the years anthropologists have detected more and more logical defects in this "class system." One, for example, is that within a few generations so many Stinkards would have to marry into the upper classes that the Stinkards would cease to exist.

Without going into the details of a complicated scholarly argument, most of these logical defects fall away when we see that the social principles which ordered Natchez society were about the same as those elsewhere in the Southeast, with these exceptions: no other Southeastern society that we know reasonably well had a kin group as preeminent as the Natchez Suns; and the Natchez Great Sun commanded more veneration and held more power than other Southeastern chiefs, though he may not have been as powerful as the French thought he was.

The Great Sun clearly commanded veneration. The Natchez believed that the first Suns were a man and a woman from the Upper World who had come down to govern men and to teach them how to live better. The man was known as the younger brother of the Sun. He commanded men to build a temple, and he brought down pure fire from the Sun and placed it in the temple where it burned perpetually. It was fed by three hickory logs of pure wood, from which the bark had been removed, tended by eight fire tenders who watched it in turn. He explained to the people the principles by which his successor should be chosen. In the end, he turned himself into stone to prevent his body from being corrupted in the earth. The French heard from the Natchez that they kept a stone statue in a wooden box, but the French were never able to see it. It was probably a statue like those found at Etowah and elsewhere in the Southeast (see fig. 92).

The Great Sun was responsible for making sure that the sacred fire burned perpetually. All the Natchez were obliged to show him deference. When anyone approached the Great Sun, he had to show deference by uttering a loud "*hou*" three times; and when he retired

208

from the Great Sun's presence, he had to walk backward uttering the same cries. If the Great Sun spoke to a man, the man uttered "*hou*" before answering. The Natchez greeted other members of the Sun family with a single "*hou*," and members of the Sun family had to greet the Great Sun with a single "*hou*." The couch on which the Great Sun sat and slept was situated to the right of the doorway to his house. Women, children, and undistinguished men were not permitted to enter his house. A man coming to see the Great Sun entered without looking to the right, proceeding at once to circle a small stone in the center of his house and coming around to face the Great Sun. Then the visitor raised his arms and shouted "*hou*" three times and approached the Great Sun, who, if he wished to speak to the man, gave him some slight sign of recognition. If a man happened to walk into sight of the temple, he had to hold his arms above his head in a ceremonial gesture and shout "*hou*." Children were taught to do this at an early age, and those who failed to do so were punished. All of the Suns looked down on the other Natchez as their inferiors. None could eat with the Suns nor touch the vessels out of which they ate. A Sun could not be put to death for a crime, and none of them were supposed to die violently. As we shall see in chapter 6, when a Sun died his spouse, retainers, and certain other individuals offered themselves to be ritually killed to accompany him to the other world.

The subjects of the Great Sun, the people of all the Natchez villages, were conspicuous in giving the Great Sun large presents of food, not so much as a tax, but as an expression of their devotion. The head warriors, in fact, cultivated a sacred field of corn, tended entirely by their own labor, and the corn from this field was stored along with other food in the Great Sun's storehouse. However, the Great Sun did not keep all of this food for himself, but redistributed it to his people. Above all, the Great Sun was supposed to be generous. He had the power to command his subjects to donate their labor in public works. But aside from having the right to live in a special house, the only thing distinctive about the Great Sun with respect to wealth was that he wore a special feather headdress. It was made with a netted crown, with a red diadem embellished with white beads or seeds, surmounted with a row of white feathers. These feathers were about eight inches high in front and four inches high in back. Each was tipped with a small red tuft of hair and a tassel. It had much the same shape as the crown of a Plains Indian war bonnet.

The actual degree of real political power possessed by the Great Sun is not easy to determine. Because of all the deferential behavior his people displayed toward him, the French thought him to be an absolute monarch. He did apparently have the power to name the holders of some of the main political and ceremonial offices. And the Great Sun was said to have had the power to condemn any of his subjects to death, but the real circumstances under which he could do this are not clear. In one recorded instance he sentenced to death a "bad woman" who was almost certainly a witch, but witches were sentenced to death elsewhere in the Southeast. Some were executed as late as the nineteenth century. But despite this supposedly despotic power, we know that the Great Sun, like other Southeastern chiefs, had a council of elders and warriors to whom he listened and whose advice he greatly respected. And we know that during the last of the wars between the French and the Natchez it became apparent that the chiefs of some of the Natchez villages acted independently of the wishes of the Great Sun.

Thus it would seem that the Great Sun reigned more than he governed. That is, he did command elaborate ceremonial deference from his people; he and his blood relatives were supported at least partly by food produced by his people, but he was obliged to redistribute some of this food at feasts and probably in other ways. His actual political power, however, may have been more limited and perhaps more fragile than he himself believed. In fact, in the year 1720, or thereabouts, the White Woman confessed to the Frenchman Le Page du Pratz that she was afraid that the Suns would become extinct because they were unable to make their subjects obey them. Perhaps one can say that the Great Sun was less powerful than the French believed, but more powerful than James Adair realized.[31]

We shall never know the full details of the Southeastern Indians' political organization at the height of their development in Mississippian times, but we know a good deal about how their chiefdoms were organized in the latter half of the eighteenth century. Each of these chiefdoms had at least one town containing a ceremonial center where political issues were discussed, religious rituals were held, and games were played. Just as in the Mississippian tradition, these towns were located along the margins of rivers and large streams, usually situated on a high bank or hill. This location along rivers had many advantages, the most important of which was nearness to the rich, easily tilled bottom land which lay along the streams. The elevated location protected the town from winter and spring floods and conferred a military advantage in case of attack.[32] Only some of the members of the chiefdom lived in the town itself; other small hamlets and homesteads, probably containing lineages and lineage segments, were scattered up and down the river and its tributaries for several miles.[33]

James Adair describes one Chickasaw chiefdom in 1720 which occupied an area about one mile wide and six miles long; another was one mile wide and four miles long; and another chiefdom or series of affiliated chiefdoms occupied an area one to two miles wide and ten miles long.[34] But the territory claimed by these chiefdoms probably extended much wider than these dimensions specified by Adair. Some evidence from the de Soto expedition suggests that the territories of the chiefdoms were separated by large rivers and by uninhabited areas.[35] But it should be understood that these were not boundaries in the modern sense; raiding parties could cross them when they chose to take the risk, and they frequently did. The chiefdoms were surrounded by buffer zones rather than precisely demarcated boundary lines.

We know from the earliest European observers in the Southeast —from de Soto in 1539–43 to those in the seventeenth century— that the larger towns in the Southeast were surrounded by palisades; some of these were rectangular in plan, while others were more irregular to take advantage of the lay of the terrain. This agrees with what the archaeologists tell us about Mississippian towns. The largest of the fortifications observed by de Soto was the town of Mabila, which is thought to have been located somewhere in southern or central Alabama. Mabila was surrounded by a wall of thick logs set vertically, side by side in the ground, reaching up to a height of sixteen feet or so. Smaller poles were bound to the outside of these upright logs and the whole thing was covered with a mixture of mud and grass so that it had the appearance of stucco. Loopholes for archers were situated at intervals around the wall, and towers were built along the wall at intervals of fifty yards. Each tower held seven or eight fighting men. Mabila could be entered by two gates, one on the east and the other on the west. Inside there were many houses and a large central plaza surrounded by mounds and important houses and buildings. Judging from large sites, such as Moundville, some of these Mississippian towns may have had more than one plaza. In addition to being palisaded, some of the towns were also surrounded by moats of water. On the fringes of the Southeastern area these palisades were usually circular in form and somewhat smaller in size than those in the Southeastern heartland. A Carolina Algonkian village with a circular palisade is depicted in a John White watercolor (fig. 50), a similar Timucuan palisade is depicted in a de Bry engraving, and similar structures were built in Cherokee

Figure 50. Carolina Algonkian town of Pomeiock, surrounded by a circular palisade. John White drawing. Courtesy, Trustees of the British Museum.

212

territory in the period A.D. 1000–1500.[36] In addition to these defensive palisades, the Southeastern Indians sometimes built small, rather insubstantial palisades around mounds and public buildings for reasons which are not well understood.[37] Perhaps they were meant to keep children and dogs out of sacred places.

The Southeastern Indians built few of these palisaded towns after the early decades of the eighteenth century. But the Creeks continued to lay out their towns according to the old pattern. That is, the center of the town was a plaza or commons surrounded by public buildings and the houses of townspeople. According to William Bartram's account, this plaza was carefully built and maintained, and the households were neatly arranged in rectangular blocks along wide streets leading into the square (fig. 51).[38] To date we have relatively little archaeological confirmation of Bartram's description of the town, so we must allow for the possibility that it was atypical.[39]

Each block of houses in the town described by Bartram probably consisted of a household comprising a matrilineage or a segment of a matrilineage. The Creek household (*huti*) was a matrilineal extended family, consisting of a matron, her daughters, and her unmarried sons. The husbands of the matron and her daughters lived there, but the households with which their allegiance lay were those of their sisters and other matrilineal relatives. The household might also include some aged or dependent members of the matron's lineage. A large household could include an orphan or one or more individuals captured in war who had been adopted into the lineage. Other households in the neighborhood were probably headed by the woman's sisters and her mother and grandmother, if alive.[40]

Eighteenth-century Creek, Cherokee, Chickasaw, and Choctaw households typically consisted of clusters of buildings. At a minimum these consisted of a summer house and a winter house, and large households in some places added a third and even a fourth building for storage and other uses. The extent to which this pattern of multiple houses extends back into Mississippian times is not definitely known, but some evidence indicates that the pattern was indeed old.[41] Although the winter temperature drops below freezing in the Southeast, the Indians wore relatively little clothing. Instead they preferred to build small, heavily insulated houses for use in bitter cold weather, and when they were outside they made it a virtue to tolerate being cold and wet.[42] The winter house (called the "hot house" by early European observers) of the Chickasaws, Choctaws, and Cherokees had a circular floor plan. The floor of the Chickasaw winter house was dug into the earth two or three feet, with a low cylindrical wall around this, and the whole thing was topped off with a conical roof supported in the center by four large pine posts laid out in a square. The roof structure was made of notched poles interwoven with split saplings or white oak splints. This was then plastered inside and out with six or seven inches of clay mixed with dried grass or Spanish moss. Before this clay covering dried, they covered the roof with shingles made of pine bark or grass thatch, laid down in circular courses starting at the bottom and ending at the top. Each course was held down by a ring of split saplings tied to the roof structure below. To the top of this the Chickasaws sometimes attached a pole with a carved eagle on top. The only opening was a small door—usually about four feet high— entered through an L-shaped or curved passageway six or seven feet long which kept out cold winds and discouraged enemies from

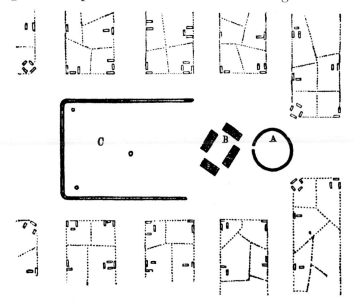

Figure 51. Creek town plan. A, the town house. B, the square ground. C, the chunkey yard. From William Bartram, "Observations on the Creek and Cherokee Indians, 1789," *Transactions of the American Ethnological Society*, vol. III, pt. 1, 1853, fig. 4, p. 55. Courtesy, University of Georgia Libraries.

Figure 52. Large Chitimacha split cane mat. It is 7 ft. long and 6 ft. 3 in. wide. Courtesy, Museum of the American Indian, Heye Foundation.

stealing in. Their couches, on which they sat and slept, were arranged along the wall. Raised up on posts two to three feet high, they were, as Adair observed, high enough that fleas could not reach them in one jump. The framework of the couches were made of saplings, white oak splints, and cane. The frame was covered with split-cane mats (fig. 52) and animal skins. In cold weather the women built a large fire of dry wood in the center of the floor of the winter

215

house. They allowed this to burn half way, then covered it with ashes. When more heat was needed, they would take a piece of cane and knock off a few ashes.[43] Fresh wood was added in the morning, and while it blazed, the winter house filled with smoke. Europeans who visited these winter houses complained of smoke and poor ventilation, but these buildings were able to retain heat efficiently. A small blaze or a few coals kept the winter house as warm as an oven. In fact, James Adair described the winter house as being like a "Dutch stove." Beneath their beds they stored pumpkins, winter squash, and other vegetables to protect them from frost. For some reason, the Creeks differed from the Cherokees, Chickasaws, and Choctaws in that they built their winter houses with a rectangular floor plan. But the Creek winter house served the same purposes.

The summer houses of the Chickasaws, Choctaws, Cherokees, and Creeks all had rectangular floor plans and gabled roofs. The Chickasaws built theirs on a framework of rot-resistant pitch pine or black locust posts set into the earth. The roof was made out of a framework of saplings, cane, and white oak or hickory splints. The eave boards and doors were made out of poplar, which is easily split and carved. The sides were then framed up using clapboards split out of cypress or pine. They covered the roof with shingles made of cypress or pine bark, weighting them down with poles and logs tied across the roof.[44] In some places the gable ends were left open to allow fresh air to flow through. At other places the only opening into the summer house was the small doorway, the purpose of this evidently being to keep out insects. The walls were usually white-washed inside and out with powdered oyster shells or white clay. From Henry Timberlake's early account we know that the Cherokee summer house was distinctive in that some of them were sixty or seventy feet long, housing many people. Some of them were two stories high, with part or all of the upper walls left open to provide a cool place for social life in hot weather.[45]

Along the Gulf Coast and in Florida the weather was warmer and the houses simpler. The Timucuans often used a single house with a circular floor plan the year around. The Natchez also appear to have used a single house all year, but theirs had a square floor plan with a domed roof. In the more tropical areas the houses sometimes lacked walls, consisting only of a floor and a roof of palmetto leaves. This kind of house, which the Seminoles call čikì• (anglicized as "chic-

Figure 53. Seminole chickee. Late nineteenth century. Negative no. 1178–N–8–1. Courtesy, Smithsonian Institution, National Anthropological Archives.

kee"), has only recently been abandoned by them in favor of modern housing (fig. 53).

According to William Bartram, the eighteenth-century Creek household consisted of up to four rectangular buildings arranged around the four sides of a square courtyard about a quarter acre in size (see fig. 51). As we have already seen, one of these houses was a summer house and a second was a winter house. A third was commonly two stories high—like the Cherokee summer house—with each story divided into two rooms. The lower room of one end of the house was used to store roots and other vegetables that would suffer from frost; the upper room at this same end was what Bartram called "the council." Both the upper and lower stories of the other end of the house were without walls. The lower room was used for storing tools and equipment, while the upper room was used as a pavilion where the head of the household could entertain guests in hot weather. The fourth house was used as a storage house for deer skins and furs. Only the larger, wealthier households owned four buildings; smaller families made do with three, two, or even one building. It is probable that the number of buildings owned by a household correlated with its developmental cycle. That is, developed households headed by an older married couple and their adult children owned more buildings than newly married couples with young children.[46]

The important eighteenth-century Creek towns, the ceremonial centers of the chiefdoms, were built around plazas. A plaza contained three structures (see fig. 51): (1) a *tcokofa* or town house (also called the rotunda or hot house), (2) a square ground or summer council house, and (3) a chunkey yard. The town house was identical in form to the winter house of the Chickasaws, Choctaws, and Cherokees, but it was larger. It commonly measured 25 feet in diameter and 25 feet from the floor to the apex of the roof. Some were much larger. The town house at the eighteenth-century Cherokee town of Chota is described as having been able to hold 500 people.[47] A series of broad beds or couches raised up from the floor on wooden posts was built around the entire circumference of the interior. Each bed was about seven feet wide and a little over seven feet in length. In some cases the town house had two or three tiers of these beds. They were sometimes inclined towards the wall, so that if a person fell asleep he would not roll off onto the floor. Having no windows, a small smoke hole, and a low door, the town house was quite dark inside.[48] When council meetings were held, a small fire was built in the center of the building out of pitch pine, splinters of dry cane, or dry wood with the bark peeled off. These were laid down in a continuous series of X's to form a spiral, the flame going round and round until it burned out; or it was arranged in a circle, with an attendant continuously replenishing the end of the circle opposite the flame. This small fire was enough to keep the earth-covered building quite hot. Archaeologists have turned up the remains of town houses at such Mississippian sites as Ocmulgee and Hiwassee Island.

The council of the chiefdom met in the town house in cold or inclement weather to settle grievances among members of the chiefdom, to give audience to ambassadors and strangers, and to

218

consult and plan activities such as agriculture and the construction of new buildings. In addition, the people met in the town house for music, feasts, dances, and other diversions. Men could freely enter the town house, but women and children were frequently excluded. People who were traveling through and who had no kinsmen in the town were permitted to sleep in the town house. And the same privilege was extended to old men and women who had no relatives to care for them.

Figure 54. Diorama of a Creek square ground. Courtesy, The American Museum of Natural History.

In warm weather the Creek square ground or summer council house served the same functions as the town house (fig. 54). This summer council house actually consisted of four sheds or arbors arranged around a square in a pattern identical to Bartram's description of ordinary Creek households. The Creeks referred to these sheds with a word which literally means "bed," or better, "bench"—the same word they used to refer to the couches in their houses. The square itself consisted of an area of half an acre, more or less, depending upon the size of the town. The sacred fire with four logs was built in the center of the square. The buildings were rectangular, one story high, and about thirty feet long. They were constructed with a wooden frame, a gabled or slanted roof, and wattle-and-daub walls. The fronts of the buildings were left completely open, facing each other across the square ground. The ends were walled in, and so was the back, but with a space of about two feet just below the roof to serve as an open window and to allow for air circulation. The sheds were sometimes divided into three compartments or "cabins," separated by low clay partitions, and making in all twelve compartments around the square ground; this was not an invariable rule, since some sheds were divided into two compartments. Some sheds had two or three tiers of benches in each cabin. These benches were of about the same dimensions as the benches in their houses and in the town house, and they were covered with the same kind of cane mats (see fig. 52).

The four corner openings to the square ground were sometimes oriented to the points of the compass, but more frequently the buildings themselves were oriented in these cardinal directions. Each compartment was allotted to a particular clan or set of linked clans, and the clan symbols were sometimes painted on boards hanging above the cabins. At the same time, specific seats in the front of the sheds were reserved for particular office holders, regardless of their clans. Ritual objects, such as eagle feathers, swan wings, scalping knives, war clubs, herbs, and so forth, were hung beneath the roofs. Pictures of creatures with mixed human and animal features, uktenas, and other designs were often painted on the supporting timbers. The main building, on the west side of the square, was particularly likely to have animals symbolizing the chiefdom carved on the posts. For Cowetas this was a bird of prey with blood dripping from its mouth, for Tukabahchees it was an alligator, for Koasatis it was the garfish, and for Atasis it was a serpent.[49]

The chief and his assistants sat in the shed on the west side of the square ground. In James Adair's time, in the back of this shed there was a small room in which they kept sacred utensils and objects. James Adair called this chamber their *sanctum sanctorum*, their "holy of holies." The warriors used to stick an *atasa*—a notched wooden war club—in the ground in front of their seats in the north shed. Notched sticks were apparently used in the same way, and some towns were said to use sticks in the shape of axes instead of in the shape of war clubs.[50]

The square ground was evidently a relatively late innovation which developed out of a prehistoric Mississippian precedent. All of our historical descriptions of square grounds date after 1700, while the archaeologists have turned up none of them at Mississippian sites. But archaeologists have turned up large rectangular buildings, often with entrances at the corners, built atop mounds. Many of these buildings were divided by a partition into two rooms, with a smaller rear room and a larger front room with a central fireplace and benches around the walls. The rear room was probably the *sanctum sanctorum*, while the front room was where the men held council. Therefore, it is reasonable to suppose that the square ground with its four small sheds, or arbors, evolved out of this large rectangular building after the Southeastern Indians ceased building mounds. This is supported by the fact that the Creeks sometimes called the entire square ground *tcoko-thlako*, or "big house," and referred as we have seen, to the individual sheds as "benches." Moreover, in some Creek towns a light cane framework was built over the square ground making a kind of roof and giving the effect of a single building instead of four. The Mississippian ancestor of the square ground was probably built atop the largest mounds; these were usually situated on the western or northwestern side of the plaza facing east or southeast onto the plaza. Since this was the building the de Soto chroniclers evidently referred to as the "chief's house," the chief may have in fact lived in it. The Great Sun of the Natchez lived in such a structure.[51]

The third part of the Creek ceremonial center was the chunkey yard. When the weather was good, it was a public place for games, dances, ritual, and public spectacle. The chunkey yard consisted of a carefully cleared area of ground surrounded on two or more sides with a low bank of earth. Sometimes it was actually sunk two or three feet into the earth. As its name suggests, this was where they played chunkey, a game in which a disc of stone was rolled across the yard and a pole or stick thrown at it to see who could hit the closest to the place where it stopped. In the center of the chunkey yard there was a pole thirty or forty feet high, sometimes with a low mound around its base, which was used in several games played by the Indians, but most notably it was used for the single-pole ball game played between men and women. Slave posts were sometimes positioned in two corners of the yard. These were decorated with the scalps of slain enemies, and prisoners of war were sometimes tied to them. The skulls of slain enemies were sometimes placed on top of these posts.

William Bartram evidently observed both the old Creek town layout and the new layout which emerged in the eighteenth century. In the old pattern, the town house was atop a circular mound nine or ten feet high built at one end of the chunkey yard, while the square ground was atop a square mound about the same height at the opposite end of the chunkey yard (fig. 55).[52] But in the new town arrangement, both the town house and the square ground were built at ground level, and both were situated at one end of the chunkey yard (see fig. 51).[53] Perhaps then as later both of them were situated northwest of the chunkey yard, where they faced southeast onto the chunkey yard.[54]

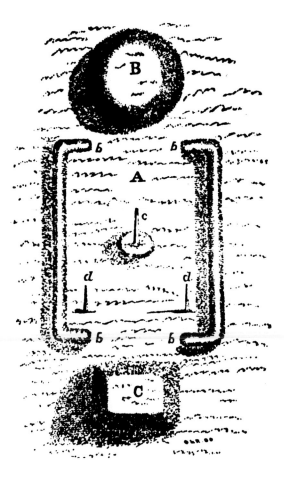

Figure 55. Ancient Creek ceremonial center. *A*, chunkey yard surrounded by (*b*) banks of earth. *B*, mound on which the town house stood. *C*, mound on which the square ground stood. *c*, "chunk pole". *d*, slave posts. From William Bartram, "Observations on the Creek and Cherokee Indians, 1789." *Transactions of the American Ethnological Society*, vol. III, pt. 1, 1853, fig. 2, p. 52. Courtesy, University of Georgia Libraries.

Among the Southeastern Indians disputes arising within a lineage were settled by the older, more experienced members of the lineage. The senior members of the lineage also managed some affairs between different lineages, particularly those involving marriage, so long as no serious disputes were involved. Serious disputes between lineages could not be satisfactorily settled by the lineages themselves. These were precisely the kind of disputes which fell within the province of the council of the chiefdom.

Among the Creeks, the executive officer of the council of the chiefdom was the miko, (Muskogee *mí•kko*) or chief. Among the Cherokees he was called *uku* (perhaps *uguku*, "hoot owl"). As we have already seen, sixteenth- and seventeenth-century European observers noted that the leaders among the Southeastern Indians received great deference from their people, so much so that the Europeans frequently called them "kings." But in the latter half of the eighteenth century, when our documentation is far more ample, the power of the Creek miko was far more limited. The miko was in charge of dispensing food from the public granary. He received all ambassadors, deputies, and strangers who visited the chiefdom, and in turn he usually represented his chiefdom in negotiations with other chiefdoms and other peoples. After a successful hunt, he alone was entitled to hold a public feast for the chiefdom. To announce this feast to his people, messengers were sent out to spread the word, the miko's standard was placed in front of his house, and a banner was flown from the pole in the chunkey yard.

Although the miko had more power in some chiefdoms than in others, the office itself was not vested with truly coercive power. He could persuade, but he could not command. The miko always conferred with his council before making any important decision, and he could be put out of office if the chiefdom's affairs went too badly. The miko could come from either a white clan or a red clan, but he was usually chosen by representatives of the white clans. Usually, the man who was selected expressed reluctance at taking the office, but the others prevailed upon him to accept. In the installation ceremony he was seated on an unsmoked white buckskin, his face was painted with white clay, and a member of a white lineage instructed him in his duties. He was specifically told that he must always be devoted to the white path of peace and that he must never shed human blood. After being installed, the miko sometimes selected an assistant to help him with some of his duties, particularly those having to do with internal affairs of the chiefdom. Some chiefdoms had several lesser mikos.[55]

The miko and his assistants occupied seats of honor in the town house and in the square ground. In the square ground his seat was situated in the center compartment of the shed on the west side. The shed to the north—the red shed—was occupied by warriors, and the building to the south—the white shed—by the "Second Men," a group to be discussed presently. The shed to the east was occupied by a variety of people, including youths, elders, visitors, and so on.

The Second Men who sat in the south shed were chosen primarily from white clans and were responsible for overseeing public works and such internal affairs of the town as the building of houses for newly married couples and the working of the communal fields. They were also in charge of preparing black drink, as will presently be described. A Second Man sometimes accompanied the miko on missions of official business, and collectively the Second Men acted as advisors to the miko.[56]

The council of the chiefdom was a thoroughly democratic body. Anyone who wanted to could speak, no matter how distasteful his views to the others, and all the people would listen politely until he had finished. The council did not meet to legislate or to adjudicate —they met to reach consensus. And they reached consensus not by voting, but by dissolving the opposition. If a man could not agree with an emerging consensus, then he either compromised or withdrew from the situation and said no more. Those who did not agree were ignored, but they were not punished. The council did not coerce people, it simply sought harmony by conciliating differences.[57] A good man was a man who avoided conflict with his fellows. He asserted his own rights cautiously; he avoided situations which might entail conflict; and he withdrew from men who were contentious or disrespectful.[58] Harmony was essential. This social ethic frustrated and angered Europeans. When a European asked a Cherokee a question which might lead to open disagreement, the Cherokee would give an evasive answer or no answer at all. As a consequence, the European concluded that the Cherokee was either untruthful or stubborn. The Cherokee, on the other hand, saw his evasion or refusal to answer as a sanction against the European's behavior, and he concluded that the European was stupid because he did not realize that it was a sanction.[59]

The Creek military was organized into three grades of warriors: the war chiefs (*tástánáigi*), the big warriors (*imáta táká'lgi*), and the little warriors (*imáta lábotskálgi*). All three grades received their titles in recognition of their having performed warlike feats, the war chiefs having accomplished the most. One of the war chiefs was designated as "Great Warrior" (Creek, *tástánági táko*) and had the duty of leading his chiefdom in war. When war was declared, it was announced by the Great Warrior. He also arranged with the Great Warriors of other chiefdoms to have ball games. These ball games, called "the younger brother of war," were not mere games, but had important political functions. The war chiefs carried out the will of the miko, although their ability to coerce was very limited. The Great Warrior had some power in matters of war, but relatively little in other matters. Both grades of warriors acted as assistants and messengers of the war chiefs. Below the warriors were the men who had not yet distinguished themselves in war. The Cherokee red organization was structured along similar lines.[60]

A further category of men on the Creek council were the "Beloved Old Men" (*isti átcagági*). They consisted of old men from the chief's clan, old war leaders, and men who had distinguished themselves in other ways. Although they were exempted from dancing and performing other duties in the Green Corn Ceremony, or busk, they were said to be the "brains of the busk." This meant that they were valued for their knowledge. Each chiefdom had only a few of them, and they sat scattered about in the different sheds in the square ground. The miko appears to have valued the advice of the Beloved Old Men over that of the Second Men.[61]

Two lesser officials of the council were the interpreter (*yatika*) and the war speaker (*hotibonaya*). The interpreter was usually selected from the miko's clan, but he could come from any other clan as well. He usually sat beside the miko during meetings and ceremonies. The interpreter was not so much a translator as he was an individual who delivered the miko's speeches, thus insulating the miko from direct confrontation with his people. The war speaker usually sat among the warriors and addressed the council on matters concerning war. He was said to be the most eloquent speaker in the chiefdom. Several European observers were impressed with the oratorical ability of the Southeastern Indians, particularly their delight in using metaphors and verbal flourishes in urging their people to right action. [62]

The council of the chiefdom met in the square ground or in the town house every day, beginning early in the morning. They discussed affairs of the chiefdom and made decisions on various issues that came before them. This seldom took all day, and so the men also smoked their pipes and occasionally diverted themselves with games.

Black drink, a ritual beverage, was a necessary part of all important council meetings. [63] We have already seen that the Southeastern Indians were greatly concerned with purity, recognizing certain rules and prohibitions which, if broken, threatened the well-being of the individual and his people. Many of these rules were dietary: certain foods were forbidden. This is the reason why the black drink ceremony was performed before every important meeting of the council. Black drink purified men of pollution, served as a symbolic social cement, and it was an ultimate expression of hospitality. Apparently, it was drunk only by mature men—never by women or young boys.

In their own language the Indians called the brew "white drink" because white symbolized purity, happiness, social harmony, and so on, but the Europeans called it "black drink" because of its color. It was made from the leaves of a variety of holly (*Ilex vomitoria* Ait.), which grows along the Atlantic and Gulf coasts and which the Indians in the interior sometimes transplanted so that it would be close at hand. Black drink is essentially like *maté*, a beverage made from the leaves of *Ilex paraguayensis* and drunk in many parts of modern Latin America. The main active ingredient of both black drink and *maté* is caffeine. To make black drink, the Indians first dried the leaves and twigs and put them in an earthen container and parched them over a fire to a dark-brown color. This roasting made the caffeine more soluble; coffee beans are roasted for the same reason. They placed the roasted leaves and twigs in water and boiled it until it was a dark-brown liquid. The drink then was poured through a strainer and into vessels to cool. As soon as it could be poured over one's finger without scalding, it was ready to be consumed. Drinking it hot heightened its effect: caffeine is thirty times more soluble in boiling water than in water at room temperature.

Black drink is a tea whose bitter taste and caffeine content increase as it is made stronger. In addition to being a stimulant, the beverage also acts as a diuretic, causing increased perspiration. And the Indians sometimes used it as an emetic. On these occasions they would drink it in large quantities, and in a quarter to half an hour they would vomit. Sometimes they would hold their arms across their chests and expel the contents of their stomachs six or eight feet. The Timucuans would drink repeatedly, vomiting it up each time (fig. 56). The precise cause of this emetic effect is not known. All *Ilex* species contain ilicin and ilicic acid, both of which are turpentine-like compounds which produce an expectorant effect, causing increased bronchial secretion. The mere volume ingested

Figure 56. Timucuan Indians drinking and vomiting black drink. Engraving by Theodore de Bry after an original painting by Jacques Le Moyne de Morgues. Negative no. 57,569. Courtesy, Smithsonian Institution, National Anthropological Archives.

227

might have caused the vomiting—even large amounts of ingested water can cause vomiting. Moreover, the Southeastern Indians sometimes mixed other ingredients into the drink, and this may have caused the vomiting. In any case, the emetic effect was more the exception than the rule. The Indians would often sit in council and drink black drink for hours at a time with no marked physical reactions.

The physiological effects of black drink are mainly those of massive doses of caffeine. Caffeine stimulates the central nervous system, exciting it at all levels. In fact, caffeine is the only true cortical stimulant known to modern medicine. It enables a person to have a more rapid and clearer flow of thought, makes him capable of more sustained intellectual effort, and sharpens his reaction time. It also increases his capacity for muscular work and lessens fatigue. Moreover, some evidence suggests that large doses of caffeine speed up blood clotting. These effects are pronounced with doses of 0.5 to 1.0 grams—the equivalent of three to six cups of strong coffee. When consumed in large quantities, black drink could have delivered at least this much caffeine, and perhaps as much as 3.0 to 4.0 grams. These effects from large quantities of black drink could have been important and even decisive factors in activities such as the ball game or warfare. And repeated use of black drink, as far as we know, entailed no more risk than daily use of strong coffee. Early European colonists in the South adopted black drink, using it as a stimulant, but they discontinued its use as coffee and tea became more easily available.

But the Southeastern Indians drank black drink for ideological reasons as well as practical reasons. Meetings of the councils of chiefdoms were preceded both by drinking black drink and by smoking tobacco. The order in which the men partook of the black drink and tobacco followed a rigid prestige hierarchy. William Bartram observed a black drink ceremony at a Creek council meeting in a town house. Before the council meeting began, black drink was brewed in an open shed directly opposite the door of the town house and about twenty or thirty yards away. Next, bundles of dry cane were brought in and arranged in a counterclockwise spiral around the center pole of the town house. By the time this was done it was night, and all of the chiefs, warriors, and old men took their proper seats. Then the canes were ignited, and the fire circled the pillar like the sun, giving off a cheerful, gentle light. Next two men came in through the door, each with a very large conch shell (see fig. 35) full of black drink. They walked with slow, measured steps and sang in a low voice. They stopped when they were within six or eight paces of the miko and members of white clans sitting to his right, and they placed the conch shells on little tables. They then picked them up again and, bowing low, advanced toward the miko. The conch shell was then handed to the miko; the servant solemnly sang in sustained syllables, *Ya-ho-la*, while the miko held the shell to his lips. After the miko was finished drinking, everybody else in the town house drank. Soon tobacco stuffed in a pouch made from the skin of the miko's clan animal was brought out and laid with a pipe at the miko's feet. He filled the pipe and lit it, blowing smoke first toward the east and then toward the other three cardinal directions. Then the pipe was passed to the principal member of the white clans, then to the Great Warrior, and thence through the ranks of the warriors and back to the miko. In the meantime, all the others were taking black drink and smoking tobacco.

Although each chiefdom had a council as its central political body, its actual powers were severely restricted. The Cherokees, in particular, were opposed to any form of coercion within the chiefdom, and they carried this principle to amazing lengths. They would not even coerce their children; they were horrified at British headmasters who caned their pupils. They would not even use coercion when it was in their public interest to do so. In 1760, a Cherokee war party killed some settlers in Carolina and Virginia. When the British seized Cherokee hostages, threatening to kill them and also to mount a punitive expedition unless the killers were surrendered, the Cherokees did not hand over the killers even though they wanted to. Only the clansmen of the killers could have done so, and they refused. As a result the British retaliated in accordance with their threat, and many Cherokees lost their lives. But though they lacked public sanctions, they did have effective means of private sanctions, including withdrawal, ostracism, public scorn, and ridicule.[64]

Perhaps the best indication of decentralization and lack of coercion within the Southeastern Indian chiefdoms is the fact that serious crimes, such as killing a person and adultery, were punished by the clans rather than by agents of the council. The crime of killing a person was punished in accordance with the law of retaliation, *lex talionis* as the lawyers call it. Under this law, the most important legal principle in the Southeast, if a person was killed, it was the duty of his male blood relatives (his brothers, sisters' sons, and mother's brothers) to kill either the killer or some other member of the killer's lineage. As in the Old Testament, it was an eye for an eye and a tooth for a tooth. The Southeastern Indians applied this principle with amazing consistency. Even if one little boy happened "accidentally" to wound another, the wounded boy would carefully await an opportunity to inflict a similar wound in retaliation. If he succeeded, then "all was straight," and the matter was settled.

The principle of retaliation may even be seen in the Cherokee theory of illness, which represents man as suffering from illnesses caused by the revenge of animals he killed without having taken the precaution of begging their forgiveness. And perhaps the bear was not accorded the same consideration given other animals because in the myth about the origin of disease and medicine (see chap. 3) the bear, after at first failing to find a way to exact revenge on man, foolishly gave up. Thus any creature too foolish to revenge the death of one of his brothers may be killed with impunity.[65]

Technically speaking, when one Southeastern Indian killed one of his fellows it was not murder, because the Southeastern Indians did not recognize types or degrees of homicide. The only thing that mattered was that one man caused the death of another, and technically speaking this was not mitigated by intent, malice, accident, or any other consideration. Thus the manslayer (and his clan) was not so much "guilty," as we use the term, as he was liable for the killing. If a Cherokee loaned his horse to a friend, and if the horse threw him and killed him, then the horse's owner would have been liable for the death. If a man was attacked by another, and if he killed his attacker in self defense, he would be liable for his death. If one man injured another in a fight, and if the injured man died months or even years later, then the other man might be held responsible for his death. In all of these cases, the soul of the man who had been killed could not rest until his clansmen had exacted revenge.[66]

It was this principle of retaliation which prevented a killing from causing a "civil war" between two clans. Thus the function of the principle of retaliation was not to exact justice as we understand it, but to keep the peace. In order for the principle to work, the clan of the manslayer had to pull away from him and allow him or some other man in their clan to be killed by members of the clan of the dead person, and this death would go unavenged. One factor that led them to do this was their knowledge that any of them, particularly the close kin of the manslayer, could be killed in his place; hence they were not anxious to help the manslayer escape. At the same time, there are several documented instances of brothers and maternal uncles offering themselves to be killed in place of a kinsman. A man who escaped death in this way might be regarded as a coward for the rest of his life, but the liability for the original killing was erased with the death of his brother or maternal uncle. Moreover, the manslayer's realization that his brother or uncle might be killed in his place frequently led him to surrender himself and accept his fate. A man who went to death in this way was something of a martyr, dying with the knowledge that it was for the good of his kinsmen.[67]

In several ways the Southeastern Indians committed acts which we regard as murder, but which they did not consider to be criminal. They sometimes put to death their old people who became decrepit or ill and who begged to be put out of their misery. This they regarded as an act of compassion. In addition, they sometimes practiced infanticide. Among the Natchez, an unmarried girl could put her newborn infant to death if she chose to do so. If a Creek woman gave birth to an infant who was deformed, or if she were unable to care for the child, she had the right to put it to death until it was a month old. However, the father of the child, being of a different clan, could not commit infanticide on his own child because he would have been held responsible for a death under the law of retaliation.

One of the great legal problems entailed in the law of retaliation was what to do with a person who killed one of his own clansmen, particularly when brother killed brother. One way in which they dealt with this was to define the crime as the most horrible act a man could commit—so horrible that it was almost unthinkable.[68] Thus deliberate killings of this kind would have been rare. If such a killing did occur, the response of the killer's fellow clansmen was not well defined. In some cases he was put to death, but in other cases, because of their reluctance to lose another clansman, he was forgiven.

In fact there was always the possibility that forgiveness might enter in to soften the principle of retaliation. If any blood relatives of a manslayer were married to members of his victim's clan, these persons might plead for mercy in behalf of their kinsman. In the case of killings that were clearly accidental, the chief or members of the council might intercede and seek forgiveness by the aggrieved clan for the manslayer. In some cases a manslayer was forgiven after he presented a captive or the scalp of an enemy to the aggrieved clan. But the aggrieved clan might or might not accept these as compensation. In some cases, if the close kin of the dead man agreed to it, the aggrieved clan would accept a payment of wealth in lieu of blood revenge.[69]

As we have already seen, among the Creeks adultery was punished by the offended lineage. Actual punishment included public humiliation, severe beatings, having one's hair cut off, or having one's nose or ears mutilated. Some evidence suggests that in the remote past adulterers might even have been killed, particularly if the relationship were incestuous. If the adulterer escaped, the punishment could be inflicted on one of his male relatives. Premarital intercourse was not punished. The Creeks indulged in it without shame or secrecy. They said that it was a woman's right "to make use of her body." Natchez girls also enjoyed all the sexual liberty they wanted until they were married. None could interfere with their behavior. In fact, Natchez girls were warned that they would not be free after they were married, so they should enjoy sexual liberty while they were single, and they were further told that if they were too stingy with their favors it would be hard for their souls to enter the other world after they died.

Among the Creeks, the council of the chiefdom could impose mild punishment. All members of the chiefdom were required without exception to attend the Green Corn Ceremony. Those who did not do so were punished by a fine. People who did not participate in public works were similarly punished. Another rule was that all were supposed to plunge into the water the first thing in the morning to purify themselves. Any who failed to do so were threatened with being "dry scratched" with a piece of wood to which several slivers of bone or garfish teeth were attached (see fig. 98). Though these scratches were not deep, they were somewhat painful. However, the punishment was not so much the pain as it was the

232

humiliation of having the scratches for all to see.

As we have seen, the Creek chiefdom was a group of people who had their own ceremonial center with a town house, square ground, and chunkey yard. The chiefdom might include only one town or settlement of people, or it might include several, along with individual households scattered up and down the river. Some Creek chiefdoms were relatively autonomous, while others were related to each other in various ways. Some chiefdoms, said to be mother and daughter chiefdoms, were formed by segmentation. The exact nature of the economic and social causes of segmentation are not well understood. Perhaps the soil in the vicinity of a town became too exhausted for good agricultural production, or perhaps the firewood supply became too depleted, or perhaps some intrinsic feature in the social organization of the Southeastern Indians caused segmentation. But whatever the precise nature of the cause, the towns sometimes split, sometimes amicably and sometimes not, with one faction moving away to establish a new town. Initially the town continued to be a part of the chiefdom, but in time it might acquire a social identity of its own, acquiring its own ceremonial center and performing its own Green Corn Ceremony. When this happened, the new town, and perhaps its satellite settlements, became a chiefdom in its own right.[70]

This process could also work in reverse. That is, if a chiefdom became too small to be viable, for whatever reason, it could fuse with another chiefdom. For example, after removal to Oklahoma the Creek chiefdoms of Okchai, Łutogułga, and Asi lanabi fused into a single chiefdom and called themselves Okchais. But in time a dispute arose, and one group split off and established an independent ceremonial center, taking the name Asi lanabi. Still later another group split off from the Okchais, taking the name Łutogułga. The people who split off evidently had no clear-cut connections with the original populations of Asi lanabi or Łutogułga.[71]

We know of one instance in which two chiefdoms fused but did not merge. In the early decades of the eighteenth century, the Cherokee chiefdoms of Great Tellico and Chatuga, on the exposed northwestern frontier of Cherokee territory, occupied the same areas with their populations intermixed, but they maintained two separate councils in two separate town houses. They lived in the same community, but they were separate corporate entities. In 1756,

Great Tellico decided to affiliate more closely with the French and fight in their interest, but Chatuga decided to remain in the British interest. Thus it could have happened that from the same community a Great Tellico man could have collaborated with French Indians in killing Englishmen, while his neighbor, a Chatuga man, could have aided the British in killing French Indians.[72]

The Southeastern Indians also used marriage as a way of forming affiliations between larger social entities. Several of the Timucuan towns de Soto passed through were linked in this way.[73] And in the early colonial period, Creek chiefs sometimes gave their sisters and sisters' daughters for marriage to white traders as a means of forming alliances. This happened in the case of Emperor Brims, an important chief among the Lower Creeks, who oversaw the marriage of his sister's daughter to an English trader. This was Mary Musgrove, later Mary Bosomworth, who in time acquired great influence among the Lower Creeks and played an important role in the early history of Georgia.[74]

DUAL ORGANIZATION

Just as the Southeastern Indian belief system was interlaced with a series of oppositions and polarities, these same structural patterns were evident in the social organization of the Indians. This can be seen most dramatically in the institution of dual chiefs: one to lead in affairs of peace, and the other to lead in affairs of war. The wider social relationships of the Southeastern Indians took the form of dual organization, a social arrangement that is fairly common in preliterate societies. Dual organization is "a system of antithetical institutions with the associated symbols, ideas, and meanings in terms of which social interaction takes place."[75] Thus a Southeastern Indian frequently found himself in a situation in which his group was set against a second group opposite his own. In general the dual organization of the Southeastern Indians seems to have been similar to the dual organization of other North American Indians, but we shall never understand all of the intricacies which lay behind it. This kind of understanding could only have been gained from intensive firsthand field work among living people by an investigator who could have grasped the inner subtleties of the Southeastern Indian belief system.[76] No one did this, and it is impossible to do it now.

234

Our only recourse is to examine relevant historical documents and try to make sense of them.

In historic times Creek chiefdoms formed alliances with each other which they symbolically expressed by saying that they were "of the same fire." A person from a chiefdom of one's own fire was identified as "my friend" (*anhissi*), while a person of an opposite fire was "my enemy or opponent" (*ankipa•ya*).[77] The Creeks invited people of the same fire to their Green Corn Ceremonies, but they never invited people of an opposite fire. Historically, this might have begun with alliances being formed among a series of old, established chiefdoms. These chiefdoms would have been thought of as "white" because in the Southeastern belief system white is the color of that which is old, established, pure, peaceable, holy, united, and so forth. Later, the Creek confederacy of historic times was perhaps formed when outlying chiefdoms and tribal groups were dislocated by white colonists and forced to form alliances with these "white" chiefdoms. From the point of view of the white chiefdoms, however, these newcomers would have been potential and sometimes actual enemies. They were therefore designated as "red," the color associated with conflict, war, fear, disunity, and danger. While the white chiefdoms were linked together with each other in various ways, the red towns were rather individualized and isolated from each other. Thus the white and red divisions were not symmetrical, but this lack of symmetry is not unusual in other societies with dual organization.[78]

The significance of this division shows up in the ball game, a form of lacrosse played with much aggressiveness and roughness (see chap. 7). Among the Creeks this game was only played between chiefdoms of opposite fire. A chiefdom could play any chiefdom of the opposite fire, but each chiefdom usually had a particular rival or rivals. When two chiefdoms had never previously played each other, either could challenge the other to a game. But when two teams had previously played, the loser of the last game was expected to challenge the winner. The game was preceded by several weeks of formal negotiations about the conditions under which the game would be played and with the players preparing themselves for the contest; indeed, the game was so important that originally a chiefdom only played one game each year, though they might play many practice games. A loss was a very serious matter. The losers were ashamed to talk about it afterwards, and they were most anxious to win a rematch in order to "bring the game back." They played with the understanding that if a team were to lose three or four consecutive games, then that team and its chiefdom became of the same fire as the winner. In this way it was possible for a chiefdom to shift from one fire to another, and some chiefdoms evidently changed several times.[79] Thus like other societies with dual divisions, Creek divisions were not inflexible.[80]

This distinction between two opposed groups of people—the insiders on the one hand, and affiliated but divided outsiders on the other—also existed *within* Creek towns. Within Creek towns the lineages were classified into two divisions—the Muskogean-speaking *Hathagálgi* or "white people" (also called "those who stick together") and the *Tcilokogálgi* or "people of different speech." The Creeks also applied this latter term to tribes such as the Hitchitis, Alabamas, and Yuchis, who spoke languages other than Muskogean.[81] An Indian attempted to explain the origin of these divisions to John Swanton by referring to the myth about the ball game between the birds and the four-footed animals. The implication of this is that the Creeks thought of differences between the divisions as analogous to the differences between the birds and the four-footed animals. Among the Seminoles, at the Green Corn Ceremony members of the two divisions divided into two semicircles and sat around a single fire, with the members of the dominant clans in each division sitting opposite each other. Within a division, the members of the dominant clan were addressed as "mother's brother" by the other clans of the division.[82]

These divisions existed between groups of lineages in particular chiefdoms. It was not a division between clans because the affiliation of some lineages varied from one chiefdom to another. The lineages of the Wind and Bear clans were almost always in the white division, and the Potato, Aktayatci, and Raccoon lineages were almost always *Tcilokogálgi*, but the Bird, Beaver, Alligator, Deer, and Cougar lineages belonged to different divisions in different chiefdoms. Like the white chiefdoms, it is probable that the lineages in the white division were relatively old, while the *Tcilokogálgis* were relative newcomers. Consistent with this, the mikos of the white chiefdoms were usually from white clans, and the mikos of red chiefdoms were usually from *Tciloki* clans.

236

Towns, speaking the Atali dialect, were on the Tellico River and on the lower course of the Little Tennessee River; and the Valley Towns, also speaking the Atali dialect, were on the Hiwassee River. These dialectical differences were great enough to make it difficult for a speaker of one to understand a speaker of another.

The chiefdoms within these four regions remained largely independent of each other. More than anything else, it was the clans which linked the chiefdoms with each other. When Cherokee chiefdoms of a region did cooperate with each other it was only when some crisis forced them to cooperate, and even then they often acted with no regard for other regions. In the early 1750s, for example, the Lower Towns were suffering from savage Creek attacks, and they were trying to make peace with the Creeks, while at the same time the Overhills were forming an alliance with the Shawnees to attack the Creeks. Because of the independent nature of these Cherokee divisions, the British found it easy to play one against the other to their own advantage.[85] But at other times, when the British wanted the cooperation of all the Cherokees, they found this lack of unity maddening. They had to treat *all* Cherokee chiefs with equal respect.[86] The Cherokees as a whole were not a body politic until the late eighteenth and early nineteenth centuries, when they formed a state organization to resist being removed from their native soil.

One further feature of Southeastern political organization has been the source of much misunderstanding. Widespread in the Southeast were chiefdoms in which there were towns called old-beloved, ancient, holy, or white towns. An example was the Cherokee town of Chota on the Little Tennessee River. It was said that no human blood was ever shed in white towns, and that they were places of sanctuary for people whose lives were in danger. This, however, is something apart from the division between white and red chiefdoms in connection with the ball game. The white sanctuary towns were "mother" or "grandmother" towns from which several daughter towns had split off. They were not necessarily larger in population than the daughter towns, but simply older. In most unilineal societies, mediation or peacemaking is symbolized or secured by going up the descent line to the nearest common ancestor of the disputing parties. Thus the parent mediates the dispute between brothers, and the grandparent mediates between first cousins. Beyond this the ancestor is unlikely to be living, but mediation can still be carried out in his name. This may have been the principle involved in the sanctuary aspect of the white towns, for they would have been the towns with the oldest ceremonial centers. This does not mean that all white towns were sanctuaries—just the old, beloved white towns. People who eloped before the mourning period was over, adulterers, and people accused of other crimes could presumably find sanctuary in these towns until a busk had been performed. The towns were also places where a manslayer could find temporary sanctuary while he and his clan desperately sought ways to secure forgiveness from the clan of the man he had killed. If the people of the sanctuary town allowed him to enter, and sometimes they did not, he found time to bargain for his life and to seek intermediaries to try to persuade the aggrieved clan to forgive him or to accept compensation.[87]

WAR

The warfare pattern of the Southeastern Indians in historic times was not warfare in the European sense. More than anything else it resembled clan retaliation, which as we have seen was the custom by which one clan sought revenge for the murder of one of its members by killing the manslayer or one of his clansmen. Warfare differed from clan retaliation in that it occurred between independent peoples, and when a killing occurred between independent peoples, one death could lead to many. Another difference was that one of the main objects of warfare was to terrorize the enemy. In clan retaliation, on the other hand, one death revenged another, and the matter was settled, at least in principle. Thus some "wars" between Southeastern Indians were prompted by events which we would have considered to have been accidents. Also, it sometimes happened that the wrong Indian group was blamed for a killing. The British never really understood the principle of retaliation, and this was a source of deep misunderstanding. If a British colonist killed a Cherokee, the Cherokees were likely to go to war against the British people, but if a Cherokee killed a British colonist, the British did not usually go to war against the Cherokees, but demanded instead that the Cherokees hand over the man who did the killing, a demand that was as frustrating as it was incomprehensible to the Cherokees.[88]

Since revenge or retaliation was the dominant motive in historic

Southeastern warfare, it was not waged for the purpose of territorial acquisition or to gain economic advantage. The main exception to this may have occurred in the Mississippian tradition, when in some instances territories were evidently invaded, taken, and then defended by people bearing Mississippian culture.[89] This expansionist impulse shows up in the oral traditions of the Natchez. In their story of how the Great Sun came to earth to govern men, the Great Sun agrees to govern only if the people agree to move to better country, which he would show them. Expansionism is also implied in the fact that after bringing down sacred fire from the Upper World the Great Sun commanded them to build a second temple at the other extremity of the country so that if the fire were extinguished at one place it would survive at the other.[90] And in their migration legend the Natchez spoke of warfare between themselves and the "ancients of the country," implying that there was competition between themselves and people who were aboriginal and who were culturally and socially more conservative. They told of migrating to the place they then lived, carrying sacred fire with them, which they then housed in a temple they built. According to the legend, the Suns did not follow until later, presumably when it was safe for them to do so.[91] While we may doubt the historical veracity of some of these oral traditions, we have no reason to doubt their implication that the Natchez, and Mississippian people in general, were expansionist. It should be understood, however, that the purpose of this expansionism was to acquire new land, not to conquer and incorporate their enemies into an empire.[92]

Aboriginal Southeastern warfare was seasonal. According to James Adair, the English colonists had a saying that the Indians were out seeking blood when the snakes were out.[93] In other words, the Indians waged war in late spring, summer, and early fall, while in late fall, winter, and early spring they turned to other pursuits, such as hunting.

Young men gained war names—a form of social honor—by their exploits in warfare. Until they acquired these names they had to perform menial tasks, tending fires, lighting pipes, and serving the other men. Undoubtedly, it was this behavior which led the French to conclude that the Natchez "Stinkards" were a servile class, whereas they were more likely to have been men who had not distinguished themselves in warfare. Warfare was the "beloved occupation" of Southeastern Indian men, and they could not imagine themselves without war. In 1725 the Cherokees were fighting the Creeks, Choctaws, Senecas, some northern Indians affiliated with the French, and probably the Chickasaws.[94]

In warfare as in other social institutions, the marginal Indians along the western Gulf Coast differed from the Southeastern Indians in the interior. According to Cabeza de Vaca, when a dispute broke out within a village, they struck and beat each other until they were worn out, but they never used the bow and arrow against each other.[95] Much of the bloodshed among these people occurred because of quarrels over women. When threatened by an outside enemy they were adept at guarding against surprise attack. They would build fires inside their houses, but would sleep outside, to fool their enemies. If they suspected that an enemy was about, they would lie awake all night with their bows strung. Frequently, they would get up and go outside to look about. They fought in a crouching position, darting from side to side to elude arrows, shouting insults back and forth at each other. After all their arrows were shot, the two hostile parties would return home. One party would not follow the other even if it had the advantage.[96]

Indian groups became hostile toward each other and sometimes remained so for many years. The Cherokees and the Iroquois, for example, conducted raids against each other almost perpetually. Iroquois war parties consisting of one or two or a few men were said to be able to reach Cherokee country in as little as five days. The purpose of the raiding was, as always, retaliation, terrorization, and war honors. Occasionally the raiding was punctuated by periods of peace. The following story, collected by Henry Schoolcraft, conveys something of the character of Cherokee-Iroquois hostilities.

> *The Seneca Peacemakers.* In the course of the long war with the Cherokee it happened once that eight Seneca determined to undertake a journey to the south to see if they could make a peace with their enemies. On coming near the border of the Cherokee country they met some hunters of that tribe to whom they told their purpose. The latter at once hurried ahead with the news, and when the peacemakers arrived they found themselves well received by the Cherokee chiefs, who called a council to consider the proposition. All but one of the chiefs favored the peace, but he demanded that the eight delegates should first join them in a war party which was just preparing to go against a tribe farther south, probably the Creeks. The Seneca agreed, and set out with the war party

for the south; but in the fight which resulted, the Seneca leader, The Owl, was captured. The other seven escaped with the Cherokee.

A council was held in the enemy's camp, and it was decided that the Owl should be burned at the stake. The wood was gathered and everything made ready, but as they were about to tie him he claimed the warrior's privilege to sing his death song and strike the post as he recited his warlike deeds. The request pleased his enemies, who put a tomahawk in his hands and told him to begin.

He told first his exploits in the north, and then in the west, giving times and places and the number of scalps taken, until his enemies were so pleased and interested that they forgot the prisoner in the warrior [sic]. It was a long story, but at last he came to the battle in which he was taken. He told how many relatives he had killed of the very men around him, and then, striking the post with his tomahawk, "So many of your people have I killed, and so many will I yet kill," and with that he struck down two men, sprang through the circle of warriors, and was away. It was all so sudden that it was some moments before his enemies could recover from their surprise. Then they seized their weapons and were after him through the woods, but he had had a good start and was running for his life, so that he outran the chase and finally reached the Cherokee camp in safety and rejoined his seven companions.

On this proof of good will the Cherokee then concluded the treaty, and the peacemakers returned to their own country.[97]

When a killing occurred between groups who lived closer together, particularly when the killing was by an irresponsible young warrior, the group to which the killer belonged would sometimes send a peace envoy from a neutral group to talk with the slain man's group. They would beg them to forgive the manslayer and to accept compensation for the man's life. They would tell them that the killing was not sanctioned by the council and that the two groups should remain friends. If the council of the slain man's group agreed with this proposal, they accepted a payment, or they accepted the death of the manslayer or some other member of his group.[98] However, if the slain man were a man of high standing, or if his relatives insisted on retaliation, the War Chief might insist on war. The other leaders might very well object to this, but the War Chief would walk out of the town house and all those supporting him would follow. Volunteers would come not only from the dead man's clan, but from other clans as well; however, the decision to wage war was almost never unanimous in a Creek town. With this development, the council then sent the messengers suing for peace back to their people with the news that blood had to be revenged with equal blood. They put out a war club painted red for all to see, and they flew a red flag announcing the declared hostilities. The Natchez hung their flag from a red war pole some seven or eight feet long, stuck in the ground and pointed in the direction of the people they were going to attack.

Among the Chickasaws, once the decision for hostilities had been made, the War Chief, or Great Warrior, would announce his intention of invading enemy territory; he then walked around his winter house three times in a direction opposite the course of the sun, beating a drum. The Great Warrior or an old and respected warrior gave an impassioned speech to the young warriors, urging them to action. Speeches like the following were given by old warriors among the Natchez:

> My comrades . . . Oh, that I were young enough and strong enough to accompany you to this war and to do against our enemies now as I did against a nation from which I have taken three scalps, against another nation from which I have taken five, and four from such another. And how many blows of the war club have I made against our enemies in order not to be taken? I made so many efforts that I gave time for the other warriors to succor me, to set me at liberty and take me away with them, for I much prefer to die fighting than to allow myself to be taken and die in the frame.
>
> So, my comrades, leave with great courage, always have strong hearts, walk on the toes, keep the eyes open, never shut your ears, have no fear of the cold, do not hesitate to throw yourselves into the water in order to escape if it is necessary, and in that case conceal your retreat well. Especially never fear the arrows of the enemy and let it be seen that you are men and true warriors. Finally, if you find the occasion for it, use all your arrows on the enemies and afterward strike, kill, until your war clubs are drunk with the blood of the enemies.[99]

The Great Warrior was then joined by other warriors, particularly from the clan of the murdered man. The women then sang war songs, inflaming the men even further. The warriors were volunteers; no one coerced them into going to war. They all went into the Great Warrior's winter house, where they remained for three days and nights (not counting the first day), fasting and drinking potions made of certain herbs, chiefly the bitter emetic button snakeroot in warm water. This was to purify them and protect them from danger. They also abstained from sexual relations during this period. They believed that their success in war was directly related to the strictness with which they observed their ritual precautions. The older men kept a particularly close eye on the young warriors, whom they feared might break the ritual rules and endanger them all. To heighten their martial spirit the older warriors told stories about their war exploits. All of the men sang death songs and performed warlike dances. The Natchez ate a war feast of deer meat for speed and dog meat to symbolize the care with which they would follow their war chief.

After they were purified and ready for combat they painted themselves with red and black paint, the colors of conflict and death, and set out. The typical Chickasaw raiding party consisted of about twenty men, and rarely as many as forty. They were led by a war leader who carried on his back a square wooden "ark" or medicine bundle, measuring about one foot by one and one-half feet, filled with holy objects and vessels made by old women. The medicine bundle also contained what were said to be the horns from the Uktena and bones from the Water Cougar. They believed that the horns would make them immune from wounds. The medicine bundles also contained sprigs of cedar and button snakeroot. The Cherokees carried in their medicine bundle some live coals from a war fire built especially for the occasion and carried in a rectangular clay container with a lid, and a crystal to be used for divining.[100]

They departed from the town with great bravado, yelling, shouting, and singing a solemn war song. They traveled single file, three or four steps apart. Once in the woods they became as quiet as they could be, and extremely cautious. If anything unusual happened that might be interpreted as a bad omen, they immediately returned home, individually or collectively, and the town approved of their actions. Such an omen would be, for example, a dream of a particular bird that was a messenger of bad omens. The Cherokees consulted their crystals for omens (see fig. 47). One way was to set a crystal on top of a red post in the sunlight. Each warrior had to pass before it, and if the crystal failed to sparkle in the sunlight, that warrior went home.[101] The British regarded this behavior as both capricious and cowardly.[102]

One of the de Soto chroniclers reports that the Indian warriors used "pikes, lances, darts, [wooden] halberds, slings, clubs, [wooden] broadswords, sticks, and the like," but that their favorite weapon of war was the bow and arrow (see fig. 27). These bows were so strong the Spaniards could not pull the string back to their face, while the Indians could pull the string to their ears.[103] Indian boys were given little bows when they were about three years old, and they began a lifetime of archery by shooting their arrows at mice, lizards, and insects.[104] De Soto's men were awed by their skill. While a Spanish soldier was reloading a crossbow or arquebus, an Indian could get off six or seven arrows.[105] The Spanish soldiers' chain mail offered them little protection against the Indians' arrows, which simply splintered against the mail and went through to the flesh. Thus they soon took to wearing heavy quilted coverings three or four fingers thick to protect themselves and their horses.[106] They performed an autopsy on one of their horses killed by an arrow, finding that the arrow entered the horse's thigh, penetrated its bowels and intestines, and lodged in its chest cavity.[107] When the Indians ran out of arrows, they used their bows as clubs, swinging them with both hands.[108] But expert as they were with the bow and arrow, soon after the deerskin trade began they replaced it with the gun.

If the bow and arrow was the main weapon of war in the aboriginal Southeast, the war club was the main symbol of war. Even after the Southeastern Indians adopted small European hatchets or tomahawks in the eighteenth century in place of their traditional war clubs, they would still sometimes carry a small war club stuck through their belts. The war clubs were carved out of dense wood in several shapes. Most of them measured between twenty and thirty inches in length. Among the Timucuans the distal ends of their war clubs were carved in a flat, spatulate shape with sharp edges. The Natchez war club was shaped like a cutlass, but with a three-inch ball carved on the back of the distal end of the club (fig. 57). Several kinds of war clubs are depicted on Southeastern Ceremonial Complex motifs (fig. 58). The Indians must have worked hard at developing finesse in using these clubs. While de Soto was passing through central Georgia, Patofa, one of the local chiefs, gave a demonstration of his skill at using the war club. His gracefulness and rhythm was compared to that of a European fencing master.[109] Over one and one-half centuries later, John Lawson seems to have witnessed

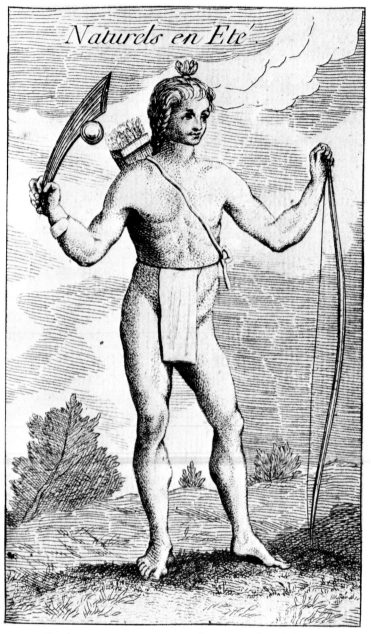

Figure 57. Natchez warrior in summer dress armed with bow and arrows and a war club. Le Page Du Pratz, *Histoire de la Louisiane*, Paris, 1758, vol. 2, p. 308. Negative no. 1168–b–4. Courtesy, Smithsonian Institution, National Anthropological Archives.

246

much the same thing in a dance performed in a town house in the South Carolina back country. Lawson describes dancers who performed with wooden "falchions" like those used by European stage fencers.[110]

The use of the war club as a symbol of warfare may explain the significance of the bi-lobed arrow, one of the more perplexing of the Southeastern Ceremonial Complex motifs. It has been suggested that the bi-lobed arrow represents a spear-thrower and that it symbolized masculinity or a man's exploits in battle.[111] But it would seem more plausible that it represented a war club, perhaps with spatulate celts attached. The war club consistently symbolized warfare. In some cases raiding parties would leave a red war club at the scene of a killing so their enemy would know who had perpetrated the raid. Important warriors among the Natchez had a war club tattooed on their right shoulder.[112] Thus the individuals whose remains were found at Etowah with bi-lobed arrows made of copper near their heads were probably warriors of the first rank (see fig. 93).

Southeastern Indian warriors traveled almost naked, dressed only in a breechcloth and moccasins. In aboriginal times a warrior carried with him a bow and arrows, a knife, and a war club stuck through his belt. Other than this, the warriors carried only a pack containing an old blanket, a small bag of parched corn meal, a wooden cup, perhaps some dried cornbread, and leather and cord to repair their moccasins. Before the gun was introduced, they used armor and shields made of woven cane and bison leather (see fig. 91).

The warriors continued observing ritual precautions while on the move. The Great Warrior chose a particular warrior to serve as waiter, and he and the other men would eat or drink only when served by this man. The warriors would eat and drink only at certain specified times, and then sparingly. They observed strict rules of comportment. They would never lean against anything to rest when sitting or standing. Among the Cherokees, if a man snapped a twig while going through the woods, he had to pick it up and carry it with him until nightfall.[113] They would sit only on fallen logs or on stones, and never directly on the earth. Similarly, the medicine bundle of holy objects carried by the Great Warrior was never placed directly on the earth, but on a pedestal made of stones or pieces of wood, and it was never touched except by the Great Warrior and his waiter. But the Great Warrior was more a leader than a commander; his

247

Figure 58. Copper celts mounted in war clubs. The portion of the club in which the celt is mounted is carved in the form of a crested woodpecker with its beak open and its tongue extended. Spiro, Oklahoma. Courtesy, Museum of the American Indian, Heye Foundation.

men fought more or less as individuals.[114] For this reason the Indians could not be strategists in the European sense. The best way to see this difference today is to observe a Cherokee or Choctaw ball game and compare it to football.

The whole object of a raid was to kill by surprise attack, and they were capable of great ingenuity in achieving this end. They often split up into several groups, each group traveling in single file, stepping in each others' tracks to make it appear that the tracks were made by a single person. They communicated with each other by imitating animal sounds, which they could closely mimic. The Cherokee war party sent out four scouts. In front went the Great Warrior, or "Raven," who imitated the sound of a raven if he caught sight of the enemy. To the right of the war party the scout was an "Owl," who imitated the sound of an owl if he saw the enemy; to the left a "Wolf"; and a "Fox" brought up the rear. All of these men were known by these animal titles, and they were entitled to wear the skins of these animals around their necks.[115] Chickasaw war parties would sometimes send out scouts ahead and to the rear who would fasten buffalo hooves or bear paws to their feet, leaving the tracks of these animals to confuse the enemy. When a war party became convinced that they were being followed, they fanned out in a semicircle and waited in ambush for their pursuers.

It was not easy for them to achieve surprise because the Southeastern Indians always moved cautiously, especially when in the woods. For example, if three men were traveling together, they would always take care to sit in a triangle, so that each faced in a different direction, to guard against being surprised. When a war party was discovered by the enemy, the party often returned home without shedding blood, surprise being essential. But sometimes they shouted insults and threats at each other, bragging about the barbarities they had committed against each other. Then, if they became sufficiently angry, their Great Warriors blew their war whistles and they commenced fighting. If a man was killed, the attackers tried to get his scalp. They did this by cutting an incision around the head, usually with a small cane knife, and by placing their feet on the victim's neck, they were able to pull off the scalp. Later the scalp was tied to a small hoop, painted red, and preserved. They sometimes hung these scalp hoops from the ends of long poles (fig. 59). The dead man's fellows tried just as strenuously to keep him

249

Figure 59. Buffalo Tamer, chief of the Tunicas. He wears facial war paint and holds a pole with three scalp locks. Drawing by A. De Batz, 1732. Courtesy, Peabody Museum, Harvard University.

from being scalped. When one side began losing—and this occurred after just one or a few losses—they would attempt to retreat into a wooded area too thick for effective pursuit.

Scalping was evidently an old practice in the Southeast. The first Europeans to encounter it were de Soto's soldiers, who saw it inflicted on their fallen comrades as they entered Apalachee territory in northern Florida. They observed that the Apalachees sometimes tied scalps to their bows as decorations.[116] We have at least some prehistoric evidence of scalping. At Moundville, for example, the skull of a young woman was found to have a shallow groove at approximately the hairline which ran horizontally all the way around the vault. She was probably scalped and then survived to suffer an infection at the line where the incision was made.[117] Other evidence of scalping in the Mississippian period may be the so-called oblong gorget (fig. 60), which usually consists of a scalloped circle with a tear-shaped protuberance. These oblong gorgets probably represented scalps attached to circular frames with the hair flowing down.[118]

The Southeastern Indians also occasionally cut off the heads of their enemies and carried them back to their villages. They sometimes placed these heads on posts outside their public buildings. The Timucuans of northern Florida sometimes dismembered the bodies of their victims and hung their limbs on trees. This was done to terrorize their enemies.[119] The skulls and longbones in Southeastern Ceremonial Complex motifs may refer to some of these practices. One pottery vessel from Moundville, for example, has incised on it skulls, armbones with hands, and an oblong gorget.

When a war party happened to surprise a small number of individuals of an enemy tribe and kill them all, they would usually leave behind some identifying mark. Sometimes it was a small wooden war club marked with appropriate symbols. Other times the symbols were simply carved in a tree. The Natchez left a small wooden tablet with symbols on it along with two red arrows stuck in the ground to form an X. Other Southeastern Indians left pictographs and other signs so that there would be no doubt as to who the killers were, taunting the other side to retaliate (fig. 61).[120]

When warriors arrived home after an unsuccessful raid they came in quietly; but if they were successful they shouted war whoops which were said to have been audible for one mile or more. The

251

Figure 60. Copper oblong gorget from Moundville. Courtesy, The University of Alabama, Museum of Natural History, Mound State Monument.

medicine bundle was placed on pieces of wood at the foot of the war pole, opposite the door of the Great Warrior's winter house. The Great Warrior, as before, circled the house three times, and then they all entered in order to be purified, because the shedding of human blood was polluting, and they fasted for three days under the guidance of the Great Warrior. Each night, the women lined up at the entrance to the winter house in two rows facing each other and sang songs. The success of the raid was thought to depend on the purity of the Great Warrior in particular. If any men were lost, the raid was thought to have been a failure and the failure was blamed on the Great Warrior. If several men were lost, he might be stripped of his war whistle, his drum, and his war names, and demoted to the position of a mere boy without war honors. It was primarily this attitude that led to such caution on a raid. And because a war party that brought back two or three scalps was thought successful, they frequently returned home after killing just one or two or a few of the enemy.[121]

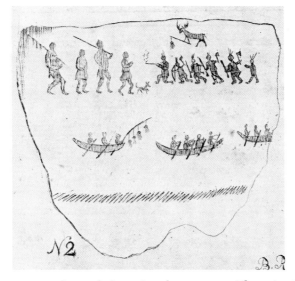

Figure 61. Pictographs made by a Creek war party. They signify that ten members of the deer clan came upon and ambushed four Choctaws (two men and two women) and took away their scalps. From Bernard Romans, *A Concise Natural History of East and West Florida*, 1775, vol. 1, p. 102. Pictograph 8. Courtesy, Smithsonian Institution, National Anthropological Archives.

The fate of captives among the Southeastern Indians varied immensely. Sometimes they were adopted and treated exactly as blood kinsmen, sometimes they were put in the precarious and uncertain position of a "slave," and sometimes they were tortured to death in a most horrible manner. When captives were enslaved, it was not slavery in the economic sense as practiced by the Europeans. In a subsistence economy a slave cannot turn a profit for his master. It was rather slavery in a social sense. The captive, or "slave," belonged to the man who captured him in war. He lived in the warrior's home and thereby became another mouth to feed. He performed menial tasks, such as gathering firewood and processing deer skins, but his primary value to his "master" seems to have been prestige—the captive was a sort of living scalp (fig. 62). He was not usually bound or in any way restricted in his movement around the village or its environs. But escape was not a viable option, either because he was too deep inside enemy territory to hope to make it out without being recaptured, or else because his master had taken the precaution of maiming him in some way to keep him from being able to run fast enough to elude his pursuers. His position was forever uncertain. He could be given as a gift to another master. He could be sold—or more accurately, bartered. Or for any of a number of reasons beyond his control he could be put to death, either by the swift, merciful blow of a war club or hatchet, or else by slow torture. From the earliest Spanish accounts it is clear that the Indians killed some of their captives brutally. Women and children who were

Figure 62. Various Indians living along the Mississippi River. The woman at lower left is an enslaved Fox; she is evidently processing an animal skin. The Negro boy was evidently captured and adopted. Drawing by A. De Batz, 1735. Courtesy, Peabody Museum, Harvard University.

taken as captives were frequently adopted and led free and relatively normal lives. But male captives, particularly the older ones who had accumulated some war honors, were frequently tortured to death in the spirit of vengeance.

In addition to torturing prisoners for vengeance, there was evidently an old pattern of sacrificial killing in the Southeast dating back to the Woodland tradition. This is supported not only by archaeological evidence, but also by early historical evidence of sacrificial killings by Indians from the lower Mississippi River eastward along the Gulf coast to Florida. The custom was practiced by the southern Caddoans, Natchez, Taensas, Tunicas, Koroas, Calusas, Timucuans, and perhaps by the people of the Carolina piedmont and coastal plain. The Taensas are reported to have sacrificed an infant when one of their public buildings was struck by lightning and destroyed by fire. And we shall see in the next chapter that when a member of the Natchez Sun lineage died, his or her spouse, retainers, and certain other individuals voluntarily offered themselves to be killed to accompany the dead Sun to the other world. The Calusas are reported to have sacrificially killed one prisoner each year as a "propitiatory" offering.[122]

When the Natchez decided to torture a captive to death, they first constructed a framework made of two poles about ten feet long, set into the earth about five feet apart. A crosspiece was then tied between the poles about two feet above the ground, and another crosspiece was tied about five feet above this, forming a square frame. The victim was tied to the foot of the frame and was fed his last meal. Everyone then assembled and the man who captured the victim uttered a death cry and struck him at the base of his neck with a war club, knocking him unconscious. He was then scalped and tied to the frame, with his wrists and ankles at the four corners of the frame, forming an X (fig. 63). His scalp was taken to relatives of slain Natchez, and they used it to "wipe tears from their eyes." He was then tortured with torches of burning cane applied to various parts of his body, all this being done in the spirit of revenge. Throughout it all the victim was expected to sing a death song. Sometimes the torture lasted for several days.[123]

More widespread in the Southeast than the Natchez frame method was the method of simply tying the victim to a post or stake. When the Chickasaws executed a captive by torture, he was tied to

Figure 63. Natchez Indians scalping a prisoner and torturing another on a frame. Woodcut from Le Page Du Pratz, *Histoire de la Louisiane*, Paris, 1758, vol. 2, opp. p. 429. Negative no. 1168–b–6. Courtesy, Smithsonian Institution, National Anthropological Archives.

the pole in the center of the chunkey yard for all to see.[124] He was stripped naked and black bearskin moccasins were placed on his feet and a burning firebrand was tied to the pole over his head, fire and the color black signifying death. He was then released from the pole and his arms tied to his sides. A strong grape vine was tied to his neck and the other end to the top of the pole, allowing him about fifteen yards of free play around the pole. They placed clay on his head to protect his scalp from being damaged by fire. The women then began torturing him by beating him with sticks and burning him with firebrands made of cane. The prisoner was supposed to show contempt for all this by singing a war song and bragging about his exploits against them. He then rushed around among his torturers trying to knock them down, kicking, and biting. When he fainted, they would throw cold water on him to revive him. When he finally died they scalped and dismembered him. No pity was shown a condemned prisoner. The women sang songs and the crowd of spectators often roared with laughter, especially if the victim showed fear.

It is not known whether this kind of torture was practiced before the arrival of the Europeans. The practice of tying prisoners to a post and torturing them with fire is reminiscent of European practices, and such torture was used against the Indians by early Spanish, French, and English colonists, most particularly by de Soto. Thus it is possible that the Indians adopted it from the Europeans, perhaps at first in retaliation for what the Europeans had done to their comrades. It is perhaps instructive that James Adair compared Chickasaw torture to the Spanish Inquisition.[125]

After a raid warriors would cut the scalps of their victims into pieces, fix them to green pine twigs, and put them on the tops of the winter houses of the murdered men for whom the blood revenge had been carried out. This final act, believed to appease the souls of the murdered men, was performed with great solemnity. The women sang songs of rejoicing, and the warriors shouted the death whoop. They then danced for three days and nights, rejoicing in the victory. In the dances, the men imitated the movements of cougars stalking their prey and the movements they made while on the raid. Soon after this the warriors who had distinguished themselves on the raid were honored and given war names (see chap. 6).

When the Southeastern Indians achieved peace, it was not peace as we know it. It meant little more than a temporary relief from the fear of enemy raids. When one party decided to sue for peace, they would send peace emissaries to their enemy. In general these peace emissaries were given safe conduct, but this was not assured, so that it was a dangerous undertaking. The emissaries sang songs of peace as they went along the way, and they carried tokens of peace with them, including strips of beads, tobacco, pipes, and white feathers. They would meet with their enemies in council, and the two sides would deliver lengthy orations which seem not to have been important for their substance, but for the general feeling they engendered. No treaty would be agreed to; no specific agreement would be reached. But if an amicable feeling could be attained, then peace in their terms would have been achieved. It might not, however, endure for long.[126]

CHAPTER FIVE

SUBSISTENCE

The way in which preliterate people wrest a living from their environment—their means of subsistence—is often considered to be a matter of simple fundamentals. People assume that the subsistence techniques of preliterate people are relatively unsophisticated economic responses to fundamental biological needs—they require little skill and less knowledge. But in making intensive studies of the subsistence techniques and belief systems of preliterate people, modern anthropologists have come to understand that such people possess remarkably detailed knowledge of their environment. We have learned, for example, that the Hanunóo of the Philippines know 10 basic and 30 derivative soil and mineral categories; they know 1,500 useful types of plants, including 430 cultigens; and they possess a wealth of knowledge about the structure of plants. Time and again throughout the world we have found that the techniques of preliterate people, which seem at first so inefficient and haphazard, are, in fact, likely to be intelligent solutions to problems posed by local social and environmental conditions.[1]

The Southeastern Indians were no exception. Because our research in this area is almost altogether archaeological and historical, we shall never have as full an understanding of their subsistence pattern as we would wish. But we do know some of the fundamental dimensions of their techniques and knowledge. We know that the Southeastern Indians were unusual in that they possessed a way of making a living which combined in fairly even proportions the hunting and gathering of wild foods with the cultivation of domesticated foods. They were both hunters *and* farmers, though we shall probably never know the precise degree to which they relied on each of these two subsistence techniques. All we can say with assurance is that both were important.

We also know that the belief system of the Southeastern Indians left its mark on their way of making a living just as it left its mark on all other areas of life. This is seen most clearly in two fundamental oppositions which gave structure to the knowledge, techniques, and behavior involved in their subsistence pattern: men as opposed to women, and the cold season as opposed to the warm season. The Southeastern Indians conceived of men and women as two radically different forms of humanity, and they consequently assigned to them contrasting roles in subsistence activities. The primary responsibility of the men was to provide meat, which they obtained by hunting and fishing, and the primary responsibility of the women was to provide vegetable food, which they obtained by cultivating domesticated foods and collecting wild foods.

Women worked hard and constantly, enjoying little leisure. But they did not complain. Among the Natchez, young girls were warned that if they were lazy they would not be able to marry a desirable husband. The men, on the other hand, did not always work so hard or so constantly; but their tasks of clearing land, hunting, and warfare required considerable strength, endurance, courage, and the ability to tolerate physical discomfort. To early European observers, who as intensive agriculturalists valued unremitting labor, it seemed that Indian women were hard workers, but that the men were incurably lazy. This, however, was a culturally biased judgment. The roles of men and women were indeed different, but each was demanding in its own way.

The activities of men and women varied according to the two divisions of the year—the cold season and the warm season. The men made their primary contribution to subsistence in the cold season, when they hunted, while the women made theirs in the warm season, when they cultivated the crops. These were seasonal emphases rather than a sharp dichotomy, because subsistence was a year-round pursuit for both sexes. The men fished and hunted a little in the warm season (and they helped a bit with the farming), and the women contributed significantly to the food supply with the food they collected in the cold season. These oppositions between men's work and women's work, and between warm weather work and cold weather work arose out of the basic structure of the subsistence pattern of the Southeastern Indians.

MEN AND WOMEN

The division of labor among the Southeastern Indians was relatively simple, with few specialized roles to be filled. As we have seen, the men were somewhat specialized among themselves in their political, religious, and military roles, and they ranked themselves serially with respect to each other. Except for kinship roles, the women were relatively undifferentiated. Like the men, the women ranked themselves with respect to each other, but the basis for their ranking is not well understood. The fundamental division of labor among the Southeastern Indians was between men and women. Indeed, the roles of men and women were so different that the two sexes were almost like different species. Consistent with this basic assumption, men and women kept themselves separate from each other to a very great extent. They seem, in fact, to have preferred to carry out their day-to-day activities apart from each other. During the day the women worked with each other around their households, while the men resorted to their town house or square ground. Separation was most important in activities which in their view epitomized sexual identity. We have already seen, for example, that warriors kept themselves apart from women for three days before going on a raid. And women kept themselves apart from men when they menstruated and gave birth. This ideological separation of the sexes was further reflected in their value on sexual abstinence. The Creeks, for example, believed that a warrior should not sleep with a woman too much, else it would sap his vitality and make him unfit for manly endeavors.

The Southeastern Indians symbolized the man/woman dichotomy in many ways. The two sexes behaved with respect to different rules of comportment. Among the Natchez, for example, the Great Sun sat with his legs crossed, presumably in the lotus position, while his women seated themselves "on their knees," presumably with their legs tucked beneath them in the sitting position used by the Japanese.[2] Although we cannot be certain, these sitting positions probably were used by all Natchez men and women. Moreover, these sitting positions go back to at least the Mississippian tradition. The male and female statues found at Etowah show precisely these same respective sitting positions (see fig. 92).

The difference between men and women was expressed in clothing and adornment. The basic item of men's clothing was the breechcloth. This was a rectangular piece of leather about five feet long and about eighteen inches wide worn between the legs with the ends hanging over a belt and falling down before and behind (see figs. 57, 59, 62). In the southern part of the Southeast, the breechcloth was sometimes made out of woven grass or fiber. In addition, the men sometimes wore decorative sashes tied around their waists with long tasseled ends falling down at their sides (see figs. 93, 102). Later they wore these sashes over one or both shoulders, draped across their chests, and tied at the hip, again with the tasseled ends hanging down at their sides (see fig. 66).[3] The men wore moccasins made of a single piece of deerskin, with one seam up the back of the foot, and another on top of the foot, with the material drawn up over the foot and toes and puckered (figs. 64, 66). They wore these moccasins only when the weather was cold or when they were out traveling. The rest of the time they went barefoot. To protect their legs from being scratched they also wore deerskin leggings when traveling (see fig. 106). These were not tailored pants but rather two separate garments, one for each leg, worn suspended from the belt. The Indians gathered them in below the knees with

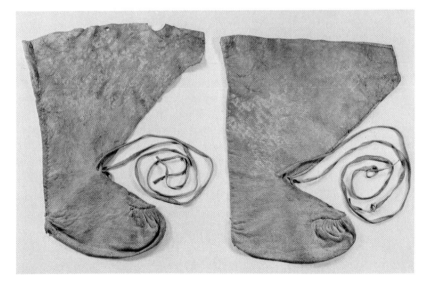

Figure 64. Chitimacha moccasins. Collected before 1885. The upper parts were wrapped about the ankles and legs and bound with the leather thongs. Negative no. 41980. Courtesy, Department of Anthropology, National Museum of Natural History, Smithsonian Institution.

fringed or woven garters, and tucked them into their moccasins below.[4] When it rained the Indians sometimes removed their moccasins and leggings to keep them from getting wet.

The traditional cold weather garment for men was a mantle or "matchcoat," this latter name coming to us from an Algonkian word. This matchcoat was made of animal skins and was worn draped over one or both shoulders (fig. 65). It extended down to the knees. The Indians used bison skins for matchcoats when they could get them, but they also sewed several beaver or muskrat skins together, and they undoubtedly used other kinds of skins as well.[5] When the weather was not so cold they wore matchcoats of deerskin, often with red, yellow, and black designs painted on them.[6] Another kind of matchcoat, described in more detail a few pages hence, was made of feathers attached to a fiber net. Natchez men sometimes wore a long shirt that reached halfway down their thighs. It was made of two deerskins and evidently had short sleeves.[7] Soon after European colonization, Southeastern Indian men began wearing cloth shirts like those worn by the frontiersmen. The Seminoles developed these shirts into distinctive garments, and when they acquired sewing machines at about the beginning of this century, they developed the distinctive patchwork designs for which they are today well known (see figs. 112, 113).[8]

In earlier times, Southeastern Indian men wore a small pouch suspended from their belt, but soon after the Europeans arrived they began suspending the pouch from a sash worn across one shoulder. In Southeastern Ceremonial Complex motifs men are sometimes represented wearing pouches with a peculiar pointed shape (see fig. 32). The men wearing these pouches are often depicted with birdlike features, and the pouches may in fact have been made to have the shape of the underside of a bird, perhaps a hawk or an eagle (see figs. 35, 93).[9] But later, probably in imitation of the pouches worn by the Europeans, they began making their pouches in a rectangular shape. In the historic period the Indians used these pouches to carry tobacco, a pipe, flint and steel for starting fires, ammunition, and sometimes a whetstone.[10]

Ordinarily, the men wore nothing on their heads, but on ceremonial occasions, probably as symbols of rank or of office, they wore head gear which could be quite elaborate. They wore feathers of various kinds, many having specific meanings. The complex head

262

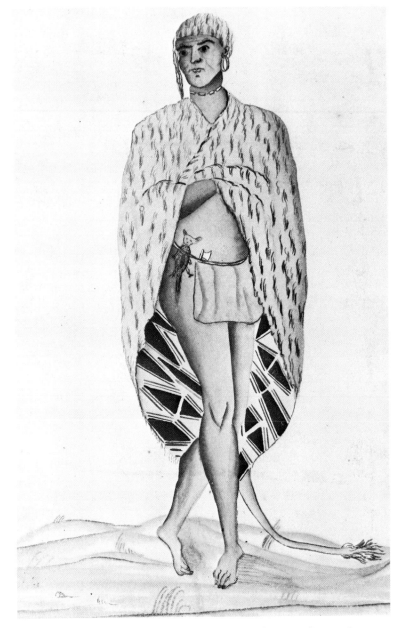

Figure 65. Southeastern Indian wearing a bison skin matchcoat. Geometric designs are painted on the inside. Drawing by A. De Batz, 1735. Courtesy, Peabody Museum, Harvard University.

ornamentation worn by men in Southeastern Ceremonial Complex motifs is not well understood (see fig. 93). In a few cases the men are depicted wearing bird or animal skins wrapped around their heads. Perhaps this was the forerunner of the turbans the Southeastern Indian men began wearing after they acquired cloth. Seminole men, in particular, came to wear elaborate turbans that were sometimes encircled with silver bands holding feathers of exotic birds (figs. 66, 112).[11]

The basic item of women's clothing was a short deerskin skirt which covered a woman from her waist to her knees (see figs. 59, 62). Timucuan women wore skirts made of Spanish moss (see fig. 56). One can only surmise about how they might have dealt with the chiggers (or red bugs) which often infest Spanish moss. In warm weather the women wore nothing above the waist, though like the men, they wore feather or skin matchcoats in cold weather. A woman's matchcoat, however, was worn differently from a man's. It was worn under the right arm with the two upper corners tied above the left shoulder, leaving both arms free and exposing the right breast. Women's moccasins were essentially like those worn by the men. They wore nothing on their heads.

Young boys and girls generally went naked in warm weather (see fig. 59). When Natchez girls were eight or ten years of age they began wearing a kind of fringed apron that was woven out of white mulberry threads and attached to tasseled cords. At puberty they began wearing women's clothes. Boys began wearing men's clothing at the age of twelve or thirteen.[12]

The duties of women and men were even more distinctive than their clothing. The women did all the work involved in running the households, including cooking and making pottery and basketry. The women were responsible for working the kitchen gardens situated near the houses, for cultivating the large agricultural fields, and for making corn into meal with a mortar and pestle. Women were also responsible for gathering most of the wild food they used. It was their task to fetch the firewood, and in the old towns which were surrounded by exhausted land, they often had to go several miles to find a suitable supply. Natchez women carried firewood and other burdens using two strips of bearskin, each about the width of a hand. One band went across the shoulders and the other across the forehead.[13]

Figure 66. Mikasuki Seminole men's clothing about 1890. *Left:* Tommy
Jumper. *Right:* Billie Stewart. Note the diamond motif on the sashes worn
by Stewart. Negative no. BAE 45331–E. Courtesy, Smithsonian
Institution, National Anthropological Archives.

The women cured animal skins and used them to make most of the clothing. The men skinned the animals they killed and dressed the skins in a preliminary way, but from this point on women were responsible for processing them. The women's first step in processing these skins was to remove all the remaining flesh from the skin and dry it in the sun. Then they punched holes all around the skin and immersed it in water for two or three days. After this it was wrung dry and hung over an inclined log and all the hair was scraped off with a piece of flint set into the notched end of a stick, or else with a drawing knife made of hardwood or the leg bone of a deer. Hair was not removed from buffalo and bear skins. The skin was then soaked in a vessel of water to which pulverized deer brains had been added.

Figure 67. Fragments of woven cloth from Spiro. The warp is probably *Arundinaria tecta* fibers; the weft is apparently rabbit hair. Courtesy, Museum of the American Indian, Heye Foundation.

266

After this the women sometimes pounded the skin to soften it. Then it was stretched on a frame and dried. The next step was to dig a shallow pit and fill it with corncobs, dried animal dung, and rotten wood. A small dome of saplings was erected over this, and the skin was pegged down and stretched over it. The contents of the pit were burned to produce dense clouds of smoke. After having been smoked on one side, the skin was turned over and smoked on the other. The Natchez sewed skins together using sinew and an awl made from the leg of a heron.[14] The skins were usually dyed yellow, red, blue, green, or black. When exposed to water the skins shrank but remained supple.

The Southeastern Indians did not possess the true loom, but the women were skilled at twining, plaiting, and weaving with their fingers, and they wove mantles on an upright loom with suspended threads (fig. 67). The most important animal fibers used in weaving were buffalo hair, though it was not always available, and opossum hair; from these they made textile pouches, garters, and sashes. They made considerable use of vegetable fibers derived from Indian hemp (*Apocynum cannabinum*) and various nettles, which they used to make cord and rope. They also used mulberry fiber, which they got from shoots four or five feet tall growing up around the stumps of cut mulberry trees. They removed the bark, dried it in the sun, beat it into a fiber, and bleached it. Using thread spun from this fiber, they made feather matchcoats by fashioning nets to which small turkey, swan, or duck feathers were attached in courses (as one would lay shingles on the roof of a house), producing a very light and warm garment (fig. 68).[15]

The principal occupations of the men were hunting, the ball game, politics, war, and the ceremonies connected with the entire round of social life. They manufactured the tools and paraphernalia used in these endeavors, and they constructed all buildings, both domestic and public, and cleared the land used for building and cultivation. When buildings were needed, the men generally erected them in spring and fall, always preferring to avoid hot weather. When a large structure such as a town house was to be built, the men got together and traced out its exact dimensions, assigning specific jobs to specific individuals. Then, when the day came to build it, all the work was done in a single day with each man performing precisely the job assigned to him. Men did the heavy

Figure 68. Reconstructed feather matchcoat. Made in the 1940s by Molly Adams, a Mataponi Indian of Palls, Virginia. Courtesy, Museum of the American Indian, Heye Foundation.

work in clearing the large fields for cultivation, and they sometimes helped the women tend them.

It would be rash to say that men were preeminent over women in the Southeast. The women, after all, owned the houses and possibly the agricultural fields, and although they had to work hard, they enjoyed considerable security and economic independence. Although women could not hold offices, they could and did participate in councils.[16] But men unquestionably came first in most ritual contexts. Among the Natchez, for example, food was always served first to the men, and even the youngest boy present would be served before the oldest, most respected woman.[17] The ideal woman was supposed to be docile and submissive. In fact, men appear to have symbolically associated women with buffalo or deer. Men, in some sense, "hunted" women just as they hunted buffalo or deer. Perhaps this explains why Southeastern Indian women sometimes wore a string made of buffalo hair around their legs.[18] This may also explain why the deer and the buffalo are seldom if ever portrayed in Southeastern Ceremonial Complex motifs. The men portrayed the animals whose qualities they feared or admired—not the ones they hunted.

The Southeastern Indians had very little choice about what they wanted to be in life. Basically, they could either be a man or a woman. The man's role was unusually demanding, and to be admired one had to possess great strength, agility, endurance, tolerance for pain, and courage. Perhaps for this reason some men became transvestites. They chose to play the woman's role rather than the man's. So it was that the French were shocked to find a few Timucuan men dressing as women and doing the things that women did. The same was true of Natchez transvestites, who cultivated fields and carried burdens along with women. Without supplying any details, the French who observed this custom among the Natchez make it plain that Natchez transvestites also played the woman's role in sexual intercourse.[19]

In the same vein, Southeastern Indian women sometimes played a man's role. Nancy Ward, an eighteenth century Cherokee woman, fought like a man in battle and the men gave her the title of "war woman" or "beloved woman." She spoke in Cherokee councils and in 1781 even conducted negotiations with an invading American army. Years before, her uncle, Little Carpenter, had attended a council in Charles Town, where he was shocked when he found no women present among the representatives of the British colonists. When Little Carpenter asked whether it was not true that "White Men as well as the Red were born of Women," he left the British stammering for an answer.[20]

THE COLD SEASON AND THE WARM SEASON

The year was not a continuous span of time for the Southeastern Indians. It was rather sharply divided into two seasons. Food was most abundant in late summer and early fall, allowing the people the leisure to hold festivities, games, and celebrations. The months were named for changes in the weather and for the ripening and availability of wild foods, so that for the Creeks, October was "big chestnut month," February was "wind month," June was "black-berry month," and so on. They celebrated the appearance of each new moon with varying degrees of formality. They counted months in terms of the passage of moons, and years in terms of the passage of summers or winters. By our standards their means of conceptualizing time were not very elaborate, although they may have been more elaborate in some places during the Mississippian period. At the Cahokia site, for example, archaeologists have unearthed the remains of large circles of posts whose alignments may have been used for simple astronomical observations.[21]

The two seasons of the Southeastern year can be called the cold season and the warm season. The Cherokee cold season (*gola*) ran from the new moon in October to the new moon in April, and their warm season (*gogi*) ran from April to October.[22] The activities of the Southeastern Indians differed rather sharply according to season, and their seasons had different symbolic associations. In the cold season, the time of the eagle, the men held council in the town house and they were occupied with hunting, mostly for deer, while the women were occupied with gathering wild foods, particularly nuts. In the warm season, the time of the snake, the men held council at the square ground and they were mainly occupied with war and the ball game, while the women tended their fields.

After the festivities of the Green Corn Ceremony and a period of leisure in late summer and early fall, the Indians foraged through the woods hunting game and gathering wild foods. The Southeastern Indians had an exact knowledge of the country around them. This is evident in Cherokee mythology where many of the events take place at specific locations, as, for instance, at a particular place on a particular mountain or at a certain spot by a certain river. These geographic features frequently have names which resonate with the myths. For example, *dakwa i*, literally "*dakwa* place," was located on the French Broad River about thirty miles below Asheville, North Carolina, and it was believed to be the home of a monstrous fish (a *dakwa*).[23] *Datle yasta i*, literally "where they fell down," was a site on the Tuckasegee River, so named because two Uktenas were once seen to lift themselves out of a deep hole in the river, to struggle with each other, and then to fall back into the water.[24] The Indians' knowledge of terrain was fairly detailed. Several early historical sources tell about their tracing accurate maps in the ashes of a fire or on the ground. Others drew maps for Europeans on paper or deerskin. In some cases these maps were visual representations of social relationships (fig. 69), but in other cases they were true maps indicating the courses of rivers and streams which the Europeans subsequently found to be reasonably accurate.[25]

This knowledge of terrain was essential in their hunting because in the historic period the Southeastern Indians sometimes ranged as far as two or three hundred miles away from their towns. These hunts were conducted by the men accompanied by their able-bodied women and some of their children. The people who were too

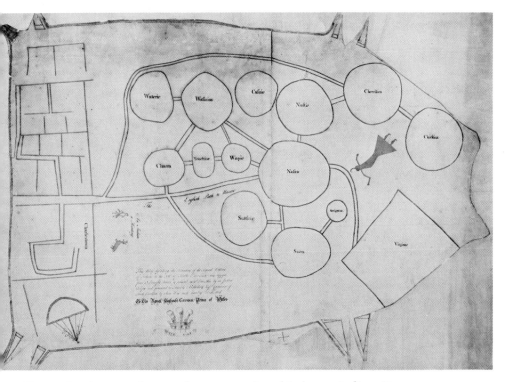

Figure 69. A copy of a map drawn on a deerskin by an Indian. It was presented in 1725 to Francis Nicholson, governor of South Carolina. The rectilinear design to the left represents the Indian's image of the streets of Charleston, with a ship in the harbor at the lower left. The remainder of the map is a schematic portrayal of the trade routes from South Carolina and Virginia to the Catawbas (Nasaw), and thence to other Indians. Sloane MS. 4723. Reproduced by permission of the British Library Board.

271

old to go out in the woods stayed behind in the town along with some of the women and children, and they kept in touch with the hunting parties through runners sent back and forth. In historic times the winter hunt lasted from November or December until February or March, when the hunters returned to their people with a supply of skins and smoked meat. This period of time may have been longer than the winter hunts that took place before European contact because after the introduction of the deerskin trade, the hunters had to stay longer in the woods in order to obtain enough skins to trade for the European goods on which they quickly became dependent.

The winter hunts were followed by spring fishing trips. As soon as herring, sturgeon, and other fish began running upstream to spawn, the Indians went to their favorite fishing spots, some of the best places being at the rapids along the fall line. When the weather was warm enough, in April or May, the first crops were planted, and these were tended and cultivated through the summer mainly by the women. While the women were busy with the crops, the men set off on raids against their enemies. Between raids they occupied themselves by playing their favorite games of skill. This continued throughout the summer until the Green Corn Ceremony and the harvest, when a new year began and the cycle started all over again.

HUNTING, FISHING, AND GATHERING

The Southeastern Indians enjoyed a diversified food supply that included both wild and domesticated foods, and it is important to realize that wild food was historically the more basic of the two. Their way of exploiting the food resources of their environment had a long history with origins far back in the Archaic tradition. Thus some of their hunting, fishing, and gathering techniques could have been more than nine thousand years old. It is no wonder, then, that their methods were so sensitively and effectively adapted to their environment and that although they depended on the cultivation of corn, beans, and squash as an important source of food, agriculture influenced rather than shaped the fundamental nature of their cultural and social organization.

As with all hunting people with simple technology, the main hunting strategy of the Southeastern Indians was not so much concerned with skillfully hitting the animal from a distance as it was in getting so close to the animal that they could not miss. Before British traders made the gun generally available to them, their main hunting weapon was the bow and arrow. The Southeastern Indians usually made their bows out of black locust, ash, and osage orange, when they could get it (see fig. 27). They usually strung their bows with strips of buckskin that had been stretched and twisted. They often made arrows out of the small variety of cane, tipping them with flint points or simply by sharpening the ends of the cane shafts. They also made arrow shafts out of red dogwood and other kinds of wood. For hunting buffalo or deer, the Natchez tipped their arrows with sharp bone points that were bound to the shafts with sinew and glue made from deer antlers or fish. They sometimes used the tough scales of garfish for arrow points. Arrows were finished with either two or three feathers attached with fish glue.[26] Hunters protected their wrists from the bowstring with a wristguard made of leather or bark. They were very accurate with the bow and arrow at distances up to forty yards, and they sometimes hit their mark from over one hundred yards away. They shot with such force that Cabeza de Vaca reports that the Apalachee Indians of northwestern Florida could shoot arrows to penetrate oak trees as thick as the calf of a man's leg.[27]

Boys and young men used blowguns to kill squirrels and birds and other small game. The blowgun was made of a hollowed piece of cane cut to a length of seven to nine feet (see fig. 106). The darts they used were about 10 to 22 inches long and were round in cross section. They were made of hard wood and had several inches of thistledown or animal hair tied to one end to form an air seal in the blowgun. The Cherokees were accurate with the blowgun up to 40 or 60 feet. Their darts had sufficient velocity to penetrate the bodies of birds, but with larger game they shot for the eyes, and reportedly with good success. We have no evidence that they used any kind of poison on these darts.[28]

In hunting as in other important matters, the right words were as important as the right tools. The Cherokees, for example, possessed a series of prayers and songs which they uttered and sang before a hunt. On the evening before a hunt, a Cherokee would go to the bank of a river and recite the following prayer addressed to the two principal deities of the hunter—Long Man, the river, and Sacred Fire.

Give me the wind. Give me the breeze. Yu! O Great Terrestrial Hunter, I come to the edge of your spittle where you repose. Let your stomach cover itself; let it be covered with leaves. Let it cover itself at a single bend, and may you never be satisfied.

And you, O Ancient Red, may you hover above my breast while I sleep. Now let good dreams develop; let my experiences be propitious. Ha! Now let my little trails be directed, as they lie in various directions. Let the leaves be covered with the clotted blood, and may it never cease to be so. You two [Long Man and Sacred Fire] shall bury it in your stomachs. Yu![29]

In the prayer the hunter asks that the wind be in his favor so his quarry will not scent him. "Great Terrestrial Hunter" refers to the river, which sends its smaller streams and rivulets out "hunting" in the forest. "Let your stomach be covered with leaves" refers to the hunter's wish that the blood-stained leaves from the game he kills and washes in the river will cover the surface of the water. The hunter also wishes that he will find sufficient game trapped in a single bend of the river so he will not have to hunt widely through the woods. "Ancient Red" refers to Sacred Fire. The hunter rubbed ashes on his chest before going to sleep, thus having Sacred Fire "hovering above his breast." He asks that it bring him good dreams as omens of a successful hunt. Slaughtered game was washed in the river and a piece of it thrown into the fire, both acts being sacrificial offerings to Sacred Fire and the Long Man, thus "filling their stomachs." The hunter would start out before daybreak, eating no food the entire day. After sunset he would eat a light meal and go to the river's edge again. Daybreak and sunset were the best times for hunting deer.

Other hunting songs were specific to particular animal species. The Cherokees had a series of deer songs, bear songs, fishing songs, and so on. These songs were valuable pieces of knowledge. They had to be purchased from hunters or priests who knew them, and they were relatively expensive. The Cherokees even had a short formula they uttered to themselves when they took aim and released an arrow or pulled a trigger: "Instantly the Red *Selagwutsi* strikes you in the very center of your soul—instantly. Yu!" The missile was unleashed on "Yu!" *Selagwutsi* was a reed (*Erianthus* Michx.) out of which arrows were made.[30]

The white-tailed deer (*Odocoileus virginianus*) was by far the most important game animal in the Southeast, providing from 50 to

90 percent of the animal protein eaten. This deer occurs all over the Southeast and in all areas adjacent to the Southeast. It is a moderately large animal, weighing from 50 to as much as 350 pounds, but a deer over 250 pounds is unusually large. Today deer are solitary or travel in small herds of ten to twenty, but in the early colonial era some reports mention herds numbering as many as two hundred. This social flexibility on the part of the deer is rather remarkable, and it is partly responsible for the successful survival of the species.

In any but the rutting season it is hard to get in close range of a deer. They have sharp senses, are frightened easily, and are extraordinarily swift and agile. If a deer decides not to run away from a hunter, it holds its tail down and melts into the foliage, and one can walk quite close to it without seeing it. In fact, the deer manages to stay hidden most of the time. But if it decides to flee, its white tail goes up like a flag, a signal to all other deer in its vicinity, and it literally bolts away. Deer have been known to jump over obstacles as high as eight feet and for distances of as far as twenty-nine feet. They can achieve a top speed of thirty-five miles an hour, and they can sustain a speed of twenty-five miles an hour for several miles.

Several aspects of the deer's seasonal cycle led the Indians to hunt them most avidly and most successfully in late fall and winter. The rutting season for deer is from late September through November, and during this time the bucks relax their usual defenses and become aggressive; they will charge at anything, even bushes and low-hanging tree limbs. At the same time, the acorns have fallen, and because this is their favorite winter feed, the deer become concentrated in oak forests. The Indians would not have failed to notice that it is during this time that deer reach their maximum weight.

Odd as it seems, the Southeastern Indians did the deer a favor by hunting them so effectively. Deer have such a high reproductive capacity that had they not been hunted they would have overpopulated to such a degree that they would have overgrazed their habitat, and this would have made them vulnerable to famine, disease, and predation.[31]

The Southeastern Indians had two favorite techniques for hunting deer: the decoy technique and the fire surround. The decoy technique was used by individual hunters during the rutting season. They would make a deer-head decoy by removing the skin from the head and neck of a deer (see fig. 11). They cured the skin and stuffed it, stretching the neck over a framework of cane hoops. The antlers were hollowed out in back so that the entire apparatus was extremely light. The hunter carried it tucked in his belt, and when he sighted a deer, he leaned over and put the decoy about his head and shoulders. He held his bow or gun in his left hand, sticking his right arm through the neck of the decoy and manipulating the head with his right hand. He then imitated the motions of a deer with the decoy head, moving it rapidly from side to side, lowering it to browse on the grass, and occasionally reaching back to lick as deer often do when they are nervous. In addition, he would sometimes imitate a deer's call or rustle the limb of a tree, so that aggressive bucks would approach looking for a fight. When a deer came into easy range, the hunter dropped the decoy, took aim, and fired. Usually the hunter would have to track down the wounded deer using its bloody trail as a guide.[32]

The deer decoy method of hunting had its peculiar hazards. One was that bucks are aggressive and can be quite dangerous during the rutting season. The chief danger, however, came not from overzealous (or overamorous) bucks, but from other hunters. The Indians were so expert at using the decoys to imitate the movements of deer that other hunters sometimes shot them by mistake.

The fire surround was a communal hunting technique used in fall and early winter, when the leaves had fallen and were dry. A group of hunters—often as many as two or three hundred—would go into the woods and set the leaves on fire in a circle of up to five miles in circumference. This forced deer and others animals into a small area where they could be easily shot. In some cases deer were forced into a river and killed as they swam. After the Southeastern Indians acquired firearms, communal hunting declined. With a gun an individual hunter could kill far more effectively than with a bow and arrow, and the reason for killing deer changed.[33] Hunters began taking only the skins, leaving the meat to rot.

Not all burning by the Indians was directly connected with fire-surround hunting. Some evidence suggests that they intentionally burned portions of the woods in winter as a matter of course. There were several benefits to be derived from this practice. Not only did it reduce the threat of serious forest fires by reducing the accumulation of dead wood and litter on the forest floor, but it also laid down a bed of ashes, a soil nutrient, and it kept the forest open by clearing out underbrush, tree seedlings, and saplings. This stimulated the growth of open meadows and plant life on which deer could browse, it probably made acorns and chestnuts easier to find, and this in turn would have increased both the deer and the turkey populations. In view of this practice of regular light burning, it is not so difficult to explain why early Europeans in the Southeastern uplands reported seeing large parklike meadows with widely separated large trees and herds of deer and flocks of turkeys which seem to us to have been unnaturally large.[34]

Perhaps it could even be said that the Southeastern Indians accomplished a semidomestication of the deer by artificially increasing its numbers. The deer seems well suited to semidomestication, as is evidenced by the fact that Magdalenian hunters in Upper Paleolithic Europe attached themselves to herds of wild reindeer, following them and systematically exploiting them.[35] Francisco of Chicora, the Southeastern Indian captured by the Spanish in the sixteenth century, told the historian Peter Martyr that his people kept deer as domesticated animals. This is probably not so much a false assertion as it is Martyr's garbled version of Francisco's attempt to explain the semidomesticated status of the deer.[36]

The Indians probably also used their dogs to hunt deer, though we know relatively little about how they did it. Dogs hunt deer more or less naturally, and they are good at it—so good, in fact, that in most parts of the Southeast today it is illegal for hunters to use dogs to hunt deer. The wolf, a near relative of the dog, was evidently an important deer predator during the Mississippian period.

Most Indians in the Southeast hunted deer by the techniques we have seen, but variations occurred not only through time but also from place to place. Cabeza de Vaca reports that the Indians of the coast near the "Island of Ill Fate," probably Louisiana, would hunt deer by running them from morning to night, until they were so exhausted that they could be approached and killed.[37] These Indians lay outside the Mississippian sphere of influence, where they evidently retained an Archaic or Woodland way of life. The French observed among the Natchez what may have been a cultural survival of this ancient technique. In preparation for a "deer dance" or simply as a diversion for young men, a party of men would go out in the woods in a U-shaped formation. When they flushed up a deer,

Figure 70. Natchez U-shaped formation for hunting deer. Woodcut from Le Page Du Pratz, *Histoire de la Louisiane*, Paris, 1758, vol. 2, opp. p. 71. Negative no. 45,068. Courtesy, Smithsonian Institution, National Anthropological Archives.

they would shout and make gestures so that the deer would dart from one side of the U-formation to the other (fig. 70). Some deer were able to escape through the open end of the formation, but often the men at the points were able to frighten them back. The men gradually closed the circle and ran the deer until it was completely exhausted. When it fell, they picked it up and carried it to the Great Sun. Afterwards they killed and quartered it, presenting the meat to the Great Sun, who in turn distributed it to the men who organized the hunt.[38]

On the western margin of the Southeastern Culture Area the white-tailed deer was less prevalent than in the east, and the buffalo (*Bison bison bison* L.) was more prevalent and hence more important in the economy. Early historic documents contain reports of moderately large herds of buffalo in Tennessee, and buffalo were occasionally seen in other parts of the Southeast. The Natchez hunted buffalo with some regularity, but even by the 1700s few were being killed in their immediate vicinity, and their rituals indicate that the deer was more important to them than the buffalo.[39] The small herds of buffalo east of the Mississippi River were as nothing compared to the enormous herds one-half million or more on the other side.[40] The Caddoans lived west of the Mississippi. They were like the Southeastern Indians in many respects, with a mixed agricultural and hunting economy, but for them the buffalo was the most important game animal. The Caddoans' subsistence pattern was intermediate between the Southeast and the Plains.[41] To the north and west of them, outside the Southeastern Culture Area, in the vast grassy expanses of the prairie and plains, the buffalo dominated not only the economy but, after the introduction of the horse, the entire lives of the Plains Indians.

The black bear was a valued game animal in the Southeast, but it was valued in a different way than the deer. Because the bear has a low reproductive rate, it was a scarce animal, and the number of bears the Indians killed was negligible compared to the number of deer they killed. But whereas the deer was killed as a staple food, the bear was killed mainly for the oil that could be extracted from its fat.

The preferred season for hunting bear was winter, for then the bears were spending most of their time sleeping. The females were particularly fond of hibernating high up in the trunks of hollow trees. The Indians would locate them by finding claw marks on the tree.

One of the hunters would imitate the sound of a bear cub in distress, and the female bear would reveal herself. A man would then climb a nearby tree and throw a bundle of burning canes into the hollow tree, and when the bear was driven out by the fire and began descending the tree, it was an easy matter for the hunters to shoot and kill it. If, however, they only succeeded in wounding the bear, all the hunters would run and climb saplings that were too small for the bear to climb in pursuit.[42]

Several birds were important in the Southeastern hunting economy: the wild turkey (*Meleagris gallopavo silvestris* Vieillot, and in Florida *M. g. osceola*), the passenger pigeon (*Ectopistes migratorius* L.), and several species of waterfowl. The wild turkey is a large bird; adult males weigh an average of 17 pounds and adult females weigh an average of 11 pounds. It was especially numerous in the aboriginal Southeast. It has been estimated that the aboriginal turkey population in the state of Georgia alone was in the neighborhood of six hundred thousand. Early historical accounts commonly report flocks containing several hundred turkeys.[43] The passenger pigeon, now extinct, was even more numerous than the turkey. Early observers of the migratory flights of these birds left many accounts of flocks which darkened the sky and which took several hours to pass overhead. Passenger pigeons roosted in trees in such numbers that limbs were broken off under their weight. They roosted only in certain areas, and the Indians hunted them in winter, going out at night with torches to blind them and long poles to knock them from their perches.[44]

Like the passenger pigeon, waterfowl were not hunted everywhere in the Southeast, but only in restricted areas and only in certain times of the year. The Indians killed them in considerable numbers from the middle of October until the middle of April along the Mississippi flyway, the route along which millions of waterfowl migrate each year. The methods used by the Indians to hunt waterfowl are not well understood. It is known that they killed far more species which fed in shallow water and on land than species which fed by diving beneath the water. Whether this difference reflects something about their hunting techniques or something about their belief system is not known.[45]

The deer, the bear, the turkey, the passenger pigeon, and the waterfowl were important game animals to the Southeastern Indians, but they also hunted most of the smaller game animals, including rabbits, squirrels, raccoons, and opossums. Of these smaller animals, the raccoon and the opossum were the most important sources of meat. Small game animals were often trapped with snares and other devices. And just as the Indians on the western fringes of the Southeast exploited the buffalo, the Indians on the southern fringes were known to have preyed upon the animals peculiar to their region. The Timucuans, for example, impaled alligators on long poles thrust down their throats, and Indians on the Florida coast sometimes killed the sea cow. Even an occasional whale was taken if it ventured too close to the beach.

The Southeastern Indians lived in an area which enjoyed some of the best fresh- and salt-water fishing in North America. Fishing was especially good along the Atlantic Coast and its rivers, in all of Florida, along the Gulf Coast, and along the lower Mississippi River and its tributaries. In one respect fishing in these areas was even better than in the Northwest Coast Area of the northwestern United States and Canada, where fishing dominated the entire Indian economy. Unlike the Northwest Coast, which greatly depended upon seasonal migrations of salmon, fishing was good in the Southeast the year around.[46] But good fishing did not automatically produce fishermen. Only in southern Florida and along the Gulf Coast was fishing the most important source of food. Fishing was important to a somewhat lesser extent along the Mississippi River, particularly in the oxbow lakes and along the Atlantic Coast, but in the remainder of the Southeast fishing was clearly less important than agriculture and hunting.[47] The reasons for the underutilization of fish in the Southeast are not entirely clear, but they seem to have been largely cultural.[48] It is striking that the Timucuans (and probably the Calusas) on the edge of the Southeastern Culture Area embroidered fishing with elaborate rules and avoidances, while in the Southeast proper no such cultural elaboration existed.[49] Indeed, the Cherokees were decidedly ambivalent about fish as a food. The idea of decayed fish revolted them, and to dream of decayed fish was a nightmare portending evil.

The Southeastern Indians fished for some of the largest freshwater fish in North America. Probably the most important of these were several varieties of catfish. It was not uncommon for blue cats (*Ictalurus furcatus* [Lesueur]) and channel cats (*Ictalurus punctatus*

[Rafinesque]) to weigh in excess of one hundred pounds, and catfish ranks with salmon in having the highest caloric content of any fish.[50] Other large fish were the spoonbill cat, or paddlefish (*Polyodon spathula* [Walbaum]); the common sturgeon (*Acipenser oxyrhynchus* Mitchill and *A. brevirostrom* Leseuer), a large and delicious fish of the Atlantic coast; and gar pikes (*Lepisosteus osseus* [L.], *L. platyrhinchus* DeKay, *L. spatula* Lacepede). They also caught several varieties of smaller fish, including shad, suckers, bass, perch, sunfish, and mullet.

One of their most effective fishing techniques was the use of various kinds of fish traps and weirs (fig. 71). They built these in shallow tidewater along the Atlantic Coast by driving small poles into the bottom of the ocean near the shore, interweaving them with reeds or oak splints. These weirs were arranged so that it was easy for fish to swim into them, but difficult or impossible to escape. One method was to build a weir all the way across a small tidal creek, so that fish were trapped at low tide after the water went out. In rocky rivers, particularly near the fall line where the current was swift and the water shallow, the Indians made fish traps out of rocks. They piled them up to form a V-shaped dam across the river, with the V pointing down stream. They placed conical fish traps at the apex of the V in such a way that fish were forced into them by the current and impeded from swimming back out. Some of the remains of these rock fish traps still exist in the Southeastern rivers today. The Choctaws made an ingenious cylindrical fish trap out of a fresh buffalo hide. The fresh blood from the hide attracted catfish. When a fisherman saw a catfish enter, he pulled a string to close the trap.[51]

Fish were also caught in several kinds of nets. A favorite was the dip net, which consisted of a long pole with a hoop attached to one end and a net affixed to the hoop. The fisherman caught fish simply by dipping the net into the water. In some coastal areas large, coarse-mesh gill nets were used with perforated shells as sinkers and small pieces of wood or gourds as floats. These were extended out into the water from the beaches, and fish became entangled in them.[52]

The Southeastern Indians also caught fish by spearing them. They used green cane spears with sharpened points and spears tipped with spikes taken from the tails of horseshoe crabs and stingrays. They frequently used spears while floating along in their dugout

The manner of their fishing.

Figure 71. Fishing techniques of Carolina Algonkian Indians. A weir across a channel is pictured at upper left. The dugout canoe contains a fire basin; the man at the rear is probably wielding a multiple pronged fish spear; a small dip-net rests against the stern. The two Indians in the background are spearing fish. John White drawing. Courtesy, Trustees of the British Museum.

canoes, and they probably also used them in the shallow waters at rapids and shoals. When they struck a large fish, they sometimes let the spear go, allowing its buoyancy to tire the fish and float it to the top of the water. In some places they hunted fish at night with fires built in clay basins in their dugout canoes. These basins were elevated so that the fire burned a couple of inches above the top of the dugout, attracting and illuminating the fish. One man tended the fire while others speared the fish. They also killed fish with the bow and arrow, impaling them with arrows with lines attached to wooden floats which kept the fish from escaping and which exhausted them.[53]

The Southeastern Indians used a fishhook with a straight (see fig. 10) shank and a rather heavy U-shaped hook made from deer and turkey bones. They evidently used most of these hooks on "trot lines," where a line was stretched in the water across a stream with several short lines, each with a baited hook, attached to it. Several times a day a fisherman inspected his trot line, pulling himself along the line in a dugout canoe, removing fish and rebaiting hooks. The use of hooks on a pole and line was apparently uncommon.[54]

In late summer, when the water in small rivers and streams was low, the Indians caught fish by poisoning them. The two favorite poisons were the buckeye (*Aesculus* L.) and the root of the plant "devil's shoestring" (*Tephrosia virginiana* [L.] Pers.). The buckeyes were pounded up and placed in pools of water; when the poison took effect, fish would float to the top of the water with their bellies up. The Indians pounded up devil's shoestring on posts resting on the bottom of the water, allowing the pieces to fall in. The active ingredient in devil's shoestring is the same as that in rotenone, an organic poison. The poison attacked the nervous system of the fish and did not spoil the meat in any way.

The Indians used a rather dramatic technique to catch the sturgeon, which in former times swam up southern rivers to spawn. They simply dropped a lasso over the tail of one of the large, sluggish fish and then held on for dear life. They were sometimes dragged into and beneath the water as the fish struggled to escape, but if they could hold on until the fish was exhausted, they could land it.

The Southeastern Indians fully exploited most of the animal life their environment had to offer, and their exploitation of plant life was just as thorough. We recall that in their belief system plants were considered to be friends of man. The Indians had a keen interest in plants, and they were astute botanical observers. This is reflected in some of the names the Cherokees gave to plants. They called mistletoe *udali* "it is married," because mistletoe always has its roots in the bark of another tree or shrub. Bear grass (*Eryngium* L.) was called *salikwayi* "greensnake," because of its long slender leaves. The lady's-slipper (*Cypripedium* L.)—a wild flower—was called *gugwe ulasula* "partridge moccasin." The shield fern (*Dryopteris* Adans.) was called *yan-utsestu* "the bear lies on it," presumably because bears like to sleep in fern beds. Many other examples could be cited.[55]

Among the Southeastern Indians women, old people, and smaller children had the job of collecting wild vegetables, berries, fruits, nuts, and seeds, and there were some of these to be collected in every season of the year. The Southeast abounded in a variety of wild plant foods, which constituted an important part of the Indian diet. The most important wild vegetables were roots and tubers of various kinds. The roots which the Creeks called red coontie were particularly important. These are the large tuberous roots which grow on several species of *Smilax* L., a bristly green briar that twines about trees throughout most of the Southeast. *Smilax pseudo-china* L. is easiest to gather because it has the least thorns, but the roots of all species are edible. The roots are best when collected in the fall, winter, or spring.[56] The food which the Seminoles called white coontie was the starchy root of *Zamia*, which grows in many places in southern Florida.[57]

"Indian potatoes" or "ground nuts" (*Apios americana* Medic.) are about the size of walnuts. They can be collected throughout the year, but they are best from late summer to spring.[58] The "wild sweet potato" (*Ipomoea pandurata* L.), more generally known as wild morning glory, has a large taproot which can weigh as much as fifteen to thirty pounds. The best time to collect it is from fall to spring.[59] They collected "swamp potatoes" from the root of arrowhead (*Sagittaria* L.), which grows in wet swamps and shallow waters. The best time to collect it is in late summer and fall.[60] The crisp, tuberous roots of Jerusalem artichoke (*Helianthus tuberosus* L.), a relative of the sunflower, could be collected in fall and winter.

The Southeastern Indians enjoyed a variety of wild fruits and berries. The most important fruit was the persimmon (*Diospyros* virginiana L.), a small tree-borne fruit that is highly astringent until late fall or early winter, when it develops a delicious datelike flavor. Eating an underripe persimmon is an unforgettable experience; they should be gathered after they have fallen to the ground and are soft and pulpy. The Indians gathered several varieties of wild grapes—muscadines and scuppernongs—which mainly grow in swamps and along the banks of rivers. They also ate wild cherries, papaws (Asimina triloba L.), tart crab apples (Malus coronaria [L.] Mill.), and small, reddish-orange wild plums (Prunus L.). Where available, they ate prickly pears (Opuntia Mill.) and maypops (Passiflora incarnata L.).

They picked and ate large quantities of berries during the summer months, including blackberries, gooseberries, raspberries, and small but sweet wild strawberries. From trees they picked huckleberries, tart black gum berries, mulberries, serviceberries, and palmetto berries.

In the fall they collected huge quantities of nuts. The most important were chestnuts (Castanea dentata [Marsh.] Borkh.), now almost extinct since the chestnut blight of 1905, chinquapins (C. pumila [L.] Mill.), a small variety of chestnut, pecans (in the northwestern part of the Southeast), several kinds of hickory nuts, and black walnuts. Along the Atlantic and Gulf coasts they ate the acorns of the live oak (Quercus virginiana Mill.), and in the interior certain other oak trees had acorns with bitter but edible kernels, especially the post oak (Quercus stellata Wang.) but also the white oak (Quercus alba L.), chestnut oak (Quercus prinus L.), and a few others. The acorns of the live oak were the least bitter of all the oaks, and from them the Indians derived an oil with a flavor similar to almond oil. Nuts were unusually important in the Indian diet. When the United States negotiated its first treaty with the Seminoles in 1823, the Seminoles were informed that they would have to abandon their villages along the Suwannee and Apalachicola rivers and move to the interior below Tampa Bay. They objected strenuously, saying among other things that hickory nuts, acorns, and persimmons did not grow there, and they could not get along without them. [61]

The Southeastern Indians collected several kinds of seeds which could readily be stored for use in winter. Cockspurgrass (Echinochloa Beau V.) produces an abundant seed from midsummer to fall which can be parched and ground into a meal. [62] The nelumbo, a large water lily (*Nelumbo lutea* [Willd.] Pers.) produces a large seed which can be collected in summer and fall, and the roots and young leaves of this plant are also edible.[63] Both the small and large varieties of cane (*Arundinaria tecta* [Walt.] Muhl., and *A. gigantea* [Walt.] Muhl.) produce an edible seed. But the small variety of cane only produces seed every three or four years, and the large variety produces seed even more irregularly.[64] Chenopodium produces large quantities of small black seeds which can be ground into a meal, and its tender leaves can be cooked to make a delicious spinach.[65] One species, "Mexican tea" or "worm seed" (*Chenopodium ambrosioides* L.) is mildly poisonous; the Indians used it to rid themselves of worms.[66]

The Southeastern Indians seem to have made relatively little use of mushrooms, although the Natchez ate a variety which grew at the foot of walnut trees, and in more recent times the Cherokees are known to have eaten several varieties.[67] Along the coast the Indians ate the crisp new growths from the top of the cabbage palmetto (*Sabal palmetto*); these can be eaten raw or cooked. Salt was collected and refined at the salt licks in various parts of the Southeast. The Indians sometimes added to their food hickory ash, the ashes of animal bones, or the ash of a certain moss. The sweet pulp from the pod of the honey locust tree (*Gleditsia triacanthos* L.) is edible, and the Indians sometimes dried it, ground it up, and used it as a sweetener.

Extensive as it seems, this account of the wild animal, fish, and vegetable foods exploited by the Southeastern Indians is incomplete. Their hunting and gathering represented the accumulated knowledge of the several millennia of Archaic and Woodland prehistory. We shall never know the full extent of their exploitation of wild foods because both the archaeological and historical records are incomplete. Perhaps we can gain some inkling of it from the Indians of the Upper Great Lakes, who utilized an estimated 400 to 500 plants, approximately 20 percent of all the vascular plants in their environment.[68] The Southeastern Indians may have used an even greater number of plants because a greater number of plant species was present in their environment.

On the margins of the Southeast, something of the old Archaic and Woodland patterns survived into the early historic period. Perhaps the closest example we have of an Archaic Culture was observed on

287

Galveston Island by Cabeza de Vaca, who was marooned there for several years. But because the island lacked the abundance of plant and animal life found in the Southeastern heartland, the way of life of this isolated group of Indians is only a partial guide to the Southeastern Archaic way of life. Even when we keep in mind that Cabeza de Vaca was experiencing this life as an outsider from a vastly different cultural tradition, we can still see that the Indians of Galveston Island had a hard time making a living.

From the time he left Aute on the lower Apalachicola River in western Florida, Cabeza de Vaca met no agriculturalists along the entire Gulf Coast. The Indians along the coast were organized into small kin groups apparently with no real chiefs. The only exception may have been a group of Indians that he met near Mobile Bay. Here he encountered five or six chiefs who were different in appearance from the rest, and who had probably come down from the interior.[69] When he reached Galveston Island, he was marooned, and so he took up life with the Indians. They had the bow and arrow, but they seldom killed large game. Their main food was a small fish, which they caught and dried.[70] From October until the end of February they subsisted mainly on small roots with a nutlike flavor which they dug out of swampy areas. Cabeza de Vaca's hands became so tender from digging these roots from beneath the waters that they would bleed, he said, if touched by a straw. In spring, when these roots began to sprout, they could no longer be used as food. When the weather became too inclement for fishing or digging roots, the Indians simply went hungry.[71] From February to April they went to the coast of the mainland and ate oysters, erecting mat-covered huts on the piles of oysters shells. Then for about one month they ate the blackberries which came ripe. For most of the summer they ate prickly pears and regarded them as a great delicacy. They kept the bones of small animals and ground them into meal, which they ate.[72] When worst came to worst, they ate spiders, ant pupae, lizards, and snakes.

This is perhaps the only written account of the kind of food-gathering economy from which the Mississippian cultural tradition arose. Though there is little doubt that life for food gatherers in the interior would have been less bleak, it is also easy to see the importance to the Southeastern Indians of the development of agriculture. Yet agriculture did not replace food gathering in the

288

Southeast, but existed side by side with it, making life more pleasant and secure.

RIVERINE AGRICULTURE

The domesticated foods of the Southeastern Indians were all vegetable, with the exception of the dogs they sometimes ate. At Guaquili, somewhere on the headwaters of the Savannah River, the

Figure 72. Negative painted dog effigy pot. Noel Cemetery, Nashville. This possibly represents the small dogs mentioned by the chroniclers of the de Soto expedition. Courtesy, Thruston Collection, Vanderbilt University.

289

Indians gave de Soto and his men several small dogs specially bred to be used as food. These dogs are reported to have been unable to bark, but little else is known about them (fig. 72).[73] Moreover, we have seen that in their feasts preparatory to war, Natchez warriors would roast a large dog and eat it to symbolize the fidelity with which they would follow the leader of their raiding party.[74] The Southeastern Indians did not possess the domesticated turkey, as did the Indians of the Southwest. But as we have already seen, even if the deer and turkey cannot be regarded as semidomesticated, the Southeastern Indians unquestionably increased their numbers by their practice of burning the woods.

The story is widespread, almost an article of faith, that in 1621 an Indian named Squanto taught the Plymouth colonists to fertilize their corn fields with fish. But it now appears that this practice was European in origin rather than Indian. Squanto was captured in 1614 and taken to Spain and England, and later he returned and lived in the Guy Colony in Newfoundland. Fish fertilizer was used both in Europe and in the Guy Colony; Squanto probably learned of it there and later passed his knowledge on to the Plymouth colonists.[75]

We have no evidence that the Southeastern Indians fertilized their fields. Ordinarily this would have meant that after growing crops on a field for a number of years the soil would have become exhausted, and they would have had to allow the land to lie fallow for several years until it recovered its fertility. The early history of the Southeast is full of reports of Indian "old fields"—abandoned agricultural fields—and this could be evidence that they did not practice permanent cultivation. But contrary to what anthropologists once thought, the Southeastern Indians do not seem to have practiced the kind of agriculture known as "forest-fallow" or "swidden" agriculture, in which a field is cropped for one to three years and then allowed to lie fallow for as long as ten or twenty years until the fields gradually become reforested and renewed.[76] The towns and villages of the Southeastern Indians were both large and, for the most part, rather permanent, and in the Mississippian period they had a rather complex political organization. Swidden agriculture can support such large and stable settlements only when the main crop is a root vegetable, such as manioc, sweet potatoes, or yams, for these are easy to cultivate and do not make great demands on soil fertility.

But the staple of the Southeastern Indians was corn, a seed crop which quickly exhausts the soil unless the soil can be renewed.[77]

Southeastern Indian agriculture might seem therefore to be something of a puzzle. It resembled swidden agriculture in some respects, but its main vegetable was corn, which exhausts land quickly, yet it supported a large and stable population. Several observations illuminate the situation even if they do not resolve it completely. For one thing, the Southeastern Indians relied on agriculture for only part of their food, obtaining a significantly large proportion by hunting, fishing, and gathering wild foods.[78] Consequently, their need for agricultural land was not as great as it would have been had they depended primarily on agriculture. Another factor is that the land they used for their fields was the rich bottom land along the courses of rivers. This riverine land was ideal for corn: it was rich in the nutrients that corn requires, it was light and easily tilled with simple tools, and it possessed the good drainage properties that are necessary for corn. When fallowed, it would have recovered rather quickly. Furthermore, while not wishing to draw a hasty analogy with archaic systems of farming in Egypt and Mesopotamia, the rivers in the Southeast did flood periodically, and in those places where backwaters stood, silt would have been deposited and the land would have thereby been renewed without having to lie fallow for many years.[79]

For all of these reasons, the term "riverine" seems appropriate for the type of agriculture practiced by the Southeastern Indians.[80] It was a type of agriculture that was intensive, in that a sizable quantity of food was grown on a rather small quantity of land, and only these favored riverine soils were farmed. The Indians avoided the yellow and red clays that predominate in the Southeast because these soils would have been difficult to work with simple tools and would have lost their nutrients quickly, requiring, in effect, swidden cultivation.

The loamy alluvial soil that was preferred for farming occurred in bands of varying widths along rivers throughout the Southeast. Before it was cleared this land was usually covered with canebrakes, making it noteworthy that corn and cane thrive on the same kinds of soil. These canebrakes were often bordered by a river on one side and a swamp on the other, this being due to the process by which the levee ridges were formed. When the river flooded and the land was covered with backwater, the coarser particles, including sand, were the first to fall out of suspension, and ridges were thereby formed next to the river. As the floodwater backed further onto the shore, soil consisting of finer particles was deposited, and the poor drainage properties of this soil caused the formation of swamps. Along the Mississippi River these rich levee ridges were sometimes as high as twenty-five feet and as wide as three miles. Along smaller rivers and streams they were, of course, proportionately smaller.

The Southeastern Indians generally preferred to build their villages and towns on ridges or bluffs above the flood level of the rivers. The size of the Caddoan villages, on the western margins of the Southeastern Culture Area, was more or less determined by the availability of riverine land and an adequate supply of firewood.[81] The same was probably true for the Indians in the rest of the Southeast. The dispersal of Cherokee villages in the narrow Appalachian valleys, for example, seems to have been governed by these same factors. In Creek towns, and probably in Indian settlements throughout the Southeast, the women cultivated kitchen gardens in addition to the large fields in the river bottoms, and these were located in and around the town itself. Towns were occasionally moved, and it is possible that this was in part owing to the fact that the land for these garden plots would gradually become exhausted, as would the firewood supply. As the town became surrounded by more and more useless land, the women would have to walk farther and farther to tend their gardens and gather firewood until at last the town would become an undesirable place to live.

The main agricultural crops of the Southeastern Indians were several varieties of corn, beans, and squash. At the time of European colonization two basic races of corn (Zea mays L.) were cultivated in the eastern United States: the tropical flint corn, which reached the eastern United States at around 200 B.C., and eastern flint corn, which reached the eastern United States around A.D. 800 to 1000. Because this eastern flint corn could germinate in a cool, moist climate, it came to be preferred over the older, less adaptable tropical flint corn, particularly in the central Plains and in the Northeast, where this was the first type of corn which could be successfully raised. In time the Indians in the Plains and the Northeast developed this eastern flint corn into a hard northern flint corn which was especially adapted to a short growing season.[82] Today descendants of the tropical flint corn are grown in many places as popcorn.[83] A third race of corn, dent corn—so called because each kernel has a dent in it—was definitely cultivated by the Natchez in the early 1700s, but was a late import from Mexico.[84] For the Natchez, dent corn was their favorite for making hominy meal.[85] A fourth kind of corn, sweet corn, was also grown in some places in North America.[86]

If the Southeastern Indians were like the Iroquois and the Indians of the Upper Missouri River, they would have distinguished by name several different strains of corn on the basis of color, shape, size, and so on.[87] We shall probably never know the particulars of how they classified their corn, but we do know that they distinguished two broad categories: early corn and late corn. The early corn ripened in ten to twelve weeks, growing on a stalk six or seven feet high and producing small ears four or five inches long. They picked this early corn when it was green. The late corn, on the other hand, ripened in about fourteen weeks, growing on a stalk as high as ten feet and producing ears seven inches or more in length.[88]

Indians in the eastern United States began cultivating beans at about the same time they began cultivating the eastern flint corn, at around A.D. 800 to 1000.[89] The common bean (*Phaseolus vulgaris* L.) occurs in hundreds of varieties, including kidney, navy, pinto, snap, and pole beans. Some of these beans grow on bushy plants, while others grow on vines, requiring that they be planted alongside cornstalks or poles.[90] Most of these varieties ripen in about ten weeks. We know that the Southeastern Indians grew several varieties of beans, but we do not know precisely how many.

Indians in the eastern United States began cultivating squash perhaps as early as 1000 B.C., far earlier than they began cultivating corn and beans. They planted the northern species, *Cucurbita pepo* L., a species comprising pumpkins and summer squashes.[91] Squash is a good vegetable because it is relatively easy to grow and it is highly productive. Some varieties of squash could be stored in a cool, dry place and kept through the winter.

Corn, beans, and squash were unusually well suited to each other. When grown in the same field they complemented each other, and in recognition of their basic compatibility the Iroquois called them the "three sisters." All three thrive in a moist environment with a moderately high temperature, and all three can tolerate the acidic soils that predominate in the Southeast. Corn and beans are particularly suited to each other, because while corn removes nitrogen from the soil, beans replace nitrogen, and the soil is therefore exhausted more slowly. Moreover, beans and corn complement each other in a dietary sense. Corn supplies some of the protein which is essential for good nutrition, but it lacks the amino acid lysine, which, as it turns out, is relatively abundant in beans. Thus when eaten together corn and beans are a relatively good source of vegetable protein.[92]

To some extent the Southeastern Indians continued cultivating or utilizing the plants of the old Eastern Agricultural Complex, namely sunflower, sumpweed,[93] chenopodium,[94] pigweed, knotweed, giant ragweed, and canary grass. The Natchez planted a small seed which may have been chenopodium, but this plant is so prolific it would probably have come up in the disturbed soil of their gardens whether they planted it or not.[95] All of these plants probably lost ground after the cultivation of corn and beans became widespread. Of the three, sunflowers remained the most important, yielding large quantities of oily seeds rich in vitamins. With their hard shells, sunflower seeds would have been easy to store for use in winter. And considering the importance of the sun in their belief system, the Southeastern Indians would not have failed to notice that the sunflower turns to face the sun when it rises, and then follows it across the heavens to where it sets in the west.

A final plant which was important in the agriculture of the Southeastern Indians was the bottle gourd (*Lagenaria siceraria*), one of the oldest plants cultivated in North America, dating to before 1000 B.C.[96] They cultivated it not for food, but for a truly remarkable variety of material uses. The bottle gourd grows to different sizes, ranging from a few inches to as much as fourteen inches in diameter. Its form varies from a small globular shape with a long neck to a large globular shape with a vestigial neck. Its most important property is that when cured it has a hard shell that is superior to pottery in that it is break resistant and very light. From the bottle gourd the Southeastern Indians made water vessels, dippers, ladles, cups, bowls, bird houses, rattles, masks, and many other things. The large gourds made especially good water vessels. These were made simply by cutting a hole a few inches in diameter on one side of the gourd near the top (fig. 73). This was both the mouth of the vessel and the handle, for the Indians could carry it by hooking their fingers into the hole. Water would soak very slowly through the walls of the

294

gourd, but this was desirable, for as it evaporated it cooled the water inside.[97]

The Southeastern Indians readily adopted several fruits and vegetables from the European colonists. Within a few years they were cultivating large orchards of fig and peach trees, and they became particularly fond of watermelons.[98] They also readily adopted chickens, pigs, horses, and to a lesser extent cattle from the colonists, but centuries passed before these domesticated animals supplanted wild meat in their diet.

The Southeastern Indians initially cleared their fields of large trees by girdling them with rings cut into the bark. Before contact they used stone axes for this, but European steel axes were so superior that they quickly became one of the items which were most desired by the Indians. After the girdled trees died, they were either burned or simply left to stand and rot. Fields that had been used the year before had to be cleared in the spring of the weeds and cane that had grown up in the past season. Although agriculture was principally a woman's occupation, the initial clearing of the fields was done by men.

The time when the crops were planted depended upon the climate. In the southerly parts of the Southeast, the first planting of early corn usually came in March or April; in the northerly parts the first planting usually came in May. They planted the early corn as soon as the threat of frost had passed, but they waited another month or so before planting the late corn because by that time there were wild foods available to deflect the attention of crows and other pests. Early corn was planted in the garden plots in and around the town, and late corn was planted in the large fields in the river bottoms. The garden plots were planted by the women, while the large fields were planted by both sexes. The labor in the large fields was communal. Early in the morning of a working day, one of the old leaders would stand on top of a mound or in the plaza and call all of the people out to work. Those who failed to come had fines imposed upon them. Before the Natchez planted seed, they took it to the Great Sun to have it sanctified.[99] This may have been done in one form or another throughout the Southeast.

Although labor was communal, the large fields were divided into individual allotments. Each household or lineage had its own plot, separated from the others by a strip of untilled soil. All the people

Figure 73. A Carolina Algonkian woman and her daughter. The woman holds a large bottle gourd; the girl holds an Elizabethan doll. John White drawing. Courtesy, Trustees of the British Museum.

worked together on one plot until it was worked up and planted, and then they moved on to another. In some cases an entire field would be cultivated by the people of a chiefdom and its produce turned over to the chief to use for ritual occasions and for redistribution to people in need.[100] Planting had a festive quality, and there was always a great deal of singing and joking. They worked the soil with digging sticks and with short hoes that had wooden handles and blades made of shell, flint, or the shoulder blade of a large mammal.[101] The Indians did not till the entire field, but instead worked up small "hills" a foot or more in diameter. This both prevented soil erosion and preserved the fertility of the soil longer than did the plow-agriculture introduced by the European colonists.[102] Hills were laid out in straight lines and spaced three or four feet apart in both directions. Laying out the corn in a regular pattern made weeding easier later on. In each hill the Indians made a cluster of four to six holes spaced about one or two inches apart. Seed that had been soaked for a day to hasten germination was dropped in, one grain to a hole. A little hill of dirt was then piled over each group of seeds. Some of the Indians carefully planted just four grains of corn in each cluster; others probably planted more and thinned out the less robust stalks after they came up.

The kind of soil suitable for riverine agriculture was scarce, and because of its scarcity, the agricultural strategy of the Southeastern Indians was designed to produce maximum yield from relatively small fields. They accomplished this by two techniques: intercropping and multiple cropping.[103] Intercropping was the planting of several kinds of vegetables mixed together in the same field. As we have seen, corn, beans, and squash complemented each other. The Indians planted corn and beans together so that as the bean vines grew up they twined around the corn stalks. In between the hills of corn and around the edges of the field they planted gourds, squash, pumpkins, and sunflowers, and chenopodium came up wherever they allowed it to grow.[104]

Multiple cropping was the planting of two successive crops on the same field in one season. The Southeastern Indians used this technique on their early corn, which ripened early and was picked and eaten green. As soon as they could clear the field of the first crop, they planted another crop in the same field to be eaten later in the season. Along with several other Indian gardening techniques, multiple cropping is still used today by some Southern gardeners. In the North, where the growing season is too short to allow multiple cropping, the Iroquois and Algonkians staggered the planting of their corn. That is, they planted a field in several stages, a couple of weeks apart, so that the corn would not all come ripe at the same time.[105] It is easy to see that this would have produced less corn per acre than the multiple cropping technique in the Southeast.

In their large fields, the Southeastern Indians planted only a single crop of late corn. This was not because it took late corn that much longer to ripen, but because late corn had to be allowed to mature and dry out before it could be harvested. Some late corn was eaten green, but most of it was dried for use later in making hominy.

After they planted their corn, cultivation consisted of "hilling" the corn, keeping predators away, and keeping the weeds down. After the corn came up a few inches, the Indians hilled it by piling loose dirt around the roots. Corn requires a large quantity of water during its growing season, but it also needs good drainage so that the plants do not drown. Hilling helps satisfy both of these requirements. Furthermore, corn has roots that are relatively weak and shallow for its size, and hilling helps keep the stalks from being blown over by the wind.

An unusual variant of hilling has been found at several Mississippian sites. At Ocmulgee and at two sites in Illinois archaeologists have found evidence of agricultural fields in which the topsoil was heaped up into parallel ridges. At Ocmulgee these ridges were about 20 centimeters high and 30 to 50 centimeters apart. The advantages of this type of cultivation are not well understood. One possibility is that it may have been an adaptation to water-logged soil.[106]

People stayed on watch in the fields during the day in order to frighten away bird and animal pests. At night fires were sometimes built around the fields for the same purpose. This job of watching the fields usually fell to old women, or to young boys under the supervision of old men. Watching the fields was a rather dangerous and sometimes fatal occupation because enemies would seize upon the watchman's lack of protection for a surprise attack.

Some of the Southeastern Indians employed a particularly clever way of keeping pests out of their gardens. They placed poles around the gardens and on the poles they hung gourd houses for purple martins. Purple martins not only consume large numbers of insects each day, but they are also aggressive toward crows and blackbirds, both of which are especially destructive of newly planted corn. Some evidence suggests that the Indians may also have encouraged the nesting of swifts and wrens, which also eat insect pests and chase away crows and blackbirds.[107]

When the corn was about one foot high, the Indians went through their fields with hoes, cutting down the weeds. Some repeated this weeding several times during the summer, but others were less meticulous, letting the weeds grow up to compete with their crops. Each time they weeded the corn, they hilled it a little more, until by the end of the summer a noticeable mound of earth was piled around the bases of the stalks. Some of the Indians "suckered" their corn by breaking off the secondary shoots which grew at the bases of the stalks. This was to make the ears grow larger, increasing the yield. In August, after growth had stopped, the ears of the late corn were bent down against the stalk to keep water from running into the husk and rotting the corn.

They harvested this late corn as soon as it was dry enough, usually in September or October. Each household or lineage harvested its own plot of corn, though in some places the plot assigned to the chief was harvested with volunteer labor from the entire town. They went through the fields collecting the ears of corn in large pack baskets carried on their backs (see fig. 106). In some places each household or lineage contributed a portion of its crop to the chief's store.

The last essential step in raising a crop of corn was storing it and keeping it safe from field mice and other animals. In some places the Indians stored their corn in cribs raised seven or eight feet from the ground on posts which were polished so mice could not climb them. The crib itself was plastered inside and out with mud. The only entrance was a small door which was sealed with mud each time it was used. They stacked the ears of corn in rows, with the better corn near the back of the crib, and the poorer corn near the entrance where it could be used first. In other places the Southeastern Indians stored their corn in special rooms in the houses in which they lived. The Choctaws sometimes protected ears of dried corn from insects by wrapping each one with grass and then plastering it all over with wet clay mixed with grass. In this manner they were able to keep corn from one year to another.[108]

PRESERVING AND COOKING FOOD

Acquiring food was only part of the total subsistence pattern of the Southeastern Indians; food also had to be preserved for use in the future and cooked to make it edible or more palatable. The Indians' favorite way of preserving food, whether meat or vegetable, was by drying it. They dried some of their fruits and vegetables in the heat of the sun. After squeezing persimmons into a pulp, they spread the pulp out in flat loaves about half an inch thick; when dried in the sun it made a sort of candy which would keep for weeks or even months, depending on how dry they made it. They also sundried wild plums, berries, and grapes. A quicker way to dry food was to put it on hurdles placed over a fire. A hurdle was simply a horizontal frame-work of woven saplings and canes resting on four posts (see fig. 74). Some foods, such as wild fruits, pumpkins, fish, and meat were dried directly on the hurdles, but others, such as wild roots, corn, oysters, and probably beans were first boiled for a short time before being dried.

The Indians cut buffalo and deer meat into moderately thin slabs, speared them on spits made of cane or saplings, and placed them over a fire, cooking them until they were quite dry. When removed from the spits, each piece of dried meat was left with a hole through which a cord could be strung, and the meat could thereby be easily stored or carried. Meat which was prepared this way would keep for at least four to six months without spoiling, and it sometimes kept for as long as one year.[109] The Indians frequently built a smoky fire, often using green hickory wood, to give a smoked flavor and aroma to the meat dried over it. Oysters and fish were smoked in this fashion along the Gulf Coast. After the oysters were quite dry, they were put in a bag to protect them from insects and hung in a dry place. All of this dried food, both domesticated and wild, was kept by the Indians in their food storehouses.

Bear meat, with its thick layers of fat, was treated differently. First the Southeastern Indians separated the fat from the lean meat, cooking or drying the lean portion like any other meat.[110] The fat was cooked in earthen pots and an oil was extracted from it. The Indians stored this oil in large earthen containers and in gourds. They used it as a condiment, a cooking oil, and even as a cosmetic. For use as a cosmetic, they mixed a red pigment into it and scented it with fragrant sassafras and wild cinnamon. They rubbed it into their hair and onto their bodies. Some Southeastern Indians stored bear oil in bags made from whole deerskins.[111]

Nutmeats were extremely important in the Southeastern diet. Nuts could be cracked and eaten raw, they could be stored for a time in their shells, and they could also be dried and preserved for a longer period of time. In addition, black walnuts, hickory nuts, and acorns provided another source of oil. The Indians were particularly fond of oil from hickory nuts, which they made by first pounding a quantity of the nuts into small pieces on nut stones—stones with several small depressions for cracking a handful of nuts at a time. They then stirred the pieces, shell and all, into a pot of water. In time the shells sank to the bottom and the oil floated to the top as a milky emulsion to be skimmed off and preserved. One hundred pounds of hickory nuts would produce about one gallon of oil. The Europeans called it "hickory milk." The Indians used it for cooking and seasoning. Hickory milk was said to impart a particularly delicious flavor to venison and to corn bread.[112]

The Southeastern Indians thoroughly cooked all the meat they ate; they never ate it raw. They used two methods of cooking it: broiling and boiling. Small animals received a minimum of dressing before cooking. Sometimes they did not gut such animals as raccoon, opossum, rabbit, and squirrel; they simply skinned them and cooked them whole. They barbecued fish, small animals, and pieces of meat of larger animals by impaling them on one end of a sharpened stick; the other end of the stick was stuck in the ground with the stick inclined toward the fire (fig. 74). They turned the stick from time to time to cook the meat evenly.[113] They impaled larger pieces of meat on spits, suspending them on two forked sticks and turning the spits as the meat cooked. The Cherokees often used spits made of sourwood (*Oxydendrum arboreum* [L.] D.C.); it imparted a pleasing flavor to the meat and was thought to repel witches.

They were fonder than we of soups and stews. After barbecuing fish, squirrel, or ground hog, they would make it into a stew, adding a little cracked hominy or hominy meal.[114] They boiled meat and fish with vegetables to make a soup. Bear and deer meat, for example, were boiled along with squash and kernels cut from ears of green corn (fig. 75). They were especially fond of kidney beans boiled with meat and seasoned with bear oil. The milky pulp of green corn was sometimes added to boiled venison to make a kind of hash. The Indians shredded or pounded dried meat before boiling it in soups, and they also ate dried meat after adding bear oil to it, much as we add mayonnaise to dry luncheon meat.

The belief system of the Southeastern Indians affected their way of thinking about food just as it affected all other realms of life. This was particularly noticeable in food prohibitions. For example, meat and vegetables could be cooked in the same pot, as could different kinds of four-footed animal meat, but they would not cook the flesh of birds and four-footed animals in the same pot. This was simply another manifestation of their insistence on keeping This World and the Upper World separate.

Corn was by far the most important single vegetable food in the

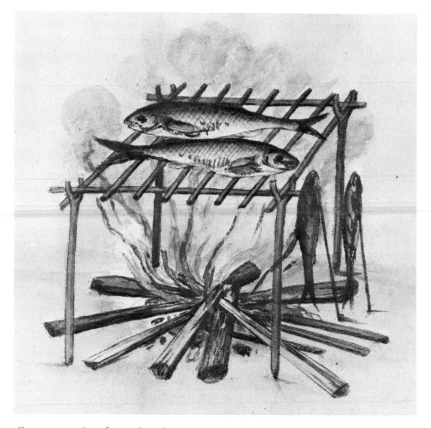

Figure 74. Carolina Algonkian method of broiling fish over an open fire. John White drawing. Courtesy, Trustees of the British Museum.

diet of the Southeastern Indians. The Natchez cooked at least forty-two different named dishes using corn, and other Southeastern Indians must have been able to do the same.[115] The simplest way to eat corn was to pick it green and roast it in the coals of a fire. They ate their early corn and some of their late corn this way. Roasted green corn was a particular favorite at the Green Corn Ceremony.[116]

Figure 75. Carolina Algonkian method of cooking food in a large pot with a conical base. John White drawing. Courtesy, Trustees of the British Museum.

The staple food of the Southeastern Indians, their staff of life, was hominy. Its manufacture required several special implements, including a mortar and pestle (see fig. 111). In historic times, and probably in prehistoric times as well, a mortar was made from a section of a hickory, oak, or beech log some twelve to twenty inches in diameter and about two feet long. The Indians rested this on one end, and in the other end they burned out a conical hole about eight inches deep. For a pestle they cut a section from a tree, preferably hickory, about six inches in diameter and five or six feet long. They trimmed this down to about two inches in diameter for about four-fifths of its length, leaving the remainder as a weight at the upper end of the pestle. The small end was used to pound the corn in the mortar, while the large, weighted end added force to the pounding. Wood-ash lye was also needed in making hominy. The Indians made it by placing hardwood ashes in a container with a small hole in the bottom. They filled the container with the ashes and poured in a quantity of cold water. The yellow liquid which dripped out of the hole was lye.

This technique of processing corn with wood-ash lye has been found to reduce some of its essential amino acids, but it dramatically increases the amount of the amino acid lysine and also the amount of niacin. Thus this treatment of corn enhances its nutritional value selectively. For people whose diet depended heavily on corn, this technique probably reduced the incidence of pellegra.[117]

Cracked hominy was one of the most important items in the Southeastern Indian diet. The process of its manufacture began with the placing of a quantity of thoroughly dry kernels of corn into a vessel filled with cool water to which was added a cup of wood-ash lye. After soaking it overnight, the corn was drained and placed in a mortar and lightly pounded with a pestle to crack the grains and loosen the hulls. The cracked grain was then separated from the hulls in a fanner, a large flat basket with a shallow pocket on one side. The corn was placed, a little at a time, on the flat part of the fanner. When the fanner was agitated, the heavier pieces of hominy rolled into the pocket while the lighter husks remained on the flat part to be flipped away. The cracked hominy was then emptied from the pocket and the process repeated until all the hulls had been separated out.

From cracked hominy the Indians made a kind of soup by putting it in a pot of water and cooking it about four hours, stirring frequently and adding enough water to keep the mixture thin. For flavor, they sometimes added a little wood-ash lye until the hominy began to turn yellow. When the hominy was done they poured it in a large earthen jar, taking out portions to eat when they wanted it. The Creeks called this dish *sá•fki* ("sofkee"), the Cherokees called it *ganohe•ni*, and the Choctaws called it *tanfula*. They often set jars of it in a moderately warm place and allowed it to sour or ferment slightly. They usually drank it cold. The Choctaw dish *pishofa* was made by boiling together one part meat and two parts cracked hominy. Cracked hominy was a hospitality food. The Cherokees served it to visitors. Inside their houses the Choctaws kept a bowl of it with a spoon alongside and a visitor who failed to eat a little of it was considered impolite.[118]

When the Southeastern Indians made bread, they usually began by processing dry corn in the same way they did to make hominy. But instead of only cracking it in the mortar, they pounded it up into a fine meal, which they further refined by sifting it through a sifter, a loosely-woven basket made of cane. The fine meal that passed through the sifter was kept for making bread; the coarse meal which did not pass through was put into the mortar for more pounding or else kept out to be added to meat and vegetable dishes or to hominy soup.

The Southeastern Indians had three different ways of making bread: frying, boiling, and baking. In each of these they began by mixing boiling hot water with fine hominy meal to form a batter. For fritters a thin batter was fried in hot bear grease in a flat-bottomed pot. For baked bread they made a thick batter and formed it into small loaves or into a flat, round pone. They placed the loaves in a flat-bottomed pot, which was covered with an inverted pot, which in turn was covered with hot coals, making in effect a small Dutch oven.[119] A variant of this was pumpkin bread, made by adding cooked and mashed pumpkin pulp to the batter.[120] The Choctaws baked a dish called "bread in shucks" (*paluska holbi*) in a simpler way. They formed the thick batter into small loaves or rolls which they wrapped in dried corn shucks that had been softened in hot water. They tied the ends and middle of each loaf with strips of shuck. Then they buried the loaves in hot ashes and cooked them for about an hour.[121] The Creeks baked something they called "hard

305

bread" (*chuto-ahake*). They formed the batter into doughnut shapes, baked them until they were thoroughly done, and then put them in the sun until they had dried as hard as wood. They would then string them on a piece of cord and carry them to eat on their travels. They were so hard they had to be stewed before they were edible.[122]

The Southeastern Indians cooked several forms of boiled corn bread, each requiring a thick batter. They made one kind by shaping lumps of batter into rolls and wrapping them with corn shucks; these were dropped into boiling water and allowed to simmer for about an hour. They could be eaten freshly cooked, or they could be dried and kept for long periods of time. This was another of the foods they carried with them on their travels.[123] Another way of making boiled bread was to form the batter into balls or flat cakes and drop them into boiling water to make a kind of dumpling.

To vary their corn breads they frequently added to the batter seeds of various kinds, particularly sunflower seeds, and also such things as nuts, berries, and wild sweet potatoes. The type of corn bread they considered their greatest delicacy was chestnut bread, which they made by adding chopped chestnuts or chinquapins to the batter. Their most nutritious corn bread, and another of their favorites, they made by adding boiled beans.[124] As we have already seen, corn and beans together provide a reasonably good vegetable source of protein. One unusual condiment was made by placing bean hulls in a pot which was put over a fire until the hulls were reduced to ashes. When this ash was added to corn batter it turned it a greenish color and gave it a special flavor.[125]

In addition to cracked hominy and hominy meal, the Southeastern Indians had a different process for making something they called "cold meal" (Choctaw, *botah kapussa*; Cherokee, *gʌwi•sida*). They made this by shelling corn from the cob at the stage when the kernels were firm but not dry. It could also be made from dry corn by steeping the kernels in warm water overnight. They put the kernels of corn in a pot of ashes and parched the corn until it was brown, stirring it frequently to keep it from scorching. When it was brittle enough to be broken between the fingers, it was placed in a mortar and pounded into a fine meal. The final step was to put the meal on a fanner to remove the hulls.[126] Cold meal would keep for a long time, and to make it keep even longer they would sometimes dry the meal

306

further over a smoky fire. They ate it by simply adding it to twice its volume of cold water; in a few minutes the meal would swell up to form a thin gruel, which they drank. It could also be eaten dry. Cold meal was another of the foods they carried with them when they traveled. They stored and carried it in bags made of dressed animal skins.[127]

The Southeastern Indians had several ways of cooking beans. Their standard way was to boil them in water and season them, often with meat or bear oil. They made succotash by boiling together hominy and beans, sometimes adding some pumpkin to the pot.[128] After the Indians boiled their beans, they sometimes put them in a mortar and mashed them to a pulp which they formed into small loaves.

They cooked pumpkin and squash by boiling or broiling. They preserved pumpkin by cutting it into round slices which they peeled and dried.[129] Pumpkin and squash seeds could of course be roasted and eaten.

The wild roots the Southeastern Indians collected were usually made into a meal or a powder. Swamp potatoes (*Sagittaria* L.), for example, were baked in a Dutch oven or in the ashes of a fire and then put in a mortar and pounded into a meal. They used this meal as they would use hominy meal, relying on it especially during winter famines.[130] They made "red" coontie (Seminole, *kontí•*) out of the large roots of *Smilax*. They first chopped the roots into pieces and pulverized them in a mortar. They put this in a pot filled with cold water, stirring vigorously. After it settled for a time, they dipped out the liquid, leaving in the bottom of the pot a residue which they dried into a reddish powder. When this starchy powder was added to boiling water it turned into a kind of jelly and was a favorite food for infants and old people. It was also mixed with hominy meal to make fried bread. In most of south Florida the Seminoles made a "white" coontie out of the roots of plants of the genus *Zamia*. The large tuberous roots of this plant are poisonous, as are its stems, leaves, and seeds, but the Seminoles were able to extract enough poison from the root to make it edible. To do this, they first chopped the root into pieces and pounded it to a pulp in a mortar. They then saturated the pulp with water making a starchy liquid that was squeezed out of the pulp into a receptacle and allowed to settle. The water was skimmed off the top and the starchy sediment allowed to ferment. After a few days it was put in the sun to dry into a yellowish white flour that was used in much the same way as red coontie. Its taste has been described as insipid, but not unpleasant.[131]

Acorns were another interesting feature of the Southeastern Indian diet. In addition to extracting an oil from acorns, the Indians occasionally made the nut meats into a meal. Live oak acorns were best for this, but the several species of white oak were almost as good, and even the black and red oaks could be used if necessary. The primary problem in processing acorns was to extract the bitter-tasting acid from the nutmeats.[132] Some acorns were edible after merely being parched, but others had to be boiled in water to remove the tannic acid.[133] These were then pounded into a pulp which was dried into a meal and used in much the same way hominy meal was used. The Choctaws relied heavily on acorn meal in years when their corn crop was poor, suggesting, perhaps, that before the cultivation of corn began in earnest, acorns may have been the staple food.[134]

One way in which the cuisine of the Southeastern Indians differed sharply from our own is that while they would eat fresh fruit and nuts, they did not ordinarily eat uncooked vegetables.[135] The concept of a garden salad would probably have been repugnant to them. Slight exceptions to this may have been wild onions (*Allium cernuum* Roth), wild garlic (*Allium canadense* L.), and in the Appalachians wild leeks or "ramps" (*Allium tricoccum* Ait.). These were among the very few green vegetables available from late fall to early spring.[136] Modern Cherokees fry ramps in a pan with a little grease, but they also occasionally eat them raw, the rule being that *everyone* has to eat them so they can tolerate each other's breath—an extraordinary halitosis which can last for several days.[137] When de Soto was marching northward through Georgia, the Indians at one of the towns came out to meet him carrying small bundles of wild onions or garlic, suggesting that they had already learned something about Spanish food preferences.

We have little historical documentation of Southeastern Indian beverages, but we may assume that many of the beverages made from herbs and fruits by modern Indians are the same or similar to those made in earlier days by their ancestors. The roots of sassafras, for example, have probably long been used to make a fragrant hot tea. The roots are best when dug early in spring, and the bark from the roots has the strongest flavor. The young leaves and young pith of sassafras are highly mucilaginous. The Choctaws dried them and ground them into a powder which they used to thicken soups, this being the forerunner of Southern gumbo.[138] The Cherokees made a hot tea out of the dried leaves, twigs, and young buds of spicebush (*Lindera benzoin* [L.] Blume).[139] Another Cherokee drink is made of maypops (*Passiflora incarnata* L.) by boiling them in water until they become soft. The pulp is then squeezed out and put through a strainer. The Cherokees drink it while it is hot.[140] Another beverage that is still made by Cherokees today was made from the ripe pods of honey locust (*Gleditsia triacanthos* L.), which contain a kind of paste with a delicate sweet-sour flavor. The Indians split the pods in half, soaked them in water which was hot but not boiling, and strained it through a cloth. They drank it as both a hot and cold beverage.[141] White and black Southerners used to make this honey locust drink and ferment it, making a kind of beer. While it is conceivable that the Southeastern Indians made honey locust beer before European colonization, we have little evidence that they did. They evidently made little or no use of alcohol as a narcotic until they were introduced to rum in the days of the deerskin trade.

When faced with the prospect of starvation, the Southeastern Indians knew techniques for eating snakes, lizards, frogs, snails, and insects.[142] Indeed, into the present century some Cherokee women knew a recipe for making a soup out of yellow jacket larvae and a recipe for fried locusts.[143]

The Southeastern Indians did not eat regular meals. They ate whenever they were hungry. Except at feasts, the Natchez seldom ate together, and even at feasts the men and women ate separately from each other.[144] They ate food from pottery or gourd containers or from shallow wooden bowls carved out of gum, poplar, box elder, sycamore, or elm. They ate with large spoons made from gourds, wood, or bison horn, and they also ate with their fingers.

The reader will no doubt have noticed that many of these Southeastern Indian dishes live on today as the basic foods in traditional Southern cooking. This in fact is true to a far greater extent than most people have ever realized, as we will see in chapter 8.

ECONOMICS

We know far more about how the Southeastern Indians built their houses, hunted game, and raised their crops than we know about the manner in which they owned and exchanged property and goods. Like other preliterate people, their economic institutions were quite different from ours. One important difference was that they had no currency. All of their economic exchanges were in the form of barter, payment in kind, or gifts. The modern Cherokees have a word (ade•la) that means both "beads" and "money," but this does not necessarily mean that they formerly used beads for money, as is so often assumed. It may simply mean that the Cherokees saw a similarity between beads and money. Beads, like money, were not useful in themselves but were highly valued nonetheless. Beads, shell gorgets, and other ornaments undoubtedly were often used in barter, as in the example given by John Lawson when he reported that Indians in the Carolinas would trade three or four dressed buckskins for a well-made shell gorget.[145] But there is no evidence that beads were in any way an actual equivalent of money. We may be sure that in Mississippian times the Southeastern Indians exchanged labor for labor and goods for goods. Even the British deerskin trade was mainly conducted by means of barter.

As in other simple economic systems, most of the economic exchanges among the Southeastern Indians must have been governed by the principle of reciprocity. That is, person A would donate his labor or a share of his food to person B as a "gift," without specifying any kind of return. At some time in the future, person B would return an equivalent amount of labor or food to person A. These exchanges would have taken place in the spirit of gift-giving, with no haggling. And the exchanges would have been between equals. Undoubtedly, this is the reason why the Indians insisted on exchanging gifts with the European colonists when anything serious had to be negotiated. In their way of thinking, this put the two parties on an equal footing.[146]

Lacking currency, the Southeastern Indians did not have a system of taxation, but they did donate labor and goods to enable the chiefdom to function. We have already seen that each chiefdom had officials whose responsibility it was to make sure that the town house, square ground, and other public edifices were kept in good repair. These men were empowered to organize volunteer labor for public works. The Southeastern Indians also donated some of the food they produced to underwrite the operation of the chiefdom. The Natchez donated food for the sustenance of the Great Sun, and perhaps for his blood relatives as well, and they also made monthly donations of food for the support of the men who tended the sacred fire. Moreover, the Natchez and other Southeastern Indians made donations of food to the chief to be used for public purposes—to feed men embarking on a raid or some other mission, to feed visitors, and to feed members of the chiefdom who were in need. In Creek chiefdoms this food was kept in a public granary, but the Cherokees evidently donated food to the chief as occasion demanded.[147] This kind of redistributive economic system has been observed in chiefdoms in other parts of the world. It is called redistributive because while it requires the people to make gifts of food to their chief, the chief in turn is required to be a paragon of generosity and is obliged to give most of the donated food to others as need dictates.

Donations were made to the chief as voluntary gifts, but people who did not give were undoubtedly criticized for being stingy, a reproach for which they would have gone to great lengths to avoid. We know of an instance in which the Great Sun of the Natchez used this principle in exhorting his people to donate meat for some visiting Frenchmen. The occasion was a harvest feast in which the Great Sun was entertaining French colonial officials. After a feast in which more than 350 bowls and vessels of all kinds of food—mostly corn dishes—were served, the Great Sun assembled his men and asked them whether they were not ashamed for having failed to provide their French guests with meat, the food to which they were accustomed. The men left instantly. In about two hours they returned in a procession, single file, bearing pieces of fresh and smoke-dried buffalo, bear, and deer meat. They threw the meat on a clean mat on the floor until the pile was a foot and a half high.[148] In this act, the Great Sun was no doubt affirming his social position both in the eyes of the French and in the eyes of his own people.

An important difference between the economic system of the Southeastern Indians and modern capitalistic economics is that the Indians placed no value on the accumulation of wealth. They held, in fact, a contrary value. While some of them were undoubtedly better off than others, the differences would never have been very great because to them a good person was a generous person, and one of the

311

worst things of which a person could be accused was stinginess. They would have understood better than we the Biblical dictum that it is better to give than to receive. The social pressures to be generous would have been strongest among lineage and clan members, but this generosity also extended to non-kin. When Cherokee warriors were given presents by the British for their services in military actions, they would share their gifts with other Indians and with white soldiers who took part in the actions.[149] The early European explorers and traders were constantly astonished by the generosity of the Indians.[150] It was one of the traits which led the Europeans to believe that the Indians had a childlike nature. The Southeastern Indians, for their own part, were baffled by the acquisitiveness and stinginess of the European colonists, whom they compared to cougars. The cougar, they said, is an animal that will sometimes kill two deer at one time, more than it can possibly eat, and yet it will lie between the two carcasses, too greedy to be willing to share its surplus. The Indians saw no point in piling up more property and goods than they could use, and if they did have a surplus, the only decent thing was to share it with others.[151]

The ways in which the Southeastern Indians defined property and ownership are not as clear as we would wish. They did have a concept of private property. After the deerskin trade began, the men owned their guns, and they undoubtedly owned their bows and arrows and war clubs before they had guns. Men and women owned the clothes they wore, and they owned the deerskins and food they produced. When they traded with the British they evidently traded as individuals. In general, they appear to have acquired ownership of a thing through investing their skill or labor into it. Much of an individual's privately owned property was interred with him when he died.[152] Though the Southeastern Indians owned some things individually, they did not carry the principle of private property to the lengths to which we carry it. They would not, for example, have carried it to the point of denying food and shelter to an impoverished relative or neighbor.

One feature of the Southeastern Indian economic system which set them apart from the British colonists was that unlike their British counterparts, Indian women could own property over which their husbands had no control. Indeed, in the early colonial period, British traders and soldiers who went among the Cherokees bought food such as corn, chickens, wild fruit, and pork from women, for they were the ones who produced and therefore owned it.[153] As we have already seen, the women owned the houses in which they lived, but whether the rights of ownership were vested in individual women or the women of a lineage is not well understood. In the latter half of the nineteenth century, American jurists used the Cherokee woman as a model in their arguments for the emancipation of white married women.[154]

Women also appear to have "owned" the agricultural fields they cultivated, but here it was not necessarily a case of private ownership as we know it. Before the arrival of European colonists, the Southeastern Indians evidently owned land communally, but because there was both a surplus of land and no incentive for a person to accumulate land, their concepts and laws concerning communal ownership were more or less implicit. Only after the Europeans arrived and began trying to gain control of the land did the Indians have a need to codify their notions of communal ownership. The Cherokees, for example, just before and after the American Revolution, made it illegal for a Cherokee to sell land to a colonist without having the approval of all the Cherokees, thereby effectively preventing the sale.[155] It might be said that agricultural land was, in effect, privately controlled but communally owned.

TRAVEL AND TRADE

The Southeastern Indians could satisfy almost all of their material wants without traveling far from home. But they did travel for three purposes: to hunt, to wage war, and to trade. As we have seen, in the cold season they sometimes traveled rather long distances to good hunting grounds, and in the warm season they traveled surprisingly long distances to exact blood vengeance against their enemies. In the Mississippian tradition as well as in the colonial period they traveled for the purpose of trading, but we know relatively little about the nature of this Mississippian trade.

Before the Europeans introduced the horse, the Southeastern Indians traveled primarily on foot, walking and running. They would journey hundreds of miles in this fashion, traveling at times with remarkable speed. James Adair tells us, for example, about a famous Choctaw warrior, Red Shoes, who ran for a distance of fifteen miles to kill a French trader escaping on a horse.[156] The aboriginal Southeast was covered with a network of trails stretching from Richmond, Virginia, to the lower Mississippi River, and from St. Augustine, Florida, northward to Ohio and the Great Lakes. Some of the trails the Indians used were made by buffalos and other large animals. Many of these led to salt licks in the Southeast, and some of the trails were as much as four feet wide and one to two feet deep.[157] Many trails, however, were made solely by the Indians. Some of them were located high in the mountains, far above the habitat of large game animals. Indian trails were considerably more numerous above the fall line than they were below it; below the fall line, in the coastal plain, travel by foot was laborious because of the many rivers and swamps.

When Southeastern Indians were traveling on foot and encountered a stream of water too deep for wading, they had several ways of getting to the other side. The most common way was to make a raft by lashing together lengths of the large cane that grew along the water's edge.[158] A second solution was to make a temporary canoe out of hickory, cypress, or elm bark. These were not the strong, graceful birchbark canoes of central and eastern Canada, but rather a crudely constructed vessel made for this one crossing and then discarded, or perhaps laid aside for use on a return trip.[159] A third solution was to kill a large animal and make a crude, bowl-shaped boat (a coracle) by stretching the skin of the animal over a framework of saplings. The white fur traders seem to have adopted this technique in their practice of carrying along on their travels a skin to be used for a boat. With this a trader had only to cut several small poles to fashion a keel, gunwales, and ribs and attach the skin covering to it.[160]

The Southeastern Indians had elaborate rules of hospitality which promoted travel among friendly towns. To be accused of being stingy with food was one of the worst things that could be said about a person. When a traveler arrived in a town, he greeted the first person he saw with: "I am come." To this the person simply replied: "You are; it is good." The traveler was offered tobacco, food, and refreshment and was taken to the square ground or town house to be greeted by the important men of the town. After these formalities they would talk, exchanging news. If the traveler found members of his clan in the town, he spent the night in one of their households; if

314

not, he spent the night in the town house. The Indians were as undemonstrative in saying goodbye as they were in saying hello. When a man was ready to depart, he rose and said: "I go." And his hosts simply replied: "You do."

The Indians also used the extensive rivers, creeks, and swamps of the Southeast as avenues of transportation. Water travel was most extensive on the Mississippi and its tributaries and on the other Southeastern rivers below the fall line, where travel by foot was difficult. Above the fall line the frequent occurrence of rapids made water travel more difficult, though it was done to some extent. The principal craft was the dugout canoe, which was fashioned from a single log of bald cypress, poplar, or pine. Aboriginally the Indians made these out of logs from trees felled by storms or, if none were available, from trees they took down by burning. They also used fire to hollow out the logs, controlling the burning by placing clay over the areas they did not want burned and by fanning the flames where they wanted the burning accelerated. At intervals they extinguished the fire and scraped out the charred wood with a shell or stone tool. The Southeastern dugout canoe had a flat bottom, straight sides, and it was frequently as long as 30 or 40 feet (see fig. 71).[161] It was propelled by paddling or poling, depending on the nature of the water.

Along the lower Mississippi River the survivors of the de Soto expedition were attacked by Indians in truly enormous canoes. The largest of them was propelled by twenty-five paddlers on each side and held twenty-five to thirty additional warriors, carrying in all seventy-five or eighty men. The Indians in these canoes sang rhythmic songs as they paddled, and the canoes moved along at the speed attained by a running horse. Some of these canoes were painted, each a particular color with the warriors on board wearing costumes and carrying weapons of the same color. Obviously, these were war canoes manned by oarsmen and warriors who were thoroughly familiar with fighting on the water.[162]

In the swamps of Louisiana and Florida, where small groups of Southeastern Indians still remain, the dugout canoe has survived into modern times. Among the Florida Seminoles dugouts are still manufactured and used.[163]

After the arrival of the Europeans, the Southeastern Indians became familiar with a new mode of transportation—the horse.

They did not take to the horse as completely as did the Plains Indians, but they did begin riding and using horses as pack animals. The Seminoles, Chickasaws, and Choctaws even developed breeds of their own.[164]

Trade among the Southeastern Indians is a fascinating aspect of their aboriginal lives, and we hope someday to know more about it. Archaeologists have found substantial evidence that they engaged in some kind of trading at a very early date, but from archaeological evidence alone it is difficult to determine whether this was a deliberate, systematic trade, or a trade that was merely occasional and incidental to other activities. We have some historical evidence of aboriginal trade in the early contact period, but this too leaves many questions unanswered.

Evidently, the most important circuit of exchange was between the coast and the interior. The coastal people traded salt, dried fish, sea shells, and the leaves of *Ilex vomitoria* (used to make black drink) to the people of the interior in exchange for red ocher, red root, flint, hard cane, feather cloaks, pottery, and animal skins.[165] Shells were prized in the interior, particularly the conch shell, used as a dipper and as a trumpet, and also the screw-shaped core of the conch shell which they used in necklaces and wore in holes in their ear lobes. Salt was traded with some regularity and was obtained along the coast and also from salt deposits in Louisiana, Arkansas, Tennessee, Kentucky, and other places.[166] Other items frequently traded were soapstone (steatite), copper, mica, and wood for making bows.

Soon after the British colonists established themselves, they initiated a trade in deerskins. For the Southeast this trade began earliest in Virginia, from whence a trade route southward through the piedmont quickly opened up. But the deerskin trade was heaviest after the founding of Charleston. From this port, English traders infiltrated the Southeast bringing guns, powder and shot, woolen cloth, hatchets, kettles, knives, vermillion, beads, and rum. These traders employed Indians to do various kinds of work for them, and some of the Indians themselves became traders or middlemen. But the deerskin trade was the beginning of the end for the Southeastern Indians. They soon became dependent on the colonists for trade goods, and the colonists took advantage of this to increase their power rapidly over the Indians, eventually dispossessing them of all their land.

CHAPTER SIX

CEREMONY

The categories and beliefs that gave substance and order to the social world of the Southeastern Indians were not merely thought out but acted out as well. Their belief system was expressed in all phases of their lives, but nowhere was it more apparent than in their ceremonies. Their entire social life was embellished with ceremony, but the kinds of ceremony that held particular importance were: rites of passage, ceremonies to achieve purity and balance with the social and natural world, and large communal ceremonies.

Repetition and formal correctness are defining characteristics of ceremony, and among the Southeastern Indians there were several ritual devices and motifs that occurred repeatedly. As among other preliterate peoples, one of the most important of these ritual devices was separation. That is, they had rules stipulating that things belonging to radically opposed categories had to be kept apart, physically and otherwise, so that, for example, in certain situations male had to be kept apart from female, birds from four-footed animals, fire from water, and so on. When men failed to keep such opposing forces apart, dire consequences could be expected to result. Related to this tradition was the Southeastern Indians' concern with maintaining purity and avoiding pollution, a concern, in fact, that was so extreme that it strikes us as having been almost obsessive.[1] Quite simply, purity was maintained when separation was successful, and pollution occurred when separation failed. Much of the ceremony of the Southeastern Indians can be understood as a means of maintaining separation and as a means of overcoming pollution when separation failed.

One rule of separation was that fire, the earthly representative of the sun, was never to be polluted with water. Thus they never extinguished fires with water, except in funerary ceremonies in an act which symbolized death. Fire was itself the ultimate symbol of man's struggle against pollution. The belief was held among many Southeastern Indians that the Sacred Fire in the town house became polluted when people disobeyed rules, and that as a consequence of human frailty this fire became progressively more polluted as the year wore on. Thus we will see that the newly lighted fire in the Green Corn Ceremony replaced the old fire which was polluted after a year of social wear and tear, and that this symbolized the beginning of a new year with a purified social structure. Smoke was considered to be closely associated with fire, and the smoke of tobacco (*Nicotiana rustica* L.) was particularly important in ceremonial and ritual contexts. Puffs of smoke were blown toward the three divisions of the cosmos or in the four cardinal directions. Bits of tobacco leaf expressed the same idea when sprinkled on a fire or when tossed into the air.

Because the Southeastern Indians insisted that things belonging in different categories should maintain a rigid separation, it necessarily followed that in the course of their lives they would occasionally encounter things that fit into more than one category. These they regarded as anomalies or abominations, and their efforts to deal with them formed the basis for many of their taboos. For example, birds that ate flesh—such as eagles, crows, buzzards, swallows, and owls—were abominations and could not ordinarily be used as human food. The same was true of animals that ate flesh, such as the cougar, wolf, and fox. (The bear was regarded as a unique animal and was an exception to this rule.) Any animal that fit into two categories was an abomination and was to be avoided, especially by children. This included the bat (a four-footed animal that could fly), the mole (a four-footed animal that was blind and that lived entirely underground), frogs and other amphibious four-footed animals (animals of this world which could enter and live in the watery Under World), and all reptiles. In addition to these food avoidances, the Indians would not eat the flesh of any animal that died of disease or unknown causes, this presumably being evidence of something unnatural. It should be understood that these were the rules of normal times: when faced with starvation, they ate to stay alive.

As important as purity, as an abstract notion running through Southeastern Indian ceremonial life, was the concept of balance. The cosmos was conceived of as consisting of parts which were in

318

opposition to each other, so that, for example, the forces of the north were opposed to the forces of the south, the forces of the east were opposed to the forces of the west, the forces of the Upper World were opposed to the forces of the Under World, men were opposed to women, and some people were opposed to other people, as white is opposed to red. As a consequence, misfortunes were often interpreted as having been caused by one force prevailing over its opposite. Their ritual specialists frequently attempted to restore the balance by enlisting the aid of the force which was opposed to the one that was out of hand. The aboriginal Southeastern Indians would have understood traditional Chinese cosmology with its opposed Yang and Yin forces far better than they would have understood our own prevailing philosophy that man should conquer nature by tampering with it in a thousand new and unheard of ways.

RITES OF PASSAGE

Like preliterate people in other parts of the world, the Southeastern Indians gave ceremonial recognition to the passage of individuals through society, particularly when that passage involved the relinquishing of one role and the assuming of another. Such ceremonies are called rites of passage, and the most important rites of passage for the Southeastern Indians were those which took place at birth, marriage (see chap. 4), and death. There were other junctures in a man's life that were also ceremonially marked, particulary when he earned names and war honors. For a woman, it was her passage through the female reproductive cycle that occasioned ritual treatment.

We have already seen that one of the fundamental categories of opposition in Southeastern thought was the man/woman dichotomy. Men and women were regarded as very different beings, and there were certain occasions when special care was required to ensure separation and thereby avoid pollution. Women, perhaps because of their procreative powers, were particularly likely to cause pollution, and they had to take special care when they menstruated and when they were pregnant. A menstruating woman possessed an especially powerful female nature, and she was forbidden to do anything that might cause a man to be polluted by it. For example, she was forbidden to bathe upstream from a man or even to stand upwind from him. In principle, a woman who broke these rules was thought to have committed a crime approaching the severity of adultery or even murder. It was believed that such a breach of conduct could offset the efficacy of the medicines and ritual precautions of the priests, thereby making the community vulnerable to misfortune. If it became known that a woman had broken one of these rules, she might subsequently be blamed for having caused an illness or misfortune suffered by someone in the community. The Southeastern Indians required menstruating women to stay apart from other people in small huts built especially for this purpose. No one was permitted to touch them or even go near them, and they ate their food from special bowls and containers. At the end of her isolation a woman emerged from the hut, bathed herself in fresh water, and put on clean clothing; she could then reenter the community.

Because we hold the equality of men and women as an ideal in our society, this custom strikes us as harsh and oppressive. But it should be considered that the Southeastern Indians may have recognized at least implicitly some sound social and psychological principles. Psychologists have amply verified what folk knowledge tells us about menstruation, namely that many women become depressed, hostile, anxious, and even socially disruptive just before and during menstruation, when their levels of the hormones estrogen and progesterone are lowest. The causes of their psychological changes are not altogether biological—they are mitigated by social and cultural factors. But whatever their nature, most women *do* experience mood changes during menstruation.[2] We have to remember that the Southeastern Indians lived in communities in which each individual had intense social relationships with many people. In such a community, a psychological mood change which might seem slight by our standards would have had the potential for serious social disruption. It was therefore something to be avoided if possible. It is likely, in fact, that except when it greatly upset their plans, the women looked forward to menstrual isolation each month and the relinquishment of responsibilities that accompanied it.

Nor was this requirement of temporary social isolation completely discriminatory. Men who were about to embark on a raid had to isolate themselves for three or four days from the company of other people. It was during this period of time that the men heightened each other's sense of solidarity, aggressiveness, and hatred for their enemy. And when they returned from a successful raid they observed a similar period of isolation while they underwent a period of purification. Other members of the community were probably quite willing to have these hyperaggressive males off to themselves where they could not cause social trouble within the community. As with the women, the men were ritually isolated when they were most completely men.

Another time in which women are most clearly women is when they are pregnant, and the Southeastern Indians surrounded pregnancy and childbirth with many rules and avoidances. The Cherokees believed that conception could take place only if during intercourse a man and woman reached sexual climax simultaneously. They believed that the child was formed by a mixture of substances from both the mother and father. They believed that in some cases these substances became mixed soon after intercourse, so that the baby would be born in a few months, but in other cases the substances might not become mixed for several months, so that the birth of the baby would be delayed.

As soon as a Cherokee woman learned that she was pregnant she informed her husband and her friends, and soon the entire community knew about it. At several monthly intervals during her pregnancy she and her husband went to water with a priest who attempted to learn whether the child would be born alive or dead, whether it would be a boy or a girl, and so on. Each time she went to water she drank an infusion made of (1) slippery elm bark (*Ulmus rubra* Muhl.) to make her slippery inside so that delivery would be easy, (2) spotted touch-me-not stems (*Impatiens capensis* Meerb.) to frighten the baby and make it "jump down" when the proper time came, (3) roots of common speedwell (*Veronica officinalis* L.), and (4) the cones of prickly pine (*Pinus pungens* Lamb.); both of the latter were thought to convey health and longevity to the infant.

A pregnant Cherokee woman was supposed to observe certain avoidances. She was not to eat squirrel, because if she did when her baby was about to be born it might go up instead of coming down, just as a frightened squirrel climbs a tree. She should not eat speckled trout else her baby might have birth marks. She should not eat rabbit, else her baby might sleep with his eyes open or his eyes might be ridiculously large. She should eat salt sparingly because it makes meat swell. She should never loiter in a doorway else the

321

baby might be slow in "jumping down." She should not wear a neckerchief, else the umbilical cord might be wrapped about the baby's neck. And there were many others.[3]

Southeastern Indian women were generally required to give birth in the menstrual hut, attended by one or more midwives.[4] Before a newborn baby was allowed to suckle, his mother took him to a creek or spring where she sprinkled water on him or even dipped him into the water. Then she rubbed him all over with bear's oil, repeating this frequently throughout his infancy; this gave some protection from insects and was believed to toughen his skin.[5] When he was about one month old, he was taken back to fresh water and bathed all over, and in winter he might be rolled in the snow to make him hardy. The father of a newborn child fasted for four days. For as much as three months after giving birth to a child, the mother was not allowed to prepare her husband's meals, and she was forbidden to sleep with him or even to touch him. The birth of twins was regarded in a special light. They were thought to be especially likely to have unusual powers and were said often to become priests or witches. This was most likely to be true of the younger twin, they believed.[6]

From the moment of birth the two sexes were treated differently. Male infants were wrapped in cougar skins while females were wrapped in deer or bison skins, which was perhaps a way of saying that men "hunted" women just as cougars hunted deer and bison. An infant spent most of the first year of life bound to a cradle board (fig. 76). These cradle boards, made of light rectangular frames of wood or basketry, made it easier for the mother to carry her infant, and it helped protect the infant from the weather and from injury. A wad of soft moss absorbed the infant's excrement.[7] The Southeastern Indians were probably like other American Indians in thinking that confining their infants to cradle boards made them grow straight and strong, a belief for which there is at least some confirmation.[8] The Natchez mother placed two sections of cane as rollers beneath the cradle board so that she could rock her baby by rolling it back and forth. And as we have already seen, most of the Southeastern Indians used the cradle board to shape the skulls of their infants. A person whose skull had been shaped in this way was believed to have superior vision.[9] The Indians discontinued this custom of headshaping early in the colonial period.

Figure 76. Seminole mother with an infant on a cradle board. George Catlin drawing. Courtesy, Western Americana Collection, Yale University Library.

The Indians were indulgent parents. A child was allowed to nurse as long as he pleased, or until his mother became pregnant again. Although mothers were primarily responsible for their children during their first four or five years of life, they were not supposed to punish them physically, particularly their sons. Boys fell under the discipline of one of their mother's older brothers. Ordinarily, the disciplinarian was the oldest, most influential male in the mother's lineage. Girls, on the other hand, remained under the supervision of the women of their clan. If physical punishment had to be administered to a boy, it was usually done by lightly scratching his dry skin with a sharp, pointed instrument. This was called "dry-scratching." Dry-scratching was especially humiliating because it left scratches or light scars on the skin for several days or weeks so that all could see them and tease the child about them. This scratching was a punishment, but it was also thought to "lighten" or lessen the child's blood, and it was believed that this made him healthier and less troublesome.[10] In other words, it was the Southeastern Indian version of punishing a child for his own good. The usual way of punishing less serious instances of misbehavior was by ridicule, a device which can be an especially powerful sanction in a small community.

Little girls learned how to play a woman's role by helping the older women with housework, tending the gardens, keeping the fire going, making pottery and basketry, and so on. Little boys learned how to hunt by doing it. They spent most of their day roaming through the woods and shooting at targets and small animals with their bows and arrows. Boys often competed with each other in seeing who could stand the most pain, as, for example, who was able to tolerate the most stings by yellow jackets. Later the boys learned to play chunkey and the ball game. Perhaps the boys' favorite sport was running foot races. If a man was to be a good warrior and a good hunter, he had to be able to run rapidly and for long distances.[11]

One of the principal ceremonial means of overcoming pollution in the Southeast was by bathing in creeks and rivers. The rule was that early in the morning, before eating any food, everybody was supposed to go to the river to swim and bathe.[12] In some places they were supposed to plunge into the water four times. This rule included men and women, young and old, although women and old men did not always live up to the rule. By overcoming pollution, bathing was believed to increase longevity. They were supposed to make these early morning visits to the river the year around. In fact, they preferred to bathe in cold water, even breaking through ice when necessary. Natchez young people made a great noise as they splashed into the water, partly to keep warm and partly to scare the alligators away. In summer, when the water was too warm to suit them, they would often forgo this custom of early morning bathing. Bathing was used in several other ceremonies in which pollution was to be overcome. We recall that after a widow had mourned her husband, she was then ceremonially bathed before reentering society as a marriageable woman.

One of the main preoccupations of Southeastern Indian men was the acquisition of war names and titles. A man had to perform the menial tasks of a child until he had won war titles. The Chickasaw male, for example, had a personal name assigned to him when quite young that was based on some aspect of his temperament, personal appearance, or some other circumstance. Thus a man might be named *Choola*, "Fox," because of some resemblance to foxes. But a man won additional names by displaying bravery and daring in war, so that *Choola* might earn the right to be called *Tannip-Abe*, "A Killer of the Enemy," or *Minggáshtàbe*, "One Who Killed a Very Great Chieftain."[13]

Among the Creeks war titles were owned by particular clans and assigned to men in recognition of demonstrated bravery. Creek war titles were compound in form. The first word was the name of a totemic animal or the name of a tribe or town, while the second name was usually one of the following: *hadjo*, "mad, crazy, fearless (in battle),"*fiksiko*, "heartless (in battle)," *yahola* (in reference to the ceremonial black drink cry),[14] *imata*, *tàstànàgi*, *heniha*, or *miko*, the last four being military and political titles. Examples of these Creek war titles are *Itco fiksiko*, "Heartless Deer," *Tcito hadjo*, "Crazy Snake," *Fus hàtci miko*, "Bird Creek Chief," and *Yufala tàstànàgi*, "Yufala Warrior." These names evidently connoted different degrees of merit or honor and were earned in sequence for increasingly meritorious acts. Thus a Creek might first earn a title ending with *hadjo*, next *tàstànàgi*, and finally *miko*.[15]

The Chickasaws assigned war names and titles on a designated day after a raid. All of the men who were to be honored awaited this day anxiously. On the appointed day all of the warriors to be honored appeared at the ceremonial ground with their bodies glistening with bear's oil, with red moccasins on their feet and fine collars of white feathers around their necks, and with their faces painted various colors. The air was filled with music, and red colors were displayed. The ceremony began with two old priests who appeared carrying white wands and crowns made of white feathers for the warriors who were to be honored. The two old men alternately delivered long orations with great feeling, commending the warriors for their observance of purity while on the raid and saying how necessary it was for people to emulate dead heroes. The orations over, one of the old men called in a loud voice one of the warriors by his new name or war title. After he repeated this three times, the warrior answered with a whoop, running over to the old man and circling him three times. The old man placed a wand in his hand and a crown on his head. Then the warrior returned to his place, and another warrior was called up to be honored. The ceremony ended with further orations admonishing the warriors always to behave honorably, in accordance with their station, and to value personal honor and the welfare of their people more than life itself.[16]

The Creeks had an even more impressive ceremony for initiating a man as war chief (tástánági). The French adventurer Louis LeClerc Milfort claims to have undergone this initiation in May of 1780, and we know of the ceremony from his description.[17] It began with a delegation of men coming to get Milfort at the house in which he lived. They placed him on a litter covered with a bearskin and borne by four men (see fig. 49). The procession was led by two men, one shaking a rattle and the other beating time on a drum. They were followed by several young warriors who carried eagle tails attached to wands and danced along shouting terrifying cries. Old war chiefs walked before, behind, and on both sides of the litter, each carrying in his hand an eagle tail, half of which was painted red. At the rear of the procession were six priests wearing loose deerskin garments about their shoulders,[18] each carrying a white bird's wing in one hand and in the other hand a sprig of the herb they used to make their war medicine.

The procession halted when they approached the square ground. Two warriors came out carrying war medicine in large gourds which had been painted red. A priest dipped his hands into the war medicine, sprinkled it about, and sang an invocation. Then the highest ranking war chiefs marched out from the square ground, dipped their hands in the war medicine and wet their faces with it. The six priests then came around from behind the litter, held the war medicine herb up against the faces of the highest ranking war chiefs, and passed the swan wings across their faces as if to wipe them. Then the war chiefs went back to the square ground and the

326

whole procession followed. Inside the square ground they refreshed themselves with black drink. Then for twenty-four hours they took nothing but the war medicine, a powerful emetic.

The next day all the men took off their clothing and went into a circular building used as a sweat house, where the heat and steam was so intense Milfort was afraid he would not be able to endure it. They remained there about half an hour, and then to Milfort's consternation all ran to plunge into a river a short distance away. After staying in the water a short time, they dressed and returned to the square ground to eat a magnificent meal. The young people were then allowed to enter the square ground to dance around the fire.

The ceremony lasted three days, during which time none of the men were allowed to leave the square ground and none, including Milfort, were allowed to sleep. When Milfort became drowsy they would splash cold water on his face. In the end he was carried back to his house on the litter, and they explained to him that the ordeals he had been through were to make him understand that he would have to endure cold, heat, and hunger, but that he should be undaunted by all of these in execution of his duties as war chief.

From the point of view of the Southeastern Indians, the most important of all the rites of passage were the mortuary ceremonies which marked the transition from life to death. We know from archaeological evidence that the Indians of the eastern United States began attaching great ceremonial importance to death in the early Woodland tradition. More than anything else, it is this mortuary complex which in Southeastern prehistory marks the division between the Woodland and the Archaic traditions. The mortuary rites of the Southeastern Indians differed from place to place and from earlier times to later times, but several features of these rites were both general and durable. First of all, the Southeastern Indians believed that some part of a person, which we may call his spirit, lived on after death. Second, the living had to show respect to spirits and take their wishes into account. Third, some individuals were accorded far more ceremony at death than others, and in some cases, after their bodies had lain in a grave or on a raised platform for some time, their bones were removed and placed in a temple or ossuary.

The Southeastern Indians were greatly concerned with what happened to their bodies after they were dead. For this reason, it posed a problem when men were killed while raiding enemies or while far away from home. Warriors would sometimes scalp one of their dead comrades themselves so that their enemies could not take the scalp. When it was possible to return and reclaim the remains of comrades fallen among the enemy, they would do so; when they could not, they wept and mourned the death of these men far more than for men who had the benefit of proper mortuary rites.[19] It was deeply disgraceful to have one's body dismembered or left to be devoured by animals. For example, when a famous Natchez war chief died, an old woman who blasphemed him and who was probably a witch, was ordered by the Great Sun to be executed. He directed his men to behead her, to leave her body to be devoured by animals, and to carry her head several miles away and throw it into a cypress swamp.[20] Thus she was given the antithesis of a proper funeral.

Archaeologists have recovered abundant evidence of the Southeastern mortuary complex from the large Mississippian sites,[21] but the best eyewitness accounts of its last vestiges are from the French who observed Natchez mortuary customs in the early 1700s. As one would expect, the Natchez lavished the greatest ceremony on the funerals of Suns, and this was especially true in 1725 on the occasion of the death of Tattooed-Serpent, an honored war chief who was a brother of the Great Sun. What impressed the French most was that when a Sun died, other individuals offered themselves to be killed so their spirits could accompany the dead Sun to the other world. This was altruistic suicide—death for a high moral purpose. Difficult as it is for us to understand, these individuals not only went to their deaths voluntarily, but they would even attempt to surmount obstacles which might get in the way of their sacrifice. For example, women with small infants were exempted, but they would sometimes try to find nurses for their infants so they could go ahead with the suicide, or they would even put their infants to death to clear the way for themselves.

Some of the people who committed suicide on the occasion of the death of a Sun were automatically chosen for this duty. These included the husband or wife of a Sun and certain people closely associated with a Sun. It was their duty to die, and in the act of dying they expressed their devotion to the dead Sun. Thus when Tattooed-Serpent died, two of his wives, one of his sisters (La Glorieuse), his first warrior, his "doctor," his head servant and speaker (whose wife accompanied him in death), his nurse, and a

328

man who made war clubs were all killed. Indeed, the Great Sun himself, crushed with sorrow over the death of his brother, wanted also to die, and his death would have in turn entailed the deaths of many others, but the French prevailed upon him to remain alive.

The readiness of women to go to the grave with their husbands explains why female remains are found in Mississippian sites where one would expect to find only the remains of high status males.[22] In a fascinating revelation, the favorite wife of Tattooed-Serpent explained why this could be.

> I know that my husband and I were great friends of the French, because we also loved you much, although I have never eaten with them, because I am a woman. But I am able to eat with them now, because I am going to the country of the spirits. Let them, then, bring us food to eat, so that I may eat with the French chiefs.[23]

In death the social distinctions which were so important in life were dissolved. Women could eat with men, and they could be buried in ground which in life had been the province of men.

The favorite wife of Tattooed-Serpent saw that the French were distressed about so many of their friends dying. She tried to explain why they should not be sad.

> French chiefs and nobles, I see that you regret my husband's death very much. It is true that his death is very grievous, as well for the French as for our nation, because he carried both in his heart. His ears were always full of the words of the French chiefs. He has always traveled the same road as the French, and he loved them more than himself. But what does it matter? He is in the country of the spirits, and in two days I will go to join him and will tell him that I have seen your hearts shake at the sight of his dead body. Do not grieve. We will be friends for a much longer time in the country of the spirits than in this, because one does not die there again. It is always fine weather, one is never hungry, because nothing is wanting [for one] to live [there] better than in this country. Men do not make war there anymore, because they make only one nation. I am going and [I] leave my children without any father or mother. When you see them, Frenchmen, remember that you have loved their father and that you ought not to repulse the children of the one who has always been the true friend of the French.[24]

Not all people under obligation to die, however, went to death so willingly. Toward the end of the de Soto expedition a sixteen- or seventeen-year-old boy voluntarily joined the Spaniards. It turned out that he was an orphan and that his adoptive father was about to die. Because the adoptive father was so fond of him, he was to be buried with him, and this he wanted to avoid.[25] A similar case involved a Natchez man named Ette-actal. He was married to a Sun woman, but when she was on her death bed, he fled to escape suicide and placed himself under the protection of Bienville, the French commandant-general. However, when Tattooed-Serpent died, Bienville was in France, and so the Natchez seized Ette-actal, brought him to the scene of the funeral, and made it plain to him that he was to die. Ette-actal began to weep bitterly, and when the favorite wife of Tattooed-Serpent saw this, she said:

> "Are you not a warrior?"
> "Yes," said he, "I am one."
> "Nevertheless you weep," she replied. "[Y]our life is then dear to you? If it is so, then it is not good that you come with us. Go away with the women."
> "Certainly life is dear to me," he replied. "I have no children. It is well that I travel some time longer on the earth until the death of the Great Sun and die with him."
> "Go away, I tell you," said she, "it is not good that you come with us and that your heart remain behind you on the earth. Once more, take yourself away from here, and let me see you no more."

Ette-actal was away in a flash. But later the same day two old women, probably members of his clan, "extremely aged and wearied of life," came to offer themselves to die in his place.[26] Similarly, the mother of La Mizenne, a Sun woman who had been under obligation to die but had not, offered herself to die in her daughter's place.[27] One other old woman who had lost the use of her legs offered herself to die, but for what reason we are not told.

The deaths which most shocked the French were those of infants who were strangled by their parents. On one occasion, at the death of a female Sun, the French report that twelve infants were strangled, but only one infant was killed at the death of Tattooed-Serpent. After bringing their dead infant to Tattooed-Serpent's house and throwing it at the feet of the corpse, the mother and father stood outside his house, leaning against the wall with eyes downcast, standing with their feet resting on wads of Spanish moss. Their motive for killing their infant and their reasons for this unusual behavior that accompanied the event are not entirely clear. One of the French observers says that the death of this infant was "a forfeit which purchased their lives at the death of the Great Sun, ennobled them, and raised them from the grade of Stinkards." Thus it may be that one or both of them were under obligation to die, and they avoided doing so by sacrificing their infant.[28]

Until the time of the mortuary ceremony Tattooed-Serpent lay in state dressed in his finest clothing, with his face painted vermillion, wearing a feather headdress of red and white feathers, and wearing moccasins as if to go on a journey. His weapons lay beside him. Nearby was a pole, peeled and painted red, from which hung a chain made of small, red cane hoops, each standing for an enemy whom Tattooed-Serpent had killed. Also nearby were all the pipes of peace presented to him during his life. As the ceremony began, some of the people brought food to him, treating him as if he might still be sentient. After placing food by his bed they said: "You no longer wish, then, to take what we present you? Are these things no more to your taste? Why is it, then, that you rebuff us and our services do not please you any more? Ah! You do not speak as usual. Without doubt you are dead. Yes; it is done. You are going to the country of the spirits, and you are leaving us forever."[29] They then uttered a distinctive, anguished, death cry, and all who heard it echoed it, and it passed to all the other Natchez villages. This death cry was periodically repeated until the mortuary ceremony came to an end.

The body of Tattooed-Serpent lay in state for three days. When the time for the ceremony came, a priest came wearing a headdress with red feathers, with the upper part of his body bare. His arms were painted red, his belt was ornamented with red and black feathers, and he carried a red baton in the shape of a cross with a cluster of black feathers attached to one end. Some men brought out the body of Tattooed-Serpent on a bed made of cane and covered with mats and placed it on poles to form a litter which was borne by six temple guardians. Other men carried chests full of his possessions. The priest led the procession, followed by the oldest of the war chiefs, who carried in one hand the pole on which the scalp-rings hung and in the other hand a pipe. Then came the men bearing the litter. They first circled the dead man's house three times, and then started for the temple. They would walk forward about ten paces and then go around in a circle, then another ten paces and another circle, and so on to the temple. Each time they made a circle the body of the infant who had been sacrificially killed by his parents was thrown down and they trampled upon it. Those who were to die followed next with red pigment daubed in their hair. Each carried in his left hand a pipe and in his right hand what the French describe as a large river mussel shell some seven inches long by three or four inches wide.[30] Each was accompanied by eight of the closest male kinsmen, wearing red feathers on their heads and with their hands colored red; these eight were to do the killing. One of them waved a red war club as if to strike and kill the person who was to die, thus symbolizing the fact that a death was about to occur.

When the procession reached the temple, a mat was spread for each person who was to die. The mats of the two wives were placed on either side of the door, and the others were placed six or seven feet apart in rows on either side of the road to the temple (fig. 77). The people who were to die sat down on the mats, their eight relatives uttered the death cry, and each of those who were to die swallowed several pellets of what appeared to be tobacco, washing them down with water from a bottle.[31] When the tobacco had stupefied them, their relatives again uttered the death cry, placed a deerskin over their heads, restrained them by holding them down, and placed a cord with a running knot around their necks. Two men on either end of the cord pulled until each person was dead.

Tattooed-Serpent was buried along with his possessions inside the temple in a trench dug into the floor on the right side; his two wives were buried with him. His sister, La Glorieuse, was buried outside, to the right of the doorway. His head servant and his wife were buried outside to the left of the door. Then, as was the custom, Tattooed-Serpent's house was burned to the ground. The others who died were placed on litters and carried back to their villages for burial.

Months later the bodies of Tattooed-Serpent and the others who died were to be dug up so that their bones could be cleaned and placed in baskets which were to be kept inside the temple.[32] De Soto observed temples with bones stored inside all through the Southeast. In some of these temples, such as Talomico, each basket or chest of bones was accompanied by a wooden statue carved in the likeness of the dead person. The Algonkians of the piedmont and coastal Virginia were somewhat different in that they slit the corpse down the back, removed the skin, and dried it; they also dried the

Temple.

Figure 77. Mortuary ceremony for Tattooed-Serpent. Woodcut from Le Page Du Pratz, *Histoire de la Louisiane*, Paris, 1758, vol. 3, opp. p. 55. Negative No. 1168–b–1. Courtesy, Smithsonian Institution, National Anthropological Archives.

skeleton after removing the flesh and then put it back into the skin along with some sand. These remains were then placed in a temple where they were kept for a time.[33] It is likely that this treatment was accorded only to important people.

The French tell us less about Natchez mortuary ceremonies for people who were not Suns. Evidently, their bodies were placed on wooden platforms raised on posts three feet from the ground. These platforms were eight feet long and about one and one-half feet wide. The body was enclosed in a vault made of saplings curved over and covered with "plaster." The vault at the foot of the corpse was left open and food was periodically placed here by the mourners. After the bones were dried, they were placed in a basket and stored.[34]

In their mortuary customs, as in other respects, the Natchez were not as unique as many have supposed. The altruistic suicides of the spouses, relatives, and close associates of dead Suns are unusual when compared to what we know about historic Cherokees, Creeks, Choctaws, and Chickasaws. But the other deaths during Tattooed-Serpent's mortuary rites were instances of infanticide, mercy killing of old people, and forfeiture of one's life for the life of a kinsman; and as we have already seen, all of these customs were widespread in the aboriginal Southeast. Likewise, other people in the Southeast in later times were similar to the Natchez in having a distinctive death cry, in leaving food and water with a corpse, in interring personal possessions with a corpse, and in preserving the bones of the dead in a basket or chest for a time and then re-interring them at a later date.

The Cherokees retained a few oral traditions about mounds even into the late nineteenth century when James Mooney lived among them. The most striking of these is the story of the spirit defenders of the Nikwasi mound (chap. 3), in which in the remote past and again during the Civil War a horde of spirit warriors came out of the side of a mound to defend the Cherokees against their enemies. One has only to see the description of the warrior burials at Mound C at Etowah, with their magnificent Mississippian trappings, to realize that the people of Etowah could have told a story very much like the one told to Mooney.[35]

The Natchez were the last of the Southeastern Indians to retain something approximating the full Mississippian mortuary complex. But other Southeastern Indians retained distinctive mortuary practices well into the historic period. James Adair, for example, describes Chickasaw mortuary customs in some detail. When a Chickasaw died or was killed some distance from home, his body was placed upon a raised platform and covered with logs to protect it from wild animals and birds. When the flesh had decayed and the bones had dried, the relatives returned to the site and bundled the bones in a white deerskin. They carried them back to the town and placed them before the house of the dead man's family. His female relatives then gathered around and wept for an hour or so. Afterwards the bones were carried into the house, where the relatives again wept, and the bones were then buried in the house floor with great solemnity. This ceremonial wailing was repeated at intervals. Some women were particularly adept at it and were encouraged to wail at the funerals of important men. According to several accounts, the Southeastern Indians also wailed in the same manner when they saw people they had not seen for a long while: one suspects that seeing them was a reminder of all the people who had died in their absence. Mourners frequently cut off their hair, allowing what remained to become disheveled.

When a Chickasaw died in the town in which he lived, all diversions such as music, dances, and games were given up for three days and nights. When it became obvious that a man was dying, he was anointed with bear's oil and his face was painted red. When death occurred, his relatives and neighbors yelled and made noises in the town to scare his spirit away. A male relative of the dead man took a firebrand in his right hand, brandished it around his head and, lamenting, thrust it into water, thus extinguishing it and symbolizing death. In addition, the fire in the house was extinguished and a new one ignited. The corpse was quickly washed, again anointed with bear's oil and the face painted red, and taken out of doors to prevent pollution of the house. They put down animal skins opposite the door of the house and placed the corpse in a sitting position as if it were alive. A eulogy was said over the body, and it was carried in a circular path around the house three times. The body was then taken inside the house and placed in a sitting position in a grave dug in the floor of the house with the face turned to the east. The dead man was dressed in his finest clothing, and his favorite possessions were placed in the ground with him. These offerings might include his pipe, a bow and arrows, his war club, and pottery vessels. In some cases these objects were intentionally broken. Favorite pets were sometimes killed and buried with their master. The dead man's tomb was covered with logs, then with several layers of cypress bark, and finally with clay. The relatives who handled the body became polluted in so doing, and they had to purify themselves by bathing and by living apart from other people for several days. The relatives were sometimes required to sleep over interments in house floors as a reminder that the death had to be revenged. In general, corpses were buried only by relatives. Thus when epidemics of European diseases broke out among the Southeastern Indians, killing whole families, the bodies were often left unburied where they lay. When an important man died, his friends took the black drink on eight successive mornings, eating sofkee made without salt. Reminiscent of Natchez custom, the man's house was sometimes abandoned and a new one built.[36]

PURITY AND BALANCE

The Southeastern Indians lived in a world which they perceived to be for the most part orderly and predictable. Their world view assumed the existence of spiritual beings who were just and consistent in their dealings with men. So long as men behaved properly and remained pure, and so long as they did not cause the forces in nature to become unbalanced, things went well in human affairs. But if men became impure and let things get out of balance, then they could expect to suffer from misfortune and illness. When things did begin going badly, however, the Southeastern Indians did not resign themselves to a passive acceptance of death and disaster. They went instead to see a ritual specialist whom they believed could discern the causes of misfortune and straighten things out. Some of these ritual specialists also were believed to be able to foretell events in the future.

Not all ritual specialists were the same with respect to the nature and scope of their knowledge and powers. They ranged from the Natchez Great Sun, whose main function appears to have been controlling the weather and the sun itself, to men and women who only knew how to work simple cures. After the French crushed the Natchez, who were the last people to represent something of the old Mississippian pattern, no Southeastern Indian ever again held ritual power comparable to the Great Sun. But the Southeastern Indians

did have religious specialists who were powerful men in their communities, particularly the men James Adair called "Archi-magi."
"Priests" is perhaps the best word for them because they had to
undergo a period of instruction and they were men who were valued
for what they knew rather than for some innate ability or power.[37]
But terminology is difficult because the social definition of these
ritual specialists has changed historically, so that today, living in
predominantly Protestant communities, they are not what they
were when they lived among people who were relatively untouched
by Christianity. Modern Southeastern Indians call contemporary
ritual specialists "conjurers" and "medicine men" (Cherokee, *di-
da:hnʌwi:sg(i)*).[38] We, however, shall be speaking historically, and
we shall call them "priests."

In addition to their priests, or men of knowledge, the Southeastern Indians had ritual specialists who were born with unusual abili-
ties. The Timucuans had men who could go into ecstatic trances, and
in so doing became so contorted that they hardly looked like human
beings; when they returned to normal they revealed prophesies.
Among the Creeks a *kiła*, or diviner (literally a "knower"), was a born
ritual specialist. The Creeks and other Southeastern Indians believed that the younger of a set of twins was likely to be a diviner,
though some thought that unless he was carefully supervised he lost
this ability at the age of eight or ten. When people fell ill they went to
a diviner and asked him to diagnose their disease. If a cure was
necessary, the patient went elsewhere to get it; the diviner was not a
healer. In addition to being able to diagnose disease, a diviner was
believed to be able to locate stolen objects, to do miraculous things
like making beads or bullets swim on top of the water, and to
determine whether a man's life would be short or long. And some of
them were believed to be able to control the weather.[39]

As late as the early decades of this century, John Swanton was told
about an Alabama diviner who could make it rain by fasting and
putting medicine in a creek. He was told about another who was said
to be able to dive beneath the water and feed fish to horned serpents, thus causing it to rain.[40] Irregularities in the weather were
believed to have been caused by men becoming impure through
improper behavior. For the Southeastern Indians, as with other
agricultural people, it was important to get the right amounts of rain
during spring and summer, and for corn the right amounts had to

come at the right times. A drought could cause the crop to fail, and too much rain could cause destructive flooding. Reflecting the importance of rain was the Indians' belief that when rain began to fall, one should not seek cover too quickly, else the rain would stop. Controlling the weather was a difficult business and often a dangerous one. A weather controller, for example, had to be careful not to be too successful when calling for rain. Adair heard about a weather controller who had been killed because as a presumed result of his efforts a river had overflowed its banks in August, causing great damage to the crops.[41] A weather controller's best protection when he failed to produce favorable results was to place the blame on wicked people in the community who had broken sacred rules.

Among the Cherokees the weather was controlled not by men who specialized in weather control, but by priests, the same ritual practitioners who performed other ceremonies. To deflect a storm which threatened the young corn crop, the Cherokee priest faced the storm, stretching one hand toward it and reciting this prayer:

Yuhahí, yuhahí, yuhahí, yuhahí, yuhahí.
Yuhahí, yuhahí, yuhahí, yuhahí, yuhahí–Yu!

Listen! O now you are coming in rut. Ha! I am exceedingly afraid of you. But yet you are only tracking your wife. Her footprints can be seen there directed upward toward the heavens. I have pointed them out for you. Let your paths stretch out along the tree tops on the lofty mountains and you shall have the paths lying down without being disturbed. Let your path as you go along be where the waving branches meet. Listen!

Then the priest waved a blade of corn and blew his breath gently in the direction in which he wanted the storm to go. The prayer addresses the storm as if it were an animal in the rutting season, directing it to follow its female to a quieter place in the tree tops of the mountains, where they will be undisturbed.[42]

Quite different from the Creek diviners were the priests of the Creeks, who were called isti poskálgi, "fasting men," because they fasted to attain purity. These priests were trained and instructed in a ceremony called pōskita, "to fast," a name which the Creeks also gave to their Green Corn Ceremony. According to information collected by John Swanton, a group of not more than four young Creeks would go to an old priest and ask him to instruct them. If he agreed to do so, they all went to a stream of water in a densely

338

wooded place where they would not be disturbed. They piled up green boughs to shield themselves completely from the eyes of intruders.

The young candidates dug up "red root" (*miko hoyanīdja*), to be discussed presently, pounded it up into a pulp, and put it in a pot of water. The old priest then blew his breath into the medicine and sang over it. The young men drank this four times before noon of the first day of instruction. This medicine was an emetic, causing them to vomit, and they ate no food.[43] Later in the afternoon, when the sun was just above the western horizon, the old priest came back and instructed them in the most elementary knowledge a priest had to know. In this instruction, they placed a high value on the ability to memorize information. The Cherokees believed that their priests should be able to memorize a sacred formula or song after hearing it just once. This was not as difficult as it sounds because the formulas and songs followed regular, structured patterns.

The first thing the candidates were taught was how to treat various kinds of wounds. The old priest taught them the proper songs to sing and the formulas to recite to make their medicine potent. The young men had to learn these word for word, and the old priest observed and criticized their performances. After this the young men were taught how to deal with other disorders. The fasting was expected to induce dreams or visions in the young men, and the old priest would interpret them. After four days of instruction, the young men went into a makeshift tent. They put hot stones on the ground and poured water over them, making clouds of steam. After they had been sufficiently steamed, they immersed themselves in the cold water of the creek. Then they went home.

After one or two months had passed and they had absorbed what they had learned, they would hold another four-day period of instruction. After five or six of these periods of instruction, a candidate would ask the old priest for an eight-day session, and finally a twelve-day session, which completed the instruction, though few of the candidates went this far. With the instruction complete, the old priest would dig a hole in the earth in which the young man was placed with a hollow cane through which he could breathe. He was then completely covered with earth. This was a ritual way of saying that the young man was dead and buried. Before uncovering the young man, the old priest covered the grave with a thin layer of leaves and set fire to them. After this, the novice's preparation was complete—he was a priest.

A Creek priest who had gone through all the instruction was entitled to wear the feather of a horned owl in his headdress. Some of the priests even carried a stuffed owl. Consistent with this, priests who had gone through the entire course of instruction were believed to have extraordinary night vision. A priest who could cure a wound was entitled to wear a buzzard feather, because buzzards are unaffected by exposure to death and impurity, and a priest who could cure snakebite was entitled to wear a fox's skin, because foxes are able to kill and eat snakes.[44] According to earlier writers, such as Adair and Bartram, each town had a head priest, whom Adair called "Archi-Magus." Needless to say, the Indians believed that these men were essential not only in healing, but also in warfare and other important matters.[45]

The Southeastern Indians believed that vengeful animal spirits were by far the greatest cause of illness. Recalling the Cherokee myth about how the animals, angered at man's cruel practice of killing their fellows, met and devised various illnesses as revenge (chap. 3), we can understand why the Indians assumed that the animals were hostile toward man. For this reason the Indians took special care not to offend the animals, and when they had to kill animals they were careful to beg their pardon. Thus when a hunter killed an animal, he sacrificed a part of the flesh to the "chief" of that particular species. On both the winter and summer hunt, they usually sacrificed the entire carcass of the first deer they killed. Moreover, when they ate meat, they would throw a bit of it into the fire as an offering.

Creek hunters were often afflicted with deer disease. The eye of a deer could cause eye troubles and the tongue of the deer caused throat troubles. But the most frequent symptoms of deer disease were rheumatic pains and arthritis. As with other animal diseases, they attempted to cure deer disease with a medicine made of various plants and trees, for these were the allies of man. The most important of these herbal medicines used by the Creeks were:[46]

1. *Miko hoyanïdja*, made from the inner bark of the root of a species of willow (possibly *Salix tristis*, the dwarf gray willow). This was a purgative of great importance.[47] Often called "red root," this was one of the most important Creek medicines. They soaked this

inner bark in cold water and drank it, and patients were sometimes bathed in it. They used it for rheumatism, nausea, fever, malaria, swellings, and many other ailments, as well as for purification.

2. *Pāsa*, popularly known as "button snakeroot" and "bear's grass" (*Eryngium yuccifolium* Michx.).[48] This medicine was also made from a root which was pounded up and mixed with water. Second in importance only to *miko hoyanîdja*, it was used for neuralgia, kidney troubles, snakebite, rheumatism, as a spring tonic, and for many other purposes. It was an expectorant and an emetic.[49]

3. *Hilis hátki*, literally "white medicine," was ginseng (*Panax quinquefolium* L.). The roots of ginseng were boiled in water and made into a potion. This was primarily used for shortness of breath, to stop the flow of blood from a wound, and to keep ghosts away. The Creeks believed that its medicinal virtues could be offset by the presence of a woman, particularly a menstruating woman. The Chinese, as is well known, have used ginseng for thousands of years, and they make great claims for it. Western doctors have been hostile toward it, but the Russians have recently been doing research on its medicinal properties.[50]

4. *Notosa*, angelica (*Angelica atropurpurea* L.). The aromatic root was chewed and the juice swallowed for stomach ache, hysteria, worms, and pains in the back.

5. *Wilāna*, wormseed (*Chenopodium ambrosioides* L.). This was used as a means of purification, as a spring tonic, and for fever. It was a mild poison effective for expelling worms and amebae which must have been a serious health problem to the Southeastern Indians.[51]

6. *Atcina*, red cedar (*Juniperus virginiana* L.). This was boiled and drunk as a spring tonic, and it was applied externally to places where aches and pains were felt. It was also used as incense. Cedar is an evergreen with a distinct fragrance and with an unusual red, decay-resistant wood with a distinctive grain. It was the wood out of which important ritual objects were made. The Cherokees would not use cedar as firewood.[52]

7. *Kapapāska*, spicebush, (*Lindera benzoin* [L.] Blume). A liquid made from boiling spicebush branches in water was drunk to purify the blood. They also used it as a tea, a casual beverage.

8. *Kofûtcka tako*, horsemint (*Monarda punctata* L.). This was made into a liquid and drunk to induce perspiration It was also used

to cure swellings in the legs. After a death, they drank it to ward off rheumatism.

These are but a few of the herbal medicines used by the Creeks. They were frequently used in combination with each other. For example, if a man caught deer disease, he drank a medicine made from a mixture of *pāsa*, *atcina*, a small piece of the tender end of a summer grapevine, and other herbs. In some cases specific herbal medicines were used for specific illnesses. Thus if a person had "blood-of-the-bear" disease, whose symptom was vomiting blood, he drank *miko hoyanīdja*. When a person had eagle disease, with severe cramps in the muscles of the neck, as if caught in the talons of an eagle, the eagle was "driven off" with *atcina* fumes. A person with millipede disease, a hoarse cough, drank a warm concoction of ginseng.

The Cherokee herbalist generally gathered his herbs just before they were to be used. When he found the plant he was searching for, he walked around the plant either once or four times, reciting the proper verbal formula. For example, when hunting ginseng, the herbalist addressed the mountain on which he stood as the "Great Man," assuring him that he was only going to take a small piece of his flesh. He then pulled up the plant, root and all, and dropped a red or white bead, whichever was appropriate, into the hole. Then he covered it up. He collected bark from the east side of the tree, and roots and branches were likewise taken from the eastern side, the reason being that they had absorbed the greatest potency from the rays of the sun. After he collected the herbs, he would tie them into a bundle and take them to a stream of water where he would say some words and drop the bundle into the water. If it floated, this was taken as a good sign and the medicine was used. But if it sank, this presumably being a sign that it was not sufficiently opposed to the Under World, it was thrown away and new herbs were gathered.[53]

In selecting appropriate herbals for particular illnesses, Cherokee priests frequently relied on analogy. That is, they prescribed herbals because they resembled some feature of an illness or condition. We have already seen, for example, that the Cherokee priest prescribed slippery elm bark to expectant mothers to make them slippery inside, thus making their deliveries easier. The Cherokee word for biliousness was *dalo•ni*, and their word for "yellow" was *dalo•nige•ʔi*. Hence they treated biliousness with medicine made of

342

herbs having either a yellow root, bark, or flower, and all of these were also called *dalo•ni*.[54]

In addition to illnesses caused by animal spirits, there were also illnesses that resulted from the violation of various rules and avoidances. For example, if a child touched a mole, it was thought that it might cause the child to go blind. If a menstruating woman carelessly came into contact with a man, the Southeastern Indians believed that the man would develop pain in his lower legs, nosebleed, headache, and severe depression. If a Creek man fell ill with this, he was treated with a decoction of *miko hoyanĭdja*, which he drank, bathed in, and used to make steam in a sweat bath.

The Creeks believed that exposure to dead bodies could be particularly dangerous. People who had the task of burying the dead were likely to suffer from illness, and it was dangerous even to step on the dirt of a grave. The symptoms of illness from exposure to a dead person were pains in the back, a chilly feeling, and fatigue in the lower limbs. The person suffering from exposure to a dead person was treated with medicine made from *miko hoyanidja* and spicebush. The medicine was divided into two parts, one heated and the other used cold, and the sufferer's affected parts were treated alternately with the hot and cold medicines. The Southeastern Indians attempted to avoid this kind of illness by using incense from burning twigs of cedar, which was thought to repel ghosts.

When a Cherokee fell ill he would first try to cure his illness with means that were known by everyone, but particularly by the old people of his lineage. If they could not cure him, then someone in his lineage would summon a priest. An ill person's husband or wife, not being a blood relative, was not expected to call in a priest. When called in to cure an illness, the priest was not paid in the usual sense, though he was paid for certain other services which had nothing to do with curing. But whenever the priest had to use beads or crystals in his cure, the patient or his blood relatives gave the priest a deerskin or a piece of cloth.[55] At the close of the ceremony the priest rolled up the beads in the cloth and took it away with him. The priest was forbidden by custom to give this cloth to any members of his own family, but he could give it to a nonrelative in exchange for something else. A new piece of cloth had to be given to a priest each time such a ceremony was repeated. If a particular cure was not successful and another cure became necessary, the patient was required to give the priest additional cloth of greater quality or quantity.

When he went to see a patient, the Cherokee priest would first try to determine the cause of the disease. If the patient had violated some rule or avoidance, the cause of his illness was easy to establish. But if this was not the case, the priest asked his patient to tell him about his dreams. Dreams were thought to be warnings of things to come. For example, the Creeks believed that if a person dreamed of fire, it meant that he and his family might fall ill with fever. When a man dreamed of fire, his whole family took a dose of red root and bathed in the creek four times as a precaution. When a man dreamed of fishes, it meant that he might suffer internal disorders. To dream of a snake meant that the dreamer or someone in his family might suffer snakebite, and as a precaution he and his family were all treated as if they had already been bitten.

The Seminoles believed that when a person fell asleep his soul left his body through his anus and went to the north where it had dream-experiences.[56] Normally, it returned when the person awoke, but sometimes it refused to come back, and this caused a person to fall ill, particularly when the soul went from north toward the east. A priest was called in to coax the soul back to its owner. If a person's soul went all the way east, and thence to the west, the person would die. But the person was not completely dead until four days later, when a second soul left his body and went to the west.[57]

In the event of a serious illness, a Cherokee priest would put his patient into seclusion. Everyone was kept away from him except members of the man's household. This was primarily to keep the patient from being polluted by a menstruating or pregnant woman. Even the presence of a man or child who had been exposed to such a woman could be polluting and would neutralize the priest's medicine.[58] In some cases the patient would be removed from his house and taken to the town house, where he remained until he either recovered or died.

The priest was also likely to impose certain dietary prohibitions on his patient. He usually forbade his patient hot food, salt, and wood-ash lye that was used as a food seasoning. Additional prohibitions might be imposed depending on the nature of the illness. Thus if the disease were rheumatism, the patient was forbidden to eat the limbs of any animal, because it was thought that they might make the condition worse.

344

As a further attempt to overcome pollution, the Cherokee priest often prescribed a sweat bath followed by a cold bath. The patient went into a winter house (or a small sweat house) where water mixed with pounded roots of wild parsnip was poured over hot stones producing clouds of steam. The man took off all of his clothing and remained in the steam until he was sweating profusely. Then he went to a stream of fresh water where he submerged himself beneath the water four or seven times. Bathing in fresh water was believed to be especially purifying when performed just at daybreak, when the red sky of dawn was reflected in the water. An especially good season for bathing was autumn, when fallen leaves in the water imparted to it their medicinal virtues.

The actual therapy administered by a priest consisted of manipulation, herbal medicines, and singing or reciting the appropriate verbal formulas. One manipulation often used was scratching. The priest first rubbed water on his patient's body to keep the skin from tearing.[59] Then he administered the scratches with a small comblike instrument with a series of sharp teeth (see fig. 98). The scratching was just deep enough for blood to color the scratches or flow slightly. The Seminole rationale for this therapeutic scratching was that one's blood could become too abundant or too "heavy," and this condition caused one to become ill, socially troublesome, or violent.[60] When William Bartram was traveling through Seminole territory in 1774, it so happened that a large rattlesnake crawled into a Seminole village. The Seminoles were afraid of the snake, but they did not dare kill it, because, as we have already seen, any man who needlessly killed a snake would suffer vengeance from snake spirits. When Bartram killed the snake, the Seminoles came to him and offered to scratch him and relieve him of some of his blood, because he obviously had too much and hence was a danger to himself and to others around him.[61]

Another form of therapeutic manipulation was rubbing. When a patient had pains or swellings in his abdomen, the Cherokee priest rubbed his abdomen with the tips of his fingers or the palm of his hand. When a patient was ill because of snakebite or from dreaming of snakes, the priest rubbed his body in a circular motion from left to right because snakes were believed always to coil themselves from right to left. This was said to "uncoil" the snake. Before rubbing a patient, the priest sometimes warmed his hands over a fire built especially for this purpose.[62] In some cases the priest blew his breath on the patient's body. In some of the Cherokee formulas the priest blew first upon the patient's right hand, then upon his left foot, then upon the left hand, and finally upon the right foot, forming an X, an old Southeastern Ceremonial Complex motif.[63]

For the Cherokees and probably other Southeastern Indians, the main strategy in a curing ceremony was to cure the illness by invoking the spiritual enemies of whatever was causing the illness.[64] Thus if a disease was thought to have been caused by a fish, the priest would invoke a spiritual fish-hawk or heron to come and seize the invader. Another general strategy was to achieve ceremonial completeness, so that the Cherokee priest usually called spiritual helpers from all of the four directions, and he repeated certain ceremonies and formulas four times. To make sure that the invaders causing a disease were completely exorcised, at the end of the ritual the priest would sometimes call in a spiritual whirlwind to "clean up" any remaining traces of the disease or its cause.

All of these ritual strategies and devices may be seen in the following Cherokee ceremony used to treat rheumatism or arthritis, an illness which afflicted many Southeastern Indians and which they greatly feared.[65] As we have already seen, they thought that this affliction was caused as a result of having killed a deer without having taken proper ritual precautions. The hunter was supposed to recite a formula begging the deer's pardon for having killed him, or else he was to build a fire on his path to keep the vengeful deer spirit from following him. As a further precaution some Indians cut portions out of the hamstrings of the rear legs of the deer, perhaps to keep the deer's spirit from following. If a hunter failed to take these precautions, the vengeful deer spirit might follow him to his home and afflict his limbs with rheumatism or arthritis.

Prior to treating his patient the priest prepared his medicine by boiling the roots of "bear's bed" fern (*Dryopteris* Adams.), "crow's shin" fern (*Adiantum pedatum* L.), and at least three other kinds of fern. Both the priest and his patient had to fast for the duration of the therapy.

The first ceremony began just as the sun came up. A terrapin shell containing two white beads was placed near the patient. After the patient took off his clothes and lay down, the priest rubbed the warm medicine on his body while reciting the following formula.

Listen! Ha! In the Sun Land you repose, O Red Dog, O now you have swiftly drawn near to hearken [*sic*]. O great *adáwĕhĭ*, you never fail in anything. O, appear and draw near running, for your prey never escapes. You are now come to remove the intruder. Ha! You have settled a very small part of it far off there at the end of the earth.

Listen! Ha! In the Frigid Land you repose, O Blue Dog. O now you have swiftly drawn near to hearken. O great *adáwĕhĭ*, you never fail in anything. O, appear and draw near running, for your prey never escapes. You are now come to remove the intruder. Ha! You have settled a very small part of it far off there at the end of the earth.

Listen! Ha! In the Darkening Land you repose, O Black Dog. O, now you have swiftly drawn near to hearken. O great *adáwĕhĭ*, you never fail in anything. O, appear and draw near running, for your prey never escapes. You are now come to remove the intruder. Ha! You have settled a very small part of it far off there at the end of the earth.

Listen! On *Wáhală* you repose, O White Dog. O now you have swiftly drawn near to hearken. O great *adáwĕhĭ*, you never fail in anything. O, appear and draw near running, for your prey never escapes. You are now come to remove the intruder. Ha! You have settled a very small part of it far off there at the end of the earth.

Listen! On *Wáhală* you repose, O White Terrapin. O now you have swiftly drawn near to hearken. O great *adáwĕhĭ*, you never fail in anything. Ha! It is for you to loosen its hold on the bone. Relief is accomplished.[66]

The priest recited this formula in a low whisper or murmur, uttering *Ha!* in a louder tone of voice. After reciting the formula and rubbing the medicine on his patient's body, the priest blew his breath on the affected parts. He repeated this ceremony three more times, replicating it exactly, with the only variation coming after the fourth performance when he blew his breath on the affected parts four times. The priest repeated this entire four-part performance again after the sun was above the horizon, again at mid-morning, and for a fourth time at noon.

In the formula recited by the priest east is called "the Sun Land," north is called "the Frigid Land," west is called "the Darkening Land," and south is called "*Wáhală*," after a mountain of that name which they believed was located in the south. An *adáwĕhĭ* was a human or spiritual being with great power. Only the very greatest priests and spiritual beings were regarded as being *adáwĕhĭ*. Since the illness was caused by a deer, the priest invokes from the four quarters spiritual dogs, natural enemies of deer, flattering them by calling them "great *adáwĕhĭ* who never fail." Each is called in from afar to come and take away a portion of the illness. Finally, the white terrapin, who had great influence in curing illness, is called in to loosen the illness from the patient's bones. The white beads in the terrapin shell symbolized relief and happiness. People suffering from rheumatism and arthritis were usually forbidden salt, wood-ash lye (as seasoning), and hot food, and moreover they were forbidden even to touch a squirrel, bison, cat, or any animal that "humps" itself into a rheumatic-like posture.

Although the medicinal and therapeutic practices of the Southeastern Indians seem strange to us today, they did not seem so terribly strange to the European colonists who lived alongside the Indians in the eighteenth century. European medicine was not greatly advanced beyond the Indians' medicine at that time, and the Europeans frequently admired the Indian curers. John Lawson, for example, takes some pains to document what he believed to be Indian successes in healing. He was particularly impressed with the way they were able to cure "scald head" with acorn oil, the "pox" with a "berry that salivates as mercury does," and with their ability to heal burns. He pointed out that they had several herbal remedies for toothache, and if these failed, they extracted the tooth by setting against it a piece of cane with a pad of leather on the end and by hitting the cane with a sharp blow to knock the tooth out. Lawson says that this method of extraction was less painful than pulling a tooth with instruments in the European manner. Lawson knew about both the emetic and diuretic properties of black drink, and he took pains to learn the medicinal properties of other herbs used by the Indians.[67]

Indeed, two hundred years later, at the time James Mooney did field work among the Cherokees, Western medical doctors still made considerable use of herbal remedies. For poor white and black people in the South this was virtually the only kind of medicine available, and even today herbalism survives in the South to some extent. In Mooney's day many people believed that Indian healers had remarkable curative powers.[68] Perhaps as a consequence of this James Mooney took the claims of Cherokee herbalists seriously, and he compared their use of herbs with the way his medical contemporaries used the same herbs. Using a sample of twenty of the most important Cherokee herbs, Mooney reports that about 25 percent of these herbs were used by the Cherokees in the same way medical doctors used them; 15 percent were of uncertain benefit by medical standards; and 60 percent had no known curative properties according to the best available medical knowledge.[69]

Thus it might seem that their reliance on analogy in selecting herbal medicines for particular complaints often led them into error, and that their use of medicine was relatively unintelligent when compared to our own. But the matter is not so simple. In early 1971 the United States Food and Drug Administration published a report on the results of tests of some 2,000 medicines sold in drug stores. Only about 39 percent of these drugs were found to be effective, and for some of them this was with qualifications. The FDA was able to substantiate only about 20 percent of the *claims* made for these drugs. The report also makes it plain that more than a few of these medicines are known to have undesirable, sometimes lethal, side effects.[70] Seen in this light, the Southeastern Indians' use of herbal medicines seems to be no less intelligent than the use of chemical medicines in our own society.

The Southeastern Indians used some of their best medicines very effectively. We have already seen that they used the caffeine in their black drink to best advantage. The same is true of *miko hoyanīdja*, the most important Creek medicine. Willow bark contains salicin, the same drug that we take in synthetic form in aspirin. Aspirin is by far the single most frequently used medicine in our own society,[71] and in fact, when we consider the number of ailments for which aspirin is effective, we can see that it is one of the most important "wonder drugs" man has thus far discovered.

The Southeastern Indians could not of course cure cancer, but since it has been estimated that from 80 to 90 percent of all cancer is caused by social and environmental factors of our own making, cancer was probably a rare illness for them.[72] As late as 1944 cancer and heart disease were virtually unknown among the Seminoles.[73] The Southeastern Indians could not cure epidemic diseases like smallpox, but it was the Europeans who first introduced such diseases.[74] In short, when all things are considered, it may be that their ways of treating illness were far more effective than we have previously assumed.

Their priests and diagnosticians were possessed of a good sense of drama, and this was among people for whom the dramatic element in healing was important. John Lawson was an appreciative observer at a session in which an old Tuscarora priest attended a man who was severely ill. The old priest stood above his patient holding in his fingers the end of a string of beads, with the other end just touching his patient's abdomen. Then the old priest began talking, and to Lawson and the others it truly seemed that he was talking to another person or being whom they could not see. To everyone's excitement the lower end of the string of beads turned up and began to rise up toward his motionless hand, "as an Eel would do," and all the beads ended up in a clump beneath his outstretched hand. Then the string of beads returned to their full length and the old priest told his patient that his "distemper" would settle in his leg, but that he would recover. According to Lawson, who was hardly willing to believe his own eyes, all of this later came to pass.[75]

The Southeastern Indians must have appreciated these dramatic interludes in their lives, but it would be a mistake to conclude that this was mere showmanship or chicanery. We have known for some time that many of man's illnesses are caused or worsened by psychosomatic factors. That is, purely psychological problems can cause one to have physiological symptoms. But we are just beginning to appreciate the fact that an unknown number of these illnesses are actually "sociosomatic." That is, people become ill because of something that is disordered in their social relationships. And we are also learning that in several preliterate societies which have been thoroughly studied by modern social anthropologists, the dramatic element in therapy is often used by a therapist to bring pressure to bear on the patient's relatives and neighbors, and in this way they can often alleviate their patient's sociosomatic complaints.[76] Thus it is likely that some of the drama in Southeastern Indian therapy was, in fact, curative.

When they fell ill the Southeastern Indians turned to their belief system for an explanation and a course of action. The organizing principles in this belief system were purity and balance, analogy, and opposition, all of which seem metaphysical or magical to us. Because our own belief system starts from such different assumptions, from such different organizing principles, our first impulse is to deny the Southeastern Indian belief system any truth or sense. And it makes very little difference whether we deny their beliefs' validity and meaning outright or under the guise of one or another functionalist or structuralist explanation. By this is meant explanations which take the form, "such and such a practice is silly, but it functions to heighten the solidarity of the society, and this is the reason for its existence," or "such and such a belief is silly, but it has a perceptible shape or structure, and this explains its existence." In that some of their herbal medicines and therapeutic techniques have been found to be eminently practical and effective, it would seem to be only prudent that we examine the particulars of their beliefs and practices before passing judgment on their validity or sense. More than one philosopher and historian of science have observed that people have explained valid observations and practices with theories which later proved to be false or inadequate.

CONJURY AND WITCHCRAFT

The Southeastern Indian concern with purity and balance was based upon the assumption that man lived in a just, well-ordered universe. So long as a man lived by the rules, which were known to him, he could expect to avoid misfortune. Yet all was not justice and order, and the Southeastern Indians knew this very well; they allowed for events whose causes were indirect, covert, and frequently unjust. They believed that these "wild" events in their lives were caused by conjury and witchcraft.[77] Conjury was the use of oral formulas and ritual acts to affect spiritual beings, including those that governed the weather, game animals, cultivated plants, and most especially the health and well-being of people. Witchcraft, on the other hand, was the intrinsically evil action of mystical means to cause human suffering and death. Any normal person might resort to conjury to attain his ends, but witchcraft was peculiar to witches, who were not human beings at all, but were heartless monsters who only appeared to be human.

We are probably safe in assuming that conjury was universally practiced among the Southeastern Indians, but our knowledge of what was entailed in conjury is reasonably complete only for the Cherokees. After Sequoyah invented his syllabary, Cherokee priests began writing their formulas down in notebooks and on pieces of paper. In these extraordinary beginnings of a sacred literature, we have been able to learn something of their assumptions about how their natural and social world was put together and of how they coped with it through ceremonial means (see fig. 3).

The first thing we must understand about conjury among the Cherokees is that it was not resorted to only in unusual circumstances. Every normal Cherokee adult probably knew and used formulas in his day-to-day affairs. A woman might utter a formula to make her food cook more quickly; a man might utter a formula to make his wind-blown cornstalks aright themselves. But some problems were more difficult than others, and it was the priests who possessed the knowledge of the formulas and ritual means of dealing with the difficult problems of life. However, the difference between formulas which were more or less common knowledge and those which were known only by the priests was for the most part a matter of degree.

Likewise, it is impossible to draw a stark line between "white" and "black" conjury among the Cherokees. One can scarcely imagine them finding fault with a person who used a formula to avoid evil or to bring about good luck. And they must have generally approved of people using conjury to rid themselves of illness. But what about a case in which a man was suffering an illness which was inflicted upon him in revenge by a person whom he had wronged? His own blood relatives would undoubtedly have approved of his conjuring to rid himself of the illness, but the relatives of the person whom he had wronged would have seen his conjuring in a different light, especially if it resulted in the illness being turned back upon the one who had sent it. People who were kin to neither the ill man nor the person he had wronged would probably have been ambivalent or noncommittal. The Cherokees possessed formulas which they believed would cause discord between man and wife, which would cause friends to quarrel, which would cause people to fall ill, and they even had formulas which were believed to cause death. But neither these formulas nor their use were intrinsically evil; their moral value depended upon the circumstances under which they were used. It was only the witch, that being who was outside the realm of humanity, that heartless wretch who senselessly attacked people, who was categorically evil.

The essential part of an act of conjury was a verbal formula (i:gawé:sdi, literally "to say one"). These formulas consisted of one or more phrases which could be spoken or sung, but the truly critical act was to think them. It was thought which made them active; the act of uttering them or other ritual acts accompanying their being uttered merely augmented or directed them.

Many of the truly serious acts of conjury required the use of "ancient tobacco" (Cherokee, *tso:lagayʌ:li*). This was not the *Nicotiana tabacum* L. with which we are familiar, but rather *Nicotiana rustica* L., a small variety of tobacco which was present in the Southeast for an unknown period of time before European contact.[78] This was one of the most important herbs used by the Southeastern Indians. They smoked it to suppress hunger, used it as a medicine, and they smoked it as a kind of spiritual facilitator before councils of war and peace and before performing rituals and ceremonies. The Southeastern Indians sometimes experienced mind-altering effects from smoking *Nicotiana rustica* L., far more than is experienced in our use of commercial *Nicotiana tabacum* L. The reason for this difference is not clear. Perhaps *Nicotiana rustica* L. contains a higher concentration of nicotene than does *Nicotiana tabacum* L., or it may be that the Indians held the smoke longer in their lungs to absorb more nicotene.[79] Another possibility is that some of the mind-altering effects could have come from other substances which they added to the tobacco. The most frequent additive was the bright red leaves of dried sumac (*Rhus glabra* L.), but the explanation they gave to Europeans for adding sumac leaves was that it reduced the harshness of the tobacco.[80]

In the memory of Cherokees in Oklahoma this ancient tobacco was grown on tiny patches of ground made ready for planting by having pieces of lightning-struck wood burned on them. These patches were hidden in the woods, where none but those growing the tobacco could see them. This ancient tobacco had no intrinsic spiritual properties; it was only an herb. It gained its power by virtue of the ritual act of "remaking" (Cherokee, *go:dhlʌhi:so ʔhnʌ:hi*, literally "remade it") which infused it with thought and power. It was this act of remaking which transferred thought to the herb, making it into a medium through which one person could affect another. Tobacco was generally remade at dawn at the bank of a stream or at a spring. A conjurer would face the sun rising in the east, hold up the tobacco in his left hand and recite a formula while kneading the tobacco in a counterclockwise direction with four fingers of his right hand. The conjurer often blew his breath or rubbed his spittle on the tobacco. If the tobacco was to be used for an antisocial purpose, it was sometimes remade at dusk or at midnight, and it was rubbed in a clockwise direction. Remade tobacco could be used in four ways: it could be smoked near the person who was the target of the conjury, so that the smoke would actually touch him; it could be blown in the direction in which he was likely to be located; it could be smoked so that the smoke would pervade and affect everyone in a general area; and bits of tobacco leaf could be left where the person to be affected would come into contact with them.[81]

Other substances besides tobacco could be remade. The Oklahoma Cherokees used the roots of the anomalous insect-devouring Venus's-flytrap (*Dionaea muscipula* Ellis) and pitcher plant (*Sarracenia purpurea* L.) as talismans and for a variety of other purposes. When remade, these roots, which they called *yú:gwil(a)*, were believed to have great power. In fact, they were believed to have the power to move of their own volition, so that one might find them in a different place from where one left them. The Indians kept these roots in small deerskin bags. When a person was embarking upon a venture in which he needed good luck, he would rub his hands over the bag containing the roots and then pass his hands over his face and body. Because *yú:gwil(a)* was unusually sensitive to influences from corpses and from menstruating or pregnant women, it was kept hidden in some out-of-the-way place.[82]

Obviously, one way to prevail over people and events is to know where they are in time and space. The Cherokees attempted to do this by using several means of divination. Some of these means were very simple, and probably known by almost everyone, while others were more complicated, requiring the services of a specialist. We have already seen that the Southeastern Indians believed that their dreams were full of meaning about events in the future, and everyone probably paid close attention to his dreams. Plummets were commonly used to divine the location of a lost object or person. A plummet was a small lump of red ocher or some other earth substance tied to a short length of string. The end of the string was held between the thumb and index finger of the right hand. The left hand was held, with fingers extended, in front of the right. A formula would be uttered, and in time the plummet would begin to swing, and the direction in which it swung most strongly would be the direction in which to search. They would then proceed in this direction for some distance, and if the thing or person was not found, another reading was taken with the plummet and they set out in another direction.[83]

The river was often used for divining into the future and for discovering the causes of illness. One method was to cut a stick of wood about two or three feet long. The diviner stood in the water, moistened one end of the stick in his mouth, then put the opposite end of the stick into the water for about half of its length and made a counterclockwise circle, about two feet in diameter, uttering a formula as he made each circle. Then he brought the stick to the center of the circle and let it rest there. Now he studied the water within the circle. If a crayfish or minnow darted into the circle it was an indication that a conjurer was at work. A bird flying overhead might mean that witchcraft was involved. If a leaf floated through the circle it meant that the person whose condition was being divined would die.[84] The river was also used for divination when Cherokees went to water upon the occasion of a new moon. While all the members of a household stood gazing into the river, the priest recited a formula asking for long life. But if anything appeared in the water—a leaf, a twig, a fish—it might mean that illness or death lay in the future.[85] Finally, in order to determine the outcome of an illness, the priest might cause his patient to vomit into the river. If the vomit sank, the patient was doomed; if it floated on top of the water he would recover.[86]

Like water, fire could also be used as a means of divination. If a person were seriously ill, and hence likely to be attacked by witches, a person protecting him would try to determine if witches were in the vicinity by using tobacco and fire. He would go to the fireplace and rake all the smouldering coals together into a cone-shaped heap. Then he would sprinkle a little ancient tobacco on the heap of coals. Wherever a spark flared up it meant that there was a witch in that direction and at a distance indicated by the distance of the spark from the top of the cone. If the tobacco particles happened to cling together and fall on top of the heap of ashes, they would often flare up with a loud burst. This meant that the witch was actually inside the house. If so, the burst of tobacco of itself was believed to be enough to kill the witch.[87]

One of the more esoteric means of divination was to use two beads: a black bead held in the left hand signifying death, illness, or disaster, and a red or white bead held in the right hand signifying health, long life, and success. A priest held these beads between the thumbs and index fingers of his hands (fig. 78). The beads moved along the first two phalanges of the index fingers, and the relative strength of this motion gave a favorable or unfavorable reading.[88] If the red or white bead had the stronger motion, it was favorable, but if the black bead had the stronger motion, it was unfavorable. Exactly what caused the movement in the beads is unclear. James Mooney thought that the movements were caused by involuntary contractions in the priest's fingers. The beads moved slowly and for only a short distance at first, then faster and faster, coming all the way down to the first joint on the index finger. The beads would come down and then go back up in an irregular serpentine motion, moving from side to side.[89]

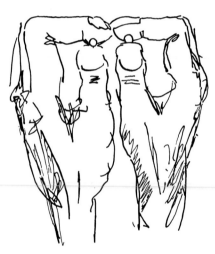

Figure 78. Cherokee method of holding beads for divination. Drawn by Frans M. Olbrechts. Negative no. 75–5993. Courtesy, Smithsonian Institution, National Anthropological Archives.

The means of divination which the Cherokees regarded as most authoritative entailed the use of certain crystals, presumably quartz. They believed that these crystals came from the scales of the Uktena (cf. chap. 3). Men who were going to war went to a priest and tried to learn of their fate in advance. The priest would gaze into his crystal, and depending upon where he saw an image in the crystal, would predict whether they would live or die. When the relatives of a sick man consulted a priest for a prognosis, he would look for the image of the sick man in his crystal. He would instruct the relatives to kill some game and prepare a feast. Later, when the feast was held, the priest would look into the crystal, and if he saw the sick man join the feast, it meant that he would recover; if not, he was doomed.

The crystals used for seeing into the future also had power in their own right. The Creeks called them *sapiyá*, believing that they brought power to a man, especially in matters of hunting and love. The Creeks ascribed power to five kinds of crystals: white, blue, red, yellow, and black. The yellow and red crystals were male, the strongest of all, while the white and blue crystals were female, and black was presumably neuter. They were said to flash and gleam like living things, and on occasion they would even move. A man kept his crystal in a circular piece of buckskin along with some powdered red pigment. When he went hunting, he put a bit of this red pigment on each cheek. When a hunter failed to kill a deer as the day wore on, he untied his buckskin pouch and let the sun's rays fall upon the crystal, and he sang a song to make it wriggle in the pigment. This was believed to charm the deer and make them come directly to the hunter. Crystals had to be handled carefully. They were hidden away in a dry place until they were actually used, and they were never kept inside one's house. To do so would sexually excite all the members of the family, especially the women, and make them behave like deer in the rutting season.

For the Cherokees the most powerful crystal of all was the ulunsuti stone which they believed came from the forehead of an Uktena (see chap. 3). The Cherokees themselves evidently debated about how many of these crystals existed. Some said that only a single man ever succeeded in capturing one. Others said that there were several. But they agreed in telling James Mooney and Frans Olbrechts that no priests at that time had possession of an ulunsuti. It was said that one could gaze into an ulunsuti and see it fill with either a streak of whitish fluid or else a vein of blood.[90]

Conjury consisted not only of trying to learn about people and events hidden in time and space, but it also consisted of acts which were aimed at influencing the lives of people and modifying the outcome of events. Like all of the Southeastern Indians, the Cherokees expended great care and psychic energy in carefully managing their relationships with kinsmen and neighbors. Some measure of this care can be seen in the fact that the Cherokees had several formulas which a person could use to create a feeling of good will among a group of people in which he was going to be present. In some cases a man used a formula which was specifically meant to overcome the ill will that a particular member of a group held for him. If a person in the group was known to hold a bitter grudge, then it would become necessary to "remake" some tobacco and smoke it in his presence. The following is a particularly powerful formula.

> Now! Nearby here the Great Red Uktena now
>   wends his way.
> Now! Now the glare of the Purple Lightning will
>   dazzle the Red Uktena.
> Also this Ancient Tobacco will be as much of a
>   thorough-going Wizard.
> Now! The Seven Reversers looking at me will be
>   dazzled by the Great Red Uktena.

In this formula a conjurer infuses the Red Uktena into the tobacco to bedazzle any Cherokee who was working against him or who held enmity toward him.[91]

The Cherokees went to great lengths to avoid causing feelings of enmity in other people. This is why they so frequently met strangers with silence rather than with the joking and small talk that we ourselves resort to in such situations. If they did happen to offend someone, they had special formulas which they believed would cause the person to forget the slight or insult. Such formulas could also be used to subdue dissension within a family and in any other situation in which one could gain an advantage in having someone else forget something.[92]

In affairs of the heart the Cherokees used formulas, often strikingly beautiful ones abounding in bird symbolism. Used by both sexes, many of the formulas were meant to attract members of the opposite sex.[93] Just as one could remake tobacco, one could invoke the red cardinal, red hummingbird, and red Tlanuwa and remake oneself, surrounding oneself with a spiritual aura which was irresistible to members of the opposite sex. The following formula was recited by a man who wished to gain a particular woman's attention at a dance. He recited it while bathing in a stream.

358

Listen! O, now instantly, you have drawn near to hearken, O *Ageyaguga* (i.e. the moon). You have come to put your red spittle upon my body. My name is _____. The blue had affected me. You have come and clothed me with a red dress. She is of the _____ clan. She has become blue. You have directed her paths straight to where I have my feet, and I shall feel exultant. Listen![94]

The formula refers to the moon because the moon was believed to have a great effect on women, and the color red attracted women irresistibly. The allusion to the moon's spittle, the essence of its being, refers to the fact that in some of the formulas a person would actually spit on his hands and rub the saliva over his face and other parts of his body.[95] The color blue represents a type of loneliness that made one susceptible to the opposite sex.

The Cherokees also had formulas which guarded against alienation of affection. A man might be worried about his young wife who could be attracted by other men. At night, after she had fallen asleep, the man would sing the following song in a low voice.

Listen! O, now you have drawn near to hearken.
—Your spittle, I take it, I eat it. (first night)
—Your body, I take it, I eat it. (second night)
—Your flesh, I take it, I eat it. (third night)
—Your heart, I take it, I eat it. (fourth night)

Listen! O, now you have drawn near to hearken, O, Ancient One. This woman's soul has come to rest at the edge of your body. You are never to let go your hold upon it. It is ordained that you shall do just as you are requested to do. Let her never think upon any other place. His soul has faded within him. He is bound by black threads.[96]

On four successive nights, the man would moisten his fingers with spittle and rub it on his wife's breast while singing this formula. The second line of the formula was repeated four times. The last two sentences are curses on any would-be seducer. Cherokee priests claimed that if a man performed this ritual, he need never fear for his wife.

To deal with still another affair of the heart, the Cherokees had a formula which a jealous suitor could use to separate two lovers or even husband and wife. A man either smoked tobacco or threw it in the fire before reciting the following formula.

Yu! On high you repose, O Blue Hawk, there at the far distant lake.

The blue tobacco has come to be your recompense. Now you have arisen at once and come down. You have alighted midway between them where they two are standing. You have spoiled their souls immediately. They have at once become separated.

I am a white man; I stand at the sunrise. The good sperm shall never allow any feeling of loneliness. This white woman is of the _____ clan; she is called _____. We shall instantly turn her soul over. We shall turn it over as we go toward the Sun Land. I am a white man. Here where I stand her soul has attached itself to mine. Let her eyes in their sockets be forever watching for me. There is no loneliness where my body is.[97]

The Blue Hawk is invoked because it brings trouble with it, separating the lovers and spoiling their souls for each other. The man uttering the formula says that he is a "white man," meaning that he is happy, attractive, fortunate, and never lonely.

The conjury feared most by the Southeastern Indians was that which was done in the spirit of vengeance. They believed that a priest could cause a person to fall ill by magically intruding small objects, such as bits of cloth, flint, or charcoal, into his body. The Cherokee word for a priest who did this was *dida:hnese:sg(i)*, literally a "putter-in and drawer-out of them."[98] When Cherokees felt small rheumatic pains or stitches in their sides, they would suspect that they were being attacked by conjury. If they subsequently fell ill they would go to a priest who would make small incisions over the affected part of the body with a piece of briar, a sliver of flint, or a rattlesnake tooth. Then he would suck the object out.

Or a person seeking vengeance could go to a priest and hire him to perform conjury that would cause his enemy to go mad. Here is a particularly chilling formula to induce madness.

Your Pathways are Black: it was wood, not a human being!
Dog excrement will cling nastily to you.
You will be living intermittently. "*Wo?!*" You will be saying along
    toward the Nightland.
Your Black Viscera will be lying all about. You will be lonely.
You will be like the Brown Dog in heat. You are changed: you have
    just become old. This is your clan _____.
In the very middle of the Prairie, changed, you will be carrying dog
    stools. "*Wo?!*" you will be saying.
Your Pathway lies toward the Nightland![99]

360

In this formula the victim is turned into a wooden thing with no feeling. In his madness he will behave like a dog, befouled with excrement, making the sounds of a dog—Wo?!.

In addition to intruding objects into his victim's body a priest was believed to be able to cause his victim to fall ill or even to die by "changing his saliva," i.e., by causing it to change into lizards or plants inside his body. Mooney collected a formula from Swimmer which was believed to accomplish this. The priest first followed his victim around until he chanced to spit on the ground. Then he collected a little of the victim's spittle on the end of a stick and placed it inside a hollow joint of wild parsnip, a poisonous plant. Into this same hollow joint he also placed seven earthworms beaten into a paste and several splinters from a tree which had been struck by lightning, thus thoroughly confounding and mixing things of the Upper World and Under World. The priest then took this tube into the forest to a tree which had been struck by lightning. At the base of the tree he dug a hole, placing a large yellow stone slab in the bottom. He placed the tube in the hole along with seven yellow pebbles. Then he filled the hole with earth, built a fire over it, and recited the following formula.

> Listen! Now I have come to step over your soul. You are of the
> _____ clan. Your name is _____. Your spittle I have put at rest under the earth. Your soul I have put at rest under the earth. I have come to cover you over with the black rock. I have come to cover you over with the black cloth. I have come to cover you with the black slabs, never to reappear. Toward the black coffin of the upland in the Darkening Land your paths shall stretch out. So shall it be for you. The clay of the upland has come to cover you. Instantly the black clay has lodged there where it is at rest at the black houses in the Darkening Land. With the black coffin and the black slabs I have come to cover you. Now your soul has faded away. It has become blue. When darkness comes your spirit shall grow less and dwindle away, never to reappear. Listen![100]

Throughout this entire procedure, the priest and his client had to observe a strict fast. The statement that the victim's soul was blue means that he should begin to feel ill and experience troubles. The repeated uses of black signify death. If this ceremony were properly carried out, the victim was supposed to begin to feel the effects at once, and if he did not employ counter magic his soul was supposed to shrivel up and death would come within seven days. The priest and his client observed the man closely. If nothing happened to him they would assume that he had used counter magic, and perhaps that he had even succeeded in turning the curse back upon them—a serious matter.

As a precaution, after the ceremony the priest and his client went to a lonely spot in the mountains where there was a suitable stream of water; there they built a temporary shelter of bark and poles. Then they went down to the stream, the priest taking with him two pieces of cloth, one black and one red, and seven red and seven black beads. The priest then laid the two pieces of cloth on the ground, placing the red beads on the red cloth and the black beads on the black cloth. The priest then took a red bead, representing his client, between the thumb and index finger of the right hand and a black bead, representing the victim, between the thumb and index finger of the left hand. The priest faced the east, holding up the beads and looking at the red bead invoking blessings on his client in a low chant, his voice rising and falling at intervals. Then he held up the black bead, calling down curses on the victim. Finally, addressing the stream as "Long Person," he implored it to protect his client. With this the client dipped up water and poured it over his head and shoulders seven times, or else immersed himself seven times. This done, the priest made a small hole in the earth, dropped in the black bead, and buried it with a stamp of his foot.

While held aloft the beads moved in the priest's fingers. If the red bead was the more lively in its movements, the priest predicted success for his client. But if the black bead prevailed, he predicted that the victim had strong counter magic and that their efforts would fail. With this, the whole ceremony had to be repeated until the movements of the red beads prevailed, or until they showed that the victim had access to magic that was too strong to be overcome. In this case the client usually went to another priest.

An intrinsically vague and uncertain distinction existed between a priest who used conjury to cause a man to fall ill, go mad, or die and a witch who could do the same. As we have already seen in chapter 3, the witch was the epitome of ambivalence in human affairs. Witches appeared to be ordinary human beings, but their viscera were full of lizards and other Under World creatures which forced them to steal the time remaining in people's lives and add it to their own. Here was the difference between a priest and a witch. The priest used

conjury to attack people in accordance with legal and moral pre-
cepts, while the witch attacked people involuntarily and uncontroll-
ably. The priest was moral, the witch was amoral. Because witches
were believed to steal years of life away from their victims and add
them to their own, it followed that witches were likely to be very old.

The Cherokees believed that witches could read a person's
thoughts, and that they could cause evil to happen by merely
thinking it. They were believed to have the ability to transform
themselves into other shapes, particularly into the guise of a
purplish ball of fire, a wolf, a raven, a cat, or an owl. The Cherokees
had several euphemisms for witches—including "owl," "raven-
mocker," and "night-walker," the latter referring to the witch's
abnormal propensity for moving about at night, either flying
through the air or burrowing beneath the earth. As a way of keeping
witches from stealing the soul of a person who was ill, a priest would
blow a circle of smoke from remade ancient tobacco all around the
house and recite the following formula.

> Now! No one is to climb over me!
> His soul itself over there will be broken as the
>   Sun rises, this Thinker of me; in the very middle
>   of the light of the setting Sun he will be broken,
>   this Thinker of me!
> I will have emerged from the Seven Clans.
> Then I have just come to strike you with Small Arrows,
>   with Small Arrows I have just come to strike you!
> Then I have just come to strike you with Lightning!
> Then I have just come to strike you with Thunder!
> Then with Clay your soul will be broken![101]

Fire and lightning, the principal means of achieving purity, were
especially powerful against witches.

If it were established that a priest had killed someone through
conjury, then presumably the Cherokees would have judged and
punished him in accordance with their law of retaliation. But when
witches were proved to be witches, they were summarily executed.
Precisely how they proved that a person was a witch is unknown, but
they most definitely did. In 1765 an old Chickasaw conjurer told
James Adair that he had determined that a child who had died
suddenly had been bewitched by an old woman; the old conjurer
had then executed the old woman without fear of sanction.[102] Being

outside the pale of humanity, the witch was not protected by the law of retaliation. Her kinsmen would not avenge her death. Witchcraft remained a capital offense among some of the Southeastern Indians until well into the nineteenth century. In 1824, for example, the Arkansas Cherokees passed a law making it illegal to kill a suspected witch.[103]

It is the realm of conjury and witchcraft wherein we have the greatest difficulty in intellectually identifying with the Southeastern Indians. What we must remember above all is that they lived out their lives in small, intense, social worlds, where disordered relationships could cause grave difficulties. And getting at the root of such troubled relationships could be a murky business indeed. Seen in this light, it is altogether likely that the means of divination used by the priests might have actually helped to free their minds from thinking in the accustomed channels, thus helping them come up with unusual solutions to what was troubling their patients. This is suggested in a remarkable formula:

> May I have Your attention now? Thunder, I obey You, and You love
> me for it.
> You feed upon my soul.
> All night long I am filled with Your Spirit, which is life itself.
> No evil can come to me.
> Make my consciousness weightless and free, like the movements of
> that agile insect, the Water Strider.
> Well! You know I have a duty to perform: to find out something.
> You know me; for I am _____.[104]

Here the priest asks that his mind be made as agile as the "water strider" so that he can hit upon solutions which are not obvious. Could a modern psychotherapist wish for more?

But after all this explanation one may still ask questions of why the Southeastern Indians believed the world was put together the way it was, of why they believed it was full of sentient spiritual beings that could be influenced by conjury. Why did the Southeastern Indians, who were so sensible and practical in most things, resort so enthusiastically to beliefs and behavior which seem to us to have been so foolish and ineffective? Even if this question could be satisfactorily answered, it would still be difficult for us, with our own notions of how the world is put together, to bridge the gap in understanding which is essential if we are truly to understand the Southeastern

364

Indians in their own terms. It is instructive to learn, however, that to eighteenth-century Europeans this world view was not nearly so alien. James Adair, for example, tells us that conjury and witchcraft were favorite topics of conversation among the Southeastern Indians, and that the traders who became conversant with them came themselves to believe in the existence of witches.[105] In other words, these beliefs made good sense in the social and cultural context in which they existed.

THE GREEN CORN CEREMONY

In addition to rites of passage and other ceremonies performed on behalf of individuals and kin groups, the Southeastern Indians celebrated a series of seasonal ceremonies and festivals attended by entire chiefdoms or groups of affiliated chiefdoms. The most important of these occurred between early spring and late summer. The Natchez celebrated each new moon of their lunar calendar with a ceremonial feast. Each of these ceremonial feasts featured a particular kind of food. Hence the ceremonial cycle was the ritual counterpart of the yearly food-getting cycle of the Southeastern Indians. Here, in the words of an eighteenth-century observer, is an outline of the Natchez ceremonial calendar:

> The first moon [i.e., the month of March] is that of the Deer.[106] The renewal of the year spreads universal joy. In order to render this feast more distinguished they then represent an event of interest to them of which they guard the memory preciously . . . .
>
> The second moon, which corresponds to our month of April, is that of the Strawberries. The women and children collect them in great quantities, and as strawberries abound in this country it may be judged whether the great Sun lacks them. The French also avail themselves of this harvest. The warriors then make their presents of wood ducks, which they have provided by a hunt made expressly for the purpose.
>
> The third moon is that of the Little Corn. This month is often awaited with impatience, their harvest of the great corn never sufficing to nourish them from one harvest to another.
>
> The fourth is that of the Watermelons, and answers to the month of June. This month and the preceding are those in which the sardines [?] run up against the current of the river.
>
> The fifth moon is that of the Peaches. It answers to our month of July. In this time grapes are also brought in if the birds have left any of them to ripen.

The sixth moon is that of the Mulberries. It is in the month of August. At this feast birds are also brought to the great Sun.

The seventh moon is that of Maize or the Great Corn.

The eighth moon is that of the Turkeys and corresponds to our month of October. It is then that this bird comes out of the thick woods to enter the open woods in order to eat nettle seeds, of which it is very fond.

The ninth moon is that of the Bison. Then they go hunt this animal. As it always stays some leagues from the cantons inhabited by men, precaution is taken to send forward to find it in order to know on what side it has thrown itself. When this is known everyone sets out, young and old, girls and women, unless they have little children, for this hunt being rough there is work for everyone. Many nations wait until later before going, in order to find the bison in greater numbers and the cows fatter. I have said before that the natives, not knowing enough to cut off the back parts of the males as soon as they have killed them, only kill them when they are fat, in order to get the tallow, without taking away the flesh, which is good to eat only when this precaution has been taken.

The tenth moon is that of the Bears. In these hunting seasons the feasts are not large, because the warriors, being all away from home, take away many of the people with them.

The eleventh moon, which corresponds to our month of January, is that of the Cold Meal. At this time many bustards, ducks, and other similar kinds of game are to be had.

The twelfth moon is that of the Chestnuts. This fruit has already been collected a long time ago, but nevertheless this month bears the name.

Finally the thirteenth moon is that of the Nuts. It is added to complete the year. It is then that the nuts are broken in order to make bread, mingling it with corn meal.[107]

Most of these seasonal ceremonies declined in importance in the eighteenth century and thereafter, but the one held in late summer, the Green Corn Ceremony, corresponding to the Natchez feast of the Great Corn, remained important. Throughout the entire history of the Southeastern Indians, from very earliest times until the recent past, the Green Corn Ceremony has been by far the most important of their seasonal ceremonies. The precise time at which it was held varied from group to group and from time to time. It was supposed to coincide with the ripening of the crop of late corn, and this could be anywhere from late July to early September. Among the Seminoles, because of their southerly location, it often came as early as May or June.[108] In one form or another the Green Corn Ceremony was celebrated by virtually all of the Indians in the eastern United

States. The one element that was embodied in the Green Corn Ceremony wherever it was practiced was that it was a rite of thanksgiving, an expression of man's gratitude that the corn crop was successful.[109] Beyond this, additional meanings and functions of the Green Corn Ceremony varied from one group to another.

In the Southeast the Green Corn Ceremony was an important vehicle in the Indians' quest for purity. The early European colonists in the Southeast called the Creek Green Corn Ceremony the "busk," after its Creek name *poskita*, literally "to fast." With fasting being one of the principal means of attaining purity among the Southeastern Indians, this is an important clue to what the ceremony meant to them. Namely, they thought of it as a means of purifying their social order.

The first act of the Chickasaws in initiating their Green Corn Ceremony was to decide on the precise day on which the ceremony was to begin.[110] They picked the time when the moon first became full after the ears of their late corn had filled out.[111] If they were like other Southeastern Indians, they would have then made up a quantity of pieces of split cane about the size of matchsticks. They would have tied these into bundles, with the sticks representing the number of days remaining until the ceremony was to begin. A messenger was sent with one of these bundles to every town which was invited to the ceremony.[112] The miko of the town threw one of these sticks away until only one remained, and this signaled the day on which the ceremony was to begin. They all departed their towns in good time and converged upon the place where the ceremony was to be held.

After all of the people from the various towns had assembled at the site of the ceremony, their first order of business would have been to arrange places to live for the duration of the ceremony. In some cases they would have stayed with fellow clansmen who lived in or near the town where the ceremony was to be held. But if room were scarce, or if the ceremony were being held away from a town, as was the custom among the Natchez,[113] and later the Seminoles,[114] the various clans would have had to erect temporary shelters.

On the first day they ate a great quantity of food in preparation for a long fast. But they were careful not to eat any of the current crop of vegetables. This was particularly true of the men. After this feast was over, all scraps of food were carefully removed from the square ground, the area which was the focus of the ceremony. On this day they also set about getting their public buildings in good order. The men plastered the miko's cabin on the square ground with white clay, and they plastered the warriors' cabin with red clay or else they painted it with the juice of a certain red root; then they tied cedar twigs to the posts of the cabins around the square ground. The town house was carefully swept clean, and the old ashes from the fireplace were carried out. Sometimes they spread a layer of white sand on the square ground. Others had the task of covering the seats on the square ground with new mats woven of split cane. The high priest, along with some of his assistants, dug up the fireplace in the square ground and swept it out. Then the high priest placed a few pieces of button snakeroot, some leaves of ancient tobacco, and some ears of corn and other vegetables into the bottom of the pit; next some of his men covered it with a layer of white clay and wet it down with clean water. Then they swept the square ground clean.

In the late prehistoric period the Southeastern Indians renewed and refurbished their public buildings more extensively than in the historic period. Archaeologists have long known that many Mississippian mounds began as a public building at ground level, then at a later date this building was either burned or torn down, a mantle of earth was placed over this, and a new building was built on top of the mantle of earth. The precise nature of the occasions on which the Indians decided to enlarge the mound with a mantle of earth is not well understood. At least occasionally the public buildings were struck by lightning and burned down, and the Southeastern Indians interpreted this as a sign that something was seriously wrong in their relationship with their deities.[115] We know from events which happened when the de Soto expedition reached Cofitachequi that the Indians sometimes succeeded in desecrating the public buildings of their enemies, and this may have occasioned the rebuilding of them. The death of a chief or some other important man may also have required the burning and rebuilding of a public building.[116]

While the men repaired the public buildings, the women cleaned their houses and their cooking vessels, and renewed their hearths. Everyone was forbidden to eat salt until the last day of the busk. Men were forbidden to touch any female, including infants, for the duration of the ceremony. The Creeks had a rule that when the men wanted to refer to women, they were not to use the word which meant "woman"; instead, they had to use appelations such as "food preparer" (*hōmpita haya*) or "one who has a house" (*tcukoléidji*). Perhaps the most stringent prohibition was that no one was permitted to eat any of the late corn before the Green Corn Ceremony was performed. This rule was most strictly observed by men; it was usually relaxed in the case of women, and often relaxed in the case of children and sick people. The early corn, being of a different category, could be eaten freely.

In the next phase of the Chickasaw Green Corn Ceremony all of the priests, political officials, warriors, and other honored men were called into the square ground by the miko's speaker to begin a fast. All children, undistinguished men, and women were excluded from the square ground. Women were strenuously excluded with the exception of some old prestigious women who took part in one of the ceremonies. Women and children were required to speak in a gentle tone of voice and to preserve harmony. Four sentinels stood at the four entrances to the square ground to keep out animals and impure people. Any dogs, for example, that happened to enter the vicinity of the square were supposed to be shot.

From the afternoon of the first day until the second sunrise the men observed a strict fast. That is, they fasted for a day and two nights. On the second day of the ceremony, while they were fasting, the priests boiled a quantity of *pasa* (button snakeroot), a bitter emetic, which all of the men took repeatedly to purge themselves of impurity. Later in the day, one of the old men would place a large quantity of ancient tobacco just outside the square ground. One of the old, prestigious women would pick it up, taking it to all of the men who could not be in the square ground because of illness, impurity, or lack of attainment. They ate the bitter leaves to purify themselves. The head priest fasted for three days prior to the first day of the Green Corn Ceremony, taking button snakeroot and ancient tobacco. Then, after fasting with the others, he was noticeably emaciated and weakened. In thus purifying themselves, the head priest and the other men believed that they ensured happiness and well-being to the people during the coming year.

Tuckabahchee, an important Lower Creek chiefdom, had an unusual feature in its Green Corn Ceremony. Tuckabahchee possessed a number of sacred objects in the form of brass and copper plates. Some of these plates were circular, and others were cut in the shape of celts or axes. The brass objects were definitely acquired from Europeans, but the copper celt-form objects may have been made from native metal (see fig. 58). One of the celt-shaped copper plates has been recovered from a grave near the Coosa River in Alabama.[117] These Tuckabahchee plates were kept hidden the entire year to be brought out during the Green Corn Ceremony on the day on which the men fasted. Women were forbidden to touch or even see them, lest they lose their potency. At dawn on this day they were ceremoniously carried down to a river or creek where they were washed and scoured. Then they were taken to the miko and put on display on a bed of white sand in the square ground.[118] On the morning of the following day they were returned to their hiding place in the earth beneath the miko's seat on the square ground.

The Florida Seminoles perhaps retain something of this old Tuckabahchee pattern of displaying sacred objects in their custom of bringing out their medicine bundles on the fast day of their Green Corn Ceremony. The Seminole medicine bundle is wrapped in a deerskin with the hair side out. It measures about one foot by two feet and is about six or eight inches thick.[119] In it are a large number of objects, each wrapped in a small piece of buckskin. Included are pieces of ginseng; hair of the white deer; small pieces of the horns of various animals, including the left horn of a horned serpent; divining crystals and other miraculous stones; the bones of Little People; rattlesnake teeth; and flint for lighting sacred fire.[120] Traditionally, each Seminole group which annually performs a Green Corn Ceremony owns a medicine bundle which is under the care of one of their medicine men. Like the Tuckabahchee plates, the Seminole medicine bundles are brought out at dawn on the morning of their fasting day. Reminiscent of a Natchez custom, a pole is stuck into the ground and the bundle is suspended from it. In the evening the medicine man takes out all the contents and examines each of them. Early in the morning of the following day, the medicine man picks up the medicine bundle and walks toward the east until he is out of sight. He returns the bundle to its hiding place for another year. In the traditional Seminole way of thinking, the medicine bundle is the "soul" of their society.

If the Chickasaws were like the Seminoles, the day on which the men fasted would also have been the day on which they discussed and attempted to settle serious crimes. Any crime which could be

370

settled at the Green Corn Ceremony was considered settled for good.[121]

On the morning of the third day of the Chickasaw Green Corn Ceremony, the women cooked a large quantity of food and placed it outside the square ground and immediately returned home. Some of the men went out and brought the food into the square ground. The men then ate the food, but not at once, because it was considered bad form to be in a hurry to break a fast of such gravity. By noon every vestige of the food was cleared from the square ground. The women carried all of the vessels to the river and washed them. As soon as the sun began declining from high noon, the chief priest ordered an attendant to announce to the town that new holy fire was about to be created, commanding all the people to stay inside their houses, to take care not to break any rules, and to extinguish every spark of their old fires. He threatened any who failed to heed these commands with dire consequences.

This was to prepare for one of the most critical acts in the ceremony—the making of new fire. For this occasion the high priest was dressed in a white buckskin "waistcoat," and he wore a white buckskin about his shoulders. Instead of going barefoot, he wore a pair of white buckskin moccasins with streaks of red painted across the toes. A tuft of blunted wild-turkey spurs was fastened above the toes. These moccasins were sewn by the high priest himself with sinews from the same animal from which the skin was taken. This was the only occasion on which he wore these moccasins. Around his neck the high priest wore a carved gorget made from a conch shell, with two holes bored through it and an otter skin thong stuck through the two holes and attached to two white buttons made of deer's horn. On his head he wore a piece of swan skin, doubled and wrapped around so that only the white feathers showed, and on the crown of his head he wore a tuft of white feathers.

When the time came to light the new fire, everyone in the square ground fell silent. The high priest and his assistant rose up and walked with a reverent, dignified step to a place where the others could not see. The high priest took a piece of dry poplar, willow, or white oak with a hole drilled partly through it and placed it between his knees. Then he took a short length of wood of a different kind and briskly drilled it between his hands for several minutes until the piece of wood between his knees began to smoke. Then he put on chips and splinters of pitch pine and fanned up flames with the wing of a white bird.[122] With the flames safely started, the high priest placed the fire in an old earthen vessel[123] reserved for this purpose and carried it out onto the square ground, placing it under an arbor whose roof was covered with a thick layer of green boughs.

The attendant fed the fire with dry wood, and a town crier was sent out to spread the good word. An old woman brought a basket of newly ripened corn and other vegetables to the square ground and placed them near the entrance. The high priest then rose from his seat and walked around the fire three times with a slow pace and a grave demeanor, rapidly speaking appropriate words in a low voice. He took a little of each of the new fruits, rubbed bear oil on them and threw them onto the fire. He also put a little black drink and button snakeroot medicine into the fire. Then he took these medicines and purified the white and red seats on the square ground. With this done, all social wrongs committed in the previous year except the crime of killing a person were forgiven. All lawbreakers who were suffering ostracism or social restriction could now return to society as full social beings.

A man went out to summon the women, who presently appeared and stood around the outside of the square ground. The high priest gave a speech to the warriors, reminding them of their responsibility to remain pure and to carry out their responsibilities bravely. Then, in much less polite language, the high priest gave a speech to the women. He told them that if any of them had failed to extinguish their old fires, or if any of them were impure, they must depart immediately or the divine fire would punish them and their relatives. He told them that they should be careful to serve only pure food to their children, lest they get worms or fall ill. He assumed a particularly sharp tone in cautioning them not to break marital or sexual rules. Then the high priest addressed all the people, and in bold, eloquent language told them to think about the new holy fire he had brought to them to purify their society. He told them that in the coming year they should endeavor to stay pure, else the divine fire would take vengeance upon them. He told them that if they behaved properly they would enjoy good health, the rainmakers would be able to bring plenty of rain, and they would be victorious over their enemies; but if they failed to keep the rules they could expect drought, captivity and death from their enemies, witchcraft,

372

and disease. His speech ended, and an attendant took some of the holy fire outside the square ground so that all of the women could get fire to light new fires in their houses.

At this point one of the high priest's assistants called in six of the old prestigious women for a dance. Each entered the square ground carrying a bundle of branches from various kinds of trees. They were dressed in their finest clothes, anointed with bear oil, and wearing tortoise shell rattles on their legs. They were joined by six old priests, each carrying similar bundles of branches pulled from the arbor over the holy fire in one hand and a wand decorated with white feathers in the other hand. The eldest priest led the dance, encircling the fire, stamping his feet with short, quick steps, and singing a sacred song to the accompaniment of pottery drums. The others followed him singing and dancing. The music thus combined drumming, the strong voices of the old priests, the shrill voices of the old women, and the sounds from the tortoise shell rattles on their legs as they danced. After about fifteen minutes the dance ended.

In the meantime a religious attendant went out to get some *Ilex vomitoria* Ait. leaves to make some black drink. The men drank this periodically throughout the remainder of the busk. The old priests, in particular, drank it to attain purity. If any of the warriors had to stay home because of wounds, a conch-shell drinking cup full of the black drink was taken to them.

The Florida Seminoles differ at this point in that their "big gathered medicine," their equivalent of the Chickasaw black drink, contains no *Ilex vomitoria* leaves. Presumably this is because *Ilex vomitoria* does not flourish in their area. Instead, their "big gathered medicine" includes a whole list of medicinal herbs, including red bay leaves (*Persea borbonia* [L.] Spreng.), blueberry leaves (*Vaccinium myrsinites* Lam.), and lizard's tail leaves (*Saururus cernuus* L.). The men drink this medicine to keep themselves from falling ill as a consequence of eating the late corn. Moreover, in the coming year it is supposed to keep their bodies strong and healthy, prevent them from gossiping, and keep them from "going crazy."[124]

After igniting new fires in their houses, the Chickasaw women outdid themselves in cooking large quantities of the new corn and vegetables for a feast on the fourth day of the busk. Ordinarily, the Indians ate sparingly, but on this feast they ate great quantities of dried meat, fish, oil, corn, beans, pumpkins, and wild fruit prepared into as many as fifty or sixty different dishes. The women carried this food to the square ground in the highest of spirits. Each man on the square ground was served food in strict order according to his rank. Later the warriors, their heads covered with white feathers and carrying white feathers in their hands, danced in three concentric circles around the sacred fire. They sang as they danced, accompanied by musicians with gourd rattles and two earthen drums covered with thin deerskins. Later the men redecorated themselves with war paint, took up their weapons and fought a mock battle. Just before the festivities drew to a close, they asked the women to join them in a dance, and they imposed a fine on any woman who refused to come. Such persuasion was seldom necessary. The women came dressed in their finest apparel, with pendants in their ears, several strings of white beads around their necks, their heads shining with bear oil, and with tortoise shell rattles attached to their legs. They joined the men dancing in three circles around the fire; they danced together for a time, and then the men and women separated.

To bring the ceremony to a close, the high priest asked one of the other priests to make an announcement to the people. The man announced that the Green Corn Ceremony was over, that all had been made pure, and that all must paint themselves and follow him. All the people immediately went to work painting themselves all over with white clay. They then followed the high priest in single file and in a strict order: after the high priest came his assistant; then the old beloved men according to seniority; next the warriors according to their reputations; the women followed them in an order of their own; they were followed by their children, who carried the little ones in their arms; and last came people who had eaten unsanctified fruits or who had broken other rules. When they reached water, the high priest immersed himself, and all the others followed suit. Afterwards they returned to the square ground for more dancing, and then the people went home. The Green Corn Ceremony was over, all was made pure, and a new year had begun.

The Green Corn Ceremony was the turning point in the Southeastern Indian year. We have nothing in our own calendar of holidays which comes close to matching it in its load of social and cultural meaning. We would have something approaching the Green Corn Ceremony if we combined Thanksgiving, New Year's festivities,

Yom Kippur, Lent, and Mardi Gras. In terms of its meaning, perhaps it comes closest to our New Year's festival, an occasion on which many people try to straighten out their affairs and make resolutions to be better people in the coming year—a year in which this attempted social tidiness will inevitably become frayed. The Southeastern Indians symbolized this wear and tear on the social order with their Sacred Fire. This was why they extinguished the old fire which had become polluted through man's inability to live up to his higher social ideals. But the Green Corn Ceremony wiped out all of this. People who were angry with each other became reconciled; people who had committed crimes were forgiven (mankillers excepted); and people who became lax in playing their social roles in good order were reminded of what their roles truly entailed.

Like nothing in our experience, the Green Corn Ceremony "cleansed" the fundamental categories in their world view, tidying up their minds and improving their mental health. This is most marked in the categorical distinction between men and women. It was during the Green Corn Ceremony that men and women played their separate roles to the hilt. Thus we find that in the afternoons throughout the Green Corn Ceremony the men and women played the one-pole ball game, and in the evenings they participated in dances. As we shall see in the next chapter, both the one-pole ball game and the Southeastern Indian dances were notable in their emphasis on sexual dichotomy.

CHAPTER SEVEN

ART, MUSIC, AND RECREATION

The ceremonies and rituals of the Southeastern Indians seem bizarre, outlandish, even irrational, until viewed against the background of their belief system. When seen in their original context, in the ideological and social soil out of which they grew, the ceremonies and rituals of the Southeastern Indians are no more irrational than our own. We encounter the same sort of problem in understanding the art forms and games of the Southeastern Indians, and likewise we find the solution to be similar. Our best road to understanding their artistic and recreational forms is to view them as the outward expressions of their belief system. Only in this way can we come to understand truly the feeling and care they lavished on their pottery, basketry, and stonework and the physical rigors they withstood in training for and playing their games.

In some ways the task of understanding the artistic and recreational forms of the Southeastern Indians is more difficult than understanding their ceremonial life. One problem is that they reached their highest artistic development in the late prehistoric and early historic period. De Soto saw architectural forms and artistic creations that surpassed anything witnessed by the Europeans who came after him, and because many of these creations were made of perishable materials, they did not survive. Hence perhaps the best Southeastern Indian art is irretrievably gone. But even when the works did survive, how can we know the standards they used to judge the expertise and creativity of the artist? Perhaps the best we can do is to describe their art forms in terms of our own aesthetic categories and to try then to show how they fit into the larger cultural and social patterns out of which they grew.

376

A further difficulty in dealing with the artistic and recreational forms of the Southeastern Indians is that all of these are intimately imbedded in other social and cultural institutions. They are neither as self-contained nor as separable from other institutions as are the art forms and games in our own culture. For instance, the Southeastern Indians placed a high value on men who could use words skillfully. Jack and Anna Kilpatrick have discussed the condensed poetry in some of the Cherokee magical formulas, some of them containing single words, compound in form, which may be likened to tiny imagist poems.[1] The most appropriate place for the presentation of these formulas, however, is not here, but in the earlier discussion of the Southeastern Indian ceremonial life. Another form of verbal artistry was oratory, the words of a gifted speaker that could move contentious men to reach consensus or the timid and hesitant to go against the enemy. And yet oratory can hardly be separated from the political institutions of the Southeastern Indians. Still another form of verbal artistry was the oral tradition, the rich and dramatic narrative whose purpose was to instruct and entertain. But here, too, it has seemed best to present a selection of these oral traditions in relation to the social institutions which elucidate them. Thus though the Cherokee story about the clan of people who were transformed into bears (chap. 3) is a good story even by our own standards, it is far more meaningful when seen in relation to the anomalous position of the bear in the Southeastern Indian belief system.

In looking at the art and recreation of the Southeastern Indians, we will often wish that we knew more about underlying social factors. For example, even though we know much about the Southeastern Indian ball game, we do not know the precise nature of the social and political forces which led them to play it with such ferocity. To a lesser extent we know the basic rules of chunkey, but what we do not understand is why the Indians would sometimes bet the last thing they owned on the outcome of a game. In general, we sense that the players of these games were motivated by social factors which lay outside the playing field, but we cannot often be specific about what they were.

ART

Like most of the aboriginal people of the New World, the South-

377

eastern Indians made great use of geometric design motifs. In the historic period they used two basic styles of geometric design, the Eastern and the Western.[2] The Eastern geometric style, frequently seen in historic Creek, Seminole, and Yuchi woven textiles, uses strings of simple diamonds, V's, and W's (see fig. 66). Finger-woven belts and garters from the eastern part of the Southeast are often completely covered with patterns composed of these simple elements. We know little of the significance of these designs, although it can be noted that for the Florida Seminoles the diamond design represents a rattlesnake.[3] In contrast, the geometric style used by Indians in the western part of the Southeast employed two types of circle motifs, both of which are rendered on a plain background. The first, the double scroll, consists of two scrolls or circles connected by a diagonal line (see fig. 86). The other motif consists of rosettes or circles spaced on a panel, with the circles enclosed in diamonds or alternated with X's and other figures. Like the Eastern motifs, these Western designs appear on finger woven textiles such as garters, sashes, and belts. Both the Eastern and Western geometric styles have some historic depth, with both occurring on prehistoric pottery recovered from the two areas.

In their use of geometric motifs the Southeastern Indians were not greatly different from other North American Indians. This, however, was not the extent of their art. They had in addition an art style that was distinctively their own.[4] It was a style unlike the austere Plains hide paintings; unlike the other-worldly, highly symbolic art of the Southwestern Indians; and unlike the intricately symbolic art of Mesoamerica. Their art style included the iconography of the Southeastern Ceremonial Complex, with such motifs as the cross in a circle, the forked eye, the barred oval (see fig. 44), the bi-lobed arrow, and so on (see fig. 32). In addition it included sprightly line drawings of animals (see fig. 39), men, and beings with mixed human and animal features (see figs. 35, 46). We know from William Bartram's observations in the Southeast that the Indians once decorated the buildings around their square ground with wall paintings of bold, well-proportioned beings with mixed human and animal features. Some of them, said Bartram, were "very ludicrous and even obscene," i.e. they were complete with male sexual organs.[5] These paintings were executed in white (using white clay or chalk) on walls which had been plastered with red clay, and in red,

Figure 79. Human head effigy pot with tattooing. Blytheville, Arkansas. Courtesy, Museum of the American Indian, Heye Foundation.

brown, and blue on walls which had been plastered with white clay. In all probability these figures of men with the heads of "duck, turkey, bear, fox, wolf, buck, &c." and of these same animals with human heads were painted in accordance with the seating arrangements of the various clans. Bartram says that the posts in front of the main cabin at the Atasi square ground were "formed in the likeness

379

of vast speckled serpents ascending upwards." Nor was Atasi the only place where Europeans saw this. The Houma temple along the lower Mississippi River is described as having a vestibule at its entrance whose walls were decorated with four "satyrs," two of which were neatly executed in relief, and all were painted in black, white, red, and yellow colors.[6] These verbal descriptions are poor substitutes for the works of art themselves, but none has survived. Fortunately, however, subjects similar to these wall paintings and carvings were inscribed in miniature on shell, stone, and pottery, all of which are more durable materials, and, as a result, many have withstood the passage of time.

Personal adornment was an important artistic medium. The men, for example, painted their bodies on all important occasions. Using red, black, and yellow pigments, the men painted elaborate designs on their faces, shoulders, and chests (see figs. 59, 62). Women, on the other hand, used body paint sparingly. Although it is difficult for us to appreciate it, the Indians of the Southeast expended much care and artistry in tattooing designs on their bodies. These were made by punching the skin with sharp needles dipped in red cinnabar or lamp black, the latter imparting a blueish color to the skin. Tattoos were worn by both men and women, but by men in particular. The designs were both geometric and representational and adorned the face, chest, arms, and legs. Bartram described the Creeks as being decorated with representations of the sun, with fanciful scrolls winding around the torso, thighs, arms, and legs, dividing the body into "tablets" which were then filled in with representations of animals, particularly serpents, military actions, and so on, all of these serving as visible marks of exploits and achievements. Bartram says that the tattooed designs were well executed, reminding him of mezzotints.[7] Fortunately, we can gain some idea of these painted and tattooed designs from human effigies made of pottery (fig. 79) and from representations of tattooed or painted people inscribed on shell, and also from a few drawings and paintings made by John White and Jacques Le Moyne de Morgues (see figs. 27, 56).

All evidence points to the fact that the Southeastern Indians were skilled at carving wood. The chroniclers of the de Soto expedition, for example, tell of religious buildings filled with wooden statuary. Yet few of these wood carvings have survived the decaying action of acidic Southern soils. Our best examples of wooden art forms come

Figure 80. Mask with deer antlers. Spiro, Oklahoma. Courtesy, Museum of the American Indian, Heye Foundation.

381

from two archaeological sites where circumstances allowed good preservation: namely, the Spiro site in Oklahoma and the Key Marco site in southern Florida. From Spiro we have a collection of full sized and miniature masks carved from red cedar with eyes, teeth, and ear spools of shell inlay. One particularly fine mask from Spiro is a man's face with graceful deer antlers on top, all of it carved from a single piece of cedar and smoothly finished (fig. 80).[8]

Figure 81. Deer mask. Key Marco. Negative no. 13256–7. Courtesy, The University Museum, University of Pennsylvania.

Figure 82. Wooden statuette of a kneeling cougar. Key Marco. Negative no. MNH 1224. Courtesy, National Museum of Natural History, Smithsonian Institution.

An even richer collection of carved wooden objects was recovered from the mud at Key Marco, Florida, in 1896. This remarkable site contained both human and animal masks, expertly carved and elaborately painted, some with eyes of shell inlay. Two particularly fine animal masks were found—one representing a deer (fig. 81) and the other representing a wolf with bared fangs. Both were painted to make them more closely resemble real animals. They were hollowed to fit the face, and holes for strings were bored through the wood on both sides. Some of the human masks were paired with animal masks and painted in identical colors, suggesting, perhaps, that a dancer or performer wore the human mask while holding the animal mask in his hand to represent dramatically his transformation into an animal.[9] Also found at Key Marco were a series of carved wooden tablets, varying in length from a few inches to almost five feet, and of uncertain meaning, though it has been suggested that they represent the head and cephalothorax of a spider. This interpretation is probably correct because, consistent with other spider representations, some of these tablets contain a cross in a circle motif. This is also consistent with the Cherokee story about the origin of fire (chap. 3). Perhaps the finest carving found at Key Marco was a six-inch statue of a cougar with realistic ears, nostrils, mouth, and paws (fig. 82).[10]

The Southeastern Indians were good basketmakers. From de Soto onward we have descriptions of baskets and mats woven with pleasing angular and curvilinear geometric designs, and a few pieces of basketry have been recovered from archaeological sites. There are two basic basketmaking techniques: weaving, in which the basket is built on a warp foundation, and coiling, in which the basket is built by over-and-under sewing with some kind of flexible material on a foundation of rods, splints, or coiled grass or straw. One of the characteristics of Southeastern Indian basketry is that almost all of it was made by weaving, and particularly by twilling. The Southeastern Indians did make some use of bark and grass in their basketry, but because of their preference for twilling, their favorite material by far was thin pieces of the outer covering of cane.[11] Some of these strips were dyed black, red, or brown and used along with natural strips to produce angular and curvilinear designs. They made a variety of baskets, including small baskets with handles; sieves and fanners for processing hominy meal; large burden baskets with

Figure 83. Choctaw basket. Double weaving may be seen through the hole at upper right. Early twentieth century. Negative no. 1102–b–25. Courtesy, Smithsonian Institution, National Anthropological Archives.

flared openings (see fig. 106); small and large hampers, often with tightly fitting covers (fig. 83); and small baskets whose bottoms came down to a point, these being somewhat reminiscent of the pointed pouches in the Southeastern Ceremonial Complex.[12] They also twilled large cane mats, usually measuring about five feet by six feet (see fig. 52). They used these mats for bedding, for carpeting, to cover the seats in the square ground, to cover the walls and roofs of their houses, to wrap the bodies of their dead for burial, and un-doubtedly for many other purposes.[13] The Chitimachas and Cherokees made particularly fine baskets. The finest Southeastern baskets are "double-weave baskets," so called because they are woven with back-to-back inside and outside fabrics, such that the surface of the basket is glossy and smooth both inside and out.

385

The finest surviving "graphic" art is that inscribed on shell. Some of these drawings occur on the conch shells that were used as dippers and as drinking cups (see figs. 35, 44, 46). Several particularly fine specimens were found at Spiro.[14] A far more frequent shell art form, as we have seen, is the shell gorget, a flat piece of shell, generally circular in shape, though other shapes were also used, and measuring between two and nine inches in diameter. The tops of these gorgets were perforated by two holes, through which the two ends of a leather thong were inserted and attached to buttons made of bone or horn, so that the gorgets could be worn about the neck. From John Lawson we learn that some of these gorgets were highly valued by the Southeastern Indians, some being worth three or four dressed buckskins.[15]

Many of the gorgets are inscribed with the iconographic symbols of the Southeastern belief system. The simpler ones are incised with fine lines into which a dark pigment was rubbed. The more elaborate ones combine incising with cutting out sections of the shell, leaving the design in outline. The most frequent overall design is a circle, or a set of concentric circles, with a cross inscribed in the center (see fig. 34).[16] In more elaborate forms, the cross in the center was made small and surrounded by a series of serrated or scalloped circles. Some of the gorgets are scalloped circles with a swastika or swastika-like figure in the center. Still others combine these motifs with a circle of human hands, sometimes with eyes in the palms.

On the more elaborate gorgets these iconographic symbols are combined with representations of animals, particularly the spider, the woodpecker, and the rattlesnake. The Southeastern Indians regarded the spider as a clever creature who caught its prey by intelligence and stealth (see fig. 38). The woodpecker was evidently admired by the Creeks for its ability to penetrate tree trunks and extract insects. And perhaps for the same reason woodpecker beaks were sometimes used by priests to "extract" objects from their patients' bodies. And the Cherokees believed that a certain type of woodpecker, the *dalala*, was terrifying to the enemy. Thus the woodpecker gorget might have been worn both by priests and by warriors (see fig. 37). The rattlesnake also had great ritual significance. Cherokee priests, for example, would coil giant spiritual rattlesnakes around the house of an ill man to keep the witches away, leaving a space between the head and the tail for the man's relatives

386

to pass through. Cherokee priests used rattlesnake fangs to make scratches before sucking out objects that were magically intruded into a person's body. One type of gorget, found mainly in Tennessee and Georgia, is a highly conventionalized depiction of a coiled rattlesnake with a huge eye (fig. 84). This design becomes a little more understandable when we learn that the Cherokee word for the Uktena meant, literally, "brilliant looker, bright-eyed."[17] Thus the rattlesnake gorget was perhaps worn as a protection against witchcraft or illness.

Figure 84. Rattlesnake gorget. McMahan Mound, Tennessee. From William H. Holmes, "Art in Shell of the Ancient Americans." *Second Annual Report of the Bureau of American Ethnology.* Washington, D. C., 1883, plate LXIII.

387

The shell gorgets that most excite our admiration are not the ones with iconographic designs, but those depicting men engaged in various activities. The drawings are sprightly, indicating a sense of movement. Men are shown fighting, running, dancing, playing games, and performing ritual acts (see fig. 32). Some of the men depicted have animal features, perhaps representing spiritual beings or men mimicking animals. A wealth of information is contained in these gorgets, much of it still not well understood.

During the Mississippian period the Southeastern Indians made pottery in an astonishing variety of utilitarian and ceremonial forms.[18] The utilitarian ware is generally plain (see fig. 30), though sometimes it is brushed, cord-marked, or incised, and it is buff, gray, brown, or black, depending on the kind of clay used and the way in which it was fired.

The finest examples of ceremonial pottery were made of blue or white clay tempered with fine sand or fresh-water shells crushed to a very fine powder. They fashioned their pottery on a small flat board which they placed on their lap, forming the vessel out of coils of clay, which they built up to form surprisingly thin walls. They smoothed the vessel inside and out with their hands, occasionally moistening their fingers in water. After the vessel was shaped they allowed it to become quite dry. Then the potter usually took a small smooth stone and polished the inside of the vessel. Then other decorations were added and the vessel was sometimes polished on the outside. When a potter had a sufficient quantity of dried vessels, she built a fire, and when there were enough hot coals, she scooped out a place in the middle, placed her vessels inside, and covered them over with hot coals to fire them.[19] Because the vessels were not glazed, water would seep slowly through the walls, and as it evaporated it cooled the vessel and its contents.

Pottery in the Southeast was a genuine art form, and like basketry it was a woman's art form. Indeed, Mississippian pottery reached a level of development that has rarely been matched by any people at a comparable level of social development. Mississippian people made a variety of bowls, finished by polishing and sometimes decorated with the addition of a red slip. They made pots large enough to hold as much as six gallons (see fig. 75). They decorated their pottery by polychromatic painting; by incising it with their fingernails, combs, and reeds; by marking it with cord and fabric; and by

388

Figure 85. Moundville jar with incised bird of prey. Courtesy, The University of Alabama, Museum of Natural History, Mound State Monument.

paddling the surface with a variety of dentate, crenulate, roulette, checker, parallel, and complicated stamp designs. Many of the finer pieces are decorated with the same iconography as that used on the shell gorgets (fig. 85). Some have incised human, animal, fish, shellfish, and vegetable motifs. Some vessels have strap handles, loop handles, lugs, plain spouts, stirrup spouts, pedestal bases, tripodal bases, and tetrapodal bases. Some of the vessels have their rims decorated with small effigies of human and animal heads (see fig. 42).

389

The ceremonial vessels included water bottles, cooking pots, jars (fig. 86), bowls, and shallow pans. The vessel that was most clearly an art form was the water bottle, a generally globular vessel with a neck and a small opening at the top. It was here that the creative hand of the potter was most free. The simplest of these water bottles have a plain globular body with an elongated neck. To this the potters added incised or painted designs. To the bases they sometimes

Figure 86. Caddoan jar. Yell County, Arkansas. Courtesy, Museum of the American Indian, Heye Foundation.

390

Figure 87. Hunchbacked human effigy bottle. It may represent an individual with rheumatoid arthritis. Recovered from a stone box grave near Nashville. Courtesy, Thruston Collection, Vanderbilt University.

added tripods. These vessels were high achievements in the potter's art, but by our standards, even finer artistic achievements were the water bottles made in the shapes of animals and men. These were made in the shape of owls (see fig. 43), frogs (see fig. 41), opossums, dogs (see fig. 72), and seated or kneeling human figures (fig. 87).

391

Some of them are so detailed that they portray hair styles and body and facial tattooing (see fig. 79).[20]

The Southeastern Indians possessed several stoneworking techniques. The oldest of these, chipping and flaking, goes all the way back to the Paleo-Indians. The technique consists of detaching flakes from the stone being shaped either by striking it with another stone or, for precise work, by exerting pressure on it with a small piece of pointed bone or antler. This was the method the Southeastern Indians used in fashioning projectile points, drills, scrapers, knives, hoes, axes, and other tools out of quartz, flint, and similar materials. Though this is an unfamiliar stoneworking technique to us, the Southeastern Indians raised it to a high art. They used it to fashion some truly extraordinary objects which they used either for ceremony or show. These were large pieces of flint shaped to mimic objects which were made out of other materials (fig. 88). The famous Duck River cache found in Tennessee includes flint reproductions of discoidals, "swords," bi-pointed knives, "batons," war clubs, and other objects. The "batons" were evidently hafted and used as actual or ceremonial war clubs. The largest of the "swords" measures twenty-seven and one-half inches, a truly extraordinary technical achievement.[21] Some of the characters inscribed on shell gorgets are shown holding bi-pointed knives and "batons."

The Southeastern Indians were also accomplished at a technique of working stone that is easier for us to appreciate. Namely, they worked stone by grinding and abrading it into a desired shape and by then polishing it to a high finish. This was the method used in fashioning stone axes and plain and spatulate celts. Some of these axes and celts are so finely made and so lacking in signs of wear that they must have been used either for ceremonial purposes or in warfare. At Spiro, Moundville, and Etowah several axes with both the celt and handle made in one piece out of finely polished stone have been found (fig. 89). These, certainly, must have been purely ceremonial or aesthetic.

Another distinctive Southeastern art form is the stone disc. These were made of polished stone, measuring 5 to 12 inches in diameter, often with scalloped edges reminiscent of some of the shell gorgets. Some of these discs have serpents, hand-eye designs, and other motifs engraved on them (fig. 90). Several of them have been found with graphite, red ocher, and other pigments on them, suggesting

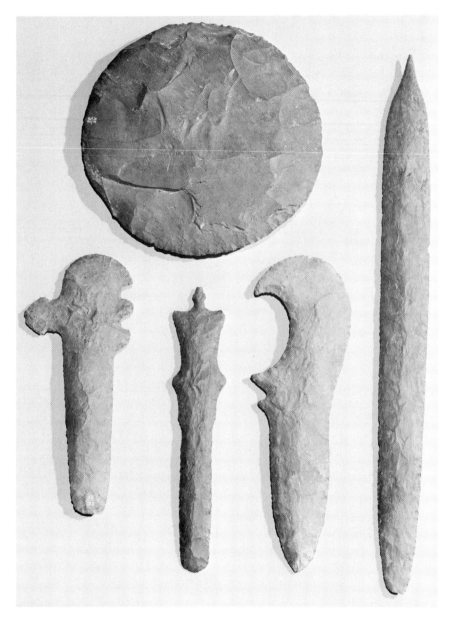

Figure 88. Selected artifacts from the Duck River Cache. *Above right:* a discoidal. *Below, from left to right:* a war club; a "baton" war club; bird of prey claw; "sword." Courtesy, Frank H. McClung Museum, University of Tennessee.

393

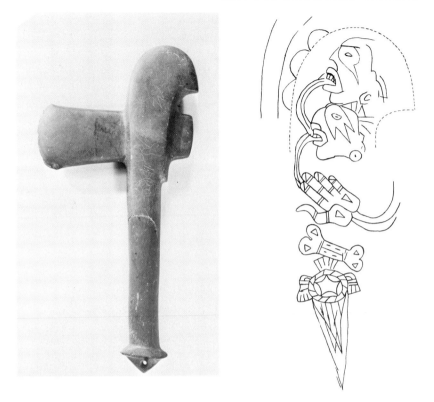

Figure 89. Monolithic axe. Recovered near Ballground, Georgia, along the Etowah River. The incised design shows two human faces with forked-eye designs, a hand, a long bone, and a scalplock on a hoop. Negative no. 38,518–A. Courtesy, Department of Anthropology, National Museum of Natural History, Smithsonian Institution. The drawing is from *The Waring Papers: The Collected Works of Antonio J. Waring, Jr.*, edited by Stephen Williams, Fig. 17, p. 80. Courtesy, University of Georgia Press and Peabody Museum, Harvard University.

that they were used as palates for preparing and mixing pigments, or were themselves painted in a ritual context.

Judged solely in terms of our own aesthetic standards, we can admire these stone tools and ritual objects from a technical standpoint, but they do not conform to what we ordinarily think of as art. The stone effigy pipes and statuary of the Southeastern Indians come closer to something that qualifies as art in our terms. Pipes for smoking tobacco were carved out of sandstone, hematite, or soapstone, and they were also made out of pottery. Some of the pipes were carved in animal forms, the most frequent being the owl, the frog, and the bear. Perhaps the finest of these pipes represent people kneeling or reclining, playing chunkey, or, perhaps humorously, themselves smoking pipes (fig. 91). Seldom more than eight or nine inches in height, the finest of these pipes are admirably executed, with the same lively quality as some of the engravings on shell cups and gorgets. Because some of the effigy pipes are quite heavy, weighing as much as eighteen pounds, the Indians must have smoked them while resting them on the ground.

The Southeastern Indians smoked tobacco both for its own sake and as a sacrament in ritual contexts, and it is no doubt for the sake of

Figure 90. Stone disc with scalloped edge. A hand-eye design is encircled by two horned serpents. Courtesy, University of Alabama, Museum of Natural History, Mound State Monument.

Figure 91. Stone effigy pipe depicting a warrior and his victim. The warrior wears a turban-like headpiece, and he appears to have some kind of armor attached to his chest and back, perhaps like that in the temple at Cofitachequi as described by the de Soto chroniclers. Spiro, Oklahoma. Courtesy, Museum of the American Indian, Heye Foundation.

396

the latter that they decorated their pipes so elaborately. James Adair says that young men tied deer trotters, turkey cock spurs, "bell-buttons" and pieces of tinkling metal to the stems of their war pipes; and they sometimes tied to the middle of the stem a piece of scalplock, smeared with red pigment, with the hair hanging down.[22] The Natchez used two ceremonial pipes or "calumets": a peace pipe and a war pipe. The peace pipe had a stem about one and one-half feet long which was covered with the skin and feathers from a wood duck. Attached to this was a fan of white eagle feathers, with black tips, and with small red tufts and tassels attached. The war pipe had the same shape as the peace pipe, but its stem was covered with the skin and feathers from the neck of a turkey buzzard. They attached a fan of flamingo feathers to the stem. These feathers were grayish-white, but they dyed them red and attached black tufts and tassels to their tips.[23]

The most impressive sculptured works of art are a series of statues which have been found mainly along the Tennessee, Cumberland, and upper Coosa-Tallapoosa rivers, and to a lesser extent along the lower Mississippi and Ohio rivers. Several dozen of them have been found, most of them carved out of sandstone, limestone, or marble, and a few out of wood. They vary from a few inches to over two feet in height. Males are represented as sitting cross-legged or else kneeling on the left knee with the right knee raised, while females are represented as sitting with their legs tucked beneath them.

In several instances pairs of the statues, representing a man and a woman, have been found interred together in stonelined graves. At Etowah archaeologists excavated a particularly fine pair carved out of white Georgia marble. Traces of white, red, black, and a greenish blue-black pigment are still evident on these statues. The woman wears a typical short skirt and has a packlike object on her back, perhaps symbolizing an infant on a cradle board (fig. 92). A particularly fine sandstone statue was found in a cave in Wilson County, Tennessee. It depicts a man kneeling on his left knee, with his right knee raised, and with his hands resting on his knees.[24]

Several early observers mention statues which were kept in temples, most of them made of wood. Peter Martyr mentions them for coastal Georgia. The descriptions of statues at Talomico from the de Soto expedition have already been described in chapter 2. James Adair tells us that the main war town among the Upper Creeks had

Figure 92. The Etowah statues. *Left:* a male, sitting cross-legged. *Right:* a female, sitting with her legs tucked beneath her. Courtesy, Historic Preservation Section, Georgia Department of Natural Resources. Photograph by David J. Kaminsky.

such a statue which he thought may "have been originally designed to perpetuate the memory of some distinguished hero, who deserved well of his country; for, when their *cussena*, or bitter, black drink is about to be drunk in the synedrion [town house], they frequently, on common occasions, will bring it there, and honor it with the first conch-shell-full, by the hand of the chief religious attendant: and then they return it to its former place."[25]

The Southeastern Indians never became very proficient at the technology of metal working, but their artistry in working metals compares favorably with that of comparable societies elsewhere in the world. With almost negligible exceptions, all of their work was in copper, a metal which occurs as nuggets in the Lake Superior region and to a lesser extent in north Georgia and in Tennessee. They used

398

this copper to make jewelry and ceremonial objects. Some of it they made into celts which were undoubtedly used in ceremonial contexts. An unusual cache of copper celts with wooden handles carved in the form of woodpeckers was uncovered at Spiro (see fig. 58).[26] The Indians also hammered the copper nuggets into thin sheets

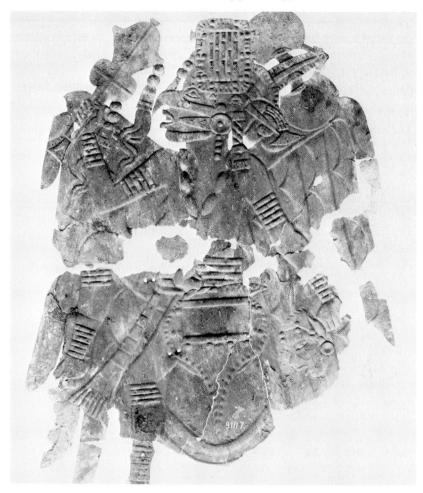

Figure 93. Repoussé copper plate from Etowah depicting a man impersonating a falcon. In his right hand he holds a "baton" war club; in his left hand he holds either a mask or a human head. Note the bi-lobed arrow and the pointed pouch. Negative no. 8094. Courtesy, Department of Anthropology, National Museum of Natural History, Smithsonian Institution.

399

which they used to cover small wooden or stone objects, such as earspools and bi-pointed knives. Sheet copper was also cut into circular gorgets and into silhouettes of "batons," "bi-lobed arrows," and feathers to be worn in headdresses. Perhaps the finest examples of metal work in the Southeast are the series of copper sheets found at Etowah with dancing men embossed on them. Each dancer is shown wearing a falcon mask, an elaborate headgear, a feathered cape, and brandishing a war club (fig. 93).

As we saw in chap. 6, the Tuckabahchees, one of the more important Creek chiefdoms, possessed a number of thin metal plates which they continued to use in ritual contexts into this century. Two or three of these were circular plates of brass; undoubtedly the Tuckabahchees obtained them from Europeans. The other four or five plates were copper sheets cut in the form of celts, similar in shape to celts found at Spiro, Etowah, and at other Mississippian sites. The Tuckabahchees kept them hidden away, bringing then out only at the time of the Green Corn Ceremony. They could only be handled by certain men, and then only when they were fasting, and they were always to be kept away from unclean women. When a truly important man died, they would bury one of the plates with him. When the Tuckabahchees were removed to Arkansas in 1836, six warriors were selected to carry the plates. Each carried on his back a single plate wrapped in a piece of buckskin. These six men spoke only with each other, and never to any of the thousands who made the walk with them to Arkansas. The six walked in single file, one mile in advance of the others. One Tuckabahchee tradition was that the Great Spirit gave them the plates when he gave them fire. He commanded them to extinguish their fires each year and to rekindle new fire by friction; and the plates were to be exhibited only at this time.[27]

MUSIC AND DANCE

As among other North American Indians, music, dance, and ritual were closely associated in the Southeast. All dances had musical accompaniments, and many of the rituals had interludes of dancing and music. Indeed, no clear line can be drawn between dancing and ritual because both were believed to contribute to the health and happiness of man. As for their musical instruments, the Southeastern Indians used the same ones that were used generally by Indians in North America. These were the drum, the rattle, and the flageolet (fig. 94).

Some of the early European accounts mention that when the Southeastern Indians went into battle they beat on a drum made of a deep wooden "platte" with the mouth tightly covered with a skin. But the favorite musical drum was made by stretching a wet deerskin over a small earthen pot, sometimes partially filling the pot with

Figure 94. Southeastern musical instruments. *Left:* Choctaw drum (negative no. 1102–b–7). *Right:* Cherokee gourd rattle (negative no. 42,432–A). *Lower:* Choctaw flageolet (negative no. 33,963). Courtesy, Department of Anthropology, National Museum of Natural History, Smithsonian Institution.

water, which was used periodically to remoisten the drumhead. Later in the historic period some Southeastern Indians made drums from hollow sections of black or tupelo gum trees, measuring about thirty inches long and fifteen inches in diameter. The drumhead was attached by means of hoops in such a way that it could easily be tightened.[28]

Rattles were commonly made of dried gourds into which a few beans, grains of corn, or pebbles had been placed, and which were affixed to wooden handles (see figs. 1, 94). In some cases these rattles were deliberately made in different sizes so that their sounds would be different. To the ends of these rattles the Cherokees sometimes fastened rattlesnake rattlers or hawk feathers.[29] Another kind of rattle was made of terrapin shells filled with pebbles and attached to heavy leather straps. The women wore these tied about their lower legs in some of the dances. In some places the women used leg rattles made of deer hooves affixed in large numbers to "stockings" they wore on their legs, so that when they danced they made a rattling sound.

Another instrument, the flageolet, was not nearly as important as the drum and the rattle. A simple wind instrument made of a length of cane or deer tibia, the flageolet was used not as an accompaniment to singing and dancing as were the drum and rattle, but rather as a kind of musical embellishment. The early European explorers were often welcomed into villages by men who came out to meet them playing flageolets. When chiefs went in procession, some of the men who went along played flageolets. In recent times the Mississippi Choctaws made flageolets out of cane, about one foot in length and with two fingerholes, and, reportedly, conjurers played them before and during ball games in order to help their side win. As elsewhere in North America, unaccompanied instrumental music was rare in the Southeast. They did, however, sometimes play the flageolet in this manner, though to European ears it produced a discordant sound. William Bartram described it as a "hideous melancholy discord."[30] In addition to the flageolet, warriors sometimes carried small whistles which they blew as they attacked their enemies.[31]

The basic unit of Southeastern music was the song.[32] Some of the present-day descendants of the Southeastern Indians still know and sing the traditional songs, and it is primarily from the performances of these people that we know anything at all about the style of the

Southeastern Indian music. The length of the songs is variable. Some are only ten seconds long, and even the longer ones last only a few minutes. A great many consist of short sections which are repeated and combined in various ways. Characteristically, the Cherokees combine these phrases in fours and sevens, the typical song consisting of seven phrases repeated four times.[33] For the most part the songs are sung using five-note and four-note scales. When the five-note scale is used in Cherokee music, only the four higher notes are extensively used in the song, while the lowest note is used almost exclusively to mark the end of a phrase or section.[34] Many of the Southeastern Indian melodies have a throbbing or undulatory movement which gradually descends. They are sung with a moderate amount of vocal tension. In their songs the Southeastern Indians are unusual among North American Indians in that they often begin and end with shouts or yells, and some of the songs employ antiphonal and responsorial techniques, in which a group of singers repeats phrases sung by a group leader.[35] Both of these devices, it should be noted, are characteristic of Negro music, and it has been suggested, though inconclusively, that they may represent an African influence.[36]

Among the Southeastern Indians music was closely tied to dance, and dance was tied to the full range of life itself. Many of the dances were named after animals, and the Indians believed that these dances affected the animals and their relations with man. Among the Alabamas, for example, there was the "horned-owl dance," the "snake dance," the "bear dance," the "bison dance," and so on. Most dances had restrictions on them. The Alabamas would not dance the horned-owl or snake dance in June, July, or August because both dances employed a serpentine movement that was believed to make snakes angry and vengeful. After participating in these particular dances the Alabamas would put their feet up close to the fire so that snakes could not see to bite them, and they would warm their hands in the fire and then rub their eyes in the belief that this would enable them to see snakes and avoid them. We can see, then, that even though dancing was an occasion of merriment and festivity, its full meaning went far beyond the event itself.

Certain features recurred regularly in Southeastern Indian dances. Dancers, for example, often arranged themselves in a circle or a spiral, frequently formed around a fire (fig. 95). The Indians

Figure 95. General dance of the Natchez Indians. From Le Page Du Pratz, *Histoire de la Louisiane*, Paris, 1785, vol. 2, opp. p. 376. Negative no. 1168–B–3. Courtesy, Smithsonian Institution, National Anthropological Archives.

almost always danced in a counterclockwise direction, the direction in which they believed a rattlesnake coils itself and the opposite direction of that followed by the sun. While going counterclockwise, the dancers would hold fans in their left hands to shield their eyes from the fire, and their right hands would be left free to do other things. When women joined in the dancing, they often formed a circle inside the men's circle and moved in a direction opposite that of the men.

The dancing itself was a simple, alternating shuffle, with the knees slightly relaxed and the body inclined forward. Men and women had different dance styles. In Cherokee dancing the women were more graceful than the men, moving their feet in a shuffle of three or four inches. The balls of their feet slid rhythmically across the ground, with only the heels being raised and lowered. Cherokee dancers held their arms limply at their sides, making few dramatic gestures.

Among the Alabamas the horned-owl dance was a great favorite. It was always danced in September, after snakes had gone in their holes for the winter. The dancers assembled and danced around a fire to the accompaniment of an old man shaking a rattle and singing. The men and women danced counterclockwise in a circle led by an old man. Each man held a handkerchief by one corner while the opposite corner was held by a woman. A woman might be followed by another woman, or by a man, but a man was never followed by another man. The men carried turkey-tail fans in their left hands. Occasionally, the dance changed and moved in a clockwise direction. The dance would end with the women standing in a row on the southeast side of the fire. One of the old men would then take up a baton made of a cane pole some twelve feet long with a hoop attached to one end; the pole had deer tails and a loaf of bread attached to it. The old man walked along letting the hoop touch the head of each woman in turn, saying, "Make bread." Another old man stood by counting off the women—"one, two, three . . ."—and when he counted the last one all of the men said "Oh!" in a high pitched voice, signifying that this portion of the dance was finished.

At this point the men departed to the woods to hunt deer. Subsequently, they brought back their venison to the dance ground and were joined by the women, who had baked large quantities of bread. They all danced once again the horned-owl dance, and afterwards the bread was distributed among the men and the venison was distributed among the women. Later, while seated, the men began to sing, led by a man shaking a rattle. They sang through a song four times and then stood up and sat down again in their places. They then stood up once again to form a circle surrounding the women. First the men danced backward with the women following them, and then the men paired off with the women. Each couple danced around the fire four times and then veered off in one of the cardinal directions. Then in an ever narrowing spiral, they danced in toward the fire again, then danced around the fire four more times, and then out in another direction. They did this for each of the four directions. The dances and the distribution of food lasted for four nights.[37]

The bawdy Cherokee booger dance was more a dramatic occasion than a dance.[38] As it was observed in the earlier part of this century, it went as follows. All of the people attending a booger dance would assemble at someone's house. For a while they would amuse themselves with ordinary social dances. Then it would be announced that some strangers were expected. The women and children would begin showing visible excitement and anxiety, a most unusual relaxation of Cherokee rules of demeanor. The air crackling with suspense, the booger gang would appear at the door. They would be four to ten men wearing blankets or sheets wrapped about their bodies and wearing masks representing Northerners, Southerners, Germans, Frenchmen, Chinese, Negroes, and Indians from other tribes.

The masks were grotesque. Most of them were carved of wood and dyed various colors using vegetable dyes. Masks of white men often had moustaches and bushy eyebrows made of opossum fur. Another type of white man mask—perhaps that of a mean man—was made of a large wasp or hornet nest that had been hollowed out from inside. Still another white man mask—representing a sex maniac —was made from a gourd. In the center, where the nose should have been, there was a pendulous length of gourd with opossum hair about its base, representing a phallus and pubic hair (fig. 96).

When the boogers came into the house, the dance leader would ask them their names. The boogers would pretend to speak languages other than Cherokee; they would whisper, clear their throats, or growl. When they did give their names, they were often obscene. Boogers might be named German, Frenchman, Black, Black Buttocks, Sooty Anus, Rusty Anus, Big Phallus, Her Puden-

Figure 96. Cherokee gourd booger dance mask with phallic nose. Negative no. 13075. Courtesy, The University Museum, University of Pennsylvania.

dum Has Long Hairs, and so on. In some cases when a booger was asked his name, he would reply with the sound of someone breaking wind, at which point everyone would laugh uproariously. Some of the boogers carried beneath their cloth wrappings elaborate phal-luses made of gourds. They would suddenly expose them and rush toward the women and girls, who would fall over one another trying to get away.

407

The boogers were hilarious because they were rule-breakers. The Cherokees had many rules of sexual restraint, but the boogers knew no restraint. They would push a man aside and try to get at his wife. Some of the boogers would act as if they were mad, falling to the floor, striking at the spectators. After the dance leader managed to quiet these boisterous "strangers," he would ask them why they had come. "Girls!" they would cry, and the women and girls would scramble out of the way again. Or they would say that they had come to fight, an overt aggressiveness which violated another fundamental Cherokee rule of behavior. Then the boogers would dance, awkwardly, like white men trying to do an Indian dance. Occasionally, a booger would rush at the women, thrust forward his buttocks and expose his gourd phallus, leaving the women screaming and giggling. Later the boogers would do a bear or eagle dance and the women, nicely dressed and behaving like upstanding Cherokee women, joined them. The boogers continued their obscene gestures, even imitating the motions of sexual intercourse. But the women were unperturbed. They pretended not to notice. The dance ended when the boogers abruptly and rudely rushed away and out the door, perhaps pausing to try to drag a screaming girl away from her laughing companions. After the boogers went out and laid their costumes and masks aside, they returned inside as ordinary, well-behaved men and joined in the dancing and merriment.

THE BALL GAME

The ball game was played in one form or another by most of the Indians in eastern North America. All the Southeastern Indians played it, with the possible exceptions of the Caddos and some of the Florida Indians. Lacrosse, the national game of Canada, is an adaptation of the game as it was played by the Algonkian Indians in northern North America, where it was played with one ball stick. The Iroquois, the Dakotas, and the Indians around the Great Lakes also played it with one stick, but the Southeastern Indians generally played with two (see fig. 100). These ball sticks were two to two and one-half feet long and were made out of a piece of hickory or pecan wood, bent into a loop at one end to form a kind of spoonlike racket. The loop was laced across with deerskin, squirrel skin, or vegetable fiber.[39] The Cherokees sometimes twisted bat whiskers in the strings and tied feathers from purple martins and crested fly-catchers to their ball sticks; this was believed to make their movements in the game swift, accurate, and deceptive to the opposing side.

The balls used in the game were made of deerskin stuffed tightly with deer or gray squirrel hair. The game was played on a cleared stretch of river bottom land, and each end of the field was marked by a goal consisting of two poles driven into the ground. The eighteenth century Chickasaw ball ground was about 500 yards long with goal posts about 3 yards apart at the base but further apart at the top. In later times the field was 150 to 200 yards long and the goal posts were 3 to 3½ feet wide with a crossbar at the top. The nineteenth century Creek playing field was 100 yards long with goals of the same form as those on our own football fields; the posts were set 4 feet apart and the crossbar was 20 feet high.[40] The object of the game was to throw the ball between the poles or to strike one of the poles with the ball. Either accomplishment scored one point. Among the Cherokees the first team to score twelve points won the game. For the Creeks the first to score twenty points won the game.

Play began when an old man (whom the Creeks called the "Ball-Witch")[41] walked out onto the field and tossed the ball up into the air between the two teams; after this the ball could only be picked up with the ball sticks. The players often struggled for eight or ten minutes before anyone gained possession of the ball. After picking it up, however, a Cherokee player could elect to discard his ball sticks and carry the ball in his hands, though the ball could be thrown for greater distances with the help of the ball sticks, which effectively lengthened the arm. The player ran with the ball, with or without the ball sticks, until he was threatened with interception by members of the opposing team, whereupon he tried to throw the ball to one of his teammates. Picking up a ball with the hands was a foul. The number of players varied, the only rule being that the sides had to be even. Mooney saw Cherokee games in which there were as few as nine players on each side, but earlier accounts describe games among both Choctaws and Creeks in which several hundred players were on the field at one time, drawing cheers from hundreds of spectators (fig. 97).[42] The game was a rough one. In 1879, W. O. Tuggle heard of one game between the Cussetas and the Cowetas (Lower Creek towns) in the Indian Territory in which one player was killed on the playing field, three died later, and fifteen were as long as a month in recovering.[43]

Figure 97. Choctaw ball game—ball up. Oil on canvas by George Catlin, 1836. Courtesy, National Collection of Fine Arts, Smithsonian Institution.

At the close of their Green Corn Ceremony the Natchez played an unusual variant of the ball game which the French called *pelotte*. The men of the red and white moieties divided themselves into two teams, with the white team wearing white feathers on their heads and the red team wearing red. The white team was the team of the Great Sun, and the red team was the team of the Great Warrior, and the goals were the Great Sun's house and the Great Warrior's house. The Great Sun and the Great Warrior began by tossing the ball back and forth between themselves, with both teams watching attentively. Then, when they least expected it, the Great Sun would throw the ball into their midst. The object of the game was to keep the ball from touching the ground, but at the same time, it was not allowed to be carried by the players—they had to keep it in the air by swatting it with the palms of their hands. Anyone who did try to

410

carry it would have it forcibly taken away by the other team and he could expect help from none of his own teammates. The game ended when the ball touched either the Great Sun's or the Great Warrior's house. A game could last as long as two hours. The winning team had the right to wear their feathers until the next ball game was played.[44]

A mere description of the rules of the game and the paraphernalia used in it does not begin to describe the social meaning it had. As we have already seen, to a large degree the ball game, "the little brother of war," was an important element in the political structure of the Creeks. From the very earliest historical accounts we learn that the Indians bet large amounts of wealth on the outcome of games. We can appreciate the game's meaning more fully when we examine the ritual and ceremony surrounding it.

James Mooney described the game as the Cherokees played it in the late nineteenth century.[45] The Cherokees called it *anetsa*. It was played exclusively by young men of the greatest athletic ability, and the reputation of being a good player conferred much prestige on a man. The young men who made up the team for a particular town had to observe a rigorous training regimen, and all the people in the town supported the team in every way they could. They all tried to stimulate the players to perform to the utmost of their ability. Young boys from eight to twelve years old played the game among themselves, hoping for the day when they would be able to play in regular games.

For the Cherokees the ball game season began in mid-summer and lasted until it was too cold to play, but the peak of the season came in the fall when the corn was ripe. The players underwent severe training during this time. The fiercely competitive foot races that were common among the Indians of the Southeast were probably regarded as training for the ball game (and warfare).[46] In addition to practicing regularly, the players had to observe several avoidances. A player could not eat rabbit because the rabbit is easily frightened and confused; he could not eat frog meat because the frog's bones are brittle and easily broken; he could not eat the sucker fish because it is sluggish in its movements; he could not eat chenopodium, nor the young of any animal for reasons similar to those already given; he could not eat hot food nor salt; and most of all, he was forbidden to touch a woman for seven or more days before a game. The ball game was a man's endeavor and if a woman even

411

touched a ball stick it rendered it unfit for use in a game. For the same reason, any man whose wife was pregnant could not play; it was thought that some of his strength went into the making of the child. It was said that in the past, men who broke these rules were put to death, but this was probably more a threat than a reality.

The ball game was always played by teams from different towns. When the rivalry between two towns became keen, and it usually did, individual players developed hatred for individual players on the opposing teams. They frequently consulted a conjurer and attempted magically to inflict illness or even death on their rivals. In this way the ball game became a contest between the conjurers in the rival towns, and in the Cherokee way of thinking the conjurers were perhaps as important as the ball players in determining the outcome of a game. It is probable that the ceremonial preparation for a ball game was similar or even identical to the preparation for war. Indeed, the game drew upon the same physical qualities which were important in their traditional warfare—speed, stamina, suppleness, deceptiveness, and strength.

On the night before a ball game the Cherokee town held a ball game dance. The dance had to be held near the town, but the exact spot was not announced until just before the dance was held. This was to prevent magical sabotage by the rival town. A conjurer from the rival town might, for example, strew the ground with a potion made from the hamstrings of rabbits, making the players who came in contact with the potion timid and easily confused. The dance began just after dark on the night before the game, and it lasted through the night until dawn. The players were required to fast from supper of the night before the game until after the game was played the next day.

In 1889, James Mooney observed a ball game dance put on by the Cherokees of Yellow Hill, who were to play the people of Raven Town the next day. The dance began about nine o'clock in the evening. It was quite dark when Mooney arrived at the scene, and he could only recognize people by their voices. Gradually all the people drifted in, some coming from as far as six or eight miles away. As Mooney approached the dance, he heard drumming and the soft voices of women singing ball game songs, punctuated by the shouts of the men. The dance was held in a grove of large trees on a narrow strip of gravelly bottom land, a place where the mountains came

412

close to the water's edge. Wild grapevines laced together the tops of the trees and hung down on all sides. A dull roar from a nearby waterfall could be heard along with the drumming and singing. Several small fires were burning. The Indians leaned against the trees or lay upon the ground. Some of the infants were wrapped in shawls and laid beneath the bushes to sleep. The men danced around a larger fire dressed only in shorts, carrying their ball sticks in their hands.

Both sexes had roles in the dance: the males were the players themselves, while the females were a group of seven women, one from each of the Cherokee clans. They danced near two upright posts connected with a crosspiece on which the ball sticks were hung. The men danced in a circle around the fire accompanied by the sound of a rattle carried by a performer who circled around the outside. The women stood side by side in a straight line a few feet away, singing and dancing to and fro, advancing toward the men and then wheeling and dancing away from them, keeping time to a drum. To one side of the ball-stick hanger there was a large flat rock under which the conjurer had placed black beads representing players on the opposing team. Periodically, the women would step on this stone to weaken the players of the opposing team by exposing them to the heaviness and sluggishness of women.[47]

In their songs the men called on various spiritual beings to strengthen them for the coming contest. They called upon one to give them endurance; another to make them quick-witted; another to make them quick and elusive; and another to make them swift runners. In contrast, the purpose of the women's songs was to take power away from the opponents. They called for victory, promising the players that tomorrow they would be able to sleep with their wives. But when they referred to their opponents in song, it was to the effect that the opponents' conjurer had miscarried a turtle, the opposing players had touched pregnant women in public, the opposing players had slept with their wives and weakened themselves, and so on.[48]

As performers, the men and the women remained distinct, each with their own dance steps and songs, but still they combined to form a harmonious whole, thus expressing the opposition between men and women but expressing at the same time the harmony of their coexistence. The seven women were relieved by other women from time to time, but the men danced the whole night long, except for the frequent intervals in which they went to water to purify themselves. Periodically the men would shout war whoops in the direction of their opponents' town. At the end of each episode of dancing, the men would rush over near the women, and the crowd of spectators shouted a prolonged "*Hu-u*."[49]

At a certain stage of the dance a man called *dalala*, "woodpecker," left the dance ground and walked a short distance in the direction of the rival town. He stood facing the direction in which the town lay, raised his hand to his mouth and uttered four yells, the last being a prolonged, peculiar quavering sound, perhaps like a woodpecker's cry. The players answered him with a chorus of yelps, sounding rather like the barking of puppies.[50] Then the *dalala* came running back to the dance ground where he shouted a single word meaning, "They are already beaten!" At the final dance they threw onto the fire boughs of pine, one of their sacred trees, and thick clouds of smoke rolled up to envelop the dancers. This smoke was believed to protect them from their opponents' conjurer and to make it difficult for their opponents to see them during the game.[51]

At sunrise the ball players dressed in their regular clothes and started out for the place where the game was to be held. They were accompanied by their conjurers and the conjurers' assistants. They usually went to the ball ground by a circuitous route to avoid the magic of the other team's conjurer.[52] On the way, the party stopped four times and "went to water." Each time they stopped, a priest performed a rite for each individual player. This consumed a considerable amount of time, so that it was usually noon before the two teams faced each other. During this time the players were forbidden to sit on a stone or a log, but only on the ground itself, and they were forbidden from leaning against anything except the back of another player; violation of these rules was thought to cause one to be defeated or to be bitten by a rattlesnake. These same rules were previously observed by Cherokee war parties on the move.

While the priest administered rites to the individual players, the others sat around twisting extra strings for their ball sticks, adjusting their clothing and decorations, and talking about the coming contest. After going to water for the fourth time, the head conjurer gave an inspirational speech to the players, telling them that all the omens were favorable, that they should play to their utmost ability, and that their victory would be applauded by their friends and relatives. This speech, given in rapid, staccato utterances, touched emotional chords in the players, who frequently interrupted with exultant yells.

When they came in sight of the ball ground, the *dalala* advanced and again gave four whoops, ending with a long quavering yell. The players answered with a shout, turning off the path to a convenient sheltered place to make their final preparations. The priest marked off a small area of ground symbolically to represent the ball ground. Then he took a small bundle of sharpened stakes about one foot long and stuck them in the ground as he told each man which position he was to occupy when the game began. Then the players stripped for the ordeal of scratching. This was performed by one of the priest's assistants with a *kanuga*, a kind of comb made of seven sharp splinters of turkey leg bone tied to a frame made out of a turkey feather (fig. 98). The turkey, we recall, was thought to be a fierce, warlike bird. Each player was scratched four times on each upper arm, inflicting scratches about six inches long between shoulder and elbow, then four times on the lower arms, between the elbow and

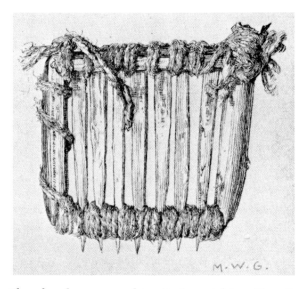

Figure 98. Cherokee *kanuga* used in ritual scratching. Negative no. 75–5992. Courtesy, Smithsonian Institution, National Anthropological Archives.

the wrist, then each leg was treated similarly above and below the knees; next, an X was scratched across the player's breast and the upper ends joined by a horizontal stroke from shoulder to shoulder, and, finally, this same design was scratched on the player's back. The scratches were shallow but painful. When it was over, a player had blood showing or trickling from nearly three hundred scratches (fig. 99). But the men endured this ordeal cheerfully, regarding it as a necessary preliminary to the game. After the scratching was done, the priest gave the men a piece of root to chew, and they spit the juice on the scratches and rubbed it in. Then they went into the water and washed off the blood. Just before playing they sometimes treated their bodies with grease (probably bear's oil, traditionally) or slippery elm bark to make it difficult for their opponents to get a hold on them.

In Mooney's day the men generally wore only a pair of shorts in the game, but formerly they wore breechcloths. In their hair they wore an eagle feather for keenness of sight, a deer's tail for swiftness, and a snake's rattle to make them terrible to their opponents, thus calling on spiritual help from all three worlds. They also marked their bodies with red and black paint. The black paint was charcoal from the dance fire, which had been made from the wood of a honey locust tree that had been struck by lightning but not killed. The Choctaws used to wear a tail made of horse hair which streamed out as they ran. The Creeks used to paint entwined serpents on their bodies, symbolizing warfare or conflict, and they would sometimes wear cougar tails.[53]

After the players were dressed and ready, they went to water for the last time. The priest selected a bend of the river where they could look toward the east while facing upstream. The men stood side by side looking down into the water with their ball sticks clasped across their breasts. The priest stood behind them while an assistant spread red and black pieces of cloth on the ground with red and black beads placed on them. There was one red bead for each player on the team, and one black bead for each of their opponents. Taking a red bead in his right hand to represent a particular player on his team, and a black bead in his left hand, the priest held them aloft, addressing "the Long Man," the river. He spoke in exaltation of the power of the river, which could toss great logs about in white foam. Beginning with one of the players, the priest asked that this player have

416

Figure 99. Ritual scratching of a Cherokee ball player. Photographed by James Mooney in 1888. Negative no. 1042. Courtesy, Smithsonian Institution, National Anthropological Archives.

the strength to toss his opponents about. The priest also called to the Red Bat to make this player elusive, to the Red Deer to give him speed, to the Red Hawk to grant him keenness of sight, and to the Red Rattlesnake to make him terrible. Then the priest raised the player to the seventh level of the world for ultimate success. Now the priest asked the player the name of his most hated opponent.

417

The player whispered it to him, and the conjurer then mentioned him by name and clan, laying a powerful curse on him, invoking Black Fog, the Black Rattlesnake, and the Black Spider to drop down his black thread from above, to wrap up his soul and drag it to the Darkening Land in the west, and there to bury it in a black coffin under black clay. The priest repeated this ceremony for each of the players and their opponents. The end of the ceremony was celebrated with an appropriate shout from the players which was believed to carry them to victory as surely as uprooted trees were carried along in the relentless current of a flooded river.

Then the players went to the ball ground in single file. There, on a field surrounded by several hundred spectators, they met their opponents. The challenging team furnished the ball, but before the game got underway, their opponents gave it a careful examination. One trick they were looking for was whether the ball had been made so small that it would slip through the netting of their ball sticks.[54] After the ball had passed inspection, the players and spectators moved about holding up articles they wanted to wager on the outcome of the game. Sometimes the betting was so competitive that people would take off some of the clothing they were wearing in order to bet it. In 1834 the Cherokee towns of Hickory Log and Coosawattee played a game near the present Jasper, Georgia, in which the chiefs of the two towns bet $1000 on the outcome of the game, an enormous sum of money for that time. When the betting was over, the two teams came onto the field shouting and lined up opposite each other, each player with his ball sticks lying on the ground in front of him pointing toward the sticks of a player of the opposing team. This was to make sure that the teams were evenly balanced.

Then an old man walked out holding the ball. He delivered a final speech to the players, telling them to remember that "the Apportioner"—the sun—was looking down on them. He told them that they should observe the rules and show good sportsmanship and that after the game each should go along a white trail to his white house; that is, the game should end in peace. Then he shouted "Ha! Taldu-gwu!" meaning literally, "Now for the twelve!" And with this he threw the ball up into the air and the game began. There was an instant clatter of ball sticks as they scrambled to get possession of the ball. When someone managed to get it, he would break out running

418

for his goal. Members of the opposing team would pursue him and try to knock the ball away from him or trip him up and make him drop it. Masses of players ended up on the ground, rolling and tumbling, trying to get possession of the ball. The action shifted back and forth from one end of the field to the other until a player succeeded in hurling or carrying the ball through the goal, thus scoring a point.

Figure 100. One on one in Cherokee ball play. Photographed by James Mooney. Negative no. 47,748–f. Courtesy, Smithsonian Institution, National Anthropological Archives.

It was an exceptionally rough game in which injuries often occurred. As in American football, the teams sometimes accused each other of going into the game with the intent of crippling or disabling the best players on the opposite side. But unlike football, the ball players did not employ elaborate team strategies. Like warriors the ballplayers were volunteers, and they were very much their own men. Like warriors on a raid they combined forces but did not elaborately coordinate their individual roles in terms of an overall strategy.[55] In some cases two players would wrestle on the ground trying to choke or injure each other even after the ball play moved to another part of the field (fig. 100); "drivers" armed with long switches would come out to whip them and force them apart. In the height of the action the players would sometimes throw down their sticks and carry the ball in their mouths or hands; sticks were later returned to their owners by the drivers or by other officials. But throughout all this rough play, the players were expected to be good sports, and from the eyewitness accounts available to us, it seems they generally were. To lose one's temper was thought to be unmanly.

After each score the ball was brought back to the center and play began anew. Throughout the game the team conjurer continued to take ritual measures to bring his team to victory. He performed his rituals in a secluded place and was kept informed of the progress of the game by an assistant, who in turn was advised by seven counselors appointed to watch the game. During the game the players were not allowed to drink water; their only drink was a sour beverage made from green grapes, wild crabapples, and several other plants.

The game ended when a team scored twelve points; this could take as little as half an hour or as long as seven or eight hours.[56] As soon as the game was over the players and spectators on the winning side claimed their bets, and the players again went to water where the priest protected them from the spiteful curses of their defeated rivals. They washed themselves clean of the dust and blood, dressed, and ate the first food any of them had tasted since supper of the previous night.

The ball game was adopted by French-speaking Cajuns in Louisiana. Called *raquette*, they played it on a field with goals about 100 yards apart. At one time it was played in the region around

Opelousas, Eunice, and Mamou. Stewart Culin tells of seeing a game between two black teams in New Orleans in 1900 in which hundreds of players participated. The game was played according to rules similar to those used by the Southeastern Indians. When the game ended, the winning team sang Creole songs.[57] Traces of the game linger on in the Southern states with place names like Ball Play, Ball Ground, or Ball Game. The ball game is still played after a fashion by modern-day descendants of the Southeastern Indians, but most of the ritual surrounding the game is no longer observed.

In addition to the ball game just described, the Southeastern Indians played another game with a ball that is sometimes called the single-pole ball game. It was played around a pole from 35 to 50 feet tall set in or near the square ground. Part of the way up the pole there was a mark, and a player who succeeded in throwing the ball and hitting the post above this mark scored one point. On top of the pole there was an object—either a square mat, some limbs from a tree, an animal skull, a wooden ball, or the carved image of a fish or eagle. Whoever succeeded in hitting this object scored as many as five points. Among the Creeks twenty points won the game.

Remains of large posts which may have been used in this game have been recovered at Cahokia, Kolomoki, and at other sites. The Timucuans are known to have played this game, betting on the outcome. James Adair says that it was played between the sexes throughout the summer months. The men evidently wagered venison and the women wagered bread. The game is still played by Cherokees, Creeks, and Seminoles in Oklahoma, and by Seminoles and Mikasukis in Florida. The general rule is that the women playing the game are allowed to pick up the ball in their hands, while the men must use their ball sticks. John Swanton was told that the men generally contrived to let the women win.[58]

CHUNKEY

In the early colonial period, the most popular game among the Southeastern Indians seems not to have been the ball game, but the game called chunkey. Always played by males, this was a variety of the hoop and pole game which was played by Indians throughout North America.[59] Chunkey was distinctive in that instead of a hoop made of wood, the Southeastern Indians used a wheel-shaped disc

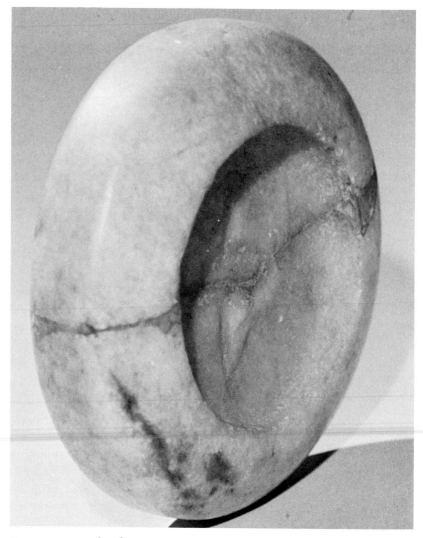

Figure 101. A chunkey stone. Diameter: 15 cm. Courtesy, Frank H. McClung Museum, University of Tennessee.

made of carefully polished stone. Similar stone discs were occasionally used by the Indians of the Northwest Coast of Canada and by the Mandans of the Missouri River region, but not nearly as often as in the Southeast.[60] Archaeologists excavating in the Southeast have found a large number of these stones, some so beautifully crafted that they are virtually works of art.

422

James Adair describes Creek and Chickasaw stones as being about two fingers in breadth and two spans in circumference. Many stones have been found at Mississippian sites which generally conform to these dimensions. Often the stones are concave on both sides. The rims of the stones vary; some are flat, some rounded, and some are beveled such that when the stone is rolled, it goes in an arc to one side (fig. 101). The game was usually played by two men at a time, with crowds of onlookers betting on the outcome. Each player had a pole. One of them rolled the stone and just as it was about to stop rolling, they both cast their poles at it, the object being to hit as near the stone as possible when it came to a rest (fig. 102). After they cast their poles, they ran along after them, perhaps empathizing with their flight in the way modern bowlers empathize with the course of their bowling balls (fig. 103).[61] Archaeologists have found several Mississippian gorgets with depictions of players casting chunkey stones.[62]

The chunkey stones were owned by the towns, or perhaps by particular clans in the towns, and they were carefully preserved. Each town had a smooth chunkey yard, sometimes covered with packed sand, where the game was played. The Cherokees scored their games in terms of how close the stone was to various marks on the pole. The Chickasaws played it with poles eight feet long which they annointed with bear oil. In the Chickasaw game the pole nearest the stone scored one point, but if it was in contact with the stone it scored two points. If both sticks were equally near, neither side scored. The Choctaws played the game on a yard that was approximately 100 feet long by 12 feet wide. Their poles were made out of hickory with four notches cut near the head, one notch in the middle of the pole, and two notches between these. The score depended on which set of notches ended up nearest the stone. The Choctaw game ended when one player scored twelve points. The players competed fiercely, the sweat drenching their bodies in the hot sun. They sometimes bet extravagantly on the game, even to the point of losing all that they possessed. In some cases they became so distraught after losing, they committed suicide.[63]

Le Page du Pratz left an account of the Natchez playing the hoop and pole game with a type of pole which he describes as having the shape of an f.[64] Fortunately, du Pratz's account is confirmed by accounts of very similar poles being used by the Pawnees. It was a

Figure 102. Chunkey player incised on a shell gorget. Eddyville, Kentucky. Negative no. MNH 14640. Courtesy, Smithsonian Institution, National Anthropological Archives.

pole with a hook on the trailing end, and with one or more crosspieces attached to the shaft. For the Pawnees the object was to cast the pole through the hoop, and if any of the crosspieces went through, it counted more.[65] Unfortunately, archaeologists cannot tell us how widely the wooden hoop was used in the Southeast, but it is probable that the chunkey stone was not the only way in which the Southeastern Indians played the game.

In the early colonial period the game of chunkey was evidently much more popular than the ball game, but this was later reversed for reasons which are not entirely clear. One possibility is that while chunkey was played by the men of a single town, the ball game was played by men of different towns, and that after European contact it became necessary for the different towns to establish closer relationships with each other for mutual self defense. Hence the ball game was one of the ways in which they could get together in peaceful conflict. Another possibility is that male prestige depended upon prowess in war, but war in the traditional sense ended when the European settlers established their supremacy, and the ball game became a substitute means of attaining prestige.[66] Another possible reason for the decline of chunkey is that it was probably bound up with traditional Southeastern beliefs and social alignments, and after these beliefs and social alignments changed, the game lost most of its meaning. The hoop was a most important symbol in the art and mythology of the Plains Indians. They sometimes wore miniature hoops as hair ornaments.[67] It is possible that some of the Southeastern Ceremonial Complex motifs referred in some way to the hoop. The shell gorgets with webbed or scalloped designs resemble some of the hoops used in the hoop and pole game. Even the cross in a circle can be seen in the hoops used by the Arapahos and Cheyennes.[68]

Figure 103. Mandan game of "tchung-kee." Oil on canvas by George Catlin, 1832. Courtesy, National Collection of Fine Arts, Smithsonian Institution.

OTHER GAMES

The Southeastern Indians played several lesser games based on chance alone or on a combination of skill and chance. An example of the latter was a Creek game called "rolling a stone." It was evidently patterned on chunkey, but of far less importance. It was played by rolling a small soapstone ball (or perhaps a small disc) along a trench

425

several feet long. At the end of the trench opposite the player lay a series of small holes dug into the earth. Some of these holes were more difficult to enter than others, and scores were determined accordingly.

Another game involving both skill and chance was the hidden ball or moccasin game. In this game a small stone or a similar object was hidden under one of four pieces of cloth or items of clothing, such as moccasins. The object of the game was to guess which one the object was under. The skill consisted in misleading the guesser by special chants, swaying from side to side, and other tricks to make him guess wrongly. They kept score with small tally sticks cut two or three inches long. This game was played widely in North America, and the Indians were amazingly adept at using subtle means of suggestion to make their opponents guess wrongly. The player, in turn, made false moves toward the moccasins to see if he could induce his opponent to give away the true location of the object. The game was adopted by the whites who reduced the number of "moccasins" to three; it became such a popular gambling game that laws were passed against it in some places. The whites generally called the game "bullet." Later it was called "the shell game."

The Southeastern Indians played several games of pure chance. The Alabamas played one such game with four gaming sticks made of cane. Each stick was about eight inches long and was made out of a section of cane split in half lengthwise. Each player threw the sticks up in the air, and the points were calculated on the basis of whether the sticks landed with their convex or concave sides up. If all of the sticks came to rest with their convex sides up it counted 10; if all had their concave sides up it counted 5; if there were three concave sides up and one convex side up, it counted 3; if two were concave and two convex, it counted 2; and if three were convex and one concave it counted 1. The Creeks, Choctaws, Natchez, and Chitimachas played similar games.

Another game of pure chance was played with half a dozen or so beans or seeds that had a light side and a darkened side, much as the two faces of a coin. The Cherokees, for example, played the game with six beans or fruit seeds. They put them in a shallow basket, shook them, and tossed them up into the air. Scoring was on the basis of the number of light or dark sides facing up. The Creeks and Choctaws played a similar game using grains of corn.[69]

426

CHAPTER EIGHT

A CONQUERED PEOPLE

The Southeastern Indians developed their way of life over the course of several millennia of living on the land in the Southeast. As a way of life it had both resiliency and vulnerability. There was a resilient strength in their belief system, which codified their knowledge and their philosophy of life, and which was structured in such a way that it could be passed from one generation to another orally and could be stored in its entirety in human memory. There was strength also in the way in which their social and cultural institutions were tied one to another with many-stranded bonds: the dualism which ran through their cosmological symbolism also played an important role in their social organization; their diversified agricultural and wild food economy was chartered by one of their most important myths; the stickball game they played with such ardor drew on the same skills and physical capabilities they used in their warfare; and in their ceremonial life they had the ritual means to set aright the imbalances, failures, and conflicts which occurred in their secular life.

But along with this resiliency there was a killing vulnerability: like other New World peoples, the Southeastern Indians before contact had been isolated through their entire history from biological and cultural developments in the Old World. They were biologically unprepared for the diseases which arrived with the European invaders; they were unprepared to deal with a people whose desire to accumulate property, resources, and land knew no limit, and who recklessly exploited the earth and its creatures; and they were unequal to a people whose use of writing enabled them to plan and coordinate aggressive political strategies and to pursue them doggedly for decades and even for centuries until they had con-

427

quered the people who stood in their way.

And so the Southeastern Indians became a conquered people. One does not think of them as such because one does not wish to, but this does not change the fact that the Southeastern Indians were conquered. It was not done quickly, nor easily, nor by a single method. Beginning with Hernando de Soto's exploration, the conquest took in all about three hundred years. In part the Indians were conquered militarily, but this was only in part, for they were able to withstand military onslaught with fair success. They were far more effectively conquered economically through a conscious effort to lead them into a dependency on European trade goods: once this was accomplished they were vulnerable to manipulation and exploitation by the unbearable economic pressures that could be brought to bear upon them.

The ultimate conquest, however, was achieved by the social system known as the Old South, a strongly hierarchical system of agricultural production using slave labor. It was a system with a voracious appetite for land, and it had not a single use for the Indians who still claimed most of the land in the Southeast at the turn of the nineteenth century. By this time military force was seldom used against the Southeastern Indians, but the threat of it along with economic sanctions were used to force them into a totally untenable position. Unable to resist effectively, the Southeastern Indians were conquered legally, legislatively, by treaties. They were "removed" from their homeland and forced to emigrate west of the Mississippi River to the Indian Territory. "Removal" is a gentle, almost antiseptic word for one of the harshest, most crudely opportunistic acts in American history. It was an act that could only have been perpetrated on a conquered people.

But there are few today who think of the Southeastern Indians as a conquered people. Perhaps it is because everything that was done to them, short of murder, was justified as having been necessary in order to help them into civilization. This was a justification for conversion to Christianity, enslavement, forced emigration, and forced enrollment in schools whose purpose was to teach the Indians to think and act as whites and to abandon their own cultures. Since all of this noble work was done in the name of civilization, the question of outright conquest hardly arises.

428

COLONIZATION

By the closing decades of the seventeenth century, Europeans had explored most of the regions of the Southeast. Spanish ships had explored the Atlantic and Gulf coasts, and Hernando de Soto had made his brutal foray through the interior. The French had explored the entire length of the Mississippi River. And less spectacularly, British explorers from Virginia had penetrated the Carolina piedmont and parts of the Appalachian Mountains.

But the Europeans had difficulty in founding viable colonies in the Southeast. All of the earliest Spanish attempts to establish colonies failed. Ponce de Leon failed almost before he set foot on the beaches of Florida; Ayllón failed on the south Atlantic coast; Narváez failed in northwest Florida; de Soto only succeeded in inflicting more horrors on the Indians than his predecessors did; and in 1559–61 Tristán de Luna failed in his attempt to establish a colony at Pensacola Bay. The Spanish colonial apparatus, which had been so successful elsewhere, failed in the Southeast in the early decades of the sixteenth century, and even later their colonial successes were only partial.

Protestant Huguenots seeking religious freedom made France's first attempt at colonization in the Southeast. A tiny contingent of Huguenots was set ashore near Beaufort, South Carolina, in 1562, but their colony, if it can be called such, survived only a few months. In 1564 René de Laudonniere led a second group of Huguenots to the mouth of the St. John's River in northern Florida where they built Fort Caroline. It was here that Jacques Le Moyne de Morgues made his drawings of the Timucuan Indians, giving Europeans their first reasonably good pictures of the natives of North America. Neither Huguenot nor Timucuan gained much from the other. The Huguenots tried to convert the Timucuans to Protestantism. The Timucuans taught the Huguenots to smoke tobacco.

When winter came the French colonists were unable to obtain food from the Indians, and they very nearly starved to death. Yet, in spite of such hardships, the colony might well have survived had not the Spanish seen this Protestant preserve in Florida as a threat to their own ambitions. In 1565, Spain sent Pedro Menéndez de Avilés to Florida to deal with the French. His first act was to establish what later became St. Augustine. Then he recruited some Timucuan

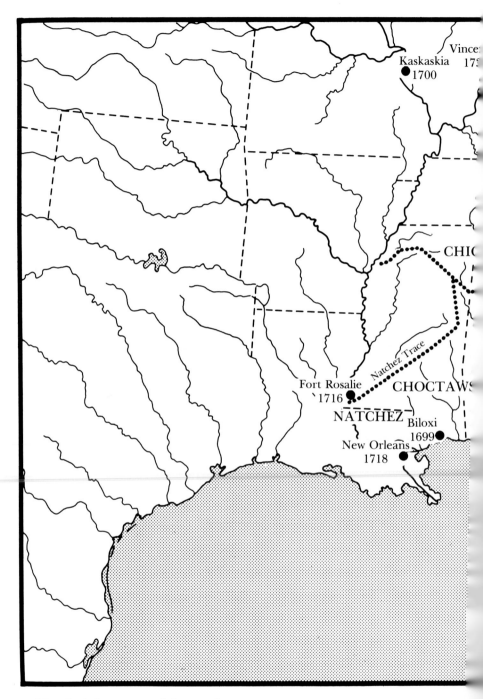

Map 6. Colonization of the Southeast.

430

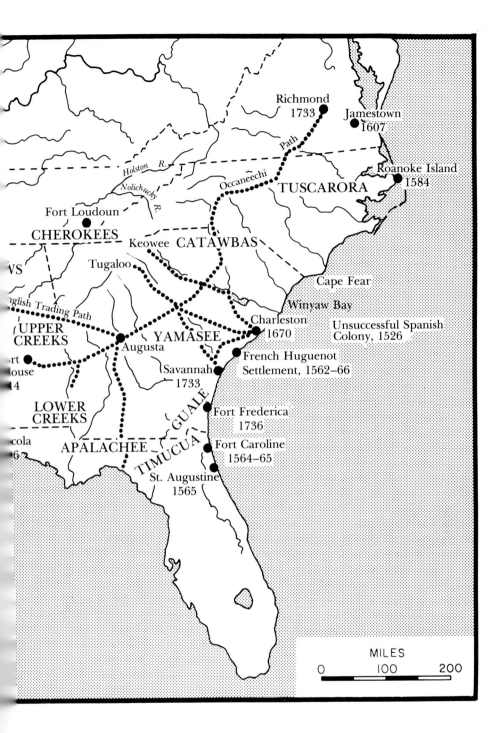

Richmond
1733

Jamestown
1607

Path

Holston R.

Nolichucky R.

Occaneechi

Roanoke Island
1584

TUSCARORA

Fort Loudoun

CHEROKEES

Keowee CATAWBAS

VS

Tugaloo

Cape Fear

English Trading Path

Winyaw Bay

Charleston
1670

Unsuccessful Spanish
Colony, 1526

UPPER
CREEKS

YAMASEE

Augusta

rt
ouse
4

French Huguenot
Settlement, 1562–66

Savannah
1733

LOWER
CREEKS

GUALE

Fort Frederica
1736

cola
6.2

APALACHEE

TIMUCUA

Fort Caroline
1564–65

St. Augustine
1565

MILES

0   100   200

allies and sailed north to Fort Caroline, where he attacked the French, defeated them, and killed every one of them who would not say that he was a Catholic.

The French did succeed in establishing a viable colony in the region along the lower Mississippi River. One purpose of this colony was to keep the area from being taken by the British. The first French settlement, Fort Maurepas (Old Biloxi), was established by Pierre Le Moyne d'Iberville at Biloxi Bay in 1699. When these French colonists explored the interior, they found some of the Indians there dying from diseases that had been brought in by Europeans, and they found Indians who were terrified after having been attacked by British traders from South Carolina and their Indian mercenaries. Some of their people had been taken away as slaves.

The French colonial effort in the Southeast was never as secure as the British. They traded with the Indians to a small extent, but they had nothing that could match the cheap trade goods the British could produce. The population of the French colony increased very slowly. Even though conditions were terrible in France at the time, Frenchmen were unwilling to emigrate to Louisiana. The French held onto their colony mainly by dealing with the Indians in an intelligent and diplomatic manner. They refrained from ridiculing Indian customs and beliefs, and they would send young French boys out to live with the Indians to learn their language and customs. Because the French colonists were so few, they could not insulate themselves from the Indians as the more numerous British colonists did.[1]

The Spanish were not able to colonize the Southeast in the way that they were able to colonize Mexico and South America, where they had found sedentary, docile populations who were accustomed to political subordination and hard labor. With such people the Spanish used the *encomienda* system, in which a number of Indians were legally bound to serve a particular *encomendero* who was supposed to give them religious instruction and to "civilize" them; he in return had the right to exploit their labor, paying a portion of his profit to Spain.

But the Southeastern Indians were neither docile nor accustomed to political subordination, and they had no taste for hard labor. In time the Spanish sought to dominate them through a mission sys-

432

tem. The manifest purpose of the mission was benevolent, even idealistic. The missionaries, through religious and humanitarian motives, undertook to both Christianize and civilize the Indians. They taught the Indians Catholic dogma and the Spanish language, and also such skills as weaving and the cultivation of new kinds of vegetables and fruits. The missionaries also served as agents of Spain in collecting and sending back information on the Indians and the territory in which they lived. And of course the missionaries acted as agents of Spain in that they constantly encouraged the Indians to adopt a more sedentary life so that they could be concentrated into villages. When persuasion failed, they occasionally tried to use force. Soldiers were sometimes quartered in the missions, or else in a nearby *presidio*.

In principle the missionaries were supposed to work themselves out of a job. That is, when they had succeeded in Christianizing and civilizing a particular group of Indians, they were supposed to move on to establish a new mission, leaving their old mission in the hands of the Indians. But in the Southeast as elsewhere this seldom if ever happened. In fact, the missions were frequently small forts. The missions were also supposed to be self-sustaining, but they seldom were, and Spain had to subsidize them. Because the missions served as buffers against the French and the British, the subsidies they received varied directly with the French and British political threat.

The first Spanish missionaries were Jesuits, who began their activities in 1566, establishing missions in coastal Florida, Georgia, South Carolina, and Virginia. But the Jesuits did not succeed in establishing a viable mission system. Some died of illnesses, others were killed by the Indians, and Spain withdrew the survivors. They were replaced by Franciscans, the first of whom arrived in Florida in 1583, and where the Jesuits failed, the Franciscans succeeded. They began by building a series of missions in northern Florida, on Jekyl Island, St. Catherines Island, and St. Simons Island, and in other locations in coastal Georgia. In the missions the Franciscans began each day by assembling the Indians for devotionals and ended each day with prayers that the Indians learned by rote memory. At least once a week they performed a mass. All of the Indians committed to memory the Ave Maria, the Credo, and the Pater Noster. The Indian children were assembled each day for schooling.

Periodically, the Indians revolted against the missionaries. In fact, the mortality rate for missionaries was rather high. But in the end the Franciscans prevailed. By 1655 they claimed to have established 38 missions in the provinces of Timucua, Guale, and Apalachee. This mission system was said to consist of 5 clerics in St. Augustine, 70 friars, and 26,000 Christianized Indians. The degree to which these Indians were Christianized is difficult to determine, but it was probably quite shallow.

The Spanish mission has been criticized on the grounds that it was oppressive and paternalistic. But in its defense it can be said that the Indians *did* have a place in the mission, whereas we shall presently see that in the British colonial system the Indians were merely objects to be exploited and got out of the way. Although they frequently failed, the Franciscans at least had the motive of preserving and protecting the Indians, albeit by destroying their cultures and by transforming them into Catholics.[2]

In the end it was the British who succeeded in colonizing the Southeast and in gaining control over the Southeastern Indians. The first British colony, founded in 1585 on Roanoke Island off the coast of North Carolina, was a failure. The colonists either died, or were killed, or were genetically absorbed among the Indians. The Jamestown colony, founded in 1607, nearly failed as a consequence of famine, disease, and Indian wars, but in the end it caught hold. The Jamestown colonists learned to grow Indian vegetables for food, and they learned to grow Indian tobacco for a cash crop. Their clearings gradually spread up the banks of the James River. In time the colonists reached the falls of the James and Appamatox rivers and opened up a trade with the Indians living in the Virginia and Carolina piedmont.

But the Virginia colony had relatively little effect on the Southeastern Indians. The real European thrust against the Southeastern Indians began in 1670, when some one hundred and fifty colonists from England and Barbados landed at the mouth of the Ashley River and built the huts and palisade of Charles Towne, thus founding the colony that was later to be South Carolina. Unlike the French and Spanish colonies in the Southeast, South Carolina was strictly a business venture sponsored by a group of British businessmen and courtiers. Moreover, Britain at the close of the seventeenth century was suffering from overpopulation and dwindling resources, and North America was a convenient outlet.

The Carolina colonists were interested in trading with the Indians at the very outset. It began in a small way as a plantation trade, with the Indians coming in to the plantations to trade their deerskins for British manufactured wares. But as time went on some of the planters provided the Indians with firearms and sent them out to capture other Indians who could then be sold as slaves. They would also arm one group of Indians and set them against any other group of Indians who threatened their conduct of trade. The first fortunes were made in this trade in deerskins and slaves, and the trade itself became one of the principal methods of British colonial expansion.

The British trade in deerskins and Indian slaves spread with amazing rapidity. Judging from the bundles of deerskins de Soto saw in Indian public buildings, the Indians may have accumulated them as objects of value in prehistoric times. In any case, when the trade began the Indians appear to have been ready for it. From Virginia the traders went down the Occaneechi trading path into the Carolina piedmont, where they traded with the "Esaws" (later called Catawbas) as early as 1673.[3] But they never had much success in reaching the Cherokees in their mountain towns. By 1690, South Carolina traders from Charleston were going up the right bank of the Savannah River to trade with the Cherokees, but this trade did not assume a great volume until later. Initially, the main Charleston trade was with the Creeks and Chickasaws. In 1698 the trader Thomas Welch went from Charleston to a Quapaw village at the mouth of the Arkansas River.[4] As we have already seen, at about this same time, when the French explored the interior near Biloxi Bay, they found the Indians in terror from just having been raided for slaves by the British. In terms of courage and adventurousness the Charleston traders rivaled the French fur traders in Canada. But we do not accord them such a heroic place in Southern history as the fur traders occupy in Canadian history, possibly because the Charleston traders were at times the scapegoats for much that went wrong in the colonies, while at other times they deserved in full measure every bad thing that was said about them.

The Spanish did not arm their mission Indians, and as the Charleston traders began penetrating the interior this Spanish policy proved to be disastrous for the Indians of the provinces of Timucua, Apalachee, and Guale. Indians from South Carolina armed with British guns constantly raided them to capture slaves.

By 1684 the Spanish missions in Guale (coastal Georgia) had collapsed. In 1702, James Moore of South Carolina systematically destroyed Spanish missions all the way down the coast to St. Augustine, and in 1704 he led what was perhaps the most devastating raid ever mounted against the Southeastern Indians. He set out on what later became known as the Lower Trading Path with an army of 50 whites and 1,000 Indian mercenaries. They moved from South Carolina across Georgia into Florida, destroying Spanish missions and fortified Apalachee towns as they went along. In all, Moore's men destroyed thirteen missions; killed several hundred Indians and Spaniards, many of whom were tortured to death; enslaved 325 men, women, and children; and relocated many more in Carolina. On a smaller scale the Carolinians continued these raids for several years. By 1710 the Apalachees, Timucuas, Calusas, and other Florida Indians were completely shattered, and Florida was unoccupied except for a few survivors huddled around St. Augustine.

In the short term the trade in deerskins and Indian slaves was a way in which the British could market some of their manufactured goods—guns, tomahawks, hoes, brass kettles, knives, rum, beads, hawk bells, and cloth (fig. 104). In the long term it was their way of reducing the Indians to dependent status and of disrupting and destroying them. As the Indians became dependent upon the traders for ammunition, cloth, and tools, they found themselves set on a disastrous course from which they could not turn back. And as the traders became economically necessary to the Indians, they found they could manipulate the Indians in innumerable ways.

But the trade with the Indians had a flaw in it. Namely, it was easy for the traders to abuse their privileges, and though the effort was made, South Carolina was never able to control them effectively. The traders were mostly poor, illiterate, and in debt, although there were exceptions, like the extraordinary James Adair, on whose work we rely for much of what we know about the Southeastern Indians. The traders lived hard and dangerous lives. More often than not the Indians hated them.[5] Spurred by economic necessity the Indians very rapidly depleted the deer population. From 1699 to 1715, Carolina exported an average of 54,000 deerskins per year. The greatest number in any one year was in 1707, when 121,355 skins were exported. The deerskin trade lasted for about one hundred years, and the slaughter of deer was tremendous. Though not so well documented, it must have been similar to the slaughter of the buffalo on the Great Plains.[6]

In addition to trading for skins, the Carolina traders continued doing a business in Indian slaves, and this assumed far greater proportions than people today realize. When the French arranged for a truce between the Chickasaws and the Choctaws in 1702, they estimated that at the instigation of the Charleston traders the Chickasaws had enslaved 500 Choctaws and had killed 1,800 of them, while having lost 800 of their own men. In 1708, when the total population of South Carolina was 9,580, including 2,900 blacks,

Figure 104. European manufactured artifacts traded to the Indians. Recovered at Fort Prince George. *Far left:* rum or wine bottle. *Upper right:* hoe; tomahawk. *Lower left:* bone-handled fork; Jew's harp; brass tinklers. Courtesy, Institute of Archaeology and Anthropology, University of South Carolina.

there were also 1,400 Indian slaves, including 500 men, 600 women, and 300 children. However, because the Indian slaves frequently escaped and because they seem to have frequently been involved in revolts and conspiracies, they were usually exported to New England or to the West Indies. The blacks, taken completely out of their cultural and natural element, were more helpless than the Indians and therefore made better slaves. In 1712 an Indian man or woman sold for 18 to 20 pounds, while a black slave sold for about twice as much.

One Carolinian justified enslaving Indians on the grounds "that it both serves to lessen their number before the French can arm them, and it is a more Effectuall way of Civilizing and Instructing [them] than all of the efforts used by the French Missionaries."[7] Another justified Indian slavery on the grounds that it saved them from cruel deaths at the hands of their enemies. To these arguments those who were opposed to Indian slavery replied that the traders endeavored "through [the Indians'] Covetousness of your gunns Powder and Shott and other European Comodities . . . to ravish the wife from the Husband, kill the Father to get the Child and to burne and Destroy the habitations of these poore people into whose Country wee were Charefully received by them, cherished and supplyed when Wee are weake, or at least never have done us hurt; and after wee have set them on worke to doe all these horrid wicked things to get slaves to sell the dealers in Indians call it humanity to buy them and thereby keep them from being murdered."[8]

As the abuses of the traders accumulated, the Indians struck back, first in the Tuscarora War of 1711, and more seriously in the Yamasee War of 1715. In North Carolina the Tuscaroras rose up and attacked colonists who were infringing on their territory. The Indians were able to hold out for a time in strongly built fortifications, but in 1713 the younger James Moore led against them an army of whites and Indians from South Carolina and dealt them a mortal blow. Many Tuscaroras were killed, and almost four hundred were taken prisoner. Most of the survivors moved north where they were accepted into the League of the Iroquois.

The Yamasee War was a widespread revolt against the Carolina traders by the Creeks, the Choctaws, some Cherokees (who later backed out), and some of the Indians who lived along the Savannah River and northward into the piedmont. After years of being

438

cheated, beaten, enslaved, embroiled in conflicts caused by the traders, having their goods stolen and their women molested and raped, the Indians had had enough. In 1711 one estimate was that the Indians were in debt to the traders to the amount of 100,000 deerskins. Putting it in other terms, this meant that each and every adult male Indian was in debt for about two years of his labor.[9]

The Yamasee War began in 1715 when the Yamasees suddenly rose up and killed Thomas Nairne, the Indian agent for South Carolina, and several traders. In a wide flung coordinated action, other traders were put to death in Creek and Choctaw towns, and the Indians attacked plantations along the coast. Charleston quickly filled up with refugees from the hinterlands. The Carolina colonists were afraid that the French and Spanish had conspired with the Indians to kill all of them, but the evidence indicates that it was a purely native revolutionary action. The Carolinians were able to win out in the end by dividing the Indians against each other. They won over the Cherokees to their interest, and when a party of Lower Creeks came to confer with the Cherokees, the Cherokees put them to death, an incident which was to cause bloodshed between Cherokees and Creeks for many years to come. The Yamasee War came to a close in 1717, when the Carolinians concluded a peace with the Creeks. The deerskin trade crumbled during the hostilities, and it was not fully rebuilt until 1722.

After the Yamasee War the rivalry between England, Spain, and France took on a different character. The Creek Confederacy gained new members, including Indians speaking both Muskogean and non-Muskogean languages. For a time British power waned, and French and Spanish power was enhanced. The Lower Creeks allowed the French to build Fort Toulouse on the Alabama River in 1717. But after this the Creeks were divided in their European loyalties, with one faction favoring the British and the other favoring the Spanish. In part these factions were engineered by the great Creek chief of Coweta Town, Emperor Brims, an astute political leader who saw more clearly than others the advantage of maintaining neutrality in the rivalry among the European colonial powers.

For about one decade after the Yamasee War the Creeks were at war with the Cherokees seeking revenge for their having sided with the British during the war and for having murdered their emissaries. The British were in no hurry to make peace between them. Indeed, they encouraged the hostilities. One Carolinian wrote: "This makes the matter of great weight to us, how to hold both as our friends, for some time, and assist them in cutting one another's throats without offending either. This is the game we intend to play if possible."[10] The French encouraged conflict between the Choctaws and the Chickasaws for the same reason. In 1725, Colonel Chicken traveled through Cherokee towns trying to prevent them from making an "unauthorized" peace with the Creeks, while at the same time trying to explain to the Cherokees why the English themselves, if they were truly friends of the Cherokees, did not go to war against the Creeks. Later in the year the English emissaries among the Creeks got wind of plans for a Creek-Choctaw raid against the Cherokees. The English then warned the Cherokees, and the latter were able to repulse the Creek-Choctaw war party. The English then told the Creeks that the Cherokees had been warned by the favorite scapegoat of that time—a trader.

As the British gradually regained their power, the position of the French was eroded. In 1724 the Natchez suddenly rose up in rebellion, killing many of the French colonists. Later the Chickasaws and the British instigated the Natchez further, and in 1729 they struck again in the "Great Natchez Conspiracy." At Fort Rosalie they killed at least 250 French men and held some 300 women and children hostage. The French retaliated in 1730, killing many of the Natchez. The survivors found refuge mainly with the Chickasaws, with a few going to live with the Cherokees, Creeks, and Catawbas. The French then repeatedly attacked the Chickasaws, but they were never able to defeat them.

In 1729, South Carolina became a crown colony and plans were immediately laid for settling several townships along the rivers into the interior. The idea was to attract poor European immigrants and to give them land allotments. The colony of Georgia was chartered in 1732 with the same goals. In 1736 the British built Fort Frederica on St. Simons Island off the coast of Georgia to defend the colony against the Spaniards. In the same year, John and Charles Wesley came to Georgia to spread Methodism among the Indians, but they soon concluded that the Indians were too corrupted by the white man's ways to be fit subjects for conversion, and God conveniently called them back to England.

In the two centuries following de Soto's exploration the South-

440

eastern Indians had greatly changed. They were much reduced in number, with many languages and societies having been completely obliterated. The groups who survived merged with each other in order to gain strength in numbers. The Southeastern Indians were still forces to be reckoned with in 1750, but many of them were demoralized. From the traders they acquired rum, which they drank in desperately immoderate amounts. Whether rum was the cause of much of the ill that befell them or simply a concomitant is arguable. Edmond Atkin, a man with twenty years of experience in the deerskin trade had this to say about Indian drinking:

> All the Indians whatever are so passionately fond of Rum, as to be unable to withstand it. The most prudent of them resolving sometimes to give a loose to it, provide Centinels who are not to taste a drop the while, to prevent any mischief they may be inclined to do when Drunk. Their Reason or Will having no share therein, they have no conception that they are culpable so far as to deserve to suffer for any mischief or outrage committed by them while in that Condition. If complained of, or up-braided for it, they say with great composure, "that they are sorry for what hath happened, But that it was not they that did it, 'twas Rum that did it." Yet being truly sensible of the great Evils produced from it by Quarrels and Acts of Violence, as well among themselves between the nearest Relations, as with the white People; they heartily lament in general the having ever known what Rum was; And have themselves pointed out to us the only Remedy possible, which is to withhold it from them. The Chiefs of every Nation finding the Evil daily increasing, and their Young Men growing untractable in their National Concerns, have at times requested the Governors of our several Colonies to restrain the Indian Traders from carrying either too much Rum, or any at all among them.[11]

Unlicensed traders from Augusta, Georgia—"the lowest people" —used to take rum and meet the Creeks and Cherokees coming in from their hunting season. They would get them drunk and cheat them out of their hard-won deerskins.[12]

In the latter half of the eighteenth century the Southeastern Indians were drawn into two bitter colonial conflicts. The first was between the French and the British for control of North America, and the second was between the American colonists and the British. France lost in the first conflict, Britain lost in the second, and the Southeastern Indians lost in both.

After 1750 the Southeastern Indians began to face a new kind of threat. In spite of their treaties with the British that set limits on colonial expansion, white intruders began settling illegally in Indian territory. Some of the "Regulators" who had just been defeated in an unsuccessful rebellion in North Carolina fled to Indian territory. Renegades who lived by plundering Indians and whites alike also moved in. When the colonists were able to apprehend these renegades, they punished them for the crimes they committed against whites, but the grand juries refused to indict them for crimes against Indians. Because of these abuses the French found a willing audience among the Southeastern Indians.

The Seven Years' War (or the Great War for Empire) between Britain and France (1756–63) was called the French and Indian War in North America. In 1759 the Cherokees were angry because Virginians fleeing this war on the Virginia frontier began settling along the Georgia and Carolina frontier where they competed with the Cherokees for land and game. The Cherokees attacked some of these people in January, 1760. The French tried to persuade the Creeks to go against the British also, but the Creeks were not willing allies. The Upper Creeks did kill eleven traders and sack their stores in May, 1760, but many other traders were warned and protected by their Indian wives. This was as far as Creek participation went, though the Creek chief Mortar (also known as Yahatastanage and as "Wolf of the Okchais") tried determinedly to form a Creek-Cherokee alliance, but the Cherokees would not agree to it.[13] In mid-August the Overhill Cherokees attacked and captured Fort Loudoun in what was perhaps the greatest Southeastern Indian military victory in the colonial period.

In 1763, at the close of the Seven Years' War, a defeated France gave up all her possessions in North America, leaving Britain in control. France ceded the province of Louisiana to Spain, while Spain ceded East and West Florida to Britain. Later, after the Americans won their Revolution, they returned Florida to Spain as a reward for her having supported them in their conflict with Britain. Subsequently, of course, the Americans again gained possession of Florida.

At the close of the French and Indian War, King George III in the Proclamation of 1763 attempted to institute a policy which would keep white men and red men separate. He proclaimed a boundary line running down the Appalachian Mountains from Maine to Geor-

442

gia. White colonists were prohibited from crossing this line, and those who had already settled to the west of the line were supposed to pull up stakes and move back. But the colonists were not to be stopped. The British never had the wherewithal to enforce the boundary, and neither colonists nor Indians took it seriously. It was little more than a line on a map.

The British colonists encroached on Indian land even more determinedly, and they began putting pressure on the Indians to cede new land. In 1763 Georgia obtained the Ogeechee territory by treaty; in 1765 the Creeks ceded a ten-mile-wide strip of land along the coast from Pensacola to Mobile; in 1773 the Creeks and Cherokees ceded a block of land extending from the Altamaha River to the Ogeechee River, to the headwaters of the Oconee, and thence to the Savannah River almost to the Cherokee towns.

The first white settlers on these frontier lands were cattlemen. They allowed their cattle to forage freely in the woods and savannahs, so that their only expense was the building of rough corrals, or "cowpens," and a crude cabin to live in. They left their families back in the safety of the settlements, where they visited periodically. This cattle-raising technology that was developed on the Southern frontier was later taken westward to the open ranges of Texas.

During the American Revolution the Southeastern Indians for the most part remained neutral. The Cherokees, however, were again angry because British colonists were encroaching into their territory along the Holston and Nolichukey rivers in northeastern Tennessee. In July, 1776, they struck out against the colonists, killing rebel and loyalist alike. In retaliation, the colonists struck back with a terrible vengeance. An army of several thousand frontiersmen stormed the Cherokee country, burning towns, destroying crops, and killing men, women, and children. The Cherokees were never the same after this. So terrible was the destruction, the Creeks could not believe the stories they heard from Cherokees who sought refuge in their towns.[14]

THE OLD SOUTH

What was the fruit of this conflict which raged throughout the eighteenth century? For the Southeastern Indians it was bloodshed, anguish, and finally dispossession. For white and black people it was

443

the social system known as the Old South. One cannot understand the history of the Southeastern Indians in the late eighteenth and early nineteenth centuries without understanding something of the sociology of the Old South, and specifically the Old South from 1800 to about 1830, before the Southeastern Indians were forced to emigrate west of the Mississippi River. After the Indians were driven out, great quantities of land were available for white occupancy, and this changed the character of Southern society.

The leading edge of the Southern frontier was dominated by the same sort of people who dominated the Old West—cattlemen grazing their herds on open ranges and people who sought to escape society, the best of whom were adventurers and poor people escaping debt, and the worst of whom were renegades and outlaws. But away from the frontier, back in the colonies, there took shape a social and economic system which later determined the contours of Southern history—the plantation. In the Old South the plantation was a large agricultural operation whose labor was under a highly centralized authority. The plantation was a kind of agribusiness whose machines were human beings.[15] This plantation agriculture expanded far more rapidly in the South than in the North because the South was blessed with an abundance of good land and a readymade water transportation system.[16] Small, self-sufficient farms dominated the North; plantations dominated the South.

Because land was so plentiful, agricultural entrepreneurs found it difficult to retain labor. If the employer of a free man became too authoritarian, the man would simply leave and obtain some land of his own. The first device used by the planters to retain labor was indenture. Ship captains in England recruited men, women, and children, mostly from the lower classes, and sold their indentures to purchasers in America. Once in America these indentured servants were supposed to serve a period of five years, or until the age of twenty-four in the case of indentured boys and girls. At the end of this period of indenture, the master was supposed to give the servant an outfit of tools and clothing and a barrel of corn. But many of these indentured servants never served out their period of indenture; many of them fell ill and died, and some of them ran away.

One consequence of indenture was that a class of poor white freedmen was created which grew ever larger as time went on. Some few of these freedmen accumulated wealth and rose socially to

compete with the plantation owners. Then as later, the less fortunate ones eventually ended up in the mountains or in the pine
barrens, while others later migrated to the frontier further south and
west. The planters considered these white freedmen a threat. In
1699, even though Virginia needed men under arms, the House of
Burgesses decided not to arm and drill the white servants (especially
the Irish) because they feared an uprising.[17]

In time the planters adopted another expedient—that of importing black slaves from Africa. At first they enslaved the Indians, but as
we have already seen, Indians did not make good slaves. However,
the African slaves were completely cut off from their social and
cultural foundations. By importing black slaves the planters created
a labor force which could not compete with them for wealth and
social position. Twenty blacks were imported into Virginia in 1619.
By 1671, Virginia had 2,000 black slaves and 6,000 indentured white
servants in a total population of about 40,000. After this the black
population rose sharply.

The plantation was organized along quasi-military lines, with the
planter serving as captain and quartermaster; the overseer and
foremen were lieutenant and sergeants; and the field hands were
privates on permanent work detail. The plantation was also a factory,
producing goods. In some cases it was a parish, and also a school: the
slaves were taught to be craftsmen, and some were taught to read
and write, even though this was technically illegal.

All of the crops raised on the plantations required large invest-
ments of labor, some of it back-breaking, some of it merely tedious.
The main crops were tobacco, indigo, rice, sugar cane, and cotton,
and of these, cotton was the crop which was to dominate the history
of the South. Unlike rice and sugar cane, which could only be grown
in restricted areas, cotton could be grown on almost any land,
including that held by the Southeastern Indians at the turn of the
nineteenth century. In growing a crop of cotton, labor was needed
primarily for plowing and hoeing, but even more for picking—a
slow, aggravating, tiring job. The first seeds of the long-fibered,
sea-island cotton were introduced into Georgia in 1786, and within a
few years it was cultivated along the coast from the Santee River to
the St. John's. The disadvantage of long-fibered cotton was that it
could only be grown on the coast and the offshore islands. The
short-fibered variety had been grown in the colonies for some time,

but it was first cultivated in considerable quantities in 1791, when it appeared that a practical cotton gin was about to be invented. This short-fibered variety could be grown inland, and its cultivation expanded very rapidly. Eventually, cotton absorbed the labor of more than three-fourths of all the slaves engaged in agriculture, as well as the labor of many whites.[18]

The social structure of the Old South was dominated by two categories of people: white masters and black slaves. Although these two categories of people play the leading roles in Southern history, there were others who lay outside this dyad, and these have suffered from historical neglect. Not all of the whites were big slaveholders. The Old South included a large and sometimes troublesome class of white "plain folk," some of whom were moderately prosperous and owned a few slaves, but others of whom were barely able to make a living. Not all of the blacks were slaves—most were, but there was a small and significant category of black freedmen. The Southeastern Indians were also more or less omitted from the structure of the Old South. They were presumed to be outside the pale of civilized society, although the fact is they were incorporated into Southern society in several ways. Lastly, in parts of the South there were small enclaves of "mixed bloods," groups of people who did not fit into any of the standard racial categories. These "mixed bloods" troubled the white planters and their racist ideology most of all.

At the apex of white society stood the planters owning vast tracts of land and many slaves. In the South wealth was more concentrated in the hands of the well-to-do than was the case in the North.[19] In tidewater Virginia, for example, about 6 percent of the population owned 60 percent of the land.[20] Their black slaves had a legal status similar to livestock. Thus the person who owned a female slave owned the children to whom she gave birth; and just as a man might force a disobedient horse into submission, he could do the same to his slaves. The way in which the slaves were treated and the rules which regulated their lives varied greatly from one plantation to another. On some plantations discipline was harsh, and the slaves would run away or would sometimes rebel; on other plantations the slaves were relatively content and apparent bonds of affection developed between master and slave.

At the close of the eighteenth century the structure of Southern society was far different from that in the North. The presence of large numbers of black slaves meant that most whites would be poor and landless. The upper class was both larger and wealthier than in the North. In the vicinity of the large plantations, virtually the only poor whites to be seen were overseers and woodcutters. In the mountains, however, almost the entire population was made up of poor whites living in isolated mountain coves, practicing subsistence agriculture, though sometimes raising considerable herds of cattle, horses, pigs, and sheep. The pine barrens were likewise heavily populated by poor whites. In many cases these poor whites were squatters, owning no title to the land on which they lived, and hence easily displaced by the rich and the powerful.[21] At least one-third of the white frontiersmen were landless workers, constantly pushed into the nooks and crannies of the Southeast.

For the Indians there was no place in the structure of the Old South. Those who still managed to hold on to a territory of their own were considered to be "nations"—fully independent entities outside the realm of Christian society. The fact is, however, that by the early nineteenth century most of the Indians were far less independent than they were believed to be. The Catawbas were considered to be a "nation" in the late eighteenth century, even though they had only about sixty or seventy fighting men, and many white squatters were living on their land.[22] Even the Indians who retained some power had their internal affairs manipulated by traders and treaty makers.

Thus the Southeastern Indians were considered to be outsiders, aliens. In actuality, however, there were several ways in which some of the Indians were incorporated into the lower orders of Southern society. As we have already seen, in the late seventeenth century and early eighteenth century they were enslaved and put to work alongside black slaves. After the Yamasee War, we hear very little about Indian slaves, and those who survived enslavement were presumably absorbed among the blacks in subsequent generations, losing their Indian identity. There were, however, several court cases in antebellum Southern courts in which slaves sued for their freedom on the grounds that their mothers were Indians.[23]

Moreover, in the early colonial period there were Indians who moved in to live near European settlements and who subsisted by performing petty services for the colonists. These were called "settlement Indians"; they lived a poor existence, often on the verge of starvation, and the whites sometimes drove them away.[24] Some of

447

them spoke English as well as their native language. We can only surmise about what happened to these people. It is likely that they intermarried with the poor whites living in the back country, with some of their progeny attaining the status of white. Others undoubtedly were absorbed into some of the "mixed blood" groups who have lived for generations in parts of the South.

The white planters used several means to create hatred and fear between the blacks and the Indians. By the beginning of the eighteenth century the blacks outnumbered the whites, and later in the same century blacks outnumbered whites by a factor of two or three to one. The whites lived in mortal fear of black insurrections, and they were even more afraid that the blacks and the Indians would combine forces. This was one reason why they ceased to use Indian slaves, thus keeping them apart from the blacks. In their treaties with the Indians the whites would insist that the Indians return any runaway slaves who might seek refuge with them. As a further precaution they made it illegal for a trader to take a black servant or worker with him into Indian territory. To heighten enmity between the races they used black troops in military actions against the Indians and likewise used Indians against blacks as slave-catchers and also to suppress slave insurrections. Settlement Indians were particularly favored for these uses. The whites were especially afraid of Maroons, escaped slaves who went into the swamps and lived by raiding the settlements as "bandits," killing whites and freeing slaves.[25]

By the end of the eighteenth century thousands of landless whites were crowding the Indian boundary at the Oconee River. And in the early nineteenth century the pressure for more land on which to grow cotton became ever stronger. The production of cotton kept expanding, and where it expanded it quickly exhausted the soil. After the forced emigration of the Southeastern Indians began, it sometimes happened that an entire frontier town would stampede from one location to another in hopes of finding better soil. By 1841 several towns were already deserted in Mississippi.[26]

By the early years of the nineteenth century the Indians were feeling everywhere the pressure for land. It was at this time that Tecumseh, the great Shawnee leader, tried to unite the Indians against the Americans on a broad front. He spoke before councils of Southeastern Indians in Mississippi, Alabama, and Georgia, stimu-

448

lating debate among the Indians but little unity. In July 1812 hostilities broke out between America and Britain. One faction among the Creeks, the Red Sticks, accepted British arms, but this led to a civil war with the other Creek faction. Some members of the rival faction fled with white settlers to the safety of Fort Mims, a frontier stockade. But the Red Sticks went against the fort in a surprise attack, routing the soldiers and killing more than 400 people. The United States quickly launched reprisals with three armies invading Creek territory from Mississippi, Georgia, and Tennessee. In the hope that they would later win favor, the Cherokees aligned themselves with the Tennessee militia under Andrew Jackson. The same motive also prompted several hundred Choctaws to join the American forces.

The Red Sticks fought with remarkable courage. At Horseshoe Bend they at first held out against the Americans and their Indian allies, forcing them to retreat several times. It was Jackson's Cherokees who turned the tide by swimming across the river and attacking the Red Sticks on their flank. More than one thousand Creeks died in the battle. At the close of the war, Jackson opened up a corridor from Tennessee to the Gulf of Mexico, thus splitting the Indians apart and isolating them one from the other.

The 1820s were a time of relative peace in the South. The Southeastern Indians realized that they could no longer oppose the Americans militarily, so they began trying to become "civilized," to meet the Americans on their own terms. The Chickasaws, Choctaws, Creeks, and Cherokees still controlled substantial areas of land. More than ever they began adopting white farming practices, building mills, accumulating property, and sending some of their children away to school. Not all of them saw this as a solution. Some of the Cherokees began to emigrate voluntarily to Arkansas at this time, becoming the first members of the group later known as the Western Cherokees.

Of all the Southeastern Indians, the Cherokees made the most concerted effort to acquire the trappings of civilization (fig. 105). It was at this time that Sequoyah invented his syllabary for writing the Cherokee language. Within three years after its invention many Cherokees, both Eastern and Western, had learned to read and write Cherokee. In 1828, with help from Samuel Worcester, a Congregational missionary, they began publishing at New Echota a bilingual newspaper, *The Cherokee Phoenix*, in Cherokee and English. This newspaper aroused interest throughout the United States and in many parts of the world. The Cherokees were the only people in the New World who had their own press. It was the highest symbol of their determination to become civilized.

The Cherokees set up a centralized government which modeled

Figure 105. Vann House. This three-story brick house was built in northern Georgia around 1804 by James Vann, a Cherokee leader. In 1834 his son and heir, Joseph Vann, was forcibly removed from the house by white men who then seized the house along with 800 acres of cultivated land, 42 cabins, 6 barns, 5 smokehouses, a grist mill, a sawmill, a blacksmith shop, eight corn cribs, a shop and foundry, a trading post, a peach kiln, a still, 1,133 peach trees, 147 apple trees, and other property. Courtesy, Historic Preservation Section, Georgia Department of Natural Resources.

450

itself after governments in surrounding Southern states. For many years escaped black slaves had sought refuge among the Cherokees as they had with other Southeastern Indians. But increasingly the wealthy Cherokees began buying black slaves to work their farms. They passed a law making it illegal for a black to marry either a white or an Indian living under Cherokee jurisdiction. In 1827 they adopted a formal constitution chartering a government with separate legislative, executive, and judiciary branches. Under their constitution, females and blacks were disenfranchised.

REMOVAL

The final assault against the Southeastern Indians came in the 1830s. Seldom in modern history has one people's aggression against another been so unforgiving, so relentless, and marked by such terrible results. The world of the Southeastern Indians changed greatly before 1830, but what happened after 1830 virtually brought it to an end. In one great political and economic crunch the Americans gained a large portion of a continent, along with all its natural resources. At little cost they forced the Indians out of their homeland, for all but the Seminoles were already too beaten to offer much resistance. The impetus for removal came not from the poor whites on the frontier, but from the Southern planters, politicians, and land speculators. Many of their countrymen opposed removal, but those who were in favor of the policy prevailed in the end, although it was at the cost of a deep sectional division in the country which eventually ended in civil war. It was with Indian removal that the seemingly perpetual availability of free land became a dominant factor in American history.

The Indians were unequal to this last contest to a far greater degree than mere numbers would lead one to expect. The Southeastern Indians were not able to combine forces. The Creek chief Mortar had tried to unite the Creeks and Cherokees, but was unsuccessful; Tecumseh later tried to unite all the eastern Indians, and he too failed. Existing cultural and social differences among the Indians were seized upon and exaggerated first by the British and later by the Americans; they deliberately aggravated existing differences. It is probable that the Indians could not conceive of the degree to which the Europeans could act in concert, nor the degree

451

to which they could plan far into the future. Even when the Indians did combine forces against the colonists, as in the Yamasee War, they failed to push their actions to a conclusion.

It was Thomas Jefferson, who professed to have the interest of the Indian at heart, who first devised a plan to move the Southeastern Indians out of the way. Jefferson had long had a scholarly interest in the Indians and their cultures. He was also a daring thinker. He proposed that poor whites and Indians should intermarry, mix, and become one people. He proposed that schools be built for the Indians so that they could be given an elementary education. But of all his proposals, only his plan for their removal was put into practice. Jefferson explicitly set forth the plan of driving the Indians further and further west, move by move, as the frontier filled with whites. His main strategy was to install "factories" (government trading posts) among the Indians, to allow them to fall in debt, and then to force them to cede land as a way of ridding themselves of debt.[27] Thus in 1805, in the Treaty of Mount Dexter, the Choctaws ceded 4,142,720 fertile acres of Mississippi in exchange for cancellation of a $48,000 trading debt and a small quantity of goods.

The main justification for Indian removal was that the whites could use the land more productively than could the Indians. The Indian, so the argument ran, was a mere heathen hunter, while the white man was a Christian farmer who could use the land efficiently, as God intended. This argument completely ignored the fact that the Indians had been agriculturalists for hundreds of years and were at that very time adopting modern agricultural techniques from the whites. Even more striking, this argument ignored the fact that some of the most important vegetable foods grown by American farmers had come to them from the Indians. Another justification was that the removal of the Indians was for their own good because it would protect them from the depredations of "unruly frontier whites." But the fact of the matter was that the local state governments in the South refused to give the Indians any legal protection, thus encouraging this very "unruliness." Other arguments were more practical: the Indians paid no taxes, and the Southern states needed room for more immigrants.

The Indians had few defenders in the South. Indeed, the political pressure for their removal was so strong that it is surprising that they had any support at all. A protest over the removal of the Choctaws

452

was organized, however, particularly in Natchez, Mississippi. The protesters pointed out that removal would break all the ties which had developed between whites and Indians. Others pointed out that removal as a benign plan to civilize the Indians was too visionary, too unproved. Still others pointed out that transportation was inadequate and that this would expose the Indians to hardships en route to the West, and moreover there was no guarantee that their new land would be safe from further white encroachments. The planter William B. Melvin of Mississippi argued that the United States had signed treaties with the Choctaws and that to violate these treaties was neither right nor just.[28] Among the strongest champions of the Indians were the Protestant missionaries, particularly the Choctaws' Cyrus Kingsbury and the Cherokees' Samuel Worcester.

Though the Americans argued that their gaining possession of North America was God's will, or a law of nature, they always took the trouble to obtain their land cessions by treaty. Some of these treaties were fraudulent, others were obtained by force, and still others were obtained by getting signatures from nonrepresentative minorities among the Indians. All too often these treaties were broken by the whites soon after they were signed.

When James Monroe became president in 1817, he appointed John C. Calhoun of South Carolina as secretary of war. One of Calhoun's tasks was to deal with the Indians, and he did so by transforming a piecemeal Indian policy into an organized program. Calhoun assumed that the Indians would have to be moved west of the Mississippi River, but he determined that it should be done as humanely as possible. Calhoun embarked on a program of "civilizing" the Indians, particularly through schooling, but at the same time he began gaining control of their land. Calhoun took the position that the Indians were not legally nations and should not be treated as such. They should be subject to the same laws as other American citizens, and he maintained that Indians who did not wish to go west should be allowed to remain as ordinary citizens. He wanted to avoid forcing his policy upon the Indians. But he told the Indians that if they attempted as nations to retain their lands, the individual states would destroy them.[29]

Georgia in particular insisted that the Indians be removed. In the middle of the 1820s nearly one-third of what is now the state of

453

Georgia was held by Creeks and Cherokees. The Cherokees flatly refused to leave, and the delegates and representatives they sent to Washington and the spokesmen they sent to other northern cities won considerable sympathy and support from clergymen, educators, and politicians. But Georgia continued to exert pressure on the Indians and had their land surveyed in preparation for a takeover. In 1827, President John Quincy Adams warned Georgia that her actions violated treaties between the United States and the Indians, and that if necessary the United States would use military force to uphold the treaties. This made the Georgians even more angry. Here was both a racial and a states' rights issue rising to divide North and South more than one-quarter of a century before the Civil War. Georgia called up its militia and occupied some of the Creek land, and the federal government, not wanting a confrontation, backed down.

The pressure to remove the Southeastern Indians assumed different proportions when Andrew Jackson was elected president in 1828. John C. Calhoun had earlier appointed Jackson as one of the commissioners to obtain a land cession from the Choctaws, but Jackson became impatient and finally angry over Calhoun's policy of moderation. Jackson preferred telling the Indians to negotiate or else, and he openly challenged Calhoun's moderation and his encouragement of the missionaries who were working among the Indians.[30]

Jackson pretended to be a friend of the Indians, claiming that his removing them from the evil effects of exposure to white civilization was for their own good. The truth was, however, that he was more than willing to push one race of people around to benefit another. It soon became plain that Jackson was a friend of the Indians only so long as he needed them, as when the Cherokees helped him fight the Creek War of 1813–14, and again when the Creeks helped him fight the Seminoles.[31] Under the guise of legality and justice, however, Jackson would strike out against the Indians on any occasion. When some Creeks had once captured a white woman, Jackson had written: "With such arms and supplies as I can obtain I shall penetrate the Creek Towns, until the captive, with her captors are delivered up, and think myself justifiable, in laying waste to their villages, burning their houses, killing their warriors and leading into Captivity their wives and children, until I do obtain a surrender of

454

the Captive and the Captors."[32] The only thing humanitarian about Jackson was that he did not order the extermination of the Southeastern Indians, as some Southerners had urged.

Once in office, Jackson appointed John Eaton, who shared his views on Indians, to the post of secretary of war. Jackson's bill requiring the Southeastern Indians to emigrate touched off one of the most bitter debates of that period. Proponents of the bill assured their opponents that force would not be used, insisting that the bill simply made it possible for the federal government to help the Indians move. Senator Theodore Frelinghuysen of New Jersey led the opposition. In the end the bill passed in the Senate by a vote of 28 in favor and 19 against. Debate was also held in the House, where the vote was 102 in favor and 97 against. Jackson signed the bill into law on June 30, 1830. It was now official. The Southeastern Indians had to move.[33]

The Choctaws, with an estimated population of 23,400, were the first of the Southeastern Indians to be removed. In 1820, Andrew Jackson had been sent to negotiate a treaty with them. He had proceeded by threatening them, telling them that if they refused to move west they would surely be destroyed. They signed the Treaty of Doak's Stand, ceding over five million acres of their homeland in exchange for thirteen million acres in Arkansas and the Indian Territory. But it turned out that white settlers were already on some of this land in the Indian Territory, and when the government began speaking of altering the boundaries of the land they were to get under terms of the treaty, the Choctaws became apprehensive and refused to leave Mississippi. In 1829, Mississippi passed an act extending the laws of Mississippi to apply to the Choctaws, and in 1830 they abolished the Choctaw government and passed other measures designed to frighten the Choctaws into leaving.

In 1830, Jackson's men bribed a minority of Choctaw leaders into signing the Treaty of Dancing Rabbit Creek, ceding all remaining Choctaw land in Mississippi. Under Article 14 of this treaty, any Choctaw who elected to do so could remain in the state of Mississippi by registering with the Indian agent within six months after the treaty was ratified. But the Indian agent, William Ward, an arbitrary, tyrannical, and insulting bully, allowed only 69 Choctaw heads of families to remain in Mississippi in token compliance with Article 14.[34]

Figure 106. Louisiana Indians Walking Along a Bayou. By Alfred Boisseau, 1847. The man carries a flintlock rifle; the boy a blowgun and two darts. One of the women carries a burden basket with a tumpline; the other carries an infant. They are possibly co-wives. Courtesy, New Orleans Museum of Art, gift of Mr. and Mrs. William E. Groves.

The Choctaws emigrated in successive parties. Some of them went individually or in small groups. A party of about 400 Choctaws departed in December of 1830, anxious to get to the new territory to claim the best land. In October of 1831 a party of about 4,000 departed, splitting up and taking several routes to the Indian Territory. En route they encountered a terrible snowstorm and many died of starvation and exposure. The survivors, tired and demoralized, reached the upper Red River in the Indian Territory in March of 1832. Another party of about 5,000 left in October of the next year. They too encountered bad weather, and an epidemic of cholera broke out.[35]

456

Some 6,000 Choctaws still remained in Mississippi. They had heard about what had happened to the earlier émigrés, and they refused to move. Some of them settled around Mobile and others worked on plantations in the cotton fields, but most of them wandered about the countryside where unscrupulous men stripped them of virtually everything they possessed. By the 1840s they were ready to do anything to escape the oppression to which they were subjected (fig. 106). Most of them emigrated between 1845 and 1854, but a few of them managed to remain in Louisiana and Mississippi and to evade emigration altogether.

The Creeks bitterly resisted removal. They did not want to leave the land where their ancestors were buried, and they had heard reports of the great number of deaths among the Choctaws when they were removed. Alabama brought pressure to bear on the Creeks by the simple expedient of giving them no legal protection. Their oaths were not accepted in court, so they had no legal redress when wrongs were committed against them. Horse thieves, renegades, and frontiersmen moved in illegally and staked claims to their land. By 1831 many of the Creeks were starving, some of them begging for food on the streets of Columbus, Georgia. Some citizens in Mobile County, Alabama, tried to get a law passed authorizing justices of the peace to seize any wild game found in the possession of the Indians. To make things worse, an epidemic of smallpox broke out among the Creeks.

On March 24, 1832, the Creeks signed the Treaty of Washington ceding all of their five million acres of territory to the United States. Out of this the United States reserved a little over two million acres to be allotted to the Creeks for plantations and farms. These parcels of land were to belong to individual Creeks who were to be given deeds after they had occupied the land for five years, or else they could sell out and move west. In addition the United States agreed to protect their lives and property and to remove white intruders and troublemakers. The United States also agreed to pay expenses for their removal to the West, and to finance their subsistence their first year there. The Creeks were explicitly assured in the treaty that they were free to stay or to emigrate. A census taken in May of 1833 showed that the Upper Towns had a population of 14,142 people, including 445 black slaves; the Lower Towns had a population of 8,552 people, including 457 black slaves.

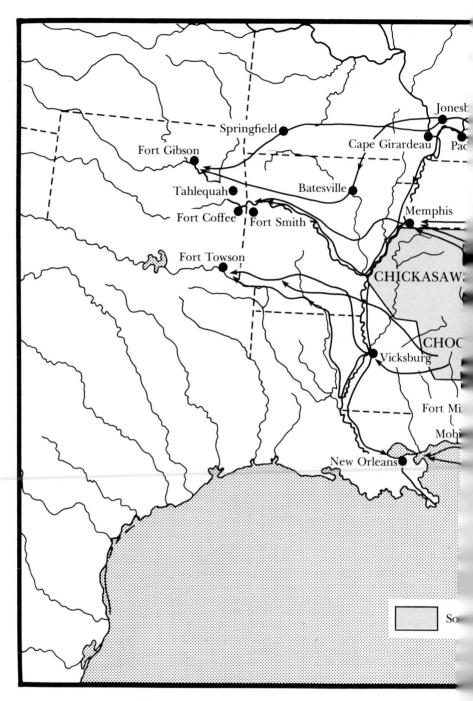

Map 7. Main Removal Routes.

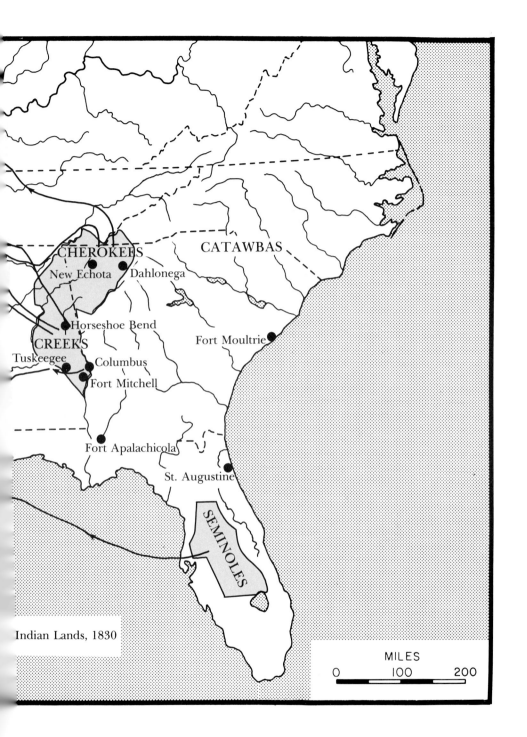

CHEROKEES

New Echota Dahlonega

CATAWBAS

Horseshoe Bend

CREEKS

Tuskeegee Columbus

Fort Mitchell

Fort Moultrie

Fort Apalachicola

St. Augustine

SEMINOLES

Indian Lands, 1830

MILES

0   100   200

The United States broke the terms of the treaty within days. Whites immediately invaded Creek land, looting, burning, raping, and killing. Alabama continued its strategy of making conditions so miserable for the Creeks that they would choose to remove. Many Creeks retreated into the swamps and forests where they tried to stay alive by eating wild food. Other whites began swindling the Creeks out of their land allotments, and land speculators formed companies to carry out the swindles even more efficiently.

In December of 1834 a party of 630 Creeks left for the West. The weather turned cold, and because they were poorly clothed they had to stop and build fires six or seven times a day to keep from freezing to death. They reached the Indian Territory in March of the next year with 469 survivors. A second group of Creeks left in December of 1835.

In May of 1836 in a reprisal against the land speculators, bands of Lower Creeks led by Eneah Emathla, Enea Micco, and Jim Henry, a Yuchi, began attacking white people and destroying their property between Tuskegee, Alabama, and Columbus, Georgia. Alarmists thought that these reprisals were the beginning of another Creek war, and this fear prompted the secretary of war to order General Thomas S. Jesup to lead an army to Alabama and to remove the Creeks by force. He captured Eneah Emathla in June and shortly thereafter about one thousand of his followers—red, white, and black—gave themselves up. The others were captured a short time later. Jesup had them manacled and chained together. In July, 2,498 Creeks (including 900 Yuchis) were put into two steamboats and taken down the Alabama River to Mobile. From there they were taken to the Indian Territory.

Just as the last group of Lower Creeks was preparing for removal, the Seminoles began hostilities, and some 700 Lower Creek men were pressed into service with the U.S. Army against the Seminoles. Their families were placed in concentration camps where they were supposedly under the protection of federal officers. But these camps were attacked by mobs from Russell County, Alabama, and Franklin County, Georgia. The mobs came in and raped the women, killed several men, and carried off some of the Indians into slavery. When some of these Creeks broke away and fled into the swamps, the Alabama militia went in and killed many of them.

In March 1837 another 4,000 Creeks were collected together at

Montgomery to be sent down river, where many of them were placed in concentration camps at Mobile. When the Creeks who fought the Seminoles returned, they found what remained of their families in these camps. The Creeks were then loaded onto steamboats to be taken west. One of the boats—the Monmouth—collided with another boat and sank. Of the 611 Indians on board, 311 drowned. By 1838, Creek removal was complete, except for some who were held in bondage as slaves in Alabama and a very few others who had escaped removal.

The Chickasaws signed the Treaty of Pontotoc Creek on October 20, 1832. They ceded all of their lands to the United States to be sold as public lands with the proceeds to be held by the government for the Chickasaws. Under the terms of the treaty the Chickasaws were supposed to have the right to remain in their homes until suitable land had been purchased in the West. But it was not until January 1837 that the Chickasaws signed the Treaty of Doaksville and at the same time purchased a suitable tract of land in the western part of the new territory held by the Choctaws. A tribal roll was prepared which listed 4,914 Chickasaws and 1,156 black slaves.

The following summer about 500 Chickasaws set out for the West. They were better outfitted and better organized than previous parties of emigrating Indians. Relatively few of the Chickasaws in the party died of disease. One of their worst problems was that a gang of horse thieves followed them, stealing horses whenever they could. In the winter of that year some 4,000 Chickasaws prepared to move, taking with them great quantities of possessions and four or five thousand horses. Most of them boarded steamboats at Memphis and were taken up the Arkansas River. Others, fearful of the boats, elected to travel overland.

Several smaller parties of Chickasaws emigrated on their own. One reason Chickasaw removal went so smoothly was that they paid for it themselves out of tribal funds from the sale of their lands, so that they had a voice in their travel arrangements. Small parties of Chickasaws continued to emigrate as late as 1850.

The Chickasaws were victimized by such swindles as being provisioned with substandard food and paying for food which they never received. But compared to the removal of the Creeks and the Cherokees, Chickasaw removal was uneventful; however, the worst hardships for the Chickasaws occurred after they reached the Indian

Territory. There they were attacked by Shawnees, Kiowas, and Comanches. Also, an acute epidemic of smallpox broke out, and over 500 Choctaws and Chickasaws died. And they suffered from hunger and malnutrition because the government did not supply them with the food due them by the treaty they had signed.[36]

Of all the Southeastern Indians, the Cherokees fought the most determined legal battle against removal. On December 19, 1829, the state of Georgia passed an act incorporating a large portion of the Cherokee Nation. The same act declared all the laws of the Cherokee Nation to be null and void. It made it a crime for any person to encourage a Cherokee to resist removal. And the crushing blow was that the act made it illegal for any Indian to testify against a white person in court. In effect, this gave the whites—any white—a license to steal and do mayhem. Soon after this the state of Georgia declared that no Indian had any right to the gold which had recently been discovered in north Georgia near Dahlonega.

Some Cherokees had voluntarily moved west in the eighteenth century. Now additional parties of a few hundred each began to emigrate to Arkansas. Several of these early groups were made up of whites with their Indian spouses, their children, and their black slaves. But as the white population of Arkansas increased, the Indians were forced to move on again to what is now Texas and Oklahoma.

The great majority of Cherokees, however, refused to leave their homeland. The white missionaries among the Cherokees were their strongest and most effective supporters. The Georgians hated them, and on December 22, 1830, Georgia passed a law making it illegal for a white person to reside in the Cherokee country without a license from the governor of the state—a license which required them to swear an oath of allegiance to the state of Georgia. The missionaries refused, and the following March, Georgia sent in the militia and arrested Samuel Worcester, Isaac Proctor, and John Thompson. They were released, but again in July they and seven others were arrested. They were beaten, put in chains, and forced to walk all the way to the jail at Lawrenceville, Georgia. When tried, all of them swore allegiance to Georgia except Samuel Worcester and Elizur Butler, who refused as a matter of principle. They were sentenced to four-years of hard labor. Worcester's lawyer took his case to the Supreme Court, arguing that he had been deprived of his constitutional rights. In this famous case—*Worcester vs. the State of Georgia*—Chief Justice John Marshall ruled that his rights had in fact been violated and that certain Georgia laws were unconstitutional. Georgia was ordered to release Worcester. But Andrew Jackson refused to enforce the ruling. He is reported to have said: "John Marshall has rendered his decision; now let him enforce it." Georgia, of course, refused to comply. In fact, Georgia was ready to take up arms over the issue, and probably would have had it not been for Jackson's contempt for the authority of the Supreme Court. Andrew Jackson, the champion of the common man, supported slavery and forced the Southeastern Indians from their homeland, and for this he was re-elected in 1832 with an overwhelming landslide, defeating Henry Clay, the man who was the Indians' last hope.

In December of 1835 the Cherokees were told that they would have to meet at New Echota, their capital, to negotiate a treaty and that any who failed to appear would be considered to be in favor of the treaty. When the meeting was held, some three to five hundred Cherokees out of a total of over 17,000 were there. Even so, the treaty was drawn up, and it was signed on December 29, 1835, mainly by one faction among the Cherokees. The treaty was obviously a fraud, a fact recognized by General Ellis Wool, who was given the job of disarming and intimidating the Cherokees. He reported that the Cherokees refused any food from the United States and that many said they would die before they would leave their homeland.

As soon as the whites got possession of Cherokee land they began instituting lawsuits to take from the Cherokees what little money they had. Because they could not testify against whites, the Cherokees automatically lost any suit instituted against them. Some of the whites resorted to less civil means. They came in and beat the Indians with "cowhides, hickories, and clubs," stripping and flogging both men and women. When General Wool attempted to protect the Cherokees, Alabama accused him of disturbing the peace and of trampling upon the rights of Alabama citizens; he was promptly court-martialed, though he was later cleared of all charges.

By May of 1838 only about 2,000 Cherokees had emigrated, leaving nearly 15,000 behind who still refused to move. General Winfield Scott was ordered to remove the remaining Cherokees by force. He brought in a contingent of about seven thousand men—

U.S. Army soldiers, state militiamen, and volunteers—and he set up his headquarters at New Echota. Stockaded concentration camps were built at several locations, and troops were sent out to arrest the Cherokees and to force them into the stockades. Men were taken from their fields, women from their kitchens, and children from their play. The Cherokees were allowed to take with them little more than the clothes they wore. The soldiers looted their homes and then burned them down. They even dug up Indian graves to steal jewelry from the corpses.

In June 1838 five thousand Cherokees departed for the Indian Territory. It was an unusually hot and dry summer. Crop losses were heavy, and the drinking water turned bad. A larger party of Cherokees waited until fall to leave, but it was only to suffer from measles, whooping cough, and exposure. Some of them were on the road for as long as six months before reaching the Indian Territory. Of some 18,000 Cherokees who were forced to emigrate, about 4,000 of them died in the process of being arrested, incarcerated in concentration camps, and marched away by force. A small number of Cherokees managed to escape removal and remain in their homeland in the mountains of western North Carolina.

The experience of the Seminoles with removal was quite different from that of other Southeastern Indians. In a sense, the Seminoles had already been removed from their homeland. The Seminoles are the descendants of Upper and Lower Creeks who moved south into Florida after the aboriginal inhabitants of Florida had been enslaved and killed. Most of these Creeks spoke Hitchiti, but a large minority spoke Muskogee, a language which was related to Hitchiti but not closely enough for the two languages to be mutually intelligible. Others spoke Alabama, Yuchi, and a few other languages. As in the Creek Confederacy, Muskogee served as a lingua franca between the speakers of different languages.

In the 1740s the Lower Creeks were using the Apalachee region as a winter hunting territory. By 1755 they had established several permanent towns. By about 1800 they had towns scattered from the Apalachicola River to the vicinity of the St. John's River, and from southern Georgia southward to the Caloosahatchee River area. As time went on these Creeks in Florida became more and more independent of the Creek Confederacy. In the 1770s the whites began calling the Creeks in the vicinity of present-day Gainesville,

Florida, "Seminoles," and they extended the term to include the Creeks living along the Apalachicola River. "Seminole" is an English version of the Muskogee word *simanó•li*, which is in turn derived from the Spanish word *cimarrón*, meaning "wild, runaway." Some modern Seminoles refer to themselves as *yàtkitiscì•* (Mikasuki) or *isticá•ti* (Muskogee), both literally meaning "red person" as opposed to a white or black person. After Horseshoe Bend as many as 2,000 or 2,500 Creeks moved south and joined the Seminoles, swelling the total population of Indians in Florida to the neighborhood of 6,000.

Another element in the Seminole population was a large group of escaped black slaves. The Seminoles owned black slaves, as did other Southeastern Indians, but the Seminoles were more benevolent toward their slaves than were the Creeks and the Cherokees. Their slaves lived in comparative freedom, their only obligation being to pay their masters a portion of their corn, livestock, or animal skins each year. Some of the blacks among the Seminoles were freedmen who enjoyed the same rights as Indians and had the same voice in community affairs.[37]

The covert motive of the United States for forcing the emigration of the Southeastern Indians was to acquire their lands, but the land held by the Seminoles was not so valuable. Much of it was swampy. What the whites wanted from the Seminoles was not their land but to gain possession of the blacks who lived among them and to close off Florida as a place to which their own slaves could escape and find refuge.

The Seminoles fought two wars against the United States. The first began in July, 1816, when Colonel D. L. Clinch and soldiers under his command joined forces with 200 Creek mercenaries under Chief William McIntosh. Together they invaded Spanish Florida and attempted to capture the blacks who were living among the Seminoles. A number of the Seminoles and their slaves took refuge in Fort Apalachicola, an old military post on the Apalachicola River. There were over 300 people in the fort, including about 30 Seminole men, 70 black men, and the rest women and children. The whites bombarded the fort, and when a cannonball hit the powder magazine, it blew up, killing 270 people and wounding the rest. The survivors were taken to Georgia and enslaved. In revenge, other Seminoles and blacks struck back at the white settlers along the Georgia-Florida boundary. In 1817 they killed a party of 40 whites who were going up the Apalachicola River. Later in the same year, Andrew Jackson invaded Seminole territory, burning their homesteads and capturing a few slaves. The war ended in 1818, and the following year the United States purchased Florida from Spain. When the treaty with Spain was ratified in 1821, the Seminoles fell under the jurisdiction of the United States. But as the white population increased, more and more black slaves escaped, and the Seminoles and blacks moved into more and more inaccessible parts of the interior of Florida.

In May 1832 the United States pressured a small number of Seminole leaders into signing the Treaty of Payne's Landing. These men were not empowered to represent the Seminoles, and the treaty was therefore clearly fraudulent. It stipulated that the Seminoles would give up their Florida lands within three years and move west to unite with the Creeks. The Seminoles well knew that the treaty was fraudulent, and the majority of them refused to move. One small party of about 150 emigrated in 1834.

The Seminoles did not want to be merged with the Creeks, and they did not want their black comrades and slaves seized by the whites—and most of all they did not want to leave Florida. The blacks in particular did not want to go west. Wiley Thompson, Indian agent for the Seminoles, told them that if they did not emigrate voluntarily, troops would be sent in to force them to emigrate. Osceola, the great Seminole leader, is said to have had a particular hatred for Thompson. One story is that it was because Thompson had seized his young wife and carried her off into slavery. On December 28, 1835, Osceola and 50 Seminoles shot and killed Thompson and a white companion. They also attacked other whites, both civilian and military. Seven miles north of the Withlacoochee River, they attacked a company of troops under Major Francis L. Dade, killing 8 officers and 102 enlisted men. Only 3 of Dade's men escaped alive. The Second Seminole War had begun.

The war proceeded by starts and stops, and the U. S. Army did not at first realize the seriousness of the conflict in which they were engaged. The Seminoles would tire of the fighting and cease hostilities, and the whites would assume that the war had ended, but then the Seminoles would strike again. Most of the actions were small. They would kill a white family and burn their homestead. The

Seminoles scattered into the swamps so that it was impossible for the U. S. Army to find them.

General Thomas Jesup mounted a brutally aggressive campaign against the Seminoles in the fall and winter of 1835. He sent several thousand troops into the interior, where they destroyed the Seminoles' food and housing. But they were able to kill or capture only a few Seminoles. When it became impossible for the Seminoles to raise crops of corn, they relied more and more on wild vegetable food. When they could not hunt with firearms for fear of being discovered, they began to hunt with bow and arrow. There is some evidence that when the U. S. Army pursued them most intensely, they killed their small infants who might cry and give away their location to the enemy.

In his desperation to win, Jesup threw away the rule book. When the Seminole leader Cooacoochee (Wild Cat) went in to St. Augustine under a flag of truce to speak with his captured father, Jesup seized Cooacoochee and put him in jail. Osceola was also seized under a flag of truce. In an amazing feat of agility, Cooacoochee and a companion escaped from prison by squeezing through a tiny window eighteen feet above the floor of their cell. Soon after this Osceola and other Seminole prisoners were taken to Fort Moultrie on Sullivan's Island, near Charleston, South Carolina, where escape was impossible. It was here that the artist George Catlin painted Osceola's portrait, and it was here that Osceola died (fig. 107).

As the war dragged on, the U. S. Army continued to suffer more casualties than did the Seminoles. The swampy environment was so hostile that the whites often ran out of food, their clothing deteriorated, and they suffered mentally from the isolation. Some of the soldiers became despondent and committed suicide. The entire army came under public criticism, and Jesup realized that he could not win a military victory. In a letter to the secretary of war, he wrote: "In regard to the Seminoles, we have committed the error of attempting to remove them when their lands were not required for agricultural purposes; when they were not in the way of white inhabitants; and when the greater portion of their country was an unexplored wilderness, of the interior of which we were as ignorant as the interior of China . . . . "[38] Jesup was relieved of his command in July, 1838.

Figure 107. Osceola. Oil on canvas portrait by George Catlin, 1838. Courtesy, National Collection of Fine Arts, Smithsonian Institution.

468

Throughout the war the Seminoles who were captured or who gave themselves up were taken to a concentration camp near New Orleans. In May of 1838 they numbered over one thousand. Nearly one third of them were blacks who were culturally Seminole. They were loaded onto steamboats and taken up the Mississippi and Arkansas rivers to the Indian Territory. Whites continued to try to take the blacks from them, but the Indians stubbornly refused to give them up. Once in the Indian Territory the Seminoles refused to be put among the Creeks because they knew the Creeks considered them to be runaways.

The Second Seminole War would not yield to a military solution. In 1840 the army tried using bloodhounds to hunt down the Indians, but even this effort failed. Some of the Seminoles surrendered in 1841, and more in 1842, and these were taken west. The Second Seminole War never really ended; it just faded away. It lasted six years; it cost the lives of 1,500 U. S. soldiers, twenty million dollars, and incalculable death and misery for the Seminoles. More Seminoles moved west in 1856, but a large group remained in Florida in the inaccessible interior of the Everglades.

The suffering of the Southeastern Indians did not end when they reached the Indian Territory. Many died there from epidemic diseases. The United States did not deliver the food and materials they promised the Indians to sustain them as they learned to make new lives for themselves. Moreover, they suffered from the physical and psychological shock of acclimating themselves to a new environment.

By the late 1830s the Southeastern Indians owned all of Oklahoma except the panhandle and a small tract in the northeastern corner. But the actual settlements of the Southeastern Indians were concentrated in the eastern part of the state, while the western part of the state was occupied by Plains Indians who were still hunting buffalo. It was here that the Five Civilized Tribes—the Cherokees, Creeks, Choctaws, Chickasaws, and Seminoles—stood in vivid contrast to the "wild" Indians who were still making their living mainly by hunting.

The Five Civilized Tribes put land under cultivation and instituted new political structures. Some of the wealthier Indians built large plantations which they worked with black slaves. The Cherokees established their capital at Tahlequah, revived their news-

469

paper, and adopted a constitutional government. The Cherokees, Choctaws, and Chickasaws quickly established their own school systems.

As time went on, other Indians sought refuge in Oklahoma. The Texans, who bitterly hated Indians, ran out the Cherokees who had built homes and farms in east Texas, and they would have massacred the Caddos had that tribe not been protected by Robert S. Neighbors, their Indian agent. The only Indians allowed to remain in Texas were a small band of Alabamas and Coushattas (Koasatis) who were given a tiny reservation.

The Civil War turned out to be a disaster for the Five Civilized Tribes. In spite of what Southerners had done to them, they generally sided with the South in the conflict. In part, no doubt, they did so because many of their leaders were slaveowners. Moreover, Arkansas lay directly to their east and Texas to their south, and the federal government was far away. The United States ceased giving the Indians monetary support during the war and thus appeared to have abandoned them.

John Ross of the Cherokees urged the Five Civilized Tribes to remain neutral. But the Choctaws and Chickasaws quickly aligned themselves with the Confederacy, and most of the Cherokees subsequently did the same. John Ross went along with them for the sake of preserving unity. One faction of the Creeks headed by Opothle Yahola and Oktarharsars (Sands) sided with the North. They were joined by some Kickapoos, Shawnees, Cherokees, Delawares, Comanches, and quite a few blacks. This group was attacked and defeated by a force of Confederates who came in from Arkansas. Many of the survivors froze to death in a blizzard as they fled to Kansas. A particularly bitter kind of guerilla warfare developed in the Indian Territory, and everyone suffered greatly.

After the Civil War ended, whites loyal to the North saw the possibility of another land grab. The Southeastern Indians were again uprooted and their homes destroyed. Some 19,000 refugees gathered around Fort Gibson and in Choctaw and Chickasaw territory. The Five Civilized Tribes were forced to cede the western half of their territory to be used by other Indians. And of course they were required to free their black slaves and to give them their rights as citizens.

In the decades following the Civil War the federal government embarked on a policy of making the Indians into white men. The government came down hard on the custom of polygyny and on native religious practices. The missionaries approved and helped implement this policy. W. O. Tuggle attended a Presbyterian camp meeting near Okmulgee, Oklahoma, which had 400 people, mostly Indians, in attendance. The people slept in tents or else out of doors, and services were held in a 50-foot-square arbor with a roof covered with prairie grass. Reminiscent of the Green Corn Ceremony, they appointed some of the boys to serve as "dog police," arming them with long switches to keep dogs out of the arbor. One of the preachers, W. S. Robertson, was married to Ann Eliza Worcester, the daughter of Samuel Worcester. She had translated several books using a Muskogee writing system. The preaching was in English, with an interpreter translating it into Muskogee. The songs they sang at this camp meeting were the same songs that were sung in camp meetings all over the South. In some places Indian preachers—usually from the Five Civilized Tribes—ministered to their own people, and sometimes they evangelized the "wild" Indians on the Plains.[39]

White land speculators continued to covet the territory of the Five Civilized Tribes. It was the owners of the railroads who paved the way to their further dispossession by circulating the story that any unassigned land in the Indian Territory could be homesteaded by whites. The railroad people collected groups of poor whites— "Boomers"—to invade the Indian Territory and stake their claims. More railroads were built through the area, and more whites, both rich and poor, moved in. In 1889 the Creeks and Seminoles sold their unassigned land to the government, and the Cherokees ceded theirs (the Cherokee Outlet) in 1891.[40]

The whites began to put pressure on the Indians to divide up their tribal holdings and to allocate parcels of land to individual Indians in fee simple title. Like all other policies forced upon the Indians, this was said to be for their own good. It was supposed to develop their pride in individual ownership and to dissuade them from their "tendency to roam." Of course, any unassigned land could be taken over by whites. Sponsored by Senator Henry L. Dawes of Massachusetts, the Dawes Act became law on February 8, 1887, dividing up the reservations into individually owned areas. But since the Five Civilized Tribes held their land under patented titles, they were exempt from the act.[41] However, more and more white immigrants settled on land owned by the Five Civilized Tribes, some legally and some illegally. By 1879 there were some 12,287 whites living on their land. In 1898, Congress passed the Curtis Act, authorizing allotment of the land owned by the Five Civilized Tribes and at the same time terminating their native governments.[42]

Land speculators immediately began defrauding them through complicated legal maneuvers. They even plundered the land holdings of orphans and other children, and this practice became particularly widespread and ugly after oil was discovered on Indian land. As they were defrauded of their lands, the poorer Indians retreated onto marginal land in the hills, living on the very edge of existence, many squatting on the land allotments of friends and relatives. In 1901 the members of the Five Civilized Tribes became citizens of the United States, and they became citizens of Oklahoma in 1907 when that state was admitted to the Union. When the Great Depression came, they almost starved to death.

The Five Civilized Tribes were said to be assimilated into the state of Oklahoma. This is both true and false. Some of the wealthy, educated mixed bloods, who gained title to the rich bottomlands along the rivers, did in time become influential citizens in Oklahoma. But the culturally conservative Indians—the "full bloods"— became second-class citizens. Most of them retreated to the marginal land in the hills and hollows. In protest many hid from enrollment parties and refused to accept their allotments. The Cherokee conservatives threatened to kill anyone who gave their names to an enrollment party. As late as 1912 nearly two thousand Cherokees still steadfastly refused to claim an allotment, even though they lived in bitter poverty.[43]

Today the descendants of the Five Civilized Tribes hold only tiny pieces of corporately owned land in Oklahoma. A surprisingly large number of them, however, are socially and culturally Indian. The Cherokees, for example, are concentrated in the northeastern corner of Oklahoma in the counties of Adair, Cherokee, Sequoyah, Delaware, and Mayes. In 1960 some 75,000 individuals in Oklahoma had some legal or political claim to being Cherokee, but only 9,500 of these are truly Cherokee in the sense of functioning socially as individuals in Cherokee communities. Many of them speak Cherokee in their homes and in fact speak relatively little English. Some

2,000 additional persons participate in Cherokee society but do not live in Cherokee communities. These 12,000 or so people are those whom Oklahomans call "full bloods," although it should be obvious that their cultural or social identity has nothing to do with their "blood," or more correctly, their genes.

The Oklahoma Cherokees live in scattered land holdings in the hills and hollows of the Ozarks. They are devout churchgoers, and their churches form the core of their communities. Most of them are Baptists, and most of those who are not Baptists are Methodists. They still maintain about half a dozen "stomp grounds," where they hold community functions. Because of recent demographic changes, with local whites moving away and with a high Cherokee birth rate, the Cherokees in this area are both becoming more distinctive and increasing in number. Because of their isolation, few white Oklahomans ever see a traditional Cherokee community. Thus quite erroneously, they say that the Cherokees are disappearing, assimilating, or "breeding out." Some are, but a larger number are not.[44]

The social factors underlying this myth of disappearing Cherokees are complex. In part the myth implies that the allotment of tribal lands was morally right and successful, and that the Indians are now assimilated into the larger society. The disappearance of the Cherokees was "tragic" but inevitable. The myth denies the existence of a viable, ethnic Cherokee community where none is supposed to exist. Moreover, the Cherokees are an ethnic group at the very bottom of the system of ranked ethnic groups in which there are fewer and fewer opportunities for social mobility. In 1963 the median per capita income of these conservative Cherokees was around $500 per year, less than half of that of their rural white neighbors. Some of them live permanently in debt, in virtual peonage.[45]

Many of the old Southeastern dances and ceremonies are still performed by Cherokees, Natchez-Cherokees, Creeks, Seminoles, Yuchis, Caddos, and Shawnees in Oklahoma. In 1974 the Oklahoma Choctaws revived some of their old dances. Most square grounds begin holding their dances in May and continue until October. For Creeks, Seminoles, and Yuchis, the peak of the ceremonial season comes in July or August at the time of the "Greencorn," their version of the old busk or Green Corn Ceremony.

They perform their dances both day and night, but especially at night around fires built on the square grounds. As in the past their

Figure 108. The ribbon dance of the New Tulsa Greencorn. 1965.
Courtesy, James H. Howard.

474

traditional dances are accompanied by musicians playing drums and hand-held rattles. The dances are often named after animals, such as the gar dance, the quail dance, and the guinea dance. Many of these dances entail complicated movements, and perhaps this is the reason why they are gradually losing out to the stomp dance, a simple dance which can be learned by the very young. In the stomp dance no drum nor hand-held rattle is used. It is led by a male leader who begins the dance by circling around the fire counterclockwise. In time others join in forming a line, including a shell-shaker girl who joins in behind the leader. On the lower part of her legs she wears leg rattles made of terrapin shells or condensed milk cans with holes punched in them. Each movement of her feet causes pebbles inside the shells or cans to make a rattling sound. In some cases additional shell-shaker girls join in, each dancing behind a male dancer. The leader vocalizes stereotyped shouts and lines of songs which the other dancers answer in unison. Some of the songs are humorous, others serious. The basic stomp dance step is a running trot in a counterclockwise direction around the fire; in quick succession one foot after the other is slapped down against the ground. Variations are often introduced as the dance proceeds. The leader may, for example, lead the line of dancers into a tight serpentine coil and then reverse himself and uncoil the line of dancers again.

The Greencorn is still celebrated at several Creek, Seminole, and Yuchi square grounds in Oklahoma. The particular way in which it is celebrated varies somewhat from one square ground to another. The Greencorn held at the New Tulsa square ground, near Spalding, Oklahoma, is representative. This square ground has four arbors laid out in the old pattern, with one in each of the cardinal directions, as well as a low earthen mound to the northeast of the square ground and an arbor for women to the southeast. On the morning of the first day of the New Tulsa Greencorn, the men refurbish the arbors and sweep the grounds, and the women perform a ribbon dance, so named because they wear combs in their hair ornamented with long trailing ribbons (fig. 108). Each of the two women who lead this dance carries a large wooden knife (*atássa*) painted with grayish-green paint, perhaps to make it resemble flint. Later they play the single pole ball game, the men playing against the women, and they end the day by stomp dancing until midnight.

On the morning of the second day the men assemble at the square

475

Figure 109. The feather dance of the New Tulsa Greencorn. 1965.
Courtesy, James H. Howard.

ground and go to water for purification. They return and perform the feather dance in honor of the birds (fig. 109). Each man holds a length of river cane six or seven feet long with two or three white feathers attached to the end. One man stands atop the earthen mound and whoops to call the birds. At different parts of this dance they shout the turkey-gobble war whoop. This dance over, they sweep away the ashes of the old year's fire and strike flint to kindle a new fire which is fed by four logs laid out in a cross. They sacrifice four perfect ears of green corn to the fire. Then the men and a few of the women take an emetic medicine, going to the edge of the square ground to vomit. Later in the day they take the emetic three more times, and the men perform the feather dance three more times. At some point men, women, and children submit themselves to ceremonial scratching on their arms and legs. In the afternoon two teams of young boys play a spirited game of stickball. At around eight-thirty they begin stomp dancing and continue all night long. All members of the town are required to participate the entire night. Just before dawn on the third day they perform the titillating drunken dance, in which the women remove their leg rattles and sing and dance along with the men, breaking down, in effect, the ritual distinction between men and women. The men all go to water, and they return whooping to the square ground. They take the emetic for the last time, and after purging themselves they eat breakfast. In the afternoon the men and women play each other in another single-pole ball game, and this brings the Greencorn to a close.[46]

THOSE WHO REMAIN

When we consider what the Southeastern Indians have gone through, it is remarkable that any of them remain on their native soil. But some do. In the 1970 census, 76,656 persons in the Southeast (Alabama, Arkansas, Florida, Georgia, Louisiana, Mississippi, North Carolina, South Carolina, Tennessee, and Virginia) told the census takers that they were Indians. This represents 9.7 per cent of the entire Indian population of the United States. The Indians in the Southeast represent only .22 per cent of the entire Southeastern population, but their number is increasing rapidly. Between 1960 and 1970 the Indian population of the Southeast increased 42 per cent, while the entire population of the Southeast increased by only

12.2 per cent. Much of this increase is not simply the result of a higher birth rate. The South is urbanizing rapidly, and Indians from other regions are being attracted to Southern cities. Another factor that should not be overlooked is that more people were willing in 1970 to identify themselves as Indians than was the case in 1960.[47]

The best known of the Indians who remain in the Southeast are the Cherokees of the Smoky Mountains of North Carolina and the Seminoles of Florida. The Choctaws of Mississippi are a surprisingly large group but not as widely known as the Cherokees and the Seminoles. Smaller and even less visible Indian groups are the Catawbas of South Carolina, the Houmas and Chitimachas of Louisiana, the Alabama-Coushattas of Texas, and a few small communities of Creeks in Alabama, Georgia, and Florida. In addition to these groups, all with unimpeachable Indian identities, there are several groups for whom Indian identity is only partial. Some of these, such as the Lumbees of North Carolina, claim to be Indians, while others, who might claim Indian ancestry on equally valid grounds, do not in fact do so.[48] These people have been variously termed "mestizos," "racial isolates," "racially mixed people," and "little races."[49]

But even the Southeastern Indians who have an unimpeachable claim to Indian identity are not all the same. Some are more "Indian" than others, and this applies to groups as well as individuals. One familiar, though erroneous, way of conceptualizing this difference is to distinguish between "full bloods," whose genetic ancestry is presumably all Indian, and "half bloods" or "mixed bloods," whose ancestry is part Indian, the implication being that full bloods are necessarily more Indian in their identity than half bloods or mixed bloods. This way of thinking ignores the fact that a person can be Indian in at least three ways, and each is more or less independent of the others: A person may be an Indian in a *genetic* sense, meaning that he is noticeably Indian in his physical appearance. A person may be an Indian in a *cultural* sense, meaning that he sees the world from a point of view whose premises are historically derived from an aboriginal belief system, and he probably also speaks an Indian language. And, finally, a person may be an Indian in a *social* sense, meaning that he occupies the status of Indian in a social system, usually as distinguished from whites and blacks.

A few people in the Southeast are Indian in all three of these

478

Figure 110. Creeks in Oklahoma. *Left to right:* Lochar Harjo; unidentified man; John McGilvry; *Ho-tul-ko-mi-ko* ("Chief of the Whirlwind"). The latter, a black man, was also called Silas Jefferson. Photographed prior to 1877. Negative no. 1164–B. Courtesy, Smithsonian Institution, National Anthropological Archives.

senses—they look like Indians, they think like Indians, and they are socially Indians.[50] These are the people who among the Cherokees, Choctaws, and Seminoles are called full bloods, but who might more properly be called "conservatives." It can easily be demonstrated that there is no necessary connection between being a genetic Indian, on the one hand, and a cultural or social Indian on the other.

At the time of removal, many Southeastern Indians owned black slaves and had freedmen living among them who spoke Indian languages fluently, and who presumably saw the world from an Indian point of view. It is said that there are today black people in

479

Oklahoma who speak Southeastern Indian languages fluently (fig. 110). Moreover, among the North Carolina Cherokees there are more than a few individuals who are considered full bloods, but who are mainly caucasoid in appearance. *Observation:* one can be a cultural Indian without being a genetic Indian.

When the last Catawba tribal roll was drawn up in 1960, just before the Catawbas terminated their status as Indians with the Bureau of Indian Affairs, it included some individuals who were caucasoid to the extent of having red hair and blue eyes. Similar individuals live among the North Carolina Cherokees, where they are called "white Indians." Some of them are from old families who can trace their lineage back well before the time of Indian Removal. *Observation:* one can be a social Indian without being a genetic Indian.

Among both the Chitimachas of Louisiana and the Cherokees of North Carolina there are Indians whose right to be on the tribal roll is unquestioned, but who speak no other language than English, and who think like the white people who live around them. *Observation:* one can be a social Indian without being a cultural Indian.

This is not to deny that most of the Southeastern Indians who still speak their native language and who still retain something of their ancestral belief system are also Indians genetically. And it is also the case that many of the Indians who speak English and retain little or nothing of Indian beliefs are racially mixed. But it is far more accurate to characterize these differences not in terms of "blood," but in terms of "conservative" Indians who speak a native language and uphold traditional beliefs and values, as opposed to "acculturated" Indians who speak the English language exclusively, and who share the culture of the non-Indians living around them. It should be understood that these two categories—conservative and acculturated—do not account for all the cultural and social variation among contemporary Southeastern Indians. Many fall between these two extremes. Some Cherokees, for example, speak both English and Cherokee, and they function in the white world while retaining some respect for the beliefs and values of conservative Cherokees.[51]

If these permutations of Indian genetic, cultural, and social components strain conventional racial categories, the "little races" of the

Southeast stretch them to their breaking point. The Lumbees of North Carolina, for example, consider themselves to be Indian, in no uncertain terms, but they are not considered to be so by some of the people who live around them. They speak no language other than English, and they retain nothing of an aboriginal culture, and they have not done so in historic times. More importantly, it is difficult to connect them clearly with indubitable Indian cultures in the historic past, though genetically they obviously have a strong Indian inheritance. There are still other little races in the Southeast who do not claim to be Indian, but who do bear some Indian genetic traits.

Of all the Indians who remain in the Southeast, the North Carolina Cherokees are the most widely known. This is partly a consequence of the role they played in American history, and partly a consequence of their living in the Smoky Mountains, where they are seen by hundreds of thousands of tourists each year. The nucleus of the Cherokees who remained in the Smoky Mountains was a small group who before removal had withdrawn from the Cherokee Nation and had been granted American citizenship. They were not required to emigrate. They were later joined by several hundred members of the Cherokee Nation who had managed to hide out in the mountains and escape removal.

After removal the Cherokees who remained in the East gained rights to land mainly through the work of a white man, William H. Thomas (1805–93), who became their agent and purchased land for them. Thomas invested everything he owned in the Southern cause during the Civil War. When he became ill toward the end of his life, the Cherokees set up a governmental apparatus with elected officials. Eventually, his creditors obtained sheriff's deeds to Cherokee land threatening them with eviction, and at that time the commissioner of Indian affairs became trustee for their lands (fig. 111). Today Eastern Cherokee land holdings total 56,574 acres in several tracts ranging from 35 acres to over 40,000 acres in size. The largest tract, the Qualla Boundary, is the one in which most of the Cherokees live, and it is here that Cherokee Village (Yellow Hill) is located.[52] The Eastern Cherokees are governed by a tribal council consisting of a chief and a vice-chief, elected every four years, and two councillors from each of their six townships, elected every two

Figure 111. A Cherokee log cabin and farmstead. Photographed by James Mooney around 1888–93. The woman on the right is pounding corn into meal. Negative no. 1000–A. Courtesy, Smithsonian Institution, National Anthropological Archives.

years. The council is responsible for regulating disputes over land, for regulating land leases, for maintaining a police force, and for maintaining tribal funds and enterprises.[53]

Several hundred thousand automobiles pass through Qualla Boundary each year, mostly carrying people on vacation or holiday. But few of these people see the real Cherokees; they see instead a series of souvenir stores with Cherokees "chiefing" in Plains Indian garb, posing for pictures, and otherwise behaving like stereotypic Indians. Tourism is the major industry for the Cherokees, but few of the restaurants, shops, motels, and so on are owned by conservative Indians. Many of them are leased to white entrepreneurs who pay a part of their proceeds to the Cherokees. In the summer months the Cherokee Historical Association operates Oconaluftee Village, in which several aspects of traditional Cherokee culture are displayed and reenacted. And the Historical Association manages a museum and the historical play *Unto These Hills*, a drama about Cherokee removal. In late September or early October the Cherokees hold their annual fair. In most respects it is like fairs everywhere, but it is different in that one can eat traditional Cherokee food and see exhibition matches of the ball game.

Few tourists see the Cherokees who live up in the hills and hollows. They are a poor people. In the middle 1950s it was estimated that the average family income was between $300 and $600 per year.[54] Until the 1940s and 1950s, most of them relied on subsistence agriculture for their living. Today most of them work for the Bureau of Indian Affairs or in the tourist industry, or else in one of the small manufacturing industries now located in Cherokee. The Cherokees are churchgoers. In 1960 they attended twenty-one churches of several denominations, with about three-fourths of them being Baptists. Their matrilineal kinship system is almost completely defunct now, with only a few of the older people remembering the old kinship terminology.

The Florida Seminoles are almost as well known as the Cherokees and for some of the same reasons. After the close of hostilities between the Seminoles and the U. S. Army, less than 200 of them remained in Florida. Andrew Jackson wanted them all out, but they were too well hidden, and it proved to be too costly to track them down. For twenty years they remained completely isolated, which they accomplished by occupying land in the Everglades and in Big Cypress Swamp, land that was useless to the whites and not easily penetrated. Little is known about what happened during this period. It is known that their two basic languages continued to exist, with about two-thirds speaking Hitchiti (now called Mikasuki) and the remainder speaking Muskogee. But although Hitchiti was spoken by the majority, Muskogee until recently continued to be the lingua franca.[55]

The Bureau of Indian Affairs began buying up land for a Seminole reservation as early as 1891, but the Seminoles were in no hurry to move onto reservation land. As late as 1930 only three or four Seminole camps were on reservation land. In the 1930s reservation lands were consolidated to form Brighton on the western shore of Lake Okeechobee, Hollywood (at first called Dania) on the lower east coast of Florida, and Big Cypress on the northeastern edge of Big Cypress Swamp. Muskogee is the predominant language at

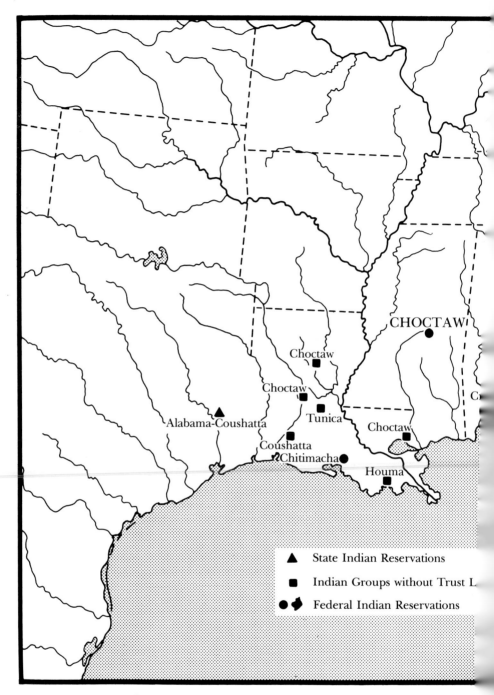

CHOCTAW

Choctaw

Choctaw

Tunica

Choctaw

Alabama-Coushatta

Coushatta

Chitimacha

Houma

C

▲ State Indian Reservations

■ Indian Groups without Trust L

●⚑ Federal Indian Reservations

Map 8. Those Who Remain.

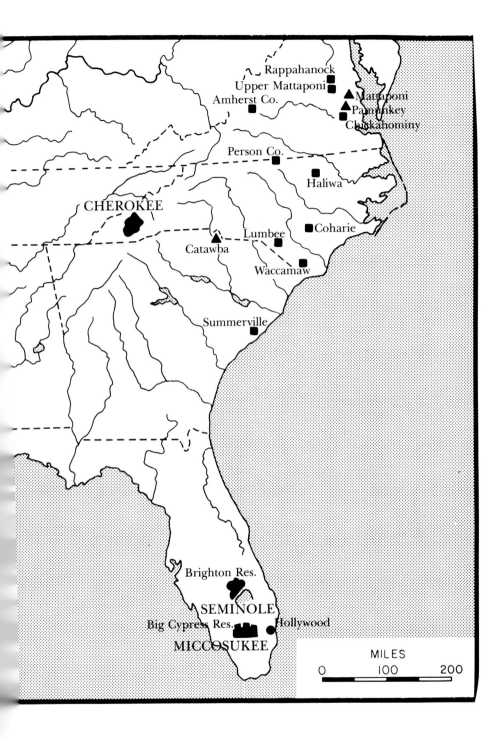

Rappahanock
Upper Mattaponi
Amherst Co.
Mattaponi
Pamunkey
Chickahominy

Person Co.

Haliwa

CHEROKEE

Coharie

Catawba
Lumbee

Waccamaw

Summerville

Brighton Res.

SEMINOLE
Big Cypress Res.
Hollywood
MICCOSUKEE

MILES

0   100   200

485

Brighton, and Mikasuki predominates elsewhere. The Bureau of Indian Affairs gradually introduced services and schooling, but the Seminoles did not take to these readily (fig. 112).[56] Now, however, almost all Seminole children attend elementary school, many have graduated from high school, and a few have been to college. English is now the lingua franca between Mikasuki- and Muskogee-speaking Indians.

Figure 112. Missionary Harriet M. Bedell with Seminole Doctor Tiger and a small boy. 1936. Negative no. 44,541. Courtesy, Smithsonian Institution, National Anthropological Archives.

486

The reservation Seminoles plus a few off-reservation Seminoles organized the "Seminole Tribe of Florida" in 1957 with a Bureau of Indian Affairs office at Hollywood. At first they were under the direct control of the Bureau of Indian Affairs, but they acquired more and more autonomy as time went on. A strong dissident faction developed among the Seminoles living along the Tamiami Trail. In 1959 they sent representatives to visit Fidel Castro in Cuba; the following year the state of Florida gave the Seminoles hunting, fishing, and frogging rights to 143,620 acres of Everglades. In 1961 the Indians living along the Tamiami Trail organized themselves as the Miccosukee Tribe of Indians of Florida. In 1965 they incorporated as a tribe distinct from the Seminoles, and a separate Bureau of Indian Affairs agency was set up for them. Later they acquired several pieces of land in various places to serve as their own reservation. They are actively trying to acquire a separate identity from the Seminole Tribe, with some of them saying that they are the true aborigines of Florida while the Seminoles are migrants from the north.

In 1967 there were 1,000 members of the Seminole Tribe of Florida, 150 members of the Miccosukee Tribe of Indians of Florida, and 200 unorganized Trail Mikasukis, a total of 1,350.[57] Many Seminoles still live in old fashioned chickees, consisting of a floor raised about three feet above the ground, with a palmetto thatch roof supported on posts, and with minimal walls (fig. 113). It is a dwelling which keeps them dry when the ground is covered with water, and it allows even the slightest breeze to come through when the weather is hot. Increasingly, though, the Seminoles are beginning to live in houses made of concrete blocks and other modern materials. These modern houses, of course, have electricity, as do most of the chickees.[58]

Most Seminoles work either on commercial vegetable farms or on cattle ranches. It is fairly easy for them to get jobs in winter, but there is relatively little for them to do in summer. They cultivate little food of their own, and they still rely on hunting to a surprisingly large extent. The deer is still their favorite game animal, but they also hunt smaller mammals and birds, and they are especially fond of turtle meat. Many Seminoles derive a portion of their income from handicrafts, such as woodcarving, sewing, and basketry, which they sell to tourists. Their average annual income is quite low, and were it

Figure 113. Seminole chickee. Circa 1921. A baby sleeps in the hammock.
Negative no. 44,353–A. Courtesy, Smithsonian Institution, National
Anthropological Archives.

not for the mild weather and plentiful game they would suffer.[59]

Modern Seminoles are truly a mixture of the old and the new.
Along with store-bought foods they still cook hominy meal to make
sofkee, and they still like to eat the inner leaves of sabal palmetto.
Many of them still prefer their ancient indirect style of social interaction, gazing at the ground or away at the horizon rather than looking
directly at the person with whom they are speaking. As in the past,
they rarely raise their voices, and they rarely punish their children.

Although the modern nuclear family is gaining in popularity, some of them still live in matrilocal extended families, and most of them know their clan affiliations. Many of them now are members of Protestant churches, mostly Baptist, but a few of the old medicine bundles still exist, and some of them still celebrate their annual Green Corn Ceremony.[60]

Although the Choctaws are not nearly so well known as the Cherokees or Seminoles, they have one of the largest populations of all the Indian groups still in the Southeast, and well over 90 percent of them still speak their native language. Over four thousand Choctaws live in the sand clay hills of east central Mississippi. Most of them live in seven counties—Winston, Noxubee, Leake, Neshoba, Kemper, Newton, and Jones—with lesser numbers living in other parts of the state. Most of them live in the communities of Bogue Chitto, Tucker, Pearl River, Red Water, Standing Pine, Conehatta, and Bogue Homo. Their existence is not well known even in the state of Mississippi.

In 1860, thirty years after removal began, some one thousand Choctaws still remained in Mississippi, and a smaller number remained in Louisiana. A tiny fraction of the Mississippi Choctaws had registered for land in accordance with Article 14 of the Treaty of Dancing Rabbit Creek. By 1860 some of them had been accepted into white society. Greenwood Leflore, for example, was elected to the Mississippi senate for two terms. But most of the Choctaws who remained in Mississippi had either evaded removal or had made their way back from the Indian Territory. A few landless Choctaws somehow managed to survive in their homeland, where their descendants live today.

The history of these landless Choctaws between 1840 and 1880 is by no means clear, but they evidently lived as squatters on marginal land. In Louisiana they sometimes lived on land loaned to them by planters. The men hunted for small game, where there was any to be had, and both men and women tended small gardens of corn, pumpkins, and potatoes. The men sometimes formed relationships with planters who became their patrons. The Indians supplied their patrons with game and provided them with petty services, such as cutting firewood, in return for a spot of land on which to live. The men avoided manual labor because that would have put them in the same category as black slaves, though in time they began to work in the cotton fields for wages. The women made handicrafts and collected wild herbs which they sold to the whites. Apparently, Louisiana Choctaws who had no planter as a patron were at the mercy of the whites who could commit crimes against them without fear of the law. Even black slaves had more legal rights than did the Choctaws during this period.[61]

After the Civil War the blacks became socially more similar to the Mississippi Choctaws than they had been previously. That is, both Choctaws and blacks were nonwhite, landless, and with little real legal protection. Both turned to wage labor for some income, but because there was little money in the South during Reconstruction, their main reliance was on sharecropping (fig. 114). That is, they raised crops on land belonging to someone else for one-half or less of what they produced. Frequently, they had to rent a draft horse or mule and purchase food from the landowner. Sharecroppers were intrinsically insecure. Their agreements with landowners were

Figure 114. John Wesley and family, Choctaws near Philadelphia, Mississippi. Early 1900s. Negative from Swanton, Vol. II, 76–B. Courtesy, Smithsonian Institution, National Anthropological Archives.

mostly spoken agreements, and it was easy for unscrupulous land-owners to defraud their tenants. Moreover, the sand clay hills of central Mississippi had been farmed to the point of exhaustion through intensive and unintelligent farming practices. Many blacks moved away, after a time, and poor whites moved in to become tenants.[62]

The Choctaws made progress. Most of them became members of Baptist, Catholic, and Methodist churches. The Catholic missionary B. J. Bekkers built a school for the Choctaws. But this came to an end when the Dawes Commission determined that all of the "fullblood" Choctaws in Mississippi were entitled to receive land allotments in Oklahoma. Private claims agents began enrolling them and trans-porting them to Oklahoma, where they then defrauded them of their land claims. Almost three-fourths of the Mississippi Choctaws moved to Oklahoma, but many of them later returned home. In 1908 and again in 1916 the Bureau of Indian Affairs sent agents to investi-gate the condition of the Choctaws. They found them without schooling, in poor health, and living in desperate poverty. Soon after this the Bureau of Indian Affairs established a Choctaw agency and began purchasing land for Choctaws to farm. By the 1940s the Bureau of Indian Affairs had purchased some 16,500 acres, but many Choctaws continued sharecropping rather than move onto reserva-tion land.[63]

Like the Seminoles, the Choctaws are a mixture of the old and the new, although they perhaps resemble their white and black neighbors to a greater degree than do the Seminoles. Sharecropping by the Choctaws began to decline in the 1950s when small farmers began to be forced away from the land by mechanization. In the late 1950s and in the 1960s several small industries opened up in the Choctaw area bringing in new jobs. But initially these jobs were not open to Choctaws. Many had to go on welfare. The younger men got jobs in dairy, poultry, or lumber operations. Wages are still low, and most Choctaws suffer from seasonal unemployment. As sharecrop-ping ended, the Choctaws fell into a cheap agricultural pool where their incomes were uncertain. For some of them life became even more difficult than the poor life they had lived as sharecroppers. By the 1970s job opportunities both on the reservation and in local industries had increased, and housing, health care, and educational opportunities had greatly improved. Some younger Choctaws are acquiring better educations, and they are moving to better jobs in urban areas. But a significant number are returning to the reservation to take white collar jobs with the Bureau of Indian Affairs and the Tribal Government (fig. 115).[64]

Besides the Cherokees, Seminoles, and Choctaws, the Alabama-Coushattas are the only other Southeastern Indians who retain parts of their aboriginal culture. In the early eighteenth century the Alabamas and Coushattas lived along the banks of the upper Alabama River. Later in the century they began moving westward until they ended up on the banks of the Sabine River near the trading post at Natchitoches. Then they moved further west to the Trinity River in Texas where they hunted in the Big Thicket. In 1854 they acquired a 1,280-acre reservation in Polk County, Texas. Today the Alabama-Coushatta reservation consists of about 4,000 acres situated some 17 miles east of Livingston, Texas. In 1960 some

Figure 115. Choctaw Woodlin Lewis teaching Mississippi Choctaw school children. Courtesy, *Choctaw Community News.*

350 Alabamas and Coushattas were living on the reservation. Most of them today speak English in their homes, but a few of the old people still speak Alabama and Coushatta. Most of them earn their income from timber-cutting and tourism.[65]

The Lumbees are the largest group of Indians in the Southeast, and in fact they are one of the largest groups in the United States. Most of them live in southeastern North Carolina in and near Robeson County. According to the 1970 census, about 30,000 Lumbees live in southeastern North Carolina, but their actual number may be somewhat higher.[66] However, even though the Lumbees are numerous, the general public has heard far less about them than about the Cherokees, Seminoles, and Choctaws. The reason for this is that the Lumbees have lost both their native language and their culture. Indeed, these Indian elements have been lost for over 200 years. When first "discovered" in the eighteenth century, all the Lumbees spoke English and lived like white frontiersmen in regard to their dress, their housing, and their drinking habits. The only thing that made them different was their racial characteristics—they were brown-skinned, like Indians. At the time of the French and Indian War they were described as "a racially mixed and lawless people."

At first the Lumbees were called Scuffletonians, after Scuffletown, a neighborhood in their territory. Some Lumbees explain their origin as having been from the survivors of the Roanoke Island Colony which was founded by John White in 1587. Within a short time after the founding of the colony, John White returned to England, and when he again visited the colony in 1590 he found it abandoned. On a tree he found the word *CROATOAN*, the name of some local Algonkian Indians. Exactly what happened to the colonists is not known. Many must have been killed by Indians and disease. But some of them may have thrown in their lot with the Indians and moved into the interior. Some scholars have doubted the veracity of this explanation of Lumbee origins, but there is no denying that the Lumbees of today bear over twenty of the surnames borne by Roanoke Island colonists. While this may perhaps explain the origin of some of the Lumbees, other elements of their population must have come from piedmont and coastal plain Indians seeking refuge from marauding frontiersmen. In addition, some Cherokees and Tuscororas may have ended up among the Lumbees. And they must have also received whites and blacks who were escaping indenture, slavery, and other colonial social institutions.

In part the Lumbees were created by geography. When the whites first came to the vicinity around the Lumber and Pee Dee rivers they found good farming land, but the country was divided up into sections by "pocosins," the unusual oval-shaped swamps in the eastern Carolinas. Travel through these swamps was very difficult. There were no roads to speak of. Hence the dugout canoe was one of the main modes of transportation. This marginal area, therefore, may have been a place of refuge for several centuries. After the Tuscarora War ended in 1713, the white frontiersmen entered the North Carolina back country in significant numbers, but they largely bypassed the Scuffletown region in favor of more accessible land further west in the piedmont.[67]

The Lumbees had little competition from the white frontiersmen until the 1760s, when Highland Scots began settling in the area. Ironically, while the Lumbees were all English-speaking at this time, these Scottish frontiersmen spoke Gaelic. The Scots were later called "Buckskins," a pejorative term with somewhat the same connotation as "redneck." The pressure for land became more and more severe, until by the time of the Civil War many Lumbees had lost their land. In fact, many of the Buckskins had lost theirs too. Neither Lumbees nor Buckskins could produce cotton as cheaply as could the planters with their slaves. As elsewhere in the South, in Scuffletown the equality of the frontier gave way to class distinctions.

Along with blacks, the Lumbees were deprived of the right to vote and to bear arms. During the Civil War they were conscripted to do labor alongside black slaves. In the process, many of them became Union sympathizers, and some of them found it necessary to hide out in the swamps to escape Confederate retribution as well as conscription labor. After the Civil War ended, and after the radical Republicans failed to transform Southern social institutions, the Southern conservatives were once again on top of the social heap. The black slave was free, but his "stomach remained a slave to the habit of eating."[68] Between the hungry man and the smokehouse full of food stood the planter with his shotgun and watch dog. Poor Southerners—red, white, and black—found themselves under the

494

power of the same people who had oppressed them before the Civil War.

It was in this climate that the Lumbee Henry Berry Lowry, then in his teens, organized a band of guerillas consisting of his kinsmen, as well as other Lumbees, whites, and blacks. They stole food and distributed it to the hungry. When they could not obtain justice through the courts, they sought retribution on their own. The band lasted for seven years. The whites defined them as outlaws and offered large rewards for their capture, but because of the inaccessibility of the swamps and popular support from the people, it became virtually impossible for the soldiers even to catch sight of the band. Henry Berry Lowry evaded being shot or captured so many times that he acquired the reputation of being bulletproof. After about seven years, however, bounty hunters began to pick off members of his band one by one.

What happened to Henry Berry Lowry is not known. Some said he accidentally killed himself with his own gun; others said he escaped. It has been said that the Lowry band failed in what it set out to do—to protect the Lumbees when power reverted back into the hands of the Southern conservatives. But in fact the Lowry band was able to keep the Lumbees from being legally placed into some half-free social position. The Lumbees fought for and established their Indian identity.[69]

When confronted by late-nineteenth-century demands to identify themselves, they called themselves "Croatans," but this was soon shortened to "Cro," and this implied "Jim Crow." They next called themselves "the Cherokees of Robeson County," but the North Carolina Cherokees complained so bitterly about this that it had to be dropped. Most recently they have taken the name "Lumbee" after the name of the Lumber River (originally the Lumbee River) which flows through Robeson County.

The Lumbees live in a society in which the whites have refused to accept them as white and have in fact tried to lump them together with blacks, but this the Lumbees have resisted. Thus the Lumbees are Indians, but with debatable and uncertain connections with known Indian ancestors in the historic past. The Lumbees, however, have had strength in numbers. For example, in January 1958 the Ku Klux Klan held a rally for the purpose of intimidating the

Lumbees. But when the rally of one hundred Klansmen began, they were suddenly surrounded by five hundred armed and angry Lumbees. Afterwards they sent the Grand Dragon a telegram: "Deepest sympathy, signed General Custer."[70]

Until recently most of the Lumbees were farmers, some owning substantial farms. But as farming has become mechanized, small farming has become economically unfeasible, and they have been forced to take jobs elsewhere. During World War II they began going north in search of work. It was at this time that they began settling in East Baltimore, where today some 2,500 Lumbees live and work. Few of them are permanent émigrés. Some stay for a while and then return to North Carolina. And even those who do become permanent residents return to North Carolina for frequent visits.

The Cherokees, Seminoles, Choctaws, and Alabama-Coushattas are Indian in every sense of the word—cultural, genetic, and social. But like the Lumbees, who are Indian mostly in a social sense and to some degree in a genetic sense, a series of small groups with similar characteristics live in various parts of the Southeast. These are people like the Catawbas, who have a small state reservation near Rock Hill, South Carolina;[71] the Houmas of the bayou country in southern Louisiana;[72] the eastern Creeks in isolated parts of Alabama, Georgia, and Florida;[73] and several smaller groups that exist elsewhere. None of these groups are Indian in a cultural sense, although some of them until recently had very old people among them who remembered something of the native language. Thus these smaller Indian groups consist of people who are not Indian culturally, except in the modern Pan-Indian sense, and many of them are not Indian in physical appearance. However, these groups do claim to be Indian with respect to the larger society, and they have clear historical grounds for doing so.

In 1968 some of the Southeastern Indians accomplished what they were never able to accomplish during the colonial period—they began cooperating for the purpose of achieving social and political ends. The Cherokees, Choctaws, Miccosukees, and Seminoles, fearful that the administration of their social, educational, and economic programs would be turned over to state and local governments, allied themselves as the United Southeastern Tribes of American Indians, Incorporated (USET). In a declaration of unity,

496

they resolved to work together to obtain a greater voice in federal programs affecting them, and to work together to alleviate poverty and bring higher standards of health and education to Southeastern Indian people. Along the same lines, in August 1970 several of the small groups of Louisiana Indians—Houmas, Coushattas, Choctaws, Tunicas, and Chitimachas—met in Baton Rouge to organize and further their common interests.[74]

In addition to groups in the Southeast who have a clear claim to Indian ancestry, there are a large number of groups whose claim is only partial. These are the "mestizos," "racial isolates," or "little races" that occur in parts of the Southeast. Because these people are said to be racially mixed, Southern whites have traditionally refused to accept them as white, and the people themselves have refused to be categorized as black. Often the whites gave them pejorative names, such as Brass Ankles, Red Bones, Dominickers, and so on.[75] Some of these people, such as the Haliwas of eastern North Carolina, are in the process of establishing for themselves an Indian identity.[76] For various social and economic reasons some of these racial isolates are now beginning to lose their distinctive identity altogether.[77] In many instances, individuals have moved away from their place of origin to other parts of the country and have been accepted as white.

Beyond these named groups of people, there are the many white Southerners who have Indians in their ancestry. Some of them are explicit about their Indian ancestry, while others speak of a vague family tradition of an Indian ancestor; some carefully conceal it, and still others may be unaware of it altogether. It is difficult to estimate the number of Southern whites and blacks with Indian ancestry, but it is probably large. When the eastern Creeks were pressing their land claims case in the 1960s, at which time people with legitimate Creek ancestry could receive a substantial sum of money, many thousands of people began arriving from all parts of the Southeast to sign up for their share. Many people who had never before acknowledged Indians in their ancestry now did so, and in some cases they attempted to do so secretly. One eastern Creek remarked of this situation: "There used to be three races of people around here: white, Indian, and colored. Now there's only two: Indian and colored."[78]

497

The influence of the Southeastern Indians on the South is greater than most people realize. It goes far beyond the genetic influence on Southern people. The Indians have influenced the South most obviously in the realm of agriculture. Tobacco, the first cash crop grown in the South, was adopted from the Indians, although the strains of tobacco now cultivated are derived from species obtained elsewhere in the New World. More notable, however, is the fact that the basic staples grown in Southern gardens today are several varieties of corn, beans, squash, and pumpkins. Moreover, not only do Southerners cultivate these Indian vegetables in their gardens, many of them also use Indian techniques of cultivation. Namely, they regularly intercrop corn and beans, allowing the beans to twine up the cornstalks, and sometimes they plant squash and pumpkins in the same area as the corn. And as they hoe their corn they often "hill" it just as the Indians did.

To a far greater degree than anyone realizes, several of the most important food dishes of the Southeastern Indians live on today in the "soul food" eaten by both black and white Southerners. Hominy, for example, is still eaten, although not as widely nor as frequently as in the past. Sofkee lives on as grits, though Southerners season their grits with a dab of butter or pork grease rather than bear's oil. All three of the Southeastern Indians' methods of cooking cornbread are used by Southern cooks. Indian fritters, fried now in pork grease instead of bear's oil, are variously known as "hoe cake," "hot-water corn bread," or "Johnny cake." This type of corn bread was and perhaps still is one of the primary breads eaten by poor people in the South. Indian baked bread is today's "corn pone" or simply "corn bread." Indian boiled cornbread is present in Southern cuisine as "corn meal dumplings," made of lumps of corn dough cooked with meat and vegetables, and as "hush puppies," boiled in oil instead of water. Contemporary Southerners do not eat boiled corn bread wrapped in husks, but during the Civil War Confederate soldiers ate quite a lot of it. They called this bread "Confederate bullets," perhaps because the bread became hard when it dried. Because these "Confederate bullets" preserved well, they were a reasonably nutritious food when there was no other to be had. Moreover, frontiersmen in the South ate a bread called "ash cake" which they learned to make from the Indians. The frontiersmen made them by forming cornmeal dough into flat cakes which they wrapped in corn husks. They put these in the fireplace and covered them with a cloth and then with ashes and hot coals to cook them.[79] Corn bread has traditionally been *the* bread of the South, and it remains important to this day.[80]

Southerners cook their beans and field peas by boiling them, as did the Indians, but seasoning them with pork fat instead of bear fat. They make succotash by boiling beans and corn together. Like the Indians they cure their meat and smoke it over hickory coals, and they have a particular regard for meat barbecued on a spit or a framework above a bed of wood coals. Another striking survival of Indian cookery in the modern South is "corn on the cob" or "roastin' ears"—green ears of corn roasted over wood coals or boiled in water; it is a great favorite for picnics and outdoor feasts.

In the not-too-distant past most of the vegetables eaten by Southerners in winter were preserved by drying, the same technique which the Indians used. Green corn was cut off the cob and dried; beans were shelled and dried, and they were also dried in the pod (in this form they were called "leather-britches"); pumpkins were sliced into circular pieces and then dried in the sun or over hickory coals just as the Indians did; and they dried fruit the same way, although they sometimes used sulphur fumes as part of the drying process, and this was a European innovation.[81]

The folk medicine used by Southerners was a mixture of Indian herbalism along with elements of European and American culture. They got from the Indians the use of such herbs as ginseng, wild cherry bark, persimmon bark, poplar bark, lady's-slipper, poke leaves, poke root, pokeberries, sassafras, yellow root, chestnut leaves, boneset, pine needles, ferns, horsemint, peppermint, snakeroot, and pennyroyal. Other elements are clearly European and American, such as using a magnet to "draw out" arthritis, a poultice of turpentine and brown sugar to stop bleeding, raw honey and vinegar for a cough, a Bible under the pillow for nightmares, and "moonshine" whiskey for practically everything.[82]

The Southeastern Indians made some rather surprising contributions to Southern folklore. In 1881 William O. Tuggle collected the following story from Cusseta-fixico, a Creek Indian living in the Indian Territory.

499

A man missed peas from his garden & after various efforts to catch the thief, he made a tar-person & put it in the garden near the peas.

A rabbit had been coming every night for the peas & the tar-person was quickly discovered by him. Stopping near he said, "Who's that, What's your name?" and receiving no reply he hopped close to the figure and said "If you don't speak I'll hit you." He struck the tar-person and his foot stuck. Again he asked, "Why don't you speak: Turn my foot loose or I'll hit you harder." The second foot stuck as he hit him again. "I've got another foot, stronger than these, & I'll hit you still harder," & the third time he hit the tar-person. "I've got one more foot, & I will have to kill you, if you don't turn my feet loose." The last foot kicked & stuck fast. The rabbit then struck with his head & it stuck.

The next morning the man came into his garden & when the rabbit saw him, he called out, "Oh, I have caught the thief who's been taking your peas. Here he is."

"Yes, I see the thief," replied the man, "and I intend to kill him." Seizing the rabbit he pulled him loose from the tar-person and carried him to a stake near the pig pen. There he securely fastened the rabbit to the stake saying, "I will go to the house & get some boiling water to scald you."

As soon as the man left, a wolf came along and seeing the rabbit tied asked what it meant.

"Oh, this man wanted me to eat up all these pigs in the pen and because I couldn't do it he tied me here."

"I can eat them for him; let me take your place." "All right," responded the rabbit, so the wolf untied the rabbit & took his place at the stake & was in turn tied by the rabbit, who ran away & crawled in a hollow tree. When the man returned & saw the wolf, "So," said he, "You are at your tricks & have changed yourself to look like a wolf. Well, I will scald you anyway." He poured the boiling water on the wolf who howled in pain & finally broke the string and ran off. He sat at the foot of the very tree in which the rabbit was concealed & as he licked his scalded hide, the rabbit reached down & stuck a splinter in him.

Jumping up, the wolf exclaimed, "I wish the ants would stop biting me and adding to my afflictions."[83]

This is obviously a precursor of the Uncle Remus "Wonderful Tar Baby Story." Joel Chandler Harris was a friend of the Tuggle family, and he read William O. Tuggle's collection of Indian myths in manuscript. Several other stories published by Harris follow Tuggle's stories almost to the letter.[84]

Other Southern folk beliefs are European in origin but perhaps have been reinforced by Southeastern Indian beliefs, as for example, some Southern beliefs about snakes. Many Southerners avoid places that look "snakey," and for good reason, for rattlesnakes reach formidable size in the South. The annals of Southern folklore are full of stories about fabulous snakes, as for example a story about a snake that bit a dog two hours after the snake's head had been cut off; or of how deer kill snakes by whirling around and pounding them to pieces; of black snakes fighting rattlesnakes in fierce battles; and of "coachwhip" snakes that wrap themselves around you and whip you with their tails. A Southern story with a definite Indian flavor tells of a man who teased a rattlesnake until it got so angry it bit itself, and then he saw it crawl away to eat button snakeroot as an antidote for its own poison.

It has often been observed that something of the frontier still lingers on in the culture of the South. Partly this came about because of the isolation of the South during the Civil War, and partly it is because of the bitter poverty in the South for many decades afterwards. Southerners continued their frontier ways after such ways were abandoned elsewhere because they could not afford any other. Is it stretching things too far to see a hint of the Southeastern Indian in some of this frontier heritage? Is there something of it in the Southerner's love of hunting and fishing?[85] And is there something of it in the Southerner's admiration of wild and reckless bravery?

NOTES

CHAPTER 1. INTRODUCTION

1. Charles Hudson, "Introduction," in *Red, White, and Black*, ed. Charles Hudson, Southern Anthropological Society Proceedings no. 5 (Athens; Ga.: Univ. of Georgia Press, 1971), 1–2.

2. Vine Deloria, Jr., *Custer Died for Your Sins: An Indian Manifesto* (New York: Avon, 1970), 10–12.

3. J. H. Elliott, *The Old World and the New, 1492–1650* (Cambridge: At the University Press, 1970), 1–53.

4. Edward G. Bourne, ed., *Narratives of the Career of Hernando de Soto* (New York: A. S. Barnes, 1904), vol. I, p. 66.

5. The coastal Indians did salvage and use the remains of wrecked ships at an early date. For example, in 1528 members of the Pánfilo de Narváez expedition found Indians in the vicinity of Tampa Bay using pieces of canvas, iron objects, and cargo boxes from a wrecked ship. They were using the cargo boxes as coffins. Alvar Nuñez Cabeza de Vaca, *The Journey of Alvar Nuñez Cabeza de Vaca*, ed. Ad. F. Bandelier (New York: Allerton, 1904), 12–13.

6. John R. Swanton, *The Indians of the Southeastern United States*, Bureau of American Ethnology Bulletin, no. 137 (Washington, D. C., 1946), 11–12. Swanton's delineation of the Southeast differs slightly from my own.

7. Henry F. Dobyns, "An Appraisal of Techniques with a New Hemisphere Estimate," *Current Anthropology* 7(1966):395–416.

8. James Mooney, "Myths of the Cherokee," *Nineteenth Annual Report of the Bureau of American Ethnology* (Washington, D. C., 1900), 16–17.

9. Charles Hudson, *The Catawba Nation* (Athens, Ga.: Univ. of Georgia Press, 1970).

10. Arrell M. Gibson, *The Chickasaws* (Norman, Okla.: Univ. of Oklahoma Press, 1971).

11. John R. Swanton, *Source Material on the History and Ethnology of the Caddo Indians*, Bureau of American Ethnology Bulletin no. 132

(Washington, D. C., 1942).

12. John R. Swanton, *Source Material for the Social and Ceremonial Life of the Choctaw Indians*, Bureau of American Ethnology Bulletin no. 103 (Washington, D. C., 1931); John H. Peterson, Jr., "The Mississippi Band of Choctaw Indians: Their Recent History and Current Social Relations." Ph.D. dissertation, Univ. of Georgia, 1970.

13. John R. Swanton, *Early History of the Creek Indians and Their Neighbors*, Bureau of American Ethnology Bulletin no. 73 (Washington, D. C., 1922). At different times the Yuchis lived in several locations in the Southeast. Their ethnological position has been debated at length. They consider themselves to be the "original inhabitants" of the Southeast. See W. O. Tuggle, *Shem, Ham & Japheth: The Papers of W. O. Tuggle*, ed. Eugene Current-Garcia with Dorothy B. Hatfield (Athens, Ga.: Univ. of Georgia Press, 1973), 52.

14. William C. Sturtevant, "Creek into Seminole," in *North American Indians in Historical Perspective*, ed. Eleanor B. Leacock and Nancy O. Lurie (New York: Random House, 1971), 92–128.

15. John M. Goggin and William C. Sturtevant, "The Calusa: A Stratified Nonagricultural Society (with Notes on Sibling Marriage)," in *Explorations in Cultural Anthropology*, ed. Ward H. Goodenough (New York: McGraw-Hill, 1964), 179–219.

16. Joffre L. Coe, "The Cultural Sequence of the Carolina Piedmont," in *Archaeology of Eastern United States*, ed. James B. Griffin (Chicago: Univ. of Chicago Press, 1952), 306–8; James Mooney, *The Siouan Tribes of the East*, Bureau of American Ethnology Bulletin no. 22 (Washington, D. C., 1894); Hudson, *Catawba Nation*, 5–28.

17. T. J. C. Brasser, "The Coastal Algonkians: People of the First Frontiers," in *North American Indians in Historical Perspective*, eds. Eleanor B. Leacock and Nancy O. Lurie (New York: Random House, 1971), 64–91.

18. Preston Holder, *The Hoe and the Horse on the Plains: A Study of Cultural Development Among North American Indians* (Lincoln, Neb.: Univ. of Nebraska Press, 1970).

19. Swanton, *Early History of the Creek Indians*, 317–20.

20. Bourne, *Hernando de Soto*, vol. I, pp. 137–40.

21. G. S. Garcilaso de la Vega, *The Florida of the Inca*, trans. and ed. J. G. Varner and J. J. Varner (Austin, Tex.: Univ. of Texas Press, 1951), 514–20; Bourne, *Hernando de Soto*, vol. I, pp. 176–80.

22. John R. Swanton, "The First Description of an Indian Tribe in the Territory of the Present United States," in *Studies for William A. Read*, ed. Nathaniel M. Caffee and Thomas A. Kirby (Baton Rouge, La.: Louisiana State Univ. Press, 1940), 326–38.

23. Lawrence C. Wroth, *The Voyages of Giovanni da Verrazzano, 1524–1528* (New Haven and London: Yale Univ. Press, 1970).

24. James B. Griffin, "Eastern North American Archaeology: A Summary," *Science* 156(1967):175.

25. David J. Hally, "The Archaeology of European-Indian Contact in the Southeast," in *Red, White, and Black*, ed. Charles Hudson, Southern Anthropological Society Proceedings no. 5 (Athens, Ga.: Univ. of Georgia Press, 1971), 55–66.

26. James Mooney and Frans M. Olbrechts, *The Swimmer Manuscript: Cherokee Sacred Formulas and Medicinal Prescriptions*, Bureau of American Ethnology Bulletin no. 99 (Washington, D. C., 1932).

27. James Mooney, "The Sacred Formulas of the Cherokees," *Seventh Annual Report of the Bureau of American Ethnology* (Washington, D. C., 1886), 301–97.

28. Mooney, "Myths of the Cherokee," 237.

29. Map no. 2 is adapted from Nevin M. Fenneman's "Physiographic Divisions of the United States," *Annals of the Association of American Geographers*, 3d ed. (revised and enlarged), vol. 18 (1928): 261–353; and from Edwin H. Hammond's map of physical subdivisions in *The National Atlas of the United States*, ed. Arch C. Gerlach, United States Department of the Interior (Washington, D. C., 1970), 61.

30. Gerlach, *National Atlas*, 121.

31. Garcilaso, *Florida*, 553–62.

32. Cabeza de Vaca, *Journey*, 92–93.

33. Gerlach, *National Atlas*, 63, 91, 111.

34. Modern geographers no longer give the fall line the physiographic significance they once did. They now argue that although the fall line represents a sharp geological division, it is not nearly so fundamental with respect to surface configurations (Gerlach, *National Atlas*, 61). That is, the surface of the lower piedmont differs only in degree from the surface of the upper coastal plain. But while this may very well be true, the fact remains that the fall line was important to the Indians in the late prehistoric era. It must have been attractive to them for several reasons, some of which are not entirely clear to us today.

35. Swanton, "First Description," 327–28.

36. John Lawson, *A New Voyage to Carolina*, ed. Hugh Talmage Lefler (Chapel Hill, N. C.: Univ. of North Carolina Press, 1967), 50–51.

37. Ibid., 53, 120–21; Tom McHugh, *The Time of the Buffalo* (New York: Knopf, 1972), 24–26.

38. Gerlach, *National Atlas*, 102–3.

39. Ibid., 96–97.

40. Ibid., 110–11.

41. William Bartram, *The Travels of William Bartram*, ed. Francis Harper (New Haven: Yale Univ. Press, 1958), 217.

42. Mary R. Haas, "Southeastern Indian Linguistics," in *Red, White, and Black*, ed. Charles Hudson, Southern Anthropological Society Proceedings no. 5 (Athens, Ga.: Univ. of Georgia Press, 1971), 44–54; Mary R. Haas, "The Southeast," in *Current Trends in Linguistics*, vol. 10, pt. 2, ed. Thomas A. Sebeok (The Hague: Mouton, 1973), 1210–49; James M. Crawford, "Southeastern Indian Languages," in *Studies in Southeastern Indian Languages*, ed. James M. Crawford (Athens, Ga.: Univ. of Georgia Press, 1975), 1–120.

43. Haas, "Southeastern Indian Linguistics," 49; Haas, "The Southeast," 1227.

44. Alexander Lesser and Gene Weltfish, "The Composition of the Caddoan Linguistic Stock," *Smithsonian Miscellaneous Collections*, vol. 87, no. 6 (1932): 1–15; Wallace L. Chafe, "Siouan, Iroquoian, and Caddoan," in *Current Trends in Linguistics*, vol. 10, pt. 2, ed. Thomas A. Sebeok (The Hague: Mouton, 1973), 1164–68.

45. James M. Crawford, "The Mobilian Trade Jargon," paper read at the 1972 meeting of the Southern Anthropological Society, at Columbia, Missouri.

46. Willard Walker, "Notes on Native Writing Systems and the Design of Native Literacy Programs," *Anthropological Linguistics* 11 (1969):148–66.

47. T. D. Stewart, "A Physical Anthropologist's View of the Peopling of the New World," *Southwestern Journal of Anthropology* 16(1960):259–73; Jesse D. Jennings, *Prehistory of North America* (New York: McGraw-Hill, 1968), 50–53.

48. Wroth, *Verrazzano*, 134.

49. Georg K. Neumann, "Archaeology and Race in the American Indian," in *Archaeology of Eastern United States*, ed. James B. Griffin (Chicago: Univ. of Chicago Press, 1952), 13–34. The older long-headed type is sometimes called "Paleoamerindian," and the more recent round-headed type is called "Mesoamerindian."

50. Charles E. Snow, "Indian Skeletons from the Museum Burials at Moundville," *Alabama Museum of Natural History, Museum Paper*, no. 15, pt. 1 (University, Ala., 1941), 7–52.

51. Tuggle, *Shem, Ham & Japheth*, 57; James Mooney, "The Cherokee Ball Play," *American Anthropologist* 3(1890):105–32.

52. The use of the cradle board does not by itself cause cranial deformation. Archaic people (see chap. 2) were evidently using cradle boards, but with little or no cranial deformation. But it shows up strongly in Adena and Hopewell populations and continues in Mississippian populations.

53. Lawson, *Voyage to Carolina*, 39–40.

54. Joseph K. Long, "A Test of Multiple-Discriminant Analysis as a Means of Determining Evolutionary Changes and Intergroup Relationships in Physical Anthropology," *American Anthropologist* 68(1966): 444–64.

55. William S. Pollitzer, "Physical Anthropology of Indians of the Old South," in *Red, White, and Black*, ed. Charles Hudson, Southern Anthropological Society Proceedings no. 5 (Athens, Ga.: Univ. of Georgia Press, 1971), 31–43.

CHAPTER 2. PREHISTORY AND EARLY HISTORY

1. Robert Wauchope, *Lost Tribes and Sunken Continents: Myth and Methods in the Study of the American Indians* (Chicago: Univ. of Chicago Press, 1962), 3.

2. Robert Silverberg, *Mound Builders of Ancient America: The Archaeology of a Myth* (Greenwich, Conn.: New York Graphic Society, 1968).

3. Millard F. Compton, "History of the Moundbuilders," published by Marshall County Council, Parent-Teacher Assoc., Moundsville, W. Va., 1938.

4. John Lear, "Ancient Landings in America," *Saturday Review* 18 July 1970, pp. 18–19, 34; Cyrus H. Gordon, *Before Columbus: Links Between the Old World and Ancient America* (New York: Crown Publishers, 1971), 89–105. For a scholarly treatment of the important problem of pre-Columbian contact between the Old World and the New, see Carroll L. Riley et al., eds., *Man Across the Sea: Problems of Pre-Columbian Contacts* (Austin, Tex.: Univ. of Texas Press, 1971).

5. Gordon Willey, *An Introduction to American Archaeology* (Englewood Cliffs, N. J.: Prentice-Hall, 1966), vol. I, 4–8.

6. Hansjürgen Müller-Beck, "Paleohunters in America: Origins and Diffusion," *Science* 156(1966):1191–1210; C. Vance Haynes, Jr., "The Earliest Americans," *Science* 166(1969):709–15.

7. Matthew Lively, "The Lively Complex: Announcing a Pebble Tool Industry in Alabama," *Journal of Alabama Archaeology* 11(1965):103–22.

8. Richard S. MacNeish, "Early Man in the Andes," *Scientific American* 224(1971):36–46.

9. C. Vance Haynes, Jr., "The Calico Site: Artifacts or Geofacts?" *Science* 181(1973):305–10.

10. Müller-Beck, "Paleohunters," 1207.

11. C. Vance Haynes, Jr., "Elephant Hunting in North America," *Scientific American* 214(1966):104–12; Larry Lahren and Robson Bon-

nichsen, "Bone Foreshafts From a Clovis Burial in Southwestern Montana," *Science* 186(1974):147–50.

12. Joe Ben Wheat, "A Paleo-Indian Bison Kill," *Scientific American* 216(1967):44–52.

13. Ibid.

14. Haynes, "Elephant Hunting"; Paul S. Martin, "The Discovery of America," *Science* 179(1973):969–74.

15. Griffin, "Eastern North American Archaeology," 156–57.

16. Wheat, "Bison Kill"; Joe Ben Wheat, "Lifeways of Early Man in North America," *Arctic Anthropology* 8(1971):22–31.

17. Willey, *American Archaeology*, 60.

18. Jennings, *Prehistory*, 110.

19. Griffin, "Eastern North American Archaeology," 178.

20. Ibid.

21. Willey, *American Archaeology*, 61.

22. Ibid., 64.

23. Thomas M. N. Lewis and Madeline Kneberg Lewis, *Eva: An Archaic Site* (Knoxville: Univ. of Tennessee Press, 1961).

24. Jennings, *Prehistory*, 117–18.

25. Fiber-tempered pottery also occurs from 3000 to 2500 B.C. on the coast of Colombia in South America. Others have argued that it was introduced into North America from Asia or Scandinavia. Cf. Jennings, *Prehistory*, 185, 189–90.

26. Joffre L. Coe, *The Formative Cultures of the Carolina Piedmont*, Transactions of the American Philosophical Society, vol. 54, pt. 5 (1964); Willey, *American Archaeology*, 265–66.

27. Richard A. Yarnell, *Aboriginal Relationships Between Culture and Plant Life in the Upper Great Lakes Region*, Univ. of Michigan Anthropological Papers no. 23 (Ann Arbor: Univ. of Michigan Press, 1964), 85–86.

28. Willey, *American Archaeology*, 267.

29. Joseph R. Caldwell, "Eastern North America," in *Courses Toward Urban Life*, eds. R. J. Braidwood and Gordon R. Willey (Chicago: Aldine Publishing Co., 1962).

30. Charles H. Faulkner, *The Old Stone Fort: Exploring an Archaeological Mystery* (Knoxville: Univ. of Tennessee Press, 1968).

31. Stuart Struever, "Middle Woodland Culture History in the Great Lakes Riverine Area," *American Antiquity*, vol. 31, no. 2 (1965):211–23; Stuart Struever and Kent D. Vickery, "The Beginnings of Cultivation in the Midwest-Riverine Area of the United States," *American Anthropologist* 75(1973):1197–1220; Patty Jo Watson, ed., *Archaeology of the Mammoth Cave Area* (New York: Academic Press, 1974); Richard A. Yarnell,

"Early Plant Husbandry in Eastern North America." Paper read at the 1975 meeting of the Southern Anthropological Society, at Clearwater Beach, Florida.

32. Jennings, *Prehistory*, 192–93; Yarnell, *Plant Life*, 102–104, 118.

33. Caldwell, "Eastern North America."

34. Yarnell, *Plant Life*, 44.

35. Griffin, "Eastern North American Archaeology," 180.

36. Jennings, *Prehistory*, 206.

37. Ibid., 213–14; Clarence H. Webb, "The Extent and Content of Poverty Point Culture," *American Antiquity* 33(1968):297–321.

38. Jennings, *Prehistory*, 191, 201.

39. Martha A. Potter, *Ohio's Prehistoric People* (Columbus: Ohio Historical Society, 1968).

40. Ibid.

41. Jennings, *Prehistory*, 200–1.

42. William H. Sears, *Excavations at Kolomoki: Final Report*, Univ. of Georgia Series in Anthropology no. 5 (Athens, Ga.: Univ. of Georgia Press, 1956).

43. Goggin and Sturtevant, "Calusa"; William H. Sears, "Food Production and Village Life in Prehistoric Southeastern United States," *Archaeology* 24(1971):322–29.

44. In the northeastern United States some elements of Hopewell culture can be seen in such archaeological manifestations as Point Peninsula, Owasco, and even historic Iroquois. See Jennings, *Prehistory*, 209–11.

45. Willey, *American Archaeology*, 293.

46. Caldwell, "Eastern North America."

47. Charles H. Nash and Rodney Gates, Jr., "Chucalissa Indian Town," *Tennessee Historical Quarterly* 21(1962):103–21.

48. Garcilaso, *Florida*, 170–71.

49. Swanton, "First Description," 330.

50. Garcilaso, *Florida*, 436. Archaeologists have described several sites similar to the one described here. Cf. Hester A. Davis, "An Introduction to Parkin Prehistory," *The Arkansas Archaeologist* 7(1966).

51. Garcilaso, *Florida*, 416.

52. Yarnell, *Plant Life*, 104–20; Willey, *American Archaeology*, 293; James B. Griffin, "Mesoamerica and the Eastern United States in Prehistoric Times," in *Archaeological Frontiers and External Connections*, eds. G. Ekholm and G. R. Willey, Handbook of Middle American Indians, vol. IV (Austin, Tex.: Univ. of Texas Press, 1966), 111–31.

53. Coe, "Cultural Sequence of the Carolina Piedmont," 301–11.

54. William H. Sears, "The Southeastern United States," in *Prehistoric*

Man in the New World, eds. Jesse D. Jennings and Edward Norbeck (Chicago: Univ. of Chicago Press, 1964), 284.

55. Melvin L. Fowler, "Cahokia: Ancient Capital of the Midwest," *Addison-Wesley Module in Anthropology*, no. 48(1974); Glenn A. Black, *Angel Site: An Archaeological, Historical, and Ethnological Study*. 2 vols. (Indianapolis: Indiana Historical Society, 1967).

56. Sears, "Southeastern United States," 281.

57. Willey, *American Archaeology*, 302–3.

58. Christopher S. Peebles, "Moundville and Surrounding Sites: Some Structural Considerations of Mortuary Practices, II," in *Approaches to the Social Dimensions of Mortuary Practices*, ed. James A. Brown, *American Antiquity*, vol. 36, no. 3, pt. 2 (1971):68–91.

59. Antonio S. Waring and Preston Holder, "A Prehistoric Ceremonial Complex in the Southeastern United States," *American Anthropologist* 47(1945):1–34. According to James Griffin, the Southeastern Ceremonial Complex has its closest affinities to the Mixteca-Puebla art style in the Postclassic period in Mexico ("Mesoamerica," 127–30). Some evidence suggests a Mesoamerican influence in the Southeast much earlier, perhaps as early as 500 B.C. to A.D. 1. Cf. David S. Phelps, "Mesoamerican Glyph Motifs on Southeastern Pottery," *Verhandlungen des XXXVIII Internationalen Amerikanisten Kongressen*, vol. 2 (Stuttgart-Munich, 1968), 89–99. And it has even been argued that Mississippian temple mounds developed out of precedents in the Woodland. Cf. Nelson A. Reed, "Monks and Other Mississippian Mounds," in *Exploration into Cahokia Archaeology*, ed. Melvin L. Fowler, Illinois Archaeological Survey Bulletin no. 7 (Urbana, Ill.: Univ. of Illinois Press, 1969), 31–42.

60. Phelps, "Mesoamerican Glyph Motifs."

61. Griffin, "Eastern North American Archaeology," 190.

62. Cabeza de Vaca, *Journey*, 128–75.

63. Robert L. Carneiro, "A Theory of the Origin of the State," *Science* 169(1970):733–38.

64. Willey, *American Archaeology*, 61.

65. Sears, "The Southeastern United States," 284.

66. Elliott, *The Old World and the New*, 12–14.

67. Stefan Lorant, ed., *The New World: The First Pictures of America* (New York: Duell, Sloan, and Pearce, 1965).

68. Elliott, *The Old World and the New*, 41–43.

69. Ibid., 44–53.

70. Wroth, *Verrazzano*, 133–43.

71. Garcilaso, *Florida*, 126.

72. Lawson, *Voyage to Carolina*, 18–19.

73. John Wesley, *The Journal of the Rev. John Wesley* (New York: E. P.

Dutton, 1906), vol. I, p. 34.

74. David B. Quinn, ed., *North American Discovery, Circa 1000–1612* (Columbia, S. C.: Univ. of South Carolina Press, 1971), 1–2.

75. Swanton, *Indians of the Southeast*, 34–35.

76. Quinn, *Discovery*, 79–81.

77. Swanton, "First Description," 326–38.

78. Wroth, *Verrazzano*, 141.

79. Quinn, *Discovery*, pp. xxii–xxiii; Alfred W. Crosby, Jr., *The Columbian Exchange: Biological and Cultural Consequences of 1492* (Westport, Conn.: Greenwood Press, 1972), 35–63.

80. Cabeza de Vaca, *Journey*, 25.

81. Ibid., 33.

82. Ibid., 68–70.

83. Garcilaso, *Florida*, 42.

84. Bourne, *Hernando de Soto*, vol. II, p. 60.

85. Garcilaso, *Florida*, 259.

86. Ibid., 185.

87. Bourne, *Hernando de Soto*, vol. II, pp. 87–88.

88. Ibid., 89.

89. Garcilaso, *Florida*, 299.

90. Bourne, *Hernando de Soto*, vol. II, pp. 99–100.

91. Ibid., 101.

92. Waring and Holder, "Prehistoric Ceremonial Complex," 1–34, fig. II-t, u, v; Emma Lila Fundaburk and Mary D. F. Foreman, *Sun Circles and Human Hands* (Luverne, Ala., 1957), plate 47.

93. Waring and Holder, "Prehistoric Ceremonial Complex," fig. III-a; Fundaburk and Foreman, *Sun Circles*, plate 48.

94. One of these is possibly depicted in Waring and Holder, "Prehistoric Ceremonial Complex," fig. II-w. Clubs like these are used today by Japanese riot police.

95. Bourne, *Hernando de Soto*, vol. II, p. 101.

96. Garcilaso, *Florida*, 314–26.

97. Bourne, *Hernando de Soto*, vol. I, pp. 70–73.

98. Ibid., vol. II, p. 108.

99. Ibid., 120–21.

100. Ibid., 123.

101. Garcilaso, *Florida*, 385–86.

102. Bourne, *Hernando de Soto*, vol. II, p. 140.

103. John R. Swanton, "Historic Use of the Spear-Thrower in Southeastern North America," *American Antiquity* 4(1938):356–58.

104. Quinn, *Discovery*, 91–92.

105. Mary Ross, "With Pardo and Boyano on the Fringes of the Georgia

Land," *The Georgia Historical Quarterly* 14(1930):267–85.

106. Swanton, *Indians of the Southeast*, 75–77.

107. William P. Cumming, *The Southeast in Early Maps* (Chapel Hill, N. C.: Univ. of North Carolina Press, 1962).

CHAPTER 3. THE BELIEF SYSTEM

1. Mary Douglas, *Purity and Danger* (London: Routledge and Kegan Paul, 1966).

2. Mooney, "Myths of the Cherokee," 234–35; John Swanton, *Myths and Tales of the Southeastern Indians*, Bureau of American Ethnology Bulletin no. 88 (Washington, D. C., 1929), *passim*.

3. Some evidence, however, indicates that the Creeks thought that the island was square in shape.

4. James H. Howard, *The Southeastern Ceremonial Complex and Its Interpretation*, Missouri Archaeological Society Memoir no. 6 (Columbia, Mo., 1968), 9, 10, 20. But note the different value assigned to the circle and cross in David Phelps's "Mesoamerican Glyph Motifs," 89–99.

5. John R. Swanton, "Religious Beliefs and Medical Practices of the Creek Indians," *Forty-second Annual Report of the Bureau of American Ethnology* (Washington, D. C., 1928), 477–78.

6. Mooney and Olbrechts, *Swimmer Manuscript*, 30.

7. Waring and Holder, "Prehistoric Ceremonial Complex," 1–34.

8. Swanton, "Religious Beliefs of the Creeks," 481.

9. John R. Swanton, "Sun Worship in the Southeast," *American Anthropologist* 30(1928):206–13.

10. John Witthoft, "Some Eastern Cherokee Bird Stories," *Journal of the Washington Academy of Science* 35(1946):177–80.

11. Mooney and Olbrechts, *Swimmer Manuscript*, 19–22.

12. Howard, *Southeastern Ceremonial Complex*, 19–26. The Cherokees originally made their sacred fires with seven logs; the Natchez made theirs with three.

13. Mooney, "Myths of the Cherokee," 256–57.

14. James Adair, *The History of the American Indians* (London, 1776), 65n.

15. Mooney and Olbrechts, *Swimmer Manuscript*, 23–24. Restrictions on the use of the true name of spiritual beings occur in many cultures. Among the ancient Hebrews, for example, only priests could utter "Yahweh," the name of God, whereas ordinary people avoided uttering it for fear of taking it in vain and in so doing incurring God's anger.

16. In our own world view the closest analogue we have to this polarity is the contrast between "left" and "right" in a political and philosophical

sense. The conservative right is of the Upper World, and the radical left is of the Under World. Another analogue is the Freudian super ego (Upper World) and id (Under World).

17. James Mooney, "The Cherokee River Cult," *The Journal of American Folklore* 13(1900):1.

18. Howard, *Southeastern Ceremonial Complex*, 37–39.

19. Swanton, "Religious Beliefs of the Creeks," 498–501.

20. James Howard has pointed out that to a distant observer the peregrine falcon appears to kill in this fashion. *Southeastern Ceremonial Complex*, 44.

21. Ibid.

22. John Witthoft has this as the red-headed woodpecker (*Melanerpes erythrocephalus*), but the cry of this bird in no way resembles *dalala*, whereas the cry of the red-bellied woodpecker, a rather startling, hoarse trill, does resemble it rather closely. Witthoft, "Birdlore of the Eastern Cherokee," *Journal of the Washington Academy of Science* 35(1946): 372–84.

23. Howard, *Southeastern Ceremonial Complex*, 45–49.

24. Ibid., 48–49.

25. Mooney and Olbrechts, *Swimmer Manuscript*, 21–26.

26. John R. Swanton, "Social Organization and Social Usages of the Indians of the Creek Confederacy," *Forty-second Annual Report of the Bureau of American Ethnology* (Washington, D. C., 1928), 35. In our own culture we attach relatively little symbolic meaning to directions. However, in Southern cemeteries corpses are sometimes interred with their heads pointed toward the west, and statues of Confederate soldiers are almost always facing defiantly northward. For Southern whites as well as for Southern Indians, trouble came from the north.

27. Mooney, "Myths of the Cherokee," 239–40.

28. It should be noted that seven was the total number of Cherokee directions: the four cardinal directions plus up, down, and right here in the center. Four and seven were evidently not the only ritual numbers in the Southeast. The number three appears to have been important among the Natchez and among the Chickasaws. The number six was a ritual number among the Timucuans. Jerald Milanich and William C. Sturtevant, eds., *Francisco Pareja's 1613 Confessionario: A Documentary Source of Timucuan Ethnography* (Tallahassee, Fla.: Division of Archives, History, and Records Management, Fla. Dept. of State, 1972), 44.

29. Mooney, "Myths of the Cherokee," 240–42.

30. This place actually exists. It is on the Little Tennessee River between the historic Cherokee towns of Chota and Citico, about half a mile from the mouth of Citico Creek. If the Tennessee Valley Authority has its

way with the Tellico Dam project, this site, along with the sites of at least twelve 18th-century Cherokee towns, will be destroyed; and both we and the Cherokees will be robbed of a part of our historical heritage.

31. Mooney, "Myths of the Cherokee," 315–16.

32. Douglas, *Purity and Danger*.

33. The bear is a special animal in many cultures. It is the object of particular ceremonial importance among indigenous peoples in the circumboreal regions of both the Old and New Worlds. Europeans, particularly the Russians, are fond of circus bears who do such manlike feats as riding bicycles and motorcycles. Cf. A. I. Hallowell, "Bear Ceremonialism in the Northern Hemisphere," *American Anthropologist* 28(1926):1–175.

To the layman the bones of bear forepaws closely resemble human handbones. The resemblance is so close the FBI saw fit to issue a bulletin detailing the differences. T. D. Stewart, "Bear Paw Remains Closely Resemble Human Bones," *FBI Law Enforcement Bulletin*, vol. 30, (1959), no. 7.

34. Jack F. Kilpatrick, and Anna G. Kilpatrick, *Run Toward the Nightland: Magic of the Oklahoma Cherokees* (Dallas: Southern Methodist Univ. Press, 1967), 83–87.

35. William Service, *Owl* (New York: Knopf, 1969).

36. Howard, *Southeastern Ceremonial Complex*, 53–54.

37. The similarity between Uktena and Quetzalcoatl of the Valley of Mexico is obvious. Uktena is also similar in form and to some degree in meaning to the dragon in Asian mythology. While the similarity between Uktena and Quetzalcoatl might be explained as an actual historical connection, there is no evidence of such a connection in late prehistoric times between Uktena and the Asian dragon. It is of course possible that there is a remote historical connection. That is, it is possible that both Uktena and the Asian dragon are historical outgrowths of a world view held by Asian people before the migration of some of them to the New World. This is not as far-fetched as it might sound. Because of the abstract, formal nature of the categories of thought which give meaning to the Uktena, they would have been relatively impervious to experience, and hence could endure with little change.

38. Just as Uktenas occurred on the margins of the known world of the Cherokees, Renaissance cartographers used to decorate the margins of their maps with anomalous monsters.

39. Rattlesnakes do have bad breath, a fact reflected in the belief held by some Appalachian whites that to smell a rattlesnake makes some people so sick they can hardly walk. See Eliot Wigginton, *The Foxfire Book* (New York: Anchor Books, 1972), 297.

40. Howard, *Southeastern Ceremonial Complex*, 49–52.

41. Ibid., 42.
42. Ibid., 53.
43. Ibid., p. 50, fig. 14D.
44. William C. Sturtevant, quoted in Howard, *Southeastern Ceremonial Complex*, 53.
45. Adair, *History*, 237–38.
46. Ibid.
47. Robin Horton, "African Traditional Thought and Western Science," *Africa* 38(1967):50–71, 177–87.
48. We in our own culture are so little interested in anomalies it is difficult for us to appreciate fully their role in the thinking of preliterate people. We retain something of it in the freak shows in rural carnivals, and in Robert Ripley's *Believe it or Not*. The ancient Hebrews were very much interested in them, as may be seen in the books of Leviticus and Deuteronomy. See Douglas, *Purity and Danger*.
49. The precise reason why Selu violated a rule here is unclear. It was perfectly all right for men to take animals they had killed to the river bank to wash the blood from them. Perhaps washing game in the river was defined as a manlike act and therefore forbidden to women. Another possibility is that this may be an oblique way of saying that Selu put menstrual blood into the river, and that this act was polluting.
50. In effect, they made a cross in a circle. This suggests that the Mississippian cross in a circle gorget was believed to protect the wearer from evil.
51. This was evidently one of the wheel-shaped stones used in the game of chunkey. See chap. 7.
52. Here the boys break a rule by bragging. They claimed to be men, but they were mere boys. In fact, the Thunder Boys probably epitomize the unruliness of youth.
53. The significance of this episode, aside from showing that the boys were rule-breakers, is not clear. Perhaps it is a somewhat garbled explanation of how the cougar got his whiskers, and why it is that the cougar avoids man.
54. The asterisks below and the ones a paragraph hence are Mooney's. They evidently mean that he collected parts of the story from several sources, later putting them together in connected form.
55. Mooney, "Myths of the Cherokee," 242–49.
56. The Yuchi and Creek oral traditions collected by W. O. Tuggle are far more fragmentary than Mooney's, but similar to this Cherokee oral tradition in several respects. Tuggle, *Shem, Ham & Japheth*, 283–85, 287–88.
57. When on top of the ground some grubworms do crawl on their

backs, with their legs wiggling in the air. Perhaps this odd feature is one reason why the grubworm was chief of the council. In addition, the grubworm is white, and it is a creature which metamorphoses itself into a flying insect, and hence the grubworm in their way of thinking was anomalous.

58. Mooney, "Myths of the Cherokee," 250–52.

59. Charles Hudson, "The Cherokee Concept of Natural Balance," *The Indian Historian* 3(1970):51–54.

60. I am grateful to Mr. Harold Cable for this remarkable observation and hypothesis.

61. Mooney, "Myths of the Cherokee," 325–26.

62. Tuggle, *Shem, Ham & Japheth*, 308–9.

63. Ibid., 171.

64. But in the Creek version of this story the bat sided with the four-footed animals and won it for them. Tuggle, *Shem, Ham & Japheth*, 289–90.

65. Agility and deceptiveness are important in the ball game, so that players who are physically small can nonetheless be great ball players. The same must also have been true of aboriginal warfare.

66. Mooney, "Myths of the Cherokee," 286–87.

67. Adair, *History*, 272–73.

68. Ibid., 12.

69. Cf. Douglas, *Purity and Danger*.

70. Ground-hog's Mother was a "Shawano" whom the Cherokees captured. They were about to torture him to death when he saved himself by promising to go out and capture the Ulunsuti. Mooney, "Myths of the Cherokee," 298–300.

71. Ibid., 297–98.

72. Howard, *Southeastern Ceremonial Complex*, 79–80.

73. James Howard has suggested that the hand and eye design had something of the meaning the hand design had for the Plains Indians in more recent times. Namely, that it was associated with warfare, and that it might have meant, as among the Omahas and Dakotas, that the warrior wearing it had been struck or wounded by the enemy (*Southeastern Ceremonial Complex*, 29–34). Like the anomalous feathered serpent, the use of the hand and eye design also occurs in the art of the Northwest Coast and in Mesoamerica, with some similarity to art motifs in China during the Shang and Early Chou dynasties. Cf. Robert L. Rands, "Comparative Notes on the Hand-Eye and Related Motifs," *American Antiquity* 22(1957):247–57.

74. Mooney, "Myths of the Cherokees," 336–37. The Nikwasi mound may be seen today at Franklin, North Carolina, surrounded by filling stations, restaurants, and asphalt. While one would wish for a more pleas-

ing setting, we can take some consolation in knowing that the mound has not yet been bulldozed in the name of progress.

75. John Witthoft and Wendell S. Hadlock, "Cherokee-Iroquois Little People," *Journal of American Folklore* 59(1946):413–22.

76. Tuggle, *Shem, Ham & Japheth*, 121.

77. Ibid., 124–25.

78. Mooney and Olbrechts, *Swimmer Manuscript*, 28–29.

79. Adair, *History*, 102.

80. Ibid., 118, 163.

81. Ibid., 232.

82. Ibid., "Preface."

83. In terms of our own psychology we see this as paranoid behavior. Although it is ethnocentric and misleading to characterize another culture in terms of our own notions of psychopathology, one is tempted to describe witchcraft as a kind of institutionalized paranoia. That is, any person who was *not* paranoid in such a society would be out of line.

84. Mooney, "Myths of the Cherokee," 349–50.

85. This site can be seen from the Blue Ridge Parkway.

86. Mooney, "Myths of the Cherokee," 316–19.

87. Ibid., 468.

88. Milanich and Sturtevant, *Pareja's* Confessionario, 23, 26.

89. Adair, *History*, 26.

90. According to Mooney, ravens sometimes dive, fold one of their wings, and turn a somersault, or more precisely, what pilots call a barrel-roll. "Myths of the Cherokee," 505.

91. A stream of water would of course be the appropriate place in which to dispose of something that was polluted.

92. Mooney, "Myths of the Cherokee," 401–3.

93. Adair, *History*, 36.

94. Raymond D. Fogelson, "An Analysis of Cherokee Sorcery and Witchcraft," in *Four Centuries of Southern Indians*, ed. Charles Hudson (Athens, Ga.: Univ. of Georgia Press, 1975), 113–31.

95. Mooney and Olbrechts, *Swimmer Manuscript*, 33.

96. Ibid., 130.

97. Ibid., 131.

98. Ibid., 30.

99. Ibid., 131.

100. Mooney, "Myths of the Cherokee," 335.

CHAPTER 4. SOCIAL ORGANIZATION

1. Goggin and Sturtevant, "Calusa," 189.

2. Swanton, "Social Organization of the Creek Confederacy," 96. To a far lesser extent we also use kinship terms in a metaphorical sense, in speaking of God as "father," of a member of one's fraternity as "brother," and of England as the "mother" country. But this carries far less weight in our thinking than it did in the thinking of the Southeastern Indians.

3. David S. Corkran, *The Creek Frontier, 1540–1783* (Norman, Okla.: Univ. of Oklahoma Press, 1967), 30–31.

4. See William S. Willis, "Patrilineal Institutions in Southeastern North America," *Ethnohistory* 10(1963):250–69. In some of the cases cited by Willis the British may have simply been mistaken in concluding that some of these sister's sons were own sons. See, for example, John Reid, *A Law of Blood: Primitive Law of the Cherokee Nation* (New York: New York Univ. Press, 1970), 91. If any of the Southeastern Indians recognized patrilineal descent in aboriginal times, it was probably some of the marginal groups. The Shawnees were patrilineal, as were most of the Plains Indians on the western margin of the Southeast. The Indians of the Gulf Coast appear to have been patrilocal. Cabeza de Vaca, for example, says that some of these Gulf Coast Indians explained their custom of female infanticide on the grounds that it kept their enemies from becoming too numerous. This implies that their daughters left their natal group upon marriage, moving in with their husband's people, and this in turn implies patrilocality. Cabeza de Vaca, *Journey*, 88. In the historic period, particularly in the 19th century, as a consequence of white influences many Southeastern Indians began emphasizing descent through the male line. Cf. Fred Eggan, "Historical Changes in the Choctaw Kinship System," *American Anthropologist* 39(1937):34–52.

5. Swanton, "Social Organization of the Creek Confederacy," 85.

6. William Harlen Gilbert, Jr., *The Eastern Cherokees*, Bureau of American Ethnology Bulletin no. 133 (Washington, D. C., 1943), 218. The Choctaws and Chickasaws also had Crow terminology, the Yuchis may have had it, and we do not have enough evidence to determine what kind of terminology the Natchez had, although they were definitely matrilineal. Cf. Eggan, "Historical Changes."

7. The term *posi* also applied to the grandmother's sisters and to her female ancestors back as far as memory reached. Swanton, "Social Organization of the Creek Confederacy," 80.

8. Gilbert, *Eastern Cherokees*, 245–53.

9. Reid, *Law of Blood*, 37–48.

10. "Father" is not consistent with Creek matrilineal organization. Log-

ically, members of the Rabbit and Skunk clans would have thought of Wind as mother's brother. This discrepancy may be a late development in this story as a consequence of the Creek kinship system's having changed to resemble the kinship system of whites.

11. Swanton, "Social Organization of the Creek Confederacy," 112–13.

12. Ibid., 109.

13. Ibid., 107–8.

14. An exception to this rule of exogamy occurred among the Calusas, where chiefs evidently married their full sisters. This custom of sister marriage has occurred elsewhere in the world, though rarely, and usually only among the elite in highly stratified societies. So far as we know, this custom did not occur elsewhere in the Southeast. Cf. Goggin and Sturtevant, "Calusa."

15. Swanton, "Social Organization of the Creek Confederacy," 368–77.

16. Merwyn S. Garbarino, *Big Cypress: A Changing Seminole Community* (New York: Holt, Rinehart and Winston, 1972), 66.

17. Gilbert, *Eastern Cherokees*, 243–45.

18. Cherokee terminology was similar, except that mother's brother's wife was called by a term which applied only to her and to mother's mother's sister's son's wife. Ibid., 225.

19. W. O. Tuggle heard of a case of this as late as 1879 in the Indian Territory. *Shem, Ham, & Japheth*, 88–89.

20. Reid, *Law of Blood*, 114–16.

21. Adair, *History*, 186–87.

22. Swanton, "Social Organization of the Creek Confederacy," 377–84.

23. Elman R. Service, *Primitive Social Organization: An Evolutionary Perspective*, 2d ed. (New York: Random House, 1971), 99–169; Morton H. Fried, *The Evolution of Political Society: An Essay on Political Anthropology* (New York: Random House, 1967), 109–84.

24. Adair, *History*, 389, 421.

25. Waring and Holder, "Prehistoric Ceremonial Complex"; Antonio J. Waring, Jr., "The Southern Cult and Muskhogean Ceremonial," in *The Waring Papers: The Collected Works of Antonio J. Waring, Jr.*, ed. Stephen Williams (Athens, Ga.: Univ. of Georgia Press, 1965), 30–69; Howard, *Southeastern Ceremonial Complex*.

26. James A. Brown, "The Dimensions of Status in the Burials at Spiro," *American Antiquity*, vol. 36, no. 3, pt. 2 (1971):92–112; Lewis H. Larson, Jr., "Archaeological Implications of Social Stratification at the Etowah Site, Georgia," *American Antiquity*, vol. 36, no. 3, pt. 2 (1971):58–67. The mere

fact that women and children are sometimes found buried in mounds and accompanied by Southeastern Ceremonial Cult materials does not necessarily indicate the existence of social class. It could have been that these women and children shared the rank of their husbands and fathers. In the same vein, that important men were sometimes buried with their relatives and retainers, who were ritually killed for the occasion, does not necessarily indicate the existence of social class.

27. Bourne, *Hernando de Soto*, vol. II, p. 97.

28. Adair, *History*, 211.

29. The kings of some African states live in constant fear of assassination: E. E. Evans-Pritchard, "The Divine Kingship of the Shilluk of the Nilotic Sudan," in *Social Anthropology and Other Essays* (New York: Free Press of Glencoe, 1962), 192–212. And cf. the fragile, fluid relationship between Burmese principalities and the highland chiefdoms on their borders in Edmund R. Leach's *Political Systems of Highland Burma: A Study of Kachin Social Structure* (Cambridge, Mass.: Harvard University Press, 1954).

30. Roy S. Dickens, Jr., "The Appalachian Summit: A.D. 1000 to Bartram," in *The Southeast*, ed. Raymond Fogelson, vol. XIII of the *Handbook of North American Indians*, ed. William C. Sturtevant (Washington, D. C.: Smithsonian Institution, in press).

31. John R. Swanton, *Indian Tribes of the Lower Mississippi Valley and Adjacent Coast of the Gulf of Mexico*, Bureau of American Ethnology Bulletin no. 43 (Washington, D. C., 1911); Jeffrey P. Brain, "The Natchez 'Paradox'," *Ethnology* 10(1971):215–22; Douglas R. White, George P. Murdock, and Richard Scaglion, "Natchez Class and Rank Reconsidered," *Ethnology* 10(1971):369–88.

32. Garcilaso, *Florida*, 533–54. The problem of flooding was greatest along the middle and lower courses of southern rivers, particularly the Mississippi River. Flooding probably did not greatly trouble the Cherokees, in their narrow mountain valleys; and it probably was not much of a problem for Indians living in the piedmont, except, of course, to the degree that travel was difficult when the rivers were high.

33. Dickens, "Appalachian Summit"; Garcilaso, *Florida*, 122.

34. Adair, *History*, 352–53.

35. Garcilaso, *Florida*, 168.

36. Lorant, *The New World*, 95, 190; Dickens, "Appalachian Summit." This circular village pattern may represent an old Woodland trait.

37. Dickens, "Appalachian Summit."

38. William Bartram, "Observations on the Creek and Cherokee Indians, 1789," *Transactions of the American Ethnological Society*, vol. 3, pt. 1 (1853), 55.

39. Some confirmation of Bartram is now turning up in archaeological research in southeastern Missouri and northeastern Arkansas, as, for example, at the Snodgrass site, and perhaps also at the King site in northern Georgia.

40. Swanton, "Social Organization of the Creek Confederacy," 170–71.

41. Dickens, "Appalachian Summit."

42. Adair, *History*, 227.

43. Ibid., 419–20.

44. Ibid., 417–19.

45. Henry Timberlake, *Memoirs, 1756–1765*, ed. Samuel Cole Williams (Marietta, Ga.: Continental Book Co., 1948), 84.

46. Bartram, "Observations," 38.

47. Timberlake, *Memoirs*, 59.

48. Ibid., 63–65.

49. Swanton, "Social Organization of the Creek Confederacy," 243.

50. These "axes" may have been related to the bi-lobed arrows described later in this chapter.

51. Waring, "The Southern Cult," 54–57.

52. Bartram, "Observations," 52.

53. Ibid., 54; Howard, *Southeastern Ceremonial Complex*, 130–41.

54. Waring, "The Southern Cult," 58–62.

55. Swanton, "Social Organization of the Creek Confederacy," 276–93.

56. Ibid., 293–96.

57. Reid, *Law of Blood*, 30–31.

58. Ibid., 237.

59. Ibid., 240.

60. Ibid., 297–98; Gilbert, *Eastern Cherokees*, 348–50.

61. Swanton, "Social Organization of the Creek Confederacy," 301–5; Gilbert, *Eastern Cherokees*, 323.

62. Swanton, "Social Organization of the Creek Confederacy," 296–97.

63. Harold Cable, Charles Hudson, and William Merrill, "The Black Drink of the Southeastern Indians," paper read at the 1971 meeting of the American Society for Ethnohistory, at Athens, Ga.

64. Reid, *Law of Blood*, 63–71.

65. Ibid., 73–75, 98, 100.

66. Ibid., 76–77.

67. Ibid., 78–84.

68. This, of course, is the moral of the story of Cain and Abel in the Old Testament.

69. Reid, *Law of Blood*, 93–112.

70. John R. Swanton, "The Social Significance of the Creek Confederacy," *Proceedings of the 19th International Congress of Americanists*

(Washington, D. C., 1915), 327.

71. Ibid., 327–28.

72. Reid, *Law of Blood*, 30–31.

73. Garcilaso, *Florida*, 73, 93.

74. Corkran, *Creek Frontier*.

75. Alfonso Ortiz, "Dual Organization As an Operational Concept in the Pueblo Southwest," *Ethnology* 4(1965):389–96.

76. Alfonso Ortiz, *The Tewa World: Space, Time, Being, and Becoming in a Pueblo Society* (Chicago: Univ. of Chicago Press, 1969).

77. Mary R. Haas, "Creek Inter-Town Relations," *American Anthropologist* 42(1940):479.

78. Ortiz, *Tewa World*.

79. Haas, "Inter-Town Relations."

80. Ortiz, *Tewa World*.

81. Swanton, "Social Organization of the Creek Confederacy," 157; Swanton, *Indian Tribes of the Lower Mississippi Valley*, 103, 111–12. Some Natchez officials were in pairs, suggesting that they represented moieties.

82. Garbarino, *Big Cypress*, 76.

83. Swanton, "Social Organization of the Creek Confederacy," 165.

84. The temple mound at the Mississippian site of Hiwassee Island had a town house with two rooms and an open porch in front. This same mound had a second, lower mound attached to it, containing a structure with an identical floor plan. Antonio J. Waring, Jr., has argued that this may represent dual organization ("The Southern Cult," 56) although one could also argue that this may have represented the joining of two chiefdoms, as with Great Tellico and Chatuga in historic times.

85. Reid, *Law of Blood*, 12–13.

86. Ibid., 58–59.

87. Ibid., 93–112.

88. Ibid., 153–55.

89. Lewis H. Larson, Jr., "Functional Considerations of Warfare in the Southeast During the Mississippi Period," *American Antiquity* 37(1972):383–92; Jon L. Gibson, "Aboriginal Warfare in the Protohistoric Southeast: An Alternative Perspective," *American Antiquity* 39(1974):130–33.

90. Swanton, *Indian Tribes of the Lower Mississippi Valley*, 170.

91. Ibid., 182–83.

92. Gibson, "Aboriginal Warfare."

93. Adair, *History*, 347.

94. Reid, *Law of Blood*, 201.

95. Cf. Napoleon Chagnon, *Yanomamö* (New York: Holt, Rinehart and

Winston, 1968), 113–17.

96. Cabeza de Vaca, *Journey*, 118–22.

97. Mooney, "Myths of the Cherokee," 365.

98. Reid, *Law of Blood*, 170–72.

99. Swanton, *Indian Tribes of the Lower Mississippi Valley*, 130.

100. Gilbert, *Eastern Cherokees*, 352–53.

101. Ibid.

102. Reid, *Law of Blood*, 177–78.

103. Garcilaso, *Florida*, 17.

104. Ibid., 234.

105. Ibid., 180.

106. Ibid., 236.

107. Ibid., 258.

108. Ibid., 265.

109. Ibid., 278. And see Harold L. Peterson's *American Indian Tomahawks*, Contributions from the Museum of the American Indian, Heye Foundation, vol. 19 (Glückstadt, Germany: J. J. Augustin, 1965).

110. Lawson, *Voyage to Carolina*, 44.

111. Howard, *Southeastern Ceremonial Complex*, 26–27.

112. Swanton, *Indian Tribes of the Lower Mississippi Valley*, 57.

113. Gilbert, *Eastern Cherokees*, 353.

114. Reid, *Law of Blood*, 177.

115. Gilbert, *Eastern Cherokees*, 348, 353–54.

116. Garcilaso, *Florida*, 257.

117. Charles E. Snow, "Possible Evidence of Scalping at Moundville," *Alabama Museum of Natural History, Museum Paper*, no. 15, pt. 2 (University, Ala., 1941), 55–59.

118. Howard, *Southeastern Ceremonial Complex*, 68.

119. Garcilaso, *Florida*, 120.

120. Reid, *Law of Blood*, 174.

121. Ibid., 179.

122. Nathaniel Knowles, "The Torture of Captives by the Indians of Eastern North America," *Proceedings of the American Philosophical Society* 82(1940):151–225.

123. Swanton, *Indian Tribes of the Lower Mississippi Valley*, 131–32.

124. Adair, *History*, 390–91.

125. Ibid., 391.

126. Reid, *Law of Blood*, 201–15.

CHAPTER 5. ECOLOGY AND ECONOMICS

1. Harold C. Conklin, "Shifting Cultivation," *Annals of the New York*

Academy of Sciences 17 (1954):133–42; Robert McC. Netting, "The Ecological Approach in Cultural Study" (Reading, Mass.: Addison-Wesley Module, 1971).

2. Swanton, *Indian Tribes of the Lower Mississippi Valley*, 53.

3. William C. Sturtevant, "Seminole Men's Clothing," in *Essays on the Verbal and Visual Arts*, 1966 American Ethnological Society Proceedings, ed. June Helm (Seattle: Univ. of Washington Press, 1967), p. 170.

4. Ibid., pp. 161–62, 170.

5. Cabeza de Vaca, *Journey*, 45.

6. Swanton, *Indian Tribes of the Lower Mississippi Valley*, 53.

7. Ibid., 52–53.

8. Sturtevant, "Seminole Clothing," 171–72.

9. Howard, *Southeastern Ceremonial Complex*, 39.

10. Sturtevant, "Seminole Clothing," 170.

11. Ibid.

12. Swanton, *Indian Tribes of the Lower Mississippi Valley*, 53.

13. Ibid., 65.

14. Ibid., 64–65.

15. Ibid., 63.

16. Reid, *Law of Blood*, 67–69.

17. Swanton, *Indian Tribes of the Lower Mississippi Valley*, 89.

18. Adair, *History*, 169.

19. Swanton, *Indian Tribes of the Lower Mississippi Valley*, 100.

20. Reid, *Law of Blood*, 69.

21. Warren L. Wittry, "The American Woodhenge," in *Explorations into Cahokia Archaeology*, ed. Melvin L. Fowler, Illinois Archaeological Survey Bulletin no. 7 (Urbana, Ill.: Univ. of Illinois Press, 1969), 43–48.

22. Gilbert, *Eastern Cherokees*, 325.

23. Mooney, "Myths of the Cherokee," 404–15.

24. Ibid.

25. David I. Bushnell, "The Account of Lamhatty," *American Anthropologist* 10(1908):568–74.

26. Swanton, *Indian Tribes of the Lower Mississippi Valley*, 58–59.

27. Cabeza de Vaca, *Journey*, 32–33.

28. Frank G. Speck, "The Cane Blowgun in Catawba and Southeastern Ethnology," *American Anthropologist* 40(1938):198–204.

29. Mooney, "Sacred Formulas," 369–71.

30. Ibid., 372–73.

31. Roger A. Caras, *North American Mammals* (New York: Meredith Press, 1967), 428–40; Bruce D. Smith, "Middle Mississippi Exploitation of the White-Tailed Deer," *Proceedings of the 30th Southeastern Archaeological Conference*, in press.

32. Swanton, *Indian Tribes of the Lower Mississippi Valley*, 69–70; Lorant, *The New World*, 85; Smith, "Mississippian Exploitation of the Deer."

33. T. N. Campbell, "Choctaw Subsistence: Ethnographic Notes from the Lincecum Manuscript," *Florida Anthropologist* 12(1959):9–24.

34. Calvin Martin, "Fire and Forest Structure in the Aboriginal Eastern Forest," *The Indian Historian* 6(1973):38–42, 54. Burning off the forest would have reduced the numbers of reptiles and insects, but we do not know whether the Indians consciously sought this when they burned the woods. The Cherokees gathered chestnuts after they burned the woods, probably roasting them in the process (Mooney, "Myths of the Cherokee," 317.)

35. Grahame Clark, *The Stone Age Hunters* (New York: McGraw-Hill, 1967), 62–66.

36. Swanton, "First Description," 326–38.

37. Cabeza de Vaca, *Journey*, 91.

38. Swanton, *Indian Tribes of the Lower Mississippi Valley*, 70–71.

39. Ibid., 71. Later the Choctaws occasionally journeyed across the Mississippi River to hunt buffalo. Cf. Campbell, "Choctaw Subsistence," 11–12.

40. Tom McHugh, *The Time of the Buffalo*, 14–17.

41. Holder, *The Hoe and the Horse*, 35–36.

42. Swanton, *Indian Tribes of the Lower Mississippi Valley*, 67–69; Bruce D. Smith, "Middle Mississippi Exploitation of Animal Populations: A Predictive Model," *American Antiquity* 39, no. 2, pt. 1 (1974):288.

43. A. W. Schorger, *The Wild Turkey: Its History and Domestication* (Norman, Okla.: Univ. of Oklahoma Press, 1966), 86, 50–61.

44. A. W. Schorger, *The Passenger Pigeon: Its Natural History and Extinction* (Madison, Wis.: Univ. of Wisconsin Press, 1955), 133–34; Lawson, *Voyage to Carolina*, 50–51.

45. Smith, "Mississippian Exploitation of Animal Populations," 281–88.

46. Erhard Rostlund, *Freshwater Fish and Fishing in Native North America*, Univ. of California Publications in Geography, vol. 9 (Berkeley: Univ. of California Press, 1952), 72, 303.

47. Ibid., 304.

48. Ibid., 148, 155–56.

49. Milanich and Sturtevant, *Pareja's* Confessionario, passim.

50. Rostlund, *Freshwater Fish*, 4, 33–34, 272–74.

51. Campbell, "Choctaw Subsistence," 14.

52. Rostlund, *Freshwater Fish*, 81–100.

53. Swanton, *Indian Tribes of the Lower Mississippi Valley*, 58–59.

54. Rostlund, *Freshwater Fish*, 120–26.

525

55. Mooney, "Myths of the Cherokee," 420–21.

56. Merritt Lyndon Fernald and Alfred Charles Kinsey, *Edible Wild Plants of Eastern North America* (Cornwall-on-Hudson, N. Y.: Idlewild Press, 1943), 140–43. *Smilax* is called cat-brier, bull-brier, green-brier, saw-brier, bamboo-vine, blaspheme-vine, and probably other names.

57. William C. Sturtevant, "History and Ethnography of Some West Indian Starches," in *The Domestication and Exploitation of Plants and Animals*, eds. Peter J. Ucko and G. W. Dimbleby (London: Gerald Duckworth and Co., 1969), 177–99.

58. Fernald and Kinsey, *Edible Wild Plants*, 252–55.

59. Ibid., 326.

60. Ibid., 86–89. It is also called duck potato and swamp potato.

61. Grant Foreman, *Indian Removal: The Emigration of the Five Civilized Tribes of Indians* (Norman, Okla.: Univ. of Oklahoma Press, 1932), 318.

62. Fernald and Kinsey, *Edible Wild Plants*, 104–5.

63. Ibid., 200–2.

64. Ibid., 91–92.

65. Ibid., 177–79. It is also called pigweed. Cf. Swanton, *Indian Tribes of the Lower Mississippi Valley*, 76.

66. Fernald and Kinsey, *Edible Wild Plants*, 180.

67. Swanton, *Indian Tribes of the Lower Mississippi Valley*, 177; Mary Ulmer and Samuel E. Beck, eds. *Cherokee Cookery* (Cherokee, N. C.: Museum of the Cherokee Indian, 1951), 47, 49, 55.

68. Yarnell, *Plant Life*, 44.

69. Cabeza de Vaca, *Journey*, 47–48.

70. These fish reminded Cabeza de Vaca of "Ruffs," a small European perch (*Acerina cernua*).

71. Ibid., 63–64.

72. Ibid., 89–90.

73. Bourne, *Hernando de Soto*, vol. II, p. 103.

74. Swanton, *Indian Tribes of the Lower Mississippi Valley*, 129. In appearance the Natchez dog resembled the wolf which was native to the South, but its bark was said to be different. Ibid., 73.

75. Lynn Ceci, "Fish Fertilizer: A Native North American Practice?" *Science* 188(1975):26–30.

76. Netting, "Ecological Approach," 20.

77. David R. Harris, "Swidden Systems and Settlement," in *Man, Settlement and Urbanism*, eds. Peter J. Ucko, Ruth Tringham, and G. W. Dimbleby (London: Gerald Duckworth and Co., 1972), 245–62.

78. The precise proportion of domesticated to wild food in the Southeastern Indian diet has not yet been established.

79. Charles Hudson, *The Catawba Nation* (Athens, Ga.: Univ. of Georgia Press, 1970), 20–21; Christopher Murphy and Charles Hudson, "On the Problem of Intensive Agriculture in the Aboriginal Southeastern United States," *Working Papers in Sociology and Anthropology* 2(1968): 24–34; Douglas C. Wilms, "Cherokee Settlement Patterns in Nineteenth Century Georgia," *Southeastern Geographer* 14(1974):46–53.

80. If future research shows, on the contrary, that Southeastern Indian agriculture was but a variety of a more general type of agriculture practices elsewhere in the world, then this term *riverine* should be set aside.

81. Holder, *The Hoe and the Horse*, 35.

82. Yarnell, *Plant Life*, 101–20; Walter C. Galinat, "The Evolution of Corn and Culture in North America," *Economic Botany* 19(1965):350–57.

83. Hugh C. Cutler and Leonard W. Blake, "Travels of Corn and Squash," in *Man Across the Sea: Problems of Pre-Columbian Contacts*, eds. Carroll L. Riley et al., (Austin, Tex.: Univ. of Texas Press, 1971), 369.

84. Ibid., 371; Swanton, *Indian Tribes of the Lower Mississippi Valley*, 74.

85. The ancestors of modern hybrid corn were developed about 100 years ago by crossing dent corn with Northern flint. Galinat, "Evolution of Corn."

86. Cutler and Blake, "Travels," 370–71.

87. William N. Fenton, *Parker on the Iroquois* (Syracuse, N. Y.: Syracuse Univ. Press, 1968), 43; George F. Will and George E. Hyde, *Corn Among the Indians of the Upper Missouri* (Lincoln, Neb.: Univ. of Nebraska Press, n. d.), 284–317.

88. Swanton, *Indian Tribes of the Lower Mississippi Valley*, 74; Swanton, *Indians of the Southeast*, 304–10.

89. Yarnell, *Plant Life*, 108–10.

90. Lawrence Kaplan, "Archaeology and Domestication in American Phaseolus (Beans)," *Economic Botany* 19(1965):358–68.

91. Cutler and Blake, "Travels," 372.

92. Kaplan, "American Phaseolus." Kaplan points out that corn and beans are an adequate source of protein for active people but they are not adequate for "the more protein sensitive members of the population, lactating mothers and young, recently weaned children."

93. Yarnell, *Plant Life*, 102–105; Yarnell, "Early Plant Husbandry."

94. William C. Sturtevant, "Historic Carolina Algonkian Cultivation of Chenopodium or Amaranthus," *Proceedings of the 21st Southeastern Archaeological Conference* (1965), 64–65.

95. Swanton, *Indian Tribes of the Lower Mississippi Valley*, 76.

96. Thomas W. Whitaker, "Endemism and Pre-Columbian Migration of the Bottle Gourd, *Lagenaria siceraria* (Mol.) Standl.," in *Man Across the*

Sea: Problems of Pre-Columbian Contacts, eds. Carroll Riley et al. (Austin, Tex.: Univ. of Texas Press, 1971), 320–27.

97. Frank G. Speck, *Gourds of the Southeastern Indians* (Boston: The New England Gourd Society, 1941).

98. Campbell, "Choctaw Subsistence," 16.

99. Swanton, *Indian Tribes of the Lower Mississippi Valley*, 166.

100. Ibid., 75.

101. Campbell, "Choctaw Subsistence," 16–17; William C. Sturtevant, "Lafitau's Hoes," *American Antiquity* 33 (1968):93–95; Swanton, *Indian Tribes of the Lower Mississippi Valley*, 75.

102. G. Melvin Herndon, "Indian Agriculture in the Southern Colonies," *The North Carolina Historical Review* 44 (1967):287.

103. Murphy and Hudson, "Intensive Agriculture," 28.

104. Herndon, "Indian Agriculture," 291. Modern advocates of organic gardening claim that intercropping helps retard damage from insects, but we do not definitely know whether this worked to the advantage of the Southeastern Indians.

105. Fenton, *Iroquois*, 26. This technique is nicely illustrated in one of John White's drawings.

106. Melvin L. Fowler, "Middle Mississippian Agricultural Fields," *American Antiquity* 34 (1969):365–75.

107. Speck, *Gourds*, 40–41.

108. Campbell, "Choctaw Subsistence," 18–19.

109. Ulmer and Beck, *Cherokee Cookery*, 46.

110. Ibid., 60.

111. Adair, *History*, 3; Swanton, *Indian Tribes of the Lower Mississippi Valley*, 69.

112. H. B. Battle, "The Domestic Use of Oil Among the Southern Aborigines," *American Anthropologist* 24 (1922):171–82.

113. Swanton, *Indian Tribes of the Lower Mississippi Valley*, 72.

114. Ulmer and Beck, *Cherokee Cookery*, 47, 54, 55.

115. Swanton, *Indian Tribes of the Lower Mississippi Valley*, 74.

116. Campbell, "Choctaw Subsistence," 17.

117. M. H. Wright, "American Indian Corn Dishes," *Chronicles of Oklahoma* 36 (1958):155–66; S. H. Katz, M. L. Hediger, and L. A. Valleroy, "Traditional Maize Processing Techniques in the New World," *Science* 184 (1974):765–73.

118. Campbell, "Choctaw Subsistence," 18.

119. Wright, "Corn Dishes," 160.

120. Ibid., 160, 163, 164–65.

121. Ibid., 160.

122. Ibid., 165.

123. Campbell, "Choctaw Subsistence," 17.

124. Swanton, *Indian Tribes of the Lower Mississippi Valley*, 75; Wright, "Corn Dishes," 160, 163.

125. Wright, "Corn Dishes," 158–59.

126. Ibid., 161, 162.

127. Campbell, "Choctaw Subsistence," 17; Ulmer and Beck, *Cherokee Cookery*, 59.

128. Ulmer and Beck, *Cherokee Cookery*, 59.

129. Ibid., 54.

130. Ibid., 55.

131. Frederick W. Sleight, "Kunti, a Food Staple of Florida Indians," *Florida Anthropologist* 6 (1953):46–52.

132. Fernald and Kinsey, *Edible Wild Plants*, 159–61.

133. Swanton, *Indians of the Southeast*, 273. Indians in the western United States who relied greatly on acorns sometimes neutralized the acid by adding wood ashes to the water. In view of their frequent use of wood ashes in cooking and processing food, we are probably safe in assuming the Southeastern Indians also used wood ashes in making acorns edible, but I know of no documentary proof of this.

134. Campbell, "Choctaw Subsistence," 15.

135. Swanton, *Indian Tribes of the Lower Mississippi Valley*, 78.

136. Fernald and Kinsey, *Edible Wild Plants*, 127–30.

137. Ulmer and Beck, *Cherokee Cookery*, 54, 58.

138. Fernald and Kinsey, *Edible Wild Plants*, 209–11. An overdose of sassafras oil is said to have a narcotic effect.

139. Ulmer and Beck, *Cherokee Cookery*, 47.

140. Ibid., 48, 58.

141. Ibid., 58.

142. Campbell, "Choctaw Subsistence," 13.

143. Ulmer and Beck, *Cherokee Cookery*, 56.

144. Swanton, *Indian Tribes of the Lower Mississippi Valley*, 78, 90.

145. Lawson, *Voyage to Carolina*, 203.

146. Edmond Atkin, *Indians of the Southern Colonial Frontier: The Edmond Atkin Report and Plan of 1775*, ed. Wilbur R. Jacobs (Columbia, S. C.: Univ. of South Carolina Press, 1954), 28, 30.

147. Reid, *Law of Blood*, 138–39.

148. Swanton, *Indian Tribes of the Lower Mississippi Valley*, 119.

149. Reid, *Law of Blood*, 124.

150. Adair, *History*, 431.

151. Reid, *Law of Blood*, 124–25.

152. Ibid., 144.

153. Ibid., 129.

154. Ibid., 140.   155. Ibid., 131–35.

156. Adair, *History*, 318.

157. William E. Meyer, "Indian Trails of the Southeast," *Forty-second Annual Report of the Bureau of American Ethnology* (Washington, D. C., 1928), 741–42.

158. Swanton, *Indian Tribes of the Lower Mississippi Valley*, 67.

159. Edwin T. Adney and Howard I. Chapelle, *The Bark Canoes and Skin Boats of North America*, United States National Museum Bulletin no. 230 (Washington, D. C.: Smithsonian Institution, 1964), 212–20; Meyer, "Indian Trails," 745.

160. Wilfred T. Neill, "Coracles or Skin Boats of the Southeastern Indians," *Florida Anthropologist* 7 (1954):119–26.

161. Swanton, *Indian Tribes of the Lower Mississippi Valley*, 66–67. One of these large canoes, probably of Cherokee manufacture, was preserved and was found by a Tennessee farmer. It may be seen at the McClung Museum at the Univ. of Tennessee. Several smaller dugout canoes, mostly fragmentary, have been found elsewhere in the Southeast.

162. Garcilaso, *Florida*, 575–76.

163. Wilfred T. Neill, "Dugouts of the Mikasuki Seminole," *Florida Anthropologist* 6 (1953):77–84.

164. Jared V. Harper, "The Adoption and Use of the Horse among the Southeastern Indians," paper at the 1974 meeting of the Southern Anthropological Society, at Blacksburg, Va.

165. Cabeza de Vaca, *Journey*, 74–75.

166. Garcilaso, *Florida*, 449–50.

CHAPTER 6. CEREMONY

1. Using the language of psychopathology to characterize normal customs and institutions in other societies is undesirable and misleading. But we have few analogues of this quest for purity in our own society. Orthodox Jewish dietary rules are comparable. An even better example in our own culture is the racial ideology originally formulated by reactionary European philosophers such as Arthur de Gobineau. In the racist world view, the differences between races are absolute, and any intimacy between members of different races (particularly black and white) raises the possibility of cosmic disorder. The main point here is that intimacy between people of different races makes people who hold this racist world view extremely anxious, just as the Southeastern Indians must have become anxious when their rules of separation failed.

2. Karen E. Paige, "Women Learn to Sing the Menstrual Blues," *Psychology Today* 7(1973):41–46.

3. Frans M. Olbrechts, "Cherokee Belief and Practice with Regard to

Childbirth," *Anthropos* 26 (1931):17–24.

4. Lawson, *Voyage to Carolina*, 196.

5. Swanton, *Indian Tribes of the Lower Mississippi Valley*, 86–87.

6. Olbrechts, "Cherokee Childbirth," 31–33.

7. Lawson, *Voyage to Carolina*, 197.

8. Charles Hudson, "Isometric Advantages of the Cradle Board: A Hypothesis," *American Anthropologist*, vol. 68, no. 2, pt. 1 (1966):470–74.

9. Lawson, *Voyage to Carolina*, 40.

10. Gabarino, *Big Cypress*, 77; James O. Buswell, "Florida Seminole Religious Ritual: Resistance and Change," Ph.D. dissertation, St. Louis University, 1972, pp. 183–87.

11. Swanton, *Indian Tribes of the Lower Mississippi Valley*, 87–88.

12. Ibid., 88.

13. Adair, *History*, 191–93.

14. "Osceola," the name of the great Seminole leader, is an English corruption of *Asi yahola*. *Asi* is the Seminole word for black drink.

15. Swanton, "Social Organization of the Creek Confederacy," 97–107.

16. Adair, *History*, 397–99.

17. Louis Le Clerc Milfort, *Memoirs, or a Quick Glance at My Various Travels and My Sojourn in the Creek Nation*, trans. and ed. Ben C. McCary (Savannah, Ga.: The Beehive Press, 1972), 99–102.

18. Milfort calls this garment a "chasuble."

19. Swanton, *Indian Tribes of the Lower Mississippi Valley*, 143.

20. Ibid., 146. As late as 1938 the Seminoles executed one of their number for murder, and they left his body unburied. Cf. Louis Capron, "The Medicine Bundles of the Florida Seminole and the Green Corn Dance," *Anthropological Papers no. 35, Bureau of American Ethnology Bulletin* no. 151 (Washington, D. C., 1953), 197.

21. Brown, "Burials at Spiro"; Larson, "Etowah"; Peebles, "Moundville."

22. Larson, "Etowah," 66.

23. Swanton, *Indian Tribes of the Lower Mississippi Valley*, 147–48.

24. Ibid., 145.

25. Garcilaso, *Florida*, 511–12.

26. Swanton, *Indian Tribes of the Lower Mississippi Valley*, 146–47.

27. Ibid., 152.

28. Ibid., 145. The remains of infants have been found alongside high status burials at Cahokia.

29. Ibid., 144. The Seminoles believed that a person had two souls. One left the body at death, but the other remained near the body for four days before going away. Robert F. Greenlee, "Medicine and Curing Practices of the Modern Florida Seminole," *American Anthropologist* 46 (1944):319.

30. Swanton, *Indian Tribes of the Lower Mississippi Valley*, 146. In view of the role of conch shell drinking cups in Mississippian burials, it is at least questionable that these were river mussel shells.

31. It is possible that these pellets contained jimson weed (*Datura stramonium* L.), a powerful, frequently poisonous narcotic, whose dried leaves superficially resemble tobacco.

32. Swanton, *Indian Tribes of the Lower Mississippi Valley*, 143–57.

33. William C. MacLeod, "Priests, Temples, and the Practice of Mummification in Southeastern North America," *Proceedings of the International Congress of Americanists*, 22d Congress, vol. 2 (Rome, 1926), 210.

34. Swanton, *Indian Tribes of the Lower Mississippi Valley*, 143.

35. Larson, "Etowah."

36. Adair, *History*, 177–85.

37. Greenlee, "Curing Practices of the Seminole," 318.

38. Kilpatrick and Kilpatrick, *Run Toward the Night-land*, 4.

39. Swanton, "Religious Beliefs of the Creeks," 615–16.

40. Ibid.

41. Adair, *History*, 86.

42. Mooney, "Sacred Formulas," 387–88.

43. In addition, Swanton quotes Benjamin Hawkins as saying that they also drank an infusion made with the bitter root of "*sou-watch-cau*," which caused them to become intoxicated and go mad. Swanton, "Religious Beliefs of the Creeks," 619.

44. Tuggle, *Shem, Ham, & Japheth*, 64.

45. Swanton, "Religious Beliefs of the Creeks," 617–21.

46. Unless otherwise noted, these are from Swanton, "Religious Beliefs of the Creeks," 655 ff.

47. William C. Sturtevant, "The Medicine Bundles and Busks of the Florida Seminole," *Florida Anthropologist* 7(1954):54. As their most important medicine, the Seminoles used the bark of southern red willow (*Salix amphibia*) instead of dwarf gray willow, probably because the latter does not grow in their area. Cf. Sturtevant, "Medicine Bundles," 52.

48. The Seminoles used *Eryngium synchaetum*. Ibid.

49. Virgil J. Vogel, *American Indian Medicine* (Norman, Okla.: Univ. of Oklahoma Press, 1970), 371.

50. Vogel, *Indian Medicine*, 307–10; Swanton, "Religious Beliefs of the Creeks," 656.

51. Vogel, *Indian Medicine*, 325–26; Greenlee, "Curing Practices of the Seminole," 327.

52. Vogel, *Indian Medicine*, 329–30. The Seminoles used *Juniperus silicicola* (Small) Bailey. Sturtevant, "Medicine Bundles," 54.

53. Mooney, "Sacred Formulas," 339–40.

54. Mooney, "Cherokee Theory and Practice of Medicine," *Journal of American Folklore* 3(1890):47; Mooney and Olbrechts, *Swimmer Manuscript*, 53.

55. Greenlee, "Curing Practices of the Seminole," 318.

56. Capron, "Medicine Bundles of the Florida Seminole," 174.

57. Greenlee, "Curing Practices of the Seminole," 319.

58. Mooney, "Cherokee Theory," 48.

59. Sturtevant, "Medicine Bundles," 56.

60. Ibid., 56–58; Buswell, "Florida Seminole Religious Ritual," 182–91.

61. Bartram, *Travels*, 164–66.

62. Mooney, "Cherokee Theory," 47–49.

63. Ibid., 49.

64. Ibid., 47.

65. Greenlee, "Curing Practices of the Seminole," 327; Charles Hudson, Ronald Butler and Dennis Sikes, "Arthritis in the Prehistoric Southeastern United States: Biological and Cultural Variables," *American Journal of Physical Anthropology* 43(1975):57–62.

66. Mooney, "Sacred Formulas," 345–49.

67. Lawson, *Voyage to Carolina*, 226–30.

68. Mooney, "Cherokee Theory," 44.

69. Mooney, "Sacred Formulas," 328–29.

70. Henry E. Simmons, "The Drug Efficacy Study: Its Effects on Therapeutics in America," Speech before the American College of Physicians, March 31, 1971, Denver, Colorado.

71. Vogel, *Indian Medicine*, 136–37, 380.

72. Philip H. Abelson, "Prevention of Cancer," *Science* 182(1973):973.

73. Greenlee, "Curing Practices of the Seminole," 328.

74. Crosby, *The Columbian Exchange*, 35–63.

75. Lawson, *Voyage to Carolina*, 225.

76. Charles Hudson, " 'Sociosomatic' Illness," manuscript.

77. This difference in terminology accords with the usual anthropological distinction between sorcery and witchcraft. In place of *sorcery* I have used *conjury* because this word has been used in the South to refer to this pattern of belief and behavior since the early colonial period.

78. Kilpatrick and Kilpatrick, *Run Toward the Nightland*, 8.

79. Swanton, *Indian Tribes of the Lower Mississippi Valley*, 79.

80. Ibid.

81. Kilpatrick and Kilpatrick, *Run Toward the Nightland*, 8–12.

82. Ibid., 83–86.

83. Ibid., 113–14; Frans M. Olbrechts, "Some Cherokee Methods of Divination," *Proceedings of the 23rd International Congress of Americanists* (New York, 1930), 547–48.

84. Kilpatrick and Kilpatrick, *Run Toward the Nightland*, 117–18.
85. Olbrechts, "Cherokee Divination," 549.
86. Ibid., 550.
87. Ibid., 550–51.
88. Ibid., 548–49.
89. Mooney and Olbrechts, *Swimmer Manuscript*, 304–5.
90. Olbrechts, "Cherokee Divination," 549–50.
91. Kilpatrick and Kilpatrick, *Run Toward the Nightland*, 149–53.
92. Ibid., 139–44.
93. And cf. Greenlee, "Curing Practices of the Seminole," 324.
94. Mooney, "Sacred Formulas," 378–79.
95. Kilpatrick and Kilpatrick, *Run Toward the Nightland*, 56.
96. Mooney, "Sacred Formulas," 380–81.
97. Ibid., 381–82.
98. Kilpatrick and Kilpatrick, *Run Toward the Nightland*, 4.
99. Ibid., 127.
100. Mooney, "Sacred Formulas," 391–95.
101. Kilpatrick and Kilpatrick, *Run Toward the Nightland*, 158–59.
102. Adair, *History*, 177.
103. Fogelson, "Cherokee Sorcery and Witchcraft," 114.
104. Kilpatrick and Kilpatrick, *Run Toward the Nightland*, 119–20; and for a fictionalized account see Joyce Rockwood, *Long Man's Song* (New York: Holt, Rinehart and Winston, 1975).
105. Adair, *History*, 36.
106. It is at least doubtful that the Natchez counted the months of their year beginning with March. Du Pratz may have listed them in this way following the old European calendar. It is rather more likely that the Natchez thought of their "Great Corn moon" as the first or last month of their year.
107. Swanton, *Indian Tribes of the Lower Mississippi Valley*, 109–10.
108. Sturtevant, "Medicine Bundles," 45.
109. John Witthoft, *Green Corn Ceremonialism in the Eastern Woodlands*, Occasional Papers from the Museum of Anthropology of the Univ. of Michigan, no. 13 (Ann Arbor: Univ. of Michigan Press, 1949).
110. Unless otherwise noted, this description of a Green Corn Ceremony is taken from Adair's *History*, 82–84, 100–8, and passim.
111. Sturtevant, "Medicine Bundles," 45.
112. Swanton, "Religious Beliefs of the Creeks," 554.
113. Swanton, *Indian Tribes of the Lower Mississippi Valley*, 114.
114. Sturtevant, "Medicine Bundles," 47.
115. Swanton, *Indian Tribes of the Lower Mississippi Valley*, 266–68.
116. Waring, "The Southern Cult," 57–58.

117. E. S. Greer, Jr. "A Tukabahchee Plate from the Coosa River," *Journal of Alabama Archaeology* 12(1966):156–58.

118. Swanton, "Religious Beliefs of the Creeks," 564, 569–70.

119. Capron, "Medicine Bundles of the Florida Seminole," 171.

120. Sturtevant, "Medicine Bundles," 35–41.

121. Ibid., 50–51.

122. These chips and splinters of pitch pine came from the resinous, highly combustible wood from old pine stumps. In the South it is called "rich pine," "fat lighter," and other terms.

123. Placing new fire in a bowl is consistent with the Cherokee myth about the origin of fire, in which the water spider brought back fire in a bowl on her back (see chap. 3).

124. Sturtevant, "Medicine Bundles," 52–55.

CHAPTER 7. ART, MUSIC, AND RECREATION

1. Jack F. Kilpatrick and Anna G. Kilpatrick, *Walk in Your Soul: Love Incantations of the Oklahoma Cherokees* (Dallas: Southern Methodist Univ. Press, 1965); Kilpatrick and Kilpatrick, *Run Toward the Nightland*.

2. John M. Goggin, "Style Areas in Historic Southeastern Art," in *Indian Tribes of Aboriginal America*, vol. 3, ed. Sol Tax. Proceedings of the 29th Congress of Americanists (Chicago: Univ. of Chicago Press, 1952), 172–76.

3. William C. Sturtevant, quoted in Howard, *Southeastern Ceremonial Complex*, 49.

4. Waring, "The Southern Cult," 32.

5. Bartram, "Observations," 18; *Travels*, 288.

6. Swanton, *Indians of the Southeast*, 617.

7. Bartram, "Observations," 19.

8. Fundaburk and Foreman, *Sun Circles*, plate 142.

9. This dramaturgical device was frequently used by masked dancers on the Northwest Coast.

10. Frank H. Cushing, "Exploration of Ancient Key Dwellers' Remains on the Gulf Coast of Florida," *Proceedings of the American Philosophical Society* 35(1896):382–89.

11. Otis T. Mason, *Aboriginal American Basketry: Studies in a Textile Art Without Machinery*, Annual Report of the Board of Regents of the Smithsonian Institution for 1902, (Washington, D.C., 1904), 386.

12. Ibid., plates 132–34.

13. Swanton, *Indians of the Southeast*, 602–3.

14. E. K. Burnett, *The Spiro Mound Collection in the Museum*, Contributions from the Museum of the American Indian, Heye Foundation,

vol. 14 (New York: Museum of the American Indian, Heye Foundation, 1945), plates XXVII–LVIII.

15. Lawson, *Voyage to Carolina*, 203.

16. Fundaburk and Foreman, *Sun Circles*, passim; William H. Holmes, "Art in Shell of the Ancient Americans," *Second Annual Report of the Bureau of American Ethnology* (Washington, D. C., 1883), 267–93.

17. Mooney, "Myths of the Cherokee," 541.

18. William H. Holmes, "Aboriginal Pottery of the Eastern United States," *Twentieth Annual Report of the Bureau of American Ethnology* (Washington, D. C., 1903).

19. Vladimir J. Fewkes, "Catawba Pottery-Making, with Notes on Pamunkey Pottery-Making, Cherokee Pottery-Making, and Coiling," *Proceedings of the American Philosophical Society* 88 (1944):69–124.

20. Holmes, "Pottery," 80–98.

21. Fundaburk and Foreman, *Sun Circles*, plates 91–92.

22. Adair, *History*, 7.

23. Swanton, *Indian Tribes of the Lower Mississippi Valley*, 128–29.

24. Fundaburk and Foreman, *Sun Circles*, plates 97, 98.

25. Adair, *History*, 22–23.

26. Burnett, *Spiro*, 38.

27. Howard, *Southeastern Ceremonial Complex*, 65–74.

28. Swanton, *Indians of the Southeast*, 624–26. A similar drum is indigenous to West Africa.

29. Ibid., 626–28; Frank G. Speck and Leonard Broom, *Cherokee Dance and Drama* (Berkeley: Univ. of California Press, 1951), 21–22.

30. Bartram, *Travels*, 320.

31. Swanton, *Indians of the Southeast*, 628–29.

32. A number of recordings of Southeastern Indian music are now available: *Delaware, Cherokee, Choctaw, Creek* (L37), Archive of Folksong, Library of Congress; *Songs of the Muskogee Creek*, 2 records, Taos, N. M.: Indian House; *Songs of the Seminole Indians of Florida*, Folkways FE 4383.

33. Marcia Herndon, "The Cherokee Ballgame Cycle: An Ethnomusicologist's View," *Ethnomusicology* 15(1971):342.

34. Ibid.

35. Bruno Nettl, *North American Indian Musical Styles*, Memoirs of the American Folklore Society, vol. 45 (Philadelphia: American Folklore Society, 1954), 33–36.

36. Frances Densmore, "Choctaw Music," *Anthropological Paper* no. 28, *Bureau of American Ethnology Bulletin* no. 136 (Washington, D. C., 1943), 101–88. James Howard regards Densmore's suggestion of an African influence to be an absurdity, saying that these devices were too widespread

at an early date to have been an African borrowing.

37. Swanton, "Religious Beliefs of the Creeks," 524–27.

38. Speck and Broom, *Cherokee Dance and Drama*, 24–39.

39. Stewart Culin, "Games of the North American Indians," *Twenty-fourth Annual Report of the Bureau of American Ethnology* (Washington, D. C., 1907), 562.

40. Tuggle, *Shem, Ham & Japheth*, 55.

41. Ibid.

42. Ibid., 36.

43. Ibid.

44. Swanton, *Indian Tribes of the Lower Mississippi Valley*, 117.

45. Unless otherwise noted, this account of the ball game as it was played by the Cherokees is drawn from Mooney's "Cherokee Ball Play."

46. Milanich and Sturtevant, *Pareja's Confessionario*, 30.

47. Raymond D. Fogelson, "The Cherokee Ballgame Cycle: An Ethnographer's View," *Ethnomusicology* 15(1971):333; Speck and Broom, *Cherokee Dance and Drama*, 60. One suspects that this act of "stepping" on the enemy by the women may also have been a symbolic way of exposing them to menstrual blood.

48. Marcia Herndon, "Cherokee Ballgame Cycle," 344–45.

49. This *"Hu-u"* is reminiscent of the sound which the Natchez uttered when greeting or addressing the Great Sun and his relatives.

50. This is reminiscent of the Natchez custom of eating cooked dog meat as part of the ritual prior to warfare. See chap. 4.

51. Fogelson, "Cherokee Ballgame Cycle," 335.

52. Ibid., 331.

53. Tuggle, *Shem, Ham & Japheth*, 55.

54. Modern Cherokees generally play the game using a small, red, rubber ball. They now use one ball stick instead of two.

55. Reid, *Law of Blood*, 181.

56. Fogelson, "Cherokee Ballgame Cycle," 332.

57. Culin, "Games," 604–5. James Howard tells me that the game was revived in the 1950s at a Cajun festival in Louisiana.

58. Howard, *Southeastern Ceremonial Complex*, 62–63, 144–48.

59. Culin, "Games," 420.

60. Ibid., 421.

61. Ibid., 485–86.

62. Fundaburk and Foreman, *Sun Circles*, plates 47, 50.

63. Culin, "Games," 486.

64. Swanton, *Indian Tribes of the Lower Mississippi Valley*, 90–91.

65. Culin, "Games," 463–69.

66. Cf. Fogelson, "Cherokee Ballgame Cycle," 330–31.

67. Culin, "Games," 428–31.
68. Ibid., 441, 445.
69. Swanton, *Indians of the Southeast*, 684–86.

CHAPTER 8. A CONQUERED PEOPLE

1. John A. Caruso, *The Southern Frontier* (Indianapolis and New York: Bobbs-Merrill, 1963).
2. Herbert E. Bolton, "The Mission as a Frontier Institution in the Spanish-American Colonies," *American Historical Review* 23(1917):42–61; John T. Lanning, *The Spanish Missions of Georgia* (Chapel Hill, N. C.: Univ. of North Carolina Press, 1935).
3. Verner W. Crane, *The Southern Frontier, 1670–1732* (Ann Arbor: Univ. of Michigan Press, 1929), 13.
4. Ibid., 45–46.
5. Edmund Atkin, *Indians of the Southern Colonial Frontier*, 8.
6. Crane, *Southern Frontier*, 110–12.
7. Ibid., 114.
8. Ibid., 139–40.
9. Ibid., 165–67.
10. Quoted in Crane, *Southern Frontier*, 263.
11. Atkin, *Indians of the Southern Colonial Frontier*, 26.
12. Ibid., 35.
13. Corkran, *Creek Frontier*.
14. Ibid., 298–99.
15. Ulrich B. Phillips, *Life and Labor in the Old South* (Boston: Little, Brown, 1929), 21–23.
16. Jackson Turner Main, *The Social Structure of Revolutionary America* (Princeton, N. J.: Princeton Univ. Press, 1965), 44.
17. Phillips, *Old South*, 29.
18. Ibid., 95.
19. Main, *Revolutionary America*, 44.
20. Ibid., 54–55.
21. Ibid., 48–49.
22. Hudson, *Catawba Nation*, 59.
23. Charles Crowe, "Indians and Blacks in White America," in *Four Centuries of Southern Indians*, ed. Charles Hudson (Athens, Ga.: University of Georgia Press, 1975).
24. Hudson, *Catawba Nation*, 56.
25. William S. Willis, "Divide and Rule: Red, White, and Black in the Southeast," *The Journal of Negro History* 48(1963):157–76.
26. Phillips, *Old South*, 100–101.

27. Arthur H. DeRosier, Jr., *The Removal of the Choctaw Indians* (Knoxville: Univ. of Tennessee Press, 1970), 23–28.

28. Ibid., 106.

29. Ibid., 38–52.

30. Ibid., 49–55.

31. F. P. Prucha, "Andrew Jackson's Indian Policy: A Reassessment," *Journal of American History* 56(1969):530.

32. Quoted in Prucha, 529.

33. DeRosier, *Choctaw Indians*, 111–12.

34. Ibid., 135–36.

35. Unless otherwise noted, the following pages on removal are drawn from Grant Foreman's *Indian Removal*.

36. Arrell M. Gibson, *The Chickasaws*, 173–81.

37. Sturtevant, "Creek into Seminole," 101–11; John W. Blassingame, *The Slave Community: Plantation Life in the Antebellum South* (New York: Oxford Univ. Press, 1972), 120–24.

38. Quoted in Foreman, *Indian Removal*, 360.

39. Tuggle, *Shem, Ham & Japheth*, 61–65, 82, 126–28.

40. Angie Debo, *A History of the Indians of the United States* (Norman, Okla.: Univ. of Oklahoma Press, 1970), 248–50.

41. Ibid., 251–52.

42. Ibid., 258–61.

43. Ibid., 264.

44. Albert L. Wahrhaftig, "The Tribal Population of Eastern Oklahoma," *Current Anthropology* 9(1968):510–18.

45. Albert L. Wahrhaftig and Robert K. Thomas, "Renaissance and Repression: The Oklahoma Cherokee," *Trans-action* 6(1969):42–48.

46. Howard, *Southeastern Ceremonial Complex*, 80–119; Claude Medford, Jr., "Notes" to *Songs of the Muskogee Creeks*, 2 records, (Taos, N. M.: Indian House); Frank G. Speck, "The Creek Indians of Taskigi Town," *American Anthropological Association Memoirs*, vol. 2, pt. 1 (1907):134–44. I am grateful to James Howard for giving these passages on contemporary Southeastern ceremonialism a critical reading and for allowing me to use some of his unpublished materials.

47. J. Anthony Parades and Kaye Lenihan, "Native American Population in the Southeastern States, 1960–1970," *Florida Anthropologist* 26(1973):45–56.

48. Brewton Berry, *Almost White* (New York: Macmillan, 1963).

49. Edgar T. Thompson, "The Little Races," *American Anthropologist* 74(1972):1295–1306.

50. John Gulick, *Cherokees at the Crossroads* (Chapel Hill, N. C.: Institute for Research in Social Science, 1960), 128.

51. Ibid., 128–29.

52. Ibid., 4–7.

53. Ibid., 9–11.

54. Ibid., 18–20.

55. Sturtevant, "Creek into Seminole," 108–12.

56. Ibid., 117–18.

57. Ibid., 120.

58. Garbarino, *Big Cypress*, 17–19.

59. Ibid., 19–29.

60. Ibid., 30–83.

61. John H. Peterson, Jr., "Louisiana Choctaw Life at the End of the Nineteenth Century," in *Four Centuries of Southern Indians*, ed. Charles Hudson (Athens, Ga.: Univ. of Georgia Press, 1975), 101–12.

62. John H. Peterson, Jr., "Mississippi Band of Choctaw Indians," 24–59.

63. Ibid., 60–139.

64. Ibid., 197–218.

65. Aline Rothe, *Kalita's People: A History of the Alabama-Coushatta Indians of Texas* (Waco, Tex.: Texian Press, 1963).

66. Parades and Lenihan, "Native American Population," 50.

67. W. McKee Evans, *To Die Game: The Story of the Lowry Band, Indian Guerillas of Reconstruction* (Baton Rouge, La.: Louisiana State Univ. Press, 1971), 20–31.

68. Ibid., 55.

69. Ibid., 196–259.

70. Ibid., 255–56.

71. Hudson, *Catawba Nation*.

72. Local whites call them "Sabines," a term which they consider to be derogatory. Ann Fischer, "History and Current Status of the Houma Indians," in *The American Indian Today*, eds. Stuart Levine and Nancy O. Lurie (Baltimore: Penguin Books, 1970), 212–35.

73. J. Anthony Parades, "The Emergence of Contemporary Eastern Creek Indian Identity," in *Social and Cultural Identity: Problems of Persistence and Change*, ed. Thomas Fitzgerald, Southern Anthropological Society Proceedings, no. 8 (Athens, Ga.: Univ. of Georgia Press, 1974), 63–80.

74. Alvin M. Josephy, Jr., *Red Power: The American Indians' Fight for Freedom* (New York: American Heritage Press, 1971), 155–66; Jesse Burt and Robert B. Ferguson, *Indians of the Southeast: Then and Now* (Nashville and New York: Abingdon Press, 1973), 241–63.

75. Berry, *Almost White*.

76. J. K. Dane and B. Eugene Griessman, "The Collective Identity of Marginal Peoples: The North Carolina Experience," *American An-*

thropologist 74(1972):694–704.

77. Lynwood Montell, *The Saga of Coe Ridge: A Study in Oral History* (Knoxville: Univ. of Tennessee Press, 1970); Lynwood Montell, "The Coe Ridge Colony: A Racial Island Disappears," *American Anthropologist* 74(1972):710–19.

78. Parades, "Contemporary Eastern Creek Indian Identity."

79. Phillips, *Life and Labor*, 349.

80. Sam Hilliard, "Hog Meat and Cornpone: Food Habits in the Ante-Bellum South," *Proceedings of the American Philosophical Society* 113(1969):8.

81. Wigginton, *Foxfire Book*, 167–84.

82. Ibid., 230–48.

83. Tuggle, *Shem, Ham & Japheth*, 171–72.

84. Ibid., 276.

85. Wild game was regularly and extensively used as food in the South until the Civil War, and it was of some importance for many years thereafter. See Hilliard, "Hog Meat and Cornpone," 1–2, 7–8. Some old Southern hunting techniques are almost certainly Indian, as for example, the turkey call made from the small bone from a turkey's wing. See Wigginton, *Foxfire Book*, 260.

BIBLIOGRAPHY

Abelson, Philip H. "Prevention of Cancer." *Science* 182(1973):973.

Adair, James. *The History of the American Indians.* New York: Johnson Reprint Corp., 1968. First published in 1775.

Adney, Edwin T., and Chapelle, Howard I. *The Bark Canoes and Skin Boats of North America.* United States National Museum Bulletin, no. 230. Washington, D. C.: Smithsonian Institution, 1964.

Atkin, Edmond. *Indians of the Southern Colonial Frontier: The Edmond Atkin Report and Plan of 1755.* Edited by Wilbur R. Jacobs. Columbia, S. C.: Univ. of South Carolina Press, 1954.

Bartram, William. "Observations on the Creek and Cherokee Indians, 1789," *Transactions of the American Ethnological Society*, vol. 3, pt. 1 (1853):1–81.

————. *The Travels of William Bartram.* Edited by Francis Harper. New Haven: Yale Univ. Press, 1958. First published in 1791.

Battle, H. B. "The Domestic Use of Oil Among the Southern Aborigines." *American Anthropologist* 24(1922):171–82.

Berry, Brewton. *Almost White.* New York: Macmillan, 1963.

Black, Glenn A. *Angel Site: An Archaeological, Historical, and Ethnological Study.* 2 vols. Indianapolis: Indiana Historical Society, 1967.

Blassingame, John W. *The Slave Community: Plantation Life in the Antebellum South.* New York: Oxford Univ. Press, 1972.

Bolton, Herbert E. "The Mission as a Frontier Institution in the Spanish-American Colonies." *American Historical Review* 23(1917):42–61.

Bossu, Jean-Bernard. *Travels in the Interior of North America, 1751–1762.* Translated and edited by Seymour Feiler. Norman, Okla.: Univ. of Oklahoma Press, 1962.

Bourne, Edward Gaylord, ed. *Narratives of the Career of Hernando de Soto*, vols. I and II. New York: A. S. Barnes and Co., 1904.

Brain, Jeffrey P. "The Natchez 'Paradox'." *Ethnology* 10(1971):215–22.

Brasser, T. J. C. "The Coastal Algonkians: People of the First Frontiers." In *North American Indians in Historical Perspective*, edited by Eleanor

B. Leacock and Nancy O. Lurie. New York: Random House, 1971.

Brown, James A. "The Dimensions of Status in the Burials at Spiro." *American Antiquity*, vol. 36, no. 3, pt. 2 (1971):92–112.

Burnett, E. K. *The Spiro Mound Collection in the Museum*. Contributions from the Museum of the American Indian, Heye Foundation, vol. 14. New York: Museum of the American Indian, Heye Foundation, 1945.

Burt, Jesse, and Ferguson, Robert B. *Indians of the Southeast: Then and Now*. Nashville and New York: Abingdon Press, 1973.

Bushnell, David I., Jr. "The Account of Lamhatty." *American Anthropologist* 10(1908):568–74.

Buswell, James O. "Florida Seminole Religious Ritual: Resistance and Change." Ph.D. dissertation, St. Louis Univ., 1972.

Cabeza de Vaca, Alvar Nuñez. *The Journey of Alvar Nuñez Cabeza de Vaca*. Edited by Ad. F. Bandelier. New York: Allerton Book Co., 1904.

Cable, Harold; Hudson, Charles; and Merrill, William. "The Black Drink of the Southeastern Indians." Paper read at the 1971 meeting of the American Society for Ethnohistory, at Athens, Ga.

Caldwell, Joseph R. "Eastern North America." In *Courses Toward Urban Life*, edited by R. J. Braidwood and Gordon R. Willey. Chicago: Aldine Publishing Co., 1962.

Campbell, T. N. "Choctaw Subsistence: Ethnographic Notes from the Lincecum Manuscript." *Florida Anthropologist* 12(1959):9–24.

Capron, Louis. "The Medicine Bundles of the Florida Seminole and the Green Corn Dance." *Anthropological Papers*, no. 35, *Bureau of American Ethnology Bulletin*, no. 151. Washington, D. C., 1953, pp. 155–210.

Caras, Rogert A. *North American Mammals*. New York: Meredith Press, 1967.

Carneiro, Robert L. "A Theory of the Origin of the State," *Science* 169(1970):733–38.

Caruso, John A. *The Southern Frontier*. Indianapolis and New York: The Bobbs-Merrill Co., 1963.

Ceci, Lynn. "Fish Fertilizer: A Native North American Practice?" *Science* 188(1975):26–30.

Chafe, Wallace L. "Siouan, Iroquoian, and Caddoan." In *Current Trends in Linguistics*, vol. 10, pt. 2, edited by Thomas A. Sebeok. The Hague: Mouton, 1973, pp. 1164–1209.

Chagnon, Napoleon A. *Yanomamö: The Fierce People*. New York: Holt, Rinehart and Winston, 1968.

Clark, Grahame. *The Stone Age Hunters*. New York: McGraw-Hill, 1967.

Coe, Joffre L. "The Cultural Sequence of the Carolina Piedmont." In *Archaeology of Eastern United States*, edited by James B. Griffin.

Chicago: Univ. of Chicago Press, 1952, pp. 301–11.

———. *The Formative Cultures of the Carolina Piedmont*. Transactions of the American Philosophical Society, vol. 54, pt. 5(1964).

Compton, Millard F. "History of the Moundbuilders." Moundsville, W. Va.: Marshall County Council, Parent-Teacher Associations, 1938.

Conklin, Harold C. "Shifting Cultivation." *Annals of the New York Academy of Sciences* 17(1954):133–42.

Corkran, David H. *The Creek Frontier, 1540–1783*. Norman, Okla.: Univ. of Oklahoma Press, 1967.

Crane, Verner W. *The Southern Frontier, 1670–1732*. Ann Arbor: Univ. of Michigan Press, 1929.

Crawford, James M. "The Mobilian Trade Jargon." Paper read at the 1972 meeting of the Southern Anthropological Society, at Columbia, Missouri.

———. "Southeastern Indian Languages." In *Studies in Southeastern Indian Languages*, edited by James. M. Crawford. Athens, Ga.: Univ. of Georgia Press, 1975.

Crosby, Alfred W., Jr. *The Columbian Exchange: Biological and Cultural Consequences of 1492*. Westport, Conn.: Greenwood Press, 1972.

Crowe, Charles, "Indians and Blacks in White America." In *Four Centuries of Southern Indians*, edited by Charles Hudson. Athens, Ga.: Univ. of Georgia Press, 1975.

Culin, Stewart. "Games of the North American Indians." *Twenty-fourth Annual Report of the Bureau of American Ethnology*. Washington, D. C., 1907.

Cumming, William P. *The Southeast in Early Maps*. Chapel Hill, N. C.: Univ. of North Carolina Press, 1962.

Cushing, Frank H. "Exploration of Ancient Key Dwellers' Remains on the Gulf Coast of Florida." *Proceedings of the American Philosophical Society* 35(1896):382–89.

Cutler, Hugh C., and Blake, Leonard W. "Travels of Corn and Squash." In *Man Across the Sea: Problems of Pre-Columbian Contacts*, edited by Carroll L. Riley et al. Austin, Tex.: Univ. of Texas Press, 1971.

Dane, J. K., and Griessman, B. Eugene. "The Collective Identity of Marginal Peoples: The North Carolina Experience." *American Anthropologist* 74(1972):694–704.

Davis, Hester A. "An Introduction to Parkin Prehistory." *The Arkansas Archaeologist* 7(1966).

Debo, Angie. *A History of the Indians of the United States*. Norman, Okla.: Univ. of Oklahoma Press, 1970.

Deloria, Vine, Jr. *Custer Died for Your Sins: An Indian Manifesto*. New York: Avon, 1970.

Densmore, Frances. "Choctaw Music." *Anthropological paper*, no. 28, *Bureau of American Ethnology Bulletin*, no. 136. Washington, D. C., 1943, pp. 101–88.

DeRosier, Arthur H., Jr. *The Removal of the Choctaw Indians*. Knoxville: Univ. of Tennessee Press, 1970.

Dickens, Roy S., Jr. "The Appalachian Summit: A.D. 1000 to Bartram." In *The Southeast*, edited by Raymond Fogelson. vol. XIII of *Handbook of North American Indians*, edited by William C. Sturtevant. Washington, D. C.: Smithsonian Institution, in press.

Dobyns, Henry F. "An Appraisal of Techniques with a New Hemisphere Estimate." *Current Anthropology* 7(1966):395–416.

Douglas, Mary. *Purity and Danger*. London: Routledge and Kegan Paul, 1966.

Eggan, Fred. "Historical Changes in the Choctaw Kinship System." *American Anthropologist* 39(1937):34–52.

Elliott, J. H. *The Old World and the New, 1492–1650*. Cambridge: At the University Press, 1970.

Evans, W. McKee. *To Die Game: The Story of the Lowry Band, Indian Guerillas of Reconstruction*. Baton Rouge, La.: Louisiana State Univ. Press, 1971.

Evans-Pritchard, E. E. "The Divine Kingship of the Shilluk of the Nilotic Sudan." In *Social Anthropology and Other Essays*. New York: Free Press of Glencoe, 1962.

Faulkner, Charles H. *The Old Stone Fort: Exploring an Archaeological Mystery*. Knoxville: Univ. of Tennessee Press, 1968.

Fenneman, Nevin M. "Physiographic Divisions of the United States." *Annals of the Association of American Geographers*. 3d ed., revised and enlarged, 18(1928):261–353.

Fenton, William N. *Parker on the Iroquois*. Syracuse, N. Y.: Syracuse Univ. Press, 1968.

Fernald, Merritt Lyndon, and Kinsey, Alfred Charles. *Edible Wild Plants of Eastern North America*. Cornwall-on-Hudson, N. Y.: Idlewild Press, 1943.

Fewkes, Vladimir J. "Catawba Pottery-Making, with Notes on Pamunkey Pottery-Making, Cherokee Pottery-Making, and Coiling." *Proceedings of the American Philosophical Society* 88(1944):69–124.

Fischer, Ann. "History and Current Status of the Houma Indians." In *The American Indian Today*, edited by Stuart Levine and Nancy O. Lurie. Baltimore: Penguin Books, 1970.

Fogelson, Raymond D. "The Cherokee Ballgame Cycle: An Ethnographer's View." *Ethnomusicology* 15(1971):327–38.

————. "An Analysis of Cherokee Sorcery and Witchcraft." In *Four*

Centuries of Southern Indians, edited by Charles Hudson. Athens, Ga.: Univ. of Georgia Press, 1975.

Foreman, Grant. *Indian Removal: The Emigration of the Five Civilized Tribes of Indians*. Norman, Okla.: Univ. of Oklahoma Press, 1932.

Fowler, Melvin L. "Middle Mississippian Agricultural Fields." *American Antiquity* 34(1969):365–75.

————. "Cahokia: Ancient Capital of The Midwest." *Addison-Wesley Module in Anthropology*, no. 48(1974).

Fried, Morton H. *The Evolution of Political Society: An Essay on Political Anthropology*. New York: Random House, 1967.

Fundaburk, Emma Lila, and Foreman, Mary D. F. *Sun Circles and Human Hands*. Luverne, Ala., 1957.

Galinat, Walton C. "The Evolution of Corn and Culture in North America." *Economic Botany* 19(1965):350–57.

Garbarino, Merwyn S. *Big Cypress: A Changing Seminole Community*. New York: Holt, Rinehart and Winston, 1972.

Garcilaso de la Vega, G. S. *The Florida of the Inca*. Translated and edited by J. G. Varner and J. J. Varner. Austin, Tex.: Univ. of Texas Press, 1951.

Gerlach, Arch C., ed. *The National Atlas of the United States*. United States Department of the Interior. Washington, D. C., 1970.

Gibson, Arrell M. *The Chickasaws*. Norman, Okla.: Univ. of Oklahoma Press, 1971.

Gibson, Jon L. "Aboriginal Warfare in The Protohistoric Southeast: An Alternative Perspective." *American Antiquity* 39(1974):130–33.

Gilbert, William Harlen, Jr. *The Eastern Cherokees*. Bureau of American Ethnology Bulletin, no. 133. Washington, D. C., 1943, pp. 169–413.

Goggin, John M. "Style Areas in Historic Southeastern Art." In *Indian Tribes of Aboriginal America*, vol. 3, edited by Sol Tax. Proceedings of the 29th Congress of Americanists. Chicago: Univ. of Chicago Press, 1952.

Goggin, John M., and Sturtevant, William C. "The Calusa: A Stratified Nonagricultural Society (With Notes on Sibling Marriage)." In *Explorations in Cultural Anthropology in Honor of George Peter Murdock*, edited by Ward H. Goodenough. New York: McGraw-Hill, 1964.

Gordon, Cyrus H. *Before Columbus: Links Between the Old World and Ancient America*. New York: Crown Publishers, 1971.

Greenlee, Robert F. "Medicine and Curing Practices of the Modern Florida Seminole." *American Anthropologist* 46(1944):317–28.

Greer, E. S., Jr. "A Tuckabahchee Plate from the Coosa River." *Journal of Alabama Archaeology* 12(1966):156–58.

Griffin, James B. "Mesoamerica and the Eastern United States in Prehistoric Times." In *Archaeological Frontiers and External Connections*, edited by G. Ekholm and G. R. Willey. Handbook of Middle American Indians, vol. IV. Austin, Tex.: Univ. of Texas Press, 1966.

————. "Eastern North American Archaeology: A Summary." *Science* 156(1967):175–91.

Gulick, John. *Cherokees at the Crossroads*. Chapel Hill, N. C.: Institute for Research in Social Science, 1960.

Haas, Mary R. "Creek Inter-Town Relations." *American Anthropologist* 42(1940):479–89.

————. "Southeastern Indian Linguistics." In *Red, White, and Black: Symposium on Indians in the Old South*, edited by Charles Hudson. Southern Anthropological Society Proceedings, no. 5. Athens, Ga.: Univ. of Georgia Press, 1971.

————. "The Southeast." In *Current Trends in Linguistics*, vol. 10, pt. 2, edited by Thomas A. Sebeok. The Hague: Mouton, 1973, pp. 1210–49.

Hallowell, A. I. "Bear Ceremonialism in the Northern Hemisphere." *American Anthropologist* 28(1926):1–175.

Hally, David J. "The Archaeology of European-Indian Contact in the Southeast." In *Red, White, and Black: Symposium on Indians in the Old South*, edited by Charles Hudson. Southern Anthropological Society Proceedings, no. 5. Athens, Ga.: Univ. of Georgia Press, 1971.

Harper, Jared V. "The Adoption and Use of the Horse among the Southeastern Indians." Paper read at the 1974 meeting of the Southern Anthropological Society, at Blacksburg, Va.

Harris, David R. "Swidden Systems and Settlement." In *Man, Settlement and Urbanism*, edited by Peter J. Ucko, Ruth Tringham, and G. W. Dimbleby. London: Gerald Duckworth and Co., 1972.

Haynes, C. Vance, Jr. "Elephant Hunting in North America." *Scientific American*, 214(1966):104–12.

————. "The Earliest Americans." *Science* 166(1969):709–15.

————. "The Calico Site: Artifacts or Geofacts?" *Science* 181(1973): 305–10.

Herndon, G. Melvin. "Indian Agriculture in the Southern Colonies." *The North Carolina Historical Review* 44(1967):283–97.

Herndon, Marcia. "The Cherokee Ballgame Cycle: An Ethnomusicologist's View." *Ethnomusicology* 15(1971):339–52.

Hilliard, Sam. "Hog Meat and Cornpone: Food Habits in the Ante-Bellum South." *Proceedings of the American Philosophical Society* 113(1969):1–13.

Holder, Preston. *The Hoe and the Horse on the Plains: A Study of Cultural Development Among North American Indians*. Lincoln, Neb.: Univ. of Nebraska Press, 1970.

Holmes, William H. "Art in Shell of the Ancient Americans." *Second Annual Report of the Bureau of American Ethnology*. Washington, D. C., 1883.

_____. "Aboriginal Pottery of the Eastern United States." *Twentieth Annual Report of the Bureau of American Ethnology*. Washington, D. C., 1903.

Horton, Robin. "African Traditional Thought and Western Science." Two parts. *Africa* 38(1967):50–71; 177–87.

Howard, James H. *The Southeastern Ceremonial Complex and Its Interpretation*. Missouri Archaeological Society Memoir, no. 6. Columbia, Mo., 1968.

Hudson, Charles. "Isometric Advantages of the Cradle Board: A Hypothesis." *American Anthropologist* vol. 68, no. 2, pt. 1 (1966):470–74.

_____. *The Catawba Nation*. Athens, Ga.: Univ. of Georgia Press, 1970.

_____. "The Cherokee Concept of Natural Balance." *The Indian Historian* 3(1970):51–54.

_____. ed. *Red, White, and Black: Symposium on Indians in the Old South*. Southern Anthropological Society Proceedings, no. 5. Athens, Ga.: Univ. of Georgia Press, 1971.

_____. " 'Sociosomatic' Illness." Manuscript.

_____. "Catawba." In *The Southeast*, edited by Raymond Fogelson. Handbook of North American Indians, vol. 13. Washington, D. C.: Smithsonian Institution, forthcoming.

Hudson, Charles; Butler, Ronald; and Sikes, Dennis. "Arthritis in the Prehistoric Southeastern United States: Biological and Cultural Variables." *American Journal of Physical Anthropology* 43(1975):57–62.

Jennings, Jesse D. *Prehistory of North America*. New York: McGraw-Hill, 1968.

Josephy, Alvin M., Jr. *Red Power: The American Indians' Fight for Freedom*. New York: American Heritage Press, 1971.

Kaplan, Lawrence. "Archaeology and Domestication in American Phaseolus (Beans)." *Economic Botany* 19(1965):358–68.

Katz, S. H.; Hediger, M. L.; and Valleroy, L. A. "Traditional Maize Processing Techniques in the New World." *Science* 184(1974):765–73.

Kilpatrick, Jack F., and Kilpatrick, Anna G. *Walk in Your Soul: Love Incantations of the Oklahoma Cherokees*. Dallas: Southern Methodist Univ. Press, 1965.

_____. "Eastern Cherokee Folk Tales Reconstructed from the Field Notes of Frans M. Olbrechts." *Anthropological Paper*, no. 80, *Bureau of American Ethnology Bulletin*, no. 196. Washington, D. C., 1966.

_____. *Run Toward the Nightland: Magic of the Oklahoma Cherokees*. Dallas: Southern Methodist Univ. Press, 1967.

Knowles, Nathaniel. "The Torture of Captives by the Indians of Eastern North America." *Proceedings of the American Philosophical Society* 82(1940):151–225.

Lahren, Larry, and Bonnichsen, Robson. "Bone Foreshafts From a Clovis Burial in Southwestern Montana." *Science* 186(1974):147–50.

Lanning, John T. *The Spanish Missions of Georgia.* Chapel Hill, N. C.: Univ. of North Carolina Press, 1935.

Larson, Lewis H., Jr. "Archaeological Implications of Social Stratification at the Etowah Site, Georgia." *American Antiquity*, vol. 36, no. 3, pt. 2 (1971):58–67.

————. "Functional Considerations of Warfare in the Southeast During the Mississippian Period." *American Antiquity* 37(1972):383–92.

Lawson, John. *A New Voyage to Carolina.* Edited by Hugh Talmage Lefler. Chapel Hill, N. C.: Univ. of North Carolina Press, 1967.

Leach, Edmund R. *Political Systems of Highland Burma: A Study of Kachin Social Structure.* Cambridge, Mass.: Harvard University Press, 1954.

Lear, John. "Ancient Landings in America." *Saturday Review*, 18 July 1970, pp. 18–19, 34.

Lesser, Alexander, and Weltfish, Gene. "The Composition of the Caddoan Linguistic Stock." *Smithsonian Miscellaneous Collections*, vol. 87, no. 6(1932):1–15.

Lewis, Thomas M. N., and Lewis, Madeline Kneberg. *Eva: An Archaic Site.* Knoxville: Univ. of Tennessee Press, 1961.

Lively, Matthew. "The Lively Complex: Announcing a Pebble Tool Industry in Alabama." *Journal of Alabama Archaeology*, 11(1965):103–22.

Long, Joseph K. "A Test of Multiple-Discriminant Analysis as a Means of Determining Evolutionary Changes and Intergroup Relationships in Physical Anthropology." *American Anthropologist* 68(1966):444–64.

Lorant, Stefan, ed. *The New World: The First Pictures of America.* Rev. ed. New York: Duell, Sloan, and Pearce, 1965.

McHugh, Tom. *The Time of the Buffalo.* New York: Alfred A. Knopf, 1972.

MacLeod, William C. "Priests, Temples, and the Practice of Mummification in Southeastern North America." *Proceedings of the International Congress of Americanists*, 22d Congress, vol. 2, Rome, 1926.

MacNeish, Richard S. "Early Man in the Andes." *Scientific American*, 224(1971):36–46.

Main, Jackson Turner. *The Social Structure of Revolutionary America.* Princeton, N. J.: Princeton Univ. Press, 1965.

Martin, Calvin. "Fire and Forest Structure in the Aboriginal Eastern Forest." *The Indian Historian* 6(1973):38–42, 54.

Martin, Paul S. "The Discovery of America." *Science* 179(1973):969–74.

Mason, Otis T. *Aboriginal American Basketry: Studies in a Textile Art Without Machinery*. Annual Report of the Board of Regents of the Smithsonian Institution for 1902. Washington, D. C.: 1904.

Meyer, William E. "Indian Trails of the Southeast." *Forty-second Annual Report of the Bureau of American Ethnology*. Washington, D. C., 1928, pp. 727–857.

Milanich, Jerald, and Sturtevant, William C., eds. *Francisco Pareja's 1613 Confessionario: A Documentary Source for Timucuan Ethnography*. Tallahassee, Fla.: Division of Archives, History, and Records Management, Fla. Dept. of State, 1972.

Milfort, Louis Le Clerc. *Memoirs, or a Quick Glance at My Various Travels and My Sojourn in the Creek Nation*. Translated and edited by Ben C. McCary. Savannah, Ga.: The Beehive Press, 1972.

Montell, Lynwood. *The Saga of Coe Ridge: A Study in Oral History*. Knoxville: Univ. of Tennessee Press, 1970.

————. "The Coe Ridge Colony: A Racial Island Disappears." *American Anthropologist* 74(1972):710–19.

Mooney, James. "The Sacred Formulas of the Cherokees." *Seventh Annual Report of the Bureau of American Ethnology*. Washington, D. C.: 1886.

————. "The Cherokee Ball Play." *American Anthropologist* 3(1890):105–32.

————. "Cherokee Theory and Practice of Medicine." *Journal of American Folklore* 3(1890):44–50.

————. *The Siouan Tribes of the East*. Bureau of American Ethnology Bulletin, no. 22 Washington, D. C., 1894.

————. "The Cherokee River Cult." *The Journal of American Folklore* 13(1900):1–10.

————. "Myths of the Cherokee." *Nineteenth Annual Report of the Bureau of American Ethnology*. Washington, D. C., 1900.

Mooney, James, and Olbrechts, Frans M. *The Swimmer Manuscript: Cherokee Sacred Formulas and Medicinal Prescriptions*. Bureau of American Ethnology Bulletin, no. 99. Washington, D. C., 1932.

Moore, Clarence B. "Moundville Revisited." *Journal of the Academy of Natural Sciences of Philadelphia*, 2d. series, vol. 13, pt. 3(1907): 337–405.

Müller-Beck, Hansjürgen. "Paleohunters in America: Origins and Diffusion." *Science* 156(1966):1191–1210.

Murphy, Christopher, and Hudson, Charles. "On the Problem of Intensive Agriculture in the Aboriginal Southeastern United States." *Working Papers in Sociology and Anthropology* 2(1968):24–34. Mimeographed.

Nash, Charles H., and Gates, Rodney, Jr. "Chucalissa Indian Town." *Tennessee Historical Quarterly* 21(1962):103–21.

Nash, Gary B. *Red, White, and Black: The Peoples of Early America.* Englewood Cliffs, N. J.: Prentice-Hall, 1974.

Neill, Wilfred T. "Dugouts of the Mikasuki Seminole." *Florida Anthropologist* 6(1953):77–84.

———. "Coracles or Skin Boats of the Southeastern Indians." *Florida Anthropologist* 7(1954):119–26.

Netting, Robert McC. "The Ecological Approach in Cultural Study." Reading, Mass.: Addison Wesley Module, 1971.

Nettl, Bruno. *North American Indian Musical Styles.* Memoirs of the American Folklore Society, vol. 45. Philadelphia: American Folklore Society, 1954.

Neumann, Georg K. "Archaeology and Race in the American Indian." In *Archaeology of Eastern United States*, edited by James B. Griffin. Chicago: Univ. of Chicago Press, 1952.

Olbrechts, Frans M. "Some Cherokee Methods of Divination." *Proceedings of the 23rd International Congress of Americanists.* New York, 1930.

———. "Cherokee Belief and Practice with Regard to Childbirth." *Anthropos* 26(1931):17–33.

Ortiz, Alfonso. "Dual Organization as an Operational Concept in the Pueblo Southwest." *Ethnology* 4(1965):389–96.

———. *The Tewa World: Space, Time, Being, and Becoming in a Pueblo Society.* Chicago: Univ. of Chicago Press, 1969.

Paige, Karen E. "Women Learn to Sing the Menstrual Blues." *Psychology Today* 7(1973):41–46.

Parades, J. Anthony. "The Emergence of Contemporary Eastern Creek Indian Identity." In *Social and Cultural Identity: Problems of Persistence and Change*, edited by Thomas Fitzgerald. Southern Anthropological Society Proceedings, no. 8. Athens, Ga.: Univ. of Georgia Press, 1974.

———, and Lenihan, Kaye. "Native American Population in the Southeastern States, 1960–1970." *Florida Anthropologist* 26(1973):45–56.

Peebles, Christopher S. "Moundville and Surrounding Sites: Some Structural Considerations of Mortuary Practices II." *American Antiquity*, vol. 36, no. 3, pt. 2 (1971):68–91.

Peterson, Harold L. *American Indian Tomahawks.* Contributions from the Museum of the American Indian, Heye Foundation, vol. 19. Glückstadt, Germany: J. J. Augustin, 1965.

Peterson, John H., Jr. "The Mississippi Band of Choctaw Indians: Their Recent History and Current Social Relations." Ph.D. dissertation,

Univ. of Georgia, 1970.

————. "Louisiana Choctaw Life at the End of the Nineteenth Century."
In *Four Centuries of Southern Indians*, edited by Charles Hudson.
Athens, Ga.: Univ. of Georgia Press, 1975.

Phelps, David S. "Mesoamerican Glyph Motifs on Southeastern Pottery."
*Verhandlungen des XXXVIII Internationalen Amerikanisten Kongres-
sen*, vol. II. Stuttgart-Munich, 1968.

Phillips, Ulrich B. *Life and Labor in the Old South*. Boston: Little, Brown,
1929.

Pollitzer, William S. "Physical Anthropology of Indians of the Old South."
In *Red, White, and Black: Symposium on Indians in the Old South*,
edited by Charles Hudson. Southern Anthropological Society Proceedings, no. 5. Athens, Ga.: Univ. of Georgia Press, 1971.

Potter, Martha A. *Ohio's Prehistoric People*. Columbus: Ohio Historical
Society, 1968.

Prucha, F. P. "Andrew Jackson's Indian Policy: A Reassessment." *Journal
of American History* 56(1969):527–39.

Quinn, David B., ed. *North American Discovery, Circa 1000–1612*.
Columbia, S. C.: Univ. of South Carolina Press, 1971.

Rands, Robert L. "Comparative Notes on the Hand-Eye and Related
Motifs." *American Antiquity* 22(1957):247–57.

Reed, Nelson A. "Monks and Other Mississippian Mounds." In *Explora-
tions into Cahokia Archaeology*, edited by Melvin L. Fowler. Illinois
Archaeological Survey Bulletin, no. 7. Urbana, Ill.: Univ. of Illinois
Press, 1969.

Reid, John P. *A Law of Blood: Primitive Law of the Cherokee Nation*. New
York: New York Univ. Press, 1970.

Ribaut, Jean. *The Whole and True discoverye of* Terra Florida. 1563
facsimile edition by Jeanette T. Conner. Deland, Fla.: Florida Historical
Society, 1927.

Riley, Carroll L., et al., eds. *Man Across the Sea: Problems of Pre-
Columbian Contacts*. Austin, Tex.: Univ. of Texas Press, 1971.

Rockwood, Joyce. *Long Man's Song*. New York: Holt, Rinehart and
Winston, 1975.

Romans, Bernard. *A Concise Natural History of East and West Florida*.
Facsimile reproduction of the 1775 edition. Gainesville, Fla.: Univ. of
Florida Press, 1962.

Ross, Mary. "With Pardo and Boyano on the Fringes of the Georgia Land."
The Georgia Historical Quarterly 14(1930):267–85.

Rostlund, Erhard. *Freshwater Fish and Fishing in Native North America*.
Univ. of California Publications in Geography, vol. 9. Berkeley: Univ. of
California Press, 1952.

Rothe, Aline. *Kalita's People: A History of the Alabama-Coushatta Indians of Texas*. Waco, Tex.: Texian Press, 1963.

Schorger, A. W. *The Passenger Pigeon: Its Natural History and Extinction*. Madison, Wis.: Univ. of Wisconsin Press, 1955.

————. *The Wild Turkey: Its History and Domestication*. Norman, Okla.: Univ. of Oklahoma Press, 1966.

Sears, William H. *Excavations at Kolomoki: Final Report*. Univ. of Georgia Series in Anthropology, no. 5. Athens, Ga.: Univ. of Georgia Press, 1956.

————. "The Southeastern United States." In *Prehistoric Man in the New World*, edited by Jesse D. Jennings and Edward Norbeck. Chicago: Univ. of Chicago Press, 1964.

————. "Food Production and Village Life in Prehistoric Southeastern United States." *Archaeology* 24(1971):322–29.

Service, Elman R. *Primitive Social Organization: An Evolutionary Perspective*, 2d ed. New York: Random House, 1971.

Service, William. *Owl*. New York: Alfred A. Knopf, 1969.

Silverberg, Robert. *Mound Builders of Ancient America: The Archaeology of a Myth*. Greenwich, Conn.: New York Graphic Society, 1968.

Simmons, Henry E. "The Drug Efficacy Study: Its Effects on Therapeutics in America." Speech before the American College of Physicians, March 31, 1971, Denver, Colorado.

Sleight, Frederick W. "Kunti, a Food Staple of Florida Indians." *Florida Anthropologist* 6(1953):46–52.

Smith, Bruce D. "Middle Mississippi Exploitation of Animal Populations: A Predictive Model." *American Antiquity* 39, no. 2, pt. 1 (1974):274–91.

————. "Middle Mississippi Exploitation of the White-Tailed Deer." *Proceedings of the 30th Southeastern Archaeological Conference*, in press.

Snow, Charles E. "Indian Skeletons from the Museum Burials at Moundville." *Alabama Museum of Natural History, Museum Paper*, no. 15, pt. 1. University, Ala., 1941.

————. "Possible Evidence of Scalping at Moundville." *Alabama Museum of Natural History, Museum Paper*, no. 15, pt. 2. University, Ala. 1941.

Speck, Frank G. "The Creek Indians of Taskigi Town." *American Anthropological Association Memoirs*, vol. 2, pt. 1(1907):99–164.

————. "The Cane Blowgun in Catawba and Southeastern Ethnology." *American Anthropologist* 40(1938):198–204.

————. *Gourds of the Southeastern Indians*. Boston: The New England Gourd Society, 1941.

Speck, Frank G., and Broom, Leonard. *Cherokee Dance and Drama*.

Berkeley: Univ. of California Press, 1951.

Stewart, T. D. "Bear Paw Remains Closely Resemble Human Bones." *FBI Law Enforcement Bulletin*, vol. 30(1959), no. 7.

———. "A Physical Anthropologist's View of the Peopling of the New World." *Southwestern Journal of Anthropology* 16(1960):259–73.

Struever, Stuart. "Middle Woodland Culture History in the Great Lakes Riverine Area." *American Antiquity* 31(1965):211–23.

Struever, Stuart, and Vickery, Kent D., "The Beginnings of Cultivation in the Midwest-Riverine Area of the United States." *American Anthropologist* 75(1973):1197–1220.

Sturtevant, William C. "The Medicine Bundles and Busks of the Florida Seminole." *Florida Anthropologist* 7(1954):31–70.

———. "Historic Carolina Algonkian Cultivation of Chenopodium or Amaranthus." *Proceedings of the 21st Southeastern Archaeological Conference*, 1965, pp. 64–65.

———. "Seminole Men's Clothing." In *Essays on the Verbal and Visual Arts*, 1966 American Ethnological Society Proceedings, edited by June Helm. Seattle: Univ. of Washington Press, 1967.

———. "Lafitau's Hoes." *American Antiquity* 33(1968):93–95.

———. "History and Ethnography of Some West Indian Starches." In *The Domestication and Exploitation of Plants and Animals*, edited by Peter J. Ucko and G. W. Dimbleby. London: Gerald Duckworth and Co., 1969.

———. "Creek into Seminole." In *North American Indians in Historical Perspective*, edited by Eleanor Burke Leacock and Nancy Oestreich Lurie. New York: Random House, 1971.

Swanton, John R. *Indian Tribes of the Lower Mississippi Valley and Adjacent Coast of the Gulf of Mexico*. Bureau of American Ethnology Bulletin, no. 43. Washington, D. C., 1911.

———. "The Social Significance of the Creek Confederacy." *Proceedings of the 19th International Congress of Americanists*. Washington, D. C., 1915.

———. *Early History of the Creek Indians and Their Neighbors*. Bureau of American Ethnology Bulletin, no. 73. Washington, D. C., 1922.

———. "Religious Beliefs and Medical Practices of the Creek Indians." *Forty-second Annual Report of the Bureau of American Ethnology*. Washington, D. C., 1928, pp. 473–672.

———. "Social Organization and Social Usages of the Indians of the Creek Confederacy." *Forty-second Annual Report of the Bureau of American Ethnology*. Washington, D. C., 1928, pp. 25–472.

———. "Sun Worship in the Southeast." *American Anthropologist* 30(1928):206–13.

————. *Myths and Tales of the Southeastern Indians*. Bureau of American Ethnology Bulletin, no. 88. Washington, D. C., 1929.

————. *Source Material for the Social and Ceremonial Life of the Choctaw Indians*. Bureau of American Ethnology Bulletin, no. 103. Washington, D. C., 1931.

————. "Historic Use of the Spear-Thrower in Southeastern North America." *American Antiquity* 4(1938):356–58.

————. "The First Description of an Indian Tribe in the Territory of the Present United States." In *Studies for William A. Reed*, edited by Nathaniel M. Caffee and Thomas A. Kirby. Baton Rouge, La.: Louisiana State Univ. Press, 1940.

————. *Source Material on the History and Ethnology of the Caddo Indians*. Bureau of American Ethnology Bulletin, no. 132. Washington, D. C., 1942.

————. *The Indians of the Southeastern United States*. Bureau of American Ethnology Bulletin, no. 137. Washington, D. C., 1946.

Thompson, Edgar T. "The Little Races." *American Anthropologist* 74(1972):1295–1306.

Timberlake, Henry. *Memoirs, 1756–1765*. Edited by Samuel Cole Williams. Marietta, Ga.: Continental Book Co., 1948.

Tuggle, William Orrie. *Shem, Ham, & Japheth: The Papers of W. O. Tuggle*. Edited by Eugene Current-Garcia with Dorothy B. Hatfield. Athens, Ga.: Univ. of Georgia Press, 1973.

Ulmer, Mary, and Beck, Samuel E., eds. *Cherokee Cookery*. Cherokee, N. C.: Museum of the Cherokee Indian, 1951.

Voegelin, C. F., and Voegelin, F. M. "Languages of the World: Native America Fascicle One." *Anthropological Linguistics*, vol. 6, no. 6 (1964).

————. "Languages of the World: Native America Fascicle Two." *Anthropological Linguistics*, vol. 7, no. 7 (1965).

Vogel, Virgil J. *American Indian Medicine*. Norman, Okla.: Univ. of Oklahoma Press, 1970.

Wahrhaftig, Albert L. "The Tribal Population of Eastern Oklahoma." *Current Anthropology* 9(1968):510–18.

Wahrhaftig, Albert L., and Thomas, Robert K. "Renaissance and Repression: The Oklahoma Cherokee." *Trans-action* 6(1969):42–48.

Walker, Willard. "Notes on Native Writing Systems and the Design of Native Literacy Programs." *Anthropological Linguistics* 11(1969): 148–66.

Waring, Antonio J., Jr. "The Southern Cult and Muskhogean Ceremonial." In *The Waring Papers: The Collected Works of Antonio J. Waring, Jr.*, edited by Stephen Williams. Athens, Ga.: Univ. of Georgia Press,

1965.

Waring, Antonio J., Jr., and Holder, Preston. "A Prehistoric Ceremonial Complex in the Southeastern United States." *American Anthropologist* 47(1945):1–34.

Watson, Patty Jo, ed. *Archaeology of the Mammoth Cave Area*. New York: Academic Press, 1974.

Wauchope, Robert. *Lost Tribes and Sunken Continents: Myth and Method in the Study of American Indians*. Chicago: Univ. of Chicago Press, 1962.

Webb, Clarence H. "The Extent and Content of Poverty Point Culture." *American Antiquity* 33(1968):297–321.

Wesley, John. *The Journal of the Rev. John Wesley*, vol I. New York: E. P. Dutton, 1906.

Wheat, Joe Ben. "A Paleo-Indian Bison Kill." *Scientific American*, 216(1967):44–52.

————. "Lifeways of Early Man in North America." *Arctic Anthropology*, 8(1971):22–31.

Whitaker, Thomas W. "Endemism and Pre-Columbian Migration of The Bottle Gourd, *Lagenaria siceraria* (Mol.) Standl." In *Man Across the Sea: Problems of Pre-Columbian Contacts*, edited by Carroll L. Riley et al. Austin, Tex.: Univ. of Texas Press, 1971.

White, Douglas R.; Murdock, George P.; and Scaglion, Richard. "Natchez Class and Rank Reconsidered." *Ethnology* 10(1971):369–88.

Wigginton, Eliot. *The Foxfire Book*. New York: Anchor Books, 1972.

Will, George F., and Hyde, George E. *Corn Among the Indians of the Upper Missouri*. Lincoln, Neb.: Univ. of Nebraska Press, n.d. First published in 1917.

Willey, Gordon R. *An Introduction to American Archaeology*, vol. I. Englewood Cliffs, N. J.: Prentice-Hall, 1966.

Willis, William S. "Divide and Rule: Red, White, and Black in the Southeast." *The Journal of Negro History* 48(1963):157–76.

————. "Patrilineal Institutions in Southeastern North America." *Ethnohistory* 10(1963):250–69.

Willoughby, Charles C. "History and Symbolism of the Muskhogeans." In *Etowah Papers*, edited by Warren K. Moorehead. New Haven: Yale Univ. Press, 1932.

Wilms, Douglas C. "Cherokee Settlement Patterns in Nineteenth Century Georgia." *Southeastern Geographer* 14(1974):46–53.

Witthoft, John. "Birdlore of the Eastern Cherokee." *Journal of the Washington Academy of Science* 35(1946):372–84.

————. "Some Eastern Cherokee Bird Stories." *Journal of the Washington Academy of Science* 35(1946):177–80.

————. *Green Corn Ceremonialism in the Eastern Woodlands*. Occasional Paper from the Museum of Anthropology of the Univ. of Michigan, no. 13. Ann Arbor: Univ. of Michigan Press, 1949.

Witthoft, John, and Hadlock, Wendell S. "Cherokee-Iroquois Little People." *Journal of American Folklore* 59(1946):413–20.

Wittry, Warren L. "The American Woodhenge." In *Explorations into Cahokia Archaeology*, edited by Melvin L. Fowler. Illinois Archaeological Survey Bulletin, no. 7. Urbana, Ill.: Univ. of Illinois Press, 1969.

Wright, M. H. "American Indian Corn Dishes." *Chronicles of Oklahoma* 36(1958):155–66.

Wroth, Lawrence C. *The Voyages of Giovanni da Verrazzano, 1524–1528*. New Haven and London: Yale Univ. Press, 1970.

Yarnell, Richard A. *Aboriginal Relationships Between Culture and Plant Life in the Upper Great Lakes Region*. Univ. of Michigan Anthropological Papers, no. 23. Ann Arbor: Univ. of Michigan Press, 1964.

————. "*Early Plant Husbandry in Eastern North America*." Paper read at the 1975 meeting of the Southern Anthropological Society, at Clearwater Beach, Fla.

INDEX

Musgrove, Mary, 234
Music, 401–8; black influence on, 537;
instruments for, 65, 72, 165, 326,
373, 374, 401–2; in ritual, 229, 325,
413; songs, 402–3; in Oklahoma today, 473, 475
Muskogees, 23, 195, 464, 465, 483, 486.
See also Creeks; Seminoles

Nairne, Thomas, 439
Names, 325
Narváez, Panfilo de, 105–7, 113
Natchez: burial customs of, 328–34;
clothing among, 262, 264; cultural
distinctiveness of, 97, 336; decoration
of pipes among, 141; deer dance of,
277–79; destruction of, 122, 440; eating customs of, 309; games among,
410–11, 426; going to water among,
324; hierarchy among, 240; houses of,
216; invaded by de Soto, 116; kinship
among, 195, 518; language of, 23; location of, 5; manner of carrying burdens, 264; moieties among, 237, 522;
in Oklahoma, 473; oral traditions of,
240; political organization of, 206–10;
public giving by, 311; ritual numbers
of, 513; sacrificial killings among, 255;
seasonal ceremonies of, 365–66, 367,
410, 534; sewing among, 267; subsistence of, 279, 287, 293, 303; tattooing, 203; transvestites among, 269;
use of bone arrow points by, 273; war
flag of, 243
Natchitoches, town of, 118
Neighbors, Robert S., 470
New Echota, 449, 463, 464
Nikwasi Mound, 169–71, 516
Numbers, ritual, 134, 346, 347, 512,
513
Nuts, 286, 301, 308, 366. *See also* Food;
Gathering

Obsidian, 66, 72
Ocale Indians, 8
Occaneechi Indians, 8
Occaneechi trading path, 435
Osceola, 466, 467, 531
Ochuse, town of, 116
Ocmulgee site. *See* Macon Plateau site
Oconaluftee Village, 482

Ocute, town of, 109
Ofo language, 24
Okchai, town of, 233
Oklahoma, Five Civilized Tribes in,
469–77
Oktarharsars, 470
Old fields, 290
Old people: allowed to sleep in town
house, 219; role in Green Corn
Ceremony, 369, 372, 373; mercy kill-
ing of, 231, 330; role in subsistence,
285, 298; as witches, 362. *See also*
Beloved Old Men
Old Stone Fort, 57–59
Omahas, 9
Omens. *See* Divination; Dreams
Oneota culture, 91
Osage, 9
Oral traditions: Ball Game of Birds and
Animals, 164; contributions of, to
Southern folklore, 499–500; First
Fire, 135; geographic specificity in,
270; How Rabbit won His Wife's Sis-
ter, 162; How the World was Made,
132; The Nest of the Tlanuwa, 136;
Origin of the Bear, 161; Origin of
Corn and Game, 149; origin of Creek
clans, 194; Rabbit and the Tar-
person, 499; Raven Mocker, 179; The
Seneca Peacemakers, 241;
similarities of, among Southeastern
Indians, 122; Spear-finger, 176; Spirit
Defenders of Nikwasi, 170; Why the
Possum Grins, 163
Oratory, 225–26; in ball game, 414–15,
418; eulogy, 335; peacemaking, 257;
in war, 243, 325–26
Ornamentation: in Archaic tradition,
44, 52, 54; in barter, 310; of buildings,
111, 220; in Mississippian tradition,
88; of pipes, 397; of priests, 371; of
slave posts, 221; of Under World beings, 127; of weapons, 111; of women,
374; in Woodland tradition, 57,
64–65, 68, 72, 74
Ortiz, Juan, 107–8, 115

Pacaha, town of, 115
Paint: on art forms, 384, 386, 388, 397;
on buildings, 367, 378–79, 380; on
clothing, 262; on face and body, 30,

The Southeastern Indians was set on the Variable Input Phototype-setter in eleven-point Caledonia with two-point spacing between the lines. Centaur was selected for display. The book was designed by Jim Billingsley, composed by Moran Industries, Inc., Baton Rouge, Louisiana, printed by Thomson-Shore, Inc., Dexter, Michigan, and bound by John H. Dekker & Sons, Inc., Grand Rapids, Michigan.

THE UNIVERSITY OF TENNESSEE PRESS · KNOXVILLE